The Human Brain and Possible Areas Linked to Mental Disorders in Children

The human brain does not reach full cognitive and emotional maturity until a person reaches his or her 30s.

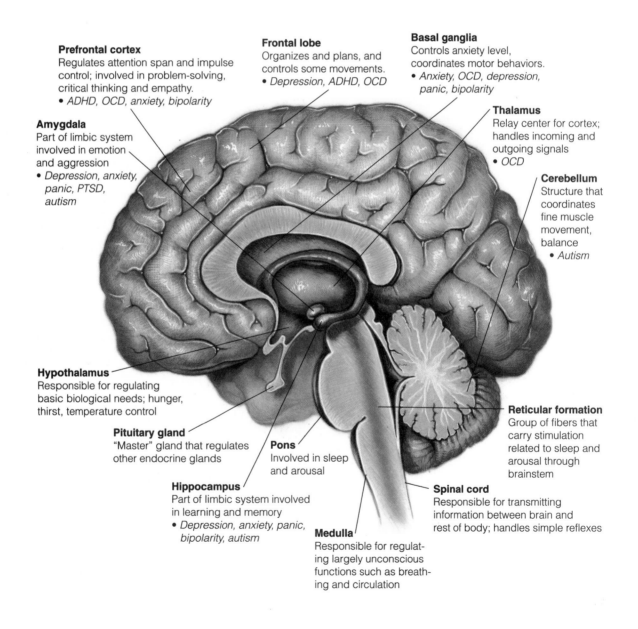

Prefrontal cortex
Regulates attention span and impulse control; involved in problem-solving, critical thinking and empathy.
• *ADHD, OCD, anxiety, bipolarity*

Amygdala
Part of limbic system involved in emotion and aggression
• *Depression, anxiety, panic, PTSD, autism*

Frontal lobe
Organizes and plans, and controls some movements.
• *Depression, ADHD, OCD*

Basal ganglia
Controls anxiety level, coordinates motor behaviors.
• *Anxiety, OCD, depression, panic, bipolarity*

Thalamus
Relay center for cortex; handles incoming and outgoing signals
• *OCD*

Cerebellum
Structure that coordinates fine muscle movement, balance
• *Autism*

Hypothalamus
Responsible for regulating basic biological needs; hunger, thirst, temperature control

Pituitary gland
"Master" gland that regulates other endocrine glands

Pons
Involved in sleep and arousal

Reticular formation
Group of fibers that carry stimulation related to sleep and arousal through brainstem

Hippocampus
Part of limbic system involved in learning and memory
• *Depression, anxiety, panic, bipolarity, autism*

Spinal cord
Responsible for transmitting information between brain and rest of body; handles simple reflexes

Medulla
Responsible for regulating largely unconscious functions such as breathing and circulation

Abnormal Child Psychology

Abnormal Child Psychology

SIXTH EDITION

ERIC J. MASH

**Oregon Health & Science University
and
University of Calgary**

DAVID A. WOLFE

**Centre for Addiction and Mental Health
and
University of Toronto**

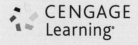
CENGAGE
Learning·

Australia · Brazil · Mexico · Singapore · United Kingdom · United States

CENGAGE
Learning·

Abnormal Child Psychology, **Sixth Edition**
Eric J. Mash and David A. Wolfe

Product Director: Jon-David Hague

Product Manager: Timothy Matray

Content Developer: Tangelique Williams-Grayer

Product Assistant: Nicole Richards

Media Developer: Jasmin Tokatlian

Marketing Manager: Melissa Larmon

Content Project Manager: Michelle Clark

Art Director: Vernon Boes

Manufacturing Planner: Karen Hunt

Production Service: Lynn Lustberg, MPS Limited

Text and Photo Researcher: Lumina Datamatics

Copy Editor: Debbie Stone

Illustrator: MPS Limited

Text Designer: Liz Harasymczuk

Cover Designer: Denise Davidson

Cover Image: Dave Nagel/Getty Images

Compositor: MPS Limited

© 2016, 2013 Cengage Learning

WCN: 01-100-101

For product information and technology assistance, contact us at
Cengage Learning Customer & Sales Support, 1-800-354-9706.

For permission to use material from this text or product,
submit all requests online at **www.cengage.com/permissions.**
Further permissions questions can be e-mailed to
permissionrequest@cengage.com.

Library of Congress Control Number: 2014936450

Student Edition:
ISBN-13: 978-1-305-10542-3
ISBN-10: 1-305-10542-7

Cengage Learning
20 Channel Center Street
Boston, MA 02210
USA

Cengage Learning is a leading provider of customized learning solutions with office locations around the globe, including Singapore, the United Kingdom, Australia, Mexico, Brazil, and Japan. Locate your local office at **www.cengage.com/global.**

Design element: © an_ju/Shutterstock.com

Cengage Learning products are represented in Canada by Nelson Education, Ltd.

To learn more about Cengage Learning Solutions, visit **www.cengage.com.** Purchase any of our products at your local college store or at our preferred online store **www.cengagebrain.com.**

Printed in the United States of America
Print Number: 01   Print Year: 2014

Brief Contents

Contents

12 | Trauma- and Stressor-Related Disorders 400

Case by Chapter

Cases by Clinical Aspect

Preface

We are delighted with the momentous success of *Abnormal Child Psychology,* leading to the release of this sixth edition. Over the past 15 years, we have become closely connected to the diversity and significance of topics covered by this vibrant and active field, which (in our humble opinion) has established essential core knowledge for students interested in the many diverse areas of psychology that are influenced by normal and abnormal developmental processes. To keep pace with this expanding knowledge base, we have reviewed literally thousands of new studies across major and minor areas in this field, resulting in the most up-to-date and comprehensive text on the market.

The positive reception to previous editions of our book and the helpful feedback from students and instructors continues to shape *Abnormal Child Psychology* into a comprehensive yet student-friendly textbook. The sixth edition maintains its focus on the child, not just the disorders, while continuing to keep the text on the cutting edge of scholarly and practical advancements in the field. Because reading textbooks can be demanding, we think you will find that the full color presentation, graphics, and artwork increase your engagement with and enjoyment of the material from the moment you pick up the book.

Major changes in diagnostic terminology and criteria are reflected in the new organization and content of the sixth edition, consistent with the *Diagnostic and Statistical Manual of Mental Disorders,* 5th edition (DSM-5). For example, chapters on specific disorders are organized developmentally, beginning with Neurodevelopmental Disorders (i.e., intellectual disability, autism spectrum disorder, communication and specific learning disorders, and attention-deficit/hyperactivity disorder). A new chapter on Trauma- and Stressor-Related Disorders was added to reflect the DSM-5 consensus that such disorders are distinct from other behavioral and emotional disorders. Also, this edition continues to expand on important new developments over the past few years. Recent findings on diagnosis, prevalence, causes, subtypes, comorbidity, developmental pathways, risk and protective factors, gender, ethnicity, evidence-based treatments, and early intervention and prevention are noted throughout. A recent upsurge of research into the role of genes and gene–environment interactions (G×E) as well as new studies of brain structure, functioning, and connectivity have contributed enormously to our understanding of the childhood disorders covered in this book.

At the same time, the sixth edition retains the hallmark features that make it one of the most successful texts in courses on child psychopathology, abnormal child and adolescent psychology, developmental psychopathology, atypical development, and behavior disorders of childhood and adolescence. Among these features are engaging first-person accounts and case histories designed to create powerful links between key topics and the experiences of individual children and their families. The features that follow are also foundational to the text.

ATTENTION TO ADVANCES IN ABNORMAL CHILD AND ADOLESCENT PSYCHOLOGY

The past decade has produced extraordinary advances in understanding the special issues pertaining to abnormal child and adolescent psychology. Today, we have a much better ability to distinguish among different disorders of children and adolescents, as well as increased recognition of common features and underlying mechanisms for these supposedly different disorders. Research advances have given rise to increased recognition of poorly understood or underdetected problems such as intellectual disabilities, autism spectrum disorder, communication and specific learning disorders, attention-deficit/hyperactivity disorder, motor disorders, oppositional and conduct disorders, depressive and bipolar disorders, teen suicide and substance abuse, anxiety disorders, obsessive–compulsive disorder, trauma- and stressor-related disorders, feeding and eating disorders, and disorders stemming from chronic health problems. Similarly, the field of abnormal child psychology is now more aware of the ways children's and adolescents' psychological disorders are distinguishable from those of adults, and how important it is to maintain a strong developmental perspective in understanding the course of childhood disorders over the life span.[1]

In a relatively short time, the study of abnormal child and adolescent psychology has moved well beyond the individual child and family to consider the roles of community, social, and cultural influences in an integrative

---

[1] Note: *Abnormal Child Psychology* (6th ed.) spans the age period from infancy through young adulthood. "Child" often is used as shorthand for this broader age range.

and developmentally sensitive manner. Similarly, those of us working in this field are more attuned to the many struggles faced by children and adolescents with psychological disorders and their families, as well as to the demands and costs such problems place on the mental health, education, medical, and juvenile justice systems.

A FOCUS ON THE CHILD, NOT JUST THE DISORDERS

We believe that one of the best ways to introduce students to a particular problem of childhood or adolescence is to describe a real child. Clinical descriptions, written in an accessible, engaging fashion, help students understand a child's problem in context and provide a framework in which to explore the complete nature of the disorder. In each chapter, we introduce case examples of children and adolescents with disorders from our own clinical files and from those of colleagues. We then refer to these children when describing the course of the disorder, which provides the student with a well-rounded picture of the child or adolescent in the context of his or her family, peers, community, and culture.

In addition to clinical case material, we use extracts, quotes, and photos throughout each chapter to help the student remain focused on the real challenges faced by children with disorders and their families. First-person accounts and case descriptions enrich the reader's understanding of the daily lives of children and adolescents with problems and allow for a more realistic portrayal of individual strengths and limitations.

A COMPREHENSIVE AND INTEGRATIVE APPROACH

To reflect the expansion of this field, the causes and effects of various childhood disorders are explained from an integrative perspective that recognizes biological, psychological, social, and emotional influences and their interdependence. This strategy was further guided by a consideration of developmental processes that shape and are shaped by the expression of each disorder. Considering the broader contexts of family, peers, school, community, culture, and society that affect development is also important for understanding child and adolescent disorders; they are a critical feature of this text.

We use both categorical and dimensional approaches in describing disorders because each method offers unique and important definitions and viewpoints. Each topic area is defined using DSM-5 criteria accompanied by clinical descriptions, examples, and empirically derived dimensions. The clinical features of each disorder are described in a manner that allows students to gain a firm grasp of the basic dimensions and expression of the disorder across its life span. Since children and adolescents referred for psychological services typically show symptoms that overlap diagnostic categories, each chapter discusses common comorbidities and developmental norms that help inform diagnostic decisions.

ATTENTION TO BOTH DEVELOPMENTAL PATHWAYS AND ADULT OUTCOMES

To provide balance, we approach each disorder from the perspective of the whole child. Diagnostic criteria are accompanied by added emphasis on the strengths of the individual and on the environmental circumstances that influence the developmental course of each disorder, which is followed from its early beginnings in infancy and childhood through adolescence and into early adulthood. We highlight the special issues pertaining to younger and older age groups and the risk and protective factors affecting developmental pathways. In this manner, we examine developmental continuities and discontinuities and attempt to understand why some children with problems continue to experience difficulties as adolescents and adults and others do not.

EMPHASIS ON DIVERSITY

The importance of recognizing diversity in understanding and helping children with problems and their families is emphasized throughout. New research continues to inform and increase our understanding of the crucial role that factors such socioeconomic status (SES), gender, sexual orientation, race, ethnicity, and culture play in the identification, expression, prevalence, causes, treatments, and outcomes for child and adolescent problems. To sharpen our emphasis on these factors, we were fortunate to receive input from Sumru Erkut, Ph.D., of Wellesley College, an expert in diversity and abnormal child development. As a result of Dr. Erkut's input, we examine differences related to SES, gender, race, ethnicity, and culture for each childhood problem under discussion. In addition, we also recognize the importance of studying distinct groups in their own right as a way of understanding the processes associated with specific problems for each gender, ethnic, or cultural group. While emphasizing new knowledge about diversity issues and childhood disorders, we also caution throughout this text that relatively few studies have examined the attitudes, behaviors, and biological and psychological processes of children and adolescents with mental disorders and problems across different cultures, and we indicate places where this situation is beginning to change.

COVERAGE OF TRAUMA- AND STRESSOR-RELATED DISORDERS, CHILD MALTREATMENT, AND RELATIONSHIP-BASED DISORDERS

A distinguishing feature of this textbook is its expansion and emphasis on several of the more recent and important areas of developmental psychopathology that do not easily fit into a deficits model or a categorical approach. One of these new areas concerns trauma- and stressor-related disorders, which are now recognized in DSM-5 as specific disorders stemming from many forms of tragic events that affect children's development and life course. The sixth edition expands on the role of stressful and traumatic events in children's lives and how such events may be direct or contributing causes to psychological disorders. We discuss the nature of child maltreatment to illustrate how major forms of childhood stress and trauma often stem from unhealthy relationships with significant others. Along with recognition of the importance of biological dispositions in guiding development and behavior, we discuss the strong connection between children's behavior patterns and the availability of a suitable child-rearing environment and how early experience can influence both gene expression and brain development. Students are made aware of how children's overt symptoms can sometimes be adaptive in particular settings or in caregiving relationships that are atypical or abusive and how traditional diagnostic labels may not be helpful.

INTEGRATION OF TREATMENT AND PREVENTION

Treatment and prevention approaches are integral parts of understanding a particular disorder. Applying knowledge of the clinical features and developmental courses of childhood disorders to benefit children with these problems and their families always intrigues students and helps them make greater sense of the material. Therefore, we emphasize current approaches to treatment and prevention in each chapter, where such information can be tailored to the particular childhood problem. Consistent with current health system demands for accountability, we discuss best practice guidelines and emphasize interventions for which there is empirical support.

A FLEXIBLE, EVEN MORE USER-FRIENDLY TEXT

The book is organized into a logical four-part framework to facilitate understanding of the individual disorders and mastery of the material overall. Following the introductory chapters that comprise Part I, the contents can be readily assigned to students in any order that suits the goals and preferences of the instructor. The following is an overview of the book's four parts:

I. Understanding Abnormal Child Psychology (definitions, theories, clinical description, research, assessment, and treatment issues);

II. Neurodevelopmental disorders (intellectual disability, autism spectrum disorder and childhood-onset schizophrenia, communication and specific learning disorders, attention-deficit/hyperactivity disorder);

III. Behavioral and Emotional Disorders (conduct problems, depressive and bipolar disorders, anxiety and obsessive–compulsive disorders, trauma- and stressor-related disorders);

IV. Problems Related to Physical and Mental Health (health related and substance-use disorders, feeding and eating disorders)

The overall length of the text is completely student-centered and manageable without sacrificing academic standards of content and coverage. Dozens of first-person accounts and case histories help students grasp the real-world impact of disorders. Two guides—"Cases by Chapter" and "Cases by Clinical Aspect"—have been provided at the front of the text to help teachers and students navigate the book as easily as possible.

In addition, chapters are consistently organized to help instructors avoid assigning sections of each chapter (e.g., biological causes) that may not appeal to the level of their students or that address particular subtopics that fall outside the parameters of a given course (e.g., childhood-onset schizophrenia or pediatric bipolar disorder). For instructors wanting a more detailed presentation of research findings, supplementary readings can be drawn from the many up-to-date citations of original research.

Related but less critical information that enhances each topic appears in the "A Closer Look" features, so that students can easily recognize that the material is presented to add further insight or examples to the major content areas of the chapter.

Finally, chapters provide many useful pedagogical features to help make students' encounters with and learning of the material an agreeable experience: *key terms* are highlighted and defined where they appear in the text, listed at the chapter's end, and defined in a separate glossary at the back of the book to help students grasp important terminology; DSM-5 tables are provided in addition to general tables to summarize diagnostic criteria; *bullet points* guide students to key concepts throughout the chapters; and interim "Section Summaries" help students consolidate each chapter's key concepts. In addition to the lists of key terms, students will find a listing of "Section Summaries" at the end of each chapter for easy reference while studying.

SUMMARY OF KEY FEATURES

- ▶ "A Closer Look" features, mentioned above, are found throughout the book to draw students into the material and enrich each topic with engaging information. Some examples include: "What Are the Long-Term Criminal Consequences of Child Maltreatment?" "Common Fears in Infancy, Childhood, and Adolescence," and "Did Darwin Have a Panic Disorder?"
- ▶ Visual learning aids such as cartoons, tables, and eye-catching chapter- and section-opening quotes, as well as numerous photos and figures, in full color, illustrate key concepts throughout the text to complement student understanding.
- ▶ The authors' in-depth coverage of the role of the normal developmental process in understanding each disorder, as well as their close attention to important sex differences in the expression, determinants, and outcomes of child and adolescent disorders, promote greater understanding.
- ▶ Current findings regarding the reliability and validity of DSM diagnostic criteria for specific disorders are discussed, with attention to issues, features, and disorders that are new to DSM-5.

NOTABLE CONTENT CHANGES AND UPDATES IN THE SIXTH EDITION

Highlights of the content changes and updates to this edition include the following:

- ▶ The most current information concerning prevalence, age at onset, and gender distribution for each disorder, including a discussion of issues surrounding the reported increase in the prevalence of autism spectrum disorder.
- ▶ Enriched coverage of gender and culture, including exciting new findings related to the expression, development, and adolescent outcomes for girls with attention-deficit/hyperactivity disorder (ADHD), conduct problems, and anxiety and mood disorders and for children from different ethnic and cultural groups.
- ▶ The most recent theories about developmental pathways for different disorders, including the childhood precursors of eating disorders.

- ▶ Integrative developmental frameworks for ADHD, conduct problems, anxiety disorders, depressive disorders, autism spectrum disorder, and child maltreatment.
- ▶ Exciting new findings on the interplay between early experience and brain development, including how early stressors, such as abuse, alter the brain systems associated with regulating stress and how they place the child at risk for developing later problems, such as anxiety or mood disorders.
- ▶ Recent genetic discoveries regarding neurodevelopmental disorders such as autism spectrum disorder, ADHD, and specific learning and communication disorders.
- ▶ Findings from neuroimaging studies of ADHD, autism spectrum disorder, anxiety, and depression that illuminate neurobiological causes.
- ▶ New information on family factors in externalizing and internalizing disorders, and on developmental disabilities.
- ▶ New findings on different presentation types, dimensions, and specifiers for disorders such as ADHD, oppositional defiant disorder, and conduct disorders.
- ▶ Recent findings on the development of precursors of psychopathy in young people.
- ▶ Recent findings on patterns of use and misuse of medications for treating ADHD and childhood depression.
- ▶ New definitions of intellectual disabilities and adaptive behavior.
- ▶ Current findings from neuroimaging studies showing the harmful effects of abuse and neglect and similar forms of stress and trauma on neurocognitive development.
- ▶ Discussion of the new DSM-5 categories Reactive Attachment Disorder (RAD) and Disinhibited Social Engagement Disorder (DSED).
- ▶ The most recent follow-up findings from groundbreaking early intervention and prevention programs, such as early interventions for children with autism spectrum disorder, Fast Track for conduct disorders, and the Multimodal Treatment Study for Children with ADHD.
- ▶ An enhanced focus on evidence-based assessment and treatments including:
  - Advances in early identification and new treatments for autism spectrum disorder (Chapter 6)
  - Descriptions of new/revised communication and learning disorders, such as social (pragmatic) communication disorder

- Behavior therapy, psychopharmacological, and combined treatments for ADHD (Chapter 8)
- Parent management training, problem-solving skills training, and multisystemic therapy for oppositional and conduct disorders (Chapter 9)
- Cognitive–behavioral therapy and interpersonal therapy for depression (Chapter 10)
- Cognitive–behavioral therapy, exposure, and modeling for anxiety disorders (Chapter 11)
- Treatment for child and adolescence substance-abuse problems (Chapter 13)
- Treatment outcome studies with anorexia and bulimia (Chapter 14)
▶ Added coverage on important, contemporary topics including:
  - Presentation types of disorders such as the predominantly inattentive presentation of ADHD and new findings on emotional impulsivity (Chapter 8)
  - Temperament and personality disorders (Chapters 2 and 4)
  - Different symptom clusters for oppositional defiant disorder (Chapter 9)
  - Parenting styles (Chapters 2, 9, 10, 11, and 12)
  - The stigma of mental illness (Chapters 1 and 4)
  - The interplay between research findings in abnormal child psychology and public policy implications throughout the book.
▶ Coverage of many significant reports from the Surgeon General, the World Health Organization, and others that will shape the future of research and practice in children's mental health (Chapters 1 and 2)
  - Support organizations for parents and children are now listed in the Instructor's Manual, along with a greatly expanded selection of multimedia and interactive learning resources, foremost among these numerous new video clips—selected by the authors. Unique in this market, these current, high-interest videos focus on topics such as ADHD, autism, bullying, life skills, and Down syndrome.

A COMPREHENSIVE TEACHING AND LEARNING PACKAGE

Abnormal Child Psychology, sixth edition, is accompanied by an array of supplements developed to facilitate both the instructors' and the students' best possible experience, inside as well as outside the classroom. Supplements continuing from the fourth edition have been thoroughly revised and updated; other supplements are new to this edition. Cengage Learning invites you to take full advantage of the teaching and learning tools available to you and has prepared the following descriptions of each.

Instructor's Manual with Test Bank

The Instructor's Manual with Test Bank closely matches the text and consists of lecture outlines and notes, learning objectives, myriad activities and handouts, video and website recommendations, "Warning Signs" transparency masters, and new listings of support organizations for parents and children. In addition to a comprehensive test bank, this resource also includes a set of extras called "Five Minutes More," which comprises additional lecture ideas, transparency/digital slide masters, and activities on selected topics such as the brain, day care, and bilingualism. The Instructor's Manual is available in print and in electronic format on the book's companion website (password-protected).

CourseMate

Abnormal Child Psychology, sixth edition, includes Psychology CourseMate, a complement to your textbook.
Psychology CourseMate includes:

▶ An interactive eBook, with highlighting, note taking and search capabilities
▶ Interactive learning tools including:
  - Quizzes
  - Flashcards
  - Videos
  - and more
▶ Engagement Tracker, a first-of-its-kind tool that monitors student engagement in the course

Go to cengagebrain.com to access these resources.

ACKNOWLEDGMENTS

One of the most rewarding aspects of this project has been the willingness and commitment on the part of many to share their knowledge and abilities. With great pleasure and appreciation, we wish to acknowledge individuals who have in one way or another contributed to its completion, while recognizing that any shortcomings of this book are our responsibility alone.

In Calgary, Alison and Megan Wiigs, as creative and talented a mother-and-daughter team as there is, have contributed enormously to every phase of this project through six editions. For their devotion to the project, they have our special gratitude. We also thank Carlie Montpetit and Camille

Popovich for their perceptive and useful feedback from a student perspective and generous help in locating resource material and references. In Toronto, Anna-Lee Straatman and Debbie Chiodo deserve rich praise for their skilled efforts at locating resource material and checking the manuscript. We are also grateful to colleagues who generously provided us with case materials and other information for this and previous editions, including Thomas Achenbach, Ann Marie Albano, Russell Barkley, David Dozois, Scott Henggeler, Giuseppe Iaria, Charlotte Johnston, Alan Kazdin, Philip Kendall, David Kolko, Ivar Lovaas, Margaret McKim, Robert McMahon, Douglas Murdoch, Joel Nigg, Gerald Patterson, John Pearce, William Pelham, John Piacentini, Phyl and Rachel Prout, Jerry Sattler, David Shaffer, Rosemary Tannock, and Fred Weizmann. Many thanks again to Sumru Erkut, Ph.D., Associate Director and Senior Research Scientist at Wellesley College's Wellesley Centers for Women, for her expert review of this text's previous edition focusing on diversity. We extend our special thanks to the many students in our courses and those from other universities who provided us with helpful feedback on this edition. Dr. Jeff St. Pierre in London, Ontario, deserves special thanks for his devoted attention to improving ways of teaching abnormal child psychology using our textbook.

The production of a textbook involves many behind-the-scenes individuals who deserve special thanks. Tim Matray, project manager, gave his support in launching this sixth edition. Tangelique Williams-Grayer and Jasmin Tokatlian, senior content developer and media developer, contributed creative ideas, valuable assistance, and friendly reality checks from start to finish. The rest of the devoted and talented staff at and associated with Cengage Learning, including Michelle Clark, content production manager; Vernon Boes, art director; Lynn Lustberg, MPS Limited Project Manager; Nicole Richards, editorial assistant; Veerabhagu Nagarajan, photo researcher; and Pinky Subi, permissions researcher, all deserve our thankful recognition for their contributions toward making the sixth edition of this text top quality.

Once again, we wish to thank our families, whose steadfast support and tolerance for the demands and excesses that go into a project such as this were critically important and exceedingly strong. The preparation of this textbook placed a heavy burden of our time away from them, and we are grateful for their unyielding support and encouragement. Eric Mash thanks Heather Henderson Mash, his wife and soul mate, for her love and support, tolerance of the time that a project like this takes away from family life, and her wise advice on many matters relating to this book. David Wolfe thanks his three children, Amy, Annie, and Alex,

who were incredible sources of inspiration, information, humor, and photographs(!). His wife, Barbara Legate, has been a touchstone throughout every edition for her intellectual and emotional support.

REVIEWERS

A critical part of writing this textbook involved feedback from students, teachers, and experts. We would like to thank several dedicated reviewers and scholars who read most of the chapters for this book and provided us with detailed comments and suggestions that were enormously helpful in shaping the final manuscript of this edition:

Rebecca Ezechukwu, Miami University
Jill Norvilitis, Buffalo State College
Brian Fisak, University of North Florida
Nicole McCray, University of Montana
Jan Weiner, Hunter College

We also wish to again acknowledge and thank the reviewers whose insights helped us in previous editions: Daniel M. Bagner, Florida International University; Paul Bartoli, East Stroudsburg University; Greg Berg, San Jose State University; Kristin Christodulu, University at Albany, State University of New York; Mary Ann Coupland, Sinte Gleska University; David Day, Ryerson University; Maria Gartstein, Washington State University–Pullman; Claire Novosad, Southern Connecticut State University; Robert Weisskirch, California State University–Monterey Bay; Debora Bell-Dolan, University of Missouri-Columbia; Richard Clements, Indiana University Northwest; Nancy Eldred, San Jose State University; Robert Emery, University of Virginia; Virginia E. Fee, Mississippi State University; Paul Florsheim, University of Utah; Gregory Fouts, University of Calgary; Laura Freberg, California Polytechnic State University–San Luis Obispo; Gary Harper, DePaul University; Casey A. Holtz, Wisconsin Lutheran College; Yo Jackson, University of Kansas; Christopher Kearney, University of Nevada–Las Vegas; Elizabeth J. Kiel Luebbe, Miami University; Janet Kistner, Florida State University; Bertha Kondrak, Central TX University; Marvin Kumler, Bowling Green State University; June Madsen Clausen, University of San Francisco; Patrick McGrath, Dalhousie University; Kay McIntyre, University of Missouri–St. Louis; Clark McKown, University of California–Berkeley; Robert McMahon, Simon Fraser University; Richard Milich, University of Kentucky; Susan K. Marell, St. Thomas Aquinas College; Martin Murphy, University of Akron; Jill Norvilitis, Buffalo State College; Narina Nunez, University of Wyoming; Stacy Overstreet,

Tulane University; Lauren Polvere, Clinton Community College; Michael Roberts, University of Kansas; Donald T. Saposnek, University of California, Santa Cruz; Dana Schneider, M.A., MFT, Sonoma State University; Michael Vasey, Ohio State University; Carol K. Whalen, University of California, Irvine; and Eric A. Youngstrom, Ph.D., University of North Carolina.

Our thanks also go to Paul Florsheim's students at the University of Utah: Trisha Aberton, Julie Blundell, Josh Brown, Kimbery Downing, Jaime Fletcher, Jeff Ford, Nick Gilson, Regina Hiraoka, Trisha Jorgensen, Michael Lambert, Monica Stauffer, Matthew Warthen, Heather Woodhouse, Kristen Yancey, and Matthew Zollinger.

Finally, we offer a special thanks to Nancy Eldred of San Jose State University for pilot-testing the text with her students. The comments were quite helpful in sharpening the student focus of subsequent editions, and we are grateful to her for volunteering for this mission! Thank you Gabriela Beas, Maria Brown, Sara Carriere, Gina Costanza, Gera-Lyne Delfin, Julene Donovan, Brieann Durose, Shelly Gillan, Rochelle Hernandez, Keri Kennedy, Doris Lan, Maggie Lau, Christine McAfee-Ward, Deisy Muñoz, Shirat Negev, Kristi Pimentel, Veronica Rauch, Sandra Ronquillo, Becky Schripsema, Dianalin Stratton, Loyen Yabut, Melissa Zahradnik.

Eric J. Mash

David A. Wolfe

1

Introduction to Normal and Abnormal Behavior in Children and Adolescents

Mankind owes to the child the best it has to give.

—UN Convention on the Rights of the Child (1989)

A FTER CENTURIES OF SILENCE, misunderstanding, and outright abuse, children's mental health problems and needs now receive greater attention, which corresponds to society's recent concern about children's well-being. Fortunately, today more people like you want to understand and address the needs of children and adolescents. Perhaps you have begun to recognize that children's mental health problems differ in many ways from those of adults, so you have chosen to take a closer look. Maybe you are planning a career in teaching, counseling, medicine, law, rehabilitation, or psychology—all of which rely somewhat on knowledge of children's special needs to shape their focus and practice. Whatever your reason is for reading this book, we are pleased to welcome you to an exciting and active field of study, one that we believe will expose you to concepts and issues that will have a profound and lasting influence. Child and adolescent mental health issues are becoming relevant to many of us in our current and future roles as professionals, community members, and parents, and the needs for trained personnel are increasing (McLearn, Knitzer, & Carter, 2007).

Let's begin by considering Georgina's problems, which raise several fundamental questions that guide our current understanding of children's **psychological disorders**. Ask yourself: Does Georgina's behavior seem abnormal, or are aspects of her behavior normal under certain circumstances?

How would you describe Georgina's problem? Is it an emotional problem? A learning problem? A developmental disability? Could something in her environment cause these strange rituals, or is she more likely responding to internal cues we do not know about? Would Georgina's behavior be viewed differently if she were a boy, or African American or Hispanic? Will she continue to display these behaviors and, if so, what can we do to help?

GEORGINA

Counting for Safety

At age 10, Georgina's strange symptoms had reached the point where her mother needed answers—and fast. Her behavior first became a concern about 2 years ago, when she started talking about harm befalling herself or her family. Her mother recalled how Georgina would come home from the third grade and complain that "I need to finish stuff but I can't seem to," and "I know I'm gonna forget something so I have to keep thinking about it." Her mother expressed her own frustration and worry: "As early as age 5, I remember Georgina would touch and arrange things a certain way, such as brushing her teeth in a certain sequence. Sometimes I'd notice that she would walk through doorways over and over, and she seemed to need to check and arrange things her way before she could leave a room." Georgina's mother had spoken to their family doctor about it back then and was told, "It's probably a phase she's going through, like stepping on cracks will break your mother's back. Ignore it and it'll stop."

But it didn't stop. Georgina developed more elaborate rituals for counting words and objects, primarily in groups of four. She told her mom, "I need to count things out and group them a certain way—only I know the rules how to do it." When she came to my office, Georgina told me, "When someone says something to me or I read something, I have to count the words in groups of four and then organize these groups into larger and larger groups of four." She looked at the pile of magazines in my office and the books on my shelf and explained, matter-of-factly, that she was counting and grouping these things while we talked! Georgina was constantly terrified of forgetting a passage or objects or being interrupted. She believed that if she could not complete her counting, some horrible

Even at age 5, Georgina's strange counting ritual was a symptom of her obsessive–compulsive disorder.

tragedy would befall her parents or herself. Nighttime was the worst, she explained, because "I can't go to sleep until my counting is complete, and this can take a long time." (In fact, it took up to several hours, her mother confirmed.) Understandably, her daytime counting rituals had led to decline in her schoolwork and friendships. Her mother showed me her report cards: Georgina's grades had gone from above average to near failing in several subjects. (Based on Piacentini & Graae, 1997)

When seeking assistance or advice, parents often ask questions similar to these about their child's behavior, and understandably they need to know the probable course and outcome. These questions also exemplify the following issues that research studies in abnormal child psychology seek to address:

▶ Defining what constitutes normal and abnormal behavior for children of different ages, sexes, and ethnic and cultural backgrounds

▶ Identifying the causes and correlates of abnormal child behavior

▶ Making predictions about long-term outcomes

▶ Developing and evaluating methods for treatment and/or prevention

How you choose to describe the problems that children show, and what harm or impairments such problems may lead to, is often the first step toward understanding the nature of their problems. As we discuss in Chapter 11, Georgina's symptoms fit the diagnostic criteria for obsessive–compulsive disorder. This diagnostic label, although far from perfect, tells a great deal about the nature of her disorder, the course it may follow, and the possible treatments.

Georgina's problems also illustrate important features that distinguish most child and adolescent disorders:

▶ *When adults seek services for children, it often is not clear whose "problem" it is.* Children usually enter the mental health system as a result of concerns raised by adults—parents, pediatricians, teachers, or school counselors—and the children themselves may have little choice in the matter. Children do not refer themselves for treatment. This has important implications for how we detect children's problems and how we respond to them.

▶ *Many child and adolescent problems involve failure to show expected developmental progress.* The problem may be transitory, like most types of bedwetting, or it may be an initial indication of more severe problems ahead, as we see in Georgina's case. Determining the problem requires familiarity with normal, as well as abnormal, development.

▶ *Many problem behaviors shown by children and youths are not entirely abnormal.* To some extent, most children and youth commonly exhibit certain problem behaviors. For instance, worrying from time to time about forgetting things or losing track of thoughts is common; Georgina's behavior, however, seems to involve more than these normal concerns. Thus, decisions about what to do also require familiarity with known psychological disorders and troublesome problem behaviors.

▶ *Interventions for children and adolescents often are intended to promote further development, rather than merely to restore a previous level of functioning.* Unlike interventions for most adult disorders, the goal for many children is to boost their abilities and skills, as well as to eliminate distress.

Before we look at today's definitions of abnormal behavior in children and adolescents, it is valuable to discover how society's interests and approaches to these problems during previous generations have improved the quality of life and mental health of children and youths. Many children, especially those with special needs, fared poorly in the past because they were forced to work as coal miners, field hands, or beggars. Concern for children's needs, rights, and care requires a prominent and consistent social sensitivity and awareness that simply did not exist prior to the twentieth century (Aries, 1962). As you read the following historical synopsis, note how the relatively short history of abnormal child psychology has been strongly influenced by philosophical and societal changes in how adults view and treat children in general (Borstelmann, 1983; V. French, 1977).

HISTORICAL VIEWS AND BREAKTHROUGHS

These were feverish, melancholy times; I cannot remember to have raised my head or seen the moon or any of the heavenly bodies; my eyes were turned downward to the broad lamplit streets and to where the trees of the garden rustled together all night in undecipherable blackness; . . .

—Robert Louis Stevenson, describing memories of childhood illness and depression (quoted in Calder, 1980)

We must recognize children as valuable, independent of any other purpose, to help them develop normal lives and competencies. Although this view of children should seem self-evident to us today, valuing children as persons in their own right—and providing medical, educational, and psychological resources to encourage their progress—has not been a priority of previous societies. Early writings suggest that children were considered servants of the state in the city-states of early Greece. Ancient Greek and Roman societies believed that any person—young or old—with a physical or mental handicap, disability, or deformity was an economic burden and a social embarrassment, and thus was to be scorned, abandoned, or put to death (V. French, 1977).

Prior to the eighteenth century, children's mental health problems—unlike adult disorders—were seldom mentioned in professional or other forms of communication. Some of the earliest historical interest in abnormal child behavior surfaced near the end of the eighteenth century. The Church used its strong influence to attribute children's unusual or disturbing behaviors to their inherently uncivilized and provocative nature (Kanner, 1962). In fact, during this period, nonreligious explanations for disordered behavior in children were rarely given serious consideration because possession by the devil and similar forces of evil was the only explanation anyone needed (Rie, 1971). No one was eager to challenge this view, given that they too could be seen as possessed and dealt with accordingly.

Sadly, during the seventeenth and eighteenth centuries, as many as two-thirds of children died before their fifth birthday, often because there were no antibiotics or similar medications to treat deadly diseases (Zelizer, 1994). Many children were treated harshly or indifferently by their parents. Cruel acts ranging from extreme parental indifference and neglect to physical and sexual abuse of children went unnoticed or were considered an adult's right in the education or disciplining of a child (Radbill, 1968). For many generations, the implied view of society that children are the exclusive property and responsibility of their parents was unchallenged by any countermovement to seek more humane treatment for children. A parent's prerogative to enforce child obedience, for example, was formalized by Massachusetts' Stubborn Child Act of 1654, which permitted parents to put "stubborn" children to death for misbehaving. (Fortunately, no one met this ultimate fate.) Into the mid-1800s, specific laws allowed children with severe developmental disabilities to be kept in cages and cellars (Donohue, Hersen, & Ammerman, 2000).

The Emergence of Social Conscience

"It is easier to build strong children than to fix broken men."

—Attributed to Frederick Douglass

Fortunately, the situation gradually improved for children and youths throughout the nineteenth century and progressed significantly during the latter part of the twentieth century. However, until very recent changes in laws and attitudes, children (along with women, members of minority groups, and persons with special needs) were often the last to benefit from society's prosperity and were the primary victims of its shortcomings. With the acuity of hindsight, we now know that before any real change occurs, it requires a philosophy of humane understanding in how society recognizes and addresses the special needs of some of its members. In addition to humane beliefs, each

society must develop ways and means to recognize and protect the rights of individuals, especially children, in the broadest sense (UN Convention on the Rights of the Child, 1989). An overview of some of these major developments provides important background for understanding today's approaches to children's mental health issues.

In Western society, an inkling of the prerequisites for a social conscience first occurred during the seventeenth century, when both a philosophy of humane care and institutions of social protection began to take root. One individual at the forefront of these changes was John Locke (1632–1704), a noted English philosopher and physician who influenced present-day attitudes and practices of childbirth and child-rearing. Locke believed in individual rights, and he expressed the novel opinion that children should be raised with thought and care instead of indifference and harsh treatment. Rather than seeing children as uncivilized tyrants, he saw them as emotionally sensitive beings who should be treated with kindness and understanding and given proper educational opportunities (Illick, 1974). In his words, "the only fence [archaic use, meaning "defense"] against the world is a thorough knowledge of it."

Then, at the turn of the nineteenth century, one of the first documented efforts to work with a special child was undertaken by Jean Marc Itard (1774–1838). A Closer Look 1.1 explains how Itard treated Victor (discovered living in the woods outside Paris) for his severe developmental delays rather than sending him to an asylum. Symbolically, this undertaking launched a new era of a helping orientation toward special children, which initially focused on the care, treatment, and training of the people then termed "mental defectives."

As the influence of Locke and others fostered the expansion of universal education throughout Europe and North America during the latter half of the nineteenth century, children unable to handle the demands of school became a visible and troubling group. Psychologists such as Leta Hollingworth (1886–1939) argued that many mentally defective children were actually suffering from emotional and behavioral problems primarily due to inept treatment by adults and lack of appropriate intellectual challenge (Benjamin & Shields, 1990). This view led to an important and basic distinction between persons with intellectual disability ("imbeciles") and those with psychiatric or mental disorders ("lunatics"), although this distinction was far from clear at the time. Essentially, local governments needed to know who was responsible for helping children whose cognitive development appeared normal but who showed serious emotional or behavioral problems. The only guidance they had previously had in distinguishing children with intellectual deficits

Victor of Aveyron

Victor, often referred to as the "wild boy of Aveyron," was discovered in France by hunters when he was about 11 or 12 years old, having lived alone in the woods presumably all of his life. Jean Marc Itard, a young physician at the time, believed the boy was "mentally arrested" because of social and educational neglect, and set about demonstrating whether such retardation could be reversed. Victor—who initially was mute, walked on all fours, drank water while lying flat on the ground, and bit and scratched—became the object of popular attention as rumors spread that he had been raised by animals. He was dirty, nonverbal, incapable of attention, and insensitive to basic sensations of hot and cold. Despite the child's appearance and behavior, Itard believed that environmental stimulation could humanize him. Itard's account of his efforts poignantly reveals the optimism, frustration, anger, hope, and despair that he experienced in working with this special child.

Itard used a variety of methods to bring Victor to an awareness of his sensory experiences: hot baths, massages, tickling, emotional excitement, even electric shocks. After 5 years of training by Dr. Itard, Victor had learned to identify objects, identify letters of the alphabet, comprehend many words, and apply names to objects and parts of objects. Victor also showed a preference for social life over the isolation of the wild. Despite his achievements, Itard felt his efforts had failed, because his goals of socializing the boy to make him normal were never reached. Nevertheless, the case of Victor was a landmark in the effort to assist children with special needs. For the first time an adult had tried to really understand—to feel and know—the

mind and emotions of a special child, and had proved that a child with severe impairments could improve through appropriate training. This deep investment on the part of an individual in the needs and feelings of another person's child remains a key aspect of the helping orientation to this day.

Source: From A History of the Care and Study of the Mentally Retarded, by L. Kanner, 1964, p. 15. Courtesy of Charles C Thomas, Publisher, Springfield, Illinois.

from children with behavioral and emotional problems was derived from religious views of immoral behavior: children who had normal cognitive abilities but who were disturbed were thought to suffer from moral insanity, which implied a disturbance in personality or character (Pritchard, 1837). Benjamin Rush (1745–1813), a pioneer in psychiatry, argued that children were incapable of true adult-like insanity, because the immaturity of their developing brains prevented them from retaining the mental events that caused insanity (Rie, 1971). Consequently, the term *moral insanity* grew in acceptance as a means of accounting for nonintellectual forms of abnormal child behavior.

The implications of this basic distinction created a brief yet significant burst of optimism among professionals. Concern for the plight and welfare of children with mental and behavioral disturbances began to rise in conjunction with two important influences. First, with advances in general medicine, physiology, and neurology, the moral insanity view of psychological disorders was replaced by the organic disease model,

which emphasized more humane forms of treatment. This advancement was furthered by advocates such as Dorothea Dix (1802–1887), who in the mid-nineteenth century established 32 humane mental hospitals for the treatment of troubled youths previously relegated to cellars and cages (Achenbach, 1982). Second, the growing influence of the philosophies of Locke and others led to the view that children needed moral guidance and support. With these changing views came an increased concern for moral education, compulsory education, and improved health practices. These early efforts to assist children provided the foundation for evolving views of abnormal child behavior as the result of combinations of biological, environmental, psychological, and cultural influences.

Early Biological Attributions

The successful treatment of infectious diseases during the latter part of the nineteenth century strengthened the emerging belief that illness and disease, including

Masturbatory Insanity

Today, most parents hardly balk at discovering their child engaging in some form of self-stimulation—it is considered a normal part of self-discovery and pleasant-sensation seeking. Such tolerance was not always the case. In fact, children's masturbation is historically significant because it was the first "disorder" unique to children and adolescents (Rie, 1971). Just over a hundred years ago, *masturbatory insanity* was a form of mental illness and, in keeping with the contemporaneous view that such problems resided within the individual, it was believed to be a very worrisome problem (Rie, 1971; Szasz, 1970).

By the eighteenth century, society's objections to masturbation originated from religious views that were augmented by the growing influence of science (Rie, 1971; Szasz, 1970). Moral convictions regarding the wrongfulness of masturbation led to a physiological explanation with severe medical ramifications, based on pseudoscientific papers such as *Onania, or the Heinous Sin of Self-Pollution* (circa 1710) (Szasz, 1970). The medical view

of masturbation focused initially on adverse effects on physical health, but by the mid-nineteenth century the dominant thought shifted to a focus on the presumed negative effects on mental health and nervous system functioning. With amazing speed, masturbation became the most frequently mentioned "cause" of psychopathology in children.

Interest in masturbatory insanity gradually waned toward the end of the nineteenth century, but the argument still remained tenable as psychoanalytic theory gained acceptance. Eventually, the notion of masturbatory insanity gave way to the concept of neurosis. It was not until much later in the twentieth century that the misguided and illusory belief in a relationship between masturbation and mental illness was dispelled. Let this example remind us of the importance of scientific skepticism in confirming or disconfirming new theories and explanations for abnormal behavior.

Source: Based on author's case material.

---

mental illness, were biological problems. However, early attempts at biological explanations for deviant or abnormal behavior were highly biased in favor of the cause being the person's fault. The public generally distrusted and scorned anyone who appeared "mad" or "possessed by the devil" or similar evil forces. A Closer Look 1.2 describes masturbatory insanity, a good illustration of how such thinking can lead to an explanation of abnormal behavior without consideration of objective scientific findings and the base rate of masturbation in the general population. The notion of masturbatory insanity also illustrates how the prevailing political and social climates influence definitions of child psychopathology, which is as true today as it was in the past. Views on masturbation evolved from the moral judgment that it was a sin of the flesh, to the medical opinion that it was harmful to one's physical health, to the psychiatric assertion that sexual overindulgence caused insanity.

In contrast to the public's general ignorance and avoidance of issues concerning persons with mental disorders that continued during the late nineteenth century, the mental hygiene movement provides a benchmark of changing attitudes toward children and adults with mental disorders. In 1909, Clifford Beers, a layperson who had recovered from a severe psychosis, spearheaded efforts to change the plight of others also afflicted. Believing that mental disorders were a form of disease, he criticized society's ignorance and indifference and sought to prevent mental disease by

raising the standards of care and disseminating reliable information (M. Levine & Levine, 1992). As a result, detection and intervention methods began to flourish, based on a more tempered—yet still quite frightened and ill-informed—view of afflicted individuals.

Unfortunately, because this paradigm was based on a biological disease model, intervention was limited to persons with the most visible and prominent disorders, such as psychoses or severe intellectual disability. Although developmental explanations were a part of this early view of psychopathology, they were quite narrow. The development of the disease was considered progressive and irreversible, tied to the development of the child only in that it manifested itself differently as the child grew, but remained impervious to other influences such as treatment or learning. All one could do was to prevent the most extreme manifestations by strict punishment and to protect those not affected.

Sadly, this early educational and humane model for assisting persons with mental disorders soon reverted to a custodial model during the early part of the twentieth century. Once again, attitudes toward anyone with mental or intellectual disabilities turned from cautious optimism to dire pessimism, hostility, and disdain. Particularly children, youths, and adults with intellectual disability were blamed for crimes and social ills during the ensuing alarmist period (Achenbach, 1982). Rather than viewing knowledge as a form of protection, as Locke had argued, society returned to the view that mental illness and retardation were diseases that could spread if left unchecked. For the next two decades, many communities opted to segregate or institutionalize people with mental disabilities and to prevent them from procreating (eugenics). We will return to these important developments in our discussion of the history of intellectual disability (formerly known as mental retardation) in Chapter 5.

Early Psychological Attributions

To conceptualize and understand abnormal child psychology, biological influences must be balanced with important developmental and cultural factors, including the family, peer group, and school. Of course, this perception was not always the case. The long-standing, medically based view that abnormal behavior is a disorder or disease residing within the person unfortunately led to neglect of the essential role of a person's surroundings, context, and relations, and of the interactions among these variables.

The recognition of psychological influences emerged early in the twentieth century, when attention was drawn to the importance of major psychological disorders and to formulating a taxonomy of illnesses. Such recognition allowed researchers to organize and categorize ways of differentiating among various psychological problems, resulting in some semblance of understanding and control. At the same time, there was concern that attempts to recognize the wide range of mental health needs of children and adults could easily backfire and lead to the neglect of persons with more severe disorders. This shift in perspective and increase in knowledge also prompted the development of diagnostic categories and new criminal offenses, the expansion of descriptions of deviant behavior, and the addition of more comprehensive monitoring procedures for identified individuals (Costello & Angold, 2006). Two major theoretical paradigms helped shape these emerging psychological and environmental influences: psychoanalytic theory and behaviorism. We'll limit our discussion here to their historical importance, but additional content concerning their contemporary influence appears in the Chapter 2 discussion of theories and causes.

Psychoanalytic Theory

In Sigmund Freud's day, near the beginning of the twentieth century, many child psychiatrists and psychologists had grown pessimistic about their ability to treat children's mental disorders other than with custodial or palliative care. Freud was one of the first to reject such pessimism and raise new possibilities for treatment as the roots of these disorders were traced to early childhood (Fonagy, Target, & Gergely, 2006).

Although he believed that individuals have inborn drives and predispositions that strongly affect their development, he also believed that experiences play a necessary role in psychopathology. For perhaps the first time, the course of mental disorders was not viewed as inevitable; children and adults could be helped if provided with the proper environment, therapy, or both.

Psychoanalytic theory significantly influenced advances in our ways of thinking about the causes and treatment of mental disorders. Perhaps the most important of these advances from the perspective of abnormal child psychology was that Freud was the first to give meaning to the concept of mental disorder by linking it to childhood experiences (Rilling, 2000). His radical theory incorporated developmental concepts into an understanding of psychopathology at a time when early childhood development was virtually ignored by mainstream child psychiatry and psychology. Rather than focusing on singular, specific causes (a hallmark of the disease model in vogue at the time), psychoanalytic theory emphasized that personality and mental health outcomes had multiple roots. Outcomes depended to a large degree on the interaction of developmental and situational processes that change over time in unique ways (Fonagy et al., 2006). In effect, Freud's writings shifted the view from one of children as innocent or insignificant to one of human beings in turmoil, struggling to achieve control over biological needs and to make themselves acceptable to society through the microcosm of the family (Freud, 1909/1953).

Contributions based on Freud's theory continued to expand throughout the early part of the twentieth century, as clinicians and theorists broke from some of his earlier teachings and brought new insights to the field. His daughter, Anna Freud (1895–1982), was instrumental in expanding his ideas to understanding children, in particular by noting how children's symptoms were related more to developmental stages than were those of adults. Anna Freud's contemporary, Melanie Klein (1882–1960), also took an interest in the meaning of children's play, arguing that all actions could be interpreted in terms of unconscious fantasy. The work of both women made possible the analysis of younger children and the recognition of nonverbal communication for patients of all ages (Mason, 2003).

In recent years, psychoanalytic theory's approach to abnormal child psychology has had less influence on clinical practice and teaching, largely because of the popularity of the phenomenological (descriptive) approach to psychopathology (Costello & Angold, 2006). Nevertheless, it is important to remember that current **nosologies** (the efforts to classify psychiatric disorders into descriptive categories) are essentially nondevelopmental in their approaches. Rather than attempting, as the Freudian approach does, to describe the development of the disease in the context of the development of the individual, nosologies such as those in the *Diagnostic and Statistical Manual of Mental Disorders* (DSM-5; American Psychiatric Association, 2013) attempt to find common denominators that describe the manifestations of a disorder at any age (Achenbach & Rescorla, 2006). Despite valid criticism and a lack of empirical validation of the content of psychoanalytic theory and its many derivatives, the idea of emphasizing the interconnection between children's normal and abnormal development retains considerable attraction as a model for abnormal child psychology.

Behaviorism

The development of evidence-based treatments for children, youths, and families can be traced to the rise of behaviorism in the early 1900s, as reflected in Pavlov's experimental research that established the foundations for classical conditioning, and in the classic studies on the conditioning and elimination of children's fears (Jones, 1924; J. B. Watson & Rayner, 1920). Initially, John Watson (1878–1958), the "Father of Behaviorism," intended to explain Freud's concepts in more scientific terms, based on the new learning theory of classical conditioning.

Ironically, Watson was perhaps more psychoanalytically inspired by Freud's theories than he intended. As he attempted to explain terms such as *unconscious* and *transference* using the language of conditioned emotional responses (and thereby discredit Freud's theory of emotions), he in fact pioneered the scientific investigation of some of Freud's ideas (Rilling, 2000). A Closer Look 1.3 highlights some of Watson's scientific ambitions and his famous study with Little Albert, as well as some of the controversy surrounding his career.

Watson is known for his theory of emotions, which he extrapolated from normal to abnormal behavior. His infamous words exemplify the faith some early researchers—and the public—placed in laboratory-based research on learning and behavior: "Give me a dozen healthy infants . . . and I'll guarantee to take any one at random and train him to become any type of specialist I might select—doctor, lawyer, artist, merchant-chief and, yes, even beggar-man and thief, regardless of his talents, penchants, tendencies, abilities, vocations, and race of his ancestors." (J. B. Watson, 1925, p. 82)

Beyond the work in their lab, the Watson household must have been an interesting place. Consider the following contrasting views and advice on raising children from one of America's first "child experts" and his wife:

John Watson (1925): Never hug and kiss them, never let them sit in your lap. If you must, kiss them once on the forehead when they say goodnight. Shake hands with them in the morning.

Rosalie Rayner Watson (1930): I cannot restrain my affection for the children completely. ... I like being merry and gay and having the giggles. The behaviorists think giggling is a sign of maladjustment, so when the children want to giggle I have to keep a straight face or rush them off to their rooms.

This example and the study of Little Albert illustrate the importance of keeping in perspective any new advances and insights that at first may seem like panaceas for age-old problems. As any soiled veteran of parenting would attest, no child-rearing shortcuts or uniform solutions guide us in dealing with children's problems—raising children is part skill, part wisdom, and part luck. Nonetheless, families, communities, and societal and cultural values play a strong role in determining how successful current child-rearing philosophies are at benefiting children.

Evolving Forms of Treatment

Compared with the times that followed, the period from 1930 to 1950 was a quiet time for research and treatment in abnormal child psychology. A few reports in the 1930s described the behavioral treatment of isolated problems such as bed-wetting (O. H. Mowrer & Mowrer, 1938), stuttering (Dunlap, 1932), and fears (F. B. Holmes, 1936). Other than these reports, psychodynamic approaches were the dominant form of treatment during this period. As a carryover from the 1800s, most children with intellectual or mental disorders were still institutionalized. This practice had come under mounting criticism by the late 1940s, when studies by René Spitz raised serious questions about the harmful impact of institutional life on children's growth and development (R. Spitz, 1945). He discovered that infants raised in institutions without adult physical contact and stimulation developed severe physical and emotional problems. Efforts were undertaken to close institutions and place dependent and difficult children in foster family homes or group homes. Within a 20-year period, from 1945 to 1965, there was a rapid decline in the number of children in institutions, while the number of children in foster family homes and group homes increased.

During the 1950s and early 1960s, behavior therapy emerged as a systematic approach to the treatment of child and family disorders. The therapy was originally based on operant and classical conditioning principles established through laboratory work with animals. In their early form, these laboratory-based techniques to modify undesirable behaviors and shape adaptive

Little Albert, Big Fears, and Sex in Advertising

Most of us are familiar with the story of Little Albert and his fear of white rats and other white furry objects, thanks to the work of John Watson and his graduate assistant (and then wife) Rosalie Rayner. However, understanding the times and background of John Watson helps put these pioneering efforts into a broader historical perspective, and highlights the limited concern for ethics in research that existed in his day.

Watson's fascination with and life dedication to the study of fears may have stemmed from his own acknowledged fear of the dark, which afflicted him throughout his adult life. His career break arrived when he was given an opportunity to create a research laboratory at Johns Hopkins University for the study of child development. Instead of conditioning rats, he could now use humans to test his emerging theories of fear conditioning. However, at that time the only source of human subjects was persons whose rights were considered insignificant or who had less than adequate power to protect themselves, such as orphans, mental patients, and prisoners. Just as he had studied rats in their cages, Watson now studied babies in their cribs.

Clearly, his method of obtaining research subjects and experimenting with them would be considered highly unethical today. To demonstrate how fear might be conditioned in a baby, Watson and Rayner set out to condition fear in an 11-month-old orphan baby they named Albert B., who was given a small white rat to touch, toward which he showed no fear. After this warm-up, every time the infant reached to touch the rat, Watson would strike a steel bar with a hammer. After repeated attempts to touch the rat brought on the same shocking sounds, "the infant jumped violently, fell forward and began to whimper." The process was repeated intermittently, enough times that eventually Albert B. would break down and cry, desperately trying to crawl away, whenever he saw the rat. Watson and Rayner had successfully conditioned the child to fear rats. They then conditioned him to fear rabbits, dogs, fur coats, and—believe it or not—Santa Claus masks (Karier, 1986).

It is disconcerting that Albert B. moved away before any deconditioning was attempted, resulting in decades of speculation as to his identity and the strange set of fears he might have suffered. In 2009 a team of psychologists tracked down Little Albert's identity and fate: he was identified as Douglas

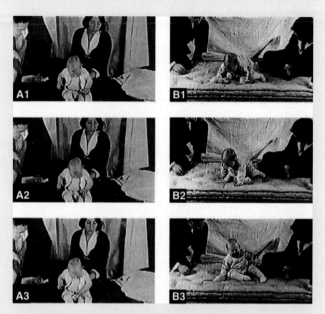

Merritte, whose mother worked at the campus hospital and was paid $1 for her baby's research participation. Sadly, the team discovered that Douglas died at age 6 of acquired hydrocephalus (Beck, Levinson, & Irons, 2009).

It is ironic, moreover, that Watson went on to develop a career in advertising after he was ousted from the university (presumably as a result of concerns over his extramarital relationship with his graduate student; Benjamin et al., 2007). His brand of behaviorism, with its emphasis on the prediction and control of human behavior, met with unqualified success on Madison Avenue. As he explained, "No matter what it is, like the good naturalist you are, you must never lose sight of your experimental animal—the consumer." We can thank John B. Watson for advertising's dramatic shift in the 1930s toward creating images around any given product that exploited whenever possible the sexual desires of both men and women.

Source: Based on Karier, 1986.

---

abilities stood in stark contrast to the dominant psychoanalytic approaches, which stressed resolution of internal conflicts and unconscious motives. Behavior therapy focused initially on children with intellectual disability or severe disturbances. Psychoanalytic practices for these children were perceived as ineffective or inappropriate. Much of this early work took place in institutions or classroom settings that were thought to provide the kind of environmental control needed to change behavior effectively. Since that time, behavior therapy has continued to expand in scope, and has emerged as a prominent form of therapy for a wide range of children's disorders (Ollendick, King, & Chorpita, 2006; Weisz & Kazdin, 2010).

Progressive Legislation

Just how far some countries have advanced in the humane and egalitarian treatment of children and youths is exemplified by the various laws enacted in the past few decades to protect the rights of those with special needs. For example, in the United States the Individuals with Disabilities Education Act (IDEA; Public Law 104–446) mandates:

► free and appropriate public education for any child with special needs in the least restrictive environment for that child;

► each child with special needs, regardless of age, must be assessed with culturally appropriate tests;

► each of these children must have an individualized education program (IEP) tailored to his or her needs, and must be re-assessed.

Similar legislation for protecting the rights of children with disabilities (and ensuring their access to appropriate resources) exists in Canada, the United Kingdom, and many other nations.

In 2007, the United Nations General Assembly adopted a new convention to protect the rights of persons with disabilities around the world. This convention represents an important shift from addressing the "special needs" of children to realizing their rights and removing the physical, linguistic, social, and cultural barriers that remain. Countries that ratify the convention agree to enact laws and other measures to improve disability rights, and also to abolish legislation, customs, and practices that discriminate against persons with disabilities. These efforts signify a paradigm shift in attitudes toward and treatment of people with disabilities—from seeing persons with disabilities as objects of charity to considering them as individuals with human rights. Specific principles addressing the needs of children with disabilities are shown in A Closer Look 1.4.

Section Summary

Historical Views and Breakthroughs

- Early biological explanations for abnormal child behavior favored locating the cause of the problem within the individual, which sometimes led to simplistic or inaccurate beliefs about causes of the behavior.

- Early psychological approaches attempted to integrate basic knowledge of inborn processes with environmental conditions that shape behavior, emotions, and cognitions.

- Greater attention to the problems of children and youths in recent years has improved their quality of life and mental health. This improvement resulted from greater societal recognition of and sensitivity to children's special status and needs since the turn of the twentieth century.

WHAT IS ABNORMAL BEHAVIOR IN CHILDREN AND ADOLESCENTS?

ADAM LANZA

Early Troubles

"You could tell that he felt so uncomfortable about being put on the spot, I think that maybe he wasn't given the right kind of attention or help. I think he went so unnoticed that people didn't even stop to realize that maybe there's actually something else going on here—that maybe he needs to be talking or getting some kind of mental help. In high school, no one really takes the time to look and think, 'Why is he acting this way?' " (Halbfinger, 2012)

"It's easy to understand why Adam Lanza felt at war with reality. Living was torture for the young boy—bright lights, loud sounds, even a touch could cause him to withdraw and become nonverbal. He became obsessed with violence to a degree that was abnormal even in today's desensitized society. Violent pictures. Violent writings. Violent poetry. Hours spent playing violent video games and researching weapons and serial killers on the Internet. Adam Lanza created a world in which he was surrounded by death."

A CLOSER LOOK 1.4

UN Convention on the Rights of Persons with Disabilities (2007)

[Article 7, pertaining to children's rights]:

1. States Parties shall take all necessary measures to ensure the full enjoyment by children with disabilities of all human rights and fundamental freedoms on an equal basis with other children.

2. In all actions concerning children with disabilities, the best interests of the child shall be a primary consideration.

3. States Parties shall ensure that children with disabilities have the right to express their views freely on all matters affecting them, their views being given due weight in accordance with their age and maturity, on an equal basis with other children, and to be provided with disability and age-appropriate assistance to realize that right.

Source: UN Convention on the Rights of Persons with Disabilities (2007). Office of the United Nations High Commissioner for Human Rights.

Lysaik (2013, December 6). Newtown massacre. Inside. Out. *Newsweek.* Available T: http://mag.newsweek.com/2013/12/06/newtown-massacre-inside-out.html

Kateleen Foy/Getty Images

Were there any clues in Adam Lanza's childhood that might suggest his violent behavior later on?

These comments were made by Olivia DeVivo reflecting on her time as a former student at Sandy Hook Elementary School with a boy named Adam Lanza. As she and other classmates noted, Lanza was considered a "loner," an odd character who was very uncomfortable around others and made no effort to connect. Despite living in the same house, he communicated with his mother by e-mail. This example reveals how children's behavior can be difficult to classify into its causes, expression, and contributing factors. It also raises several key questions: First, how do we judge what is normal? A lot of kids are "loners" during adolescence and have difficulty connecting to peers. Second, when does an issue become a problem? In this instance, did anyone sense that Lanza's social isolation might lead to or be due to potentially serious social and mental problems? Finally, why are some children's abnormal patterns of behavior relatively continuous from early childhood through adolescence and into adulthood, whereas other children show more variable (discontinuous) patterns of development and adaptation? Was there anything about Lanza's behavior in childhood that indicated that he would kill innocent children and teachers at Sandy Hook Elementary years later?

Although these questions are central to defining and understanding abnormal child behavior and warrant thoughtful consideration, no simple, straightforward answers exist. (This should be familiar ground to those of you who are psychology majors.) More often than not, childhood disorders are accompanied by various layers of abnormal behavior or development, ranging from the more visible and alarming (such as delinquent acts or physical assault), to the more subtle yet critical (such as teasing and peer rejection), to the more hidden and systemic (such as depression or parental rejection).

Moreover, mental health professionals, while attempting to understand children's weaknesses, too often unintentionally overlook their strengths. Yet, many children cope effectively in other areas of their lives, despite the limitations imposed by specific psychological disorders. An understanding of children's individual strengths and abilities can lead to ways to assist them in healthy adaptation. Also, some children may show less extreme forms of difficulty or only the early signs of an emerging problem rather than a full-blown disorder. Therefore, to judge what is abnormal, we need to be sensitive to each child's stage of development and consider each child's unique methods of coping and ways of compensating for difficulties (Achenbach, 2010).

Childhood disorders, like adult disorders, have commonly been viewed in terms of deviancies from normal, yet disagreement remains as to what constitutes normal and abnormal. While reading the following discussion, keep in mind that attempting to establish boundaries between abnormal and normal functioning is an arbitrary process at best, and current guidelines are constantly being reviewed for their accuracy, completeness, and usefulness.

Defining Psychological Disorders

The study of abnormal behavior often makes us more sensitive to and wary of the ways used to describe the behavior of others. Whose standard of "normal" do we adopt, and who decides whether this arbitrary standard has been breached? Does abnormal behavior or performance in one area, such as mood, have implications for the whole person?

Although there are no easy answers to these questions, Georgina's real-life problems require an agreement on how to define a psychological (or mental) disorder. A **psychological disorder** traditionally has been defined as a pattern of behavioral, cognitive, emotional, or physical symptoms shown by an individual. Such a pattern is associated with one or more of the following three prominent features:

▸ The person shows some degree of distress, such as fear or sadness.

▸ His or her behavior indicates some degree of disability, such as impairment that substantially interferes with or limits activity in one or more important areas of functioning, including physical, emotional, cognitive, and behavioral areas.

▶ Such distress and disability increase the risk of further suffering or harm, such as death, pain, disability, or an important loss of freedom (American Psychiatric Association [APA], 2013).

To account for the fact that we sometimes show transitory signs of distress, disability, or risk under unusual circumstances (such as the loss of a loved one), this definition of a psychological disorder excludes circumstances in which such reactions are expected and appropriate as defined by one's cultural background. Furthermore, these three primary features of psychological disorders only describe what a person does or does not do in certain circumstances. The features do not attempt to attribute causes or reasons for abnormal behavior to the individual alone. On the contrary, understanding particular impairments should be balanced with recognizing individual and situational circumstances.

Labels Describe Behavior, Not People

It is important to keep in mind that terms used to describe abnormal behavior do not describe people; they only describe patterns of behavior that may or may not occur in certain circumstances. We must be careful to avoid the common mistake of identifying the person with the disorder, as reflected in expressions such as "anxious child" or "autistic child." The field of child and adult mental health is often challenged by **stigma**, which refers to a cluster of negative attitudes and beliefs that motivates fear, rejection, avoidance, and discrimination with respect to people with mental illnesses (Heflinger & Hinshaw, 2010). Stigma leads to prejudice and discrimination against others on the basis of race, ethnicity, disabilities, sexual orientation, body size, biological sex, language, and religious beliefs. Because of stigma, persons with mental disorders may also suffer from low self-esteem, isolation, and hopelessness, and they may become so embarrassed or ashamed that they conceal symptoms and fail to seek treatment (Puhl & Latner, 2007). Accordingly, throughout this text we separate the child from the disorder by using language such as "Ramon is a child with an anxiety disorder," rather than "Ramon is an anxious child." Children like Ramon have many other attributes that should not be overshadowed by global descriptive or negative labels.

In addition, the problems shown by some children may be the result of their attempts to adapt to abnormal or unusual circumstances. Children with chronic health problems must adapt to their medical regimens and to negative reactions from peers; children raised in abusive or neglectful environments must learn how to relate to others adaptively and to regulate emotions that may, at times, be overwhelming. Therefore, the primary purpose of using terms such as *disorder* and *abnormal behavior* for describing the psychological

status of children and adolescents is to aid clinicians and researchers in describing, organizing, and expressing the complex features often associated with various patterns of behavior. By no means do the terms imply a common cause, since the causes of abnormal behavior are almost always multifaceted and interactive.

This approach to defining abnormal behavior is similar to the one most often used to classify and diagnose mental disorders, according to the guidelines in the DSM-5 (APA, 2013). We use this approach in guiding the thinking and structure of this book because of its clinical and descriptive utility. Yet, despite advances in defining abnormality and vast improvements in the diagnostic and classification systems, ambiguity remains, especially in defining a particular child's maladaptive dysfunction (Rutter, 2010; Zachar & Kendler, 2007). Boundaries between what constitute normal and abnormal conditions or distinctions among different abnormal conditions are not easily drawn. At present, the DSM-5 approach has achieved some consensus supporting its value in facilitating greater communication and increased standardization of research and clinical knowledge concerning abnormal child psychology. We consider the DSM-5 and current alternatives to classification of childhood disorders in Chapter 4.

Competence

Definitions of abnormal child behavior must take into account the child's **competence**—that is, the ability to successfully adapt in the environment. Developmental competence is reflected in the child's ability to use internal and external resources to achieve a successful adaptation (Masten, 2011). Of course, this prompts the question "What is successful?" Successful adaptation varies across culture and ethnicity, so it is important that the traditions, beliefs, languages, and value systems of a particular culture be taken into account when defining a child's competence. Similarly, some children face greater obstacles than others in their efforts to adapt to their environment. Minority children and families, as well as those with socioeconomic disadvantages, must cope with multiple forms of racism, prejudice, discrimination, oppression, and segregation, all of which significantly influence a child's adaptation and development (Children's Defense Fund, 2007).

Judgments of deviancy also require knowledge of a child's performance relative to that of same-age peers, as well as knowledge of the child's course of development and cultural context. In effect, the study of abnormal child psychology considers not only the degree of maladaptive behavior children show but also the extent to which they achieve normal developmental milestones. As with deviancy, the criteria for defining competence can be very specific and narrow in focus, or they can be as plentiful and as broad as we wish (Masten & Wright, 2010).

How do we know whether a particular child is doing well, and how do we, as parents, teachers, or professionals, guide our expectations? **Developmental tasks**, which include broad domains of competence such as conduct and academic achievement, tell how children typically progress within each domain as they grow. Knowledge of the developmental tasks provides an important backdrop for considering a child or adolescent's developmental progress and impairments. Examples of several important developmental tasks are shown in Table 1.1.

TABLE 1.1 | Examples of Developmental Tasks

Age Period	Task
Infancy to preschool 	• Attachment to caregiver(s) • Language • Differentiation of self from environment
Middle childhood	• Self-control and compliance • School adjustment (attendance, appropriate conduct) • Academic achievement (e.g., learning to read, do arithmetic) • Getting along with peers (acceptance, making friends) • Rule-governed conduct (following rules of society for moral behavior and prosocial conduct)
Adolescence 	• Successful transition to secondary schooling • Academic achievement (learning skills needed for higher education or work) • Involvement in extracurricular activities (e.g., athletics, clubs) • Forming close friendships within and across gender • Forming a cohesive sense of self-identity

Source: From *The Development of Competence in Favorable and Unfavorable Environments: Lessons from Research on Successful Children*, by A. S. Masten and J. D. Coatsworth, 1998, American Psychologist, 53, 205–220. Copyright © 1998 by the American Psychological Association. The APA is not responsible for the accuracy of this translation.

Photo Credits (top to bottom): ©Flashon Studio/Shutterstock.com; ©Gelpi JM/Shutterstock.com; ©OLJ Studio/Shutterstock.com.

Conduct is one of the fundamental domains in Table 1.1; it indicates how well a person follows the rules of a particular society. From a young age, children are expected to begin controlling their behavior and to comply with their parents' requests. (This doesn't mean they always do so. . . .) By the time children enter school, they are expected to follow the rules for classroom conduct and to refrain from harming others. Then, by adolescence, they are expected to follow the rules set by school, home, and society without direct supervision. Similar developmental progression occurs in the self-domain, where children initially learn to differentiate themselves from the environment, and to gradually develop self-identity and autonomy. In the discussion of disorders in the chapters to follow, we attempt whenever possible to balance the information on abnormal behavior with the growing awareness of children's competencies and strengths.

Developmental Pathways

Why don't children with similar early experiences have similar problems later in life? Conversely, why do children and adolescents with the same disorder sometimes have very different early experiences or family characteristics? Another aspect of judging deviancy involves deciding when a concern or issue about a child's behavior starts to become a more recognizable pattern, especially since behavior fluctuates and changes considerably as a child develops. Therefore, in addition to distinguishing between normal and abnormal adaptation, we must consider the temporal relationship between emerging concerns in early childhood and the likelihood that they will lead to problems later on.

A **developmental pathway** refers to the sequence and timing of particular behaviors and possible relationships between behaviors over time. The concept allows us to visualize development as an active, dynamic process that can account for very different beginnings and outcomes (Pickles & Hill, 2006). It helps us to understand the course and nature of normal and abnormal development. Two examples of developmental pathways are shown in ● Figure 1.1. The child in Figure 1.1(a) has experienced maltreatment at a young age. Maltreatment can significantly alter the child's initial course of development, resulting in diverse and often unpredictable outcomes, such as eating, mood, or conduct disorders. This example illustrates **multifinality**, the concept that various outcomes may stem from similar beginnings (in this case, child maltreatment).

A Multifinality

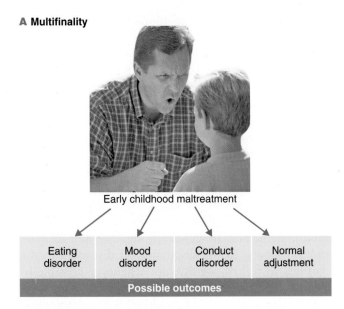

Early childhood maltreatment

Eating disorder	Mood disorder	Conduct disorder	Normal adjustment
Possible outcomes			

B Equifinality

Possible beginnings		
Genetic pattern	Familial characteristics	Environmental features

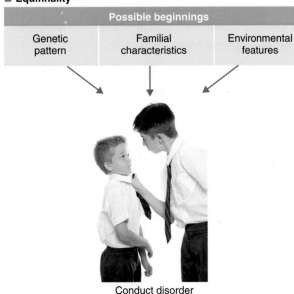

Conduct disorder

● **FIGURE 1.1** | (a) Multifinality: Similar early experiences lead to different outcomes; (b) Equifinality: Different factors lead to a similar outcome.

Photo Credits: (a) SW Productions/Jupiter Images; (b) ©iStockphoto.com/yellowsarah.

In contrast, other children might set out on their developmental journeys with very different strengths and weaknesses, but later have a similar disorder. As illustrated in Figure 1.1(b), genetic patterns, familial characteristics, and features of each child's environment represent different pathways leading to a similar outcome (conduct disorder). This example illustrates **equifinality**, the concept that similar outcomes stem from different early experiences and developmental

pathways. As we will learn in Chapter 9, children with conduct problems may have very diverse early experiences and risk factors but later show similar patterns of behavior. By looking at possible developmental pathways, we gain a better understanding of the ways in which children's problems may change or remain the same over time.

In summary, diversity in how children acquire psychological strengths and weaknesses is a hallmark of abnormal child psychology. Because no clear cause-and-effect relationship exists for each child and adolescent disorder, the following assumptions need to be kept firmly in mind (Hayden & Mash, 2014):

▶ There are many contributors to disordered outcomes in each individual.

▶ Contributors vary among individuals who have the disorder.

▶ Individuals with the same specific disorder express the features of their disturbance in different ways (e.g., some children with a conduct disorder are aggressive, whereas others may be destructive to property or engage in theft or deceit).

▶ The pathways leading to any particular disorder are numerous and interactive, as opposed to unidimensional and static.

Section Summary

What Is Abnormal Behavior in Children and Adolescents?

● Defining a psychological disorder involves agreement about particular patterns of behavioral, cognitive, and physical symptoms shown by an individual.

● Terms used to describe abnormal behavior are meant to define behavior, not to be used as labels to describe individuals.

● Defining abnormal behavior requires judgment concerning the degree to which a person's behavior is maladaptive or harmful as well as dysfunctional or impaired.

● Diversity in how children acquire psychological strengths and weaknesses is a hallmark of abnormal child psychology. The many contributors to abnormal behavior may vary within and between individuals with similar disorders.

● The study of psychological disorders involves attempts to describe the presenting problems and abilities, to understand contributing causes, and to treat or prevent them.

● Developmental pathways help to describe the course and nature of normal and abnormal development; multifinality means that various outcomes may stem from similar beginnings, whereas equifinality means that similar outcomes stem from different early experiences.

RISK AND RESILIENCE

I am convinced that, except in a few extraordinary cases, one form or another of an unhappy childhood is essential to the formation of exceptional gifts.

—Thornton Wilder (1897–1975)

RAOUL AND JESSE

Why the Differences?

Raoul and Jesse were childhood friends who grew up in the same rundown housing project, in a neighborhood plagued by drugs and crime. By the time they were 10 years old they were both familiar with domestic and community violence, and each lived with his mother and an older sibling after his parents divorced. The boys rarely saw their fathers, and when they did it usually wasn't a pleasant experience. By the time they reached grade 6 they were falling behind at school, and started to get into trouble with the police for staying out too late, hassling kids at school, and breaking into cars. Despite these problems and a struggle to keep up, Raoul finished high school and received 2 years of training in a local trade school. He is now 30 years old, works at a local factory, and lives with his wife and two children. Raoul sums up his life thus far as "dodging bullets to reach where I want to go," but he's happy to be living in a safe neighborhood and to have the hope of sending his children to college.

His friend Jesse never graduated from high school. He dropped out after being expelled for bringing a weapon to school, and has been in and out of prison several times. At age 30, Jesse drinks too much and has a poor record of finding and keeping a job. He has had several short-term relationships and fathered two children, but he rarely visits them and never married either mother. Jesse has lived in several locations over the years, mostly in his old, unchanged neighborhood. (Based on Zimmerman & Arunkumar, 1994)

These brief life histories illustrate two very different developmental paths that started out at the same place. Jesse's troubles might have been predicted based on present knowledge of abnormal development, but it is more difficult to explain how some children, like Raoul, seem to escape harm despite stress and adversity. Perhaps you are familiar with someone—from a novel, the entertainment field, or personal friendship—who seems to come out on top despite adversity and limited resources. How do you suppose individuals such as Jay Z (see Box 1.5) escape the odds and achieve their life goals?

The answer to this complicated question is coming into focus, thanks to studies that look at risk as well as protective factors affecting children's courses of

development (Compas & Andreotti, 2013). A **risk factor** is a variable that precedes a negative outcome of interest and increases the chances that the outcome will occur. In contrast, a **protective factor** is a personal or situational variable that reduces the chances for a child to develop a disorder. As you might suspect, children like Raoul and Jesse, who face many known risk factors such as community violence and parental divorce, are vulnerable to abnormal development. Acute, stressful situations as well as chronic adversity put children's successful development at risk. Chronic poverty, serious caregiving deficits, parental mental illness, divorce, homelessness, and racial prejudice are known risk factors that increase children's vulnerability to psychopathology—especially in the absence of compensatory strengths and resources (Evans, Li, & Whipple, 2013; Kim-Cohen & Gold, 2009).

Yet, like Raoul, some vulnerable children do not develop problems later. Instead, they seem resilient despite their stress-filled environments, managing to achieve positive outcomes despite being at significant risk for psychopathology. Children who survive risky environments by using their strong self-confidence, coping skills, and abilities to avoid risk situations may be considered resilient—they seem able to fight off or recover from their misfortune (Luthar, 2006). These children are also most likely to show sustained competence while under stress, or to rebound to a previously healthy level of competence following traumatic or stressful experiences (Kim-Cohen & Gold, 2009). **Resilience** is not a universal, categorical, or fixed attribute of the child; rather, it varies according to the type of stress, its context, and similar factors (Rutter, 2012). Individual children may be resilient with respect to some specific stressors but not others, and resilience may vary over time and across situations. Resilience is seen in children across cultures, despite the extraordinary circumstances that some may face (Kirmayer et al., 2011; Ungar, 2010).

The concept of resilience reminds us that a direct causal pathway rarely leads to a particular outcome. Ongoing interactions exist between protective and risk factors within the child, between the child and his or her surroundings, and among risk factors themselves. Protective factors are personal or situational variables that reduce the chances for a child to develop a disorder. Risk factors do the exact opposite—they increase the child's likelihood of developing a problem. Risk factors and protective factors should be thought of as processes rather than absolutes, since the same event or condition can function as either type of factor, depending on the overall context in which it occurs(Rutter, 2007a). For example, placing young children with another family may serve to protect them if they were being severely mistreated. However, for some children out-of-home placement could increase their vulnerability if it creates more stress due to being removed from their mother or father. Throughout each chapter, we offer similar examples of children's vulnerability and resilience in relation to particular circumstances and disorders.

● Figure 1.2 illustrates some of the better-known characteristics of children and adolescents who display resilience, which are sometimes overlooked in attempts to explain abnormal development. These characteristics constitute a protective triad of resources and health-promoting events: the strengths of the individual, the family, and the school and community (Luthar, 2006). Protective factors vary tremendously in magnitude and scope, and not all three resources are necessary. For some children, merely the availability of a supportive grandparent or teacher can effectively change the course and direction of their development. Other children may need additional or different protective factors, such as a better learning environment, community safety, or sufficient family resources.

Source	Characteristics
Individual	Good intellectual functioning
	Appealing, sociable, easygoing disposition
	Self-efficacy, self-confidence, high self-esteem
	Talents
	Faith
Family	Close relationship to caring parent figure
	Authoritative parenting, warmth, structure, high expectations
	Socioeconomic advantages
	Connections to extended supportive family networks
School and community	Adults outside the family who take an interest in promoting the child's welfare
	Connections to social organizations
	Attendance at effective schools

● **FIGURE 1.2** | Characteristics of children and adolescents who display resilience in face of adversity.

Photo Credits (top to bottom): ©Odua Images/Shutterstock.com; ©Apollofoto/Shutterstock.com; ©iofoto/Shutterstock.com.

Section Summary

Risk and Resilience

- Children's normal development may be put in jeopardy because of risk factors, which can include acute, stressful situations and chronic adversity.

- Some children seem to be more resilient in the face of risk factors. Resiliency is related to strong self-confidence, coping skills, and the ability to avoid risk situations, as well as the ability to fight off or recover from misfortune.

- Children's resilience is connected to a protective triad of resources and health-promoting events that include individual opportunities, close family ties, and opportunities for individual and family support from community resources.

THE SIGNIFICANCE OF MENTAL HEALTH PROBLEMS AMONG CHILDREN AND YOUTHS

It's up to each of us to help create a better world for our children.

—Dr. Benjamin Spock

Until very recently, children's mental health problems were the domain of folklore and unsubstantiated theories in both the popular and scientific literatures. Only a few generations ago, in the mid-nineteenth century, overstimulation in schools was seen as a cause of insanity (Makari, 1993), and only one generation ago, in the mid-twentieth century, autism was believed to be caused by inadequate, uncaring parents (Bettelheim, 1967).

We now recognize that mental health problems of children and adolescents are a frequently occurring and significant societal concern worldwide. For example, by 2020 behavioral health disorders will surpass all physical diseases as a major cause of disability throughout the world (Substance Abuse and Mental Health Services Administration [SAMHSA], 2011; World Health Organization [WHO], 2007). Perhaps most telling of all is the mounting evidence that "*many, if not most, lifetime psychiatric disorders will first appear in childhood or adolescence*" (Costello, Egger, & Angold, 2005a, p. 972, italics added; Kessler et al., 2009).

Surveys conducted in North America and elsewhere find that about one child in eight has a mental health problem that significantly impairs functioning (Costello et al., 2005a), a finding that extends even to infants and toddlers (Skovgaard et al., 2007). Many other children have emerging problems that place them at risk for later development of a psychological disorder. As surprising as it may sound, recent longitudinal studies have found that by their 21st birthday, three out of five young

In the United States, the richest country in the world, nearly one in four children (23.1%) live in poverty, ranking the United States second out of 35 developed countries in terms of child poverty (UNICEF Innocenti Research Centre, 2012).

adults meet criteria for a well-specified psychiatric disorder (Copeland et al., 2011). Some children have difficulties adapting to school or to family circumstances, so they behave in ways that are developmentally or situationally inappropriate. Others show more pronounced patterns of poor development and maladjustment that suggest one or more specific disorders of childhood or adolescence. The process of deciding which problems merit professional attention and which ones might be outgrown involves a good understanding of both normal and abnormal child development and behavior.

Despite the magnitude of children's mental health needs today, the youngest one-fourth of the population (those under age 18) have very few treatment options, and the options that are available are woefully underfunded (Weisz & Kazdin, 2010). Sadly, the majority of children and youths needing mental health services do not receive them, due largely to poor understanding of mental disorders and limited access to intervention (Mark et al., 2008; McEwan, Waddell, & Barker, 2007). The demand for children's mental health services is expected to double over the next decade because the number of child and adolescent mental health professionals is not expected to increase at the required rate (Health Resources and Services Administration, 2010). A career in children's mental health, anyone?

The chapters that follow explain that a significant proportion of children do not grow out of their childhood difficulties, although the ways in which children express difficulties are likely to change in both form and severity over time. Children's developmental impairments may have a lasting negative impact on later family life, occupations, and social adjustment, even when they no longer have the disorder.

The Changing Picture of Children's Mental Health

If all children and adolescents with known psychological disorders could be captured in a photograph, the current picture would be much clearer than that of only a generation ago. The improved focus and detail are the result of efforts to increase recognition and assessment of children's psychological disorders. In the past, children with various mental health and educational needs were too often described in global terms such as *maladjusted*, because assessment devices were not sensitive to different syndromes and diagnostic clusters of symptoms (Achenbach & Rescorla, 2007). Today, we have a better ability to distinguish among the various disorders. This ability has given rise to increased and earlier recognition of previously poorly understood or undetected problems—learning disorders, depression, teen suicide, eating disorders, conduct disorders, and problems stemming from chronic health conditions and from abuse and neglect.

Another difference in today's portrait would be the group's composition. Younger children (Skovgaard et al., 2007) and teens (Wolfe & Mash, 2006) would appear more often in the photo, reflecting greater awareness of their unique mental health issues. Specific communication and learning disorders, for example, have only recently been recognized as significant concerns among preschoolers and young school-age children. Similarly, emotional problems, such as anxiety and depression, which increase dramatically during adolescence (Rudolph, Hammen, & Daley, 2006), were previously overlooked because the symptoms are often less visible or disturbing to others than are the symptoms of behavior or learning problems.

What would not have changed in our photo is the proportion of children who are receiving proper services. Fewer than 10% of children with mental health problems receive proper services to address impairments related to personal, family, or situational factors (Costello et al., 2005a). Limited and fragmented resources mean that children do not receive appropriate mental health services at the appropriate time. Fortunately, this situation is beginning to change, with greater attention paid to evidence-based prevention and treatment programs for many childhood disorders and calls for more integrated services for children within school systems (Kirby & Keon, 2006; Weisz & Kazdin, 2010).

The children and teens in the picture would not reflect a random cross section of all children because mental health problems are unevenly distributed. Those disproportionately afflicted with mental health problems are:

- Children from disadvantaged families and neighborhoods (Brooks-Gunn, Schneider, & Waldfogel, 2013)
- Children from abusive or neglectful families (Cicchetti et al., 2010; Wekerle et al., 2006)
- Children receiving inadequate child care (Pollak et al., 2010)
- Children born with very low birth weight due to maternal smoking, diet, or abuse of alcohol and drugs (D'Onofrio et al., 2010)
- Children born to parents with mental illness or substance abuse problems (Davis et al., 2011; Mellin, 2010)

Also, the children in the picture could not easily be grouped according to these categories because children often face combinations of environmental stressors and psychosocial deprivations. Such children are especially at risk of having their healthy development compromised to the degree that they are said to show abnormal behavior or to suffer from a mental disorder.

WHAT AFFECTS RATES AND EXPRESSION OF MENTAL DISORDERS? A LOOK AT SOME KEY FACTORS

New pressures and social changes may place children at increasing risk for the development of disorders at younger ages (Obradovic et al., 2010). Many stressors today are quite different from those faced by our parents and grandparents. Some have been around for generations: chronic poverty, inequality, family breakup, single parenting, and so on. Others are more recent or are now more visible: homelessness, adjustment problems of children in immigrant families, inadequate child care available to working parents, and conditions associated with the impact of prematurity, parental HIV, and cocaine or alcohol abuse on children's growth and development (Chapman, Dube, & Anda, 2007). Even welcome medical advances can have a negative effect. Higher rates of fetal survival have contributed to a greater number of children with behavior and learning difficulties who require specialized services at a younger age.

Surveys estimate that about 1 child in 8 has a mental health problem that interferes with his or her development, and 1 in 10 has a specific psychological disorder.

©iStockphoto.com/CFutcher

It is important to remember that the manner in which one's circumstances affect the course (e.g., progression) of a disorder should be distinguished from how they may initially contribute to the problem. That is, environmental stressors, such as poverty, child abuse, or lack of safety, may act as nonspecific stressors that bring about poor adaptation or even the onset of a disorder in some vulnerable children. In contrast, these same environmental influences may affect the course of the disorder in other children by affecting the extent to which the child's problems are attenuated or exacerbated (Schreier & Chen, 2013; Williams & Steinberg, 2011). Examples of major factors in the development and expression of child psychopathology are noted next, and they resurface throughout our subsequent discussions of each disorder.

Poverty and Socioeconomic Disadvantage

The most dangerous place for a child to try to grow up in America is at the intersection of race and poverty.

—Children's Defense Fund (2007)

If you looked beyond the faces of the children in our hypothetical photo, you would note that in many cases, the background and circumstances of children and youths with mental health problems provide obvious clues to their origins. Some of the most telling clues are the experiences of poverty, disadvantage, and violence faced by many, which can have a cumulative effect on mental health.

Childhood poverty is a daily reality for about 1 in 4 children in the United States (U.S. Census Bureau, 2011a) and 1 in 7 in Canada (Statistics Canada, 2011); it is especially pronounced among Native American/First Nations and African American children (Spicer & Sarche, 2006). Growing up with poverty has a substantial effect on the well-being of children and adolescents, especially in terms of impairments in learning ability and school achievement. Moreover, low income is tied to many other forms of disadvantage: less education, low-paying jobs, inadequate health care, single-parent status, limited resources, poor nutrition, and greater exposure to violence. Any one disadvantage can impair children's developmental progress significantly (Razza, Martin, & Brooks-Gunn, 2010).

The impact of childhood poverty is telling. Children from poor and disadvantaged families suffer more conduct disorders, chronic illness, school problems, emotional disorders, and cognitive/learning problems than children who are not poor (McMahon & Luthar, 2007). These impairments may be due to the pronounced effect on prefrontal cortex development stemming from the social inequalities of chronic poverty (Kishiyama et al., 2009; Luby et al., 2013). Economic

Eighty-eight percent of homeless families in the United States are headed by women.

deprivation alone is not responsible for these higher rates because many children do succeed under harsh circumstances. Nevertheless, the greater the degree of inequality, powerlessness, and lack of control over their lives, the more children's physical and mental health are undermined (Aber, Jones, & Raver, 2007).

Poverty has a significant, yet indirect, effect on children's adjustment, most likely because of its association with negative influences—particularly harsh, inconsistent parenting and elevated exposure to acute and chronic stressors—that define the day-to-day experiences of children in poverty. For example, youths who live in inner-city areas and witness community violence are most likely to develop post-traumatic stress disorder (Kiser, 2007) as well as cognitive delays and impairments that affect both learning and mental health (Farah et al., 2006).

Sex Differences

We have known for some time that boys and girls express their problems in different ways (Zahn-Waxler et al., 2006). For example, hyperactivity, autism, childhood disruptive behavior disorders, and learning and communication disorders are more common in boys than in girls; the opposite is true for most anxiety disorders, adolescent depression, and eating disorders. What we don't understand is whether these differences are caused by definitions, reporting biases (the more "disturbing" problems are most likely to come to the attention of mental health agencies), or differences in the expression of the disorder (Martel, 2013). For example, aggressive behavior may be expressed more directly by boys (fighting) and more indirectly by girls (spreading rumors). Although mental health problems for girls have been understudied, this situation is changing; therefore, we consider the expression of problems for boys and girls in each chapter.

Sex differences in problem behaviors are negligible in children under the age of 3 but increase with age (Achenbach & Rescorla, 2006). Boys show higher rates of early-onset disorders that involve some form of neurodevelopmental impairment, and girls show more emotional disorders, with a peak age of onset in adolescence. For example, boys generally have higher rates of reading disorders, autism spectrum disorders, attention-deficit/hyperactivity disorder (ADHD), and early-onset persistent conduct problems, whereas girls have higher rates of depression and eating disorders (Copeland et al., 2011; Rutter et al., 2004).

● Figure 1.3 depicts the normal developmental trajectories for girls and boys across the two major dimensions of internalizing and externalizing behaviors.

Internalizing problems include anxiety, depression, somatic symptoms, and withdrawn behavior; **externalizing problems** encompass more acting-out behaviors, such as aggression and delinquent behavior. You'll notice from Figure 1.3(A) that externalizing problems for boys start out higher than for girls in preschool and early elementary years, and that these problems decrease gradually for both boys and girls until the rates almost converge by age 18. The opposite pattern emerges for internalizing problems. Parents report similar rates of internalizing problems for boys and girls in early childhood, but girls outpace boys in these problems over time (Bongers et al., 2003). These developmental trajectories of problem behaviors provide a useful basis for identifying deviations from the normal course, although these overall trends need to be considered in relation to a number of additional factors that we discuss throughout the text.

Finally, it is interesting to note that the types of child-rearing environments predicting resilience in the face of adversity also differ for boys and girls. Resilience in boys is associated with households in which there is a male role model (such as a father, grandfather, or older brother); structure; rules; and some encouragement of emotional expressiveness. In contrast, girls who display resilience come from households that combine risk taking and independence with support from a female caregiver (such as a mother, grandmother, or older sister; Werner, 2005).

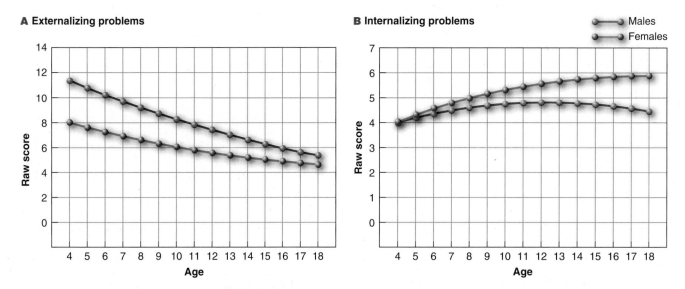

● **FIGURE 1.3** | Normative developmental trajectories of externalizing problems (A) and internalizing problems (B) from the child behavior checklist. Ages are shown on the *x* axis. The *y* axis shows the raw scores (higher score means more problems).

Adapted from "The normative development of child and adolescent problem behavior," by Bongers, I. L., Koot, H. M., van der Ende, J., & Verhulst, F. C., 2003, *Journal of Abnormal Psychology*, 112, 179–192. Copyright © 2003 by the American Psychological Association. Reprinted with permission. The APA is not responsible for the accuracy of this translation.

Race and Ethnicity

Physical variations in the human species have no meaning except the social ones that humans put on them.

—American Anthropological Association, 1998

People who are from racial or ethnic minority groups comprise a substantial and vibrant segment of many countries, enriching each society with many unique strengths, cultural traditions, and important contributions. In the United States, the number of people who are ethnic minorities is growing rapidly—by 2050, the nation's population of children is expected to be 62% minority, up from 44% today (U.S. Census Bureau, 2011b).

As reflected in the quote above, the majority of cultural anthropologists today believe that race is a socially constructed concept, not a biological one (Crisp & Turner, 2011; Sternberg, Grigorenko, & Kidd, 2005). This helps explain why very few emotional and behavioral disorders of childhood occur at different rates for different racial groups. Children from certain ethnic and racial groups in the United States are overrepresented in rates of some disorders, such as substance abuse, delinquency, and teen suicide (Nguyen et al., 2007). However, once the effects of socioeconomic status (SES), sex, age, and referral status are controlled for (i.e., the unique contributions of these factors are removed or accounted for), few differences in the rate of children's psychological disorders emerge in relation to race or ethnicity (Roberts, Roberts, & Xing, 2006). Some minority groups, in fact, show less psychopathology after controlling for SES (Nguyen et al., 2007; Roberts et al., 2006).

Even though rates of problems are similar, significant barriers remain in access to, and quality and outcomes of, care for minority children (Alegria, Vallas, & Pumariega, 2010). As a result, American Indians, Alaska Natives, African Americans, Asian Americans, Pacific Islanders, and Hispanic Americans bear a disproportionately high burden of disability from mental disorders (Agency for Healthcare Research and Quality, 2011). Specifically, the majority culture has neglected to incorporate respect for or understanding of the histories, traditions, beliefs, languages, and value systems of culturally diverse groups. Misunderstanding and misinterpreting behaviors have led to tragic consequences, including inappropriately placing minorities in the criminal and juvenile justice systems (Pumariega, Rothe, Song, & Lu, 2010).

Minority children and youths face multiple disadvantages, such as poverty and exclusion from society's benefits. This exclusion is often referred to as marginalization, and it can result in a sense of alienation, loss of social cohesion, and rejection of the norms of the larger society. Resisting the combined effects of poverty and marginalization takes unusual personal strength and family support. Since children from ethnic and racial minority groups are overrepresented in low-SES groups, we must interpret with caution the relationships among SES, ethnicity, and behavior problems that often emerge while discussing childhood disorders. We also have to keep in mind that, despite the growing ethnic diversity of the North American population, ethnic representation in research studies and the study of ethnicity-related issues receive relatively little attention in studies of child psychopathology and treatment (Coll, Akerman, & Cicchetti, 2000; Schwartz et al., 2010).

As was the case for SES and sex differences, global comparisons of the prevalence of different types of problems for different ethnic groups are not likely to be very revealing. On the other hand, investigations into the processes affecting the form, associated factors, and outcomes of different disorders for various ethnic groups hold promise for increasing our understanding of the relationship between ethnicity and abnormal child behavior.

Cultural Issues

The values, beliefs, and practices that characterize a particular ethnocultural group contribute to the development and expression of children's disorders, and affect how people and institutions react to a child's problem (Rescorla et al., 2011). Because the meaning of children's social behavior is influenced by cultural beliefs and values, it is not surprising that children express their problems somewhat differently across cultures. For example, shyness and oversensitivity in children have been found to be associated with peer rejection and social maladjustment in Western cultures, but to be associated with leadership, school competence, and academic achievement in Chinese children in Shanghai (Chen, Rubin, & Li, 1995; Rubin et al., 2006).

Because of cultural influences, it is important that research on abnormal child behavior not be generalized from one culture to another unless there is support for doing so. Some underlying processes, such as regulating emotion and its relationship to social competence, may be similar across diverse cultures (Eisenberg, Smith, & Spinrad, 2011). Similarly, some disorders, particularly those with a strong neurobiological basis (e.g., ADHD, autism spectrum disorder), may be less susceptible to cultural influences. Nonetheless, social and cultural beliefs and values are likely to influence the meaning given to these behaviors, the ways in which they are responded to, their forms of expression, and their outcomes (APA, 2013). Few studies have compared the attitudes, behaviors, and biological and psychological processes of children with mental disorders across different cultures. However, in this text, we will indicate where this situation is beginning to change.

Child Maltreatment and Non-Accidental Trauma

Children and adolescents are being neglected and abused at an alarming rate worldwide (WHO, 2010). Each year nearly 1 million verified cases of child abuse and neglect (a rate of 10 per 1,000 children) occur in the United States (U.S. Department of Health and Human Services, 2010), and more than 80,000 in Canada (Public Health Agency of Canada, 2010). U.S. phone surveys of children and youths between 10 and 16 years old estimate that more than one-third of U.S. children (6 million) in that age bracket experience physical and/or sexual assaults during these ages, not only by family members but also by persons they may know from their communities and schools (Finkelhor, 2011).

These related forms of non-accidental trauma—being the victim of violence at school or being exposed to violent acts in their homes or neighborhoods—lead to significant mental health problems in children and youths.

In a telephone survey of more than 4,000 youths between 12 and 17 years of age, 16% of boys and 19% of girls met the criteria for either post-traumatic stress disorder, major depressive episode, or substance abuse/dependence in relation to acts of violence (Kilpatrick et al., 2003). Tragically, these acts of abuse and trauma are estimated to cost $124 billion per year in the United States as a result of direct and indirect harm over the lifetime of these children (Fang, Brown, Florence, & Mercy, 2012). Because of the increasing significance of these acts, more attention is being given to developing ways to prevent maltreatment, and help youngsters exposed to maltreatment and trauma. We devote discussion to this concern in Chapter 12: Trauma- and Stressor-Related Disorders.

Special Issues Concerning Adolescents and Sexual Minority Youths

Early to mid-adolescence is a particularly important transitional period for healthy versus problematic adjustment (Cicchetti & Rogosch, 2002; Wolfe & Mash, 2006). Substance use, risky sexual behavior, violence, accidental injuries, and mental health problems are only a few of the major issues that make adolescence a particularly vulnerable period. Disturbingly, mortality rates more than triple between late childhood and early adulthood, primarily as the result of risk-taking behaviors (Centers for Disease Control and Prevention, 2010).

Late childhood and early adolescence is also a time during which youths who are lesbian, gay, bisexual, and transgendered (LGBT) face multiple challenges that can affect their health and well-being. Growing up in a society that is predominantly heterosexual—and largely biased against other sexual identities—makes adolescence a particularly difficult time for those who are not heterosexual. According to several large surveys of LGBT youths in middle and high schools, they are more likely to be victimized by their peers as well as by family members, and they report more bullying, teasing, harassment, and physical assault than other students (Kosciw, Greytak, & Diaz, 2009). For example, 81% report experiencing verbal abuse related to being LGBT, 38% have been threatened with physical attacks, 22% have had objects thrown at them, 15% have been physically assaulted, and 16% have been sexually assaulted (D'Augelli, 2006). Given the stigma and prejudice that exist in many parts of society, it is not surprising that young people who are LGBT have higher rates of mental health problems, including depression and suicidal behavior, substance abuse, and risky sexual behavior, as compared with their heterosexual counterparts (Coker, Austin, & Schuster, 2010).

In response to mounting concerns, the special needs and problems of adolescents are receiving greater attention, especially because serious consequences are preventable. For example, various health organizations and government agencies implemented campaigns in schools, community programs, and healthcare settings to reduce adolescent risk taking and experimentation (Beardslee, Chien, & Bell, 2011). Because the problems of adolescents have been neglected as compared with those of children, throughout this text we will look at the expression of each disorder in both childhood and adolescence as much as possible.

Lifespan Implications

Over the long term, the impact of children's mental health problems is most severe when the problems continue untreated for months or years. The developmental tasks of childhood are challenging enough without the added burden of emotional or behavioral disturbances that interfere with the progress and course of development. About 20% of the children with the most chronic and serious disorders face sizable difficulties throughout their lives (Costello & Angold, 2006). They are least likely to finish school and most likely to have social problems or psychiatric disorders that affect many aspects of their lives throughout adulthood.

The lifelong consequences associated with child psychopathology are exceedingly costly in terms of economic impact and human suffering. The costs are enormous with respect to demands on community resources such as health, education, mental health, and criminal justice systems; loss in productivity; the need for repeated and long-term interventions; and the human suffering of both the afflicted children and the family and community members they encounter. Fortunately, children and youths can overcome major impediments when circumstances and opportunities promote healthy adaptation and competence.

The growing recognition of the concerns presented in this chapter has led to a number of major initiatives to achieve the goals of prevention and help. These initiatives are summarized in a number of government reports that include recommendations as to how these goals can be achieved. Many of these important reports are available on the Internet (see A Closer Look 1.6), and we recommend that you familiarize yourself with these developments.

Section Summary

What Affects the Rates and Expression of Mental Disorders? A Look at Some Key Factors

- Clear understanding of both normal and abnormal child development and behavior is needed to decide which problems are likely to continue and which might be outgrown.
- About one child in eight has a mental health problem that significantly impairs functioning.
- A significant proportion of children do not grow out of their childhood difficulties, although the ways in which these difficulties are expressed are likely to change in both form and severity over time.
- Mental health problems are unevenly distributed. Children who experience more social and economic disadvantage or inequality and children exposed to more violent, inadequate, or toxic environments are disproportionately afflicted with mental health problems.
- A child's biological sex, ethnic background, and cultural surroundings are all important contributors to the manner in which his or her behavioral and emotional problems are expressed to and recognized by others.
- Many childhood problems can have lifelong consequences for the child and for society.

A CLOSER LOOK 1.6

Current Reports on Mental Health Issues Pertaining to Children and Youths

Since release of the U.S. Surgeon General's Report on Mental Health in 1999, there have been many important national and international initiatives and reports about understanding and helping children and adolescents with mental health problems. The wonders of the information age provide free access to this wealth of information (as if reading your textbook were not enough!). Below is a list of some (but by no means all) of the more important documents that are shaping the field. Your Psychology CourseMate provides live links to most of these documents.

Mental Health

U.S. Public Health Service Office of the Surgeon General. (1999). *Mental health: A report of the Surgeon General.* Rockville, MD: Department of Health and Human Services, U.S. Public Health Service.

Development and Psychopathology

Institute of Medicine. (2000). *From neurons to neighborhoods: The science of early childhood development.* Washington, DC: National Academies Press.

Children's Rights

UNICEF (2013): Convention on the Rights of the Child. Protecting and realizing children's rights. Available at: http://www.unicef.org/crc/index_protecting.html.

Culture, Race, and Ethnicity

U.S. Public Health Service Office of the Surgeon General. (2001). *Mental health: Culture, race, and ethnicity: A supplement to Mental health: A report of the Surgeon General.* Rockville, MD: Department of Health and Human Services, U.S. Public Health Service.

Children's Mental Health

Report of *Healthy Development: A Summit on Young Children's Mental Health* (2009). Partnering with communication scientists, collaborating across disciplines, and leveraging impact to promote children's mental health. Washington, DC: Society for Research in Child Development. Available at: www.apa.org/pi/families/summit-report.pdf

(continues)

(continued)

Research on Children's Mental Health
Children's Health Policy Centre: *Children's Mental Health Research Quarterly*. Available at: http://childhealthpolicy.ca/the-quarterly

Mental Health: International Perspective
World Health Organization. (2007). *The world health report 2007.* Geneva: World Health Organization.

Transforming Mental Health Care
Transforming mental health care in America. Rockville, MD: Substance Abuse and Mental Health Services Administration (SAMHSA). Available at: http://www.samhsa.gov/federalactionagenda/NFC_TOC.aspx.

   Out of the Shadows At Last: Transforming Mental Health, Mental Illness and Addiction Services in Canada. The Standing Senate Committee on Social Affairs, Science and Technology. Available at: http://www.parl.gc.ca/Content/SEN/Committee/391/soci/rep/rep02may06-e.htm

Substance Abuse
Substance Abuse and Mental Health Services Administration. (2011). *Results from the 2010 National Survey on Drug Use and Health: Summary of National Findings* (NSDUH Series H-41, HHS Publication No. (SMA) 11-4658. Rockville, MD. Available at: http://oas.samhsa.gov/nsduhlatest.htm

Suicide Prevention
U.S. Department of Health and Human Services. *Suicide Prevention: Resources and Publications.* Substance Abuse and Mental Health Services Administration. Available at: http://www.samhsa.gov/prevention/suicide.aspx

National Strategy for Suicide Prevention: Goals and Objectives for Action. A Report of the U.S. Surgeon General and of the National Action Alliance for Suicide Prevention (2012). Available at: http://www.surgeongeneral.gov/library/reports/national-strategy-suicide-prevention/index.html

Youth Violence
U.S. Public Health Service Office of the Surgeon General. (2001). *Youth violence: A report of the Surgeon General.* Rockville, MD: Department of Health and Human Services, U.S. Public Health Service.

   Centers for Disease Control and Prevention. *Injury Prevention and Control: Youth Violence.* Available at: http://www.cdc.gov/ViolencePrevention/youthviolence/index.html

Reducing Health Risks
World Health Organization. (2012, September). *What are the key health dangers for children?* Available at: http://www.who.int/features/qa/13/en/index.html

Violence and Health
World Health Organization. (2002). *World report on violence and health.* Geneva: World Health Organization. Also see: *WHO Violence and Injury Prevention.* Available at: http://www.who.int/violence_injury_prevention/violence/en

Sexual Minority Youths
Centers for Disease Control and Prevention. (2011, June). *MMWR: Sexual Identity, Sex of Sexual Contacts, and Health-Risk Behaviors Among Students in Grades 9–12—Youth Risk Behavior Surveillance, Selected Sites, United States, 2001–2009.* Available at: http://www.cdc.gov/healthyyouth/disparities/smy.htm

LOOKING AHEAD

The significance of children's mental health problems emerges over and over again throughout this text, as we consider the many different individual, family, social, and cultural influences that define abnormal child psychology. Because children cannot advocate on their own behalf, and because their mental health needs and developmental issues differ markedly from those of adults, it is important that we keep these concerns in mind. Moreover, children's problems don't come in neat packages. Many disorders discussed in the text overlap with other disorders in terms of symptoms, characteristics, and treatment needs. Once again, the importance of viewing the whole child in relation to his or her difficulties emerges as the best strategy in understanding abnormal child and adolescent psychology,

using diagnostic criteria as guideposts rather than as firm rules.

The next three chapters discuss theories, causes, research, and clinical issues. Chapter 2 looks at current ways of viewing child and adolescent disorders. It includes the exciting advances made possible by new discoveries about the brain, and notes how these discoveries have become more integrated with knowledge of the biological and psychological processes affecting children's development and disorders. Chapter 3 reviews research methods with children, youths, and families that help us understand features, causes, course, and treatment methods. Chapter 4 discusses clinical issues pertaining to children's mental health, especially current approaches to assessment, diagnosis, and treatment. Because psychological interventions vary considerably in relation to each disorder, we will describe the most recent and effective treatments for specific disorders in the context of the disorders to which they apply. This allows information on treatments and their effectiveness to be woven into our knowledge about the description and causes of the disorder.

Chapters 5 through 14 examine specific disorders and conditions affecting children and adolescents. We organize these disorders and conditions into three general categories:

▶ *Neurodevelopmental disorders.* Chapters 5 through 8 examine a broad range of disorders that appear early in development and lead to a range of impairments in personal, social, and academic functioning. These developmental deficits are often chronic and affect children's ability to learn or perform normally, including intellectual disability, autism spectrum disorder, communication and learning disorders, and attention-deficit/hyperactivity disorder (ADHD).

▶ *Behavioral and emotional disorders.* Chapters 9 through 12 cover behavioral and emotional conditions that typically emerge in mid-childhood to late childhood and adolescence. These include disruptive and conduct disorders (sometimes referred to as externalizing problems because they involve conflicts with the environment), mood and anxiety disorders (sometimes referred to as "internalizing problems" because they involve conflicts within the child that are less visible to others), and trauma- and stressor-related disorders. We also discuss child maltreatment in the chapter on trauma- and stressor-related disorders because of the significance of abuse and other forms of non-accidental trauma on children's developmental progress and course.

▶ *Problems related to physical and mental health.* Chapters 13 and 14 discuss child and adolescent disorders stemming from medical or physical conditions that may affect children's overall psychological functioning, and vice versa, such as chronic illness, substance abuse, and eating disorders and related conditions.

Far greater attention has been devoted to the description and classification of abnormality in children than to healthy child functioning and how children adapt to the challenges of growing up. In light of this imbalance, throughout this text we introduce each disorder with a discussion of normal developmental processes, such as children's normal intellectual development (in relation to intellectual disability) and the normal range of misbehavior and acting out (in reference to conduct problems). We also consider children's strengths and adaptive abilities, regardless of the presence of a particular disorder, and factors that are believed to encourage healthy adaptation regardless of other impairments. We then present the core features of each disorder (such as hyperactivity–impulsivity, sad mood, or antisocial behavior), followed by significant associated features (such as problems in self-esteem, peer relations, or substance abuse).

As you begin your journey into the field of abnormal child psychology, keep in mind that the threats facing children today—child poverty, chronic illness, maltreatment, and indifference—are no less significant than those of the past, although they sometimes fail to arouse the indignation of society to the extent that major changes are implemented and maintained. Even countries that have outlawed child labor, child abuse, and many other forms of actual and potential harm have only recently begun to recognize the profound importance of the quality of the early childhood environment for children's health, well-being, and competence. Fortunately, it is unlikely that children and youths will ever again be seen as insignificant, costly burdens on society. As each chapter in this text indicates, efforts aimed at change in policies and programs directed toward children and youths are gaining momentum.

Study Resources

SECTION SUMMARIES

KEY TERMS

2

Theories and Causes

Everything should be made as simple as possible, but not simpler.

—Albert Einstein

CHAPTER PREVIEW

AT THE RISK OF sounding vague, we must acknowledge that nearly all child and family disturbances result from multiple, interacting risk factors and processes. Contextual events in the family or school environment exert considerable influence over an individual's course of development (see the Chapter 1 discussion of risk and resilience). Therefore, a given child's problems must be considered in relation to multiple levels of influence—individual, family, community, and culture—rather than be attributed to any one factor. Since the causes of psychological disorders are significant, in this chapter we describe the primary biological and psychological influences.

In this chapter, we consider theories and research findings regarding influences that shape the child's ongoing development in many different ways. Some influences (such as biological factors and the effects of environmental factors) are contained within the child, whereas many others (such as family patterns and cultural norms) lie at various distances from the child's immediate surroundings. We will see how examining these various causal influences contribute to a better understanding of abnormal child development and how they are conceptually related to one another.

Let's begin by considering Jorge's situation and his parents' complaints, which raise important issues. Could Jorge have mild intellectual disability that impairs his learning? Is Jorge's mother right about his having a learning disability? Does Jorge have a specific communication or learning problem unrelated to intellectual disability that affects his schoolwork? Perhaps his school and family environments have contributed to his learning difficulties and fear of school. Did his parents and teachers expect him to fail? Has he been given much assistance? Has he been abused or neglected at home?

WHAT IS CAUSING JORGE'S PROBLEMS?

Suppose you were asked to interview Jorge, his teachers, and his parents to find out why schoolwork is difficult for him. How would you go about this task? What information do you feel would be essential to know, and what plan might you follow to organize and explore the many possible reasons for his problem? Most likely, you would form a working theory to help you in determining what to ask and why. At first, your theory might be very basic and unrefined. Jorge's problem in school might be connected to the negative comments and pressure he is getting from his parents and teacher. As you proceed, your theory about Jorge's problem would likely expand and become more detailed, allowing you to probe with more precise questions.

Let's briefly consider possible interrelated causes of Jorge's behavior:

1. *Biological influences.* Because we know little about Jorge's early development, we might ask his mother about her prenatal history, including major illnesses, injuries, or perhaps marital problems or undue stresses that might have affected her pregnancy. Jorge's problems also reflect a tendency toward behavioral inhibition; he may approach new or challenging situations with greater apprehension and fear than other children (Gleason et al., 2011).

Children with fears and anxiety—which are affected by levels of stress hormones circulating in the body—are more likely to have parents who had similar problems during childhood (Micco et al., 2009). Jorge may have inherited a tendency to respond to his environment with heightened arousal or sensitivity. Alternatively, his early neurological development and the patterns of connections established within his brain may have been influenced by the child-rearing styles his parents used when he was an infant. These early patterns, in turn, can influence how Jorge approaches new tasks, reacts to criticism, or relates to others (Belsky & de Haan, 2011). Another possibility is that Jorge may have inherited one or more genes that influence his phonological awareness. He may not be able to recognize and process all the English language phonemes (individual sounds) and thus suffers from a reading disorder (Scerri & Schulte-Körne, 2010).

2. *Emotional influences.* Children like Jorge not only think and behave in ways that provide clues to their distress, but also show various emotional signals that are not obvious at first. Emotional expression offers another unique window for viewing Jorge's inner world, especially his emotional reactions to challenges such as reading. Consider this possibility: As Jorge approaches his reading assignment or thinks about returning to school the next morning, he is overwhelmed by fear, bordering on panic. His heart races, his breathing quickens, and his thoughts turn to ways to escape from this dreaded situation as quickly as possible. As he is preoccupied by such feelings and worry, his concentration declines further.

Jorge's inability to regulate feelings of arousal, distress, or agitation that may surface without warning is a key element in describing his problem, but we still have not determined how it might have originated. Emotional reactivity and expression are the ways infants and young children first communicate with the world around them, and their ability to regulate these emotions as they adapt is a critical aspect of their early relationships with caregivers (Eisenberg, Smith, & Spinrad, 2011). Emotions can be powerful events,

JORGE

Not Keeping Up

Jorge was almost 14 years old when he was referred to me because of his academic problems. Since grade 4 he had been performing well below average in his classes, had difficulty concentrating, and was considered to be "too quiet and nervous." For the past four summers he had taken extra classes to improve his reading, but was currently reading at the third-grade level. As a result, his parents received a letter from the school saying he likely would not be promoted to the next grade if his work didn't improve. Everyone seemed angry at Jorge for not keeping up.

When I met with Jorge, his version of his school problems was short and to the point: "It's the teachers," he said, as he looked at the floor and squirmed in his seat. "How am I expected to learn anything when they yell at you? When I told my English teacher that I hadn't finished reading my book for class, he said I take too long 'cuz my mind wanders too much. How am I expected to learn when they think I'm dumb?" After further discussion, Jorge summed up his view of the problem in a quiet, sullen voice: "I know I'll never get anywhere with the brain I've got. I can't figure stuff out very fast, and the teachers aren't much help. Just thinking about school makes me jittery. I'm afraid I'll say something stupid in class and everyone will laugh at me."

Jorge's mother and father met with me separately and were quick to add their own opinions about why their son didn't do well in school. They had moved from their Spanish-speaking neighborhood when Jorge was in grade 2, and he struggled to learn English in school because his parents did not speak it at home. His mother admitted that she becomes aggravated and starts to yell when Jorge says he doesn't want to go to school or can't do his schoolwork,

Everyone seemed to be angry with Jorge

but she didn't think this was an issue. She quickly added, "I've read about learning disabilities and I think he's got one. He can't control his mind enough to center on anything. He's scared to go to school, and avoids homework as if his life depended on it." By the end of the interview it was evident that Jorge's parents were angry at him. They felt Jorge blamed his teachers for his own lack of effort, and that he should be in a special classroom and maybe given medications to calm him down so he wouldn't worry so much about school. (Based on authors' case material)

---

demanding that the child find ways to reduce or regulate their force. The most adaptive way is to seek comfort from a caregiver, which gradually helps the child learn ways to self-regulate. By extension, Jorge's school refusal or phobia could have emerged at a younger age from anxiety about his mother's availability, which grew to a more pronounced and generalized insecurity (Bernstein & Victor, 2010).

3. *Behavioral and cognitive influences.* Jorge has been performing below average in reading for some time. Using our knowledge of learning principles, we might investigate Jorge's current situation from the perspective of events that elicit fear or avoidance, and events that maintain such avoidance by reducing unpleasant reactions. Jorge's lack of progress may be a function of punitive events when he is criticized by his parents or singled out by his teacher.

A behavioral approach to Jorge's problem might be to try to change aspects of his environment—such as the attention he receives from his teacher or parents for his gradual, slow efforts to do his schoolwork—to see what effect this approach has on his school performance and avoidance. We might also consider the teasing or rejection by peers in his school environment that may make him fearful. By observing Jorge at school and narrowing the list of possible events that may contribute to his fears, we can begin to develop hypotheses about Jorge's learning history and, most importantly, possible ways to remedy the problem. One possibility might be to increase the likelihood of reinforcement that is contingent on Jorge's efforts to complete his schoolwork (Little, Akin-Little, & Newman-Eig, 2010).

Cognitive influences, such as a person's interpretation of events, are also important to consider. How does Jorge view the situation, and does his view accurately reflect the situation? Children with fears and worries sometimes develop a belief system that can be self-defeating, leading them to believe that they will fail at everything (Beidel & Turner, 2007). Jorge has failed in reading and other events at school, and it is plausible that he anticipates further struggles with schoolwork and with other children. His own words are quite clear in this respect: "How am I expected to learn when they think I'm dumb?" "I know I'll never get anywhere with the brain I've got." "Just thinking about school makes me jittery." Such thoughts only tend to make him more anxious and more likely to avoid school as much as possible. In short, Jorge expects to fail and be ridiculed at school, issues that certainly warrant attention. Children's self-expressions and other cognitions offer a window on their inner world, which may provide clues that we miss when observing their actions.

4. *Family, cultural, and ethnic influences.* An understanding of the possible causes of Jorge's difficulties would be incomplete without considering his family and peer relationships, his social setting, and his larger cultural and ethnic identity (Marks, Patton, & Coll, 2011). His early relationship with his parents may have contributed to a lessened ability to regulate his emotions adaptively; his current relationships with his teachers, peers, and family members offer further clues. At the family level, how sensitive are his parents to recognizing his special limitations, and how willing are they to teach him alternative strategies? His mother has high hopes and expectations for her child, as well as a life and problems of her own (including a job). Even though she wants only what's best for Jorge, and her behavior is understandable, her lack of sensitivity may still be a problem. Her pointed statement, "I've read about learning disabilities and I think he's got one," suggests that she dismisses the problem by labeling it as "his" problem. Neither parent appears to be open to considering other possible explanations. Furthermore, his mother admits to becoming exasperated and yelling at Jorge. What effect might this have on his tenuous self-concept and his attempts to regulate his fear and arousal?

All children, not only those with problems, require a parenting style that is sensitive to their unique needs and abilities and that places appropriate limits on them to help them develop self-control (Morris et al., 2011). Significant adults both within Jorge's family and at school have not been responding to him with sensitivity, so it's not surprising that Jorge's behavior has grown worse over time.

Along these same lines, it is important to consider how Jorge's behavior might be affected by culturally

specific norms and standards. That is, his family's expectations for how he should behave at school and at home may be at odds with those of his non-Hispanic peers (Trommsdorff & Cole, 2011). Children from cultural minority groups face challenges in adapting to their receiving culture—a process known as "acculturation"—and Jorge may be caught between the two. Over time, he may learn to balance these opposing demands and expectations, especially if he lives in a bicultural environment. There is growing evidence that biculturalism, in which the child or adolescent strives to adapt to both their heritage and their receiving cultures, is the most adaptive approach to acculturation (Schwartz et al., 2013).

Finally, for proper development, children require a basic quality of life that includes a safe community, good schools, proper health and nutrition, access to friends their own age, and opportunities to develop close relationships with extended family and members of their community. These opportunities and necessities are in the background of every child's developmental profile and can emerge as very significant issues for children undergoing parental divorce or living in poverty (Fabricius & Luecken, 2007; Rutter, 2003a).

Several important factors that need to be considered in addressing Jorge's problems are shown in ● Figure 2.1. There are many "strikes against Jorge" that need to be considered; clinicians and researchers often attempt to visualize the multiple causes to allow assessment and intervention to address them properly.

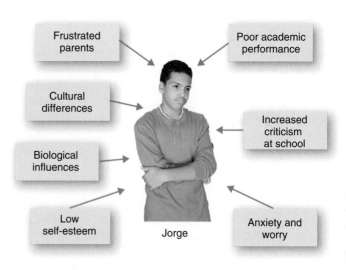

● **FIGURE 2.1** | Jorge's concerns: where do we intervene?

Photo Credit: Kin Images/Photodics/Jupiter Images

Section Summary

What Is Causing Jorge's Problems?

- Jorge's case exemplifies many interconnected factors that cause or contribute to psychological problems in children.
- The study of causes of abnormal child behavior involves theory and findings on biological, psychological, social, and cultural/ethnic factors.
- Biological factors include genetic and neurobiological contributors, among others.
- Psychological influences include the role of behavioral and cognitive processes, as well as emotional and relationship influences.
- Major social contributors to child problems involve family patterns, peer relations, community factors, and cultural expectations.
- Factors in each one of these areas impact and interact with the other areas.

THEORETICAL FOUNDATIONS

Defining what is abnormal within the context of children's ongoing adaptation and development, and sorting out the most probable causes of identified problems, is a complicated process. Very few simple or direct cause-and-effect relationships exist. The study of abnormal child behavior requires an appreciation of developmental processes as well as individual and situational events that can have a major bearing on the course and direction of a particular child's life. Studying normal development informs our theories of abnormal development, and vice versa.

Most clinical and research activity begins with a theoretical formulation for guidance and information. Theory is essentially a language of science that allows us to assemble and communicate existing knowledge more comprehensively. A theory permits us to make educated guesses and predictions about behavior based on samples of knowledge, moving us forward to explore possible explanations. Like a treasure map that provides clues and signposts, a theory offers guidance for our pursuit of causal explanations. Knowledge, skill, and evidence must be added to bring these theoretical clues to life.

The study of the causes of childhood disorders is known as **etiology**, which considers how biological, psychological, and environmental processes interact to produce the outcomes that are observed over time. Research into biological determinants has focused on possible causes such as structural brain damage or dysfunction, neurotransmitter imbalances, and genetic influences. Psychological and environmental models emphasize the role of environmental toxins, early experiences, learning opportunities, disciplinary practices, family systems, and sociocultural contexts. Although these factors are often described as possible "causes," they are, in fact, primarily risk factors and correlates associated with certain disorders—their causal role is not always clear.

Numerous theoretical models have been proposed to explain and suggest treatment for children's psychological disorders, although many of the theories have not been substantiated or even tested (Weisz & Kazdin, 2010). Until recently, most models focused on single explanations that failed to consider other influences and their interactions. One-dimensional models do not capture the complexities of abnormal child behavior that are increasingly evident from research (Kazdin & Whitley, 2006). The alternative to single-factor explanations is much more complex and informative. It considers multiple causes that can interact in various ways over time to affect normal and abnormal development. Keeping in mind this central theme of multiple, interactive causes will help you grasp the complexity of each disorder discussed within this text.

Developmental Psychopathology Perspective

Developmental psychopathology is an approach to describing and studying disorders of childhood, adolescence, and beyond in a manner that emphasizes the importance of developmental processes and tasks. This approach provides a useful framework for organizing the study of abnormal child psychology around milestones and sequences in physical, cognitive, social–emotional, and educational development. It also uses abnormal development to inform normal development, and vice versa (Cicchetti, 2006; Hinshaw, 2013). Simply stated, developmental psychopathology emphasizes the role of developmental processes, the importance of context, and the influence of multiple and interacting events in shaping adaptive and maladaptive development. We adopt this perspective as an organizing framework to describe the dynamic, multidimensional process leading to normal or abnormal outcomes in development (Hayden & Mash, 2014).

A central belief of developmental psychopathology is that to understand maladaptive behavior adequately, one must view it in relation to what is normative for a given period of development (Cicchetti, 2006). The main focus is on highlighting developmental processes, such as language and peer relations and how they function, by looking at extremes and variations in developmental outcomes. In so doing, this perspective emphasizes the importance and complexity of biological, familial, and sociocultural factors in predicting and understanding developmental changes. It draws on knowledge from several disciplines, including psychology, psychiatry, sociology, and neuroscience, and integrates this knowledge within a developmental framework (Hinshaw, 2013).

The value of theory lies not only in providing answers but also in raising new questions and looking at familiar problems in different ways. Theory, research, and practice in abnormal child psychology all require an understanding of the assumptions underlying work in this area. Let's look at three prominent assumptions derived from a developmental psychopathology perspective and how they have shaped our approach to abnormal child psychology.

Abnormal Development Is Multiply Determined

Our first underlying assumption is that abnormal child behavior is *multiply determined*. Thus, we have to look beyond the child's current symptoms and consider developmental pathways and interacting events that, over time, contribute to the expression of a particular disorder.

To illustrate this assumption, let's return to Jorge's problems. One way to look at Jorge's problems is to say that he lacks motivation. Although it is a reasonable explanation, this one-dimensional causal model, which attempts to trace the origins of Jorge's reading difficulty to a single underlying cause, is probably too simplistic. Scientific method emphasizes the need to simplify variables to those of the most importance, but focusing on one primary explanation rather than identifying and allowing for several possible explanations (e.g., genetic factors, reinforcement history, and peer problems) fails to consider the concept of developmental pathways (discussed in Chapter 1). A particular problem or disorder may stem from a variety of causes, and similar risk factors may lead to very different outcomes.

Another way to view Jorge's difficulties—the way we emphasize here—considers multiple influences, including his developmental profile and abilities, his home and school environment, and the ongoing, dynamic interactions among these factors. To address Jorge's reading problem from a multidimensional perspective, we would first assess his current abilities by using multiple sources of data on his ability to function in different settings. Even if we were interested only in his reading ability, we would consider a wide range of characteristics besides those we initially believed to be signs of reading problems. Otherwise, our assumptions about the nature of reading problems might prevent us from considering other explanations. Could criticism and yelling from Jorge's mother affect his concentration or self-esteem? Is Jorge different from

Children's comfort with their environment is shown by their actions

other children in terms of his ability to recognize language sounds from written words? These are some of the questions we would want to answer through careful observation and assessment, using a theoretically guided decision-making strategy.

Child and Environment Are Interdependent

Our second assumption extends the influence of multiple causes by stressing how the child and environment are **interdependent**—how they influence each other. This concept departs from the tradition of viewing the environment as acting on the child to cause changes in development, and instead argues that children also influence their own environment. In simple terms, the concept of interdependence appreciates how nature and nurture work together and are, in fact, interconnected (Rutter, 2011a). Thus, children elicit different reactions from the same environment; different environments, such as home or school, elicit different reactions from the same child.

The dynamic interaction of child and environment is referred to as a **transaction** (Sameroff, 2010; Sameroff & MacKenzie, 2003). The child and the environment both contribute to the expression of a disorder, and one cannot be separated from the other. A transactional view regards both children and the environment as *active contributors* to adaptive and maladaptive behavior. Most persons who know children best—parents, teachers, child care workers, and others—would probably agree that this view makes the most sense: Children act on their environment, and their environment acts on them, as in the example of Jorge. According to this transactional perspective, children's psychological disorders do not reside within the child, nor are they due solely to environmental causes. They most often emerge from a combination

"The title of my science project is 'My Little Brother: Nature or Nurture.'"

of factors, which interact in ways that follow general laws of organized development.

Although a transactional view considers general principles of development that apply to all children, it is also sensitive to individual circumstances—in the child's family or biological makeup—that influence or alter typical outcomes. Learning about such deviations from the norm is what this textbook is all about.

Abnormal Development Involves Continuities and Discontinuities

Think for a moment about how Jorge's various problems might have begun and how they might change or even disappear over time. Might his current problems of avoiding school and homework be connected to his earlier difficulties in reading? Are these qualitatively different problems, or are they different manifestations of the same problem? Are his current problems qualitatively different from those he had at a younger age because his problems today include avoiding school and homework?

Few psychological disorders or impairments suddenly emerge without at least some warning signs or connections to earlier developmental issues. This connection is apparent, for example, in early-onset and persistent conduct disorders, with which parents and other adults often see troublesome behaviors at a young age that continue in some form into adolescence and adulthood (Reef, van Meurs, Verhulst, & van der Ende, 2010). However, it is critical to note that some forms of abnormal child development may be continuous or discontinuous across childhood, adolescence, and adulthood, in either a consistent or a transformed manner (Schulenberg, Sameroff, & Cicchetti, 2006).

Continuity implies that developmental changes are gradual and quantitative (i.e., expressed as amounts that can be measured numerically, such as weight and height changes) and that future behavior patterns can be predicted from earlier patterns. **Discontinuity**, in contrast, implies that developmental changes are abrupt and qualitative (i.e., expressed as qualities that cannot be measured numerically, such as changes in mood or expression) and that future behavior is poorly predicted by earlier patterns.

As an example, consider a preschool child who uses physical aggression with peers. What would you expect that child to be like 10 years later? According to the notion of continuity, he or she would be more likely to engage in antisocial and delinquent behaviors as an adolescent and adult. That is, the pattern of problem behavior (in this case, physical aggression) is continuous across developmental periods, although it gradually changes in form and intensity. Pushing a peer may turn into striking someone with a fist or object. Importantly, continuity refers to patterns of behavior, rather than specific symptoms that remain over time. Continuity is well supported for early-onset and persistent conduct disorders, which have a significant likelihood of later evolving into serious antisocial acts (Lynam et al., 2009).

Other problem behaviors, such as eating disorders, seem to follow a more discontinuous pattern; they occur more suddenly and without much prior warning. In these cases, there are few good behavioral predictors from early childhood as to why a particular child begins to restrict eating or to purge food during early adolescence (see Chapter 14). Sometimes discontinuity can refer to an unexpected or atypical outcome, such as a child who shows normal development until about 18 months of age and then displays loss of language and reduced social engagement (characteristics of some children with autism). In such circumstances, the connection between early and later patterns seems abrupt and discontinuous, which is very baffling to parents.

As we will see throughout our discussion of each disorder, positive factors such as individual competence or social intervention, as well as negative factors such as poverty or discrimination, can influence the continuity or discontinuity of development over time (Rutter, Kim-Cohen, & Maughan, 2006). Returning to Jorge, can you think which of his behavior patterns (if any) were continuous and which seemed to be more discontinuous? Like many problems in abnormal child psychology, Jorge's current behavior pattern involves *both* continuities and discontinuities. Some of his troubles, such as school and homework avoidance, seem qualitatively different (discontinuity) from his reading disorder. His other behaviors, such as slow reading and comprehension, seem to follow (continuity) from his earlier academic problems.

Remember that the concepts of continuity and discontinuity apply to the understanding of abnormal and normal development. However, even with wide fluctuations in the way problems are expressed over time, children show some degree of consistency in organizing their experiences and interacting with their environment, whether that consistency is adaptive or maladaptive (Sroufe, Coffino, & Carlson, 2010). The degree of continuity or discontinuity will vary as a function of changing environmental circumstances and transactions between the child and the environment. These continual changes, in turn, will affect the child's developmental course and direction.

In sum, a central theme of our basic assumptions is that the study of abnormal child psychology must consider abnormality in relation to multiple, interdependent causes and major developmental changes that typically occur across the life cycle. Until recently, developmental aspects of abnormal child behavior were often overlooked in relation to children's behavioral and emotional problems (Cicchetti, 2006). To redress this imbalance, throughout this text we discuss developmental issues pertaining to the nature, symptoms, and course of each disorder.

Changes, Typical and Atypical

● Figure 2.2 presents an overview of developmental periods by age. It gives examples of normal achievements

for each period, as well as behavior problems most often reported in general population samples and the clinical disorders that typically become evident at each period. Guidelines for the typical sequence of development across several important dimensions are helpful, but we must keep in mind that age in years is an arbitrary way to segment continuous sequences of development. You may find yourself turning back to this table to reorient yourself to children's normal and abnormal development.

Children's behaviors—both adaptive and maladaptive—are interconnected with their environment and influenced by their biological makeup. Recently, the field of developmental psychopathology has taken an interest in developmental cascades to help explain why some problems in childhood go on to become major problems later on, whereas others do not (Masten & Cicchetti, 2010). **Developmental cascades** refer to the process by which a child's previous interactions and experiences may spread across other systems and alter his or her course of development, somewhat like a chain reaction (Masten & Cicchetti, 2010). This concept helps to explain how processes that function at one level or domain of behavior (such as curiosity) can affect how the child adapts to other challenges later on (such as academic performance) (Cox et al., 2010). Throughout this book, the developmental psychopathology perspective adds developmental relevance and richness to categorically based DSM-5 disorders and to early intervention possibilities.

Approximate age (years)	Normal achievements	Common behavior problems	Clinical disorders
0–2	Eating, sleeping, attachment	Stubbornness, temper, toileting difficulties	Mental retardation, feeding disorders, autistic disorder
2–5	Language, toileting, self-care skills, self-control, peer relationships	Arguing, demanding attention, disobedience, fears, overactivity, resisting bedtime	Speech and language disorders, problems stemming from child abuse and neglect, some anxiety disorders, such as phobias
6–11	Academic skills and rules, rule-governed games, simple responsibilities	Arguing, inability to concentrate, self-consciousness, showing off	ADHD, learning disorders, school refusal behavior, conduct problems
12–20	Relations with opposite sex, personal identity, separation from family, increased responsibilities	Arguing, bragging, anger outbursts, risk-taking	Anorexia, bulimia, delinquency, suicide attempts, drug and alcohol abuse, schizophrenia, depression

● **FIGURE 2.2** | A developmental overview.

Photo Credits (top to bottom): © Michael Pettigrew/Shutterstock.com; © YUYI /Shutterstock.com; © iStockphoto.com/aabejon; © iStockphoto.com/bmcent1.
Based on Achenbach, 1982; Tully & Goodman, 2007

An Integrative Approach

How do we attempt to make sense of the many environmental and individual factors that influence child behavior? Since no single theoretical orientation can explain various behaviors or disorders, we must be familiar with many theories and conceptual models—each contributes important insights into normal and abnormal development.

Even models that consider more than one primary cause can be limited by the boundaries of their discipline or orientation. Biological explanations, for instance, emphasize genetic mutations, neuroanatomy, and neurobiological mechanisms as factors contributing to psychopathology. Similarly, psychological explanations emphasize causal factors such as insecure attachments, cognitive distortions, or maladaptive reinforcement and/or learning histories. Biological and psychological models are both multicausal and distinctive in terms of the relative importance each attaches to certain events and processes. Each model is restricted in its ability to explain abnormal behavior to the extent that it fails to incorporate important components of other models. Fortunately, such disciplinary boundaries are gradually diminishing as different perspectives take into account important variables derived from other models. For example, biological influences are often taken into account when explaining how psychological factors, such as behavior or cognition, interact over time and result in a psychological disorder (Cicchetti & Curtis, 2006; Sameroff, 2010).

Over time, major theories of abnormal child psychology have become compatible with one another. Rather than offering contradictory views, each theory contributes one or more pieces of the puzzle of atypical development. As all the available pieces are assembled, the picture of a particular child or adolescent disorder becomes more and more distinct. Psychological theories are merely tools to study human behavior; the more you learn what these tools can and cannot do and which tool to use for which purpose, the more knowledgeable and skilled you will become. Remember that no single integrative theory fully captures the diversity of perspectives and findings represented by current research in abnormal child psychology.

Section Summary

Theoretical Foundations

- A theory allows us to make educated guesses and predictions about behavior that are based on existing knowledge, and it allows us to explore these possible explanations empirically.

- Developmental psychopathology provides a useful framework for organizing the study of abnormal child psychology around milestones and sequences in physical, cognitive, social–emotional, and educational development.

- A central theme of this text is the importance of considering multiple, interactive causes for abnormal behavior, in conjunction with the major developmental changes that typically occur.

- Three underlying assumptions about abnormal development are stressed: It is multiply determined, the child and the environment are interdependent, and abnormal development involves continuities and discontinuities of behavior patterns over time.

- The complexity of abnormal child behavior requires consideration of the full range of biological, psychological, and sociocultural factors that influence children's development.

DEVELOPMENTAL CONSIDERATIONS

Even though children's psychological disorders have very different symptoms and causes, they share common ground: They are an indication of adaptational failure in one or more areas of development (Rutter & Sroufe, 2000). **Adaptational failure** is the failure to master or progress in accomplishing developmental milestones. In other words, at the broadest level, children with psychological disorders differ from children their own age in some aspect of normal development. Again, such failure or deviation is rarely due to a single cause, but typically results from an ongoing interaction between individual development and environmental conditions.

The causes and outcomes of abnormal child behavior operate in dynamic and interactive ways over time, making them a challenge to disentangle. Designating a specific factor, such as Jorge's reading problem, either as a cause or as an outcome of a particular disorder usually reflects the point at which we take note of the problem.

Children's development follows an organized pattern that is nurtured through positive experiences with their caregivers

His reading problem, for example, may be viewed as a disorder in its own right (such as a learning disorder in reading), the cause of his other difficulties (such as poor study habits and oppositional behavior), or the outcome of some other condition or disorder (such as a communication disorder). As you read the following chapters and gain a better understanding of the causes of abnormal child behavior, remember that children's behavior and their environment are interconnected.

Organization of Development

Change and reorganization are fundamental aspects of biological and behavioral systems (Sameroff, 2010). An organizational viewpoint looks closely at the psychological processes that may explain how these systems influence each other. In an attempt to understand abnormal development, we may choose to focus on any or all aspects of this organizational process. In the **organization of development** perspective, early patterns of adaptation, such as infant eye contact and speech sounds, evolve with structure over time and transform into higher-order functions such as speech and language. Prior patterns of adaptation are incorporated into successive reorganizations at subsequent periods of development, much as toddlers learn to make certain speech sounds before they develop the ability to use language.

An organizational view of development implies an active, dynamic process of continual change and transformation. As the child's biological abilities unfold during each new stage of development, they interact with environmental factors to direct and redirect the course of development. Because development is organized, sensitive periods play a meaningful role in any discussion of normal and abnormal behavior. **Sensitive periods** are windows of time during which environmental influences on development, both good and bad, are enhanced (Roth & Sweatt, 2011a). Infants, for example, are highly sensitive to emotional cues and proximity to their caregivers, which assists them in developing secure attachments (R. A. Thompson & Meyer, 2007). Toddlers are sensitive to the basic sounds of language, which helps them distinguish sounds and combine them to form words (Shafer & Garrido-Nag, 2007). Sensitive periods can be enhanced opportunities for learning but are not the only opportunities; change can take place at other times. For example, children adopted from orphanages show a number of negative developmental outcomes as a result of their early institutional deprivation. However, their outcome is also affected by later experiences in the post-institutional environment (Reeb et al., 2009). Human development is a process of increasing differentiation and integration, more like a network of interconnecting pathways than one straight line.

Understanding the seemingly endless list of possible causes that influence children's normal and abnormal development is made easier by the fact that development generally proceeds in an organized, hierarchical manner (Sameroff, 2010). Simply stated, a child's current abilities or limitations are influenced by prior accomplishments, just as your progress through trigonometry or calculus depends on the command of arithmetic you acquired in elementary school. As children develop greater abilities or show signs of adaptational failure, these changes influence their further developmental success or failure. Studying abnormal child behavior within a developmental psychopathology perspective, as described previously, fosters an understanding of the interactive, progressive nature of children's abilities and difficulties.

Section Summary

Developmental Considerations

- Children's development is organized, which means that early patterns of adaptation evolve over time and transform into higher-order functions in a structured, predictable manner.

We turn now to three major perspectives on abnormal child development: (1) biological perspectives, which include both genetic and neurobiological factors that are often established (but by no means fixed) at birth or soon thereafter; (2) psychological perspectives, such as emotions, relationships, and thought processes; and (3) familial, social, and cultural influences, which set additional parameters on normal and abnormal development.

BIOLOGICAL PERSPECTIVES

Broadly speaking, a neurobiological perspective considers brain and nervous system functions as underlying causes of psychological disorders in children and adults. Biological influences on a very young child's brain development include genetic and constitutional factors, neuroanatomy, and rates of maturation. Regions of the brain are highly influenced by the availability of various biochemicals and neurohormones, which interact differently to affect an individual's psychological experiences (Cicchetti & Cannon, 1999). This process depends on environmental factors that direct or reroute ongoing brain processes. Remember that a neurobiological perspective acknowledges and recognizes the need to incorporate environmental influences in accounting for disorders.

The developing brain has long been a mystery, but its secrets are gradually being revealed. The examination of biological influences begins with the amazing process of neuronal growth and differentiation. During pregnancy, the fetal brain develops from a few all-purpose cells into a complex organ made up of billions of specialized, interconnected neurons (Johnson & de Haan, 2006). The speed and distance these emerging neurons travel is astonishing as they multiply to form various brain structures and functions. The brain stem commands heartbeat and breathing, the cerebellum controls and coordinates sensorimotor integration, and the cortex is where thought and perception originate.

Embryonic development generates an initial overabundance of neurons (Innocenti, 1982). At first these cells are largely undifferentiated, but as they reach their destinations, they become neurons with axons that carry electrical signals to other parts of the brain. These axonal connections, or synapses, form the brain's circuits and lay the foundation for further growth and differentiation. Notably, genes determine the main highways along which axons travel to make their connection; but to reach particular target cells, axons follow chemical cues strewn along their path that tell them the direction to various destinations.

By the fifth month of prenatal development, most axons have reached their general destination, although there are far more axons than the target cells can accommodate. Thus, during early childhood, synapses multiply; then selective *pruning* reduces the number of connections in a way that gradually shapes and differentiates important brain functions (Johnson & de Haan, 2006). The nervous system seems to prepare itself for new growth and demands by sending in reinforcements and then cutting back once the environment has signaled it has everything it needs. Throughout life we undergo cycles that narrow the gap between structure and function. At the level of the nervous system, the microanatomy of the brain is constantly redefined to meet the demands and requirements of an adult world. Like the pruning of a tree, this process fosters healthy growth of different areas of the brain according to individual needs and environmental demands, and eliminates connections that serve to restrict healthy growth.

How permanent are these early brain connections? This question has provoked different theories and agonized many parents who are concerned about their children's early development. For instance, if early brain functions are unlikely to change, this implies that early experiences set the course for lifetime development. Freud's similar contention implied that an individual's core personality is formed from an early age, which sets the pace and boundaries for further personality formation. To the contrary, scientists now believe that brain functions undergo continual changes as they adapt to environmental demands (Fox, Levitt, & Nelson, 2010).

Neural Plasticity and the Role of Experience

Many early neural connections are not stable; some are strengthened and become more established through use, while many others regress or disappear. Thus, the answer to the question about the permanence of early connections is that the brain shows neural plasticity throughout the course of development (Nelson, 2011). **Neural plasticity**, or malleability, means the brain's anatomical differentiation is use-dependent: Nature provides the basic processes, whereas nurture provides the experiences needed to select the most adaptive network of connections, based on the use and function of each. It is truly fascinating how nature and nurture work together to create such highly specific, extremely adaptive central nervous system functions.

Think of the developing brain as a work in progress, one in which the environment plays an essential role as supervisor of this dynamic rewiring project (see ● Figure 2.3). In fact, environmental experience is now recognized to be critical to the differentiation of brain tissue itself. Although nature has a plan for creating the human brain and central nervous system, environmental opportunities and limitations significantly influence this plan from the beginning. Thus, a transactional model explains normal and abnormal development. A

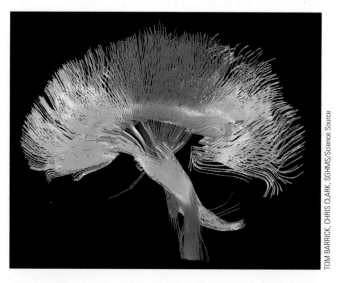

● **FIGURE 2.3** | Colored 3-dimensional magnetic resonance imaging (MRI) scan of the white matter pathways of the brain, side view. White matter is composed of myelin-coated nerve cell fibers that carry information between nerve cells in the cerebrum of the brain (top half of image) and the brain stem (bottom center). Blue represents neural pathways from the top to the bottom of the brain, green represents pathways from the front (left) to the back (right), and red shows pathways between the right and left hemispheres of the brain.

child's brain structure remains surprisingly malleable for months and even years after birth; therefore, transaction occurs between ongoing brain development and environmental experiences; neither nature nor nurture is sufficient to explain the complexity of the developing brain (Fox et al., 2010).

Experience, of course, comes in all shapes and sizes. The prenatal environment as well as childhood illness and diet count as experience, as do maltreatment and inadequate stimulation. Children's early caregiving experiences play an especially important role in designing the parts of the brain involved in emotion, personality, and behavior (O'Connor, 2006). Normal, healthy methods of child rearing, for instance, may increase children's ability to learn and cope with stress (Belsky & de Haan, 2011). In contrast, abuse and neglect can prime the brain for a lifetime of struggle with handling stress or forming healthy relationships (De Bellis, Woolley, & Hooper, 2013).

Brain maturation is an organized, hierarchical process that builds on earlier function, with brain structures restructuring and growing throughout the life span. Primitive areas of the brain, which govern basic sensory and motor skills, mature first and undergo the most dramatic restructuring, during the first 3 years of life. Moreover, these perceptual centers, along with instinctive centers such as the limbic system, are strongly affected by early childhood experiences and set the foundation for further development (Nelson, 2011). The prefrontal cortex, which governs planning and decision making, and the cerebellum, a center for motor skills, are not rewired until a person is 5 to 7 years old. Major restructuring of the brain occurs between ages 9 and 11 in relation to pubertal development, and then throughout adolescence the brain once again prunes unnecessary synaptic connections. Thus, the brain certainly does not stop changing after 3 years. For some functions, the windows of influence are only beginning to close at that age, while for others they are only beginning to open. Our brain functions undergo lifelong

renovation, with restructuring being a natural by-product of growth.

Because the brain is intrinsically shaped by the effects of early experience, the consequences of inadequate or traumatic experience may be enduring and extremely difficult to change (Glover, 2011). During this evolution of brain growth and differentiation many things can go wrong, thereby altering how neurons form or interconnect. Problems or disruptions at a younger age are typically associated with more severe organic disorders and central nervous system complications. Proper prenatal care, proper nutrition, and avoidance of tobacco or alcohol during pregnancy can go a long way in reducing the risk of such complications and lifelong disabilities.

Genetic Contributions

Genetics explains why you look like your father, and if you don't, why you should.

—Tammy, age 8

To understand genetic influences, we first must understand the nature of genes, bearing in mind that virtually any trait results from the interaction of environmental and genetic factors (Rutter, 2011a). A review of genetics terminology and function may assist our understanding of some causes of abnormal child behavior.

Each person's unique genome is established at conception and consists of approximately 20,000 to 25,000 genes (International Human Genome Sequencing Consortium, 2004). Genes contain genetic information from each parent, and they are distributed on 22 matched pairs of chromosomes and a single pair of sex chromosomes. In males, the sex chromosome pair consists of an X and a Y chromosome (XY), and in females, the sex chromosome pair consists of two X chromosomes (XX).

Genetic factors are implicated in all of the childhood disorders discussed in this text. Some genetic influences are expressed early in development, such as

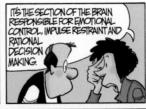

behavioral inhibition or shyness (Nigg, 2006), whereas others show up years later, such as a depressive cognitive style (Garber & Flynn, 2001). Moreover, the expression of genetic influences is malleable and responsive to the social environment. Positive environmental circumstances can help a child "beat the odds" of developing a significant disorder, despite genetic predisposition (Masten & Wright, 2010).

The Nature of Genes

A gene is basically a stretch of DNA and, by itself, it does not produce a behavior, an emotion, or even a passing thought. Rather, it produces a protein. Although these proteins are vital for the brain to function, very rarely do they cause a behavior to happen. Instead, they produce tendencies to respond to the environment in certain ways (Sapolsky, 1997). Each of us has genetic vulnerabilities, tendencies, and predispositions, but rarely are the outcomes inevitable. The lesson in all of this is simple, yet important. The false notion that genes determine behavior should be replaced with the more accurate statement: Genes influence how we respond to the environment, and the environment influences our genes. Today, researchers are highly interested in this **gene–environment interaction (G×E)**, as discussed in A Closer Look 2.1.

A CLOSER **LOOK** 2.1

Gene–Environment Interactions in Abnormal Child Psychology

Normal and abnormal child development are the result of complex interchanges between nature and nurture and are affected not only by genetic and environmental influences, but also by the timing of when they meet (Lenroot & Giedd, 2011). Researchers refer to this interplay of nature and nurture as *gene–environment interactions*, or G×E. The underlying biological changes to genetic structure result from **epigenetic** mechanisms, which involve changes in gene activity resulting from a variety of environmental factors, such as toxins, diet, stress, and many others; in other words, the environment can turn genes on and off (Roth & Sweatt, 2011b). The growing field of developmental neuroscience has shown that epigenetic changes may play a central role in the long-term impact of early life experiences, as these experiences become biologically embedded in the development of our organ systems, especially the brain (Shonkoff, 2010).

G×E helps explain why some people exhibit disorders and others do not, in the face of similar environmental events. For example, as shown in the top of the diagram below (A), children may be exposed to domestic violence or abuse in their family (a high environmental stressor), but only those who possess a particular genotype may end of showing significant problems later on. Alternatively (B), children who carry a genotype known to increase susceptibility for a particular disorder may only develop that disorder if they are exposed to specific environmental risks (i.e., a toxic prenatal or postnatal environment) (Wermter et al., 2010).

There's more to the story—epigenetic alterations may be reversible through pharmacological and behavioral interventions. Research on gene–environment interactions is opening new windows of opportunity—targeting children with particular risk factors (either genetic, environmental, or both)—that determine the best timing and strategies for early intervention (Bakermans-Kranenburg & Van IJzendoorn, 2011; Ellis et al., 2011).

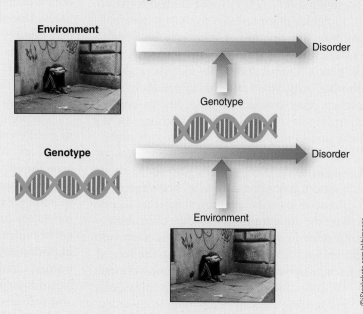

A Environmental factors, such as abuse or social isolation, only lead to a psychological disorder if the person has a specific genetic makeup.

B A person who has a susceptible genetic makeup will only develop a psychological disorder if additional environmental risk factors exist.

©iStockphoto.com/nkbimages

Calvin and Hobbes

by Bill Watterson

Behavioral Genetics

Sorting out the interactive influences of nature and nurture is the not-so-easy task of **behavioral genetics**, a branch of genetics that investigates possible connections between a genetic predisposition and observed behavior, taking into account environmental and genetic influences. Behavioral genetics researchers often begin their investigations by conducting familial aggregation studies. They look for a nonrandom clustering of disorders or characteristics within a given family and compare these results with the random distribution of the disorders or characteristics in the general population (Rende & Waldman, 2006). For example, parents of children with childhood-onset schizophrenia tend to have higher rates of schizophrenia spectrum disorders relative to normative prevalence rates.

Family aggregation studies cannot control for environmental variables that may also contribute to a particular outcome. For example, a child may be anxious because of his parents' child-rearing methods rather than their genetic contributions. To increase scientific rigor following suggestive familial aggregation studies, researchers may conduct twin studies to control for the contribution of genetic factors (Ehringer et al., 2006). Twin studies may compare identical—or monozygotic (MZ)—twins, who have the same set of genes, to fraternal—or dizygotic (DZ)—twins, who share about half of each other's genes (the same as all first-degree relatives). The crucial scientific question is whether identical twins share the same trait—say, reading difficulties—more than fraternal twins do. Studies of twins provide a powerful research strategy for examining the role of genetic influences in both psychiatric and nonpsychiatric disorders. However, the shared environment presents a potential confounding element in any twin study unless the twins are reared apart (Ehringer et al., 2006).

Molecular Genetics

No twisted thought without a twisted molecule.

—Ralph Waldo Gerard (1900–1974)

Compared to behavioral genetics, molecular genetics more directly supports the influence of genes on child psychopathology. **Molecular genetics** research methods directly assess the association between variations in DNA sequences and variations in a particular trait or traits. More than an association, variations in genetic sequences are thought to cause the variations in the trait(s) (Rutter & Dodge, 2011). As we will discuss throughout this book, molecular genetics research methods have been used to search for specific genes for many childhood disorders, including autism, attention-deficit/hyperactivity disorder, and learning disability (however, no specific gene has been identified for most of the disorders discussed in the book). Discovering that mutations in one gene or another may causally influence a particular form of child psychopathology is only the beginning. The longer-term goal is to determine how genetic mutations alter how the genes function in the development of the brain and behavior for different psychopathologies (Rende & Waldman, 2006).

The identification of specific genes has the potential to greatly enhance our understanding of a disorder and its specific components. However, identifying a specific gene for any disorder addresses only a small part of genetic risk. Similar and multiple interactive genes are a far more likely cause than a single gene. Moreover, genetic influences are probabilistic rather than deterministic; environmental and genetic factors generally have equal importance (Rutter & Dodge, 2011). Most forms of abnormal child behavior are polygenic, involving a number of susceptibility genes that interact with one another and with environmental influences, to result in observed levels of impairment (Rende & Waldman, 2006).

Neurobiological Contributions

The study of abnormal child psychology requires a working familiarity with brain structures, as shown in ● Figures 2.4, 2.5, and 2.6. This section provides an overview of major structures mentioned later in the context of specific disorders. Once you are familiar with the various areas and functions of the brain, you will have the basic vocabulary needed to understand exciting research in childhood psychopathology.

Brain Structure and Function

The brain is often divided into the *brain stem* and the *forebrain* (telencephalon) because of their separate functions. The brain stem (see Figure 2.5), located at the base of the brain, handles most of the autonomic functions necessary to stay alive. The lowest part of the brain stem, called the *hindbrain*, contains the *medulla*, the *pons*, and the *cerebellum*. The hindbrain provides essential regulation of autonomic activities such as breathing, heartbeat, and digestion, and the cerebellum controls motor coordination. The brain stem also contains the *midbrain*, which coordinates movement with sensory input. The midbrain houses the *reticular activating system* (RAS), which contributes to processes of arousal and tension.

At the very top of the brain stem is the *diencephalon*, located just below the forebrain. The diencephalon contains the *thalamus* and *hypothalamus*, which are both essential to the regulation of behavior and emotion. The diencephalon functions primarily as a relay between the forebrain and the lower areas of the brain stem.

Next is the forebrain, which has evolved in humans into highly specialized functions. At the base of the forebrain is an area known as the *limbic*, or border, *system* (see Figure 2.6). It contains a number of structures that are suspected causes of psychopathology, such as the *hippocampus, cingulate gyrus, septum,* and *amygdala*. These important structures regulate emotional experiences and expressions and play a significant role in learning and impulse control. The limbic system also regulates the basic drives of sex, aggression, hunger, and thirst.

Also at the base of the forebrain lay the *basal ganglia*, which include the *caudate nucleus*. Researchers are discovering that this area regulates, organizes, and filters information related to cognition, emotions, mood, and motor function, and that it has been implicated

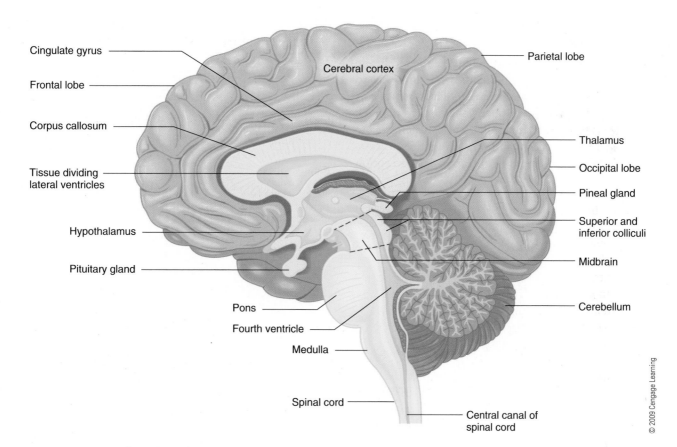

● **FIGURE 2.4** | Structures of the human brain.

Based on Kalat, *Biological Psychology*, 10E.

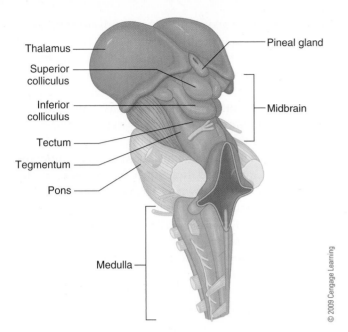

● **FIGURE 2.5** | The brain stem (cerebellum removed to reveal other structures).

Based on Kalat, *Biological Psychology*, 10E.

in attention-deficit/hyperactivity disorder (ADHD, discussed in Chapter 8); disorders affecting motor behavior, such as tics and tremors; and obsessive–compulsive disorder (OCD, discussed in Chapter 11).

The cerebral cortex, the largest part of the forebrain, gives us our distinctly human qualities and allows us to plan as well as to reason and to create. The cerebral cortex is divided into two hemispheres that look very much alike but have different functions. The left hemisphere plays a chief role in verbal and other cognitive processes. The right hemisphere is better at social perception

and creativity. Researchers believe that each hemisphere plays a different role in certain psychological disorders, such as communication and learning disorders.

Around puberty, the brain develops new brain cells and neural connections, and then once again begins to reorganize and consolidate (Benes, 2006). This new growth and restructuring results in further maturation of the lobes of the brain. ● Figure 2.7 shows the *temporal*, *parietal*, and *frontal lobes* of the brain and their important functions. The **frontal lobes** are discussed most often in subsequent chapters on disorders and are worth special attention. The frontal lobes contain the functions underlying most of our thinking and reasoning abilities, including memory. These functions enable us to make sense of social relationships and customs and to relate to the world and the people around us, which is why they have considerable relevance in the study of abnormal child psychology. Fortunately, all of these functions continue to mature well into late adolescence and early adulthood. By implication, the brain you had when you reached adolescence is not the one you have now.

Remarkably, these critical brain areas perform their functions in an integrated, harmonious fashion—aided by important regulatory systems and neurotransmitters—that permits the whole to be much larger than the sum of its parts. However, for many disorders defined in this text, one or more of these brain areas are not performing

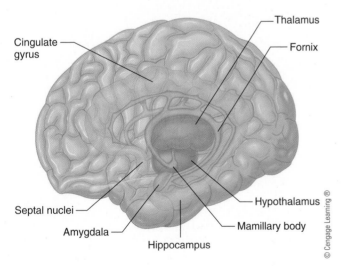

● **FIGURE 2.6** | Structures of the limbic system.

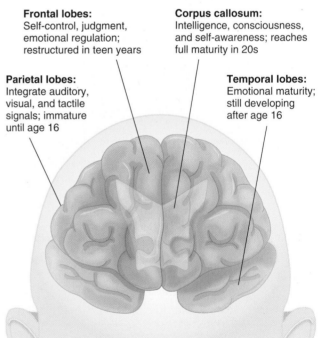

Frontal lobes:
Self-control, judgment, emotional regulation; restructured in teen years

Corpus callosum:
Intelligence, consciousness, and self-awareness; reaches full maturity in 20s

Parietal lobes:
Integrate auditory, visual, and tactile signals; immature until age 16

Temporal lobes:
Emotional maturity; still developing after age 16

● **FIGURE 2.7** | The lobes of the brain and their functions.

their functions as they should, either as a result of other problems or as a primary cause of the disorder.

The Endocrine System

The endocrine system is an important regulatory system that has been linked to specific psychological disorders, such as anxiety and mood disorders, in both children and adults. There are several endocrine glands, and each produces a particular hormone that it releases into the bloodstream. The *adrenal* glands (located on top of the kidneys) are most familiar because they produce **epinephrine** (also known as adrenaline) in response to stress. Epinephrine energizes us and prepares our bodies for possible threats or challenges. The *thyroid* gland produces the hormone thyroxine, which is needed for proper energy metabolism and growth and is implicated in certain eating disorders of children and youths (discussed in Chapter 14). Finally, the *pituitary* gland, located deep within the brain, orchestrates the body's functions by regulating a variety of hormones, including estrogen and testosterone. Because the endocrine system is closely related to the immune system, which protects us from disease and many other biological threats, it is not surprising that it is implicated in a variety of disorders, particularly health- and stress-related disorders (discussed in Chapter 13).

One brain connection that is implicated in some psychological disorders involves the hypothalamus and the endocrine system. The hypothalamus carries out the commands it receives from the adjacent pituitary gland and other hormones, such as those regulating hunger and thirst. The pituitary gland in turn stimulates the adrenal glands to produce epinephrine and the stress hormone known as **cortisol**. The hypothalamus control center, coupled with the pituitary and adrenal glands, make up a regulatory system in the brain known as the **hypothalamic–pituitary–adrenal (HPA) axis**. A Closer Look 2.2 explains how this axis has been implicated in several psychological disorders, especially those connected to a person's response to stress and ability to regulate emotions, such as anxiety and mood disorders.

Neurotransmitters

Neurotransmitters are similar to biochemical currents in the brain. These currents develop in an organized fashion to make meaningful connections that serve larger functions such as thinking and feeling. Neurons that are more sensitive to one type of neurotransmitter, such as serotonin, tend to cluster together and form **brain circuits**, which are paths from one part of the brain to another (R. R. Dean et al., 1993). Tens of thousands of these circuits operate in our brains. Brain

---

The HPA Axis and Stress Regulation

The HPA axis is a central component of the brain's neuroendocrine response to stress. The hypothalamus, when stimulated, secretes the corticotropin-releasing hormone (CRH), which stimulates the pituitary gland to secrete the andrenocorticotropic hormone (ACTH) into the bloodstream. ACTH then causes the adrenal glands to release cortisol, the familiar stress hormone that arouses the body to meet a challenging situation. This system, like many others, works on a feedback loop: Cortisol modulates the stress response by acting on the hypothalamus to inhibit the continued release of CRH (Sternberg & Gold, 1997). Researchers are discovering that this important feedback loop, which regulates our level of arousal and apprehension, can be seriously disrupted or damaged by various traumatic and uncontrollable events. These events can cause a child or adolescent to maintain a state of fear or alertness that becomes toxic over prolonged periods of time (Bremner, 2007).

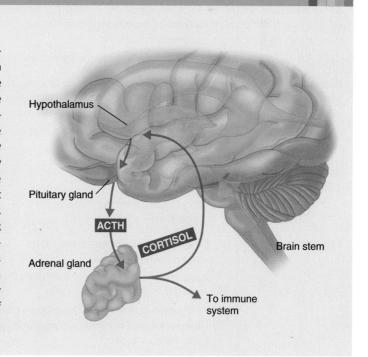

circuits and neurotransmitters relate to particular psychological disorders, permitting more targeted treatments. Psychoactive drugs work by either increasing or decreasing the flow of various neurotransmitters—for example, increasing dopamine in the case of stimulant medications for ADHD (Vitiello, 2007). However, changes in neurotransmitter activity may make people *more likely* or *less likely* to exhibit certain kinds of behavior in certain situations, but they do not cause the behavior directly. Table 2.1 summarizes the four neurotransmitter systems most often mentioned in connection with psychological disorders.

Section Summary

Biological Perspectives

- Brain functions undergo continual changes, described as neural plasticity, as they adapt to environmental demands.
- Genetic influences depend on the environment. Genetic endowment influences behavior, emotions, and thoughts; environmental events are necessary for this influence to be expressed.
- Gene–environment interactions (G×E) explain how the environment shapes our genotype through a process known as "epigenetics."

- Neurobiological contributions to abnormal child behavior include knowledge of brain structures, the endocrine system, and neurotransmitters, all of which perform their functions in an integrated, harmonious fashion.

PSYCHOLOGICAL PERSPECTIVES

Each psychological perspective described in this section has value in explaining the development of psychopathology. At the same time, each perspective has certain limitations and may be more, or less, applicable to a particular disorder or situation. Remember, transactions between environmental and individual influences cause abnormal behavior. Children's inherited characteristics coupled with the experiences and influences in their environment make them the way they are today. Also, some seemingly maladaptive behaviors, such as excessive fearfulness or watchfulness, may in fact be understandable when considered in the context of the child's environment if it involves parental abuse or school violence.

Our interest in psychological bases for abnormal behavior begins with a focus on the role of emotions in establishing an infant's ability to adapt to new surroundings. Infants use emotion to organize new information

TABLE 2.1 | Major Neurotransmitters and Their Implicated Roles in Psychopathology

Neurotransmitter	Normal Functions	Implicated Role in Psychopathology
Benzodiazepine-GABA	Reduces arousal and moderates emotional responses, such as anger, hostility, and aggression Is linked to feelings of anxiety and discomfort	Anxiety disorder
Dopamine	May act as a *switch* that turns on various brain circuits, allowing other neurotransmitters to inhibit or facilitate emotions or behavior Is involved in exploratory, extroverted, and pleasure-seeking activity	Schizophrenia Mood disorders Attention-deficit/hyperactivity disorder (ADHD)
Norepinephrine	Facilitates or controls emergency reactions and alarm responses Plays a role in emotional and behavioral regulation	Not *directly* involved in specific disorders (acts generally to regulate or modulate behavioral tendencies)
Serotonin	Plays a role in information and motor coordination Inhibits children's tendency to explore their surroundings Moderates and regulates a number of critical behaviors, such as eating, sleeping, and expressing wanger	Regulatory problems, such as eating and sleep disorders Obsessive–compulsive disorder Schizophrenia and mood disorders

Source: © Cengage Learning ®

and avoid potential harm. Early relationships between infants and caregivers further provide structure and regulation for these emotional responses. As the child develops, cognitive processes such as self-efficacy play a larger role in assisting the young child to make sense of the world and to reorganize earlier functions that may be unnecessary or even maladaptive for new challenges involving language development, peer interactions, and similar skills. As with brain development, things can go wrong at any point along this continuum of emotional and cognitive development as a function of the child's interaction with the environment.

Emotional Influences

Emotions and affective expression are core elements of human psychological experience. From birth, they are a central feature of infant activity and regulation (Sroufe, 2005). Throughout our lives, emotional reactions assist us in our fight-or-flight response. From an evolutionary perspective, emotions give special value to events and make particular actions most likely to occur. In effect, emotions tell us what to pay attention to and what to ignore, what to approach and what to avoid. Given their important job, and backed up by powerful stress-regulating hormones such as cortisol, emotions are critical to healthy adaptation.

Interest in emotional processes and their relation to abnormal child behavior has grown considerably in recent years (Arsenio & Lemerise, 2010). Children's emotional experiences, expressions, and regulation affect the quality of their social interactions and relationships and thus are at the foundation of early personality development. Researchers are discovering a wealth of information demonstrating the influential role of emotion in children's lives. Emotions not only serve as important internal monitoring and guidance systems designed to appraise events as either beneficial or dangerous, but they also provide motivation for action (Hastings, Zahn-Waxler, & Usher, 2007).

Children have a natural tendency to attend to emotional cues from others, which helps them learn to interpret and regulate their own emotions. They learn, from a very young age, through the emotional expressions of others (Bretherton & Munholland, 2008). Within the first year of life, infants learn the importance of emotions for communication and regulation; by their second year, they have some ability to attribute cause to emotional expression. Of particular interest to abnormal child psychology is the finding that children look to the emotional expression and cues of their caregivers to provide them with the information needed to formulate a basic understanding

The ability to infer another's emotional state by reading facial, gestural, postural, and vocal cues has an important adaptive function, especially for infants and toddlers

of what's going on. To young children, emotions are a primary form of communication that permits them to explore their world with increasing independence (LaFreniere, 2000).

Emotion Reactivity and Regulation

We can divide emotional processes into two dimensions: emotion reactivity and emotion regulation. **Emotion reactivity** refers to individual differences in the threshold and intensity of emotional experience, which provide clues to an individual's level of distress and sensitivity to the environment. **Emotion regulation**, on the other hand, involves enhancing, maintaining, or inhibiting emotional arousal, which is usually done for a specific purpose or goal (Perlman & Pelphrey, 2011; Southam-Gerow & Kendall, 2002). Jorge, for example, was emotionally reactive to certain academic tasks; he became upset and couldn't concentrate. This emotional reaction could lead to poor regulation, resulting in Jorge becoming distraught and difficult to manage at times. Once again, a transactional process is at work, whereby emotional reactions prompt the need for regulation, which influences further emotional expression.

A further distinction can be made between problems in *regulation* and problems in *dysregulation*. Regulation problems involve weak or absent control structures, such as Jorge's trouble concentrating in class; dysregulation means that existing control structures operate maladaptively (Izard et al., 2006). For example, a child may be fearful even when there is no reason in the environment to be fearful or anxious.

Children's emotion regulation abilities, as often shown by their emotion reactivity and expression, are important signals of normal and abnormal development. Emotions also help young children learn more about themselves and their surroundings, as part of learning to identify and monitor their feelings and behavior. The child–caregiver relationship plays a critical role in this process because it provides the basic setting for children to express emotions and to experience caring guidance and have limits placed on them. *Authoritative* parents establish limits that are both sensitive to the child's individual development and needs and demanding of the child to foster self-control and healthy regulation (Maccoby & Martin, 1983). Because of its vital role in emotional development, the child–caregiver relationship will surface again and again when we discuss childhood disorders.

Some forms of emotion dysregulation may be adaptive in one environment or at one time but maladaptive in other situations. Children who have been emotionally and sexually abused may show shallow emotions, known as "numbing," which is a symptom of a posttraumatic stress reaction that serves to protect the child from overwhelming pain and trauma (described in Chapter 12). If numbing becomes a characteristic way of coping with stressors later in life, however, it may interfere with adaptive functioning and long-term goals.

Temperament and Early Personality Styles

You hear it all the time: "She was an easy baby, right from the first day I brought her home from the hospital," or "Sleep? What's that? Since little Freddy was born, we are up all hours of the night, feeding, changing, and trying to soothe him." Unmistakably, some infants are more placid than others, some are more active, and some are more high-strung, and these differences are often recognizable in the first few days or weeks of life (Thomas & Chess, 1977). What relevance does this have to abnormal development?

The development of emotion regulation or dysregulation is thought to derive from both socialization and innate predispositions, or temperament. **Temperament** refers to the child's organized style of behavior that appears early in development, such as fussiness or fearfulness, which shapes the child's approach to his or her environment, and vice versa. Temperament is a subset of the broader domain of personality, so it is often considered an early building block of personality (Kagan, 2013). Three primary dimensions of temperament are linked to normal and abnormal child development (Rothbart & Posner, 2006):

1. *Positive affect and approach.* This dimension describes the "easy child," who is generally approachable and adaptive to his or her environment and possesses the ability to regulate basic functions of eating, sleeping, and elimination relatively smoothly.

2. *Fearful or inhibited.* This dimension describes the "slow-to-warm-up child," who is cautious in his or her approach to novel or challenging situations. Such children are more variable in self-regulation and adaptability and may show distress or negativity toward some situations.

3. *Negative affect or irritability.* This dimension describes the "difficult child," who is predominantly negative or intense in mood, not very adaptable, and arrhythmic. Some children with this temperament show distress when faced with novel or challenging situations, and others are prone to general distress or irritability, including when limitations are placed on them.

These temperament dimensions, or early self-regulatory styles, have been linked to distinct brain activity that underlies a child's cautious versus more eager approach to novel situations, which supports the conclusion that temperament is established during early brain development (Berger & Berger, 2011; Perlman & Pelphrey, 2010). Early infant temperament may be linked to psychopathology or risk conditions in several ways. In some instances, a temperamental style may be highly related to a particular disorder, such as anxiety. In other instances, the condition may develop from the features closely related to temperament, but the condition itself may appear unrelated (Rothbart & Posner, 2006). For example, an infant's extreme sensitivity to emotional stimuli may contribute to a tendency to withdraw from others as a toddler or preschooler; over time, this tendency may transform into an interpersonal style characterized by a self-reported lack of feeling toward others and, consequently, peer rejection or other risk conditions. Also, infant negative affect can contribute to maternal withdrawal or indifference, leading to insecure attachment and its associated risk conditions.

Young children with an irritable temperament may show distress when demands are placed on them

Temperament may influence later development by affecting a child's development of self-control. Notably, a fearful or cautious temperament style at a young age is linked to better self-control, presumably because the child is less impulsive and takes his or her time before making choices (Tarullo, Obradovic, & Gunnar, 2009). But like most aspects of child psychology, temperament and self-control have to achieve a reasonable balance— a high degree of self-control is a positive thing for the more exuberant toddlers, but can be problematic for more shy youngsters because others view them as socially withdrawn (White et al., 2011). Thus, a balance between emotional reactivity and self-control, known as *self-regulation*, is the best formula for healthy, normal adjustment.

Personality disorders are rarely diagnosed until late adolescence or early adulthood, by which time it is evident that the person's pattern of behavior or inner experience is enduring and problematic (Shiner, 2007). For this reason, personality disorders are not discussed in the following abnormal child psychology chapters. A brief overview is provided below to assist students in gaining familiarity with the concept of personality disorders as they may apply to children and adolescents.

As described in the DSM-5 (APA, 2013), personality disorders include antisocial, borderline, histrionic, paranoid, schizoid, schizotypal, narcissistic, avoidant, dependent, and obsessive–compulsive. These 10 types share a common set of criteria:

▶ An enduring pattern of inner experience and behavior that deviates noticeably from the expectations of the individual's culture. For example, one individual may show very different ways of thinking, feeling, and behaving as compared with others in his or her culture.

▶ This enduring pattern of unusual thinking, feeling, or behaving is inflexible and pervasive across a wide range of situations, and results in clinically significant distress or impairment in functioning.

Additional considerations should be used in diagnosing those rare cases of personality disorders among children and adolescents (APA, 2013, p. 647):

▶ Personality disorder categories may be applied to children or adolescents in those relatively unusual instances when the individual's particular maladaptive personality traits appear to be pervasive, persistent, and unlikely to be limited to a particular developmental stage or another mental disorder.

▶ To diagnose a personality disorder in an individual under age 18, the features must have been present for at least 1 year. The one exception to this is antisocial personality disorder, which cannot be diagnosed in individuals under the age of 18 years.

Remember, some personality traits that may be regarded as pathological during adulthood are considered relatively normal during adolescence (such as mood swings and impulsivity!). For this reason, the diagnostic criteria emphasize that a personality trait must *deviate markedly* from cultural expectations to be considered symptomatic of a personality disorder.

The lifelong significance of emotion reactivity and regulation is backed up by strong empirical evidence linking early behavioral styles to adult personality characteristics 30 years later, as described in A Closer Look 2.3.

Behavioral and Cognitive Influences

Behavioral and cognitive explanations for abnormal child behavior emphasize principles of learning and cognition, which shape children's behavior and their interpretation of things around them. Behavioral and cognitive approaches differ essentially in the extent to which they apply cognitive concepts and procedures to the understanding of behavior. Applied behavior analysis, at one end of this continuum, focuses primarily on observable behavior and rejects the notion that cognitive mediation is necessary for explaining behavior. At the other end is social learning theory, which relies more broadly on cognitive processes and explanations.

Most behavioral explanations assume that the child is best understood and described by behavior in a particular situation rather than in terms of stable traits. Although a child's particular learning history is of interest, behavioral methods focus on the most pragmatic, parsimonious explanation for a particular problem behavior. By the same reasoning, this approach recognizes that successfully changing a problem behavior does not imply knowledge about its origin, but rather emphasizes contemporaneous causes, referred to as *controlling variables*. Cognitive theorists, on the other hand, are interested in how certain thought patterns develop over time and how they relate to particular behavioral strategies, such as problem solving. Following is a refresher on some of the major behavioral and cognitive theories.

Applied Behavior Analysis (ABA)

Based on B. F. Skinner's classic studies, ABA examines the relationships between behavior and its antecedents and consequences, which is known as a *functional approach* to behavior. No implicit assumptions are made about underlying needs or motives that contribute to abnormal behavior; ABA describes and tests

Similarities in Children's Early Behavioral Styles and Adult Personality and Well-Being

Caspi et al. (2003) conducted a landmark study of the connection between early temperament style in children and their later personality traits as adults. These researchers observed more than 1,000 children at age 3 and evaluated their temperament along five dimensions: undercontrolled, inhibited, confident, reserved, and well-adjusted. Twenty-three years later they conducted an assessment of these same individuals as adults, and found some interesting consistencies in "personality style" over this length of time.

When observed at age 3, children classified as undercontrolled (10% of the sample) were rated as irritable, impulsive, and restless. At age 26, these same individuals scored high on personality traits linked to "negative emotionality." They were easily upset and most likely to overreact to minor events, and they reported feeling mistreated, deceived, and betrayed by others. Children classified as inhibited (8% of the sample) were considered a bit fearful and easily upset, and by age 26 they were described as unassertive and took little pleasure in life. The researchers found that the remaining three temperament groups did not display such dramatic personality profiles as adults, but a considerable amount of continuity in style did occur over time. Confident children (28% of the sample) were seen as friendly and eager to explore, and they were the least conventional and most extroverted as adults. Reserved children (15% of the sample) were described as timid and somewhat uncomfortable, and by adulthood they described themselves as unassertive and were seen by others as being introverted. Finally, the well-adjusted children (40% of the sample), who behaved in an age- and situation-appropriate manner at age 3, showed adult personality traits that closely resembled the average, well-adjusted adult.

The story doesn't end there. The researchers have continued to follow this sample and have determined that their degree of self-control as children predicted their adult health, substance use problems, personal finances, and criminal offenses in their early 30s (Moffitt et al., 2011). These findings provide the strongest evidence to date that children's early behavioral styles forecast how they will typically behave, think, and feel as adults. They also imply that tremendous benefits to individuals and society could result if large-scale programs to teach children self-control skills were offered at an early age.

© Cengage Learning ®

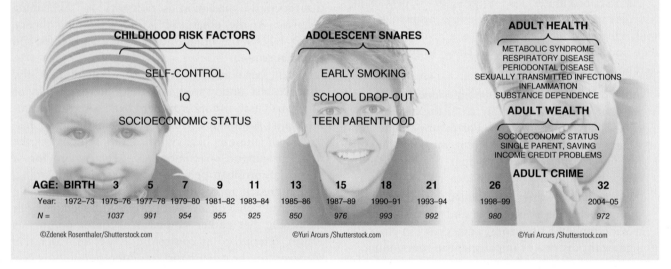

AGE: BIRTH	3	5	7	9	11	13	15	18	21	26			32
Year: 1972–73	1975–76	1977–78	1979–80	1981–82	1983–84	1985–86	1987–89	1990–91	1993–94	1998–99			2004–05
N =	1037	991	954	955	925	850	976	993	992	980			972

CHILDHOOD RISK FACTORS
SELF-CONTROL
IQ
SOCIOECONOMIC STATUS

ADOLESCENT SNARES
EARLY SMOKING
SCHOOL DROP-OUT
TEEN PARENTHOOD

ADULT HEALTH
METABOLIC SYNDROME
RESPIRATORY DISEASE
PERIODONTAL DISEASE
SEXUALLY TRANSMITTED INFECTIONS
INFLAMMATION
SUBSTANCE DEPENDENCE

ADULT WEALTH
SOCIOECONOMIC STATUS
SINGLE PARENT, SAVING
INCOME CREDIT PROBLEMS

ADULT CRIME

©Zdenek Rosenthaler/Shutterstock.com   ©Yuri Arcurs /Shutterstock.com   ©Yuri Arcurs /Shutterstock.com

functional relationships between stimuli, responses, and consequences. ABA is based on four primary operant learning principles, which explain how behaviors are acquired or changed as a result of particular consequences. These four principles are probably familiar to you: *Positive* and *negative reinforcement* are any actions that increase the target response; *extinction* and *punishment* decrease a response. Children are quite accomplished at learning the contingencies between their behavior and its consequences, and have an uncanny ability to apply some of their own! These principles of operant conditioning remain influential across a variety of applied areas—from basic experimental research to clinical treatment (DeGrandpre, 2000).

Classical Conditioning

Based on the extension of Pavlov's famous learning trials and Watson's experiments with Little Albert (see Chapter 1), classical conditioning explains the acquisition of deviant behavior on the basis of paired associations between previously neutral stimuli (such as math problems) and unconditioned stimuli (such as food or criticism). Any neutral event can become a *conditioned stimulus* if it is paired enough times with an event that already elicits a certain response. Paired associations can help explain many adjustment problems in children and adolescents, although we do not typically know what the original association may have been. In addition, more than one learning paradigm may occur at the same time. For this reason, dual learning explanations for undesirable behavior are common (that is, combinations of features of both operant and classical conditioning).

Returning to Jorge's problem, imagine that he associates reading (a neutral event) with humiliation or anxiety (unconditioned stimuli), which prompts him to escape or avoid the activity. His avoidance, in turn, is negatively reinforced by its consequences: His anxiety decreases and he avoids feelings of humiliation. This analysis considers both instrumental (operant) and respondent (classical) conditioning as part of his learning history. Can you think of possible environmental changes or contingencies that might modify Jorge's behavior in a desirable fashion?

Social Learning and Cognition

Social learning explanations consider not only overt behaviors such as Jorge's school problems, but also the role of possible *cognitive mediators* that may influence the behaviors directly or indirectly. According to Albert Bandura's (1977, 1986) social learning explanation, behavior may be learned not only by operant and classical conditioning, but also indirectly through *observational* (vicarious) learning. Children can learn a new behavior merely by watching another person model the behavior, without apparent reinforcement or practice.

Children's increasing cognitive abilities play a role in both normal and abnormal development

Ariel Skelley/Blend Images/Corbis

Social learning also incorporates the role of social cognition in acquiring desirable and undesirable behavior. **Social cognition** relates to how children think about themselves and others, resulting in the formation of mental representations of themselves, their relationships, and their social world. These representations are not fixed, but are continually updated on the basis of maturation and social interaction (Herrmann et al., 2007). Children's ongoing cognitive development in reasoning, problem solving, and making attributions helps them make sense of who they are and how they relate to their surroundings. Moreover, social learning and social–cognitive viewpoints also consider the role of affect and the importance of contextual variables, such as family and peers, in both the origins and maintenance of problem behaviors (Arsenio & Lemerise, 2010).

Like individual differences in temperament and emotion regulation, crucial differences exist in how children process information and make sense of their social worlds. Like adults, children have a natural desire to evaluate their behavior in various circumstances, especially those involving some element of possible failure, harm, or personal risk. For some children, teens, and adults, these self-appraisals may be based on faulty beliefs or distortions; for others, an attributional bias about their ability or the intentions of others leads them to reinterpret the event in a way that fits their preexisting belief ("I got a good grade in math because the exam was too easy"; "He's a jerk, so who cares if I tease him?") (Lansford et al., 2010).

Since the first description of observational learning in the early 1960s, cognitive models have grown in both richness and complexity, and their constructs appear quite often throughout this text. Cognitive distortions, insufficient cognitive mediation, and attributional styles and expectations are important determinants in the development and treatment of behavioral and emotional problems in children and adolescents (Bierman et al., 2010).

Section Summary

Psychological Perspectives

- Emotion reactivity and regulation are critical aspects of early and subsequent development, affecting the quality of children's social interactions and relationships throughout their life span.

- Three major approaches to abnormal behavior, based on principles of learning, are applied behavior analysis, principles of classical conditioning, and social learning and social cognition theories. Social learning and social cognition theories place more significance on cognitive processes than overt behavior.

FAMILY, SOCIAL, AND CULTURAL PERSPECTIVES

In addition to biological and psychological influences, children's normal and abnormal development depends on social and environmental contexts. Understanding context requires a consideration of both *proximal* (close-by) and *distal* (further-removed) events, as well as those that impinge directly on the child in a particular situation at a particular time. We consider these wide-ranging environmental conditions and learning experiences in relation to the family and peer context and the social and cultural context.

What exactly do we mean when we refer to a child's environment? Family? Peer groups? Clean air? A child's environment is constantly changing in relation to its many components, much as a lake or stream is affected by a proximal event, such as a rainstorm, as well as more distal events, such as the seasons.

Environmental influences include shared and nonshared types. **Shared environment** refers to environmental factors that produce similarities in developmental outcomes among siblings in the same family. For example, if siblings are more similar than expected from only their shared genetics, this implies an effect of the environment they share, such as being exposed to marital conflict or poverty, or being parented in a similar manner. In the example of identical twins, shared environmental influence is estimated indirectly from correlations between twins by subtracting the heritability estimate from the MZ twin correlation. **Nonshared environment**, which refers to environmental factors that produce behavioral differences among siblings, can then be calculated by subtracting the MZ twin correlation from 1.0 (Pike & Kretschmer, 2009; Pike & Plomin, 1996).

Interestingly, it is nonshared environmental factors that create differences among siblings that seem to contribute to a large portion of the variation. Environmental factors that have been postulated as nonshared include differential treatment by parents, peer influences, and school environment (Eley & Lau, 2005).

● Figure 2.8 depicts Bronfenbrenner's (1977) ecological model, which shows the richness and depth of the various layers of a child's environment by portraying it as a series of nested and interconnected structures. Note that the child is at the center of this sphere of influence, which contains various levels interconnected in meaningful ways. The child's immediate environment begins with family members and home surroundings, but it quickly grows more complex as the child enters preschool, visits neighborhood parks, and makes friends.

Social settings also affect the child even when the child does not directly experience these influences. Parents' friends and jobs, the availability of family support services such as health and welfare programs, and similar community resources and activities that are positive and negative make up the child's larger social framework (Sameroff, 2010). Finally, though far removed from the child's day-to-day activities, cultural ideology or identity governs how children should be treated (the sanctioning of corporal punishment), what they should be taught, and what goals are important to achieve (Achenbach & Rescorla, 2007). These levels of environmental influences and their reciprocal connections (they affect the child, and the child affects them) are key elements in understanding the nature of child abuse and neglect and many child and adolescent disorders.

Infant–Caregiver Attachment

The study of abnormal development has profited from extensive work on child–caregiver relationships; this has painted a dramatic picture of the importance of early caregiver attachment to a child's emotional health (Sweeney, 2007). British child psychiatrist John Bowlby (1973, 1988) integrated aspects of evolutionary biology with existing psychodynamic conceptions of early experiences to derive his theory of attachment. **Attachment** refers to the process of establishing and maintaining an emotional bond with parents or other significant individuals. This process is ongoing, typically beginning between 6 and 12 months of age, and provides infants with a secure, consistent base from which to explore and learn about their world (Sroufe, 2005).

In attachment theory, instinctive behaviors are not rigidly predetermined but rather become organized into flexible, goal-oriented systems through learning and goal-corrected feedback. Bowlby reasoned that infants are "preadapted" to engage in relationship-enhancing behaviors such as orienting, smiling, crying, clinging, signaling, and, as they learn to move about, proximity seeking. In order to survive, however, infants must become attached to a specific person (or persons) who is available and responsive to their needs. Adults are similarly equipped with attachment-promoting behaviors to respond to an infant's needs, which are complementary to the needs of the infant—smiling, touching, holding, and rocking.

The evolving infant–caregiver relationship helps the infant regulate her or his behavior and emotions, especially under conditions of threat or stress. Accordingly, attachment serves an important stress-reduction function. The infant is motivated to maintain a balance between the desire to preserve the familiar and the desire to seek and explore new information. Self-reliance develops when the attachment figure provides a secure base for exploration (Bretherton & Munholland, 2008). Moreover, a child's *internal working model* of relationships—what he or she expects

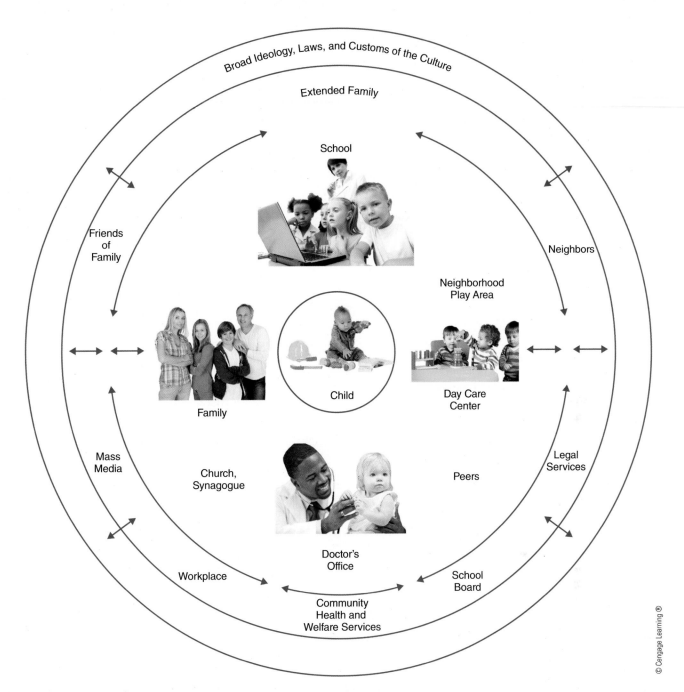

● **FIGURE 2.8** | An ecological model of environmental influences.

Photo Credits (clockwise from center and top): ©glenda/Shutterstock.com; ©Pressmaster/Shutterstock.com; ©iStockphoto.com/ lostinbids; © iStockphoto.com/Sean Locke; ©Goodluz/Shutterstock.com

© Cengage Learning ®

from others and how he or she relates to others—emerges from this first crucial relationship and is carried forward into later relationships. The three major organized patterns of attachment (and one disorganized pattern) are summarized in Table 2.2, along with their theoretical and empirical links to various forms of psychopathology. Keep in mind, however, that attachment features constitute only one aspect of human relationships. Insecure attachments have been implicated in a number of childhood disorders, but no one-to-one correspondence exists between specific patterns of attachment and particular disorders (Sroufe, 2005).

The Family and Peer Context

Child psychopathology research has increasingly focused on the role of the family system, the complex relationships within families, and the reciprocal influences among

TABLE 2.2 | Types of Attachment and Their Relation to Disordered Outcomes

Type of Attachment	Description during Strange Situation[1]	Possible Influence on Relationships	Possible Disordered Outcomes
Secure	Infant readily separates from caregiver and likes to explore. When wary of a stranger or distressed by separation, the infant seeks contact and proximity with caregiver; the infant then returns to exploration and play after contact.	Individuals with secure attachment histories tend to seek out and make effective use of supportive relationships.	Although individuals with secure attachments may suffer psychological distress, their relationship strategy serves a protective function against disordered outcomes.
Insecure *Anxious, avoidant type*	Infant engages in exploration, but with little affective interaction with caregiver. Infant shows little wariness of strangers, and generally is upset only if left alone. As stress increases, avoidance increases.	As children and adults, individuals with an insecure, *avoidant pattern of early* attachment tend to mask emotional expression. They often believe they are vulnerable to hurt, and others are not to be trusted.	Conduct disorders; aggressive behavior; depressive symptoms (usually as a result of failure of self-reliant image).
Insecure *Anxious, resistant type*	Infant shows disinterest in or resistance to exploration and play, and is wary of novel situations or strangers. Infant has difficulty settling when reunited with caregiver, and may mix active contact-seeking with crying and fussiness.	As children and adults, individuals with an *insecure, resistant* pattern of early attachment have difficulties managing anxiety. They tend to exaggerate emotions and maintain negative beliefs about the self.	Phobias; anxiety; psychosomatic symptoms; depression.
Disorganized, disoriented type (not an organized strategy)	Infant lacks a coherent strategy of attachment. Appears disorganized when faced with a novel situation and has no consistent pattern of regulating emotions.	Individuals with disorganized, disoriented style show an inability to form close attachments to others; may show indiscriminate friendliness (little selective attachment).	No consensus, but generally a wide range of personality disorders (van Ijzendoorn et al., 1999).

[1]The Strange Situation is a method of assessing infant–caregiver attachment. It involves a series of increasingly stressful separations and reunions that resemble typical daily occurrences, such as meeting strangers and being left alone (Ainsworth et al., 1978).

Note: The relationships between attachment styles and abnormal development are based on both theoretical and empirical findings, summarized in E. A. Carlson and Sroufe (1995). (Sroufe et al., 1999)

Source: © Cengage Learning ®

various family subsystems. There is a need to consider the processes occurring within disturbed families, and the common and unique ways these processes affect both individual family members and subsystems. Within the family, the roles of the mother–child and marital subsystems have received the most research attention, with less attention being given to the role of siblings (Defoe et al., 2013) or fathers (Smith et al., 2012).

Family systems theorists argue that it is difficult to understand or predict the behavior of a particular family member, such as a child, in isolation from other family members (P. A. Cowan & C. P. Cowan, 2006). This view is in line with our earlier discussion of underlying assumptions about children's abnormal development—*relationships*, not individual children or teens, are often the crucial focus. This view, however, is often at odds with mainstream psychological and psychiatric approaches to psychopathology, yet it is compatible with developmental processes.

More and more, the study of individual factors and the study of the child's context are being seen as mutually compatible and beneficial to both theory and intervention. Furthermore, the manner in which the family, as a unit, deals with typical and atypical stress plays an instrumental role in children's adjustment and adaptation. The outcome of stressful events depends in part on the nature and severity of the stress, the level of family functioning prior to the stress, and the family's coping skills and resources. Stress that is positive or tolerable, such as changing schools or a decline in family income, often brings about change, growth, and reorganization of families and is not usually harmful to children's development (Masten & Wright, 2010; Rutter, 2011a). However, some forms of stress are considered "toxic" to child development because they cause strong, frequent, and/or prolonged activation of the child's stress response in the absence of adult protection and support (Shonkoff, 2010). Some of the more influential family-related issues raised in

The "Core Story" of Development

For several years a group of neuroscientists, developmental psychologists, pediatricians, and others have been working on a "core story" of child development in an effort to translate complex ideas and findings into actions that reduce social problems and improve children's chances at successful development. We thought a brief list of their core story themes would provide a nice summary of the important issues you have read about in this chapter:

1. Child development is a foundation for community development and economic development because capable children become the foundation of a prosperous and sustainable society.
2. Brain architecture is constructed through an ongoing process that begins before birth and continues into adulthood. The quality of that architecture establishes either a sturdy or a fragile foundation for all the capabilities and behavior that follow.
3. Skill begets skill as brains are built in a hierarchical fashion, from the bottom up. Increasingly complex circuits and skills build on simpler circuits and skills over time.
4. The interaction of genes and experience shapes the circuitry of the developing brain. Young children serve up frequent

invitations to engage with adults, who are either responsive or unresponsive to their needs. This "serve and return" process is fundamental to the wiring of the brain, especially in the early years.
5. Cognitive, emotional, and social capacities are intertwined. Learning, behavior, and both physical and mental health are highly interrelated over the life course. You cannot address one domain without affecting the others.
6. Although manageable levels of stress are normative and growth promoting, toxic stress in the early years (e.g., from severe poverty, serious parental mental health impairment such as maternal depression, child maltreatment, and/or family violence) can damage developing brain architecture and lead to problems in learning and behavior, as well as increased susceptibility to physical and mental illness.
7. Brain plasticity and the ability to change behavior decrease over time. Consequently, getting it right early leads to better outcomes and is less costly, both to society and to individuals, than trying to fix it later.

Source: Based on Shonkoff & Bales, 2011.

Supported by the National Scientific Council on the Developing Child and the FrameWorks Institute.

---

discussions of childhood disorders throughout this book are parental depression, child abuse, parental substance abuse, divorce, marital violence, poverty, and parental criminality.

Although quite distinct, these major family and individual issues share a common thread in terms of their impact on child development: They disrupt, disturb, or interfere with consistent and predictable child care and basic necessities. Such disruption or impairment, in turn, interferes with children's ongoing development to such an extent that their ability to manage stress and form satisfactory relationships with peers, teachers, and other adults cascade into lifelong psychological difficulties (Cox et al., 2010; Obradović, Burt, & Masten, 2010).

A Closer Look 2.4 provides a useful summary of the concepts discussed throughout this chapter to assist readers in understanding the major processes affecting normal and abnormal development.

Section Summary

Family, Social, and Cultural Perspectives

- Attachment approaches to abnormal child behavior emphasize the evolving infant–caregiver relationship,

which helps the infant regulate behavior and emotions, especially under conditions of threat or stress.
- Children's normal and abnormal development depends on a variety of social and environmental settings, including the child's family and peer system and the larger social and cultural context.

LOOKING AHEAD

Society's understanding of children's and adolescents' healthy, normal development has been gradually evolving toward a more holistic, health-promoting orientation, which is impacting the definitions and services related to children's mental health (Barry, 2009; Lewin-Bizan, Bowers, & Lerner, 2010). This emerging dynamic, interactive view of health recognizes the importance of both individual and environmental factors in achieving positive development. The neuroscience and ecological perspectives on human health and behavior add momentum to this growing view because they consider human adaptation within its normal context.

Health and successful adaptation are today seen as worthy and appropriate aspects of the study of abnormal child and adolescent psychology. Along with an increased emphasis on **health promotion**, today's research and thinking accept the notion that various childhood disorders share many clinical features and causes. Health promotion encourages changes, opportunities, and competence to achieve one's health potential (R. M. Kaplan, 2000; Ungar, 2010). When applied to children, this view recognizes the multicausal and interactive nature of many child and adolescent psychological disorders and the importance of contextual factors. It also speaks to the importance of balancing the abilities of individuals with the challenges and risks of their environments (Kirmayer et al., 2011; Masten & Wright, 2010). Throughout the text we return to the many ways abnormal child and adolescent psychology can be studied in a developmentally sensitive, systems-oriented manner.

These conceptual shifts are gradually changing the face of mental health and educational services for children and youths, with important implications for pediatrics, psychology, psychiatry, social work, nursing, education, and child development. How individuals think about health, how daily life is organized and experienced, how social policy is developed, how social resources are allocated, and how people are trained to implement these policies have reached their greatest potential in history for achieving major improvements in services to assist younger populations who cannot speak for themselves. Although this tremendous impact on the field of mental health, and on children and youths in particular, has not yet become reality, we are encouraged by how society has progressed in addressing the needs of children.

Study Resources

SECTION SUMMARIES

KEY TERMS

3

Research

If we knew what it was we were doing, it would not be called research, would it?

—Albert Einstein (1879–1955)

IN THIS CHAPTER, WE look at the process of research and the many challenges faced by those who study children and adolescents with problems and their families. **Research** is generally viewed as a systematic way of finding answers to questions—a method of inquiry that follows certain rules.

A SCIENTIFIC APPROACH

The aim of science is not to open a door to infinite wisdom, but to set a limit to infinite error.

—Brecht, *The Life of Galileo*

Scientific research strategies can be used to understand children with problems and how they can be helped. A scientific approach is an organized way of investigating claims that improves on using common sense and casual observations. However, science is more than just organized common sense. Science requires that a claim be based on theories backed up by data from well-designed studies that test alternative explanations and that observations be checked and repeated before conclusions are drawn (Rutter & Solantaus, 2014). A scientific approach is especially important in abnormal child psychology. Although relationships between variables of interest may seem obvious when observed casually—a child consumes too much sugar and becomes hyperactive—these relationships are often not as straightforward as they seem. What we initially may think is a simple cause-and-effect connection may be obscured by complex interactions and a combination of variables. Parents and professionals who work with children have a tendency to interpret and relate information according to their own belief systems and experiences. These relationships sometimes become firmly established, independent of whether they are supported by facts. Even when new information comes along, such as studies indicating a lack of correlation between sugar and hyperactivity, one's previous views or understanding can be difficult to change.

Folklore, home remedies, and fad treatments ranging from chicken soup to swimming with dolphins are unscientific aspects of abnormal child psychology. Simple explanations, such as "sugar causes hyperactivity," or simple solutions, such as "spare the rod and spoil the child," may appeal to parents or teachers because they promise an easy answer or quick remedy for a complex problem. Folklore and fad treatments, unintentionally or otherwise, play to the vulnerabilities of parents of children with problems, parents who desperately want the best for their children. More often than not, easy answers or quick remedies do not work, and sometimes they bring unfortunate consequences and costs for children with problems and their families.

People have always been skeptical about scientific research leading to new knowledge. Consider the following comments:

> After a few more flashes in the pan, we shall hear very little more of Edison and his electric lamp. Every claim he makes has been tested and proved impracticable. (*New York Times*, January 16, 1880)

> Louis Pasteur's theory of germs is ridiculous fiction. (Pachet, professor of physiology [Toulouse, 1872])

Fortunately, the light bulb, pasteurization, and many other ideas once viewed with skepticism have clearly caught on. Nevertheless, people are skeptical about research in abnormal child psychology for good reason. First, experts on childhood problems frequently disagree. Newspapers, magazines, websites, and TV talk shows provide a steady diet of conflicting opinions. The answers we get (e.g., violence on television makes children more aggressive, daycare has a harmful effect on children's emotional adjustment) often depend on which "expert" we ask.

Second, research studies that appear in mainstream media are frequently oversimplified, and the way in which findings are presented can make them more or less believable. For example, people are more likely to agree with the findings of a study when the findings are presented with a photo of a brain image, as compared with the same findings presented without a brain image or with a bar graph (McCabe & Castel, 2008). In the absence of information about the limitations of brain-imaging procedures, findings can be misrepresented or misunderstood.

Third, research findings in abnormal child psychology are often in conflict with one another. For example, most studies find that elementary-school-age girls are more prone to depression than boys, but some studies report higher rates of depression in boys, and other studies report no differences. How do we make sense out of inconsistent and sometimes contradictory findings? As we will discuss in this chapter, conflicting findings are often the result of how different studies are conducted—for example, the way depression is defined or how children for the study are selected (e.g., from clinics vs. from the general population).

A fourth reason for skepticism is that research has led to different recommendations regarding how children with problems should be helped. In some cases the same treatment (e.g., antidepressant medication) has been shown to be helpful, to have no effect, or to be harmful. As one practitioner put it after hearing about an effective new treatment method at a conference, "I'd better hurry home and use it quickly before a new study is published to show that it doesn't work!" Many conclusions from research with children are

Abnormal child psychology can involve novel research methods, such as the possibility of using robots to help to understand, diagnose, and treat children with autism spectrum disorder.

qualified—rarely are there clear-cut answers. A moderate amount of discipline is good; too little or too much discipline is bad. Certain treatments may work for some children but not for others, for older but not for younger children, or for children with certain cultural backgrounds but not for others.

Finally, even when scientific evidence is relatively clear and produces a consensus, many parents and professionals may dismiss the findings because they have encountered an exception, usually one drawn from personal experience. For example, despite the large amount of research showing that the habitual use of harsh physical punishment by parents can have extremely negative effects on children, a parent may still say, "My father used his belt on me when I was a kid and it sure taught me how to behave properly!"

Because no single study is perfect, it is important to be an informed consumer and to keep in mind that it is the *accumulation* of findings—not one study—that advances the field. Research in abnormal child psychology using a scientific approach has led to exciting new advances in understanding children with problems and how they can best be helped. For example, in Chapter 6, we discuss studies that have identified brain abnormalities in children with autism that may tell us why these children have difficulty making social connections

with people. Other research—using home videotapes of 12-month-old infants who are later diagnosed with autism at 2 to 3 years of age—has identified early social markers for autism such as the infant "not responding to her name when called" or "rarely making eye contact." The discovery of possible biological and social markers helps identify children with autism at a younger age than ever before. This is critical, because the earlier a child with autism receives help, the better the outcome. In studies of autism and other disorders, findings from different studies do not always agree. Nevertheless, the accumulation of new findings from scientific research into the neurobiology, early social development, and intervention for children with autism has greatly advanced our understanding of this disorder and continues to suggest new ways to help these children.

When Science Is Ignored

The greatest enemy of knowledge is not ignorance, it is the illusion of knowledge.

—Stephen Hawking

The example of *facilitated communication* (FC) illustrates some of the lessons to be learned when scientific methods and evidence are ignored or dismissed. FC is a seemingly well-meant but highly controversial and misused procedure for teaching children with autism and other impairments to communicate. Using this method, a facilitator provides manual assistance by lightly holding a child's hand, wrist, or arm (see photo), while the child supposedly communicates by typing on a keyboard or by pointing to letters on an alphabet board. The alleged purpose of the manual assistance by the facilitator is to help the child press the keys that she or he wants to press—not to influence key selection. However, because the assistance is continued indefinitely, the possibility of direct influence by the facilitator exists.

Facilitated communication: Who's doing the communicating?

FC received widespread exposure in the media when it was reported that children who received it showed feats of literacy and intellectual competence far exceeding their presumed abilities (Biklen, 1990). The results were considered remarkable because the typical youngster using FC had a lifelong history of autism, profound intellectual disability, or both and had never talked (Jacobson, Mulick, & Schwartz, 1995). Proponents claim that, with this method, children with autism can generate phrases and sentences describing complex memories and feelings and demonstrate other advanced language skills (Biklen & Cardinal, 1997).

However, critics of FC view the method as quackery—no different from a Ouija board. Are the extraordinary outcomes attributed to FC fact, or are they fiction? Scientific research would indicate fiction. Controlled studies have consistently found that the child's supposed communication is being controlled by the facilitator (Mostert, 2001). In one revealing study, different questions were delivered through headphones to facilitators and individuals with autism ranging in age from 16 to 30 years (both were unaware that the questions were different). The resulting answers by the individuals with autism were found to match the questions given to the facilitator, not the client, indicating that it was the facilitator who was doing the communicating (Wheeler et al., 1993).

Unfortunately, FC continues to be used each day with thousands of youngsters with disabilities throughout the world (Grayson et al., 2012), which illustrates the potentially damaging effects of using practices not based on scientific evidence (Lilienfeld, 2007; Mostert, 2010). As reflected in the following comments by the father of a young boy with autism, parents who want the best for their children are particularly vulnerable to the false promise of questionable interventions:

> Professionals are very quick to dismiss the abilities of autistics. . . . So when facilitated communication proponents say they have found a way around the wall, parents are quick to believe. . . . But . . . the workshops can cost $250. The equipment $800 more. And what do we get for our money? Parents themselves "can't facilitate," they tell us. Our children will require facilitated communication for life, they say, and will never communicate on their own. . . . In short, the price we are asked to pay in an effort to communicate with our children is to allow strangers into our families to mediate our relationships with our own kids and to accept everything the stranger tells us on blind faith. (Mark S. Painter, Sr. [Dillon, 1993])

FC is of special interest to our discussion of a scientific approach to research because it meets many of the criteria of *pseudoscience:* demonstrations of benefit are based on anecdotes or testimonials, the child's baseline abilities and the possibility of spontaneous improvement are ignored, and related scientific procedures are disavowed. The differences between scientific and pseudoscientific claims are not simply whether or not they are based on evidence (Finn, Bothe, & Bramlett, 2005). As we discuss later in this chapter, it is the quality of the evidence, how it was obtained, and how it is presented that are crucial in evaluating whether claims are scientifically believable. Scientists are certainly capable of making incorrect claims. What distinguishes them from pseudoscientists is that they play by the rules of science, are prepared to admit when they are wrong, and are open to change based on new evidence (Lilienfeld, Lynn, & Lohr, 2003). Because a scientific approach to research is diverse and complex, many criteria, methods, and practices are necessary to depict how this approach is applied in abnormal child psychology. This will be our focus in the sections that follow, where we consider research in abnormal child psychology—from the questions that researchers who study childhood disorders typically seek to address, to the research process, to the methods and research designs used to study problems in children. In the last section, we discuss important ethical and pragmatic issues. The research that we present throughout this book emphasizes a scientific approach to abnormal child psychology. As we begin this journey, it is also important to keep in mind that science is a social enterprise undertaken by humans, and research is inevitably influenced by scientists' values (Sonuga-Barke, 2011).

Section Summary

A Scientific Approach

- A scientific approach to abnormal child psychology is a way of thinking about how best to understand and answer questions of interest, not just an accumulation of specific methods, practices, or procedures.

- Science requires that theories be backed up by evidence from controlled studies and that observations be checked and repeated before conclusions are drawn.

- Facilitated communication (FC) meets many of the criteria of pseudoscience because demonstrations of benefit are based on anecdotes or testimonials, the child's baseline abilities and the possibility of spontaneous improvement are ignored, and typical scientific procedures are disavowed.

- What distinguishes science from pseudoscience is that scientists play by the rules of science, are prepared to admit when they are wrong, and are open to change.

THE RESEARCH PROCESS

Science is not a collection of facts, any more than opera is a collection of notes. It's a process, a way of thinking, based on a single insight—that the degree to which an idea seems true has nothing to do with whether it is true, and that the way to distinguish factual ideas from false ones is to test them by experiment.

—Ferris (1998)

Research in abnormal child psychology is best characterized as a multistage process involving key decisions at various points. The process typically begins with the researcher(s) developing a hypothesis (research question) on the basis of observation, theory, and previous findings, and deciding on a general approach to research. The next stage involves identifying the sample to be studied, selecting measurement methods, and developing a research design and procedures. The research design and procedures must balance practical considerations with the adequacy of the research to address the hypotheses under investigation. The final stage consists of gathering and analyzing the data and interpreting the results in relation to theory and previous findings in an attempt to resolve the problem that initially led to the research. In this ongoing process, findings and interpretations from the study can then be used to generate future research questions and stimulate further research.

The main stages of the research process are summarized in ● Figure 3.1. Keep in mind that ethical considerations in conducting research with children and families must be considered at every stage of this process. We will discuss these ethical considerations in the final section of this chapter, "Ethical and Pragmatic Issues."

Since there is no one "correct" approach to research, most problems in abnormal child psychology are best studied by using multiple strategies and multiple methods (Rutter & Solantaus, 2014). Research is much like any decision-making process. This process requires an understanding of the conceptual, methodological, and practical considerations to make informed decisions about when certain research methods and strategies are appropriate and when they are not. To study abnormal child psychology, researchers must include research designs and methods of data analysis that can identify direct and indirect effects and different causal pathways for various disorders (Cicchetti & Hinshaw, 2003). We discuss common research questions and topics in abnormal child psychology in the sections that follow, addressing specific issues encountered at different stages of the research process.

Common Research Questions and Topics

Parents typically ask similar questions about their children, and the cases of Whitney (age 14) and Tito (age 7) provide examples.

WHITNEY

Always Sad

I don't understand why Whitney is so sad all the time. She's continually arguing with her brother, hates school, and has no friends. She's always been a moody child, but became much worse after my husband and I divorced. Is her sadness due to her moody personality, the divorce, or is something at home or at school making her feel this way? (Based on authors' case material)

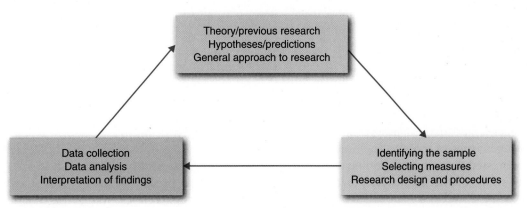

● **FIGURE 3.1** | The research process in abnormal child psychology.

© Cengage Learning®

Constantly Fighting

Tito is constantly fighting with other kids at school. He never does what we ask him to do. When things don't go his way, he has a full-blown tantrum and throws and breaks things. My husband thinks Tito's just a tough kid, and that all he needs is firm discipline. He uses his belt a lot with Tito, but it doesn't seem to make a difference. I'm really worried. Will Tito outgrow his behavior? Is my husband being too strict? What can I do about it? (Based on authors' case material)

These case examples include typical questions that parents ask about their children's problem behavior and development. They are also questions that generate abnormal child behavior research: for example, research on the impact of divorce on children's mood and behavior, as in Whitney's case, or whether fighting and destructive behavior are likely to decrease with age, as in the case of Tito. As noted above, research typically begins with a hypothesis based on a theory, which predicts certain outcomes or behavior. Research hypotheses guide the researcher's choice of methods and the research designs most appropriate for answering certain questions. Research questions and topics are often based on theories of atypical development and behavior (discussed in Chapter 2). Some studies test predictions drawn from a single theory, whereas others test predictions based on different theories. When little or no theoretical knowledge is available, investigators may also develop a research question without an explicit prediction. For example, are there more depressed children today than there were a generation ago? Is child abuse more prevalent in our society than in other parts of the world?

Nature and Distribution of Childhood Disorders

Questions regarding the nature and distribution of childhood disorders include how disorders are defined, diagnosed, and expressed at different ages and in different settings. Related questions are directed at patterns of symptoms, base rates for various child problems and competencies, and natural progressions of problems and competencies over time. Such questions are frequently addressed through **epidemiological research,** which is the study of the incidence, prevalence, and co-occurrence of childhood disorders and competencies in clinic-referred and community samples (Costello, Egger, & Angold, 2005a). **Incidence rates**

reflect the extent to which new cases of a disorder appear over a specified period (e.g., the number of youths who develop a depressive disorder during the school year). **Prevalence rates** refer to all cases, whether new or previously existing, observed during a specified period of time (e.g., the number of teens with conduct disorder in the general population during 2012 and 2013). Estimates of incidence and prevalence can be obtained over a short period, such as 6 months, or over a much longer period. For example, *lifetime prevalence* indicates whether children in the sample have had the disorder at any time in their lives.

Knowledge about the risk for, and expression of, an individual disorder over the life course helps us understand the nature of the disorder and use this understanding as the basis for prevention and treatment (Costello & Angold, 2006). For example, studies of teens over time have found depression to be a recurrent disorder with poor long-term outcomes for many youngsters. This knowledge about the course of the disorder has resulted in promising new approaches to prevent and treat depression in young people, which we present in Chapter 10, "Depressive and Bipolar Disorders."

As we noted in Chapter 1, about 10% to 20% of children worldwide have a clinically diagnosable disorder, and many more exhibit specific symptoms or subclinical problems (Belfer, 2008). However, overall rates obscure the enormous variability in reported rates from study to study. It can be very confusing when one study reports a prevalence rate of 1% and another reports a rate of 20% for the same disorder at roughly the same point in time. Similarly, rates of reported problems in children have been found to vary from 6% to 20% when reported by teachers and from 10% to 40% when reported by parents (Costello & Angold, 2006). Some studies would lead you to conclude that almost every child you encounter has a problem; for others, the problem is so rare you wonder whether it even exists. Which conclusion is accurate?

To answer this question, we must know something about epidemiological research and how estimates of the number of cases (e.g., children with a problem or disorder) are made. Cases may be defined in terms of single symptoms, multiple symptoms, or patterns of symptoms with likely causes and associated characteristics. Estimates of prevalence vary widely depending on which definition we use, with estimates based on single symptoms being much higher than those based on patterns of symptoms. It is sobering to learn that lifetime prevalence estimates of mental disorders obtained prospectively (studying the same sample of children over time and assessing them at periodic intervals) are *double* those found in retrospective studies (asking people to remember what occurred at an earlier time), which are subject to recall failure (Moffitt et al., 2010). Case definition in abnormal child psychology is complex because children do not refer themselves for treatment. Therefore, equating illness with seeking treatment can be misleading. The factors that lead to referral sometimes have more to do with the child's parents, teachers, or doctor than with the child's behavior. Therefore, it is important that we study problems in children who are not referred to clinics for treatment as well as those who are. Throughout this book you will see many examples of striking differences in prevalence rates and other research findings, depending on whether children from clinics or children from community samples are the focus of study.

Prevalence rates also vary depending on whether cases are defined in terms of patterns of symptoms, impairment in functioning (e.g., difficulties at home or at school), or both. Fewer cases are identified when both symptoms and impairment in functioning are used than when definitions are based on either one or the other.

The rate and expression of childhood symptoms and disorders often vary in relation to demographic and situational factors, such as socioeconomic status (SES) (e.g., the social, economic, and physical environment in which the child lives as reflected in measures such as family income, education, or occupation); parents' marital status; and the child's age, gender, and cultural background, to name but a few. Consequently, these variables must be assessed and controlled for in most studies. For example, children from one ethnic group may display higher rates of learning problems than those from another ethnic group and may also have a lower SES. If we don't take SES into account we might conclude that differences in learning are related to ethnicity when they are instead a function of factors associated with lower SES such as poor nutrition and fewer learning opportunities. Similarly, although conduct problems are reported to be more frequent in African American than in Caucasian youngsters (McLaughlin, Hilt, & Nolen-Hoeksema, 2007), this finding is likely an artifact related to SES. That is, conduct problems are more prevalent in low-SES families and, since African American children are overrepresented in such families in North America, it is likely that the link between race and conduct problems is accounted for by stressful conditions associated with growing up in a poor family (Bird et al., 2001). In support of this, few differences in conduct problems in African American versus Caucasian youth are reported for primarily middle-class samples (Sameroff, Peck, & Eccles, 2004). The importance of cultural differences is highlighted in A Closer Look 3.1, which shows an

Children's socioeconomic status and cultural background play an important role in the rate and expression of childhood symptoms and disorders

example of epidemiological research into the types of child behavior problems reported by parents in seven cultures.

Correlates, Risks, and Causes

Whitney, in the case at the beginning of this section, displays persistent sadness that seems to be related to several variables: her history of being a moody child, her parents' divorce, her problems at school, and her lack of friends. Do any of these variables, alone or in combination, account for her sadness? If so, in what ways? Three variables of interest in abnormal child psychology are correlates, risk or protective factors, and causes of other variables. Most research in abnormal child psychology is designed to answer questions about the relation between the three general variables and childhood disorders. Because virtually all childhood disorders are the result of multiple variables interacting with one another over time, answers to these questions are rarely straightforward.

Correlates refer to variables that are associated at a particular point in time with no clear proof that one precedes the other. For example, Whitney's having no friends is associated with her sadness. Is she sad because she has no friends, or has her sadness prevented her from making friends? Since we don't know which variable came first, her lack of friends and her sadness are correlated variables.

A *risk factor* is a variable that precedes an outcome of interest and increases the chances of a negative outcome (see Chapter 1). For example, Whitney's depressed mood got worse following her parents' divorce. Do you think parental divorce is a risk factor for the development of depression or other problems in children? Remember that a risk factor increases the chances for

Cross-Cultural Epidemiological Research: Behavior Problems Reported by Parents of Children in Seven Cultures

Widespread movements of refugees and immigrants are placing millions of children into new and unfamiliar environments. Evaluating the mental health of these children can be difficult because of cultural variations in what constitutes abnormal behavior, how to identify such behavior, and what to do about it. Crijnen, Achenbach, and Verhulst (1997) examined the 6-month prevalence rates of child behavior problems as reported by parents or parent surrogates in studies carried out in seven cultures, using the same measurement instrument—the Child Behavior Checklist (CBCL) (Achenbach, 1991a). As shown in the figure, the total problem scores of children in Puerto Rico and China were well above the overall mean. In contrast, the total problem scores of children in Germany and Israel, were well below the overall mean. This epidemiological study indicates that parents in different cultures report different rates of problem behavior in their children. However, the findings do not indicate why these differences occur. Other kinds of studies are needed to answer that question—for example, research into cultural variations in child-rearing practices or expectations for child behavior (Achenbach & Rescorla, 2007).

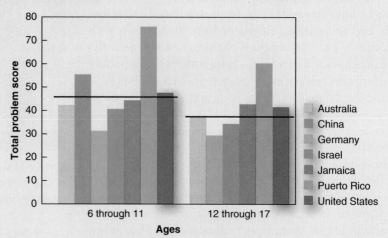

Total problem scores for children in seven different cultures. Overall mean Child Behavior Checklist (CBCL) problem scores and mean CBCL problem scores for each culture at ages 6 through 11 and ages 12 through 17. Overall mean scores across cultures for each age grouping are indicated by solid horizontal lines. China did not provide enough 12- through 17-year-olds for analysis.

Based on Journal of the American Academy of Child & Adolescent Psychiatry, 36, A.A.M. Crijnen, T.M. Achenbach & F.C. Verhulst, Comparisons of Problems Reported by Parents of Children in 12 Cultures: Total Problems, Externalizing, and Internalizing, 1269–1277.

a certain outcome. It does not mean that it will occur; its occurrence will depend on other factors. Obviously, most children of parents who divorce do not become clinically depressed. Divorce is not necessarily a cause of a youngster's depression and low self-esteem, but it can be a risk factor (Hetherington, Bridges, & Insabella, 1998). A *protective factor* is a positive variable that precedes an outcome of interest and decreases the chances that a negative outcome will occur. The close relationship enjoyed by Whitney and her mother may serve as a protective factor against future episodes of depression.

Research into risk and protective factors often requires that large samples of children be studied and that multiple domains of child functioning—physical, cognitive, psychosocial—be assessed over long periods of time. This is necessary because: (1) only a small proportion of children at risk for a problem will actually develop the disorder; (2) the areas of child functioning

that will be affected, and how they will be affected, are not known in advance; and (3) the ages at which a disorder may occur or reoccur are also not known in advance. Sometimes the effects of exposure to a risk factor during infancy or early childhood may not be visible until adolescence or adulthood. The possibility that delayed, or *sleeper,* effects will occur complicates the study of risk and protective factors, since children must be studied for many years if delayed effects are to be detected.

Finally, other variables are *causes.* They influence, either directly or indirectly through other variables, the occurrence of a behavior or disorder of interest. Tito's father uses severe punishment when his son misbehaves. Is this punishment a cause of Tito's aggressive behavior? Is Tito learning aggressive behavior from his father? Questions about causes are complicated because what qualifies as a cause will vary according to the variables of interest and how far back in time a causal chain can be traced. Because childhood disorders are the result of multiple factors acting in concert, a challenge for researchers is to identify the relative contributions of each factor and—more importantly—to determine how they combine and interact over time to produce specific outcomes (Dodge & Pettit, 2003). When it comes to childhood disorders, "with very few exceptions, there is no such thing as a single basic necessary and sufficient cause" (Rutter, 2007b, p. 378). However, scientific research can help strengthen or weaken certain inferences about the causal role of some variables versus others.

Moderating and Mediating Variables

The key difference between moderating and mediating variables is that moderators have an independent effect on the existing relationship between two variables, whereas mediators account for some or all of the apparent relationship between two variables. **Moderator variables** influence the *direction* or *strength* of the relationship of variables of interest. The association between two variables depends on or differs as a function of moderating variables, such as the child's age, sex, SES, or cultural background. For example, as illustrated in ● Figure 3.2, in a study examining the relation between adolescents' self-reported history of physical abuse and their self-reports of internalizing problems such as anxiety and depression, McGee, Wolfe, and Wilson (1997) found that the correlation between the severity of physical abuse history and internalizing problems was greater for females than for males. The child's sex was a moderator variable; that is, the relationship between two of the variables (in this case, abuse and internalizing problems) differed, depending on the third (if the adolescent was a boy or a girl).

Mediator variables refer to the process, mechanism, or means through which a variable produces a particular outcome. Mediators describe what happens at the psychological or neurobiological level to explain how one variable results from another. In one study, Snyder (1991) found that on days when mothers of 4- to 5-year-old children experienced negative moods and frequent hassles, they were most likely to respond negatively to their children's misbehavior and to reinforce their children's coercive tactics during mother–child conflicts. In turn, the use of these types of maternal discipline was related to an increase in same-day child behavior problems. As shown in ● Figure 3.3, these findings indicate that the relationship between maternal distress and child conduct problems is partly mediated by the type of discipline mothers use on days when they feel distressed. Mothers' disciplinary strategies help explain the relationship between maternal distress and child conduct problems.

Outcomes

What are the long-term outcomes for children who experience problems? Many childhood problems decrease or go away as children mature, but we need to know at approximately what age such improvements may be expected. Similarly, will other problems emerge, such as the child developing a low opinion of himself or herself because of trouble with, say, wetting the bed or worrying too much about school? Returning to Tito's oppositional and aggressive behaviors, will we expect his problems to decrease or go away as he gets older, or do they forecast continued conflict with peers, future school problems, and later difficulties in social adjustment? The study of outcomes in abnormal

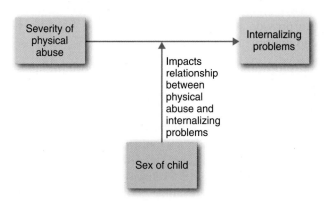

● **FIGURE 3.2** | Example of a moderator variable: Sex of the child moderates the relationship between abuse and internalizing problems.

© Cengage Learning®

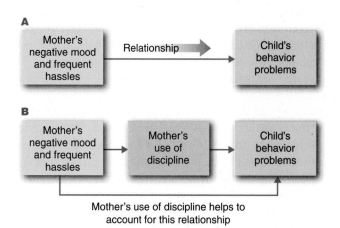

Mother's use of discipline helps to account for this relationship

● **FIGURE 3.3** | Mediating variables: The type of discipline used by mothers on days they are feeling distressed mediates the relationship between maternal distress and child behavior problems.

© Cengage Learning®

child psychology is perhaps one of the most important research topics in the field today.

Interventions

How effective are our methods for treating or preventing childhood problems? Are some types of treatment more effective than others? Questions about treatment and prevention are concerned with evaluating the short- and long-term effects of psychological, environmental, and biological treatments; comparing the relative effectiveness of differing forms and combinations of treatment; and identifying the reasons that a particular treatment works. The questions also concern identifying factors that influence the referral and treatment process; understanding how processes such as the child–therapist relationship contribute to treatment outcomes; and assessing the acceptability of equivalent forms of treatment to children, parents, and teachers.

Many treatments for children and adolescents have not been evaluated, although this situation is steadily improving (Silverman & Hinshaw, 2008). These days, numerous studies evaluate treatment outcomes using **randomized controlled trials (RCTs)**, in which children with a particular problem are randomly assigned to different treatment and control conditions. We discuss the importance of random assignment later in this chapter. Findings from controlled research studies indicate that children who receive treatment are generally better off than children who do not.

However, an important distinction needs to be made between treatment efficacy and treatment effectiveness (Chorpita et al., 2011). **Treatment efficacy** refers to whether the treatment can produce changes under well-controlled conditions. In efficacy research, careful control is exercised over the selection of cases, therapists, and delivery and monitoring of treatment. In contrast, **treatment effectiveness** refers to whether the treatment can be shown to work in clinical practice, not just in well-controlled research settings. In research on effectiveness, treatment is evaluated in clinical settings, clients are usually referred rather than selected, and therapists provide services without many of the rigorous controls used in research. The benefits of treatment for children with problems have generally been found to be lower in clinical practice settings (effectiveness trials) than in controlled research settings (efficacy trials) (Weisz et al., 2013). As a result, a high priority for intervention research is on developing and testing interventions in settings where clinical services for youths are typically provided and finding ways to strengthen the bridge between research, public policy, and clinical practice (Chorpita & Daleiden, 2014; Weisz, 2014; Weisz, Ng, & Bearman, 2014). Relatedly, there is a growing interest in the design, development, and investigation of new technologies as a service delivery vehicle that could help to reduce the gap between intervention research and clinical practice (Jones, 2014).

Section Summary

The Research Process

- Research is a multistage process that involves generating hypotheses, devising an overall plan, selecting measures, developing a research design and procedures, gathering and analyzing the data, and interpreting the results.
- One's theory of abnormal child behavior determines the variables studied, the choice of research methods, and the interpretation of research findings.
- Questions about the nature and distribution of childhood problems are addressed through epidemiological research into the incidence and prevalence of childhood disorders and competencies in clinic-referred and community samples.
- Other common research topics in abnormal child psychology focus on correlates, risk and protective factors, causes, moderating and mediating variables, outcomes, and interventions for childhood disorders.

METHODS OF STUDYING BEHAVIOR

The study of children's behavioral and emotional problems requires that the methods we use to measure these problems generate scores that are reliable and valid. This is no easy task. Children's problems must be evaluated based on samples of their behavior in different situations (e.g., home or school) that often reflect differing perspectives of adults. These evaluations are likely to be affected by the child's age, sex, and cultural background and by the assessors' personal expectations and values. As a result, no single measurement can provide a complete picture of a child's problems, and multiple measures and sources of information are needed.

Standardization, Reliability, and Validity

The methods and measures that we use to study child and family behavior must undergo careful study to determine how well they measure constructs such as depression, anxiety, and intellectual disability. The use of well-standardized, reliable, and valid measures and procedures is essential to scientific research, as depicted in ● Figure 3.4.

Standardization is a process that specifies a set of standards or norms for a method of measurement that are to

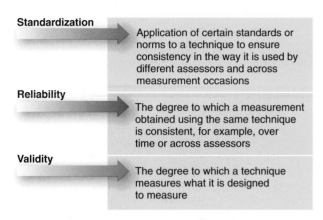

Standardization → Application of certain standards or norms to a technique to ensure consistency in the way it is used by different assessors and across measurement occasions

Reliability → The degree to which a measurement obtained using the same technique is consistent, for example, over time or across assessors

Validity → The degree to which a technique measures what it is designed to measure

● **FIGURE 3.4** | Concepts that determine the value of our methods of measurement and assessment.

© Cengage Learning®

be used consistently across different assessments of the construct of interest. These standards and norms relate to the procedures that must be followed during administration, scoring, and evaluation of findings—for example, as specified in a manual for an intelligence test. Without standardization, it is nearly impossible to replicate the information obtained using a method of measurement. In addition, results are likely to be unique to the situation in which they are obtained and will not apply to other situations. In some cases, the measure may be applied to many children who vary in age, gender, race, SES, or diagnosis. The scores are then used for comparison purposes. However, the test scores of an 8-year-old boy from a low-SES background should be compared with the scores of other children like him, not with the scores of a 16-year-old girl from an upper-SES background.

Reliability refers to the consistency, or repeatability, of results obtained using a specific method of measurement. One type of reliability, *internal consistency,* refers to whether all parts of a method of measurement contribute in a meaningful way to the information obtained. To be reliable, information must also not depend on a single observer or clinician; various people must agree on what they see. This is known as *interrater reliability.* Imagine how you might react if you took your child to see three different psychologists and received three different diagnoses and three different treatment recommendations. How would you know which one was correct? In this case, the diagnoses would not be reliable because two or more of the psychologists did not agree. Similarly, tests or interviews repeated within a short time interval should yield similar results on the two occasions. In other words, the results need to be stable over time, which is referred to as *test–retest reliability.*

Reliability alone isn't enough to determine whether a method reflects the investigator's goals—validity must also be demonstrated. The **validity** of a method refers to the extent to which it actually measures the dimension or construct that the researcher sets out to measure. Validity is not all or none but rather a matter of degree, and it can be assessed in many ways. First, the measure can be examined for its *face validity,* or the extent to which it appears to assess the construct of interest. A questionnaire that asks whether you get nervous before taking an exam would be a face-valid measure of test anxiety, whereas one that asks if you think you are a parrot would not. *Construct validity* refers to whether scores on a measure behave as predicted by theory or past research. For example, a test of intelligence has construct validity if children who obtain high scores on the test also have better grades in school, understanding of concepts, verbal reasoning, recall, and parent ratings of intelligence than do children who obtain low scores on the test. Two components of construct validity are convergent validity and discriminant validity. *Convergent validity* reflects the correlation between measures that are expected to be related—for example, a teen's report of her depression in a screening interview and her scores on a depression questionnaire. It is an indication of the extent to which the two measures assess similar or related constructs—in this case, depression. This is in contrast to *discriminant validity,* which refers to the degree of correlation between measures that are not expected to be related to one another. For example, scores on a measure designed to assess depression and another designed to assess intelligence should not correlate.

Finally, *criterion-related validity* refers to how well a measure predicts behavior in settings where we would expect it to do so—at the same time (concurrent validity), or in the future (predictive validity). For example, a child's high scores on a measure of social anxiety should predict that the child would display anxiety or avoidance in current social situations and will perhaps have difficulties making friends in the future. Criterion-related validity tells whether scores on a measure can be used for their intended purpose.

Measurement Methods

A variety of measurement method options are available to assess important dimensions of children's behavioral, cognitive, emotional, and neurodevelopmental functioning. These methods are explicit plans to observe and assess children and their surroundings in ways that will reveal relatively clear relations among variables of interest.

Among the measurement options in abnormal child psychology are interviews, questionnaires,

TABLE 3.1 | Interview, Questionnaire, and Observation

	Interview	Questionnaire	Observation
Structure of situation	Semistructured or structured	Highly structured	Structured or unstructured
Structure of responses	Probe, expand, and clarify	Highly structured; no opportunity for probes or clarification	Vary from very inclusive observation of all behaviors to highly selective coding of very specific behaviors (e.g., number of "smiles")
Resource requirements	Considerable time needed for interviewing and coding responses and scoring.	Little investigator time needed for administration	Extensive time needed for observing and for coding and summarizing observations
Sources of bias	Relies on participants' perceptions and willingness to report; responses may be influenced by interviewer characteristics and mannerisms	Relies on participants' perceptions and willingness to report	Does not rely on participants' providing specific information, but what is observed may be influenced by the presence of the observer
Data reduction	Requires analysis or recoding of narrative responses	Little data reduction needed	Highly influenced by the complexity of the observation system

© Cengage Learning®

checklists and rating scales, psychophysiological recordings, brain imaging, performance measures, and direct observations of behavior (Mash & Barkley, 2007). A variety of intellectual, academic, and neuropsychological tests are also used (Sattler, 2008). In this chapter, we focus primarily on how these methods are used in research. We talk more about their use in clinical practice and about tests and testing in Chapter 4.

As presented in a comparison of three of the most commonly used methods of gathering data—interviews, questionnaires, and observations—shows how they differ on important dimensions. Because the information we obtain from children and families often varies as a function of the method used, researchers frequently rely on several methods to define and assess the constructs of interest.

Reporting

Reporting methods assess the perceptions, thoughts, behaviors, feelings, and past experiences of the child, parents, and teachers. These instruments include relatively unstructured clinical interviews, highly structured diagnostic interviews, and questionnaires. An important question regarding reporting methods relates to who is reporting on behavior. For example, with a *self-report measure*, a child or parent will provide information about his or her own behavior, feelings, and thoughts. Alternatively, using an *informant-report measure*, a person who is well

acquainted with the child, usually a parent or a teacher, will provide information about a child's behaviors, feelings, or thoughts based on his or her observations of the child.

A concern with self- and informant-report methods is how accurately children, parents, or teachers report their own or others' thoughts, feelings, and behaviors. Inaccuracies may occur because of a failure to recall important events, selective recall or bias, and in some cases, intentional distortions. Some individuals may try to make themselves or others look better or worse than they actually are. Reporting methods also require a certain level of verbal ability and may not accurately assess individuals who have difficulty expressing themselves. Obviously, young children would fall into this category—children under the age of 7 or 8 are usually not reliable reporters of their own behavior. Individuals from a cultural background different from the one in which a reporting method was developed may have difficulty understanding and responding to certain questions. For this reason, it is essential that the reporting method used be sensitive to the language and cultural background of the person being evaluated.

Psychophysiological Methods

Psychophysiological methods assess the relationship between physiological processes and behavior to identify which nervous system structures and processes contribute to children's atypical development and behavior. Among the most common measures are autonomic nervous system activity, such as heart rate, blood pressure, breathing, pupil dilation, and electrical conductance of the skin. Changes in heart rate, for example, may be related to emotional responses. In addition, specific patterns of autonomic arousal may be associated with differences in children's temperament—their degree of shyness with people or responses to novel events (discussed in Chapter 11).

There are many limitations associated with psychophysiological measures, especially with young children. Sometimes, findings for these measures are inconsistent from one study to the next, and researchers may have to infer how the child may have processed a particular event or stimulus. Also, a child's physiological response can be influenced easily by other factors, such as the child's reaction to the recording equipment or to hunger, fatigue, or boredom. These extraneous influences must be minimized if conclusions are to be based on psychophysiological measures.

Many studies have used an *electrophysiological measure* of brain functioning, the **electroencephalogram (EEG)**, to link the brain's measurable electrical activity with ongoing thinking, emotion, or state of arousal (Rothenberger, 2009). The EEG records electrical brain activity using electrodes attached to the surface of the child's scalp. Because different EEG waves are related to different states of arousal, differential patterns of EEG activation may suggest sleep disturbances or various emotional states. For example, with respect to emotional states, a greater amount of electrical activity in the right frontal lobe of the brain as compared with the left frontal lobe is associated with anxiety and depression (McManis et al., 2002).

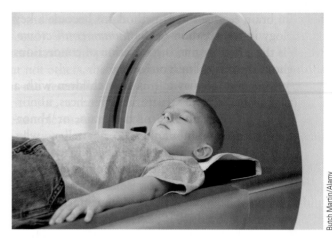

A child about to be evaluated using computed tomography (CT or CAT) scan

Neuroimaging Methods

Neuroimaging methods are used to examine the structure and/or function of the living brain (Wong, Grunder, & Brasic, 2007). These methods provide new ways of testing neurobiological and other theories for many childhood disorders—for example, by identifying abnormalities in the structure or functioning of specific brain regions or in how regions of the brain communicate with one another. These brain abnormalities, for instance, may cause the problems that children with autism have in recognizing people's facial expressions. *Structural* brain imaging procedures include *magnetic resonance imaging* (MRI) and *computed tomographic* (CT) scans. MRI uses radio signals generated in a strong magnetic field and passed through brain tissue to produce fine-grained analyses of brain structures. CT scans also reveal the various structures of the brain. As we will see in Chapter 8, findings from CT and MRI studies have led to the hypothesis of abnormal neural maturation in children with attention-deficit/hyperactivity disorder (ADHD).

Two types of functional imaging procedures are *functional magnetic resonance imaging (fMRI)* and *positron-emission tomography* (PET). fMRI is a form of MRI that registers neural activity in functioning areas of the brain. By doing so, it can show which brain areas are active during particular mental operations such as solving a specific type of problem or reacting to a fear-inducing stimulus. PET scans assess cerebral glucose metabolism. Glucose is the brain's main source of energy, so measuring how much is used is a good way to determine the brain's activity level.

Diffusion MRI (dMRI) is a magnetic imaging method that produces images showing *connections*

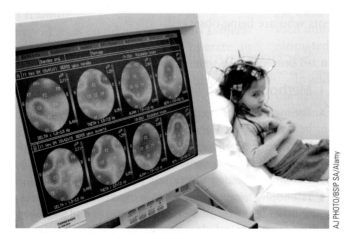

An electroencephalogram (EEG) is used to monitor electrical activity of the brain in a young girl

A failure to consider comorbidity may result in an interpretation of findings in relation to one disorder, when these findings are more validly attributed to a second disorder or to a combination of disorders. To deal with comorbidity in research samples, some researchers may select only participants with single, or pure, disorders. This strategy may yield small, atypical samples whose findings do not generalize to other populations. Although there is no single research strategy to address questions about comorbidity, studies that compare children showing single disorders with children showing comorbid disorders are needed to help disentangle the effects of comorbidity. It also needs to be recognized that much of the comorbidity among disorders may be artifactual, related more to the overlap in symptoms used to define and diagnose childhood disorders than to the co-occurrence of distinct conditions (Drabick & Kendall, 2010; Rutter, 2010).

A third issue is that we must be sensitive to the setting and source of referral of children for research.

Comorbidity: A 10-year-old girl with multiple disabilities, including intellectual disability, autism, and epilepsy.

©iStockphoto.com/ktaylorg

Random selection occurs when subjects are drawn from a population in a way that gives each individual in that population an equal chance of being selected for the study. This is rare in studies of child psychopathology. At the other end of the spectrum are studies that use *samples of convenience,* in which subjects are selected for a study merely because of their availability, regardless of whether they provide a suitable test of the questions or conditions of interest. Research samples in abnormal child psychology have been selected from numerous settings, including outpatient psychology and psychiatry clinics, schools, hospitals, day-care centers, and the community. Effects related to different settings are often confounded with effects related to different referral sources (e.g., physicians, teachers, and parents), since referral sources also differ across settings.

General Research Strategies

There are several different, yet complementary, approaches to research design that offer various advantages and disadvantages. The choice of approach frequently depends on the research questions being addressed, the nature of the childhood disorder under investigation, and the availability of resources (Hartmann, Pelzel, & Abbott, 2011).

Nonexperimental and Experimental Research

One goal of scientific research is to simplify and isolate variables in order to study them more closely. Varying or manipulating values of the variable(s) of interest while trying to control or hold constant other factors that could influence the results meets this goal. Doing this makes it possible to study the association between the particular variables of interest. The basic distinction between nonexperimental versus experimental research reflects the degree to which the investigator can manipulate the experimental variable or, alternatively, must rely on examining the natural covariation of several variables of interest. The *independent variable* is manipulated by the researcher. Based on a research hypothesis, the independent variable is anticipated to cause a change in another variable. The variable expected to be influenced by the independent variable is called the *dependent variable.* The greater the degree of control that the researcher has over the independent variable(s), the more the study approximates a true experiment.

In a **true experiment** the researcher has maximum control over the independent variable or conditions of interest and can use random assignment of subjects to groups, include needed control conditions, and control possible sources of bias. Conversely, the less control the researcher has in determining which participants will and will not be exposed to the independent variable(s), the more nonexperimental the research will be. Most variables of interest in child psychopathology cannot be manipulated directly, including the nature or severity of the child's disorder, parenting practices, or genetic influences. As a result, much of the research conducted on children with problems and their families relies on nonexperimental, correlational approaches.

In *correlational studies*, researchers often examine relationships among variables by using a **correlation coefficient**, a number that describes the degree of association between two variables. A correlation coefficient can range from −1.00 to +1.00. The size of the correlation indicates the strength of the association between two variables. A zero correlation indicates no relationship; the closer the value gets to −1.00 or +1.00, the stronger the relationship is. The sign of the correlation coefficient (plus or minus) indicates the direction of the relationship. A positive sign (+) indicates that as one variable increases in value, so does the other, whereas a negative sign (−) indicates that as one variable increases, the other decreases.

For example, a positive correlation of +0.70 between symptoms of anxiety and symptoms of depression indicates that children who show many symptoms of anxiety are also likely to display symptoms of depression. Alternatively, children who show few symptoms of anxiety are likely to display few symptoms of depression. However, a negative correlation of −0.70 between symptoms of depression and social skills, for example, indicates that children who show many symptoms of depression have fewer social skills.

The primary limitation of correlational studies is that interpretations of causality cannot be made. A correlation between two variables does not mean that one variable causes the other. If we find a relationship

Children's symptoms of anxiety and depression are often positively correlated.

between depression in children and depression in their parents, it could mean that being around a child who is depressed may lead to depression in parents, that parental depression may lead to depression in the child, or that depression in the child and parent may both be due to another, more fundamental variable, such as a shared genetic disposition to depression.

In experimental investigations, researchers must take steps to control for characteristics of participants that could decrease the accuracy of the findings. For example, if two groups of children differ with respect to education, intelligence, SES, or the presence of related disorders, it would be impossible to determine whether the independent variable or the other characteristics led to the results. **Random assignment** of participants to treatment conditions protects against this problem because the probability of a subject's appearing in any of the groups is the same. By assigning participants to groups on the basis of the flip of a coin, numbers drawn from a hat, or a table of random numbers, the chance is increased that characteristics other than the independent variable will be equally distributed across treatment groups.

As we have noted, many hypotheses in abnormal child psychology cannot be tested by randomly assigning participants to conditions or by manipulating conditions in the real world. A compromise involves the use of natural experiments, also called *quasi-experimental designs* or *known-group comparisons*. In **natural experiments**, comparisons are made between conditions or treatments that already exist. The experiments may involve children with different disorders, parents with different problems, or different family environments (e.g., children who have suffered from neglect vs. children who have not). These studies are essentially correlational, but the subjects are selected to ensure that their characteristics are as comparable as possible, with the exception of the independent variable. Despite the extreme care exercised by researchers to equate existing groups, natural experiments cannot achieve the same level of precision and rigor as true experimental research. Nevertheless, for many important questions in abnormal child psychology, natural experiments using known-group comparisons are the only option (Rutter, 2007b).

Prospective and Retrospective Research

Research designs that address questions about the causes and long-term outcomes of childhood disorders may differ with respect to the time the sample is identified and the time data are collected. In a **retrospective design**, a sample of people is identified at the current time and asked for information relating to an earlier time. Individuals are identified who already show the outcome of interest, and they are compared with controls who do not show the outcome. Assessments focus on characteristics in the past, and inferences are made about past characteristics and the current outcome. For example, a sample of young adults with a substance-use disorder might be asked to provide retrospective ratings and descriptions of their early family experiences.

Although data are immediately available in retrospective studies, they are also highly susceptible to bias and distortion in recall. Parents of teenagers diagnosed with schizophrenia may reinterpret their views of the teen's childhood, distorting their recollection of the teen's prior behavior or friendships. Moreover, retrospective designs fail to identify the individuals who were exposed to certain earlier experiences but did not develop the problem. Young adult females with an eating disorder may report more childhood experiences of sexual abuse. However, this finding could not serve as the basis for a conclusion that childhood sexual abuse is a specific precursor to eating disorders in young adulthood. The retrospective study fails to identify children who experienced childhood sexual abuse but did not develop an eating disorder as young adults.

In **real-time prospective designs**, the research sample is identified and then followed over time, with data collected at specified time intervals. The same youngsters are followed or assessed over time in order to understand the course of change or differences that may develop over time or during important developmental transitions such as middle-school entry or adolescence. For example, infants who are fearful in response to novel events may be followed over time to determine whether they later develop anxiety disorders or other problems to a greater extent than infants who are not fearful.

Prospective designs correct for several of the problems associated with retrospective research. By following a sample over time we can identify children who develop a disorder as well as those who do not. Since information is collected in real time, problems relating to bias and distortion in recall are minimized. Disadvantages of prospective designs include loss of participants over time and the extended length of time needed to collect data.

Analogue Research

Analogue research evaluates a specific variable of interest under conditions that only resemble or approximate the situation for which one wishes to generalize. Analogue studies focus on a circumscribed research question under well-controlled conditions. Often, the purpose of the research is to illuminate a specific process that would otherwise be difficult to study.

For example, Lang et al. (1989) were interested in whether the higher-than-normal rates of alcohol consumption observed in fathers of boys with attention-deficit/hyperactivity disorder (ADHD)/conduct disorder (CD) might be partly due to the distress associated with interacting with their difficult children (these researchers must have been parents, too!). Male and female single college students who were social drinkers were randomly assigned to interact with boys who were trained to perform behaviors characteristic of either typical children (friendly and cooperative) or children with ADHD/CD (overactive and disruptive). Participants also rated their own mood before and after interactions with the child. After the interaction, participants were given a 20-minute break while they anticipated another interaction with the same child. During the break, beer was freely available for their consumption. Both male and female participants reported comparable levels of elevated distressed mood after interacting with children enacting the ADHD/CD role. However, only the men who had interacted with these children drank enough to increase blood alcohol levels.

The findings suggest that interacting with a child with ADHD/CD may increase alcohol consumption in fathers. However, an analogue study only resembles the conditions of interest—the study participants were single college students, not parents of children with ADHD/CD; the children did not really have ADHD/CD; drinking was confined to an artificial laboratory setting; and only beer was available. Therefore, it is difficult to know whether similar effects would occur in real-life circumstances (despite anecdotal reports by some parents that their kids drive them to drink!). These conditions raise the question of external validity, or the generalizability of research findings.

Research Designs

Research designs are the strategies used to examine question(s) of interest. They refer to the ways in which a researcher arranges conditions to draw valid inferences about the variables of interest.

Case Study

The **case study**, which involves an intensive, usually anecdotal, observation and analysis of an individual child, has a long tradition in the study of abnormal development and behavior. Itard's description of Victor, the Wild Boy of Aveyron; Freud's treatment of a phobia in Little Hans; John Watson's conditioning of a phobic reaction in Albert B.; and many other similar case studies have played an influential role in shaping the way we think about children's problems. The case study, especially as used in the clinical context, brings together a wide range of information about an individual child from various sources, including interviews, observations, and test results. The goal is to get as complete a picture as possible of the child's psychological functioning, current environment, and developmental history. Sometimes the goal is to describe the effects of treatment on the child.

Case studies yield narratives that are rich in detail and provide valuable insights into factors associated with a child's disorder. Nevertheless, they also have drawbacks. They are typically viewed as unscientific and flawed because they are characterized by uncontrolled methods and selective biases, by inherent difficulties associated with integrating diverse observations and drawing valid inferences among the variables of interest, and by generalizations from the particular child of interest to other children. Hence, case studies have been viewed primarily as rich sources of descriptive information that provide a basis for subsequent testing of hypotheses in research using larger samples and more controlled methods. They may also provide a source for developing and trying out new treatment methods.

Despite their unscientific nature, there are compelling reasons why systematically conducted case studies are likely to continue to play a useful role in research on childhood disorders. First, some childhood disorders, such as childhood-onset schizophrenia, are rare, making it difficult to generate large samples of children for research. Second, the analyses of individual cases may contribute to the understanding of many striking symptoms of childhood disorders that either occur infrequently or are hidden and therefore difficult to observe directly. Third, significant childhood disturbances such as posttraumatic stress disorder (see Chapter 12) often develop as the result of a natural disaster, severe trauma, or abuse. These extreme events and circumstances are not easily studied using controlled methods.

Single-Case Experimental Designs

Single-case experimental designs have most frequently been used to evaluate the impact of a clinical treatment, such as reinforcement or stimulant medication, on a child's problem (Kazdin, 2011). The central features of single-case experimental designs that distinguish these from uncontrolled case studies include systematic repeated assessment of behavior over time, the replication of treatment effects within the same subject over time, and the participant's serving as his or her own control by experiencing all treatment conditions (Barlow, Nock, & Hersen, 2009). Many single-subject designs exist, the most common being the A-B-A-B (reversal) design and the multiple-baseline design carried out across behaviors, situations, or individuals.

In an **A-B-A-B reversal design,** a baseline of behavior is first taken (A), followed by an intervention phase (B), then a return-to-baseline phase during which the intervention is removed (A), and a final phase in which the intervention is reintroduced (B). When changes in behavior only occur during the intervention phases, this provides evidence that changes in behavior are due to the intervention. Findings from a study using a *reversal design* are presented in ● Figure 3.5. In this example, a behavioral intervention was used to reduce self-injurious behavior (SIB) in Ann, a 5-year-old girl with profound intellectual disability and multiple handicaps. Ann's SIB consisted of biting her hand and wrists during grooming activities, such as brushing her teeth. These behaviors were getting progressively worse and causing open wounds. During the initial baseline phase, the percentage of intervals during which Ann engaged in SIB during three brief sessions of toothbrushing ranged from 20% to 60%.

Intervention consisted of a negative reinforcement procedure in which Ann was permitted to briefly escape from the grooming activity when she performed an appropriate competing behavior (in this case, pushing a button that, when activated, played the message "Stop!"). She was also physically guided by a trainer to brush her teeth whenever she engaged in SIB. When these procedures were implemented during the intervention phase,

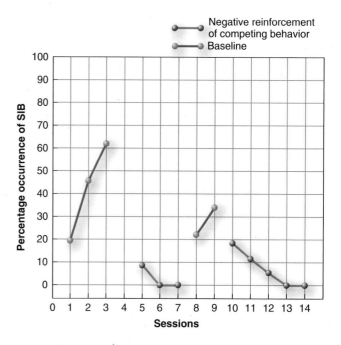

● **FIGURE 3.5** | A-B-A-B (reversal) design: treatment of Ann's self-injurious behavior (SIB).

Based on Use of Negative Reinforcement in the Treatment of Self-Injurious Behavior by M.W. Steege, D.P. Wacker, K.C. Cigrand, W.K. Berg, G.C. Novak, T.M. Reimers, G.M. Sasso & A. DeRaad, 1990, Journal of Applied Behavior Analysis, 23, 459–467.

an immediate reduction of SIB to 10% resulted, with no SIB occurring in the next two sessions. During the reversal, or return-to-baseline, phase, treatment was withdrawn and Ann's SIB increased to previous baseline levels. When treatment was reinstituted, SIB decreased again, and no biting was observed during the final two sessions. The finding that Ann's levels of SIB decreased only during the intervention phases, and not during the baseline or return-to-baseline phases, suggests that the reductions in Ann's SIB resulted from the intervention procedures.

Although the reversal design is applicable for use with a wide range of behaviors, there are limitations. One limitation is that if a treatment really works, the behavior may not reverse during the return-to-baseline phase. Do you see any other limitations of this design? Once Ann stopped engaging in SIB after intervention, do you think there was sufficient justification for reinstituting her harmful behavior for experimental purposes? We intentionally selected this example to illustrate a major limitation of the A-B-A-B design, which is the ethical concerns surrounding the return-to-baseline condition following effective treatment for undesirable or even dangerous behaviors. The

multiple-baseline design that we describe next gets around this concern, because no reversal is needed once intervention is introduced.

In a **multiple-baseline design** across behaviors, different responses of the same individual are identified and measured over time to provide a baseline against which changes may be evaluated. Each behavior is then modified in turn. If each behavior changes only when it is specifically treated, a cause-and-effect relationship between the treatment and the behavior change is inferred. Other common varieties of multiple-baseline designs involve successive introductions of treatment for the same behavior in the same individual across different situations or for the same behavior across several individuals in the same situation. The critical feature of the multiple-baseline approach is that change must occur only when treatment is instituted and only for the behavior, situation, or individual that is the target of treatment. Simultaneous changes must not occur for untreated behaviors, situations, or individuals until the time that each is, in turn, targeted for treatment.

Findings from a study using a multiple-baseline design across situations are presented in ● Figure 3.6.

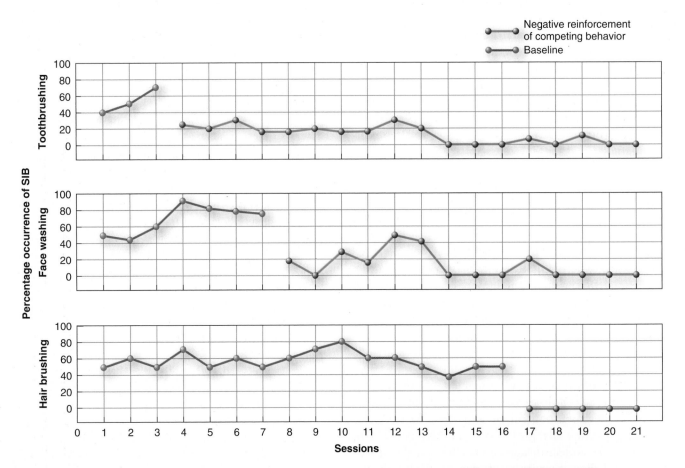

● **FIGURE 3.6** | Multiple-baseline design across situations: treatment of Dennis's self-injurious behavior (SIB).

Based on Use of Negative Reinforcement in the Treatment of Self-Injurious Behavior, by M. W. Steege, D. P. Wacker, K. C. Cigrand, W. K. Berg, G. C. Novak, T. M. Reimers, G. M. Sasso & A. DeRaad, 1990, Journal of Applied Behavior Analysis, 23, 459–467.

In this example, the same intervention procedures used with Ann were used to reduce self-injurious behavior (SIB) in Dennis, a 6-year-old boy who also had profound intellectual disability and multiple handicaps. Dennis's SIB consisted of biting his hands, wrists, or arms during grooming activities such as toothbrushing, face washing, and hair brushing. His SIB was getting worse and causing open wounds. During the initial baseline phase, the percentage of intervals during which Dennis engaged in SIB averaged 50% or more during toothbrushing, face washing, and hair brushing. When an intervention was implemented during toothbrushing, an immediate decrease in Dennis's SIB resulted, with consistently low rates of SIB maintained throughout treatment. Moreover, no changes in Dennis's SIB were observed during face washing or hair brushing until the intervention was introduced during those situations.

Because changes in Dennis's SIB occurred only when an intervention was introduced during each of the specific situations, there is support for the hypothesis that intervention led to those changes. A multiple-baseline design avoids the problem associated with the reversal design of having to return to baseline when treating dangerous or unwanted behaviors.

Several advantages and limitations are associated with the use of single-case experimental designs. These designs preserve the personal quality of the case study and offer some degree of control for potential alternative explanations of the findings, such as the effects of maturation and reactivity to observation. Single-case designs also provide an objective evaluation of treatment for individual cases, permit the study of rare disorders, and facilitate the development and evaluation of alternative and combined forms of treatment. The negative aspects of the design are the possibilities that specific treatments will interact with unique characteristics of a particular child, the limited generalization of findings to other cases, and the subjectivity involved when visual inspection rather than statistical analysis is used to evaluate the data. The findings for Ann and Dennis were fairly clear-cut. Difficulties in interpretation arise when baseline data or observed changes are highly variable.

Between-Group Comparison Designs

Many research designs are based on comparisons between one group of children assigned to one or more conditions and other groups of children assigned to one or more different conditions. When participants are randomly assigned to groups, and groups are presumed to be equivalent in all other respects, one group typically serves as the *experimental group* and the other serves as the *control group*. Any differences observed between groups are then attributed to the experimental condition.

The choice of an appropriate control or comparison group often depends on what we know prior to the study and the questions we wish to answer. For example, if an established and effective treatment for adolescent depression exists, testing a new approach against a no-treatment control group will likely answer the wrong question, not to mention that it may raise ethical concerns about withholding a proven effective treatment. We do not want to know whether the new approach is better than nothing—we want to know whether it is better than the best available alternative treatment.

In many cases, assignment of participants to groups may not be possible, particularly when one wishes to make comparisons between known or intact groups, such as children who have been referred to clinics for depression versus those with depression who have not been referred. In these types of known-group comparisons there is no assignment; rather, the selection criteria for including or excluding participants from the groups must be carefully specified.

Cross-Sectional and Longitudinal Studies

Researchers interested in developmental psychopathology need information about the ways in which children and adolescents change over time. To obtain this information, researchers extend correlational and experimental approaches to include measurements taken at different ages. Both cross-sectional and longitudinal designs are research strategies in which a comparison of children of different ages serves as the basis for research.

In **cross-sectional research**, different youngsters at different ages or periods of development are studied at the same point in time, whereas in **longitudinal research**, the same children are studied at different ages or periods of development. In cross-sectional studies, researchers do not have to worry about the many problems associated with studying the same group of children over a long period. When participants are measured only once, researchers need not be concerned about selective loss of participants, practice effects, or general changes in the field that would make the findings obsolete by the time the study is complete. Although cross-sectional approaches are efficient, they are limited in the information they generate with regard to developmental changes. Evidence about individual change is not available. Rather, comparisons are limited to age-group averages.

Longitudinal designs are conducted prospectively. Data collection occurs at specified points in time from

Longitudinal Research: Does Child Maltreatment Lead to More Peer Rejection over Time?

Dodge, Pettit, and Bates (1994a) assessed a representative sample of 585 boys and girls for physical maltreatment in the first 5 years of life and then followed them for 5 consecutive years, from kindergarten through the fourth grade. Twelve percent of the sample was identified as having experienced maltreatment. The children's peers, teachers, and mothers independently rated the maltreated children as being more disliked, less popular, and more socially withdrawn than the nonmaltreated children in every year of evaluation—and the magnitude of the difference increased over time. As shown in the accompanying figure, by grade 4 more than twice as many maltreated as nonmaltreated children were rejected by their peer group. The results suggest that early maltreatment may disrupt relationships with adults, which in turn impairs a child's ability to form effective relationships with other children.

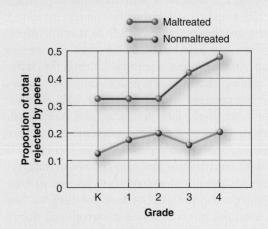

Proportions of maltreated and nonmaltreated children rejected by their peer group.

Based on Effects of Physical Maltreatment on the Development of Peer Relations by K.A. Dodge, G.S. Pettit & J.E. Bates, 1994, Development and Psychopathology, 6, 43–55.

the same individuals initially selected because of their membership in one or more populations of interest. In studies of child psychopathology, the populations of interest often consist of children at risk for developmental problems due to exposure to any one of a number of factors—for example, having a mother with depression or growing up in an abusive family situation.

The prospective longitudinal design allows the researcher to identify patterns that are common to all youngsters and to track differences in developmental paths that children follow. For example, a longitudinal study can tell that certain fears may decrease with age for all children but that some children may have an anxious disposition and show less of a reduction in specific fears with age. Because data are collected on the same individuals at time 1 and time 2, causal inferences between earlier events and later events and behavior based on temporal ordering can be made. Such inferences of causality cannot be made in cross-sectional designs, in which different individuals are assessed at the two time points. Longitudinal designs also allow for identification of individual developmental trends that would be masked by averaging data over individuals. The prepubertal growth spurt exemplifies this, where rapid accelerations in growth

occurring at different ages across the population are not reflected in growth measures averaged across adolescents. An example of a longitudinal study is presented in A Closer Look 3.2.

Despite their advantages, longitudinal designs have many practical and design difficulties (Hudziak & Novins, 2013). Practical concerns include obtaining and maintaining research funding and resources over many years and the long wait for meaningful data. Design difficulties relate to aging effects and cohort effects. *Aging effects* are general changes that occur because as participants age there are increases in physical prowess, impulse control, or social opportunity. *Cohort effects* are influences related to being a member of a specific **cohort**—a group of individuals who are followed during the same time and experience the same cultural or historical events. For example, the cohort of teens who lived in war-torn Yugoslavia in the early 1990s differ in many respects from North American teenagers living through the technological boom of the early 1990s.

The experience of being repeatedly studied, observed, interviewed, and tested may also threaten the validity of a longitudinal study. Children and adults may become more sensitized to the thoughts, feelings, and behaviors under investigation, thus thinking about them and revising them in ways that have nothing to do with age-related changes. Furthermore, with repeated testing, participants may improve as the result of practice effects, including greater familiarity with test items and better test-taking skills. Finally, changes within the field of abnormal child psychology may create problems for longitudinal studies conducted over an extended period. Theories and methods are constantly changing, and those that first led to the longitudinal study may become outdated.

Qualitative Research

Qualitative research focuses on narrative accounts, description, interpretation, context, and meaning (Denzin & Lincoln, 2011). The purpose of qualitative research is to describe, interpret, and understand the phenomenon of interest in the context in which it is experienced (Daly, 2007; Patton, 2002). This approach can be contrasted with a quantitative approach, which emphasizes operational definitions, careful control of the subject matter, the attempted isolation of variables of interest, quantification of dimensions of interest, and statistical analysis. Rather than beginning with already developed observational systems or assessment tools, qualitative researchers strive to understand the phenomenon from the participant's perspective. Qualitative data are typically collected through observations or open-ended interviewing and are recorded narratively as case study notes, for example. The observations and narrative accounts obtained are examined to build general categories and themes.

Proponents of qualitative research believe that it provides an intensive and intimate understanding of a situation that is rarely achieved in quantitative research (Denzin & Lincoln, 2011). Qualitative methods, such as the use of examples or stories, may be particularly engaging to children and enable the discussion of sensitive topics, while allowing the children a sense of control over the research situation (Barter & Renold, 2000). On the other hand, qualitative methods may also be biased by the researcher's values and preferences, and the findings cannot easily be generalized to individuals and situations other than the ones studied. Nonetheless, quantitative and qualitative research methods can be used in complementary ways (Lyons & Coyle, 2007). Qualitative methods can be used to identify important dimensions and theories that can then be tested quantitatively. Alternatively, qualitative case studies may be used to illuminate the meaning of quantitatively derived findings (Guerra et al., 2011). In addition, if qualitative data have been reduced to numbers through word counts or frequency counts of themes, the data can be analyzed using quantitative methods.

To give you a feel for qualitative research, consider a study by Petalas and colleagues (2009), who were interested in the experiences and views of siblings growing up in families that included a child with autism spectrum disorder (ASD). Eight typically developing children (9 to 12 years of age) with a brother with ASD were interviewed. Semi-structured interviews were analyzed using *interpretive phenomenological analysis* (IPA), a qualitative research approach that seeks to capture the richness and diversity of participants' accounts by uncovering central themes that emerge from their talk (Smith, Flowers, & Larkin, 2009). From this perspective, each sibling participant is seen as an expert on his or her personal experience. Each sibling interview lasted about 20 minutes on average and was audio-recorded and fully transcribed, resulting in 70 single-spaced pages of data. Analysis of these data involved reading and rereading of the transcripts until emergent themes were extracted. Briefly, one of the investigators listened to the recording and read the transcript to become familiar with the interview content. Transcripts were then read line by line, noting comments in the margins (e.g., summaries of meaning). Transcripts were then reread multiple times until themes emerging from the data were extracted by grouping sibling comments that clustered together. The themes were then checked and validated by the investigators to be sure that they were grounded in the data. This process, yielded five main themes, which are shown in A Closer Look 3.3, along with examples of a few of the sibling comments on which the themes were based.

The themes and examples highlight several features of the experiences of children growing up with a brother with ASD. You can see that siblings differ in their attitudes and interpretations of their experiences, and, to varying degrees, all mention positive aspects of having a brother with ASD. Siblings also describe different ways they were affected by having a brother with ASD, such as becoming socially isolated, changing their own behavior to cope with their brother's odd mannerisms and aggressive behavior, and having less family time for leisure and recreation. The exploratory findings from this qualitative study can be used to inform future larger-scale studies and quantitative research. They may also have implications for practice—for example, the need to develop enhanced support services for siblings of children with ASD (Petalas et al., 2009).

Qualitative Research: Siblings Talk about Their Brothers with Autism Spectrum Disorder (ASD)

Theme 1. Living with a Brother with ASD: Siblings' accounts of the impact on themselves and their families

- "I never feel like the youngest, even when I was small. … I suppose I learned how to take care of people just like if I had a younger brother." [Lizzie]
- "Jake's loud and he won't stop running into my bedroom when we're talking; and then he just wants to play with us all the time. I get very irritated and I can't get him out. That's why I have a lock on my bedroom door now. [Maddie]
- "I feel quite angry, because he has spoiled a day, which we were all enjoying to that point. I feel quite sad because my Mom and Dad spend that money on us, and then he has to go and spoil it by having a tantrum." [Kevin]

Theme 2. Others' Reactions: Implications for siblings

- "It's quite annoying because they don't see Jack for who he really is; they just see a big person that's got Asperger's and [who] is really annoying. [Leah]
- "So if he starts swearing or starts kicking, you know, it's quite embarrassing because people might think, oh, you know, their mother or father taught him to do that, so it's quite embarrassing to me to think that people sort of disrespecting my family and me and my brother." [Kevin]
- "Just sometimes they sort of—well, when you make new friends they ask what's wrong with him and I have to explain it. And they get used to it when they get to know him. You tell them more about it, and you tell them stories and stuff. [Lizzy]

Theme 3. Acceptance and Wanting Change

- "Jack's just like an average person, that he's just got this Asperger's; but he's just like a normal. He's just got Asperger's. … He's just like my normal brother; I never even think about it. I just recognize him as just another human. [Dylan]
- "… I like him the way he is. He's my brother. I'd never make him normal because I knew him like this. And I can't imagine a brother any other way. Well, not like Tyler any other way. I can't imagine him any other way, I wouldn't change anything." [Lizzy]

- "I'd like to tell him how much I appreciate him, because I don't really do that enough. He's often said to me, you're the worst brother in the world, you know, I don't like you, and I could show my appreciation more towards him than I do now." [Kevin]

Theme 4. Positive Views and Experiences

- "He's good at remembering things, like if he puts something up on his textbook, he'll remember it there, he'll remember it easier than anyone else. [Eddie]
- "I like that he always shows who he is. He always shows that he does have a personality and he is someone. And also just so he can't talk doesn't mean he doesn't have anything to say. He can sort of speak to you in a way." [Lizzy]
- "Last year, I'm not quite sure, he won a computer by doing horse riding. He didn't win, but he got it for doing so well, which I was really pleased by him for doing that. Not just for winning the computer, but because he'd done so well." [Kevin]

Theme 5. Support

- "He had someone called Lana who took him out on days out which was fun for him, and gave us as a family some time to go to places that maybe he wouldn't like to go. Like just as a family, without him, so that he would go where he liked to go, and us where we liked to go. Like just daytrips." [Lizzy]
- "I feel quite annoyed, because there's no one really to talk to about when I feel angry with Jack, and when he always gets his own way, and stuff about that. [Leah]
- "Mom went to a meeting for people who had children like Ryan and once she had to take me, and I met two other girls there, who had brothers who were autistic which is cool because you can still have a laugh with them and that, but they understand it better." [Kelsey]

From Petalas, M. A., Hastings, R. P., Nash, S., Dowey, A., & Reilly, D. (2009). "I like that he always shows who he is": The perceptions and experiences of siblings with a brother with autism spectrum disorder. *International Journal of Disability, Development and Education, 56*, 381–399.

Section Summary

Research Strategies

- Careful attention must be given to the way in which samples are identified for research in abnormal child psychology, including issues such as how the disorder of interest is defined, criteria for inclusion in the study, comorbidity, the setting from which subjects are drawn, and sample size.
- We can distinguish between nonexperimental and experimental research strategies on the basis of the degree to which the investigator can manipulate the experimental variable or, alternatively, must rely on examining the covariation of variables of interest.

- In prospective research, a sample is followed over time, with data collected at specified intervals. In retrospective research, a sample is identified at the current time and the sample members asked for information relating to an earlier time.

- Analogue research evaluates a specific variable under conditions that only resemble the situation for which the researcher wishes to generalize.

- The case study involves an intensive, usually anecdotal, observation and analysis of an individual child.

- Single-case designs involve repeated assessments of the same subject over time, the replication of treatment effects within the same subject, and the subject's serving as his or her own control. Two common examples are the A-B-A-B (reversal) design and multiple-baseline design across behaviors, situations, or individuals.

- Between-group designs compare the behavior of groups of individuals assigned to different conditions, such as an experimental group, or a comparison group and a control group.

- In cross-sectional research, different individuals at different ages or stages of development are studied at the same point in time. In longitudinal research, the same individuals are studied at different ages or stages of development.

- Qualitative research focuses on narrative accounts, description, interpretation, context, and meaning, and strives to understand the phenomenon from the participant's perspective and in the context in which it is experienced.

ETHICAL AND PRAGMATIC ISSUES

The image of overzealous scientists in white lab coats using children as guinea pigs for their experiments is a far cry from current research practices in abnormal child psychology. Researchers and policy makers have become increasingly sensitive to the possible ethical misuses of research procedures and are correspondingly more aware of the need for standards to regulate research practices (Fisher et al., 2013; Hoagwood & Cavaleri, 2010).

Research in abnormal child psychology must meet certain standards that protect children and families from stressful procedures. Any study must undergo careful ethical review before it can be conducted. Current ethical guidelines for research with children are provided through institutional review boards, federal funding agencies, and professional organizations such as the American Psychological Association and the Society for Research in Child Development.

Ethical standards for research with children attempt to strike a balance between supporting freedom of scientific inquiry and protecting the rights of privacy and the overall welfare of the research participants. Finding this balance is not always easy, especially with children. Although researchers are obligated to use nonharmful procedures, exposing the child to mildly stressful conditions such as a brief separation from their parent or exposure to an anxiety-producing stimulus may be necessary in some instances if benefits associated with the research are to be realized. Children are more vulnerable than adults to physical and psychological harm, and their immaturity may make it difficult or impossible for them to evaluate exactly what research participation means. In view of these realities, precautions must be taken to protect children's rights during the course of a study.

Informed Consent and Assent

The individual's fully informed consent to participate, obtained without coercion, serves as the single most protective regulation for research participants. **Informed consent** requires that all participants be fully informed of the nature of the research—as well as the risks, benefits, expected outcomes, and alternatives—before they agree to participate. Informed consent also includes informing participants of the option to withdraw from the study at any time, and of the fact that participation or nonparticipation in the research does not affect eligibility for other services.

Regarding research with children, protection is extended to obtaining both the informed consent of the parents or other legal guardian acting for the child and the assent of the child. **Assent** means that the child shows some form of agreement to participate without necessarily understanding the full significance of the research, which may be beyond younger children's cognitive capabilities. Guidelines for obtaining assent of the child call for doing so when the child is around the age of 7 or older. Researchers must provide school-age children with a complete explanation of the research activities in language they can understand. Factors that require particular attention when seeking children's assent include age, developmental maturity, psychological state, family factors, and the influence of the investigator seeking assent (Meaux & Bell, 2001). In addition to parents and children, consent must be obtained from other individuals who act on behalf of children, such as institutional officials when research is carried out in schools, day-care centers, or medical settings.

Voluntary Participation

Participation in research is to be voluntary, yet some individuals may be more susceptible to subtle pressure and coercion than others. Protection for vulnerable populations, including children, has received considerable attention. Families of high-risk infants and children are potentially more vulnerable, owing in part to the families' distress over their children's high-risk status. Although instructed otherwise, parents recruited from social service agencies or medical settings may still feel that their treatment or quality of care will be threatened if they do not participate in the research. Parents who mistreat their children may feel that their failure to participate in research could result in the loss of their child, a jail sentence, or failure to receive services.

The role of the researcher requires balancing successful recruiting with not placing pressure on potential participants. Volunteerism is itself a biasing factor in research. Individuals who agree to participate in research obviously differ from those who are approached but refuse. The question of whether volunteerism significantly biases findings on the variables of interest remains unanswered.

Confidentiality and Anonymity

Information revealed by individuals through participation in research is to be safeguarded. Most institutions require that individuals be informed that any information they disclose will be kept confidential and that they be advised regarding any exceptions to confidentiality. Adult informants must be told about the limits of confidentiality prior to their participation in research. In research with children, one of the most frequently encountered challenges to confidentiality occurs when the child or parent reveals past abuse or information that would suggest the possibility of future abuse of the child. Procedures for handling this situation vary across studies. They depend on the circumstances of the disclosure (e.g., by an adult within the context of therapy) and the reporting requirements of the state or province.

Nonharmful Procedures

No research procedures should be used that may harm the child either physically or psychologically. Whenever possible, the researcher is also obligated to use procedures that are the least stressful to the child and family. In some instances, psychological harm may be difficult to define, but when doubt is present, the researcher has the responsibility to seek consultation from others. If harm seems inevitable, alternative methods must be found or the research must be abandoned. In cases in which exposure of the child to stressful conditions may be necessary if therapeutic benefits associated with the research are to be realized, careful deliberation and analysis of the risks and benefits by an institutional review board are needed.

Other Ethical and Pragmatic Concerns

Sensitivity to ethical concerns is especially important when the research involves potentially invasive procedures, deception, the use of punishment, the use of participant payment or other incentives, or possible coercion. In longitudinal research, investigators must be particularly sensitive to the occurrence of unexpected crises, unforeseen consequences of research, and issues surrounding the continuation of the research when findings suggest that another course of action is required to ensure the child's well-being.

Many research problems typically addressed through standardized instructions and procedures are compounded by children's limited experience and understanding of novel research tasks and the particular characteristics of children with problems and their families. Researchers working with children with mental health problems and/or developmental disorders may face unique research challenges, such as motivating the children; keeping within time limitations; ensuring that instructions are well understood; and coping with possible boredom, distraction, and fatigue. Similarly, the families of children with problems often exhibit characteristics that may compromise their research participation and involvement. These characteristics include high levels of stress, marital discord, parental psychiatric disorders, substance-use disorders, restricted resources and/or time for research, and limited verbal abilities.

The final responsibility for the ethical integrity of any research project lies with the investigator. Researchers are advised or—in the case of research funded by government agencies—required to seek advice from colleagues. Special committees exist in hospitals, universities, school systems, and other institutions to evaluate research studies on the basis of risks and benefits. This evaluation involves weighing the costs of the research to participants in terms of inconvenience and possible psychological or physical harm against the value of the study for advancing knowledge and improving the child's life situation. If there are any risks to the safety and welfare of the child or family that the research does not warrant, priority is always given to the participants.

Section Summary

Ethical and Pragmatic Issues

- Research in abnormal child psychology must meet certain standards that protect children and families from stressful procedures, including informed consent and assent, voluntary participation, confidentiality and anonymity, and nonharmful procedures.

- To ensure that research meets ethical standards, researchers seek advice from colleagues and have their research evaluated by institutional ethics review committees. The final responsibility for the ethical integrity of any research project is with the investigator.

Study Resources

SECTION SUMMARIES

KEY TERMS

Clinical assessment is like good detective work.

environments (Mash & Hunsley, 2007). Strategies typically include an assessment of the child's emotional, behavioral, and cognitive functioning, as well as the role of environmental factors (Sattler & Hoge, 2006). These strategies—which should be based on scientific evidence and clinical expertise—form the basis of a flexible and ongoing process of hypothesis testing regarding the nature of the problem, its causes, and the likely outcomes if the problem is treated as opposed to leaving it untreated (Haynes, Smith, & Hunsley, 2011).

Clinical assessment is much broader than interviewing or testing alone. The ultimate goal of assessment is to achieve effective solutions to the problems children and their families face, and to promote and enhance their well-being. *Clinical assessments are meaningful to the extent that they result in practical and effective interventions.* In other words, a close and continuing partnership between assessment and intervention is vital; they should not be viewed as separate processes (Mash & Hunsley, 2005; Youngstrom, 2013).

The focus of clinical assessment is to obtain a detailed understanding of the *individual* child or family as a unique entity (e.g., Felicia and her family), referred to as **idiographic case formulation.** This is in contrast to a **nomothetic formulation,** which emphasizes broad general inferences that apply to large *groups* of individuals (e.g., children with a depressive disorder). A clinician's nomothetic knowledge about general principles of psychological assessment, normal and abnormal child and family development, and specific childhood disorders is likely to result in better hypotheses to test at the idiographic level (Haynes, Mumma, & Pinson, 2009).

As you can imagine, the process of decision-making is similar to studying for several exams at the same time. You must be familiar with fundamental information in areas such as childhood depression or specific learning disorders and then be able to integrate this knowledge in new ways to make it applicable to help solve a particular problem. Like studying for exams, this process at first seems like you are trying to cram everything into a funnel to distill what is most important. Unlike studying for exams, however, working with children and families and applying your training and experience to new situations is often very enjoyable!

Clinicians begin their decision making with an assessment, which can range from a clinical interview with the child and parents to more structured behavioral assessments and psychological testing. Keep in mind that assessment is not something done *to* a child or family—it is instead a collaborative process in which the child, family, and teacher all play active roles. Because adults play a critical role in defining the child's problem and providing information, it is particularly important to establish a rapport with them, and active family and teacher involvement are important for both assessment and intervention (Dowell & Ogles, 2010).

Developmental Considerations

Diversity is the one true thing we all have in common. Celebrate it every day.

—Anonymous

In assessing children and families, one needs to be sensitive to the child's age, gender, and cultural background as well as to normative information about both typical and atypical child development. Such knowledge provides the clinician with a context for evaluating and understanding the behavior and circumstances of an individual child and family.

Age, Gender, and Culture

A crucial building block for assessment and treatment is recognizing diversity within children's developmental functions and capacities at various ages. How might Felicia's age, gender, or cultural background influence our approach to assessment, diagnosis, and treatment?

School refusal in a 13-year-old like Felicia is significant because it results in missed educational and social opportunities. In contrast, a 13-year-old's refusal to travel by airplane may be inconvenient or distressing, but in most cases would not have the same serious consequences as missing school. A child's age has implications not only for judgments about deviancy but also for selecting the most appropriate assessment and treatment methods. For example, at what age can a child provide reliable information in an interview? With respect to treatment, how might time-out for misbehavior for a 3-year-old differ from time-out for a school-age child?

Like age, the child's gender also has implications for assessment and treatment. Numerous studies have reported gender differences in the rates and expression of childhood disorders (Bell, Foster, & Mash, 2005). As shown in Table 4.1, some childhood disorders and conditions are more common in males than in females, others are more common in females than in males, and still others are equally common in the two sexes (Rutter, Caspi, & Moffitt, 2003). In general, boys are about three to four times more likely than girls to display early-onset disorders such as autism spectrum disorder (ASD) and attention-deficit/hyperactivity disorder (ADHD), whereas girls are more likely than boys to display disorders that have their peak onset in adolescence, such as depression and eating disorders (Martel, 2013).

As we have emphasized, most childhood disorders are identified and defined by adults, usually because adults find the child's symptoms particularly salient or troublesome. In general, overactivity and aggression are more common in boys than in girls; girls tend to express their problems in less observable ways such as sadness, fear, and shame (Chaplin & Aldao, 2013). In fact, among the symptoms that best distinguish boys who are referred for treatment are "showing off or clowning" (as reported by parents) and "disturbing other pupils" (as reported by teachers) (Achenbach & Rescorla, 2001). Thus, boys may receive an excess of referrals, and girls may be overlooked because of their less visible forms of suffering. Our assessments and interventions must be sensitive to possible referral biases related to gender and gender differences. The difficulty in distinguishing between true gender differences and differences in reporting is illustrated by the finding that the rate of ADHD diagnoses during the early to mid-1990s increased approximately threefold among girls, as compared with twofold for boys (Robison et al., 2002). Could the rate of ADHD in girls possibly increase threefold during one decade? It is more likely that increasing recognition of the disorder and its various forms of expression in girls contributed to the dramatic increase in these ADHD diagnoses (Hinshaw & Blachman, 2005). In considering gender differences, it is critical to keep in mind that there is great variability not just between boys and girls but also within each group. In addition, gender differences in emotional expression and behavior have been shown to vary depending on the age of the child, the interpersonal context in which the child is observed, and the personal relevance and demands of the situation (Chaplin & Aldao, 2013).

The study of gender differences has contributed enormously to our understanding and assessment of childhood disorders (Rose & Rudolph, 2006). However, it is also extremely important to study both girls and boys as distinct groups in their own right. An exclusive focus on sex differences could delay careful study of the expression of and underlying processes associated with specific disorders in one group or the other (Hinshaw, 2008). For example, studies into social aggression in girls have found that when angry, girls show aggression indirectly through verbal insults, gossip, ostracism, getting even, or third-party retaliation—referred to as *relational aggression* (Crick & Rose, 2000). As girls move into adolescence, the function of their aggressive behavior increasingly centers on group acceptance and affiliation. When adjustment problems are studied in relation to the issues most salient for girls (e.g., relationships, body image), it has been shown that girls experience significant problems during childhood. These problems include relational aggression and also behaviors that are self-serving, directed outward, and intended to physically harm others. This combination of relational and physical aggression is the strongest predictor of future psychological–social adjustment problems in girls (Crick, Ostrov, & Werner, 2006). Interestingly, children who engage in forms of social aggression that are not typical of their sex (overtly aggressive girls and relationally aggressive boys) are significantly more maladjusted than are children who engage in gender-normative forms of aggression (Crick, 1997).

Finally, cultural factors must be carefully considered during assessment and treatment (Achenbach & Rescorla, 2007; Nikapota, 2009). There is a rapidly changing demographic and cultural landscape in the United States as its population becomes increasingly

TABLE 4.1 | Gender Patterns for Selected Problems of Childhood and Adolescence

More Commonly Reported among Males

Attention-deficit/hyperactivity disorder	Autism spectrum disorder
	Language disorder
Childhood conduct disorder	Specific learning disorder
Intellectual disability	Enuresis

More Commonly Reported among Females

Anxiety disorders	Eating disorders
Adolescent depression	Sexual abuse

Equally Reported among Males and Females

Adolescent conduct disorder	Feeding disorder
Childhood depression	Physical abuse and neglect

Source: Adapted from "Gender differences in the diagnosis of mental disorders: Conclusions and controversies of DSM-IV," by C. M. Hartung and T. A. Widiger, 1998, *Psychological Bulletin, 123,* 260–278. Copyright © 1998 by the American Psychological Association. Reprinted with permission. APA is not responsible for the accuracy of this translation.

Biology and socialization interact to create different interests and behavior profiles of girls and boys.

Courtesy of David Wolfe

multiracial and multicultural. By 2030, European-Americans in the United States will no longer constitute the majority among children under 18 years of age, and this is already true in children under 8 years of age (U.S. Census Bureau, 2013). Consequently, cultural sensitivity in the assessment, diagnosis, and treatment of children with emotional and behavioral problems and their families has become increasingly important (Pumariega et al., 2013). Consistent with this view is the expanded cultural emphasis in the most recent revision of the *Diagnostic and Statistical Manual of Mental Disorders* DSM (DSM-5; APA, 2013). The DSM-5 includes a framework for developing a cultural formulation of the child's disorder based on the child and family's cultural identity; their cultural concepts of distress; psychosocial stressors and cultural features of vulnerability and resilience; cultural aspects of the relationship between the child, family, and clinician; and an overall cultural assessment including a culturally appropriate plan for treatment. To assist, the DSM-5 also contains a "Cultural Formulation Interview," with a module for children and adolescents, to gather information about the impact of culture on the child's presenting problems and implications for treatment (APA, 2013; available at www.psychiatry.org/practice/dsm/dsm5/online-assessment-measures).

Cultural patterns reflect learned behaviors and values that are shared among members, are transmitted to group members over time, and distinguish the members of one group from those of another group. Culture can include ethnicity, language, religious or spiritual beliefs, race, gender, socioeconomic status (SES), age, sexual orientation, geographic origin, group history, education and upbringing, and life experiences.

Children who are ethnic minorities may have a greater risk of being misdiagnosed or underdiagnosed. For example, one study found that psychiatrically hospitalized African American adolescents were more often diagnosed with organic/psychotic disorders and less often diagnosed with mood/anxiety disorders than Caucasian teens (Kilgus, Pumariega, & Cuffe, 1995). In addition, African American and Hispanic children are less likely than white children to receive treatment (Zimmerman, 2005). Culturally competent assessment and treatment practices require that clinicians examine their own belief systems and the culturally based assumptions that guide their clinical practice.

A cultural formulation is necessary to establish a relationship with the child and family, motivate family members to change, obtain valid information, arrive at an accurate diagnosis, and develop meaningful recommendations for treatment. Ethnic identity and racial socialization are key factors to consider in the assessment of all children and families, including those from the dominant culture (Dishion & Stormshak, 2007b).

Cultural syndromes refer to a pattern of co-occurring, relatively invariant symptoms associated with a particular cultural group, community, or context (APA, 2013). For example, *mal de ojo* or the "evil eye" is a concept that is widespread throughout Mediterranean cultures and Latino communities throughout the world. A malady to which children are especially vulnerable and believed to be caused by a hateful look or glance from a malicious person, the evil eye can cause fitful sleep, crying without apparent cause, diarrhea, vomiting, and fever in children. Cultural syndromes rarely fit neatly into one Western diagnostic category (Alarcón, 2009). In addition, although the cross-cultural validity of Western diagnostic criteria varies widely depending on the disorder, data regarding their validity across cultures for many childhood disorders is lacking (Canino & Alegria, 2008). Therefore, it is important that clinicians assess the extent to which a child's cultural background and context affect the expression of both individual symptoms and clinical disorders. Although cultural syndromes may not be recognized as disorders in the culture in which they occur, distress and other illness features may still be recognized by an outside observer (APA, 2013).

What is considered abnormal child behavior may vary from one cultural group to the next (Serafica & Vargas, 2006). For example, a child's shyness and oversensitivity are likely to lead to peer rejection and social maladjustment in Western cultures, but the same qualities may be associated with leadership, school competence, and educational achievement in Chinese children (Chen, Rubin, Li, & Li, 1999). In addition, it may be difficult to engage parents from some cultures if mental health issues are seen as particularly taboo, if intervention into personal family matters by strangers is viewed negatively, or if the causes of the illness in that culture are seen as physical or spiritual (Yasui & Dishion, 2007).

In negotiating assessment and treatment plans with children and families who may not share the clinician's concept of mental illness, a clinician must recognize the diversity that exists across and within racial and ethnic groups in lifestyle and patterns of acculturation (i.e., level of adaptation to dominant culture versus background culture). Generalizations about cultural practices frequently fail to capture these regional, generational, SES, and lifestyle differences. For example, SES level is a major confound in findings of differences in rates of psychopathology between various cultures because ethnic minority cultures are frequently overrepresented in low SES populations (Glover & Pumariega, 1998). An individual's acculturation level can also significantly

Recognizing diversity across and within ethnic groups is an important role of the clinician.

impact assessment and subsequent interventions. The lower the level of one's acculturation, the higher one scores on measures of psychopathology, particularly in conjunction with low SES and education level (Cuéllar, 2000). Having an awareness of the cultural customs and values that can affect behaviors, perceptions, and reactions to assessment and treatment, as well as recognizing the major confound of SES with these factors, puts the clinician in a better position to develop a meaningful assessment and intervention strategy.

Normative Information

Felicia's school refusal and sad mood started after her mother's hospitalization. Is Felicia's reaction normal for a stressful life event? How common are these symptoms in girls her age after a brief period of separation from a parent? Felicia also withdrew from social contact and experienced sleep disturbances. Adolescence is a time of biological and social upheaval for many youths. Therefore, we need to know whether Felicia is different from other girls her age with respect to these problems; if she is different, when should we become concerned and take action?

Knowledge, experience, and basic information about norms of child development and behavior problems are the crucial beginning to understanding how children's problems or needs come to the attention of professionals. As many parents discover, figuring out what to expect of their children at various ages can be challenging. Parents are faced with determining what difficulties are likely to be chronic versus those that are common and transient, deciding when to seek advice from others, and determining what treatment is best for their child. Immigrant parents can have even more difficulty with these tasks when trying to assess their second-generation child's behavior as the child attempts to navigate at least two different cultures (Falicov, 2003).

Isolated symptoms of behavioral and emotional problems generally show little correspondence with children's overall adjustment. Usually, the *age inappropriateness, severity,* and *pattern* of symptoms, rather than individual symptoms, define childhood disorders. Also, the extent to which symptoms result in impairment in the child's functioning is a key consideration. Nevertheless, certain symptoms do occur more frequently in children referred for assessment and treatment. Table 4.2 provides examples of parent- and teacher-rated symptoms that occur more frequently or in more extreme forms in children ages 6 to 18 who are referred for treatment and that best discriminate them from same-age children who are not referred for treatment. As you can see, these symptoms are relatively common behaviors that occur to some extent in all children—sadness, a lack of concentration, and demands for attention top the list.

Purposes of Assessment

Children and families are assessed for one or more purposes. These purposes guide the assessment process, including decisions regarding the use of particular assessment methods. As described below, three common purposes of assessment are description and diagnosis, prognosis, and treatment planning (McLeod, Jensen-Doss, & Ollendick, 2013).

Description and Diagnosis

"Diagnosis is not the end but the beginning of practice."

–Fischer (1879–1962)

The first step in understanding a child's problem is to provide a **clinical description,** which summarizes the unique behaviors, thoughts, and feelings that together make up the features of the child's psychological

disorder. A clinical description attempts to establish basic information about the child's (and usually the parents') concerns at presentation, especially how the child's behavior or emotions are different from or similar to those of other children of the same age, sex, socioeconomic, and cultural background.

If you conducted an evaluation of Felicia, what information would be most important to include in your clinical description? You would start by describing how her behavior differs from normal behavior of girls her age. First, assessing and describing the *intensity, frequency,* and *severity* of her problem would communicate a sense of how excessive or deficient her behavior is, under what circumstances it may be a problem, how often it does or does not occur, and how severe the occurrences are. Second, you would need to describe the *age at onset* and *duration* of her difficulties. Some problems are transient and will spontaneously remit, while others persist over time. Like frequency and intensity, age at onset and duration of the problem behavior must be appraised with respect to what is considered normative for a given age. Finally, you would want to convey a full picture of her *different symptoms and their configuration.* Although Felicia needed help because of particular problems at school and with her peers, you need to know the full range, or profile, of her strengths and weaknesses to make informed choices about the likely course, outcome, and treatment of her disorder.

After establishing an initial picture of Felicia's presenting symptoms, you would next determine whether this description meets the criteria for diagnosis of one or more psychological disorders. **Diagnosis** means analyzing information and drawing conclusions about the nature or cause of the problem, or assigning a formal diagnostic label for a disorder. Does Felicia meet standard diagnostic criteria for a major depressive disorder and, if so, what might be the cause?

Diagnosis has acquired two separate meanings, which can be confusing. The first meaning is *taxonomic diagnosis,* which focuses on the formal assignment of cases to specific categories drawn from a system of classification such as the DSM-5 (APA, 2013) or from empirically derived traits or dimensions (discussed later in this chapter) (Achenbach & Rescorla, 2001). *Problem-solving analysis,* the second, much broader meaning of diagnosis, is similar to clinical assessment and views diagnosis as a process of gathering information that is used to understand the nature of an individual's problem, its possible causes, treatment options, and outcomes.

Thus, Felicia's assessment will involve a complete diagnostic (problem-solving) analysis to get the most comprehensive picture possible. In addition, Felicia may receive a formal diagnosis of *major depressive*

TABLE 4.2 | **Parent- and Teacher-Rated Problems That Best Discriminate between Referred and Nonreferred Children**

• Unhappy, sad, or depressed	• Poor schoolwork
• Can't concentrate	• Inattentive
• Demands attention	• Stubborn
• Disobedient at school	• Moody
• Doesn't get along with others	• Sulks
• Impulsive	• Temper
• Nervous	

Based on Achenbach, T. M. and Rescorla, L. A. (2001), Manual for the ASEBA School-Age Forms & Profiles, ISBN 978-0-938565-73-4. Burlington, VT: University of Vermont, Research Center for Children, Youth, and Families) p. 144.

"They're trying to figure out whether it's a chemical thing or I'm just a crybaby."

disorder (discussed in Chapter 10), which means that she possesses characteristics that link her to similar youths presumed to have the same disorder (taxonomic diagnosis). A secondary diagnosis of an anxiety disorder, such as separation anxiety disorder or school refusal, may be necessary for Felicia, since comorbidity of depression and anxiety is very common among girls her age. Comorbidity exists when certain disorders among children and adolescents are likely to co-occur within the same individual, especially disorders that share many common symptoms (see Chapter 3). Awareness of one disorder alerts us to the increased possibility for another disorder. Some of the more common comorbid disorders are conduct disorder and ADHD, ASD and intellectual disability, and childhood depression and anxiety (Drabick & Kendall, 2010).

Prognosis and Treatment Planning

Prediction is very difficult, especially if it's about the future.

—Attributed to Niels Bohr (1885–1962)

Prognosis is the formulation of predictions about future behavior under specified conditions. If Felicia does not receive help for her problem, what will likely happen to her in the future? Will her problems diminish as she gets older, or will they get worse?

Naturally, parents and others immediately want to know the possible short- and long-term outcomes for their child and what events might alter such projections. Remember that many childhood concerns, such as fears, worries, and bed-wetting, are common at certain ages, so any decision to treat a child's particular problem must be based on an informed prognosis. Clinicians must weigh the probability that circumstances will remain the same, improve, or deteriorate with or without treatment, as well as what course of treatment should be followed.

In addition, treatments for children and adolescents often focus on enhancing the child's development rather than merely on removing symptoms or restoring a previous level of functioning. In Felicia's case, for example, an assessment might reveal that she has poor social skills, so intervention plans might focus on efforts to teach her these skills in a concerted fashion to reduce the chances of continuing social relationship difficulties. A prognosis based on careful assessment can also serve to inform parents and others about the importance of doing something now that may reduce the likelihood of major problems later.

Treatment planning and evaluation means using assessment information to generate a plan to address the child's problem and to evaluate the effectiveness of the treatment. Felicia's mother keeps her daughter home from school when Felicia complains of stomach pains. She also does Felicia's homework. Does this information suggest a possible course of action? Felicia thinks she can't do anything well. Will helping her to change this and other irrational beliefs make a difference in her depression? When action is taken, how can we evaluate whether it is having the desired effect?

Treatment planning and evaluation may involve further specification and measurement of possible contributors to the problem, determination of resources and motivation for change, and recommendations for the treatments likely to be the most feasible, acceptable, and effective for the child and family. For example, are Felicia's parents unintentionally rewarding her physical complaints and school refusal by giving her extra attention when she doesn't go to school? Is Felicia willing to discuss with a therapist why she refuses to go to school? Are her parents willing to set limits on her behavior despite a history of struggle and failure with previous attempts?

Section Summary

Clinical Issues

- Clinical assessment is directed at differentiating, defining, and measuring the child's behaviors, cognitions, and emotions of concern, the environmental circumstances that may contribute to these problems, and the child's strengths and competencies.

- Assessments are meaningful to the extent that they result in effective interventions; a close and continuing partnership must exist between assessment and intervention.

- Age, gender, and culture influence how children's symptoms and behavior are expressed and recognized, and have implications for selecting the most appropriate methods of assessment and treatment.

(continues)

- The age inappropriateness, the severity, and the pattern of symptoms, rather than individual symptoms, usually define childhood disorders.

- Three purposes of assessment are: (1) description and diagnosis that determine the nature and possible causes of the child's problem, (2) prognosis that predicts future behavior under specified conditions, and (3) treatment planning and evaluation.

ASSESSING DISORDERS

If something exists, it exists in some amount. And if it exists in some amount, then it is capable of being measured.

–René Descartes

Not everything important can be measured, and not everything that can be measured is important.

–Albert Einstein

If you were planning to assess Felicia's problems, where would you begin and what might you include in your assessment? Should you interview Felicia, both parents, and her teacher? Do you need to observe Felicia at home? At school? Are there psychological tests or questionnaires to help you pinpoint Felicia's strengths and weaknesses, such as intelligence, emotion regulation, concentration, social skills, and learning ability?

You'll quickly recognize how massive the decision-making process can seem. In view of this complexity, many clinical settings use a multidisciplinary team approach to assessment. Psychological test administration and interpretation experts work with others to generate the most complete picture of a child's mental health needs. Multidisciplinary teams may include a psychologist, a physician, an educational specialist, a speech pathologist, and a social worker.

Some children may need to be referred for a medical exam as part of a comprehensive assessment to investigate whether a physical problem is related to their disorder. For example, a physiological problem may be causing a particular child's bed-wetting or sleep disorder. A thorough medical assessment by a physician could evaluate Felicia's stomach pains, sleep disturbances, and weight loss and be used to determine whether Felicia's depression was related to drug use or a general medical condition such as hypothyroidism (low levels of thyroid hormones).

Ideally, the clinical assessment of children experiencing difficulties relies on a **multimethod assessment approach,** which emphasizes the importance of obtaining information from different informants in a variety of settings and using a variety of methods that include interviews, observations, questionnaires, and tests. Deciding which assessment is best for a specific case is based on whether the assessment is for diagnosis, treatment planning, or treatment evaluation; on whether the problem is observable (like aggression) or internal (like anxiety); and on the child's and family's characteristics and abilities. In addition, the methods used need to be reliable, valid, cost-effective, and useful for treatment (Hunsley & Mash, 2008).

Clinical assessment consists of many strategies and procedures designed to help understand the child's thoughts, feelings, and behaviors as they occur in specific situations. Clinical interviews are usually conducted with the parents and child separately or in a family interview, and they help establish a good working relationship with the child and family. They are also extremely useful in obtaining basic information about existing concerns as viewed by the child and family members and in pinpointing directions for further inquiry. Behavioral assessments, checklists and rating scales, and psychological tests are then used in accordance with a decision-making approach. Information is also obtained from teachers and other significant individuals who interact with the child in various settings. The purpose is to obtain the most complete picture possible in order to develop and implement an appropriate treatment plan, within the limits of available resources.

A comprehensive assessment requires that some consideration be given to evaluating the child's strengths and weaknesses in areas ranging from basic language and self-care skills to coping and leadership abilities. If our detective work suggests that a particular area of functioning deserves closer scrutiny, then a more in-depth assessment of that area is warranted. However, if initial assessments indicate that certain areas of functioning are not a problem, then further assessments may not be necessary. For example, for a child who performs poorly in school, an assessment of intellectual functioning and academic performance is essential. On the other hand, for a child who experiences difficulties at home but is doing fine at school, assessment of intellectual and academic functioning may be unnecessary. Keep in mind that the most comprehensive assessment procedures will have little clinical impact if they are not practical to use in the settings in which youths with mental health problems are typically assessed. Thus, practitioners and policy makers more and more are seeking assessment protocols that are cost-effective and feasible to use in real-world service delivery settings (Ebesutani et al., 2012).

Clinical Interviews

Children and adolescents don't usually refer themselves for treatment. Typically, they are referred because of the impact of their behavior on others. Thus, they often do not understand why they are seeing a mental health profession, and in fact they may not even experience any distress or recognize any cause for concern. (To be fair, some adults are like this, too!) The initial clinical interview can be very important not only in obtaining information, but also in setting the stage for collaboration and cooperation among the child, family members, and other concerned parties.

The clinical interview is the assessment procedure usually used with parents and children. However, based on interviewers' theoretical orientations, styles, and purposes, interviews may vary considerably in terms of the kinds of information obtained and the meaning assigned to that information (Sattler & Mash, 1998). Interviews allow professionals to gather information in a flexible manner over many sessions. The findings can then be integrated with more time-consuming assessments, such as family observations or psychological testing.

Clinical interviews use a flexible, conversational style that helps the child or parent to present the most complete picture possible. Interviewees will be encouraged to tell their stories with minimal guidance, which permits the children and parents to convey their thoughts and feelings in ways that approximate how they think in everyday life. During the clinical interview, the interviewer may observe nonverbal communications by the child and parent, such as facial expressions, body posture, voice, mannerisms, and motor behavior. These informal observations can provide the clinician with additional insights into the parent–child relationship that may be relevant in determining the presenting problem and the direction for treatment planning.

Clinical interviews can provide a large amount of information during a brief period. For example, during an hour-long interview with a parent, much detail about the child's developmental history, likes and dislikes, behavioral strengths and deficits, responses to discipline, relationships with others, and school performance can be obtained—far more than would be learned by observing the parent and child interacting for the same amount of time (Sattler, 1998).

Many clinicians develop their own style for engaging school-age children and adolescents in discussing their situation. We often use video games, crafts, and similar enticements to help the child feel more comfortable. When younger children are referred, it may be more appropriate to involve one parent in a joint game or activity. Younger children are more likely to "be themselves" with their parents than with a stranger. (For this age group, drawing, coloring, and similar fun activities are almost always successful in initiating a new relationship.) Also, because of their developmental level, younger children or children with intellectual disabilities may be capable of providing only general impressions of their internal states, behavior, and circumstances.

Depending on the child's age, you may want to adopt a child-friendly approach for the interview that fits with the child's developmental status, the nature of the problem, and the interview purpose. The interview typically will attempt to elicit information about the child's self-perceptions and perceptions of others, and to obtain samples of how the child responds in a social situation with an adult. Children's views of why they were brought to the clinic, their expectations for improvement, and their understanding of the assessment situation are all important to consider, along with the manner in which they interpret significant events such as divorce or family violence. Engaging unwilling children can be difficult. Since other people typically seek help on behalf of the child, some children and adolescents may feel that they do not have a problem and therefore they see no need to be interviewed.

What questions would you ask Felicia's parents? Perhaps you want to know how long Felicia's reluctance to separate from her parents has been a concern and whether help has been sought previously. You might also want to discuss the exact nature of the problems her parents are concerned about and to provide them with some indication of the next steps in the assessment and treatment process.

Children's initial reactions to seeing a mental health professional are often ones of fear and resistance.

Developmental and Family History

Initial assessments often include a **developmental history** or **family history**, in which information is obtained from the parents regarding potentially significant developmental milestones and historical events that might impact the child's current difficulties. Often this information is gathered via a background questionnaire or interview that typically covers the following areas (Sattler, 1998):

▶ *The child's birth and related events*, such as pregnancy and birth complications or the mother's use of drugs, alcohol, or cigarettes during pregnancy

▶ *The child's developmental milestones*, such as age at which walking, use of language, bladder and bowel control, and self-help skills started

▶ *The child's medical history*, including injuries, accidents, operations, illnesses, and prescribed medications

▶ *Family characteristics and family history*, including the age, occupation, cultural background, and marital status of family members and the medical, educational, and mental health history of parents and siblings

▶ *The child's interpersonal skills*, including relations with adults and other children, and play and social activities

▶ *The child's educational history*, including schools attended, academic performance, attitudes toward school, relations with teachers and peers, and special services

▶ *The adolescent's work history and relationships*, including relationships with others of the same sex and the opposite sex

▶ *A description of the presenting problem*, including a detailed description of the problem and surrounding events, and how parents have attempted to deal with the problem in the past

▶ *The parents' expectations* for assessment and treatment of their child and themselves

Here is part of the developmental and family history given by Felicia's parents:

FELICIA

History

Her parents reported that Felicia was the result of an unplanned pregnancy following an initial miscarriage, the adoption of a son, and the birth of a sister. The pregnancy and Felicia's early life were described as uncomplicated and generally happy. Felicia reached developmental milestones late, required extra assistance with tasks, was quite reserved and uncommunicative, and experienced speech articulation problems. Her parents said they tended to "baby" Felicia, since she was seen as "slow." She was similarly described as developmentally immature by her teachers. As a result, she had repeated the first grade even though her attendance and academic performance were consistently good.

Felicia's adopted brother, age 23, attended a local college and lived at home. Her sister, age 16, also lived at home and attended high school. Felicia's mother had trained to become a registered nurse; her father held a Ph.D. in chemistry and managed the research department of a large company. No significant problems were reported for the other children, with the exception of some difficulty on the part of the brother in establishing independence.

Felicia's mother described experiencing a significant depression after each of her pregnancies and following her own father's death the previous year, a loss that was reported to have been very painful for Felicia also. Felicia's father reported no difficulties and was considered a stable and dependable person.

Based on Depression, by D. J. Kolko, 1987. In M. Hersen and V. B. Van Hasselt (Eds.), Behavior Therapy with Children and Adolescents: A Clinical Approach, pp. 163–164.

Many events presented in this developmental and family history may be relevant to the assessment of Felicia's current problems and must be explored as the assessment proceeds. For example, the babying described by Felicia's parents may reflect a more general pattern of overdependency on her parents that is contributing to her school refusal. The significant depression experienced by Felicia's mother following her pregnancies may suggest a family risk for depression. The death of Felicia's grandfather a year earlier may have been a triggering event, leading to a mood disturbance in both Felicia and her mother. During the early stages of assessment, these are hypotheses; as evidence accumulates with ongoing detective work, hypotheses can be supported or rejected as indicated by new data.

Semistructured Interviews

Most interviews with children and parents are unstructured. Clinicians use their preferred interview style and format, as well as their knowledge of the disorder, to pursue various questions in an informal and flexible manner. Unstructured clinical interviews provide a rich source of clinical hypotheses. However, their lack of standardization may result in low reliability and selective or biased gathering of information. To address this problem, clinicians sometimes use **semistructured interviews** that include specific questions designed to elicit information in a relatively consistent manner regardless of who is conducting the interview. The format of the interview usually ensures that the most important aspects of a particular disorder are covered. An appealing feature of semistructured interviews, especially for older children and youths, is that they can be administered by computer, something many children find entertaining and often less threatening at first than a face-to-face interview. The semistructured format also permits the clinician to follow up on issues of importance that may emerge during the interview. For younger children, a semistructured interactive interview using hand puppets may provide useful information about the child's emotional, behavioral, and peer problems (Ringoot et al., 2013).

The consistency and coverage of semistructured interviews may be offset by a loss of spontaneity between the child and the clinician, especially if the interview is conducted too rigidly. Under such circumstances, children and adolescents may be reluctant to volunteer important information not directly relevant to the interviewer's questions. With appropriate modifications that make the interview process easier to follow, however, semistructured interviews are reliable and very useful in assessing a wide range of children's symptoms (Edelbrock, Crnic, & Bohnert, 1999). Sample questions from a semistructured interview for young people like Felicia who are experiencing depression are presented in Table 4.3.

Behavioral Assessment

The clinical interviews described in this chapter are valuable in eliciting information from parents and school-age children. They provide an initial look at how the child and family think, feel, and behave and an initial hypothesis with regard to the factors that might be contributing to the child's problems. However, it is often necessary to obtain a firsthand look at the child's behavior in everyday life situations at home or at school or to ask someone who sees the child on a regular basis to observe the child's behavior.

Behavioral assessment is a strategy for evaluating the child's thoughts, feelings, and behaviors in specific settings, and then using this information to formulate hypotheses about the nature of the problem and what can be done about it (Haynes & Heiby, 2004). Behavioral assessment frequently involves observing the child's behavior directly, rather than inferring how children think, behave, or feel on the basis of their descriptions of inkblots or the pictures they draw.

Using behavioral assessment, the clinician or another person who sees the child regularly identifies **target behaviors,** which are the primary problems of concern, with the goal of then determining what specific factors may be influencing these behaviors. Sometimes this is a

TABLE 4.3	Semistructured Interview Questions for an Older Child or Adolescent with Depression

Depressed Mood/Irritability

- Do you feel sad?
- Do you get moody?

Loss of Interest

- Have you lost interest in doing things, like your hobbies?
- Is there anything you look forward to doing?

Self-Deprecatory Ideation

- Do you feel that you are worthless?
- Have you thought about committing suicide?

Sleep Disturbances

- Do you have trouble sleeping lately?
- Do you need more sleep than usual lately?

Change in School Performance

- Do you have trouble concentrating in school?
- Have you ever refused to go to school?

Decreased Socialization

- Have there been any changes in your relationships with friends?
- Do you feel a need to be alone?

Somatic Symptoms

- Do you get pains in your stomach?
- Do you get muscle pains and aches?

Loss of Usual Energy

- Do you feel you have less energy to do things?
- Do you often feel tired?

Change in Appetite and/or Weight

- Do you have to force yourself to eat?
- Has there been a change in your weight?

Based on Clinical and Forensic Interviewing of Children and Families: Guidelines for the Mental Health, Education, Pediatric, and Child Maltreatment Fields by J. M. Sattler, pp. 938–940.

straightforward task, as with a child who complains of illness every Monday morning and, as a result, is kept out of school for the day (sound familiar?). In other cases, the child displays multiple problems at home or school. Felicia's school refusal appears to be part of a larger pattern of difficulties that includes social withdrawal, depression, and possibly separation anxiety.

Even the seemingly simple task of identifying what is bothering a child can be a challenge. Remember that an adult usually decides that the child has a problem and that the child should be referred for an assessment. Adults often disagree about the nature of the child's problem, especially when they observe children in different settings (De Los Reyes & Kazdin, 2005). Ratings by various people may be influenced by differences between their cultures and that of the child. For example, when teachers rate youths from another cultural background, they are more likely to rate them higher on behavioral and emotional problems than are the teachers who have a similar background, the parents, or the children themselves (Skiba, Knesting, & Bush, 2002). Further, a child's presenting problem can often be very different from the one eventually identified as the target for intervention.

A commonly used and simple framework for organizing findings in behavioral assessment has been dubbed the "ABCs of assessment":

A = Antecedents, or the events that immediately precede a behavior

B = Behavior(s) of interest

C = Consequences, or the events that follow a behavior

In Felicia's case we might observe the following sequence: (A) Whenever Felicia's mother asks her to go to school (antecedent), (B) Felicia complains that she has stomach pains and refuses to go (behaviors), and (C) her mother lets Felicia stay home (consequence). This antecedent–behavior–consequence sequence might suggest that Felicia is being reinforced for her physical complaints and school refusal by not having to go to school. In addition, because there are no positive consequences for going to school and no negative ones for staying at home, Felicia might act this way on future school days. The ABCs of assessment can be used to organize information in specific contexts, as just described, or as an overall framework for assessment.

Behavior analysis or **functional analysis of behavior** is the more general approach to organizing and using assessment information in terms of antecedents, behaviors, and consequences (Hanley, Iwata, & McCord, 2003). As shown in ● Figure 4.1, functional analysis can be used to identify a wide range of antecedents and consequences that might be contributing to Felicia's school refusal and depression. The antecedents and consequences for Felicia's behavior include events in the immediate situation (a reduction in anxiety), more remote occurrences (being teased at school), events in the external environment, and Felicia's inner thoughts and feelings.

The goal of functional analysis is to identify as many factors as possible that could be contributing to a child's problem behaviors, thoughts, and feelings and to develop hypotheses for the factors that are most important and/or the most easily changed. In some cases, hypotheses can be confirmed or rejected by changing the antecedents and consequences to see whether the behavior changes. For example, we might teach Felicia to relax when thinking about going to school in order to reduce her anxiety (changing an antecedent) to see whether this decreases her school refusal. Or she could be instructed to substitute more positive self-statements ("I can succeed in school") for her negative ones ("I'm no good at anything") to see whether this decreases her depressive symptoms and raises her self-esteem. In these examples, you can see a close interplay between assessment and intervention when carrying out a functional analysis.

The process of gathering information about the child's behavior in specific settings takes many different forms. Often it involves either asking the parent, teacher, or child about what goes on in specific situations or observing the child. Clinicians develop their initial hypotheses based on information provided by the parents and the child during the interview; they pursue their hypotheses further using behavioral assessments, such as behavior checklists and rating scales and observations of behavior in real life or in role-play simulations. In general, behavioral assessment can be viewed as an approach to organizing assessment information for an individual child and developing hypotheses for treatment (Francis & Chorpita, 2004).

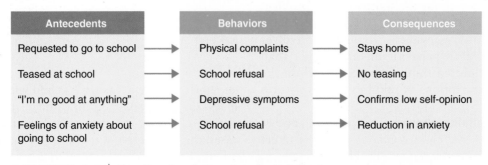

● **FIGURE 4.1** | Functional analysis: antecedents, behaviors, consequences.

© Cengage Learning®

Checklists and Rating Scales

Reports concerning child behavior and adjustment can be obtained using global checklists and problem-focused rating scales. Global behavior checklists are used to ask parents, teachers, and sometimes the youths themselves to rate the presence or absence of a wide variety of child behaviors or to rate the frequency and intensity of these behaviors.

Unlike a clinical interview, the use of a well-developed checklist is strengthened by its known degree of standardization and by the opportunities to compare an individual child's score with a known reference group of children of a similar age and the same gender (Fernandez-Ballesteros, 2004). Checklists are economical to administer and score, and they provide a rich source of information about parents' or teachers' reports about children's behavior, including possible differences in the reports by parents in the same family and differences between parent and teacher reports. Keep in mind, however, that informants may differ in their views of the child's strengths and weaknesses because they interact with the child in different surroundings and circumstances. These discrepancies are not necessarily bad because they inform the clinician about the possible range of behavior in which the child engages, the possible circumstances that increase or decrease target behaviors, and the possibly unrealistic demands or expectations placed on the child.

Nevertheless, these discrepancies underscore the importance of obtaining information from multiple observers (Grigorenko, Geiser, Slobodskaya, & Francis, 2010).

The Child Behavior Checklist (CBCL) developed by Thomas Achenbach and his colleagues is a leading checklist for assessing behavioral problems in children and adolescents ages 6 to 18 (Achenbach & Rescorla, 2001). The CBCL is widely used in treatment settings and schools, and its reliability and validity has been documented in numerous studies. One form of the CBCL, which is completed by the parent, is often used in combination with teacher-completed and youth-completed checklists, classroom observations, and interviews designed to assess the same child behavior problems (Achenbach, 2009). A notable feature of the CBCL is that it has been used to assess children in 80 or more cultural groups throughout the world and as such provides a robust measure for evaluating immigrant, refugee, and minority children from diverse backgrounds (Achenbach et al., 2008).

The scales of the CBCL can be used to create a profile that gives the clinician an overall picture of the variety and degree of the child's behavioral problems. A CBCL profile derived from a checklist completed by Felicia's mother is shown in ● Figure 4.2. The profile shows that her major areas of concern about her daughter are with respect to symptoms of *anxious/depressed*

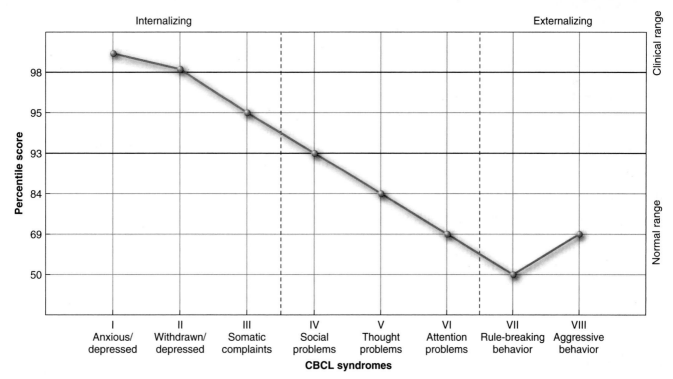

● **FIGURE 4.2** | Child Behavior Checklist (CBCL) profile for Felicia.

Based on Achenbach & Rescorla, 2001. Reference Crediting: Achenbach, T. M., & Rescorla, L. A. (2001). Manual for the ASEBA school-age forms & profiles. Burlington: University of Vermont, Research Center for Children, Youth, and Families.

disorder, we might say that she is significantly above average (often referred to as being within the *clinical range*) on the dimensions of depression and anxiety. These and other traits or dimensions are typically derived using statistical methods from samples drawn from both clinically referred and nonreferred child populations to establish ranges along each dimension (Achenbach & Rescorla, 2001).

Although they are more objective and potentially more reliable than clinically derived categorical systems, dimensional approaches based on statistical data also have limitations. First and foremost, the derived dimensions are dependent on sampling, method, and informant characteristics, as well as on the age and sex of the child (Mash & Hunsley, 2007). Consequently, integrating information obtained from different methods, from various informants, and over time or across situations can be challenging (De Los Reyes et al., 2013). Dimensional approaches may also be insensitive to contextual influences. For example, suppose you were a parent and were asked to describe whether your child "acts too young" using the scale "never, sometimes, a lot." You might want to clarify the circumstances or context under which she sometimes acts too young ("whenever I take her grocery shopping" or "when she is playing with other children"). Dimensions provide a useful estimate of the degree to which a child displays certain traits and not others, yet they often have to be tailored to the child's unique circumstances and developmental opportunities.

Many dimensions of child psychopathology have been identified through research. These include the *externalizing behavior* and *internalizing behavior* dimensions, which reflect aggressive/rule-breaking behaviors and anxious/withdrawn/depressed behaviors, respectively. Some of the most common dimensions identified in children and adolescents are presented in Table 4.5, along with examples of specific associated problem behaviors.

Although the debate about which approach is "best" has not been resolved, there is a growing consensus that each approach has value in classifying childhood disorders and that a combined approach may be needed (Pickles & Angold, 2003). In fact, to some extent, current approaches attempt to do this. For example, the DSM-5 includes dimensional ratings of severity for categorical diagnoses such as ADHD and ASD, and items drawn from empirically derived dimensions such as "anxious/depressed" have been used to develop rationally derived DSM-oriented scales identified by experts from different cultures as being consistent with DSM categories. However, it is not yet known whether combining the two approaches makes an appreciable difference in diagnosis as compared with using just one approach or the other (Ebesutani

TABLE 4.5 | **Commonly Identified Dimensions of Child Psychopathology and Examples of Items That Reflect Each Dimension**

Anxious/ Depressed	Withdrawn/ Depressed	Social Problems
Cries a lot	Would rather be alone	Too dependent
Worries	Refuses to talk	Doesn't get along with peers
Feels worthless	Secretive	
Nervous, tense	Shy, timid	Gets teased

Somatic Symptoms	Thought Problems	Aggressive Behavior
Feels dizzy	Hears things	Argues
Overtired	Sees things	Mean to others
Aches, pains	Strange behavior	Attacks people
Headaches	Strange ideas	Destroys others' things

Attention Problems	Rule-Breaking Behavior	
Inattentive	Lacks guilt	
Can't concentrate	Bad companions	
Can't sit still	Lies	
Confused	Runs away from home	

Based on Achenbach, T. M. & Rescorla, L. A. (2001). Manual for the ASEBA School-Age Forms and Profiles. (Burlington, VT: University of Vermont, Research Center for Children, Youth, and Families, 2001).

et al., 2010). Some severe forms of intellectual disability may be best conceptualized as qualitatively distinct conditions (categories), whereas most other childhood disorders, such as depression or anxiety, may be best described as extreme points on one or more continuous dimensions.

Also, depending on whether the purpose is clinical diagnosis or research, one approach may be more useful than the other. A dimensional approach to conceptualizing psychological factors such as behavior, affect, and cognitive abilities among children is compatible with research methods that determine the degree of association between two or more variables. Therefore, a dimensional approach is often preferred by those conducting psychological research. A categorical approach, on the other hand, is often more compatible with clinical purposes, for which the objective is to incorporate the whole pattern of the child's behavior into a meaningful diagnosis and treatment plan. In addition, categories are useful for communicating among clinicians, and categorical diagnoses are often required for clinical decisions—for example, to determine a child's eligibility for specialized services. In light of the different types of information provided by dimensions and categories, it is important to incorporate dimensions into current diagnostic practices while also finding feasible ways to reach categorical decisions (Rutter, 2011b).

The *Diagnostic and Statistical Manual of Mental Disorders* (DSM-5)

We begin our discussion of the DSM-5 with a brief synopsis of the evolution of current systems of diagnosis to show how far we have come in recognizing mental disorders in children and adolescents. The terminology and focus of prior systems reflected the major theoretical views of mental illness at the time; a shift to a more objective, informed approach occurred by the 1990s and continues today.

Historical Context

The slow process of formal recognition of the prevalence and significance of mental disorders began in 1948, when the *International Classification of Diseases* (ICD-6) added a section on mental disorders (WHO, 1948). Because many thought that the early ICD system was inadequate, in 1952 the American Psychiatric Association (APA, 1952) developed its own *Diagnostic and Statistical Manual of Mental Disorders* (DSM-I), which was revised in 1968 (DSM-II) (APA, 1968). These first efforts were not a huge success, but they did launch a sustained effort to improve the classification of mental disorders, an effort that continues today. Unfortunately, children and adolescents were neglected in the early versions of DSM; most childhood disorders were relegated to the adult categories, with the exception of mental retardation (intellectual disability), schizophrenia–childhood type, and transient disturbances in behavior or mood.

The DSM-III and DSM-III-R (APA, 1980, 1987) provided significant advances over the earlier versions. They discarded psychodynamic assumptions about etiology used in the earlier versions in favor of an atheoretical descriptive approach based on observable signs and symptoms. Clinical descriptions were replaced by explicit diagnostic criteria that helped to increase diagnostic reliability. In addition, they included more child categories and placed a greater emphasis on empirical data. With these changes came a shift in diagnostic systems and causal models. Less focus was put on the disorder existing within the child alone, and more emphasis was placed on the surrounding context in which the problem occurred. The DSM-III-R was developed to be a *prototypical* classification system by

which a child could be diagnosed with a certain subset of symptoms without having to meet all symptom criteria. This was an important change, especially in view of the heterogeneity of symptoms associated with most childhood disorders (Mash & Hunsley, 2007). On the other hand, it also means that individuals with the same diagnosis can and often do show very different patterns of symptoms. Consider that there were nearly 150 million different ways for an individual to meet the DSM-III-R criteria for an antisocial personality disorder (Widiger, 1993). The DSM-IV was published in 1994, followed by a revision in 2000 (DSM-IV-TR). Many changes were made to the classification system, the criteria sets for diagnosis, and the descriptive text in order to keep up with new research, correct factual errors, and provide new information.

DSM-5 Disorders

The DSM-5 was published in 2013, nearly two decades after the DSM-IV. The child and adolescent knowledge base has changed dramatically in the past 20 years. These changes necessitated conceptual, diagnostic, and procedural revisions, which are described in later chapters on disorders. We first introduce you to DSM-5 disorders that apply to children and adolescents. The first grouping, *Neurodevelopmental Disorders,* is shown in Table 4.6, and will be discussed in detail in the chapters to follow. Historically, these disorders were thought of as first occurring in childhood or as exclusive to childhood. However, it is now apparent that these early-occurring disorders continue into adolescence and adulthood for many of those affected. In addition to

TABLE 4.6 | Neurodevelopmental Disorders

Intellectual Disabilities — DSM-5
(Intellectual Disability [Intellectual Developmental Disorder] [mild, moderate, severe, profound], Global Developmental Delay)

Autism Spectrum Disorder (with or without accompanying intellectual or language impairment)

Communication Disorders (Language Disorder, Speech Sound Disorder, Childhood-Onset Fluency Disorder [Stuttering], Social [Pragmatic] Communication Disorder)

Specific Learning Disorder (with impairment in reading, written expression, or mathematics)

Attention-Deficit/Hyperactivity Disorder (predominantly hyperactive/impulsive predominantly inattentive, or predominantly combined presentation)

Motor Disorders (Developmental Coordination Disorder, Stereotypic Movement Disorder, Tourette's Disorder, Persistent (Chronic) Motor or Vocal Tic Disorder)

Source: Diagnostic and Statistical Manual of Mental Disorders, Fifth Edition. American Psychiatric Association.

faced by Felicia, her family, and other children like her, and then to promote and enhance long-term adjustments.

Cultural Considerations

Most interventions for youths with problems have failed to incorporate the unique experiences of ethnic minority children and their families (Yasui & Dishion, 2007). However, as evidence-based interventions have advanced, so has a growing awareness of the cultural context of children and families receiving psychological interventions (Huey & Polo, 2008; Scott et al., 2010). Parents from different ethnic groups and cultures have different parenting values and use different child-rearing practices. They also have different beliefs about childhood problems, how mental health services are provided, how to describe their children's problems when they seek help, and preferred interventions (Yasui & Dishion, 2007; Yeh et al., 2005). The **cultural compatibility hypothesis** states that treatment is likely to be more effective when it is compatible with the cultural patterns of the child and family. The importance of cultural sensitivity in treatment is reflected in the finding that for some problems and treatments, ethnic similarity between a child's caregiver and the therapist is associated with better treatment outcomes for the child (Halliday-Boykins, Schoenwald, & Letourneau, 2005).

Culturally competent children's mental health services may be provided in a number of ways. For example, in therapy for Hispanic children and adolescents, cultural competence may be achieved by matching children and families with clinicians of the same ethnicity; by customizing the treatment to Hispanic cultural values, beliefs, and customs (e.g., familism, spiritualism, and *respeto*); or by incorporating ethnic and cultural narratives and role play into therapy (Malgady, 2010). In recent years, existing evidence-based treatments have been successfully adapted and implemented to meet the needs of specific cultural groups—as, for example, in the case of a cognitive–behavioral intervention for trauma in American Indian youths (Goodkind, LaNoue, & Milford, 2010). Such cultural adaptations of existing treatments may include changes in treatment surface structure (e.g., changes in treatment materials, mode of service delivery, or treatment setting), as well as deep structure changes that focus on factors unique to a particular racial or ethnic group, such as cultural beliefs regarding how trauma affects health and cultural practices for treating these problems.

Treatment services for children must not only attend to the presenting symptoms but must also consider the specific values, norms, and expectations present within many cultures; the various religious beliefs and practices of each family; and other circumstances that might make what is a successful treatment for one family a failure for another (Schwoeri, Sholevar, & Combs, 2003). Cultural values and common parenting practices and beliefs for five different cultural groups are shown in Table 4.8.

Can you think of how these cultural beliefs and practices might lead us to use different treatments? One issue might be the different parenting styles cross-culturally. African American families place greater emphasis on strict discipline, whereas Latino and Native American parents are generally more permissive. In helping families establish effective rules and forms of discipline for their children, the clinician must be aware of these important cultural practices and find methods that each parent is comfortable using. As we emphasized earlier, generalizations about cultural practices and beliefs may fail to capture the diversity that exists within and across cultural groups, so we must be extremely careful not to stereotype individuals of any cultural group.

"I like to think that each generation will need a little less therapy than the generation before."

Treatment Goals

What are the typical goals of treatment? Reducing symptoms (problems), producing more substantial changes that will enhance the child's long-term functioning, or both? Since both are important, treatment goals often focus on building children's adaptation skills to facilitate long-term adjustment, rather than on merely eliminating problem behaviors or briefly

TABLE 4.8 | Cultural Values and Parenting Practices and Beliefs

	African American	Latino American	Asian American	Native American	European American
Cultural Values	Communalism Individualism Kinship relations Unity Creativity Cooperation Authenticity Racial identity	Family loyalty Interpersonal connectedness Mutual respect Self-respect	Self-control Social courtesy Emotional maturity Respect for elders	Centrality of family Sharing Harmony Humility	Independence Autonomy Individualism Initiative Acquisition of skills Self-development Standing up for one's own rights
Parenting Practices and Beliefs	Authoritarian parenting No-nonsense parenting Unilateral parental decision-making Egalitarian family structure Strict discipline Communal parenting	Authoritarian parenting Patriarchal family structure High expression of parental warmth Communal parenting Freedom	Authoritarian parenting Structural and managerial parental involvement Patriarchal family structure Strict discipline Parental control Negotiation of conflict Parent as teacher	Permissive, lax parenting Shame as discipline Patriarchal and matriarchal family structures Communal parenting	Authoritative parenting Egalitarian family structure Parent as manager Demanding

Sources: Adapted from Forehand and Kotchik, 1996; and from Yasui and Dishion, 2007.

reducing subjective distress. Other treatment goals and outcomes are also of crucial importance to the child, family, and society (Jensen, Hoagwood, & Petti, 1996; Kazdin, 1997). These include:

▶ *Outcomes Related to Child Functioning:* Reduction or elimination of symptoms, reduced degree of impairment in functioning, enhanced social competence, improved academic performance

▶ *Outcomes Related to Family Functioning:* Reduction in family dysfunction, improved marital and sibling relationships, reduction in stress, improvement in quality of life, reduction in burden of care, enhanced family support

▶ *Outcomes of Societal Importance:* Improvement in the child's participation in school-related activities (increased attendance, reduced truancy, reduction in school dropout rates), decreased involvement in the juvenile justice system, reduced need for special services, reduction in accidental injuries or substance abuse, enhancement of physical and mental health

The interlocking network of physical, behavioral, social, and learning difficulties that characterizes most childhood disorders requires a multidisciplinary approach to attain these treatment and prevention goals.

In many instances, children require medication or medical intervention that must be coordinated with psychosocial interventions, such as in connection with ADHD, ASD, eating disorders, depression, and chronic medical conditions. Thus, the use of combined treatments is common. In addition, psychological interventions for children and adolescents often require integration with effective teaching strategies, as illustrated in later chapters addressing intellectual disability, communication disorders, and specific learning disorder. Finally, some children require integration of community and social services to aid in their protection and basic needs, which we discuss in Chapter 12 in the section on child abuse and neglect.

Ethical and Legal Considerations

Many children referred for assessment and treatment experience multiple disadvantages and arguably need special help and protection. Both ethically and legally, clinicians who work with children and families are required to think about the impact that their actions will have not only on the children themselves, but also on the responsibilities, rights, and relationships that connect the children and their parents (Dishion & Stormshak, 2007a; Prout & Prout, 2007).

Cultural background is an important consideration in understanding the child's uniqueness and expectation.

Bailey, 2009). Several core ethical issues for mental health interventions with children and families versus interventions with adults are highlighted in Table 4.9. Ethical issues with children are complex because of ongoing changes in the legal status of children and a trend toward recognition of minors' constitutional rights, including self-determination and privacy (Melton, 2000). However, a more basic issue is determining when a minor is competent to make his or her own decisions, rather than determining only whether he or she has the legal right to do so. Some of the challenging issues faced by clinicians working with children include deciding when a minor can provide informed consent or refuse treatment as well as balancing the child's rights to confidentiality against the rights of the parents and the integrity of the family.

In addition to these ethical and legal concerns, much larger ethical questions concern the provision of services for children and families. Many interventions currently used to treat children with complex problems are known to be limited in scope—for example, 1 hour per week of therapy—and cannot realistically be expected to have a meaningful or lasting impact on children who are experiencing severe problems. Furthermore, a number of currently used interventions are intrusive,

TABLE 4.9 | **Ethical Issues in Clinical Work with Children and Families**

1. Children are inherently more vulnerable than adults.
2. Children's abilities are more variable and change over time.
3. Children are more reliant upon others and upon their environment.
4. Ethical principles and practices in the treatment of adults must be modified in response to the child's current developmental abilities and legal status.
5. Boundary and role issues are often more prevalent and more complex when caring for children than for adults.
6. Adult practices, and the adult knowledge base, do not transfer reliably to the care of children.
7. Practitioners must develop skills to work with families, agencies, and systems.
8. It is key to monitor one's own actions and motivations.
9. Seeking consultation and advice is helpful in difficult situations.
10. It is essential to maintain an absolute commitment to the safety and well-being of the patient.

Source: Reprinted from *Psychiatric Clinics of North America, 32,* Belitz, J. & Bailey, R. A., Clinical ethics for the treatment of children and adolescents: A guide for general psychiatrists, 243–257, Copyright 2009, with permission from Elsevier.

The ethical codes of professional organizations, such as the American Academy of Child and Adolescent Psychiatry (2009) and the American Psychological Association (2002, 2010), provide minimum ethical standards for practice, including: (a) selecting treatment goals and procedures that are in the best interests of the client; (b) making sure that client participation is active and voluntary; (c) keeping records that document the effectiveness of treatment in achieving its objectives; (d) protecting the confidentiality of the therapeutic relationship; and (e) ensuring the qualifications and competencies of the therapist. There is also an increasing emphasis on involving children, depending on their developmental level, as active partners in decision making with regard to their own psychological or medical treatment (McCabe, 1996, 2006).

In addition to these general ethical standards, there is a growing recognition of the unique challenges and ethical dilemmas associated with mental health interventions for children and their families (Belitz &

expensive, and not supported by data (Kazdin, 2000). A more fundamental and thorny ethical question in some cases is whether we should provide any treatment when we know that the treatment may not make a difference or, even worse, may have harmful effects.

Clinicians who work with children and their parents need to be aware of federal, state, and local laws that affect both assessment and treatment of children with special needs. Many of these laws apply to children with mental and physical disabilities and handicaps and are based on the recognition that disability is a natural part of the human experience and that all citizens (children included) are entitled to equal treatment and education. Two laws that have had a profound influence on services for children with disabilities are the Education for All Handicapped Children Act (1975) and its amendment, the Individuals with Disabilities Education Improvement Act (2004). The following are two of the many purposes of these laws:

▸ To ensure that all children with disabilities have available to them a free, appropriate public education that emphasizes special education and related services designed to meet their unique needs and prepare them for employment and independent living.

▸ To ensure that the rights of children with disabilities and of the parents of such children are protected.

General Approaches to Treatment

The number and diversity of treatments for children have grown tremendously; currently, more than 550 treatments are currently in use to help children (Kazdin, 2000). While we will (thankfully) not attempt to cover them all, in the remainder of this chapter we provide a brief overview of several of the major approaches. More than 70% of practicing clinicians who work with children and families identify their approach as *eclectic*; this means that they use different approaches for children with different problems and circumstances and that they see most of these approaches as having value. In light of this practice, the large number of treatments specified above likely represents a vast underestimate of the full range of treatments used with children. Let's now turn to a brief overview of some of the general approaches to treatment and see how they might apply to Felicia.

Psychodynamic Treatments

Psychodynamic approaches view child psychopathology as determined by underlying unconscious and conscious conflicts (Lesser, 1972). Therefore, the focus is on helping the child develop an awareness of unconscious factors that may be contributing to his or her problems (AACAP, 2012; Galatzer-Levy et al., 2000). With younger children, this awareness can occur through play therapy (Chethik, 2000); with older children, it occurs through verbal interactions with the therapist. As underlying conflicts are revealed, the therapist helps the child resolve the conflicts and develop more adaptive ways of coping. Research has found some support for the effectiveness of both long- and short-term approaches to psychodynamic psychotherapy with children and adolescents (Abbass et al., 2013; Midgley & Kennedy, 2011), although further controlled studies are needed.

In Felicia's case, a therapist would help her gain insight into her problems through an intensive process of psychotherapy, perhaps lasting months or even years. The therapist might explore her earliest memories of her relationship with her parents by having her recall positive and negative memories and exploring how she constructs her childhood memories and relationships. The assumption is that once she resolves the underlying problems, such as an insecure attachment to her mother, Felicia's overt symptoms of depression, social withdrawal, school refusal, and physical symptoms will be alleviated (Muratori et al., 2003).

Behavioral Treatments

Behavioral approaches assume that many abnormal child behaviors are learned. Therefore, the focus of treatment is on re-educating the child, using procedures derived from theories of learning or from research. Such procedures include positive reinforcement, time-out, modeling, and systematic desensitization (Morris & Kratochwill, 2007). Behavioral treatments often focus on changing the child's environment by working with parents and teachers.

In Felicia's case, a therapist might try to decrease her school refusal by instructing her parents to not let her stay at home when she protests and by rewarding her for going to school with praise or a preferred activity. In addition, the therapist might use modeling, role-playing, and reinforced practice to help Felicia learn more effective social skills.

Cognitive Treatments

Cognitive approaches view abnormal child behavior as the result of deficits and/or distortions in the child's thinking, including perceptual biases, irrational beliefs, and faulty interpretations (Kendall, 2011b). For example, for an attractive girl who gets A grades but thinks she is ugly and is going to fail in school, treatment emphasis is on changing these faulty cognitions. As cognitions change, the child's behaviors and feelings are also expected to change.

In Felicia's case, she may believe that she can't do well in school, that if she goes to school then harm will befall her mother, or that children at school will think she's stupid. Changing these negative views by challenging them and by helping Felicia develop more rational and more adaptive forms of thinking, should lead to changes in her behavior.

Cognitive–Behavioral Treatments

Cognitive–behavioral approaches view psychological disturbances as the result of both faulty thought patterns, and faulty learning and environmental experiences. These approaches begin with the basic premise that the way children and parents think about their environment determines how they will react to it (Meichenbaum, 1977). Combining elements of both the behavioral model and the cognitive model, the cognitive–behavioral approach grew rapidly as behavior therapists began to focus on the important role of cognition in treatment for both the child and the family (Kendall, 2011a).

Faulty thought patterns that are the targets of change include distortions in both cognitive content (e.g., erroneous beliefs) and cognitive process (e.g., irrational thinking and faulty problem solving). As you will learn, cognitive distortions and biases have been identified in children with a variety of problems, including, for example, depression, conduct disorder, and anxiety disorders.

The major goals of cognitive–behavioral treatment are to identify maladaptive cognitions and replace them with more adaptive ones, to teach the child to use both cognitive and behavioral coping strategies in specific situations, and to help the child learn to regulate his or her own behavior. Treatment may also involve how others respond to the child's maladaptive behavior. Using a cognitive–behavioral approach, a therapist would help Felicia learn to think more positively and to use more effective social skills and coping strategies.

Client-Centered Treatments

Client-centered approaches view child psychopathology as the result of social or environmental circumstances that are imposed on the child and interfere with his or her basic capacity for personal growth and adaptive functioning. The interference causes the child to experience a loss or impairment in self-esteem and emotional well-being, resulting in even further problems. The therapist relates to the child in an empathic way, providing unconditional, nonjudgmental, and genuine acceptance of the child as an individual, often through the use of play activities with younger children and verbal interaction with older youths (Axline, 1947). The therapist respects the child's capacity to achieve his or her goals without the therapist's serving as a major adviser or coach—the therapist respects the child's self-directing abilities.

In Felicia's case, being babied by her parents, who view her as slow, may have led to interference with her adaptive functioning and to low self-esteem. In treatment, a therapist would comment on what Felicia is saying and feeling to help her understand her feelings and to increase the congruence between her feelings and her behavior. In therapy, Felicia would lead the way as the clinician follows.

Family Treatments

Family models challenge the view of psychopathology as residing only within the individual child and, instead, view child psychopathology as determined by variables operating in the larger family system. Like other approaches, the many varieties of family therapy differ widely in their underlying assumptions and approach to treatment. However, nearly all of the approaches view individual child disorders as manifestations of disturbances in family relations (Rivett, 2008).

Treatment involves a therapist (and sometimes a co-therapist) who interacts with the entire family or a select subset of family members, such as the parents and child or the husband and wife. Therapy typically focuses on the family issues underlying problem behaviors. Depending on the approach, the therapist may focus on family interaction, communication, dynamics, contingencies, boundaries, or alliances. It is also essential to adapt family interventions to the cultural context of the family (Kumpfer et al., 2002).

In Felicia's case, her overall helplessness and physical symptoms may be serving to maintain her role as the baby in the family, or may be serving as the parents' way of avoiding their own marital difficulties by focusing the problem on Felicia. A therapist would assist Felicia and her family in identifying and changing these and other dysfunctional ways in which family members relate to one another.

Neurobiological Treatments

Medical models view child psychopathology as resulting from neurobiological impairment or dysfunction and rely primarily on pharmacological and other biological approaches to treatment. Examples include the use of stimulant medications for the treatment of ADHD, antipsychotic medications for the treatment of schizophrenia or serious aggressive and destructive behavior, and selective serotonin reuptake inhibitors (SSRIs) such as fluoxetine (Prozac) for the treatment of depression and anxiety, along with practice guidelines for their use (AACAP, 2009a). Although still in a very early stage, there is also a growing interest in developing pharmacological interventions that target basic mechanisms such as gene expression, neurotransmission abnormalities, and other abnormal processes underlying the child's disorder (Vitiello & Grabb, 2013). Table 4.10 provides a summary of medications and their typical uses with children and adolescents, which you may find helpful when reviewing treatment for specific disorders discussed in other chapters.

Other, much more controversial forms of biological intervention include electroconvulsive therapy (ECT) for severe depression, the administration of large doses

TABLE 4.10 | Descriptions of Common Medications for Children and Youths[a]

Type of Medication	Treatment Uses	Examples
Stimulant and non-stimulant medications for ADHD	Attention-deficit hyperactivity disorder (ADHD)	*Stimulants:* Dextroamphetamine (*Dexedrine, Adderall*), Methylphenidate (*Ritalin, Metadate, Concerta, Focalin*) *Nonstimulant:* Atomoxetine (*Strattera*)
Antidepressant medications	Depression, school phobias, panic attacks, and other anxiety disorders, bed-wetting, eating disorders, obsessive–compulsive disorder, post-traumatic stress disorder, and ADHD	*Selective serotonin reuptake inhibitors (SSRIs):* Fluoxetine (*Prozac*), Sertraline (*Zoloft*), Paroxetine (*Paxil*), Fluvoxamine (*Luvox*), Venlafaxine (*Effexor*), Citalopram (*Celexa*), and Escitalopram (*Lexapro*). *Tricyclic antidepressants (TCAs):* Amitriptyline (*Elavil*), Clomipramine (*Anafranil*), Imipramine (*Tofranil*), and Nortriptyline (*Pamelor*). *Monoamine oxidase inhibitors (MAOIs):* Phenelzine (*Nardil*) and Tranylcypromine (*Parnate*).
Antipsychotic medications	Controlling psychotic symptoms (delusions, hallucinations), disorganized thinking, motor tics, and Tourette's syndrome. They are occasionally used to treat severe anxiety and may help in reducing very aggressive behavior.	*First-generation antipsychotics:* Chlorpromazine (*Thorazine*), Thioridazine (*Mellaril*), Fluphenazine (*Prolixin*), Trifluoperazine (*Stelazine*), Thiothixene (*Navane*), and Haloperidol (*Haldol*) *Second-generation antipsychotics (also known as atypical or novel):* Clozapine (*Clozaril*), Risperidone (*Risperdal*), Paliperidon (*Invega*), Quetiapine (*Seroquel*), Olanzapine (*Zyprexa*), Ziprasidone (*Geodon*), Aripiprazole (*Abilify*), Iloperidone (*Fanapt*), Lurasidon (*Latuda*), and Asenapine (*Saphris*).
Mood stabilizers and anticonvulsant medications	Bipolar disorder, severe mood symptoms and mood swings (manic and depressive), aggressive behavior and impulse control disorders.	Lithium (lithium carbonate, *Eskalith*), Valproic acid (*Depakote, Depakene*), Carbamazepine (*Tegretol*), Lamotrigine (*Lamictil*), and Oxcarbazepine (*Trileptal*).
Anti-anxiety medications	Selective serotonin reuptake inhibitors are used to treat anxiety in children and adolescents and are included above in the section on antidepressants. Other medications (presented here) used to treat anxiety in adults are rarely used with children and adolescents, but may be helpful for brief treatment of severe anxiety.	*Benzodiazepines:* Alprazolam (*Xanax*), Lorazepam (*Ativan*), Diazepam (*Valium*), and Clonazepam (*Klonopin*) *Antihistamines:* Diphenhydramine (Benadryl), and Hydroxyzine (Vistaril) *Atypical:* Buspirone (*BuSpar*) and Zolpidem (*Ambien*).

[a]These medications are often used in association with other forms of intervention such as psychotherapy, parent training, etc.

Source: Based on Psychiatric medication for children and adolescents Part. II: Types of medications, American Academy of Child & Adolescent Psychiatry, 2004, Updated May 2012.

of vitamins or minerals to children with autism, and the scrupulous elimination of food additives and preservatives from the diets of children with ADHD. In Felicia's case, a psychiatrist might consider using SSRIs to treat her depressive symptoms. As shown in ● Figure 4.5, the use of psychotropic medications for children's mental health problems increased significantly from the late 1980s to the mid-1990s, which can be attributed to increasing public acceptance of these medications as part of the treatment of mental health problems among children and youths during that time period (Olfson et al., 2002). Growth in the use of medications for children's mental health problems has slowed or leveled off over the past decade, although the percentage of children receiving more than one class of medication has increased (Comer, Olfson, & Mojtabai, 2010). Along with increased use, concerns have been expressed about the frequent use of medications with very young children (Chirdkiatgumchai et al., 2013; Gleason et al., 2007), and their frequent misuse and abuse by adolescents (Zosel et al., 2013). The use of prescription medication also varies in relation to racial/ethnic status. For example, more than 20% of non-Hispanic white adolescents report using prescription medication for depression versus 4% to 9% of Asian, black, and Hispanic youths (Cummings & Druss, 2011).

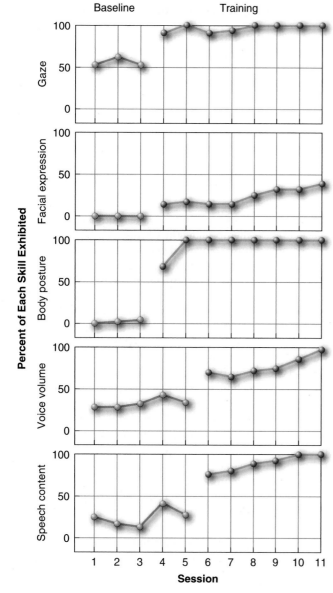

● **FIGURE 4.6** | Results of behavioral role-play intervention.

Based on Depression by D. J. Kolko, 1987. In M. Hersen and V. B. Van Hasselt (Eds.),"Behavior Therapy with Children and Adolescents: A Clinical Approach", pp. 163–164.

Best practice guidelines are systematically developed statements to assist practitioners and patients with decisions regarding appropriate treatment(s) for specific clinical conditions. These guidelines are intended to offer recommendations on the most effective and cost-effective treatments for children with particular problems and their families (March et al., 2007).

Two main approaches have been used to develop best practice guidelines. The *scientific approach* derives guidelines from a comprehensive review of current research findings. This approach emphasizes **evidence-based treatments (EBTs)**, which are clearly specified treatments shown to be effective in controlled research with specific populations (Weisz & Kazdin, 2010). Most EBTs have been evaluated in large-scale clinical trials involving large numbers of children and careful comparisons with other EBTs or other forms of treatment (e.g., medication). The *expert-consensus approach* uses the opinions of experts to fill in the gaps in the scientific literature—for example, when research is inconclusive or when there is a lack of information about multicultural issues. Thus, *evidence-based practice* is not the blind application of research findings, but rather it involves the use of the best available scientific evidence combined with good individual clinical expertise and provides for consumer choice, preference, and culture (Institute of Medicine, 2011; Sackett et al., 2000).

A number of professional organizations whose members provide mental health services to children and their families have developed excellent best practice guidelines, for example, the Society of Clinical Child and Adolescent Psychology (www.effectivechildtherapy.com) and the American Academy of Child and Adolescent Psychiatry (www.aacap.org). In the chapters that follow, we will discuss many of the best practice interventions that are recommended for youths with particular problems.

Consistent with the growing emphasis on improving outcomes, efforts to evaluate treatments for childhood disorders have intensified (Chorpita et al., 2011; Weisz & Kazdin, 2010). These efforts allow us to take a closer look at the overall effectiveness of commonly used treatment methods.

Let's begin with the good news:

▸ Changes achieved by children receiving psychotherapy are consistently greater than changes for children not receiving psychotherapy.

▸ The average child who is treated is better off at the end of therapy than at least 75% of children who did not receive treatment, particularly with respect to symptom reduction.

▸ Treatments have been shown to be effective for children with a wide range of problems, including both internalizing and externalizing disorders.

▸ Treatment effects tend to be lasting, with the effects at follow-up (usually around 6 months after treatment) similar to those found immediately after treatment.

▸ Effects are about twice as large for problems that are specifically targeted in treatment as they are for changes in nonspecific areas of functioning. This result suggests that treatments are producing focused changes in targeted areas such as anxiety rather than producing nonspecific or global effects such as changes in how the child feels (Weisz, 1998).

▶ The more outpatient therapy sessions children receive, the more improvement is seen in their symptoms (Angold et al., 2000).

So what's the bad news? Although research findings present a generally positive picture of psychotherapy with children and of behavioral and cognitive–behavioral approaches in particular, there are a number of important limitations.

First, although research generally shows that most treatments are effective in reducing symptoms such as anxiety, depression, and oppositional behavior, fewer than 20% of treatments demonstrate evidence that they reduce impairment in life functioning (Becker, Chorpita, & Daleiden, 2011). Thus, greater attention to the development and evaluation of interventions that also result in meaningful changes in the child's overall life functioning is needed. Second, we must be aware of the critical difference between research therapy that is carried out in laboratory-based outcome studies and therapy that is carried out in community-based clinics (Wagner, Swenson, & Henggeler, 2000). Most of the evidence-based treatment outcome studies for specific disorders fall into the category of research therapy. However, as compared with research therapy, clinical therapy is typically conducted with more severe cases, directed at a diverse set of problems and children, and carried out in clinic or hospital settings by professional career therapists with large caseloads (Weisz & Weiss, 1993). In general, clinical therapy is less structured and more flexible than research therapy, and it uses relatively more nonbehavioral methods, such as psychodynamic and eclectic approaches. In contrast to the findings for research therapy, similar analyses for studies of clinical therapy have resulted in minimal effects (Andrade, Lambert, & Bickman, 2000; Weisz et al., 2013). These findings suggest that conventional services for children as they are currently carried out may have limited effectiveness. However, few controlled studies exist of child therapy outcomes in settings where it is typically conducted, although this situation is changing. Thus, it is premature to draw any conclusions from the findings from clinic and community studies until more empirical data about therapy in clinical practice are available (Weisz, Jensen-Doss, & Hawley, 2006; Weisz et al., 2013).

In summary, although the efficacy of treatments for many child and adolescent mental health problems is substantial, testing of the effectiveness and cost-effectiveness of these treatments in real-world settings and dissemination of this information and its use in public settings are key issues that require further attention (Novins et al., 2013).

NEW DIRECTIONS

Knowing is not enough; we must apply

Willing is not enough; we must do

—Goethe

Despite the availability of many potentially effective assessment and treatment procedures, as many as 70% to 80% of children and families with significant mental health needs do not receive any specialized assessment or treatment services (Merikangas et al., 2011). Service rates are highest for children with ADHD and other behavior disorders, but fewer than one in five youths receive services for their anxiety, eating, or substance use disorders. This situation is even worse for youths from low-income families, ethnic minority youths, and those in the child welfare and juvenile justice systems. This raises the larger issue of whether current evidence-based practices are, by themselves, a viable way to help these large, unrecognized, and underserved groups of children and to reduce the gap between children's mental health needs and the availability and access to effective services (Kazak et al., 2010).

In response to this issue there has been a general "call to action" from many family, public, professional, and scientific organizations to address these challenges and actively promote the uptake of evidence-based assessment and treatment practices into public health, school, and mental health systems. This has led to an increasing number of opportunities for partnerships among the various stakeholders, along with financial incentives at the state and federal levels to support these efforts. The result has been several exciting new initiatives that focus on:

1. Increasing the recognition of children's mental health needs, not only on the part of laypersons, but also among education, welfare, juvenile justice, and health care professionals (Jensen et al., 2011).

2. Developing a much wider range of child mental health service delivery models based on: (a) the use of new technologies (e.g., Internet, smart phones, video-conferencing assessment and treatment services for rural youths [Duncan, Valasquez,

Prevalence

Based on available evidence and estimates, the total number of children and adults with intellectual disability is approximately 1% of the general population (Maulik et al., 2011). However, each person applies his or her own cognitive abilities in unique ways that may be more or less adaptive in her or his own environment. Thus, prevalence estimates vary across time and across countries as a result of IQ measurement problems, different definitions of ID, and varying study designs (Witwer, Lawton, & Aman, in press).

Sex Ratio

Among children with mild intellectual disability (by far the most common diagnosis), males outnumber females at a ratio of 1.6:1. Males outnumber females among the other levels of severity as well, but these ratios are inconsistent across studies and tend to be small. Similar to racial differences in the diagnosis of intellectual disability, gender differences in ID may be an artifact of identification and referral patterns rather than true differences in prevalence (Einfeld et al., 2010). If a true male excess of intellectual disability does exist, researchers suspect this may be due to the occurrence of X-linked genetic disorders such as fragile-X syndrome (discussed later in the chapter), which affect males more often than females (Handen, 2007).

Socioeconomic and Cultural Influences

It is a well-established finding that intellectual disability is more prevalent among children of lower socioeconomic status (SES) and children from minority groups (Witwer et al., in press). This link is found primarily among children in the mild intellectual disability range; children with more severe levels are identified almost equally in different racial and economic groups. Whether or not signs of organic etiology are present, diagnoses of mild intellectual disability increase sharply from near zero among children from higher SES categories to about 2.5% in the lowest SES category (APA, 2000). These figures indicate that SES factors play a suspected role both in the cause of intellectual disability and in the identification and labeling of persons with intellectual disability (Maulik et al., 2011).

The overrepresentation of minority and low-SES children in the group with mild intellectual disability is a complicated and unresolved issue. As we noted, average IQ levels for the African American population are lower than IQ levels found in the white population, resulting in more African American children among samples of children with mild intellectual disability. What specific environmental circumstances might create such an imbalance in IQ findings? To answer this question, Brooks-Gunn et al. (2003) tested the theory that the differences can be partially explained based on social and economic disadvantage. They accounted for initial IQ differences of over 17 points in African American versus white children by the independent effects of economic deprivation, home environment, and maternal characteristics. As shown in ● Figure 5.1, initial IQ differences were almost 18 points between a sample of African American and white children at 5 years of age, controlling for gender and birth weight. However, these differences were reduced by about 71% after adjusting for differences in poverty and home environment. Similar gains in IQ performance are found when children are adopted from working-class into middle-class homes, reinforcing the significant role of the environment in shaping one's intellectual and adaptive abilities (Nisbett et al., 2012). These data remind us that the likelihood of a diagnosis of intellectual disability is shaped and influenced by social and cultural forces such as racial discrimination, poverty, and cultural insensitivity (Emerson, 2012).

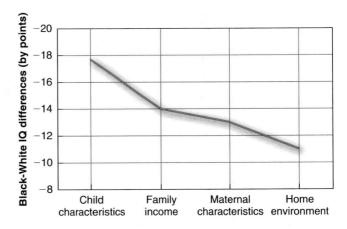

● **FIGURE 5.1** | Factors accounting for differences in IQ scores between white and African American children at 5 years of age.

Based on data from Brooks-Gunn, J., Klebanov, P. K., Smith, J., Duncan, G. J., & Lee, K. (2003). The Black-White test score gap in young children: Contributions of test and family characteristics. *Applied Developmental Science*, 7(4), pp. 239–252

Section Summary

Features of Intellectual Disabilities

- The DSM-5 criteria for intellectual disability consist of deficits in intellectual functioning (confirmed by IQ testing and clinical assessment), deficits in adaptive functioning, and onset of intellectual and adaptive deficits during the developmental period.

- Children with intellectual disability vary widely in their degree of disability and level of functioning.

- IQ scores are no longer used to determine level of impairment. Rather, DSM-5 describes four levels of severity—mild, moderate, severe, or profound—based on adaptive functioning that determines a person's level of needed supports.
- Intellectual disability occurs in an estimated 1% of the population, more often among males than females.
- Intellectual disability occurs more often among children from lower socioeconomic and minority groups. Economic disadvantage and discrimination practices often account for these findings.

DEVELOPMENTAL COURSE AND ADULT OUTCOMES

To appreciate the manner in and extent to which children with intellectual disabilities achieve various developmental milestones, consider how typically developing children express themselves. An infant exploring his or her world relies on primitive sensorimotor functions—touching, tasting, and manipulating objects—to learn about the environment. At this stage of development everything is new, and the brain is establishing literally millions of new connections each day.

Then, between 18 and 24 months of age, the toddler begins to acquire language and to draw on memories of past experience to aid in understanding the present. For an intellectually normal child, it is during this stage that the child's environmental conditions and opportunities are known to play a crucial role in fostering enthusiasm for learning and in establishing the roots of intellectual sophistication. Although the majority of children with ID progress through each developmental milestone in roughly the same manner as other children, important differences in their developmental accomplishments are evident.

Much of the knowledge about other issues involved in the developmental course and adult outcomes for children with intellectual disability is derived from studies of children with Down syndrome. Chromosome abnormalities are the single most common cause of moderate to severe intellectual disability. **Down syndrome** is the most common disorder resulting from these abnormalities. children with Down syndrome, along with their parents, have frequently participated in studies comparing their development with that of their normally developing peers.

Dan, a 15-year-old with Down syndrome, describes how his early development was similar to, but much slower than, that of his younger brother.

Dan, with moderate intellectual disability, is describing how his younger brother Brian, with normal

intelligence, caught up with him by the time Brian was 2 years old, and progressed through developmental milestones at a faster pace. Does Dan's development follow the same organized sequence as Brian's? Will his development show specific deficits in certain intellectual abilities such as language? Or will he eventually catch up? This case illustrates the developmental-versus-difference controversy (Weiss, Weisz, & Bromfield, 1986), an issue that has intrigued those in the field of child development and intellectual disability for some time. Simply stated, the **developmental-versus-difference controversy** is this: Do all children—regardless of intellectual impairments—progress through the same developmental milestones in a similar sequence, but at different rates? Or do children with intellectual disability develop in a different, less sequential, and less organized fashion?

The developmental position, which applies primarily to individuals not suffering from organic impairment, consists of two primary hypotheses: First, the *similar sequence hypothesis* argues that all children, with or without intellectual disability, pass through stages of cognitive development in an identical (invariant) order; they differ only in their rate and upper limit of development (Bennett-Gates & Zigler, 1998). Second, the *similar structure hypothesis* suggests that children with intellectual disability demonstrate the same behaviors and underlying processes as typically developing children at the same level of cognitive functioning (such as Dan and his younger brother were at ages 5 and 2). That is, if children with intellectual disability are matched to typically developing children by their mental age, then the children with intellectual disability will show equivalent performance on cognitive tasks, such as problem solving, spelling, and moral reasoning. The developmental position rejects the notion of a specific deficit or difference among children with intellectual disability and instead emphasizes how these children traverse the stages more slowly and attain a lower developmental ceiling than typically developing children (Bennett-Gates & Zigler, 1998).

In contrast, the **difference viewpoint** argues that cognitive development of children with intellectual disability differs from that of children without intellectual disability in more than developmental rate and upper limit. According to this position, even when his mental age is matched to his younger brother's, Dan will show qualitatively different reasoning and problem-solving strategies, and he may never be able to accomplish some tasks beyond a certain level.

Evidence supports the developmental hypothesis for children with familial, not organic, types of intellectual disability, but this issue has not yet been resolved. Children with familial intellectual disability generally follow developmental stages in an invariant order, the same as children with normal intellectual abilities, with the possible exception of some children with co-occurring brain abnormalities or autism (Bennett-Gates & Zigler, 1998). The similar structure hypothesis has also been supported for children with familial intellectual disability, with some exceptions. Children with familial intellectual disability show slight deficits in memory and information processing as compared with mental-age–matched children without intellectual disability (Schuchardt, Gebhardt, & Mäehler, 2010), which may be due to the children's difficulty in staying motivated to perform repetitive, boring tasks (Weisz, 1999).

The picture for children with organically based intellectual disability (such as Dan, who has Down syndrome) is more straightforward. They often have one or more specific deficit areas that cause them to perform more poorly than mental-age–matched children without intellectual disability. Thus, Dan is likely to show some differences in his performance in certain areas of development, including his expressive language. Nevertheless, he will likely pass through the same developmental sequences as his younger brother, but at a slower pace.

Motivation

Many children who fall within the range of mild intellectual disability are bright enough to learn and to attend regular schools and classrooms. However, they are more susceptible to a sense of helplessness and frustration, which places additional burdens on their social and cognitive development. As a consequence, they begin to expect failure, even for tasks they can master; in the absence of proper instruction, their motivation to tackle new demands decreases (Harris, 2006).

Ed, describing his memory of comments made by his teacher in elementary school, expresses this phenomenon well:

> Her negative picture of me stood out like a sore thumb. That's the problem with people like me—the schools and teachers find out we have problems, they notice them, and then we are abandoned. That one teacher was very annoyed that I was in her class. She had to put up with me. (Bogdan & Taylor, 1982)

Children with intellectual disability, consequently, expect little success, set lower goals for themselves, and settle for minimal success when they are able to do better, as compared with typically developing children of their same mental age (Weisz, 1999). This learned helplessness may be unwittingly condoned by adults. When they are told a child is "retarded," adults are less likely to urge that child to persist after failure than they are to urge a normal child at the same level of cognitive development. On the other hand, young children with mild intellectual disability improve in their ability to remain on task and they develop goal-directed behavior when

"Acknowledge our children's differences but respect their uniqueness." —Parent of a child with Down syndrome

provided with stimulating environments and caregiver support (Wilkins & Matson, 2009).

Changes in Abilities

Intellectual disability is not necessarily a lifelong disorder. Although it is a relatively stable condition from childhood into adulthood, the IQ score can fluctuate in relation to the level of impairment and type of intellectual disability. Children such as Matthew who have mild intellectual disability may, with appropriate training and opportunities, develop good adaptive skills in other domains and may exceed the level of impairment required for a diagnosis of intellectual disability.

The major cause of a child's intellectual disability certainly affects the degree to which his or her IQ and adaptive abilities may change. The IQ of children with Down syndrome, who are not representative of the course of intellectual disability in general, may plateau during the middle childhood years and then decrease over time. For example, from 1 to 6 years of age, children with Down syndrome often show significant age-related gains in adaptive functioning, but as they grow older, their pace of development levels off or even declines (Margallo-Lana et al., 2007). A similar deceleration is often seen in the rate of social development of these children as they grow older (Hazlett et al., 2011). This observation has been termed the *slowing and stability hypothesis* (Hodapp et al., 2011), and it affirms that children with Down syndrome may alternate between periods of gain in functioning and periods of little or no advance. Although these children continue to develop in intelligence, they do so at progressively slower rates throughout the childhood years.

Language and Social Behavior

Research on language development and social functioning among children and adolescents with Down syndrome suggests that their development follows a largely predictable and organized course (Filippi & Karmiloff-Smith, 2013). Because their cognitive development, play, self-knowledge, and knowledge of others are interrelated in organized and meaningful ways, the underlying symbolic abilities in children with Down syndrome are believed to be largely intact.

However, important differences in language development exist between children with Down syndrome and their typically developing age-mates. Perhaps the most striking difference for children with Down syndrome is the considerable delay in the expressive language development that is necessary to establish independent living skills. Their expressive language is often much weaker than their receptive language, especially as they attain communication abilities beyond the 24-month level (Filippi & Karmiloff-Smith, 2013).

Another major milestone of infancy and early childhood development is the ability to form secure attachments with caregivers. Although their attachments form more slowly than usual, many children with Down syndrome form secure attachment relationships with their caregivers by 12 to 24 months of developmental age (Dykens, Hodapp, & Evans, 2006). Still, a significant number of these children may have problems in developing a secure attachment because they express less emotion than other children. In one study, children with Down syndrome were not picked up and held by either the mother or the stranger in the strange situation to the same extent as non-delayed children. (See Table 2.2 for a description of the "strange situation" method of assessing child–caregiver attachment.) Even when these children made approaches with appropriate signals for contact, mothers and strangers rarely completed the contact, presumably because the children did not show the distress signals of crying, reaching, or holding on that typically tell the parent "I want to be picked up!" (Vaughn, Contreras, & Seifer, 1994). This finding has important implications for parents of young children with Down syndrome: Even though they may show few signals of distress or desire for contact, these infants and toddlers need to be held and nurtured just as others do.

Following the attachment period, the next important developmental milestones relate to the emergence of a sense of self, which establishes the early foundations of personality. Like other children, toddlers with Down syndrome begin to delight at recognizing themselves in mirrors and photos, although this milestone is often delayed. The experience of self-recognition in most infants is immediately met by smiles and laughter, and this experience is also found among toddlers with Down syndrome (Mans, Cicchetti, & Sroufe, 1978). This positive affect accompanying their visual self-recognition suggests that these children feel good about themselves. However, as toddlers and preschoolers, children with Down syndrome show delayed and aberrant functioning in their *internal state language*, the language that reflects the emergent sense of self and others (through the use of words such as "mad" and "happy"). Because internal state language is critical to regulating social interaction and providing a foundation for early self–other understanding, these children may be at increased risk for subsequent problems in the development of the self-system (Huck, Kemp, & Carter, 2010).

Children with intellectual disability, especially those with moderate to mild impairments, learn symbolic play—games, puppets, and sports—in much the same manner as do other children. Nevertheless, they often fail to gain their peers' acceptance in regular education settings, because they may have deficits in social skills and social–cognitive abilities (Cook & Oliver, 2011). Concerns about the social development of children with intellectual disability are increasing as a result of the movement to include children with different levels of ability in regular classrooms and schools, rather than only placing them in institutions or specialized facilities. Typically developing children seem to prefer playing with other typically developing children, and as a result, children with intellectual disability are more socially isolated from other children their age (Guralnick, Connor, & Johnson, 2011). These integrated classrooms allow children with intellectual disabilities, despite their limited social skills, to interact with typically developing peers, which in turn has a positive impact on their social status (Leffert, Siperstein, & Widaman, 2010; Siperstein, Glick, & Parker, 2009).

Emotional and Behavioral Problems

PATTIE

Disturbed or Disturbing?

Pattie was labeled mentally retarded and lived in over 20 homes and institutions before being committed to a state school at age 10. At the age of 20, she discussed some of her experiences and feelings: "I guess I was very disturbed. I call it disturbed, but it was when I was very upset. A lot of people at (the institution) … told me I was disturbed—that I was disturbed and that I was retarded—so I figure that all through my life I was disturbed. Looking at the things I done, I must have been disturbed. … Upset and disturbed are the same in my mind. Crazy to me is something else. It is somebody that is really gone. I mean really out. Just deliberately kill somebody just to do it. That is what I call crazy. I guess what I was was emotionally disturbed—yeah. Emotionally disturbed is a time when too many things are bothering me. They just build up till I get too nervous or upset. My mind just goes through all these changes and different things. So many things inside that were bothering me." (Based on Bogdan & Taylor, 1982.)

Pattie's description of her feelings while living in various institutions illuminates how "disturbing" her behavior could be. But are her feelings a function of her environment and personal limitations? Many children and adolescents with intellectual disability have to face many obstacles related to their intellectual, physical, and social impairments, and often they have little control over their own lives.

In the early 1970s, a major study was conducted to gain some understanding of the extent of psychiatric disorders among children and adults with and without intellectual disability (Rutter et al., 1976). Ratings by both parents and teachers revealed that about one-third of the children with mild intellectual disability and one-half of the children with more severe forms of intellectual disability showed major signs of emotional disturbance, suggesting that these problems are common. Since then, research has estimated that the risk of emotional and behavioral disturbances among children with intellectual disabilities is approximately three to five times greater than among typically developing children (Einfeld, Ellis, & Emerson, 2011). These problems are due largely to limited communication skills, additional stressors, and more neurological deficits faced by these children and youths (Adams & Oliver, 2011).

The nature and course of psychiatric disorders in children and adolescents with and without intellectual disabilities is likely very similar. Problem behaviors of youths with mild and moderate disabilities are similarly stable and persistent over the course of their development (de Ruiter et al., 2008; Einfeld et al., 2011). Impulse control disorders, anxiety disorders, and mood disorders are the most commonly diagnosed psychiatric diagnoses for children with intellectual disability. Although these problems are sometimes severe and often require intervention, they are considered to be part of the spectrum of problems that coexist with intellectual disability, and as not indicators of other psychiatric illnesses (Hodapp et al., 2006). By early adulthood, persons with intellectual disabilities continue to show a greater risk for psychopathology than the general population, although problems in attention and aggression show a significant decline from childhood rates (Buckles, Luckasson, & Keefe, 2013).

Adjustments usually are needed in how DSM-5 diagnostic criteria for other mental disorders are applied, however. The frequency of temper tantrums, hyperactivity, and mood disorders among these children requires consideration of what is normal or typical for other children with similar levels of intellectual disability. For example, the diagnosis of attention-deficit/hyperactivity disorder (ADHD) requires the presence of behavioral disturbance that is inappropriate for an individual's developmental level. Attention spans, distractibility, and on-task behaviors vary considerably among individuals with profound intellectual disability. An individual with profound intellectual disability must be compared with other children with profound intellectual disability for the purpose of diagnosing any other psychiatric disturbance (APA, 2013).

Internalizing Problems

Adolescence is a developmental period of increased risk for mood disorders and other internalizing symptoms, which is especially true for those with intellectual disability (Hodapp & Dykens, 2009). Like their normally developing peers, adolescents with Down syndrome and other forms of intellectual disability may show a decline in their previously sociable and cheerful behaviors, and in some cases they may suffer from significant symptoms of depression and social withdrawal.

ADHD-Related Symptoms

Teachers and parents of children and adolescents with intellectual disability commonly report ADHD-related symptoms that require adjustments in instruction and child-management strategies (Neece et al., 2013). When a teacher is present to prompt the appropriate behavior and participate in the activity, children with intellectual disability with and without ADHD generally will remain on task. However, when instructed to work without teacher assistance, differences between those with and without ADHD emerge (Handen et al., 1998). When children with intellectual disability and ADHD are placed on stimulant medication, they are able to remain on task for longer periods and their accuracy on cognitive tasks improves, similar to the responses of children with normal IQs (Simonoff et al., 2013).

Other Symptoms

Children and adults with intellectual disability may show additional symptoms that can be particularly troublesome. Pica (discussed in Chapter 14), which can result in the ingestion of caustic and dangerous substances, is seen in its more serious forms among children and adults with intellectual disability. **Self-injurious behavior (SIB)** is a serious and sometimes life-threatening problem that affects about one in five young children with ID (MacLean & Dornbush, 2012). Some common forms of SIB include head banging, eye gouging, severe scratching, rumination, some types of pica, and inserting objects under the skin. The long-term prognoses for pica and SIBs are not favorable. Emotional withdrawal, stereotypies (frequent repetition of the same posture, movement, or form of speech—e.g., head banging, hand or body movements), and avoidance of eye contact are often still evident more than 20 years later among persons with more severe forms of intellectual disability (Taylor, Oliver, & Murphy, 2011).

Thus, children with intellectual disability may show emotional and behavioral problems that require special recognition and learning strategies. In general, these problems do not constitute major psychiatric disorders, but they do reflect the greater challenges these children may have in learning to express their needs and in adapting to their surroundings. A 7-year-old girl with mild intellectual disability, for instance, may be at a developmental level comparable to that of a typically developing 4-year-old. In the classroom, therefore, she may have difficulty sitting in her seat and remaining on task. She may not always control her emotions or her behavior as well as other 7-year-olds in the class, leading to occasional outbursts of laughter or anger. It is important to keep these problems within a developmental perspective. We would not expect a 4-year-old to behave as well in the classroom as an older child, and expectations and teaching methods have to be adjusted accordingly. As expressed so well by Ed and Pattie, labeling a child with a diagnostic term that implies pathology or inability is often ill-conceived and counterproductive. Such terms must be used sparingly—only in circumstances, such as self-injurious behaviors, for which special attention is warranted.

Other Physical and Health Disabilities

Children with intellectual disabilities may also suffer other physical and developmental disabilities that can affect their health and development in pervasive ways. Such disabilities are usually related to the degree of intellectual impairment. Based on a meta-analysis of 31 studies, the prevalence of chronic health conditions in this population is much higher than in the general population (Oeseburg et al., 2011). ● Figure 5.2 shows some of the more common developmental disabilities found among children with intellectual disabilities.

Despite major co-occurring physical and intellectual disabilities, children and adults with Down syndrome now have a life expectancy approaching 60 years, largely as a result of better medical treatments for respiratory infections and congenital heart disorders (Dykens, 2013). However, most individuals with Down syndrome who live beyond the age of 40 demonstrate cognitive decline (much like Alzheimer's disease) due to gene damage on chromosome 21 (Torr et al., 2010).

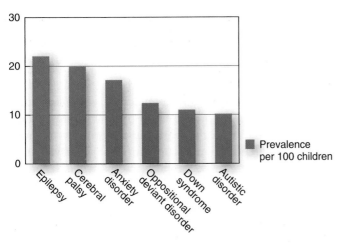

● **FIGURE 5.2** | Chronic health conditions among children with intellectual disabilities.

Based on Data from Oeseburg et al. (2011)

Section Summary

Developmental Course and Adult Outcomes

- Children with intellectual disability follow developmental stages in the same order as do typically developing children. However, their goals and motivation are reduced over time because of feelings of frustration, which often lead to expectations of failure.

- Adaptive skills and level of impairment may improve over time, especially for children with mild intellectual disability, if appropriate training and opportunities are provided.

- Developmental disabilities, such as speech and language problems and behavioral disturbances, are common. Emotional and behavioral problems are considered part of the spectrum of problems coexisting with intellectual disability, rather than indicators of mental disorder.

- Children with intellectual disability have a greater chance of having other physical and developmental disabilities, such as cerebral palsy, epilepsy, and emotional and behavioral disorders that can affect their health and development in pervasive ways.

CAUSES

It is astounding to consider that there are over 1,000 genetic disorders associated with intellectual disability, in addition to other organic causes (Hodapp & Dykens, 2009). Yet, despite the number of known causes, scientists are unsure of the causes of the majority of intellectual disability, especially mild ID. A genetic or environmental cause is known for almost two-thirds of individuals with moderate to profound intellectual disability, whereas the causes are known for only about one-quarter of the individuals with mild intellectual disability (McDermott et al., 2007; van Bokhoven, 2011). Some causes happen before birth (prenatal), as is the case with all genetic disorders and accidents in the womb. Other causes are birth-related (perinatal) insults, such as prematurity or a lack of oxygen (anoxia) at birth. Still other causes are an inflammation of the brain lining (meningitis), head trauma, and other factors that occur after birth (postnatal).

Historically, causes of intellectual disabilities were divided into two fairly distinct groups—an organic group and the cultural–familial group (Hodapp & Dykens, 2003). The causes in the **organic group** have a clear biological basis and are usually associated with severe and profound intellectual disability, whereas causes in the **cultural–familial group** have no clear organic basis and are usually associated with mild intellectual disability (Hodapp et al., 2006).

Four major categories of risk factors contribute to intellectual disabilities: biomedical, social, behavioral, and educational. These four risk factors interact across time and even across generations from parent to child and provide a more comprehensive explanation of the interacting causes of problems associated with intellectual impairments (AAIDD, 2010; Chapman, Scott, & Stanton-Chapman, 2008). The definitions, characteristics, and causes of intellectual disability on the basis of these four risk factors are summed up in Table 5.5.

Although a distinction between organic and nonorganic risk factors clarifies the underlying causes of intellectual disability, keep in mind that the distinctions are less clear in milder forms of intellectual disability than they are in more severe forms. For example, the large majority of persons at more severe levels of intellectual impairment (96%) show a clear etiology for the disorder, whereas a sizable percentage (32%) of those with mild impairments does not (Simonoff et al., 1996).

Considerable knowledge exists about organic intellectual disability because of the strong biological factors involved. Also, the increased ability to diagnose organic problems has led to increased estimates of this type of intellectual disability relative to cultural–familial causes—about one-third to one-half of all persons with intellectual disability show a clear organic cause (Hodapp et al., 2006). In stark contrast, the cultural–familial group remains somewhat of a mystery, although it comprises one-half to two-thirds of all persons with intellectual disability (Witwer et al., in press). As noted in Table 5.5, the prime suspects are environmental and situational factors such as poverty, inadequate child care, poor nutrition, and parental psychopathology, which mostly affect the psychological, and not the biological, development of the child. However, more

TABLE 5.5 | **Risk Factors for Intellectual Disability**

Timing	Biomedical	Social	Behavioral	Educational
Prenatal	1. Chromosomal disorders 2. Single-gene disorders 3. Syndromes 4. Metabolic disorders 5. Cerebral dysgenesis 6. Maternal illness 7. Parental age	1. Poverty 2. Maternal malnutrition 3. Domestic violence 4. Lack of access to prenatal care	1. Parental drug use 2. Parental alcohol use 3. Parental smoking 4. Parental immaturity	1. Parental cognitive disability without supports 2. Lack of preparation for parenthood
Perinatal	1. Prematurity 2. Birth injury 3. Neonatal disorders	1. Lack of access to prenatal care	1. Parental rejection of caretaking 2. Parental abandonment of child	1. Lack of medical referral for intervention services at discharge
Postnatal	1. Traumatic brain injury 2. Malnutrition 3. Meningoencephalitis 4. Seizure disorders 5. Degenerative disorders	1. Impaired child–caregiver interaction 2. Lack of adequate stimulation 3. Family poverty 4. Chronic illness in the family 5. Institutionalization	1. Child abuse and neglect 2. Domestic violence 3. Inadequate safety measures 4. Social deprivation 5. Difficult child behaviors	1. Impaired parenting 2. Delayed diagnosis 3. Inadequate early intervention services 4. Inadequate special education services 5. Inadequate family support

specific cause-and-effect relationships have not been determined. Accordingly, both genetic and environmental factors are implicated in milder forms of intellectual disability, but in a manner as yet to be determined (Toth & King, 2010).

The relative importance of the environment also stands out in the two-group distinction. The socioeconomic background of the organic group is about the same as that for the general population, which fits with the notion that severe forms of intellectual disability can affect anyone, regardless of SES. The familial group is overrepresented by those of lower SES and social disadvantage and is significantly related to a family history of intellectual disability. This fits with the assertion that an impoverished social environment can influence intellectual growth and ability in subtle, yet crucial, ways.

In most cases, the risk factors for intellectual disabilities have been supported empirically, with some adjustments as noted earlier in terms of nonorganic risk factors. First, the percentage of individuals with a clear organic cause has increased over the past few decades because of the greater knowledge of genetic and organic causes. Also, the original assumption that mild intellectual disability is not due to biomedical (organic) causes had to be tempered by findings that epilepsy, cerebral palsy, and other organic disorders are found more often among persons with mild intellectual disability than among those without intellectual disabilities (Hodapp et al., 2011).

Inheritance and the Role of the Environment

The study of human intelligence has received the lion's share of attention in terms of the underlying processes involved in genetic makeup and the environmental factors that influence genetic expression. Still, the long-standing debate concerning the relative contributions of genes and environment is far from being fully resolved (McDermott et al., 2007). Conceivably, genetic influences on development are potentially modifiable by environmental input, although the practicality of the modifications is another matter. Similarly, environmental influences on development involve the genes or structures to which the genes have contributed (Neisser et al., 1996). Simply stated, children do not inherit an IQ—they inherit a **genotype**, which is a collection of genes that pertain to intelligence. The expression of the genotype in the environment—the gene–environment interaction—is

referred to as the **phenotype**. The **heritability** of a trait describes the proportion of the variation of a trait attributable to genetic influences in the population (Neisser et al., 1996). Heritability of any given trait, therefore, can range from none (0%) to 100% genetically determined.

Is it possible to estimate the heritability of intelligence and, by implication, the heritability of intellectual disability? This intriguing question can now be answered with some degree of confidence, but little fanfare. The overwhelming evidence points to a heritability of intelligence of approximately 50%; that is, both genetic and nongenetic factors play powerful roles in the makeup and expression of intelligence (Davis, Arden, & Plomin, 2008).

There are so many specific genetic causes of intellectual disability that some skepticism about the importance of environmental effects still remains. The difficulty of identifying, pinpointing, and measuring specific, nongenetic variables certainly adds to this dilemma. However, considerable evidence has demonstrated that major environmental variations do affect cognitive performance and social adjustment in children from disadvantaged backgrounds (Ramey, Ramey, & Lanzi, 2007). For example, children born to socially disadvantaged parents and then adopted into more privileged homes have higher IQ scores, stronger self-esteem, and fewer acts of delinquency than siblings reared by their disadvantaged, biological parents (Juffer & van IJzendoorn, 2007; van der Voort et al., 2013).

The prenatal environment may influence IQ to a greater extent than was previously appreciated. A review of studies of twins and nontwin siblings revealed that a shared prenatal environment (i.e., all children shared the same mother) accounted for 20% of IQ similarity in twins but only 5% in nontwin siblings (Devlin, Daniels, & Roeder, 1997). These findings imply that prenatal influences such as nutrition, hormone levels, and toxic substances may be misidentified as genetic when in fact they are environmental (Rutter, 2011). The practical benefits of this research are important to consider. If early environmental (prenatal) influences have a significant impact on intellectual functioning, then expanding public health initiatives aimed at improving maternal nutrition and reducing prenatal exposure to toxins may not only improve maternal prenatal care, but may also improve children's intellectual and cognitive functioning.

Genetic and Constitutional Factors

Despite the rapid expansion of knowledge regarding the genetic mechanisms underlying conditions associated with intellectual disability, the actual biological mechanisms that cause impaired intellect are poorly understood (Hodapp & Burack, 2006). Identification of abnormal genes, or genes involving an increased risk for particular disorders, is invaluable for genetic screening and counseling, but the identification does not specify a more effective treatment mode for intellectual disability.

Because so many conditions cause intellectual disability, the focus in this section will be on several different disorders or classes of disorder, including Down syndrome, fragile-X syndrome, Prader–Willi and Angelman syndromes, and single-gene conditions. Each disorder illustrates different aspects of genetic mechanisms. The various ways in which genes may interact with environmental influences also are highlighted.

Chromosome Abnormalities

The most common disorder that results from a chromosome abnormality is Down syndrome. These abnormalities also can occur in the number of sex chromosomes, resulting in intellectual disability syndromes such as Klinefelter's (XXY, a disorder in which males have an extra X chromosome) and Turner's (XO, a disorder in which women are missing a second X chromosome). These latter disorders are somewhat common—about 1 in 400 live births—but they are generally less devastating than genetic irregularities in their effects on intellectual functioning (Simonoff et al., 1996).

The number of children with Down syndrome has gradually decreased from 1 in 700 births to 1 in 1,000 births over the past two decades, due to increased prenatal screening and termination of pregnancies diagnosed with Down syndrome (Hazlett et al., 2011; Roizen & Patterson, 2003). The syndrome produces several distinguishing physical features, including a small skull; a large tongue protruding from a small mouth; almond-shaped eyes with sloping eyebrows; a flat nasal bridge; a short, crooked fifth finger; and broad, square hands with a simian (monkeylike) crease across the palm. These physical features are sometimes inconspicuous, and they can appear in varying degrees.

In most cases of Down syndrome, the extra chromosome results from **nondisjunction**, which is the failure of the 21st pair of the mother's chromosomes to separate during meiosis. When the mother's two chromosomes join with the single 21st chromosome from the father, the result is three number 21 chromosomes instead of the normal two (known as trisomy 21). Because nondisjunction is strongly related to maternal age, the incidence of Down syndrome increases from about 1 per 1,000 live births for mothers less than 35 years old to about 20 per 1,000 when the mother is 45 years of age or older (Wu & Morris, 2013).

Although the chromosomal basis of Down syndrome is well understood, the specific cause of intellectual disability in these children is not known. Gene mapping of chromosome 21 has resulted in the belief that some genes may have localized effects on brain development (Roizen, 2007). Testing this theory from a functional perspective, researchers pinpointed differences in hippocampal function among young children with and without Down syndrome based on neuropsychological testing (Pennington et al., 2003). Because the hippocampus plays an important role in long-term memory, these findings help to explain some of the underlying processes that affect the ability of children with Down syndrome to acquire normal language skills (a fundamental aspect of IQ).

Fragile-X syndrome is the most common cause of inherited intellectual disability (Down syndrome occurs more frequently but is rarely inherited). This disorder affects about 1 in 4,000 males and 1 in 8,000 females (Hagerman, 2011). Physical features of fragile-X syndrome are more subtle than those of Down syndrome and may include a large forehead, a prominent jaw, and low, protruding ears. Intellectual disability is generally in the mild to moderate range, although some children are profoundly handicapped and others have normal intelligence (Cornish et al., 2013). Males suffer more detrimental effects of fragile-X syndrome; intellectual disability occurs in most males who have fragile-X syndrome, as compared with only about half of females (Reiss & Hall, 2007).

Children and adolescents with fragile-X syndrome, which affects twice as many boys as girls.

Although the gene for fragile-X syndrome, known as the FMR-1 gene, is located on the X chromosome, this syndrome does not follow a traditional X-linked inheritance pattern. About one-third to one-half of the females who carry and transmit the disorder are themselves affected with a variant of the syndrome and show a slight degree of cognitive or emotional impairment. Further, about 20% of males with the FMR-1 gene transmit the disorder but are not affected themselves (Fatemi & Folsom, 2011).

The behavioral characteristics of fragile-X syndrome are often subtle but distinctive. The majority of affected males have unusual social and communication patterns marked by shyness and poor eye contact, as well as significant delays in cognitive and communication development (Einfeld, 2005). Social anxiety and avoidance are also common in girls with this disorder, even if unaccompanied by intellectual disability (Gerenser & Forman, 2007). Notably, most males and about one-third of females with fragile-X syndrome show some autism-like behaviors, such as flapping hands, biting themselves, repetitive actions, and walking on toes, and close to half of children with fragile-X syndrome meet the criteria for a diagnosis of autism (McCary & Roberts, 2013).

Prader–Willi syndrome is a complex genetic disorder that includes short stature, intellectual disability or learning disabilities, incomplete sexual development, low muscle tone, and an involuntary urge to eat constantly. The syndrome is rare and estimated to affect only about 5 to 10 per 100,000 births (Dykens, Cassidy, & DeVries, 2011). Between ages 2 and 6, children with this syndrome develop extreme overeating, foraging, and hoarding. They need fewer calories than normal to maintain an appropriate

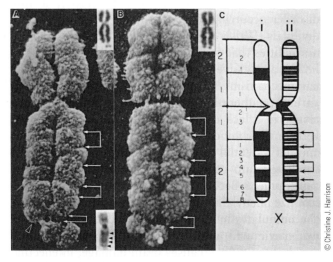

This micrograph shows the "pinched chromosome" found in fragile-X syndrome.

Lip-Philtrum (space between the nose and upper lip) Guide

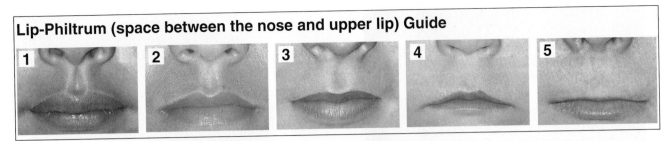

This series of photos provides a more detailed look at degrees of philtrum groove smoothness. In Photo 1, you see a normal lip-philtrum groove. As your eye moves to the right, you see philtrums that are progressively smoother. In Photo 5, you see the smoothness characteristic of FAS

The most extreme form of FASD, **fetal alcohol syndrome**, is considered to be a leading known cause of intellectual disability because of its clear link to intellectual impairment. Fetal alcohol syndrome is estimated to occur in 0.5 to 2.0 per 1,000 live births (Centers for Disease Control and Prevention, 2011c), although it is considered to be grossly underdiagnosed and may be considerably more common. Alarmingly, the incidence of this disorder is about 4 times higher among African Americans and 16 times higher among Native Americans as compared with majority populations (MMWR, 2002). Despite over two decades of public health warnings about abstaining from alcohol immediately before and during pregnancy, fetal alcohol spectrum disorders have not declined (Watson et al., 2011).

Fetal alcohol syndrome is characterized by central nervous system (CNS) dysfunction, abnormalities in facial features, and growth retardation, with affected children falling below the 10th percentile. The mechanism that causes the abnormalities is not clear but is believed to involve the *teratogenic* (damage to fetal development) effects of alcohol on the development of the central nervous system and the related damage from metabolic and nutritional problems associated with alcoholism (Niccols, 2007). On average, the IQ of children and youths with this disorder is in the mild range of intellectual disability (Streissguth, 2007). In addition to intellectual deficits, these children often have long-term difficulties that resemble ADHD, including attention deficit, poor impulse control, and serious behavior problems, which often persist into adulthood and carry high treatment costs (Amendah, Grosse, & Bertrand, 2011; Vaurio, Crocker, & Mattson, 2013).

Several teratogens other than alcohol are known to increase the risk of intellectual disability because of their effect on CNS development. Viral infections, such as rubella (German measles), contracted by the mother during the first 3 months of pregnancy can cause severe defects in the fetus. However, immunization has virtually eliminated this cause of intellectual disability in most developed countries. Syphilis, scarlet fever, tuberculosis of the nervous system, degenerative diseases of the nerves, and sometimes measles and mumps can lead to intellectual disability. ID also can be caused by x-rays, certain drugs taken by the mother during pregnancy, mechanical pressure on the child's head during birth, lack of oxygen due to delays in breathing at birth, poisons such as lead and carbon monoxide, and tumors and cysts in the head (Hodapp & Dykens, 2003). In essence, any biochemical or infectious substance that cannot be destroyed or regulated by the mother's immune system or regulatory system can pose a risk to fetal development and, in turn, intellectual ability.

Social and Psychological Dimensions

The final group of factors that cause intellectual disability, or occur in association with it, is perhaps the least understood and most diverse. Broadly defined, these factors include many environmental influences, such as deprived physical and emotional care and stimulation of the infant, and other mental disorders that are often accompanied by intellectual disability, such as autism spectrum disorder. Together these factors account for about 15% to 20% of intellectual disability. Although quite broad in scope, these influences are largely indirect and unproven because they often are embedded in different layers and degrees of individual and family circumstances. Parental deviance, such as abuse or neglect, and how it can affect intellectual and behavioral development is discussed in greater detail in Chapter 12.

Parents not only provide their children with their genes, but also provide the child-rearing environment and atmosphere that serve to direct and shape the child's psychological development right from the beginning. Consider the comments by the father of a young child with Down syndrome, who had to learn how to ask for proper assistance and to connect with other families of children with Down syndrome:

I will never forget when the nurse told us how much these children can achieve. Her advice to contact a local association for children with Down syndrome was an important beginning. Other parents at the association helped me understand that Down syndrome was a chromosomal aberration and not a disease, and [gave advice on] how to look for help. My son was hardly a month old when he began physiotherapy to help him learn and interact with others. Jake is 3 years old now and he is full of life. He walks, repeats several words, and understands directions. (Adapted from Martin, 1995)

How do families who have a child with intellectual disability contribute to the child's healthy development or, alternatively, to his or her decline? In recent years, the field of intellectual disabilities has shown a major change in how this question is addressed. Rather than focusing only on the family's negative influence, researchers are interested in learning how some families successfully cope with the additional stress and demands of raising a child with intellectual disability. As is the case when dealing with other stressors, individual members and the family unit can be affected negatively as well as positively, such as when a couple or siblings are brought closer together by caring for a child with special needs (Hodapp & Dykens, 2012; Lobato et al., 2011; Neece, Blacher, & Baker, 2010).

One way in which parents adapt successfully to having a child with special needs is to use social supports and community resources, although individual preferences regarding the type of support used may vary, and supports that help mothers may not help fathers. Mothers often are concerned about how raising a child with intellectual disability may affect their personal relationships with their husbands and about the restrictions the child's care may place on their role in the family, whereas fathers worry about not feeling close to the child. Thus, mothers and fathers differ in how they understand and relate to the child with intellectual disability, the aspects of raising the child they see as stressful, and the factors that best alleviate stress (Gerstein, Crnic, Blacher, & Baker, 2009).

Understanding how young people with Down syndrome function socially and independently has helped identify the factors that affect their adjustment to community living. Not surprisingly, early cognitive development is a strong predictor of developmental progress and self-sufficiency among such children, as shown in areas such as language (Filippi & Karmiloff-Smith, 2013). However, family factors are also important, particularly mothers' strategies for coping with their children's problems and their families' levels of social support (Gray et al., 2011).

Section Summary

Causes

- The two-group approach emphasizes the important etiological differences between organic and cultural–familial causes of intellectual disability.
- Organic causes include genetic and constitutional factors, such as chromosome abnormalities, single-gene conditions, and neurobiological influences.
- Suspected cultural–familial, or nonorganic, causes of intellectual disability include diverse social, behavioral, and educational risk factors.
- Some of the established risk factors for intellectual disability include alcohol, lead, and other toxins or injuries that affect prenatal and postnatal development. Other risk factors affect the quality of physical and emotional care and stimulation of the infant and small child, such as poverty and inadequate family supports.

PREVENTION, EDUCATION, AND TREATMENT

We plead for those who cannot plead for themselves.

—Motto of Highgate, the first public institution for persons with intellectual disability, established in London, England, October 1847

As we turn our discussion toward treatment methods for children with intellectual disability, consider for a moment how you would apply your knowledge of psychological and educational treatments to best assist a child such as Vanessa or Matthew. Would you first try to get Matthew's behavior problems under control and then teach him other skills? Would Vanessa likely benefit from individualized treatment that emphasizes gradual speech training and self-help skills?

As is true for several other disorders we have discussed, such as ADHD and some types of conduct disorders, the primary presenting problems—in this case, intellectual deficiency and limited adaptive abilities—are chronic conditions that pose limitations across many important areas of development. Consequently, programs often must be designed to fit the educational and developmental levels of each individual child even more so than, say, treatment programs for children with behavior or anxiety problems. It is useful to begin this task with an overview of major environmental and individual characteristics that may increase the risk of adjustment problems, or serve to protect the child from such problems.

A child's overall adjustment is a function of parental participation, family resources, and social supports (on the environmental side), combined with his or her level of intellectual functioning, basic temperament, and other specific deficits (on the individual side). Treatment can be designed to build on the child's existing resources and strengths in an effort to bolster particular skill areas or learning abilities. In other words, it is not necessary to focus attention primarily on what the child lacks, but rather on how best to match teaching and therapeutic methods to the child's own levels and abilities to accomplish realistic, practical goals. Thus, treatment and education for children with ID involves a multicomponent, integrated strategy that considers children's needs within the context of their individual development, their family or institutional setting, and their community (Wilkins & Matson, 2009).

The severity of intellectual disability can be prevented or reduced in some instances by taking proper precautions. Therefore, we begin this section by discussing current health care practices involving parental education and prenatal screening. These procedures, implemented in many communities, are designed to inform parents about proper prenatal care and risks and to detect abnormal fetal development. We then turn to psychosocial treatments for children with intellectual disability and their families, which have become a common part of many treatment and education plans. In short, treatment focuses on teaching the child necessary skills and abilities, such as language, personal care and hygiene, and social skills, as well as on teaching skills and providing supports to parents and other caregivers.

Psychopharmacological interventions for children and adults with intellectual disabilities have been hindered by both professional and public perceptions that psychotropic drugs are used to control behavior—a view based on unfortunate and inappropriate use in the past and on the drugs' major side effects. Although many newer classes of compounds that reduce unpleasant side effects have become available over the past decade, these compounds have not been systematically studied in treating people with intellectual disability. Nevertheless, drug treatment is beneficial in some cases. As with other childhood disorders, drug treatment can be targeted at desirable changes in specific behaviors or dimensions, such as compulsions, aggression, or self-injury, rather than at treating the underlying disorder itself (Golombek & King, 2010; Ghuman et al., 2009).

Prenatal Education and Screening

One of the best opportunities to promote healthy outcomes occurs during prenatal development (Hodapp & Burack, 2006). Although not all forms of intellectual disability can be prevented prenatally, many debilitating forms related to fetal alcohol syndrome, lead poisoning, or rubella can easily be prevented if proper

precautions are taken. A much larger number of children are positively affected by prenatal education and health care if one includes not only the prevention of specific risks, but also the promotion of proper child care, especially during the child's first 2 years.

Not too long ago, a pregnant woman would have seen her doctor for several visits prior to childbirth, and may have gained additional knowledge through reading and from family members. At that time, the focus was largely on the medical needs of the pregnancy, with little opportunity to consider what it means to raise a child and to prepare for the added stress and complexity that child care involves.

Today, almost all communities have prenatal programs for parents, and fathers have taken on a much larger role. Parents are provided with information about the different periods of fetal development and are cautioned about the use of alcohol, tobacco, nonprescribed drugs, and caffeine during pregnancy. These programs, often run by public health nurses, community colleges, churches, and other community organizations, have filled much of the gap in services between basic medical care and basic child care that parents need prior to the birth of a baby. The stresses of childbirth and postnatal adjustment are described, with opportunities for parents to consider the additional supports they may need and the changes they may need to make to ensure the child's health and safety. Many programs also include discussion of children with special needs, so that parents are not left feeling confused and alone (Ramey et al., 2007).

In providing these important prenatal services, there is an increasing multicultural focus that sensitively and appropriately considers the cultural background of the recipients (Pumariega et al., 2013). We now recognize that family members make choices based on cultural influences. To be of most help, prenatal and postnatal services must be culturally diverse and culturally sensitive. Meeting this goal involves working with informal support and assistance networks, such as churches, community and spiritual leaders, and community organizations, in ways that extend self-determination. Prenatal programs are increasingly breaking away from a set curriculum and are being modified to establish a better fit with each cultural group or community—for example, by providing information on ways to access health care and family services for persons with limited transportation, limited income, and so forth.

Prenatal screening constitutes a particular form of genetic screening that is used to determine whether a fetus has a genetic abnormality, such as Down syndrome, which would lead to a seriously handicapping condition. Ultrasound scanning can detect many conditions associated with physical defects, and testing of amniotic fluid during fetal development assists the prenatal diagnosis of chromosomal abnormalities and genetic diseases identifiable at the DNA level (Roizen & Patterson, 2003). Substantial advances in genetic screening allow for much greater precision in genetic counseling. For example, noninvasive molecular genetic techniques are replacing invasive techniques, such as amniocentesis, for women whose pregnancies are considered to be at an increased risk for certain chromosome abnormalities, which allows for quicker diagnosis of a broad range of genetic disorders (Devers et al., 2013). Ethical and practical guidelines are still under review, however, because there is a fundamental difference between using genetic information to prevent an illness or disease and altering genetic material to promote desired (or get rid of undesired) personal characteristics.

Psychosocial Treatments

The first psychosocial treatment we consider involves intensive, broad-ranging, early-intervention services for families with young children that are designed to reduce risk factors and promote healthy child development. Although expensive to deliver, these services are proving to be of considerable benefit to children and families over the long term, and they accomplish a great deal more than merely reducing intellectual deficits. We then take a close look at the existing educational and therapeutic methods that have successfully benefited children with various levels of intellectual disability. We discuss the application of behavioral, cognitive–behavioral, and family-oriented interventions, with an emphasis on the task of integrating known treatments that best match the different needs of these children.

As a prelude to the discussion of psychosocial treatments, we acknowledge the importance of community-based activities that offer people with disabilities a choice of ways to develop their interpersonal and practical skills and self-confidence. Studies find that athletes who participate in Special Olympics score higher on measures of social competence and have more positive self-perceptions than do their nonathlete counterparts (Special Olympics, 2007).

Early Intervention

For over 50 years, involving caregivers and other adults in early, intensive, child-focused activities has been one of the most promising methods for enhancing the intellectual and social skills of young children with developmental disabilities, including children with intellectual disability, learning disabilities, and lack of environmental stimulation (Wilkins & Matson, 2009). Many of these children would be described as disadvantaged or high-risk, synonymous terms referring to family circumstances such as low income, insufficient health care, and poor housing; child characteristics such as low IQ, poor adaptive abilities, and physical or health disabilities; or a combination of the two. Early educational intervention consists of systematic efforts to provide high-risk children with supplemental educational experiences before they enter school, and this intervention frequently includes other family and child services.

One of the more successful examples of an early educational intervention is the Carolina Abecedarian Project (Campbell & Ramey, 2010). The intervention was offered to children of poor families (98% of whom were African American), who were provided with enriched environments from early infancy through the preschool years. In follow-up studies of over 100 children, results showed that by age 2, the test scores of children in the enrichment group were already higher than the test scores of children in control groups, and at age 15, they remained some 5 points higher, 10 years after the end of the program. At age 15, members of the treated group were less likely to score in the intellectual disability or low-normal range of intellectual functioning. The enrichment group also outperformed the control groups in academic achievement through 10 years in school for both reading and mathematics, and there were fewer instances of grade retention or special education classes (Ramey et al., 1999, 2000). By age 30, those who received the intervention had better educational attainment, with some evidence of economic benefit as well (Campbell et al., 2002; Campbell et al., 2012; Pungello et al., 2010).

Based on these and related findings, the optimal timing for intervention appears to be during the preschool years (Hodapp & Burack, 2006). Early education programs such as the Abecedarian project are highly relevant to the issue of environmental effects in intellectual disability because they involve children from socially disadvantaged backgrounds, who have a much higher risk of intellectual disability. Although the programs show effectiveness, the lasting benefits depend on the stability and continuation of environmental changes that foster healthy child development. A Closer Look 5.3 offers a set of practical recommendations for enhancing children's lives through early intervention.

Dan's mother added some additional ideas, based on her own experiences:

> Be creative. He learns by repetition, so the more closely you follow the "house" system and coordinate all the topics of all the classes, the easier he and the other students can learn. He can learn spelling words of items he touches in science lab. He can learn history related to his library book of the week. Combine the lesson plans to touch all phases of the subject.

Practical Recommendations for Enhancing Children's Lives through Early Intervention

- *Encouragement of exploration.* Children are encouraged by adults to explore and gather information about their environments.
- *Mentoring in basic skills.* A trusted, familiar adult teaches children basic cognitive skills such as labeling, sorting, sequencing, and comparing.
- *Celebration of developmental advances.* Family and others who know the child celebrate and reinforce each of the child's accomplishments.
- *Guided rehearsal and extension of new skills.* Responsible others assist the child in rehearsing and extending newly acquired skills.
- *Protection from harmful displays of disapproval, teasing, or punishment.* Constructive criticism and negative consequences for unacceptable behaviors are used.
- *A rich and responsive language environment.* Adults provide a predictable and understandable environment for communication. Spoken and written language are used to convey information, provide social awards, and encourage the learning of new material and skills.

Source: C. T. Ramey and S. L. Ramey, 1992.

Behavioral Treatments

As noted earlier, for many years the way to deal with problems faced by persons with ID was to isolate them from society by placing them in institutions or separate schools, a practice that curtailed their ability to interact with typically developing peers. Behavioral interventions first emerged in the context of these restricted settings and were initially seen primarily as a means to control or redirect negative behaviors, such as aggression or self-injury.

Through the efforts of concerned behavioral therapists, important principles were established concerning the implementation of behavioral methods with children and other persons who are unable to provide fully informed consent. The Association for Behavior Analysis (ABA) Task Force stipulated that each individual has the right to the least-restrictive effective treatment, as well as a right to treatment that results in safe and meaningful behavior change (Van Houten et al., 1988). These efforts, coupled with continued input from parents and educators, led to a greater emphasis on positive methods for teaching basic academic and social skills in both schools and communities to help children and adolescents with intellectual disability adapt in the most normal fashion.

Vanessa's treatment plan typifies how several important behavioral methods are successfully applied. Language training often is considered a fundamental starting point for teaching more advanced skills to children with intellectual disability, and behavioral methods are well suited for this purpose (Matson, Matson, & Rivet, 2007; van der Schuit et al., 2011). The plan developed for Vanessa offers a useful example of how these methods are applied. Vanessa participated in one-to-one therapy sessions during which she was reinforced (by edibles and praise) for emitting sounds that imitated the therapist's sounds. The speech therapist used a *shaping* procedure that began by forming a list of responses (such as "ge," "ga," "oh") that were progressively more similar to the target response (in this case, the word go). After Vanessa mastered the first sound, she was reinforced only for attempts at the next sound on the list, and so on, until the desired sound or word was gradually shaped.

To encourage her speech sounds and simple words to become functional speech and language, the therapist taught Vanessa to imitate the names of pictures shown to her. If she said the name of the picture, such as "dog," within a few seconds, she received social rewards and, if necessary, tangible rewards such as candy. As Vanessa became more adept at naming the pictures, the therapist began to use some of the trained words in response to questions he would pose, such as "What is this?" Gradually, Vanessa's mother and father were brought into the sessions with the therapist to begin asking her similar questions and promoting her use of functional speech. As her speech grew, new words and short sentences were introduced—ones that would be of most use to Vanessa on a daily basis at home, at the cafeteria, and when asking to use the bathroom.

Vanessa's behavior during mealtimes also presented considerable problems for her parents. She had difficulty getting food onto her fork or spoon, so her parents were taught to use simple methods of *modeling* and *graduated guidance* to assist. After demonstrating how to hold a spoon, they would show her how to pick up her food and bring it to her mouth. They carefully demonstrated each step involved, from dipping the spoon to placing it in the mouth, each time praising her for her attempts. As required, they would guide her hand to show her how each step was done.

Unfortunately, without much warning, Vanessa would sometimes throw or spit her food, so her parents were also taught how to respond to such outbursts. Their first attempt to stop this problem was to remove her food for half a minute or so. If this tactic did not settle the behavior, or if she became more aggressive, they used time-out from reinforcement. They provided a short reprimand ("Don't throw food!")

Social and sports events are an important way of fostering independence, social competence, and self-esteem in persons with intellectual disability.

and told her why she was in time-out. Without ceremony, they turned her chair into the corner for about a minute. At the first sign of settling her behavior, they turned Vanessa around in her chair to face them and returned to a positive, guided method of helping her to learn to feed herself.

In addition to their training in basic skills to promote language and readiness to learn, many older children and adolescents with ID benefit from training in specific social skills to promote their integration into regular classrooms and other activities. As mentioned previously, individuals with intellectual disability have various degrees of difficulty in communication, self-control, anger management, correct recognition and labeling of affect in others, social problem solving, and a host of other interpersonal limitations that often lead to victimization by peers (Fisher, Moskowitz, & Hodapp, 2013).

Tailored to each student's individual needs, social skills training uses positive reinforcement strategies to teach and reward important interpersonal skills such as smiling, sharing, asking for help, attending, taking turns, following directions, and solving problems (Kemp et al., 2013). Peers without disabilities also can be taught effective ways to interact socially with children with intellectual disability, a method known as social inclusion. This method is successful in increasing the quantity and quality of interactions between children with disabilities and their peers without disabilities, and it promotes the development of friendships (Harada et al., 2011; Siperstein et al., 2009).

Cognitive–Behavioral Therapy

The same theories that led to the development of cognitive therapy techniques for children with other types of learning and behavior problems generally apply to children with intellectual disability as well. These methods are most effective for children with some receptive and expressive language skills—like the skills Vanessa acquired after careful and prolonged training through the use of visual and physical prompts. Once children are able to follow adult verbal directives and to verbally describe their own actions, they are in a position to benefit from verbal self-regulation and behavioral-inhibition training programs (Cobb et al., 2006; Bexkens et al., 2014). Self-instructional training is most beneficial for children who have developed some language proficiency but still have difficulty understanding and following directions. **Self-instructional training** teaches children to use verbal cues, initially taught by the therapist or teacher, to process information, to keep themselves on task ("I'm not gonna look. I'm gonna keep working."), and to remind themselves of how to approach a new task ("What do I have to do here? First, I have to. …").

Education of children with intellectual disability has been plagued by the fact that specific cognitive skills can be taught, yet children often lack the higher-order (metacognitive) capabilities to apply these skills in new situations. Children with intellectual disabilities use fewer, simpler, and more passive cognitive strategies in memory and learning task situations than do children without such disabilities (Hodapp et al., 2011). Therefore, instructional methods developed to assist the average or above-average learner are often ineffective. Coupled with this concern is the continued reliance on verbal instruction to teach behavioral and cognitive skills to normal and exceptional children.

Language problems may require verbal instructional techniques to be replaced by methods that capitalize on a particular child's strongest learning channels. These methods often rely less on verbal, symbolic representation and more on perceptual, visually oriented techniques such as modeling and picture cuing.

Specific learning techniques also can be used to improve memory and learning. For example, in addition to being taught various basic math skills, students learn to identify the type of math problem they confront and then to choose the appropriate strategy for solving the problem. The first goal of this training is to teach the child to be *strategical*—to use cognitive strategies—and then to be *metastrategical*—to make discriminations regarding how to apply different strategies in different situations. This method has been successful in teaching children with learning difficulties a range of adaptive skills, such as math and language (Hay et al., 2007).

behavior; (3) highly restricted, fixated interests that are abnormal in intensity or focus; and (4) hyperreactivity or hyporeactivity to sensory input or unusual interest in sensory aspects of the environment. Table 6.1 includes examples of specific symptoms for each type.

DSM-5 also specifies that a *severity* rating of current symptoms be made for each domain. Severity ratings reflect the extent to which the symptoms interfere with the child's functioning. More severe deficits are rated as requiring greater levels of support, as follows: requiring support (level 1); requiring substantial support (level 2); and requiring very substantial support (level 3). Severity level ratings should help in guiding the types of programs and services needed to help the child and family, but since symptom severity may fluctuate across situations and over time, these ratings are not intended to be used in determining the child's eligibility for services.

DSM-5 criteria for ASD provide a relatively new way of looking at autism. In light of this, we highlight several key changes in ASD criteria from DSM-IV to DSM-5 and why they were made. First, the DSM-5 organization of symptoms into two domains represents a change from DSM-IV, in which deficits in social interaction and those in communication were viewed as separate domains along with the third domain of restricted and repetitive behavior. However, research does not support viewing social interaction and communication as distinct domains (Frazier et al., 2012), and clinicians have difficulty separating the symptoms of each. For example, is difficulty engaging in two-way conversation a deficit in social reciprocity or in communication skills? (Klinger et al., 2014)

Second, DSM-5 eliminated all previous subtypes of ASD (e.g., Autistic Disorder, Asperger's Disorder, Pervasive Developmental Disorder, Not Otherwise Specified [PDD-NOS]) and substituted a single overarching category—ASD. One reason for doing this was to increase the consistency of diagnosing ASD. In DSM-IV, the criteria for autism subtypes were not well conceptualized or defined. Although clinicians could readily distinguish ASD from other neurodevelopmental disorders (e.g., intellectual disability, specific learning disorder), distinctions between subtypes were unreliable and inconsistent and were related more to where the diagnosis was made, the child's level of intellectual ability, and co-occurring conditions, than to the child's ASD symptoms (Lord et al., 2012). A second reason for using a single ASD category rather than subtypes was a recognition that changes in developmental level can lead to changes in symptom presentation. Although an ASD diagnosis is stable after 2 years of age, children often changed diagnosis from one subtype to another because of age-related changes in their social and cognitive skills (van Daalen et al., 2009). Thus, rather than representing true change, these age- and skill-related fluctuations in diagnosis are best viewed as variability within a single disorder.

The elimination of subtypes in DSM-5 does not mean that these distinctions are unimportant. As we have noted, ASD is not one thing, and there is a great deal of heterogeneity within the disorder. What is important is having a classification system that can address this variability (Rutter, 2013). To do this, DSM-5 includes the use of *specifiers* to indicate when other important conditions, such as intellectual and/or language impairment, are present and whether the child's ASD is associated with a known medical or genetic condition or with another neurodevelopmental, mental, or behavioral disorder. This provides a more detailed description of the full range and severity of the child's problems, which is critical to developing an appropriate treatment plan.

There is support for the conceptual validity of using a single ASD category. However, many individuals with ASD, their families, advocacy groups, and clinicians suggest that fewer individuals will be diagnosed, especially those with milder symptoms and normal intellectual abilities who were previously diagnosed with Asperger's disorder. Therefore, the use of DSM-5 could result in reduced eligibility for services for these children. Although research to date suggests that most children diagnosed with Asperger's disorder will receive a diagnosis of ASD using DSM-5 criteria (Huerta et al., 2012), it is not yet known whether this will be the case in clinical practice. The possibility that some individuals could be disadvantaged by changes in DSM-5 criteria will require further monitoring and evaluation (Kent et al., 2013).

ASD across the Spectrum

When we hear the term *autism*, or *ASD*, we may think of Raymond, the main character in the movie *Rain Man*, or Temple Grandin (who was the subject of an HBO film), a high-functioning and insightful woman with ASD who is a Professor of Animal Sciences, one of the top scientists and consultants in the humane livestock handling industry, and a leading advocate for persons with ASD (Grandin & Panek, 2013). Although some individuals with ASD display the abilities and special talents that are often portrayed in the movies, most do not.

ASD is defined as a **spectrum disorder** because its symptoms, abilities, and characteristics are expressed in many different combinations and in any degree of severity (Lai et al., 2013). Thus, ASD is not an "all or nothing" phenomenon. At one end of the spectrum we may find a child who is mute, crouched in a corner of his room, spinning a paper clip over and over again for hours; at the other end of the spectrum is a researcher who is also able to hold a corporate job—as long as

Dr. Temple Grandin (left) with award-winning actress Clare Danes, who portrayed her in the highly acclaimed film, *Temple Grandin*.

it doesn't require interacting with customers. Although children with ASD vary widely in intellectual ability, language, age, socioeconomic (SES), gender, and race, the majority of them display most of the core features of the disorder (Mayes & Calhoun, 2011). Nevertheless, despite the similarities in their core profile, they show enormous variability in the expression and severity of their symptoms. This variability among children with ASD applies widely across both their social communication and behavioral impairments (Jones & Klin, 2009).

Children with ASD not only differ widely in their core symptoms, but they may also, in varying degrees, display features not specific to ASD—most commonly, intellectual disability and epilepsy. Thus, children with the same diagnosis of ASD can be vastly different from one another in their intellectual ability, severity of language problem, and degree of progress. To illustrate this key point, let's compare and contrast two children, Lucy and John, both diagnosed with autism.

LUCY

ASD with Intellectual Disability

Lucy's parents watched her development right from the start because there had been so many difficulties during pregnancy and delivery. Labor began 3 weeks early and lasted 23 hours, so that forceps were needed to assist the delivery. Lucy had to have oxygen to revive her, spent 4 days in the special-care unit, and received treatment for jaundice.

Indeed, it seemed that everything in Lucy's development was troubling. For example, she was always too distressed to feed or she fed so ravenously and quickly

that she vomited. Nights were no better—she took hours to settle and always woke early. By her first birthday she had only just started to sit up, and was still not crawling. The family physician said that Lucy was indeed delayed in her development. At 14 months, she began to crawl (6 months is typical), and at 19 months she pulled herself up on the furniture (most children do this at around 12 months); she made little progress in other areas.

At 2 years of age, Lucy still did not use any words, and was unresponsive to her parents' attempts to engage her in simple games like peek-a-boo. At 30 months, she started to walk (most children walk by 14 months). However, her main sounds were a strange clicking noise made with the back of her tongue and a variety of screams. She still seemed oblivious to people around her (including her parents) unless they had something she wanted. A pediatrician thought the delay in her development might be due to the difficulties with her delivery and suggested that Lucy be checked every 12 months.

She loved to play with a particular blue and red rattle that she would shake or spin for hours. Once she had the rattle she did not look at anyone, and if someone tried to take it from her she screamed and banged her head on the floor. Understandably, this devastated her parents. Lucy took great interest in odors, sniffing food, toys, clothes, and (to her parents' embarrassment) people. She also liked to feel things, and often tried to stroke stockings on women's legs, even those of complete strangers. If they tried to stop her, she had a tantrum.

When Lucy was 4 years old, her pediatrician suspected she had ASD, and referred her to a psychologist for a detailed assessment. The diagnosis was confirmed, and her parents were told that Lucy was generally delayed in her development. They were heartbroken, but they felt that finally Lucy would get the help she desperately needed. (Autism: The Facts, by Baron-Cohen and Bolton, (1993) pp. 1–8.)

JOHN

ASD with Average Intellectual Ability

John was born after a normal pregnancy and delivery. As an infant, he was easy to feed and slept well. He seemed happy and content to lie in his crib for hours. He sat unsupported at 6 months (which is in the normal range), and soon after, he crawled. His parents saw him as independent and willful. However, his grandmother thought John lacked interest in people.

John walked on his first birthday (in sharp contrast to Lucy, who did not walk until 30 months of age); yet during his second year he did not progress as well as

(continues)

head-circumference data in ASD studies raises the important concern that previous findings could be an artifact of using outdated norms and that when current norms for early brain growth are used there are few observed differences between changes in early brain growth in infants with ASD and other children (Raznahan et al., 2013). Thus, it remains to be established whether the "accelerated" growth in head size is specific to children with ASD when contemporary norms are used or whether it also occurs in samples of healthy children and those with other psychiatric disorders (Rommelse et al., 2011).

Accompanying Disorders and Symptoms

The disorders that most often accompany ASD are ID and epilepsy (Bolton et al., 2011). Additional behavioral and psychiatric symptoms may include ADHD (Hanson et al., 2013), conduct problems (Guttmann-Steinmetz, Gadow, & DeVincent, 2009), anxieties and fears (Hallett et al., 2013), and mood problems (Magnuson & Constantino, 2011). Some children with ASD also engage in extreme, and sometimes potentially life-threatening, *self-injurious behavior* (SIB)—any self-inflicted behavior that can cause tissue damage to the child's own body (see Chapter 5). The most common forms of SIB are head banging, hand or arm biting, and excessive scratching and rubbing. Head banging, if not prevented, can be severe enough to produce bleeding or even brain injury. SIB may occur for a variety of reasons—self-stimulation, to gain attention, or to eliminate unwanted demands—or, it may occur for no apparent reason (Furniss & Biswas, 2012). Whatever the reasons, rates of emergency/hospital treatment for self-inflicted injuries in children with ASD are seven times greater than for typically developing children (McDermott, Zhou, & Mann, 2008). However, SIB may not occur more frequently in young children with ASD than in those with other forms of developmental delay. For children with ASD, ID, atypical sensory processing, need for sameness, repetitive behaviors, and impulsivity are among the strongest risk factors for SIB (Duerden et al., 2012; Richman et al., 2013).

Section Summary

Associated Characteristics of ASD

- Previous estimates were that about 70% of children with ASD also have ID. However, recent reports suggest that ID in individuals with ASD is closer to 40% to 50%, a decrease that is most likely related to increased diagnoses of ASD in higher-functioning individuals and to the effects of early intervention.

- Children with ASD display a deficit in theory of mind (ToM)—the ability to understand other people's and one's own mental states, including beliefs, intentions, feelings, and desires.
- Children with ASD display a general deficit in higher-order planning and regulatory behaviors (e.g., executive functions).
- They may display co-occurring medical conditions and physical features such as seizures, sleep problems, gastrointestinal symptoms, or increased head size.
- Children with ASD may display co-occurring symptoms of ADHD, conduct problems, anxieties and fears, and mood problems.

PREVALENCE AND COURSE OF ASD

For decades, ASD was thought to be a rare disorder, affecting about 1 per 2,500 children (Tanguay, 2000). However, recent findings worldwide indicate a much higher prevalence rate—as many as 1 per 68 children or between 1% and 2% (CDC, 2014; Elsabbagh et al., 2012). ASD affects over 2 million individuals in the U.S. and tens of millions more worldwide (Autism Speaks, 2013). In terms of economic burden, the total estimated annual societal costs of caring for children with ASD in the United States are $11.5 billion or more (Ganz, 2007; Levelle et al., 2014). Health care costs for children with ASD are at least six times higher than for those without ASD and even higher for those with ASD and a co-occurring condition such as ID, ADHD, or epilepsy (Peacock et al., 2013). Given the increasing prevalence and growing emphasis on early identification and intervention for children with ASD, it is likely that these costs will continue to rise.

Many causes for the apparent dramatic increase in ASD have been proposed—vaccines, mercury, diet, acetaminophen, caffeine, antibiotics, allergies, environmental pollutants, and electromagnetic radiation—but to date none has been scientifically substantiated. It seems likely that most, if not all, of the rise in prevalence is caused by a greater awareness among parents and professionals; a broadening of the concept and its definition over the years; greater recognition and diagnosis of milder forms of ASD; changes in diagnostic criteria and categories; diagnostic substitution (i.e., the number of children receiving special education under other diagnostic categories, primarily ID, speech impairment, and learning disabilities, has decreased as those diagnosed with ASD have increased); and better case-finding methods (King & Bearman, 2009; Wazana, Besnahan, & Kline, 2007). However, whether there is also a real increase in prevalence due to an unidentified cause remains an open question. Interestingly, in contrast to scientific opinion that the increase in ASD prevalence is mainly due to changes in awareness and diagnostic practices, many laypeople continue to believe that the increase is due to increased exposure to new environmental, medical, and technological hazards (e.g., vaccinations, cell phone towers) (Russell, Kelly, & Golding, 2009).

ASD is found in all social classes and has been identified worldwide. It is about four to five times more common in boys than in girls, a ratio that has remained fairly constant over the years, even with increasing prevalence estimates (CDC, 2014). The sex difference is most apparent among children with IQs in the average to above-average range, perhaps being as high as 10:1 in higher-functioning individuals. However, among children with ASD and profound ID, the numbers of boys and girls are similar. Thus, although girls are less often affected by ASD than are boys, when they are affected, they tend to have more severe intellectual impairments (Dworzynski et al., 2012). Girls with ASD who do not have an intellectual impairment are more likely to be formally diagnosed at a later age than boys (Giarelli et al., 2010). Girls with comparable high levels of ASD symptom severity as boys are also less likely to be diagnosed, suggesting that there is a bias in diagnosis or that in the absence of co-occurring intellectual or behavioral deficits girls may be better able to cope with the same level of ASD symptoms (Constantino & Charman, 2012). In general, the clinical manifestations of ASD are quite similar for boys and girls, although there may be some differences in their cognitive profiles (Carter et al., 2007). For example, it has been found that girls with ASD engage in more pretend play than do boys, suggesting that impairment in pretense may be less of a problem for girls (Knickmeyer, Wheelwright, & Baron-Cohen, 2008). Findings also suggest brain differences underlying ASD in males and females (Lai et al., 2013).

In considering the high ratio of males to females with ASD, Simon Baron-Cohen (2002, 2009) proposed the *extreme male brain theory of ASD*. Those with ASD are presumed to fall at the extreme high end of a continuum of cognitive abilities associated with systemizing (understanding the inanimate world), and at the extreme low end of abilities associated with empathizing (understanding our social world). Both abilities are present in all males and females, but males are presumed to show more systemizing and females more empathizing. Frequent interests and behaviors that occur among individuals with ASD (e.g., attention to detail, collecting, an interest in mathematics, mechanical knowledge, and scientific and technical information) are presumed to reflect an extreme on the systemizing dimension of the male brain, and a relative absence of empathizing (e.g., mindreading, empathy, eye contact, and communication) (Baron-Cohen et al., 2003). Interestingly, one brain study found that females with ASD displayed masculinization at the neural level (Lai et al., 2013). The extreme male brain theory is intriguing but somewhat controversial. Further research into the neurocognitive aspects of these dimensions in individuals with ASD will be needed before we can infer that they are "from Mars and not Venus."

Rates of ASD are comparable across different racial and ethnic groups. Where differences are found, prevalence is higher among non-Hispanic white children than among members of other groups, most likely because of underidentification in non-Hispanic black and Hispanic children (CDC, 2012a). Different racial and ethnic groups do not differ in core symptoms of or risk factors for ASD (CDC, 2012a; Cuccaro et al., 2007). However, African American children are nearly three times more likely than white children to receive another diagnosis such as ADHD or adjustment disorder before being diagnosed with ASD, and they are nearly three times more likely to experience delays in receiving intervention (Mandell et al., 2007). Societies differ in how they integrate ASD into their cultural frameworks. For example, in contrast to viewing ASD as a disorder, some cultures view children with ASD as having special skills or as being more in touch with the spirit world. Cultural views range from those of the Navajo, who embrace their children with ASD as being blessed (Kapp, 2011), to the South Koreans, who may hide their children with ASD to protect siblings from being considered tainted and unmarriageable (Grinker, 2007).

Age at Onset

The *diagnosis* of ASD is usually made in the preschool period or later. However, most parents of children with ASD become seriously concerned a year or more before a diagnosis is made, typically during the months preceding their child's second birthday (McConkey, Truesdale-Kennedy, & Cassidy, 2009) At this time, their child's lack of progress in language, imaginative play, and social relations stands in sharp contrast to rapid developments in these areas by other children of the same age. Although deficits of ASD become increasingly noticeable around age 2, elements are probably present and noticed earlier, as reflected in Anne-Marie's solemn reaction to her first birthday party (Yirmiya & Charman, 2010).

ANNE-MARIE

First Birthday

We were celebrating Anne-Marie's first birthday and had just paraded in, bearing the cake with much fanfare. Daniel, her big brother, almost two and a half years old, and greatly excited, joined us in singing. Anne-Marie, in her high-chair, gazed solemnly at the cake, her baby body still, her mouth unsmiling. ... I couldn't help once again making a silent comparison to her brother, who at his first birthday party had squealed with delight. ... Who knows, really, what the first sign was, at what point Anne-Marie began to slip away from us? Was it around that first celebration, or after or before? (Based on Maurice, 1993b)

At present, the period from 12 to 18 months seems to be the earliest point in development at which ASD can be reliably detected. For example, an interesting study found that children with ASD generally did not show signs of the disorder at 6 months of age, but between 6 and 12 months they failed to gain new social skills or showed a loss of previously acquired ones (Ozonoff et al., 2010). Most children with ASD showed a subtle and gradual loss of specific social skills between 6 and 18 months that went unnoticed by parents. These findings suggest that traditional views that symptoms of ASD are present at birth or that the child shows dramatic regression at a later age may not accurately depict how ASD develops. Instead, the onset of symptoms may be more accurately represented as being on a continuum based on the amount and timing of loss of previously acquired skills (Ozonoff et al., 2009). Consistent with this view are recent findings that an early decline in eye contact over the first 6 months may precede the gradual loss of specific social skills that occurs from 6 to 12 months of age. Children who later developed ASD and typically developing children did not differ in eye contact in the first month of life, but for those who later developed ASD, eye contact gradually decreased over the first 6 months of life (Jones & Klin, 2013).

Currently, diagnoses of ASD that are made around age 2 to 3 years are stable for most children (Bryson, Rogers, & Fombonne, 2003; Kleinman et al., 2008). However, with increasing research into key early indicators, systematic screening and direct observation of infants at risk for ASD (e.g., those with older siblings with the disorder), and universal screening of young infants, it is likely that ASD can and will be reliably detected at earlier ages, particularly for those with low IQ (Bryson et al., 2008; Oosterling et al., 2010; Pierce et al., 2011). Features of atypical development, that are very similar to those found in ASD but are less severe, have recently been detected in infant siblings of children with ASD by the infants' first birthday (Ozonoff et al., 2014). Possible early indicators of ASD may include: "uses few gestures to express social interest," "doesn't respond when name is called," "rarely makes eye contact when interacting," "limited babbling, particularly in a social context," and "displays odd or repetitive ways of moving hands and/or fingers" (Zwaigenbaum et al., 2009). Children with ASD have been found to differ from typically developing children on most of these indicators between the ages of 12 and 24 months. However, in one study, only early communicative gestures were found to distinguish children with ASD from those with developmental delay or language impairment (Vaness et al., 2012). As part of its campaign to raise awareness about the importance of early identification for intervention, the American Academy of Pediatrics (AAP) recommended that all children be screened for ASD at 18 months and 24 months (Hampton, 2007). The organization Autism Speaks has a video glossary on its website (www.autismspeaks.org) where you can view fascinating video clips that show some of the early red flags for ASD as well as examples of commonly used treatments. To date, efforts to implement screening approaches in community settings have had positive results. However, the extent to which these results have brought about reduced time to diagnosis and enrollment in services has not yet been tested (Daniels et al., 2013).

Course and Outcome

Children with ASD develop along different pathways. Some show abnormal behavior soon after birth; some, 25% or more, show seemingly normal development for the first year or longer followed by *regression* (the loss of previously acquired language and social skills, with an onset of ASD) (Parr et al., 2011); while others appear to improve significantly over time (Fein et al., 2013). The symptoms of children with ASD change over time. Most symptoms gradually improve with age, even though children continue to experience many problems. During adolescence, some symptoms, such as hyperactivity, self-injury, and compulsivity, may worsen (Spector & Volkmar, 2006). During later adolescence and adulthood, abnormalities such as stereotyped motor movements, anxiety, and socially inappropriate behaviors are common, even in high-functioning individuals; these individuals also often experience loneliness, social disadvantage and exclusion, and work difficulties (Howlin, 2013). Complex obsessive–compulsive rituals may develop, and talking may be characterized by idiosyncratic and perseverative speech, monotonous tone, and self-talk (Newsom & Hovanitz, 2006).

Findings from early studies of children with ASD who received limited help indicated that an overwhelming majority (70% or more) showed poor outcomes with limited progress and continuing handicaps that did not permit them to lead an independent existence (Lotter, 1978). More recent follow-up studies report slightly better, but quite similar, outcomes (Eaves & Ho, 2008; Howlin et al., 2004; Howlin et al., 2013). Very few adults with ASD achieve high levels of independence. Most remain quite dependent on their family and other support services, with few friends and no permanent job (Roux et al., 2013). These adults continue to display problems in communication, stereotyped behaviors and interests, and poor reading and spelling abilities. Overall, children with better language skills, higher intellectual ability, and higher scores on measures of reciprocal social interaction at the time of diagnosis show better long-term outcomes, but outcomes can be variable even for high-functioning individuals (Bennett et al., 2008). It is possible that better long-term outcomes will be achieved by more recent generations of children with ASD who were diagnosed at a younger age, are higher-functioning, and received intensive early intervention. However, future longitudinal research will be needed before we know. Whatever the outcome, the reality is that children with ASD grow up, and most will continue to require age-appropriate supports and services. To date, far greater attention has been given to research, programs, and services for children with ASD than to adolescents and adults with ASD. Further efforts to address the needs of older individuals with ASD are sorely needed (Bailey, 2012; Wilczynski, 2013).

Section Summary

Prevalence and Course of ASD

- ASD is a disorder that affects as many as 1 in 68 children, or between one and two percent. It is four to five times more common in boys than in girls. ASD is found across all social classes and has been identified in every country in which it has been studied.
- ASD is most often identified around age 2 years or older, although elements are present at a much earlier age.
- Children with ASD may develop along different pathways. Some show abnormal behavior soon after birth; others show seemingly normal development for the first year or longer followed by regression; while others appear to improve significantly over time.
- Most children with ASD show gradual improvement of their symptoms with age, although they continue to display social impairments that make them different from other people throughout their lives.
- The two strongest predictors of adult outcomes in children with ASD are intellectual ability and language development.

CAUSES OF ASD

No single abnormality can account for all the impairments associated with ASD, or for the many forms of the disorder, ranging from mild to severe. Although the precise causes of ASD are still not known, our understanding of possible mechanisms has increased dramatically (Klinger et al., 2014). These advances are evident when we consider that, not long ago, autism was being attributed to cold and unloving parents. It is now generally accepted that ASD is a biologically based neurodevelopmental disorder with multiple causes involving genetic and environmental risk factors (Faja & Dawson, 2013). To understand ASD, we must consider problems in early development, genetic influences, and neuropsychological and neurobiological findings.

Problems in Early Development

Children with ASD experience more health problems prenatally, at birth, or immediately following birth than do other children. Although not proven as independent risk factors, prenatal and neonatal complications such as preterm birth, bleeding during pregnancy, toxemia (blood poisoning), viral infection or exposure, a lack of vigor after birth, and others have been identified in a small percentage of children with ASD (Gardener, Spiegelman, & Buka, 2009, 2011). One study found that very preterm birth (gestational age of <26 weeks) was associated with a much higher rate of ASD, with a prevalence of 8% diagnosed by age 11 (Johnson et al., 2010). Other risk factors that affect the prenatal environment may place the fetus at increased risk for ASD. These include increased maternal age, in vitro fertilization, maternal use of prescription and nonprescription drugs, toxic chemicals in the environment during pregnancy, maternal fever or maternal illnesses such as diabetes or infections during pregnancy, chronic hypertension, and prepregnancy obesity (Szatmari, 2011). For example, with regard to parental age, a study of over 7 million children in California found that older mothers and fathers were more likely to have a child with ASD than were younger parents (Grether et al., 2009). It was found that an increase of 10 years in maternal age was associated with a 38% greater risk of ASD and that the same increase in paternal age was associated with a 22% greater risk. The relationship between increasing parental age and ASD suggests that age could be a contributing factor in the increase in ASD, and also raises questions about possible mechanisms including age-related gene variants or epigenetic dysfunction (Sandin et al., 2012). Exposure to antidepressant medication (SSRIs) during the first trimester of pregnancy has also been found to increase the risk of ASD (Croen et al., 2011). Although problems during pregnancy and birth may not be the primary cause of ASD, they do suggest that fetal or neonatal development has been compromised (Szatmari, 2011).

A controversial and widely publicized proposal was that some cases of ASD in children who speak only a few words and have other social–communicative behaviors that disappear in the second year of life might be linked to vaccinations. Two hypotheses attracted the most attention. The first incriminated the measles components of combination vaccines for measles–mumps–rubella (MMR) (Wakefield et al., 1998; *retracted* February, 2010). The second lay blame on exposure to ethyl mercury (thimerosal), a preservative used in other vaccines (Ball, Ball, & Pratt, 2001). Both hypotheses claimed that the apparent ASD "epidemic" coincided with the introduction of MMR vaccines and/or increased exposure to thimerosal as a result of the increased number of recommended childhood vaccinations in the first 3 years of life. However, current scientific evidence does not support an association between MMR vaccines or thimerosal and ASD (Fombonne, 2008; Institute of Medicine, 2004; see also The Editors of The Lancet, 2010). Nevertheless, a large number of parents of children with ASD still believe that their child's disorder was caused by vaccinations (Harrington et al., 2006).

Genetic Influences

Studies of specific chromosomal anomalies and gene disorders, findings from family and twin studies, and specific gene studies indicate a substantial role for genetic factors in ASD (Rutter, 2005). However, despite strong evidence for a genetic contribution and some noteworthy findings emerging from tests of hundreds of genes, the rate of progress in gene discovery has been slow, and the genetic architecture of ASD remains largely unknown (El-Fishawy & State, 2010).

Chromosomal and Gene Disorders

The discovery of the fragile-X anomaly (see Chapter 5) in about 2% to 3% of children with ASD led to increased attention to this and other chromosomal defects that might be related to ASD (Turk & Graham, 1997). In general, individuals with ASD have an elevated risk, about 5%, for chromosomal anomalies (Barton & Volkmar, 1998; Dykens & Volkmar, 1997). However, these anomalies alone do not indicate the specific gene sites underlying the disorder, because ASD has been associated with anomalies involving several chromosomes (Freitag et al., 2010).

ASD is also associated with *tuberous sclerosis,* a rare single-gene disorder. The manifestations of this disorder can vary widely from mild to severe; they may include neural deficits, seizures, and learning disabilities. Most cases are derived from de novo mutations, cases in which no family history of the disorder existed (Bailey, Phillips, & Rutter, 1996). About 25% or more of children with tuberous sclerosis also have ASD. This makes the association between ASD and tuberous sclerosis greater than that for any other genetically based condition.

Family and Twin Studies

Some studies have found that as many as 15% to 20% of siblings of individuals with ASD also have the disorder, a number nearly twice that seen in earlier reports (Ozonoff et al., 2011). Also, at 3 years of age, high-risk siblings who do not receive a diagnosis of ASD show greater severity of symptoms of ASD and lower levels of developmental functioning than do low-risk children (Messinger et al., 2013). In addition, family members of children with ASD display higher-than-normal rates of social and language deficits and unusual personality features that are very similar to those found in ASD but are less severe (Gerdts et al., 2013; Ozonoff et al., 2014). Referred to as the *broader autism phenotype,* these deficits include social oddities such as aloofness, lack of tact, and rigidity; pragmatic language problems such as over-communicativeness or undercommunicativeness; and poor verbal comprehension. Family members with the broader phenotype do not, however, display the atypical language (e.g., pronoun reversal), extreme stereotyped repetitive behavior, or the ID and epilepsy that are often associated with a formal diagnosis of ASD (Rutter, 2000). These findings are consistent with a general family risk for ASD that is genetically mediated. In addition, a growing number of studies have reported similar neurophysiological correlates (e.g., atypical brain activation, reduced white matter) for children with ASD *and* their "unaffected siblings," suggesting a family susceptibility to ASD involving a

ASD develops. Genetic and [...] lead to abnormalities in br[...] in turn lead to generalized [...] child processes information [...] her environment (Faja & D[...] turbances are likely to disru[...] brain development during e[...] ity (Dawson et al., 2002). [...] ship between the child's earl[...] outcomes will be mediated [...] child interacts with and ada[...] ment. For example, Wan et [...] quality of interaction betwee[...] and their caregivers at 12 [...] with an autism diagnosis at [...] on the interaction between [...] environment in which the [...] children will follow differe[...] ways. Although pathways m[...] development, the longer the [...] pathway, the more difficult [...] Thus, as we discuss in the n[...] the earlier the risk for ASD [...] sooner intervention begins, [...] that the child will have a [...] Spence, & Wang, 2006).

Section Summary

Causes of ASD

- ASD is a biologically based [...] that may result from multipl[...]
- Some children with ASD ex[...] tal complications such low [...] pregnancy, toxemia (blood [...] exposure, and a lack of vigo[...]
- ASD is a genetic disorder, [...] large effects have not been [...] a complex genetic disorder [...] and simultaneous genetic [...] Shared environmental expe[...] may also be involved.
- Nonautistic relatives of i[...] higher-than-normal rates [...] tive deficits that are simila[...] ASD, but are less severe an[...] lectual deficits or epilepsy. [...]
- Neuropsychological impair[...] functioning, including int[...] language, and executive fu[...]
- Structural abnormalities in [...] temporal lobe, prefrontal [...] tem structures have been f[...]

wide array of brain regions and networks (Barnea-Goraly, Lotspeich, & Reiss, 2010; Belmonte, Gomot, Baron-Cohen, 2010).

Twin studies have reported concordance rates for ASD in identical twins ranging from 70% to 90%, in contrast to near-zero rates for fraternal twins (Rutter, 2005). These findings indicate that the heritability of an underlying liability for ASD may be as high as 90% and suggest that almost all the variance in the expression and stability of ASD over time can be attributed to inherited genetic influences (Freitag et al., 2010; Holmboe et al., 2013; Lichtenstein et al., 2010). One exception is a finding that a large proportion of the variance in susceptibility to ASD could be explained by *shared environmental experiences* (58%), with heritability accounting for a smaller amount (38%) (Hallmayer et al., 2011). If replicated, this finding suggests that susceptibility to ASD may have a moderate genetic heritability component and a substantial shared twin environmental component. To date, the major focus of research on ASD has been on genetic influences, with minimal attention paid to environmental factors. The finding that shared environmental experiences have a significant influence on ASD susceptibility suggests that environmental risk factors occurring prior to or by the end of the first year of life could play an important role. Thus, further research into problems in early development of the type discussed previously, such as low birth weight, multiple births, maternal infections during pregnancy, and parental age, may help to advance our understanding of ASD (Hertz-Picciotto, 2011).

Molecular Genetics

New research using molecular genetics has pointed to particular areas on many different chromosomes as possible locations for *susceptibility genes* for ASD (Klinger et al., 2014). Susceptibility genes are causally implicated in the susceptibility to ASD but do not cause it directly on their own. Although several searches for major ASD genes have been undertaken, they have not yielded consistent results (Freitag et al., 2010). No single gene has been found to be relevant for most cases of ASD. Inconsistent findings in gene studies may be due to the considerable etiologic heterogeneity within ASD and the diverse ways in which it appears. Rather than a single gene, ASD is associated with rare mutations that have a strong effect for a very small proportion of individuals with ASD who have such genes, and a few common variants of small effect in several genes that seem to be a factor for many cases of ASD (Anney et al., 2012). Thus, ASD is likely to be a complex genetic disorder resulting from both rare mutations and simultaneous

genetic variations (e.g., submicroscopic deletions or insertions of segments of DNA) in multiple genes (El-Fishawy & State, 2010). Moreover, the expression of ASD gene(s) may be influenced by environmental factors (e.g., exposure to drugs, maternal illness)—a "a second hit" that occurs primarily during fetal brain development. The possible role of such gene–environment interactions (GxE) and also gene–environment correlations (rGEs) in ASD requires further study (Corrales & Herbert, 2011; Meek et al., 2013).

Finally, there are a number of situations in which epigenetic dysregulation (changes in gene expression caused by mechanisms other than changes in the underlying DNA sequence) may be associated with the development of ASD, For example, co-morbid genetic conditions such as fragile-X syndrome or genes or genomic regions exhibiting abnormal epigenetic regulation (Grafodatskaya et al., 2010) may be associated with ASD. Thus, in searching for genetic alterations responsible for ASD, it may also be necessary to look beyond mutations and variations in specific genes into epigenetic regulation of gene function (Rangasamy, D'Mello, & Narayanan, 2013).

Brain Abnormalities

Although there is no known biological marker for ASD, impressive advances have been made in documenting the neurobiological basis of the disorder (Neuhaus, Beauchaine, & Bernier, 2010; Pelphrey et al,, 2011). Current research suggests that the behavioral features of ASD may result from abnormalities in brain structure and functioning that are consistent with early disturbances in neural development, possibly tracing back to prenatal development (Minshew, Johnson, & Luna, 2000; Stoner et al., 2014; Xiao et al., 2014). Importantly, although many brain regions are implicated, the disorder does not seems to lie in an abnormality localized in one part of the brain. Rather, it results from a lack of normal connectivity across brain networks that underlie the core features of ASD (Rudie et al., 2012; Stigler et al., 2011; Waterhouse & Gillberg, 2014).

Neuropsychological impairments in ASD occur in many domains, including verbal intelligence, orienting and selective attention, memory, pragmatic language, and executive functions (Dawson et al., 2002). The widespread nature of these deficits suggests that multiple regions of the brain are involved at both the cortical and subcortical levels (Happé & Frith, 1996). The types of neuropsychological deficits also vary as a function of the severity of the child's disorder. For example, low-functioning children with ASD may show impairments in basic memory functions, such as visual recognition memory, which are mediated by the brain's

medial temporal lobe (Barth, F
1995). In contrast, high-functioni
more subtle deficits in working m
complex verbal material, suggesti
higher cortical functions (Dawsoi

Biological Findings

Brain imaging studies have look
functional abnormalities in brain
sistently localized brain lesions
symptoms of ASD (Williams &
terms of abnormal brain developi
study examined brain growth at i
from ages 1.5 to 5 years in norma
who received a confirmed diagno
4 years of age (Schumann et al., 20
ASD showed evidence of overgro
and white matter in all regions by
the time that their clinical sympt
Almost all brain regions were fou
normal rate; this finding was mor

In terms of localized brain
have consistently identified struc
the cerebellum and in the medi
related limbic system structures
2005; Courchesne et al., 2007).
atively large part of the brain l
stem, is most frequently associa
ment. However, it is also partia
lating emotion, language, execut
thought, and attention (Hodge
areas of the cerebellum are fou
smaller than normal in youngst
larly in those with a higher leve
et al., 2009). It has been propo:
normalities may underlie the j
with ASD have in rapidly shiftir
one stimulus to another (Courcl

A second localized brain
medial temporal lobe and coi
structures such as the amygd;
(Groen et al., 2010; Johnson e
& Amaral, 2009). These areas
ciated with functions that are
dren with ASD—for example,
emotion regulation (Mazefsky e
dala plays an especially impoi
ing the emotional significance
toward social stimuli, in the j
direction, and, along with the
term memory (Schulkin, 2007
scan studies suggest that there
functional abnormalities in the

their claims under close scientific scrutiny, and some may have harmful effects (Research Autism, 2013; Umbarger, 2007).

Although behavioral, educational, and medical treatments may improve learning and behavior, and may permit a few children to achieve near-normal functioning, there is no known cure for ASD. The goals for most treatments are to minimize the core problems of ASD, maximize the child's independence and quality of life, and help the child and family cope more effectively with the disorder (Myers, Johnson, and the Council on Children with Disabilities, 2007). These goals can be facilitated by treatments designed to enhance development and learning, to reduce associated maladaptive behaviors, and to educate and support parents in meeting these goals. Understanding parents' beliefs about the causes of their child's ASD may also be important for treatment (Dardennes et al., 2011).

Promising new programs of early intervention, community-based education, and community living options are all reasons for optimism about improving outcomes for children with ASD (Rogers & Wallace, 2011; Volkmar et al., 2014). The most benefit is likely to come from developmentally oriented, early behavioral interventions that involve parents and that are used along with special educational methods (Rutter, 2006b). Most children treated using these newer evidence-based methods show significant gains in language, communication, and measured IQ and a modest reduction in the severity of the core symptoms of autism (Virués-Ortega, 2010; Young et al., 2010). However, questions remain concerning how intensive the interventions need to be (e.g., 20 vs. 40 hours per week), how much change can be achieved, and the extent to which changes can be directly attributed to the intervention. Additional controlled studies are needed before long-term outcomes can be fully assessed (Charman, 2011; Vismara & Rogers, 2010).

Overview

EMILIE

A Full-Time Job

When Emilie was 2 she was diagnosed with autism, Emilie's mother recalled, her eyes brimming with tears. "We've been relying on ourselves ever since." Emilie's mother and father have read about children with autism who became accomplished scientists and musicians—but progress for Emilie, now age 4, has been slow. Two months ago they hired a specialist to teach them a new one-on-one approach for

The demands of parenting a child with ASD are considerable.

getting through to Emilie with a reward system. Pictures of food are taped to hallway walls. On the fridge is a cutout of a glass of milk. After years of shrieking and kicking for what she wants, Emilie is learning to express her needs. When she points to what she wants, she gets a reward—a potato chip or an activity she likes. Every afternoon mother and daughter spend 2 hours on the floor, face to face, their legs interlocked. "Listen to maman, Emilie. Look at me. Look at me. Say 'yes.' Say 'yes.' Do you like chips, Emilie? You can have one if you just say the word, 'yes.'"

Emilie's mother coaxes patiently, firmly, holding out a bowl of chips. But Emilie runs to the radiator and climbs it, teetering there. When her mother pulls her down Emilie shrieks, kicks, and falls to the floor crying. In a minute the episode is over, and the lesson begins again. This time Emilie looks at her mother, says "yes," and holds out her hand for a chip. "Bravo, sweetheart. You did it. I knew you could," her mother beams. Emilie's mother has used the reward system to build Emilie's vocabulary to 22 words. That, to her parents, has been a monumental breakthrough.

"We have to motivate her," says her mother, whose only respite is an evening out once or twice a month with her husband. "If we let her be, she'd just climb or hide under the cover all day long. That's my nightmare, that she'll end up in a psychiatric hospital, withdrawn from the world. I can see that we are slowly beginning to get through to her," Emilie's mother says with a deep sigh. "She didn't pay any attention to us at all before. She never showed any affection or made eye contact. But now she looks at me and says 'maman.' Sometimes she hugs me. It doesn't happen every day. But it grabs my heart when it does."

From Susan Semenak, *The Gazette*, November 21, 1996, pp. A1 and A15. Reprinted by permission.

Emilie's case captures the demands, frustrations, aspirations, and hopes of a family trying to do the best possible for their child with ASD. A number of treatments are available for helping children with ASD, such as Emilie, and their families. These treatments focus on the specific social, communication, behavioral, and cognitive deficits of ASD that we have discussed throughout this chapter. They include strategies for engaging children in treatment; decreasing disruptive behaviors; teaching appropriate social behavior, including joint attention, imitation, and reciprocal interaction; increasing functional, spontaneous communication; promoting cognitive skills such as symbolic play and perspective taking; and teaching adaptive skills that prepare the child for increased responsibility and independence. Family interventions enable parents to participate fully in their child's treatment and to cope with the substantial demands and parenting-related stress associated with raising a child with ASD (Estes et al., 2014; Rivard et al., 2014). In addition, educational interventions and speech and language therapy are commonly used. Also, for some children, antipsychotic medications (e.g., risperidone, aripiprazole) may help to decrease interfering and challenging behaviors and symptoms such as irritability, severe tantrum behavior, physical aggression, and repetitive behaviors (Volkmar et al., 2014), particularly when they are combined with intensive behavioral intervention (Arnold et al., 2012; Frazier et al., 2010). However, the effectiveness of these medications must be balanced against their known adverse effects, such as weight gain or liability to cause metabolic disorders (McPheeters et al., 2011).

Because children with ASD have great difficulty making changes and generalizing previously learned skills to new environments, these areas must be directly addressed in treatment. It is also critical that treatment be tailored to meet the needs of the individual child and the family, thus making it possible for each child to meet his or her full potential. In the following paragraphs we highlight how several of the treatment components mentioned previously are implemented.

Initial Stages

Initially, treatment focuses on building rapport and teaching the child learning-readiness skills. Various procedures help the child feel comfortable being physically close to the therapist and to identify rewards to strengthen the child's social behavior, affection, and play. Imitating the child's use of toys may increase eye contact, touching, and vocalizations directed toward the therapist. Prompting the child to engage in play with a preferred toy may decrease social avoidance.

Children with ASD must learn to sit in a chair, come when called, and attend to their teacher if they are to progress. These readiness skills are taught using two approaches. The first is a step-by-step approach to presenting a stimulus and requiring a specific response, referred to as **discrete trial training**. The second attempts to strengthen behavior by capitalizing on naturally occurring opportunities, referred to as **incidental training**. Most interventions use a combination of these approaches (Ghezzi, 2007).

Reducing Disruptive Behavior

Young children with ASD display many disruptive and interfering behaviors, such as tantrums or throwing objects, as well as self-stimulation, aggression, and self-injury. These behaviors are common reactions to demands on the child that are made early in treatment, and they must be eliminated if the child is to learn more adaptive forms of social interaction and communication. Many procedures are effective in eliminating disruptive behavior, including rewarding competing behaviors, ignoring the behavior, and mild forms of punishment.

Teaching Appropriate Social Behavior

Teaching appropriate social behavior is a high treatment priority (White, Keonig, & Scahill, 2007). The salience of social cues may be increased by pairing people with whom the child has contact with actions, activities, and events that the child finds pleasant or useful. Younger children are also taught ways to express affection through smiling, hugging, tickling, or kissing—behaviors that enable them to return the affection they receive from others. Other ways to enhance social interaction include teaching social toy play, social pretend play, and specific social skills such as initiating and maintaining interactions, taking turns and sharing, and including others in activities. Developmental and relationship approaches foster parental use of child-centered responsive interactions that embed numerous opportunities for teaching social and emotional behaviors into play. Parent-assisted Children's Friendship Training programs for school-age children with ASD target conversational skills, peer group entry skills, developing friendship networks, good sportsmanship, good host behavior during play dates, and handling teasing (Laugeson et al., 2012). Group social skills interventions have also been shown to improve social behaviors in high functioning children with ASD (Derosier et al., 2010).

One strategy for teaching appropriate social behavior to children with ASD involves teaching normal or mildly handicapped peers to interact with them. Peers are taught to initiate age-appropriate social behaviors such as playing with toys, commenting about activities, or acknowledging their partner's responses. Teachers may signal and reward the peers' social initiations with the child with ASD. Other strategies use prompts and rewards for teaching the child with ASD to initiate interactions, and in some cases to involve siblings as trainers (Kohler, Strain, & Goldstein, 2005).

Teaching Appropriate Communication Skills

Several strategies are used to help children with ASD communicate more appropriately. **Operant speech training** is a step-by-step approach that first increases the child's vocalizations and then teaches imitation of sounds and words, the meanings of words, labeling objects, making verbal requests, and expressing desires. The emphasis is on teaching the child to use language more spontaneously and more functionally in everyday life situations to influence others and to communicate better (Newsom & Hovanitz, 2006).

Executive Function Intervention

Recent interventions have also focused on the executive functioning deficits displayed by children with ASD. One such school-based program, Unstuck and On Target [UOT], uses cognitive–behavioral strategies

The mother of Max, a 4-year-old boy with ASD, spends hours each day teaching communication skills to her son.

to reduce insistence on sameness and to teach flexibility, goal-setting, and planning (Kenworthy et al., 2013). A controlled study compared third- and fifth-graders with ASD and average or above-average intellectual ability who received the UOT intervention with a comparable group of children with ASD who received social skills training. After intervention, children in both groups improved, but those receiving UOT showed significantly greater improvement in their problem-solving, flexibility, and planning/organizing skills. When observed in their classroom, children who had received UOT were better able to follow rules, make transitions, and be more flexible (Kenworthy et al., 2013). Both groups made equivalent gains in social skills. These findings are promising in showing that children with ASD with average or above-average intellectual ability can learn higher-level cognitive skills and apply them in a mainstream classroom.

Early Intervention

As methods to identify ASD at a very young age are developed, possibilities for effective early intervention with infants and toddlers increase dramatically (Wallace & Rogers, 2010). The promise of early intervention derives, in part, from the plasticity of neural systems early in development (Mundy & Neal, 2001) and the fascinating hypothesis that providing very young children with ASD with intensive and highly structured experiences may alter their developing brains in ways that permit outcomes that are not otherwise possible (Dawson, 2008). In an important investigation, Dawson et al. (2012) found that 18-to-30–month-old children with ASD who received early intervention showed significantly greater improvement than comparison children after intervention in their ASD symptoms, IQ, language, and adaptive and social behaviors. In support of the hypothesis of altering the developing brain through early intervention, at 48 to 77 months of age, children who had received the early intervention also displayed more normal patterns of brain activation when viewing faces versus objects than did comparison children, and these brain changes were associated with improved social behavior. Nowadays, whenever possible, intensive interventions for children with ASD begin before the age of 3— the earlier the intervention, the better the outcome is likely to be (Rogers et al., 2012).

Comprehensive early-intervention programs include many of the specific treatments for ASD that we have described (Harris, Handleman, & Jennett, 2005). A variety of early-intervention programs are available, some based on a learning/behavioral model (e.g., Applied Behavior Analysis; Lovaas & Smith, 2003; Smith, 2011), others based on a structured teaching model (e.g., TEACCH; Mesibov, Shea, & Schopler, 2005), and others based on developmental (e.g., Early Start Denver Model; Dawson et al., 2010) and/or relationship-focused (DIR or Floor Time; Greenspan & Wieder, 2006) approaches. Although these and other programs may differ in philosophy and emphasis, they share many common goals and features, which is why different models may result in similar outcomes when applied in standard-practice preschool or school settings (Kasari & Smith, 2013). There is a growing consensus that the most effective interventions for children with ASD include the following features (Myers et al., 2007):

▶ *Early:* Begin intervention as soon as an ASD diagnosis is seriously considered.

▶ *Intensive:* Active engagement of the child at least 25 hours a week, 12 months a year, in systematically planned, developmentally appropriate educational activities with specific objectives.

▶ *Low Student–Teacher Ratio:* Allow sufficient one-on-one time and small-group instruction to meet specific individualized goals.

▶ *High Structure:* Use predictable routines, visual activity schedules, and clear physical boundaries to minimize distractions.

▶ *Family Inclusion:* Include a family component, with parent training as indicated.

▶ *Peer Interactions:* Promote opportunities for interactions with typically developing peers.

▶ *Generalization:* Teach child to apply learned skills in new settings and situations and to maintain the use of these skills.

▶ *Ongoing Assessment:* Monitor child's progress and make adjustments in treatment as needed.

The average age of children with ASD entering early-intervention programs has been 3 to 4 years or younger. These children have an average IQ in the mid-50s, although many are not testable at the time of their intake for treatment. Early intervention provides direct one-to-one work with the child for 15 to 40 hours per week and active involvement of the family. In effect, these programs become a way of life for the family—24 hours a day, 7 days a week. Programs are carried out at home and in the preschool, and efforts are made to include the child in interactions with normal peers, especially later in treatment.

Comprehensive reviews of outcomes for children with ASD completing early-intervention programs find that many of them are able to function in regular educational placements, although the type of setting and amount of support services needed varied considerably. Most children also show developmental gains, as reflected in improvements in their social behavior and communication, IQ scores, and scores on developmental tests and as found on classroom observations (Dawson et al., 2010; Eikeseth et al., 2007; Howard et al., 2005).

The UCLA Young Autism Project

The UCLA Young Autism Project began about 50 years ago under the direction of Dr. Ivar Lovaas (1927–2010). Now referred to as the Applied Behavior Analysis (ABA) or Early Intensive Behavioral Intervention (EIBI) approach, it is the most detailed and labor-intensive of the early intervention programs and begins the earliest. It is one of the few programs that currently qualifies as an evidence-based treatment for ASD based on outcomes evaluated against control groups of similar-age children receiving less-intensive intervention (Lord & Jones, 2013; Rogers & Vismara, 2008). For these reasons, we focus on this approach, although we recognize that other potentially useful approaches have yet to be evaluated and that a few others that have been evaluated are also available.

The program includes many of the key elements of early intervention and is based on principles of applied behavior analysis, including the use of rewards and punishment and shaping by successive approximation (Lovaas, 2003; Smith, 2011). Parents are taught to act as the primary therapists for their children, with direction and help from therapists who work with them in the home. The average age of children entering the program is 32 months.

In a landmark research investigation, children with ASD were assigned to one of three groups. Although this assignment was not carried out randomly, the groups were found to be comparable with respect to age, language, intellectual functioning, and other measures prior to intervention. The experimental group of 19 children received 40 hours per week of intensive intervention. Control group 1 consisted of 19 children

Early intervention is essential for children with ASD.

Janine Wiedel Photolibrary/Alamy

parent with psychosis was combined with maternal depression during pregnancy (Maki et al., 2010). In light of the enormous number of genes, gene regulatory mechanisms associated with brain development, and mutational mechanisms that can disrupt these processes, it is possible that most affected individuals with COS have a unique genetic cause (Kuniyoshi & McClellan, 2014).

The occurrence of central nervous system dysfunction among individuals with schizophrenia, and the dramatic improvements associated with the administration of medications, suggest that schizophrenia is a disorder of the brain (Lewis & Lieberman, 2000). Brain scan studies of youngsters with COS have found enlarged ventricles and a shrinkage in brain gray matter that spreads across the brain during adolescence, beginning in the rear brain structures involved in attention and perception and spreading to the frontal parts of the brain involved in executive functions such as planning and organization (Vidal et al., 2006). The progressive loss of gray matter was accompanied by delayed/disrupted white matter growth, hippocampal volume loss, and a progressive decline in cerebellar volume. Interestingly, most of these changes were also found in the nonpsychotic siblings of the children with COS. However, siblings showed later normalization of the earlier gray matter abnormalities, suggesting a role for restorative/protective factors. In contrast, the hippocampal volume loss across age in children with COS was not shared by their siblings; thus it appears to be specific to schizophrenia (Rapoport & Gogtay, 2011). Another study found that atypical neural activity in a network of language-associated brain regions during discourse processing was associated with subsequent thought disorder severity and social outcome in youth at risk for psychosis (Sabb et al., 2010). Findings like this are important in identifying potential biomarkers for COS that may suggest strategies for intervention and prevention.

No single brain lesion has been identified in all cases of COS, and the lesions that have been found in some cases are not specific to schizophrenia (Kyriakopoulos & Frangou, 2007). In addition, atypical developmental patterns of brain development over time are often more prominent than are anatomic brain differences at any one time point (Rapoport & Gogtay, 2011). In general, brain research on COS points to a widespread developmental disruption of neural connectivity. These disrupted neural connections likely involve susceptibility genes that impact developmental processes involved in establishing connectivity within and between brain regions (Karlsgodt et al., 2008; Rapoport et al., 2012).

Environmental Factors

COS is a familial disorder, but the less than 100% concordance rates for identical twins suggest that nongenetic influences contribute to the likelihood of a child developing schizophrenia. Nongenetic factors, including exposure to infectious, toxic, or traumatic insults and stress during prenatal or postnatal development, may interact with a genetic susceptibility for schizophrenia (Arseneault et al., 2011; Lahti et al., 2009; Rapoport et al., 2005). Several nongenetic factors occurring during pregnancy and birth are associated with an increased risk for later schizophrenia, including: maternal diabetes, low birth weight, older paternal age, winter birth, and prenatal maternal stress (King, St-Hilaire, & Heidkamp, 2010). Each of these factors alone is associated with a slight increase in risk, which multiplies when they are combined with each other and/or with other risk factors. In considering other nongenetic influences, the elevated likelihood of psychiatric illness in parents of children with schizophrenia will likely have a negative effect on the ability of the affected parent to function in a parental role.

By themselves, psychosocial factors do not cause COS. However, they may interact with biological risk factors to affect the onset, course, and severity of the disorder. Parents of children with schizophrenia score higher than parents of children with depression on **communication deviance,** which is a measure of interpersonal signs of attentional and thought disturbance. Children from families with high communication deviance display the most severe impairment and the poorest attentional functioning. These findings suggest that communication deviance may be associated with a severe form of schizophrenia or that family interaction may worsen the severity of dysfunction (J. R. Asarnow, Goldstein, & Ben-Meir, 1988). Parents of children with schizophrenia are more likely to use harsh criticism of their children than are parents of depressed children or normal controls, which could be a reaction to their child's severe difficulties.

Support for the role of the family environment comes from studies showing that exposure to a poor family environment and certain patterns of communication may interact with a genetic risk for schizophrenia to further increase a child's risk for developing a schizophrenia-spectrum disorder. For example, in a longitudinal study of children of biological mothers with schizophrenia-spectrum disorders who were adopted at an early age, poor child-rearing environments and communication deviance of the adoptive parents predicted which adoptees developed a schizophrenia-spectrum disorder (Wahlberg et al., 2004; Wynne et al., 2006). Children with a dysfunctional child-rearing environment and adoptive parents who displayed high rates of communication deviance were significantly more likely to develop schizophrenia-spectrum disorder than those raised in more positive family environments. For children with a low genetic risk for schizophrenia, a poor family environment and deviant parent communication patterns did not increase the risk for the later development of a schizophrenia-spectrum disorder.

Family findings highlight the stress, distress, and personal tragedy often experienced by families of children with schizophrenia (J. R. Asarnow & Asarnow, 2003). In the words of June Beeby, the mother of 17-year-old Matthew, who was diagnosed with schizophrenia and believed that God wanted his mother and his sister to die:

> "It's quite horrendous. First of all, you've got somebody that you love, a child that you've raised. And then suddenly, the child becomes a crazy person" (M. Nichols, 1995, p. 70). On a dark and cold winter day, June Beeby arrived home to find her son dead in a pool of blood. "He had taken two ordinary dinner knives … and plunged them into his eyes until they pierced his brain" (p. 70). In a diary entry that he had made 2 years before he took his life, Matthew had described an encounter with God: "He used his power and he controlled my brain for nine months. … God wanted me to feel that I would die, in order for individuals to live forever in heaven" (p. 74).

Treatment

As a parent you feel you have a tremendous responsibility to keep a son or daughter safe. … But when your child is schizophrenic you can't do that, because the person doesn't want help.

—From "Schizophrenia: Hidden Torment," by M. Nichols, *Maclean's,* January 30, 1995

COS is a chronic disorder with a poor long-term outcome for most sufferers, although some youngsters may display more positive outcomes (McClellan et al., 2013; Röpcke & Eggers, 2005). In either case, outcomes for most afflicted individuals are vastly improved over what they once were. Current treatments emphasize the use of antipsychotic medications (e.g., clozapine, risperidone) combined with psychotherapeutic and social and educational support programs (McClellan et al., 2013; National Institute of Health and Clinical Excellence [NICE], 2013b). Although we know far less about the use of antipsychotic

medications with children than with adults, they are widely used to treat young people with schizophrenia, and a majority of youngsters with schizophrenia will spend much of their life on some medication (Findling et al., 2014). Medications help control psychotic symptoms in children with schizophrenia by blocking dopamine transmission at the D2 dopamine receptor. However, adverse effects with antipsychotic treatment are prevalent and are associated with reduced adherence to treatment. Depending on the type of medication, these side effects can be serious and may include increased levels of prolactin, motor dysfunction (e.g., tremor), weight gain, sedation, or dysregulation of glucose. Thus, it is extremely important that these side effects be carefully monitored and managed with changes in dose or type of medication as needed (Tiffin, 2007). There is also a need for psychosocial treatments, such as family intervention, social skills training, and cognitive–behavioral therapy (Addington, Piskulic, & Marshall, 2010). The need for educational support that provides factual information about the illness and its treatment within a recovery-focused discussion with the patient and family is also widely recognized in clinical practice (McDonnell & Dyck, 2004; Tiffin, 2007). Although findings from psychosocial treatments with older individuals with schizophrenia are promising, more controlled studies with children and adolescents are needed (Tiffin & Welsh, 2013).

Using a prevention framework, recent efforts have focused on a variety of pharmacological, biological, psychosocial, and family interventions for high-risk younger individuals well before the onset of psychotic symptoms. Findings to date have suggested that these interventions can be effective in reducing the risk of transition to full-blown psychosis over the short term but over the longer term may only delay transition to psychosis (Preti & Cella, 2010). Further research into the prediction and prevention of psychosis in youths at high clinical risk for psychosis is needed, particularly in relation to possible long-term benefits (Addington & Heinssen, 2012).

Section Summary

Causes and Treatment of COS

- Current views regarding the causes of COS are based on a neurodevelopmental model in which a genetic vulnerability and early neurodevelopmental insults result in impaired connections between many brain regions. This impaired neural circuitry may increase the child's vulnerability to stress.

(continues)

EVERYONE HAS IMPORTANT NEEDS and ideas. Imagine not being able to get them across. Sights and sounds surround you, but you cannot focus your attention long enough to make sense of them. When you are shown how to read or add, you find that the letters and numbers look and sound too much alike. Children and adolescents with communication and learning disorders experience these difficulties daily. Everyday tasks can be confusing and frustrating, and sometimes result in a cycle of academic failure and lowered self-esteem.

JAMES

Smart but Can't Read

James, age 9, was a growing concern for his teacher: "James is obviously a very bright boy, and he wants to do well. I've noticed that he likes art, and is always wanting to draw. But he gets really upset when I ask him to do some work in class.

He looks like he dreads coming to school. And he complains that some words he tries to read don't make sense to him. I'm worried that his increasing frustration is going to cause other problems in school or with friends. Sometimes he gets mad at something and he has trouble calming down. If he is trying to create something that doesn't turn out the way he envisioned it, he explodes and slams his fist against the wall."

What James's mother heard was all too familiar. She knew that her son would get involved in something only if he could do it his own way. Her mind wandered briefly to when he was a toddler and sometimes got so anxious and worried about something that he had trouble sleeping or felt sick. She shared with his teacher her frustration at trying to find out what the problem was: "Getting him to read at home is like pulling teeth. He won't read at all on his own because he knows he can't read many of the words." (Based on authors' case material.)

FRANCINE

Shunned and Falling Behind

Francine, age 7, was entering a new school for the second time in 2 years. The first school was too challenging, and the other kids teased her because she "doesn't know what 2 plus 2 is." She is content to play for hours by herself and is not interested in the things that other kids her age are doing. "Most of the time," her mother explained, "Francine seems sad and in a bit of a fog." Although school performance was a major concern, her mother was also quite worried about Francine's lack of friends and the way other children treated her.

Her mother and father proudly shared their daughter's early childhood history and developmental milestones with me during our first interview. "Francine walked before she was a year old, and was a very talkative baby and toddler, who picked up new words quite quickly. She was a healthy and normal baby—we can't figure out why she seems so uninterested in school and other kids." They went on to explain: "When she entered preschool and kindergarten, she seemed uninterested in making friends. The other kids basically ignored her, even though she didn't do anything to bother them. My husband and I didn't think much of it at first. In fact, we bragged about how she took an early interest in reading and would spend a lot of her time alone with a book or magazine, even when she was 4 or 5, although she didn't usually understand what she read. But we grew more concerned around age 5 because she paid little attention to popular movies, toys, and things other kids her age played with. When she was a preschooler, we also noticed that she had trouble with numbers and understanding concepts like "more," "less," or "bigger." She knows what these words mean now, but she is still confused when we ask her to count something.

Yesterday I gave her her allowance and just for the heck of it, I used pennies, nickels, and dimes to see if she could add them up. No matter how hard we tried, she became confused, switching from one coin to the other, and she thought she had a bigger allowance if I stacked the pennies up! And if you ask her to arrange something, like setting the table for dinner, you never know what you'll end up with!" (Based on authors' case material.)

Children with communication or learning disorders can learn, and they are as intelligent as anyone else. Their disorders usually affect only certain limited aspects of learning, and rarely are they severe enough to impair the pursuit of a normal life—but they can be very stressful. Consider the experiences of James and Francine: James and Francine have different learning problems. James's are with language and reading. His ability to distinguish between different language sounds (phonemes) is underdeveloped, which is the primary reason for his poor word recognition and writing ability. Francine's problems are mostly with nonverbal learning, such as math. She can read quite well, but she has difficulty understanding some of the subtleties of others' facial expressions and gestures. She also confuses terms and instructions that describe numerical or spatial relationships, such as "larger than" or "sit beside the couch."

The field of learning and communication disorders, broadly referred to as "learning disabilities," has changed dramatically during the past 50 years. For many years, learning problems were attributed to poor motivation or poor instruction. Fortunately, breakthroughs in neuroimaging techniques has led to increased recognition of the differences in the neurological makeup and development of children with problems in language and related cognitive tasks. With recent advances in detection and intervention aimed at early language development, signs of communication problems are detected at an early age and children are taught using alternative methods that build on their developmental strengths.

In this chapter, we emphasize the relationship between language development and the subsequent appearance of a learning problem once the child enters school. We put these problems in a developmental context by showing how communication disorders (diagnosed primarily in early childhood) and learning disorders (identified most often during early school years) have interconnected features and underlying causes. As a case in point, preschoolers with communication disorders are more likely to develop a learning disability by middle childhood or early adolescence (Beitchman & Brownlie, 2014).

DEFINITIONS AND HISTORY

Learning disability (LD) is still commonly used as a general term for learning problems that occur in the absence of other obvious conditions, such as intellectual disability or brain damage. In the *Diagnostic and Statistical Manual of Mental Disorder*, 5th edition (DSM-5) two more specific terms are used, *communication disorders* and *learning disorders*, but the common use of the term *learning disability* requires that it be clarified and defined.

A learning disability affects how individuals with normal or above-average intelligence take in, retain, or express information. Incoming or outgoing information can be scrambled as it passes between the senses and the brain. Unlike most physical disabilities, a learning disability is hidden and is often undetected in young children (Lovett & Lewandowski, in 2014). Thus, children with learning disabilities often must cope not only with their limitations in reading, writing, or math but also with the frustration of convincing others that their problems are as legitimate as visible disabilities.

Learning difficulties often show up in schoolwork and can impede a child's ability to learn to read, write, or do math, but they also can affect many other parts of life, including work, daily routines, family life, and friendships. Some learning problems are specific and

Slowly but surely, most children learn the letters of the alphabet and how to use them to read and write words. For children with certain learning disabilities, however, the shapes and sounds of different letters continue to be confusing.

affect a narrow range of ability, whereas others may affect many different tasks and social situations. Each type of learning disability, whether it is related to reading, writing, math, or language, is characterized by distinct definitions and diagnoses. Knowledge of communication and learning disorders is growing rapidly as a result of increased scientific interest and research support. We now recognize that a learning disability, though challenging, does not have to be a handicap. Many well-known people with learning difficulties used their talents in exceptional ways, including Albert Einstein, Winston Churchill, and Thomas Edison.

The main characteristic all children with learning difficulties share is failing to perform at their expected level in school. Otherwise, symptoms vary tremendously (Beitchman & Brownlie, 2014). Many children and adults who are unable to acquire academic skills at a normal rate have been helped by recognizing and attending to specific learning problems.

Children with learning disabilities constitute a third of all children in the United States and Canada who receive special education services (National Center for Educational Statistics, 2012). Yet, experts still struggle to adequately define learning disabilities because of their many forms and overlapping symptoms, which you will note in the following lengthy definition:

Learning disability is a lay term (not a diagnostic term) that refers to significant problems in mastering one or more of the following skills: listening, speaking, reading, writing, reasoning, and mathematics. Learning disabilities do not include visual, hearing, or physical impairments; intellectual disability; emotional disturbance; or environmental disadvantage. Emotional and social disturbances and other adaptive deficiencies may occur with learning problems, but they do not by themselves constitute a learning disability (Individuals with Disabilities Education Improvement Act [IDEA], 2004).

In Chapter 5 we described intellectual disability as involving deficits in basic cognitive abilities that include problem solving, verbal skills, and mental reasoning. But the broader concept of intelligence also includes logical, mathematical, and language abilities that reflect a pattern of relative strengths and weaknesses possessed by everyone. For example, we are all stronger in some areas of learning and performance than in others (e.g., we enjoy writing and reading, but don't ask us to fix your car). Similarly, children with specific learning disorders who have normal intelligence show a pattern of relative strengths and weaknesses that can make some learning tasks much more difficult. This pattern is noteworthy mostly because it is so extreme and unexpected for a child who otherwise shows normal cognitive and physical development.

Communication disorder is a diagnostic term that refers to deficits in language, speech, and communication (APA, 2013). Communication disorders include the following diagnostic categories:

Few realize that Albert Einstein had early speech and language difficulties, given his monumental contributions to society.

Bettmann/Corbis

- ▶ language disorder (problems using language to communicate, such as spoken words or sign language, or understanding what other people say)
- ▶ speech sound disorder (deficits in productive speech sounds)
- ▶ childhood-onset fluency disorder (problems in speech fluency, such as stuttering)
- ▶ social (pragmatic) communication disorder

These communication disorders are developmentally connected to the later onset of learning disorders.

Specific learning disorder is a diagnostic term that refers to specific problems in learning and using academic skills. The DSM-5 integrates the frequently co-occurring problems in reading, mathematics, and written expression into this one category, and uses specifiers to designate impairments in one or more of these areas. Specific learning disorder is determined by achievement test results that are substantially below what is expected for the child's age, schooling, and intellectual ability.

An unexpected pattern of strengths and weaknesses in learning was first noted and studied during the late nineteenth century by physicians who were treating patients with medical injuries (Hammill, 1993). Franz Joseph Gall, a pioneer of language disorders, was struck by what he observed among some of his brain-injured patients: They had lost the capacity to express their feelings and ideas clearly through speech, yet they did not seem to suffer any intellectual impairment. One of his patients could not speak, but had no problem writing his thoughts on paper. Because he knew that this patient had normal speech before the head injury, Gall reasoned that the problem must have resulted from brain damage that had disrupted the neurological processes related to speech. For the first time, scientists began to pinpoint areas in the brain that control the ability to express and receive language processes.

These early observations, based on known medical injuries, raised the possibility that people with learning disabilities differ from people with intellectual disability in terms of relative strengths and deficits. People with learning disabilities have normal intellectual processes in most areas but are relatively weaker in others, which is known as having an **unexpected discrepancy** between measured ability and actual performance. This premise remained the foundation of most definitions of learning disability for many years. However, researchers and practitioners eventually agreed that subaverage performance on achievement tests, rather than a discrepancy between potential and actual performance, was a better way to capture these learning difficulties (Maehler & Schuchardt, 2011).

The links between intellectual disability, organic brain damage, and learning problems fascinated scientists, who had a firmer understanding of brain–behavior relationships by the 1940s. During that time, the question still remained as to why some children who did not fit the definition of intellectual disability based on IQ had significant problems in learning. Could intellectual disability be restricted to only certain intellectual abilities? Were academic problems the same as those assessed by measures of general intelligence?

Strauss and Werner (1943) shed light on this issue by pointing out that children learn in individual ways, challenging the concept that learning is a relatively uniform, predictable process in children without intellectual disabilities. Three important concepts from this period continue to influence the field to this day (Hallahan, Pullen, & Ward, 2013):

1. Children approach learning in different ways, so each child's individual learning style and uniqueness should be recognized and used to full advantage.

2. Educational methods should be tailored to an individual child's pattern of strengths and weaknesses; one method should not be imposed on everyone.

3. Children with learning problems might be helped by teaching methods that strengthen existing abilities rather than emphasize weak areas.

By the early 1960s, the modern learning disabilities movement had begun. Parents and educators were dissatisfied that children often had to be diagnosed with an intellectual disability in order to receive special education services. A category was needed to describe learning problems that could not be explained on the basis of intellectual disability, lack of learning opportunities, psychopathology, or sensory deficits (Lyon, Fletcher, & Barnes, 2003).

Thus, the emerging concept of learning disabilities made intuitive sense to many who were familiar with the varied needs of children, and it was welcomed as states and provinces began to support special education programs and services. The domination of physicians and psychologists in the field gave way to greater input from educators, parents, and clinicians. Teacher training expanded to include new ways to teach youngsters who could not respond to typical classroom methods. Professionals trained in speech and language pathology became an important part of school-based services.

As the focus of the learning disabilities movement shifted from the clinic to the classroom, parents and educators assumed a major role in programming and placement. They were encouraged by the fact that the term *learning disabled* did not stigmatize children, but rather brought them needed services (Hammill, 1993).

The fact that these children had normal intelligence gave parents and teachers hope that difficulties in reading, writing, and math could be overcome if only the right set of instructional conditions and settings could be identified (Lyon et al., 2003). These developments led to the recent Response-to-Intervention (RTI) movement, which views LD in terms of what academic help children need rather than what disability they might have (Lovett & Lewandowski, in press). Thus, with the collaborative leadership of parents, educators, and specially trained professionals, the field of learning disabilities grew from its beginning in the 1960s to the major component of educational services it is today.

Section Summary

Definitions and History

- *Learning disability* is a general lay term for communication and learning problems that occur in the absence of other obvious conditions such as intellectual disability or brain damage.

- Children and adults with learning disabilities show specific deficits in using spoken or written language, often referred to as relative strengths and weaknesses.

- Parents and educators assumed a major role in bringing recognition and services to children with learning disabilities.

LANGUAGE DEVELOPMENT

From birth, infants selectively attend to parental speech sounds and soon learn to communicate with basic gestures and sounds of their own. Usually, by their first birthday they can recognize several words and use a few of their own to express their needs and emotions. Over the next 2 years, their language development proceeds at an exponential pace, and their ability to formulate complex ideas and express new concepts is a constant source of amazement and amusement for parents. Adults play an important role in encouraging language development by providing clear examples of language and enjoying the child's expressions.

Language consists of **phonemes**, which are the basic sounds (such as sharp *ba*'s and *da*'s and drawn-out *ee*'s and *ss*'s) that make up language. When a child hears a phoneme over and over, receptors in the ear stimulate the formation of dedicated connections to the brain's auditory cortex. A perceptual map forms that represents similarities among sounds and helps the infant learn to discriminate among different phonemes. These

From an early age, children love to express themselves.

maps form quickly; 6-month-old children of English-speaking parents already have auditory maps different from infants in non-English-speaking homes, as measured by neuron activity in response to different sounds (Kuhl et al., 2006). By their first birthday, the maps are complete, and infants are less able to discriminate sounds that are not important in their own language.

Rapid development of a perceptual map is why learning a second language after—rather than with—the first language is difficult; brain connections are already wired for English, and the remaining neurons are less able to form basic new connections for, say, Swedish. Once the basic circuitry is established, infants can turn sounds into words, and the more words they hear, the faster they learn language. The sounds of words serve to strengthen and expand neural connections that can then process more words. Similar cortical maps are formed for other highly refined skills, such as musical ability (Huss et al., 2011). A young child who learns to play a musical instrument may strengthen the neural circuits that underlie not only music, but verbal memory as well (Ho, Cheung, & Chan, 2003).

Phonological Awareness

Not all children progress normally through the milestones of language development. Some are noticeably delayed, continuing to use gestures or sounds rather than speech. Others progress normally in some areas, such as following spoken directions and attending to commands, but have trouble finding the words to express themselves clearly.

Although the development of language is one of the best predictors of school performance and overall intelligence (Sattler, 2008), delays or differences in development are not a definitive sign of intellectual disability

or cognitive disorder. Rather, such deviations from normal may be just that—deviations—and may be accompanied by superior abilities in other areas of cognitive functioning. Albert Einstein, who is considered an intellectual genius, began speaking late and infrequently, causing his parents to worry that he was "subnormal." According to family members, when his father asked his son's headmaster what profession his son should adopt, the answer was simply, "It doesn't matter, he'll never make a success of anything" (R. W. Clark, 1971, p. 10).

Since language development is an indicator of general mental development, children in whom language fails to develop or who show severe delays in acquiring language are considered at risk of having a language-based learning disability. Albert Einstein notwithstanding, early language problems are considered highly predictive of subsequent communication and learning disorders (Heim & Benasich, 2006; Williams, 2010).

Phonology is the ability to learn and store phonemes as well as the rules for combining the sounds into meaningful units or words. Deficits in phonology are a chief reason that most children and adults with communication and learning disorders have problems in language-based activities such as learning to read and spell (Larkin & Snowling, 2008; Nation, Snowling, & Clarke, 2007).

A young child is required to recognize that speech is segmented into phonemes (the English language contains about 42, such as *ba, ga, at,* and *tr*). This task is difficult for many children because speech does not consist of separate phonemes produced one after another. Instead, sounds are *co-articulated* (overlapped with one another) to permit rapid communication, rather than pronounced sound-by-sound (Liberman & Shankweiler, 1991). About 80% of children can segment words and syllables into their proper phonemes by the time they are 7 years old. The other 20% cannot, and it is these children who struggle hardest to read (S. E. Shaywitz & Shaywitz, 2013; Vellutino et al., 2004).

Generally, early language problems surface as learning problems when children enter school, because in school children are taught to connect spoken and written language. Those who do not easily learn to read and write often have difficulty learning the alphabetic system—the relationship of sounds to letters. They also cannot manipulate sounds within syllables in words, which is called a lack of phonological awareness and is a precursor to reading problems (Rvachew, 2007).

Phonological awareness is a broad construct that includes recognizing the relationship between sounds and letters, detecting rhyme and alliteration, and being aware that sounds can be manipulated within syllables in words. Primary-grade teachers detect phonological awareness as they ask children to rhyme words and manipulate sounds. For example, the teacher can say "hat" and ask the child to say the word without the *h* sound, or say "trip" and have the child say the word without the *p*. To assess the child's ability to blend sounds, teachers can say the three sounds *t*, *i*, and *n*, for example, and see whether the child can pull the sounds together to say "tin."

In addition to serving as a prerequisite for basic reading skills, phonological awareness and processing also appear highly related to expressive language development (Boada & Pennington, 2006). Readers with core deficits in phonological processing have difficulty segmenting and categorizing phonemes, retrieving the names of common objects and letters, storing phonological codes in short-term memory, and producing some speech sounds. Reading and comprehension depend on the rapid and automatic ability to decode single words. Children who are slow and inaccurate at decoding have the most difficulties in reading comprehension (Melby-Lervåg, Lyster, & Hulme, 2012).

Section Summary

Language Development

- Language development is based on innate ability and environmental opportunities to learn, store, and express important sounds in the language. It proceeds very rapidly during infancy.

- Deficits in phonological awareness—the ability to distinguish the sounds of language—have been identified as a major cause of communication and learning disorders.

COMMUNICATION DISORDERS

Children with communication disorders have difficulty producing speech sounds, using spoken language to communicate, or understanding what other people say. In DSM-5, communication disorders include the diagnostic subcategories of *language disorder*, *speech sound disorder*, *childhood-onset fluency disorder (stuttering)*, and *social (pragmatic) communication disorder*. These subcategories are distinguished by the exact nature of the child's impairment.

Recall that during development phonological problems appear before problems in language reception or expression, yet they have strong similarities. The following discussion focuses on language disorder in an effort to highlight early childhood problems that represent the fundamental features of communication

disorders. (Stuttering has a unique clinical feature and developmental course, so it is discussed separately.)

Consider Jackie's communication problems at age 3 years:

JACKIE

Screaming, Not Talking

Jackie's mother explained with no hesitation why she asked for help: "My 3-year-old daughter is a growing concern. Since she was a baby, she has been plagued by ear infections and sleep problems. Some nights she screams for hours on end, usually because of the ear infections. She has violent temper outbursts and refuses to do simple things that I ask her to do, like get dressed or put on her coat."

The child, waiting in the playroom, could be heard screaming over her mother's voice. Jackie was asking my assistant for something, but she could not make out what Jackie was saying. It was pretty obvious how frustrated both the child and her mother must feel on occasion. Her mother explained how she and Jackie's father had divorced when Jackie was less than 2 years old, and that after weekend exchanges it sometimes took a few days for Jackie's routine to return to some degree of normalcy.

I opened the letter she had brought from Jackie's preschool teacher, someone who I knew had a great deal of experience with children of this age. "Jackie is a bright and energetic child," the letter began, "but she is having a great deal of difficulty expressing herself with words. When she gets frustrated, she starts to give up or becomes angry—she won't eat her meals or she fights with staff at nap time, even if she is hungry or tired. If a new teacher at day care is introduced, it takes Jackie a long time to get used to the new person. Jackie seems to understand what she is being asked, but can't find the words to express herself, which understandably leads to an emotional reaction on her part." (Based on authors' case material.)

Language Disorder

Jackie's problems met the criteria for a **language disorder,** which is a communication disorder characterized by difficulties in the comprehension or production of spoken or written language. As a result of these deficits, Jackie showed her frustration loudly and inappropriately.

Children's language development follows specific steps, although each child may proceed through the steps at a different pace. Normal variations can make it difficult to predict that a given child's early communication problems will later become major problems in learning. A common example is the child who points to different objects and makes grunting or squealing noises that the parent quickly recognizes as "more milk" or "no peas." Prior to age 3 or so, many children communicate this way unless parents actively encourage using words and discourage nonverbal communications. Nevertheless, despite plenty of verbal examples and proper language stimulation, some children do not develop in some areas of speech and language, and they later have problems in school. This developmental connection makes the study of communication disorders highly pertinent to understanding and treating subsequent learning problems.

Table 7.1 shows the major features of the DSM-5 diagnostic criteria for language disorder. Children with a language disorder, such as Jackie, do not suffer from intellectual disability or from autism spectrum disorder, which affect speech and language. Rather, they show persistent difficulties in acquiring and using language to communicate (Criterion A). A child's ability to use language depends on both receptive skills (i.e., receiving and comprehending language) and expressive skills (i.e., production of vocal, gestural, or verbal signals). Thus, children with this disorder often show reduced vocabulary, limited sentence structure, or impairments in their ability to carry on a conversation. A child's expressive and receptive abilities may differ such that his or her language comprehension, for example, is stronger than his or her language expression. For example, when asked by her parents to go upstairs, find her socks, and put them on, Jackie was quite capable of complying. When asked by her mother to describe what she has just done, however, she might respond simply, "find socks."

The linguistic abilities of children with language disorders vary significantly, based on the severity of the disorder and the age of the child. Most often, these children begin speaking late and progress slowly in their speech development. Their vocabulary often is limited and is marked by short sentences and simple grammatical structure, as in Jackie's response. To fit the diagnostic criteria, these problems must be substantially below the abilities of other children of the same age, resulting in functional limitations in communication, social participation, or academic achievement (Criterion B). In addition, the symptoms must begin in the early developmental period (Criterion C) and not be attributable to other sensory impairments or medical conditions (Criterion D).

Although their hearing is normal, children with language disorder may have difficulty understanding particular types of words or statements, such as complex if–then sentences. In severe cases, the child's ability to understand basic vocabulary or simple sentences may be impaired, and there may be deficits in auditory processing of sounds and symbols and in their storage, recall, and sequencing. Understandably, these problems make the child seem inattentive or noncompliant, and the disorder can be easily misdiagnosed. Imagine how it would feel to be in Greece visiting an English-speaking host and her Greek husband. Unless your host is present, trying to engage in friendly conversation can be frustrating and uncomfortable. Even if both you and the husband can each understand a few words the other is saying, you probably cannot actually converse. If you have ever faced a similar communication barrier, you probably have an appreciation of the frustration and discomfort that accompany a language disorder.

When the developmental language problem involves articulation or sound production rather than word knowledge, a **speech sound disorder** may be an appropriate diagnosis. Children with this disorder have trouble controlling their rate of speech, or lag behind playmates in learning to articulate certain sounds. Typically, children learn phonemes and use intelligible speech by the age of 3 years or so, with the exception of some of the more difficult sounds such as *l, r, s, z, th,* and *ch,* which may take a few years longer to articulate (APA, 2013).

TABLE 7.1 | **Diagnostic Criteria for** Language Disorder

DSM-5

(A) Persistent difficulties in the acquisition and use of language across modalities (i.e., spoken, written, sign language, or other) due to deficits in comprehension or production that include the following:

(1) Reduced vocabulary (word knowledge and use).

(2) Limited sentence structure (ability to put words and word endings together to form sentences based on the rules of grammar and morphology).

(3) Impairments in discourse (ability to use vocabulary and connect sentences to explain or describe a topic or series of events or have a conversation).

(B) Language abilities are substantially and quantifiably below those expected for age, resulting in functional limitations in effective communication, social participation, academic achievement, or occupational performance, individually or in any combination.

(C) Onset of symptoms is in the early developmental period.

(D) The difficulties are not attributable to hearing or other sensory impairment, motor dysfunction, or another medical or neurological condition and are not better explained by intellectual disability (intellectual developmental disorder) or global developmental delay.

Source: Diagnostic and Statistical Manual of Mental Disorders, 5th edition. American Psychiatric Association.

Depending on the severity of the disorder, the speech quality of these children may be unusual, and even unintelligible. For example, at age 6, James still said "wabbit" instead of "rabbit" and "we-wind" for "rewind." Preschoolers, of course, often mispronounce words or confuse the sounds they hear, which is a normal part of learning to speak. When these problems persist beyond the normal developmental range (age 4) or interfere with academic and social activities by age 7, they deserve separate attention.

Prevalence and Course

Children usually reveal problems in speech articulation and expression as they attempt to tackle new sounds and express their own concepts. Even though prevalence estimates account for normal variations in language development and are based on individuals who meet specific diagnostic criteria, the degree of severity can vary considerably. For example, in early childhood, milder forms of speech sound disorder are relatively common, affecting close to 10% of preschoolers. Many of these children outgrow their earlier difficulties, so only 2% to 3% of preschoolers meet the criteria for speech sound disorder. However, language disorder is a bit more common, affecting about 7% of younger school-age children across studies (Beitchman & Brownlie, 2014; Heim & Benasich, 2006).

Communication disorders are identified almost twice as often in boys as in girls (Pinborough-Zimmerman et al., 2007); boys' language difficulties are more often accompanied by behavior problems, and consequently, they are referred and diagnosed with communication learning disorders more often than girls (Vellutino et al., 2004). By 4 years of age a child's individual differences in language stabilize, so problems that remain past this age are highly predictive of later outcomes. About 50% fully outgrow their problems, whereas the other 50% may show improvement but still have some degree of impairment into adulthood. Children with receptive language impairments, in particular, have a poor prognosis as compared with those with primarily expressive impairments. Receptive language problems are more resistant to treatment and are often associated with reading difficulties throughout their education (APA, 2013).

Even though language problems usually diminish with time, children with communication disorders often have higher-than-normal rates of negative behaviors that began at an early age (van Daal, Verhoeven, & van Balkom, 2007). Associated behavior problems, such as attention-deficit/hyperactivity disorder (ADHD) and social skill limitations, can add to

communication problems and further alter the course of development in terms of how these children relate to peers or keep up with educational demands (Durkin & Conti-Ramsden, 2010). To give children with special needs the opportunity to interact with typically developing children, school systems have begun to include these children in regular, rather than segregated, classrooms. **Inclusion** education strategies are based on the premise that the abilities of children with special needs will improve from associating with normally developing peers and that by doing so these children will be spared the effects of labeling and special placements.

Causes

Notable findings that support the role of genetics, brain function, and environmental risk factors associated with a higher incidence of learning disorders are discussed in the following sections.

Genetics

Language processes appear to be heritable to a significant degree, although the specific genetic underpinnings are difficult to pinpoint. About 50% to 75% of all children with a language disorder show a positive family history of some type of learning disability (American Speech–Language–Hearing Association [ASHA], 2008; Heim & Benasich, 2006). Twin studies and adoption studies also suggest a genetic connection (McGrath et al., 2007; Plomin, Haworth, & Davis, 2010; Whitehouse et al., 2011).

Scientists are zeroing in on specific deficits in brain functioning that lead to communication disorders and may be heritable. Studies comparing language-impaired children with and without an affected parent suggest that *temporal processing deficits* occur significantly more often in children with a positive family history for a language-based learning disability (Caylak, 2011; Flax et al., 2003). That is, affected children have more difficulty deciphering certain speech sounds because of subtle but important differences in the way neurons fire in response to various sounds. In a twin study, Bishop et al. (1999) found that the variation in temporal processing was due to environmental factors and not to genetics because twin–twin correlations were similar for monozygotic (MZ) and dizygotic (DZ) twins. However, what does appear to be genetic is a deficit in phonological short-term memory.

The Brain

Language functions develop rapidly and are housed primarily in the left temporal lobe of the brain

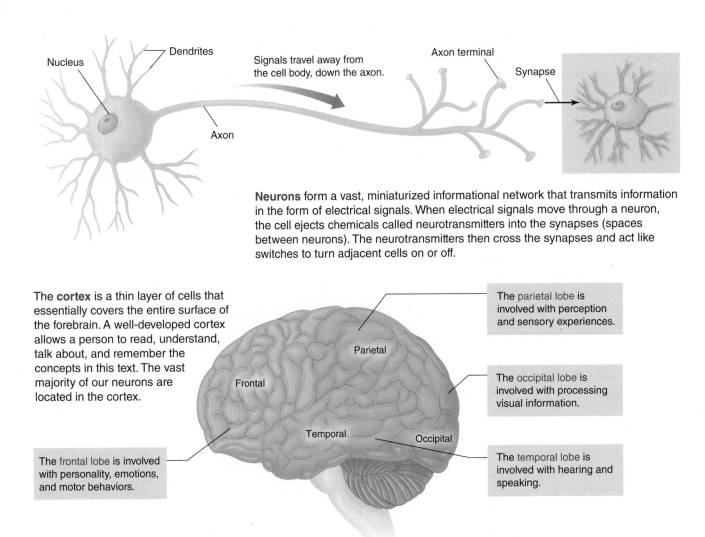

Neurons form a vast, miniaturized informational network that transmits information in the form of electrical signals. When electrical signals move through a neuron, the cell ejects chemicals called neurotransmitters into the synapses (spaces between neurons). The neurotransmitters then cross the synapses and act like switches to turn adjacent cells on or off.

The **cortex** is a thin layer of cells that essentially covers the entire surface of the forebrain. A well-developed cortex allows a person to read, understand, talk about, and remember the concepts in this text. The vast majority of our neurons are located in the cortex.

The parietal lobe is involved with perception and sensory experiences.

The occipital lobe is involved with processing visual information.

The temporal lobe is involved with hearing and speaking.

The frontal lobe is involved with personality, emotions, and motor behaviors.

● **FIGURE 7.1** | Areas of the brain involved in language functions.

From Plotnik/Kouyoumdjian. Introduction to Psychology, 9th ed. 2011 Wadsworth, a part of Cengage Learning, Inc

(see ● Figure 7.1). A circular feedback loop helps strengthen the developmental process of language reception and expression. The better children comprehend spoken language, the better they will be able to express themselves. Feedback from their own vocalizations, in turn, helps shape their subsequent expressions. Lack of comprehension and absence of feedback reduces verbal output, and thus interferes with the development of articulation skills (Vellutino et al., 2007).

Anatomical and neuroimaging studies show that deficits in phonological awareness and segmentation are related to problems in the functional connections between brain areas, not to a specific dysfunction of any single area of the brain (Lyon et al., 2006; Richlan, Kronbichler, & Wimmer, 2011). Some brain imaging studies have indicated that poor performance on tasks demanding phonological awareness is associated with less brain activity in the left temporal region, suggesting that phonological problems may stem from neurological deficits or deviations in posterior left-hemisphere systems that control the ability to process phonemes (Richlan et al., 2011; S. E. Shaywitz et al., 2009). We return to these findings on brain function later, in our discussion of reading disorders.

Recurrent otitis media (middle ear infection) in early childhood was long thought to contribute to language difficulties, because hearing loss accompanies frequent or long bouts of infections. Although otitis media that occurs often during early childhood may lead to speech and language delays, these delays improve relatively quickly and largely disappear by age 7 (Zumach et al., 2010).

In summary, although biological findings point to abnormal brain functioning, how this abnormality originates is still unclear. The best guess is that communication disorders result from an interaction of genetic influences, slowness or abnormalities of brain maturation, and possibly, minor brain lesions that escape clinical detection (S. E. Shaywitz, Morris, & Shaywitz, 2008).

Home Environment

How much does the home environment contribute to communication disorders? Do some parents fail to provide adequate examples to stimulate their children's language? Because of the important role parents play in children's development, psychologists have studied this issue carefully.

We noticed when we first visited Jackie at home that her stepfather was a very quiet man who often communicated nonverbally—a gesture, a frown, a short phrase. Her mother used very simple speech when talking to Jackie but not when talking to Jackie's 6-year-old sister. These observations match those of researchers (St. James-Roberts & Alston, 2006; Whitehurst & Lonigan, 1998) who compared verbal interactions of families with and without a child who had a language disorder. They found that parents changed the way they spoke to their children, depending on their children's abilities. When the child spoke in simple, two- or three-word sentences, the parents adjusted their speech accordingly. Note that, except in extreme cases of child neglect or abuse, it is unlikely that communication disorders are caused by parents. Parental speech and language stimulation may affect the pace and range of language development, but not the specific impairments that characterize the disorders (Glascoe & Leew, 2010; McGrath et al., 2007).

Treatment

Although communication disorders in some children may self-correct by age 6 or so, those with more severe communication and language difficulties will continue to lag behind their peers and are at risk of having behavioral or social problems if the difficulties are left untreated. Thus, parents should seek help in understanding their child's speech delays and to ensure that they are doing everything possible to stimulate language development. In general, treatment for children with communication disorders is based on three principles (Beitchman & Brownlie, 2014): (1) treatment to promote the child's language competencies; (2) treatment to adjust the environment in ways that accommodate the child's needs; and (3) therapy with the child (or youth) to equip him or her with knowledge and skills to reduce behavioral and emotional symptoms.

Specialized preschools, for example, have had good results using a combination of computer- and teacher-assisted instruction to teach early language skills to young children, which helps to pace the child's practice of new skills (Hatcher et al., 2006; Loo et al., 2010; Smith-Lock et al., 2013).

For Jackie, we designed ways that her parents and day-care teachers could build on her existing strengths. Her day-care teacher had an excellent idea: Because Jackie loved to draw and to talk about her artwork, why not use her interest in drawing to increase her enthusiasm for speaking? When I visited her class, Jackie ran up to show me her drawing, exclaiming, "I draw picture of mom, dad, kitty, and lake." We agreed that her behavior problems could be managed by simple forms of ignoring and distracting and the occasional time-out. Jackie became attached to computer graphics and images, and she soon was able to identify letters and small words and to move shapes around the screen. All the while, her expressive language improved, and by age 5 she could pronounce all the letters of the alphabet and was eager to start kindergarten.

Childhood-Onset Fluency Disorder (Stuttering)

Childhood-Onset Fluency Disorder (Stuttering) is the repeated and prolonged pronunciation of certain syllables that interferes with communication. It is quite normal for children who are still learning to speak to go through a period of nonfluency, or unclear speech, as part of their development. It takes practice and patience for a child to develop the coordination for the tongue, lips, and brain to work in unison to produce unfamiliar or difficult combinations of sounds. For most children, this period of speech development passes without notice, and for most parents it is full of wonder and amusement as their children wrestle with new words. Some children, however, progress slowly through this stage, repeating (*wa-wa-wa*) or prolonging (*n-ah-ah-ah-o*) sounds; they struggle to continue or develop ways to avoid or compensate for certain sounds or words. Four-year-old Sayad has speech problems that typify the pattern of stuttering:

SAYAD

Family Legacy

Sayad's parents had received a lot of informal advice from friends and relatives about their son's speech problems, but most of what they said was worrisome. "He'll struggle with this for most of his life," his grandmother had warned. "If something isn't done right away, he'll become a stutterer, and be so self-conscious that he won't be able to keep up in school or with his friends."

(continues)

(continued)

Sayad started repeating and prolonging some of his words when he was about 2, but now his problem had grown more noticeable. As he spoke, he pursed his lips, closed his eyes, and shortened his breathing, seeming to tense up his face. Yet his interactions with me were friendly and at ease. "M-m-m-m-y words get stuck in m-m-m-m-y m-m-mouth," he explained, "and I-I-I-I talk t-t-t-too fast. Wh-wh-wh-why can't I talk right?" I soon discovered why his grandmother was so concerned: The child's great-grandfather and great-uncle both stuttered, and Sayad's father had been a stutterer until he was a teenager.

Sayad's mother had been trying to ignore the problem and not draw attention to it, but she was growing more aware that Sayad's peers teased and imitated him. She explained why she came for an assessment: "We were on the way to the store when Sayad kept saying 'where' over and over. After I stopped the car and unfastened his seatbelt, he finished his question—'is daddy?' After that, I gave up on my 'leave it alone' notion and began trying ways to slow Sayad down a bit." (Based on authors' case material.)

DSM-5 diagnostic criteria for Childhood-Onset Fluency Disorder (Stuttering) are shown in Table 7.2. This disorder involves disturbance in the normal fluency and time patterning of speech that is atypical for the child's age and that occurs often and persists over time. Stuttering is characterized by sound and syllable repetitions, sound prolongations, pauses within a word, word substitutions to avoid problematic words, and similar pronunciation and speech difficulties. These difficulties lead to anxiety about speaking or participating in activities that require effective communication or social participation. Over time the child may develop a fearful anticipation of speaking in front of others and attempt to avoid speech situations such as talking by telephone or in class. The disorder may be accompanied by motor movements such as eye blinks, tics, tremors of the lips or face, etc. (APA, 2013).

Prevalence and Course

Stuttering is relatively common as young children learn to articulate sounds clearly and appropriately. Population-based surveys indicate that 11% of children stutter by age 4, with girls affected as much as boys (Reilly et al., 2013; Yairi & Ambrose, 2013). However, few children receive a diagnosis of childhood-onset fluency disorder because about 80% recover from stuttering as they attend school for a year or so (Packman, Code, & Onslow, 2007). The prevalence of stuttering across

the lifespan (i.e., the number of individuals of all ages who meet the diagnostic criteria at any point in time) is below 1% (Yairi & Ambrose, 2013). Higher rates of parent-reported stuttering have been noted among African American and Hispanic children in the United States, although how racial and cultural factors may affect stuttering remains unclear (Boyle et al., 2011).

Causes and Treatment

Many myths and falsehoods surround stuttering. The widely held view that stuttering is caused by an unresolved emotional problem or by anxiety is not supported by any evidence (Packman et al., 2007). Because the problem runs in families, researchers have focused on family characteristics as the major causes. However, it is not likely this behavior is acquired primarily as a function of the child's linguistic environment. Sayad's grandmother and mother would be relieved to know that the communicative behavior of mothers does not significantly contribute to the development of stuttering (Howell & Davis, 2011).

TABLE 7.2 | **Diagnostic Criteria for** Childhood-Onset Fluency Disorder (Stuttering)

DSM-5

(A) Disturbances in the normal fluency and time of patterning of speech that are inappropriate for the individual's age and language skills, persist over time, and are characterized by frequent and marked occurrences of one (or more) or the following:

(1) Sound and syllable repetitions.

(2) Sound prolongations of consonants as well as words.

(3) Broken words (e.g., pauses within a word).

(4) Audible or silent blocking (filled or unfilled pauses in speech).

(5) Circumlocutions (word substitutions to avoid problematic words).

(6) Words produced with an excess of physical tension.

(7) Monosyllabic whole-word repetitions (e.g., "I-I-I-I" see him).

(B) The disturbance causes anxiety about speaking or limitations in effective communication, social participation, or academic or occupational performance, individually or in any combination.

(C) The onset of symptoms is in the early developmental period (*Note:* Later-onset cases are diagnosed as adult-onset fluency disorder).

(D) The disturbance is not attributable to a speech-motor or sensory deficit, dysfluency associated with neurological insult (e.g., stroke, tumor, trauma), or another medical concern and is not better explained by another mental disorder.

Source: Diagnostic and Statistical Manual of Mental Disorders, 5th ed. American Psychiatric Association.

Genetic factors play a strong role in the etiology of stuttering, accounting for approximately 70% of the variance in the causes of stuttering (Dworzynski et al., 2007). Environmental factors, such as premature birth or parental mental illness, account for the remaining causal influences (Ajdacic-Gross et al., 2010). Genetic factors most likely influence speech by causing an abnormal development in the location of the most prominent speech centers in the brain, which are usually in the left hemisphere. This biological source for stuttering explains many of its clinical features, including the loss of spontaneity and occasional problems in self-esteem (Howell, 2011; Kell et al., 2009).

Since most children outgrow stuttering, one of the most frustrating problems for parents and therapists is to decide whether therapy would be intervention or interference. Therapy is usually recommended if sound and syllable repetitions are frequent, if the parent or child is concerned about the problem, or if the child shows, like Sayad, facial or vocal tension. A common psychological treatment for children who stutter is to teach parents how to speak to their children slowly and use short and simple sentences, consequently removing the pressure the child may feel about speaking (Howell, 2011; Rousseau, Packman, Onslow, Harrison, & Jones, 2007). Other beneficial treatments for stuttering include contingency management, which uses positive consequences for fluency and negative consequences for stuttering (Bothe et al., 2006; Murphy, Yaruss, & Quesal, 2007), and habit reversal procedures, such as learning to regulate breathing (Bate et al., 2011).

Social (Pragmatic) Communication Disorder

Social (Pragmatic) Communication Disorder (SCD) is a new disorder in DSM-5. It involves persistent difficulties with pragmatics—the social use of language and communication (APA, 2013). Pragmatics are culturally specific practices and skills related to social uses of language, conversational norms, and the use of nonverbal communication, such as eye contact and gestures (Beitchman & Brownlie, 2014). Pragmatic difficulties involve both expressive and receptive skills—being able to adapt one's communication to the social context and being able to understand the nuances and social meanings expressed by others.

The first requirement for a diagnosis of social (pragmatic) communication disorder involves persistent difficulties across four areas (Table 7.3):

▶ Deficits in using communication for social purposes. A child may show difficulty greeting others or sharing information appropriately.

TABLE 7.3 | **Diagnostic Criteria for** Social (Pragmatic) Communication Disorder

DSM-5

(A) Persistent difficulties in the social use of verbal and nonverbal communication as manifested by all of the following:

  (1) Deficits in using communication for social purposes, such as greeting and sharing information, in a manner that is appropriate for the social context.

  (2) Impairment of the ability to change communication to match context or the needs of the listener, such as speaking differently in a classroom than on a playground, talking differently to a child than to an adult, and avoiding use of overly formal language.

  (3) Difficulties following rules for language and storytelling, such as taking turns in conversation, rephrasing when misunderstood, and knowing how to use verbal and nonverbal signals to regulate interaction.

  (4) Difficulties understanding what is not explicitly stated (e.g., making inferences) and nonliteral or ambiguous meanings of language (e.g., idioms, humor, metaphors, multiple meanings that depend on the context for interpretation).

(B) The deficits result in functional limitations in effective communication, social participation, social relationships, academic achievement, or occupational performance, individually or in combination.

(C) The onset of the symptoms is early in the developmental period (but deficits may not become fully manifest until social communication demands exceed limited capacities).

(D) The symptoms are not attributable to another medical or neurological condition or to low abilities in the domains of word structure and grammar, and are not better explained by autism spectrum disorder, intellectual disability (intellectual developmental disorder), global developmental delay, or another mental disorder.

Source: Diagnostic and Statistical Manual of Mental Disorders, 5th ed. American Psychiatric Association.

▶ Difficulties changing their communication to match the situation or the listener, such as the classroom versus the playground.

▶ Problems following the rules of language, such as taking turns in a conversation,

▶ Difficulties understanding what someone is not explicitly saying, such as being able to make inferences based on the context of the situation.

A diagnosis of SCD is not typically made until the child is 4 or 5 years old, to determine whether he or she has shown adequate developmental progress in speech and language. Signs of language impairment, such as a history of delay in reaching language milestones, are common, but it is the specific deficits in social communication that determine this disorder. As with other communication disorders, onset must be early in development and result in functional limitations in communication, social participation, social relationships or academic functioning.

Social (pragmatic) communication disorder was added to the DSM because of the number of children who did not meet conventional criteria for an autism spectrum disorder (ASD) yet who had persistent difficulties with social aspects of communication and peer relations. SCD is differentiated from ASD largely on the basis of fewer restricted/repetitive patterns of behaviors and interests (Gibson et al., 2013). The symptoms of SCD also overlap with ADHD, social anxiety disorder, and intellectual disability in that they share problems in social, pragmatic communication. Although this diagnostic category is new, studies based on similar samples of children suggest that some children show improvement over time while others continue to show social communication deficits into adulthood. Regardless of improvements in social communication, children with SCD may suffer lasting impairments in peer relations due to their early difficulties. Thus, peer-assisted interventions are recognized as effective ways to build pragmatic communication and social skills for these children (Murphy, Faulkner, & Farley, 2014).

Section Summary

Communication Disorders

- Speech and language problems that emerge during early childhood include difficulty producing speech sounds, demonstrating speech fluency, using spoken language to communicate, or understanding what other people say.
- Even though most children with communication disorders acquire normal language by mid-to-late adolescence, early communication disorders are developmentally connected to the later onset of learning disorders.
- Language disorder is a communication disorder involving difficulties in comprehension or production of spoken or written language.
- Childhood-Onset Fluency Disorder (Stuttering) is relatively common among younger children, and declines significantly once the child enters school.
- Social (Pragmatic) Communication Disorder is new to DSM-5. Its primary characteristics involve difficulties in the social use of verbal and nonverbal communication.
- Causes of communication disorders include genetic influences and slow or abnormal brain maturation.
- Many communication disorders resolve themselves after children begin attending school. Treatment is recommended for children who show significant language delays or difficulties; it involves accommodating the child's needs to strengthen speech and language skills.

SPECIFIC LEARNING DISORDER

People do not understand what it costs in time and suffering to learn how to read. I have been working at it for eighty years, and I still can't say that I've succeeded.

—Goethe (1749–1832)

Whether we are studying Roman history or calculus, applying ourselves to the task of learning requires exertion and concentration. Like physical activities, some learning activities are more difficult than others, especially for younger children who have not developed a foundation of good study habits and successful learning experiences. Parents and teachers may notice that a child is struggling unusually hard to master a particular skill, such as reading, and wonder why. The problem may be formally assessed by an IQ test and various standardized tests that assess abilities in specific academic areas.

When achievement in reading, math, or writing is well below average for the child's age and intellectual ability, he or she may be diagnosed with a specific learning disorder (SLD). In other words, a child with a specific learning disorder is intellectually capable of learning key academic concepts of reading, writing, and math, but seems unable to do so. The phrase "unexpected academic underachievement" captures this notion that the child's learning problems are indeed *specific* and not due to intellectual disability or global developmental delay (APA, 2013).

JAMES

Strong Points Shine

The look on the 9-year-old's face said it all—he did not want to be here. "I'm tired of talking to people" was his terse greeting. I wondered for a moment whether he would talk to me at all, but as soon as he saw my computer, he brightened a bit. To allow time for him to feel more comfortable, I invited James to play a quick game or two. His skill at the action games told me a lot about his basic energy and problem-solving ability—he was a whiz at figuring out the rules of each game and getting a high score. We spoke casually during the warm-up, but it was clear to me that he preferred to concentrate on the game.

A half hour passed, with little more than a few sentences exchanged. A quick trip to the snack bar gave us the common ground we needed to open up and talk a bit. "Why does my teacher want me to come here?" he reasonably asked. As he listened and replied to my explanation, his language problems stood out. His sentences were short, simple, and rapid. Here is an example:

"James, tell me something about your favorite story or a recent movie you've seen."

"I like the movie. Lots of dogs."

"What movie is that, James?"

"Dog movie."

During testing, James often tried to start before I had finished telling him what to do. He was eager to do what I asked, but he stopped abruptly as soon as he had trouble. James could focus on only one sound at a time, so if he missed early cues or initial instructions, he would become disoriented, frustrated, and uncooperative. James wanted to do well, but I could see he was struggling. He completed the WISC-IV (Wechsler Intelligence Scale for Children, 4th ed.) in less than an hour, hurrying almost as if to escape his own mistakes. His measured general intelligence was within the normal range, but his performance abilities (performance IQ, 109) were much stronger than his verbal abilities (verbal IQ, 78). It was obvious as well that the test underestimated his true ability, as a result of his eagerness to finish and his difficulty with understanding some of the instructions.

To my surprise, James was ready to continue on to the next test after only a short computer game break. He explained why this was so: "I put things together, like puzzles. I make cars and planes at my house." As long as I gave him small breaks on the computer, he was willing to tackle the material on the tests. Some of his spelling errors stood out immediately, such as *skr* for *square*, and *srke* for *circle*. When asked to write the sentence "he shouted a warning," he wrote "he shtd a woin." He read "see the black dog" as "see the black pond," and "she wants a ride to the store" as "she was rid of the store." He seemed to use a "best guess" strategy in tackling reading, based on the sounds that he knew: When asked to write the word *bigger*, he wrote just *her*. But I noticed that James's enthusiasm picked up a bit as he began telling stories from pictures he was shown, and he marveled at his own ability to rotate shapes on the computer to complete a picture. He left my office more animated and talkative than when he arrived, which showed how nice it must have felt for him to experience success. (Based on authors' case material.)

James, at age 9, had problems primarily in reading and spelling. Contrast his reading difficulties with those of Tim, who struggles with spatial orientation and mathematical reasoning.

TIM

Warming with Interest

When I first saw Tim, he seemed aloof and disinterested. His eyes stayed focused on the floor, and his body remained expressionless, as if to say, "Leave me alone, and let me outta here." As I searched for something to say, I asked Tim to tell me a little about his family: "Do you have any brothers or sisters? Does your family like to do anything special together?" His tired response, "I have two brothers, my father works all day, mom plays piano. We want a boat," sent me a clear message as to his mood and interest in this activity. My usual ploy of turning on the computer games fell flat—"I hate computers" was Tim's preemptive response. I wondered, "Is he depressed, angry, hurt, frustrated? Just what is going on here?"

Having looked at his school record, I knew he was struggling, especially in math and physical sciences, but his speech and affect expressed more than only academic problems. His school records flashed the news that Tim had a specific learning disorder, as evidenced by his WISC-IV performance score of 79 that fell in the borderline-to-low-average range, and his verbal score of 108 that fell in the average range. The test administrator had politely described Tim's test-taking approach as "reluctant." Notes by teachers indicated that he commonly had problems on tasks involving drawing, particularly if they required memory, and his math and social skills were far below those of others in his class.

I pulled out my *Where's Waldo?* book and we began looking at it together. In addition to being fun, looking for Waldo and his friends (small figures amidst millions of figures and colors) required Tim to be patient. At first he balked, but I noticed that he improved if he used his own verbally mediated strategy to solve the problem. Tim talked to himself as he thought aloud: "Look around the edges first, then start to look closer and closer to the middle of the page. Look for Waldo's red and white shirt—look closely at each section!" The more interested he was, the more he would talk. Once he warmed up, his smile appeared, along with his admission that "this sure beats math lesson." (Based on authors' case material.)

James's pattern of strengths and weaknesses shows that although he has reading problems, other strengths compensate for this disability. He has strong talents for figuring out how things work and for drawing ideas on paper. Tim has several strengths, too, especially in linguistic skills such as word recognition, sentence structure, and reading. In contrast to James, Tim has problems primarily in the visual, spatial, and organizational spheres, which show up as difficulties with tactile (touch) perception, psychomotor activity (e.g., throwing and catching), and nonverbal problem solving (e.g., figuring out math problems and assembling things).

Both boys fit the diagnostic criteria for SLD. Note how Tim's academic problems, in particular, were almost masked by his frustration and low self-esteem.

For children with specific learning disorders, following simple instructions can be confusing and frustrating.

Emotional problems are often seen in children who are bright enough to recognize that their performance is below that of others and are frustrated with their poor performance at school. The limitations of both James and Tim can affect every aspect of their formal education as well as their interpersonal abilities; therefore, these disorders require comprehensive and ongoing treatment plans.

To understand the nature of specific learning disorders, picture yourself asking for directions to a famous monument at an information booth in an unfamiliar town. The attendant hands you a map with written directions: "Go out the driveway and turn right. Go till you reach the second light, turn left, and look for the sign to Amityville. It's about 3 miles down the road. You'll pass a cemetery and a red schoolhouse, and go under a railroad trestle before you get to Highway 18. When you see the sign, turn right." Most of us would have trouble recalling these verbal directions, so having them written in the map makes them easier to follow. However, children or adults with an SLD in reading experience confusion in these common situations that involve understanding the meaning of what is read. Specific learning problems can be difficult to recognize because, for most of us, the material in question is straightforward and simple. The child may be blamed for not listening, not paying attention, or for being "slow," which further disguises the true nature of the learning problems.

The main diagnostic feature of SLD is that the child has difficulties learning keystone academic skills of reading, writing, spelling, or math (see Table 7.4). These difficulties may appear in one or more of these

TABLE 7.4 | Diagnostic Criteria for Specific Learning Disorder

(A) Difficulties learning and using academic skills, as indicated by the presence of at least one of the following symptoms that have persisted for at least six months, despite the provision of interventions that target those difficulties: **DSM-5**

   (1) Inaccurate or slow and effortful word reading (e.g., reads single words aloud incorrectly or slowly and hesitantly, frequently guesses words, has difficulty sounding out words).

   (2) Difficulty understanding the meaning of what is read (e.g., may read text accurately but not understand sequence, relationships, inferences, or deeper meanings of what is read).

   (3) Difficulties with spelling (e.g., may add, omit, or substitute vowels or consonants).

   (4) Difficulties with written expression (e.g., makes multiple grammatical or punctuation errors within sentences; employs poor paragraph organization; written expression of ideas lacks clarity).

   (5) Difficulties mastering number sense, number facts, or calculation (e.g., has poor understanding of numbers, their magnitude, and relationships; counts on fingers to add single-digit numbers instead of recalling the math fact as peers do; gets lost in the midst of arithmetic computation and may switch procedures).

   (6) Difficulties with mathematical reasoning (e.g., has severe difficulty applying mathematical concepts, facts, or procedures to solve quantitative problems).

(B) The affected academic skills are substantially and quantifiably below those expected for the individual's chronological age, and cause significant interference with academic or occupational performance, or with activities of daily living, as confirmed by individually administered standardized achievement measures and comprehensive clinical assessment. For individuals aged 17 years and older, a documented history of impairing learning difficulties may be substituted for the standardized assessment.

(C) The learning difficulties begin during school-age years but may not become fully manifest until the demands of those affected academic skills exceed the individuals limited capacities (e.g., as in timed tests, reading or writing lengthy complex reports for a tight deadline, excessively heavy academic loads).

(D) The learning difficulties are not better accounted for by intellectual disabilities, uncorrected visual or auditory acuity, other mental or neurological disorders, psychosocial adversity, lack of proficiency in the language of academic instruction, or inadequate educational instruction.

Note: The four diagnostic criteria are to be met based on a clinical synthesis of the individual's history (developmental, medical, family, educational), school reports, and psychoeducational assessment.

(continues)

TABLE 7.4 | **Diagnostic Criteria for** Specific Learning Disorder *(continued)*

Specify if:

With impairment in reading:

Word reading accuracy

Reading rate or fluency

Reading comprehension

With impairment in written expression:

Spelling accuracy

Grammar and punctuation accuracy

Clarity or organization of written expression

With impairment in mathematics:

Number sense

Memorization of arithmetic facts

Accurate or fluent calculation

Accurate math reasoning

Specify current severity:

Mild: Some difficulties learning skills in one or two academic domains, but of mild enough severity that the individual may be able to compensate or function well when provided with appropriate accommodations or support services, especially during the school years.

Moderate: Marked difficulties learning skills in one or more academic domains, so that the individual is unlikely to become proficient without some intervals of intensive and specialized teaching during the school years. Some accommodations or supportive services at least part of the day at school, in the workplace, or at home may be needed to complete activities accurately and efficiently.

Severe: Severe difficulties learning skills, affecting several academic domains, so that the individual is unlikely to learn these skills without ongoing intensive individualized and specialized teaching for most of the school years. Even with an array of appropriate accommodations or services at home, at school, or in the workplace, the individual may not be able to complete all activities efficiently.

Source: Diagnostic and Statistical Manual of Mental Disorders, 5th ed. American Psychiatric Association.

skills, including inaccurate or slow reading, difficulty understanding the meaning of what is read, difficulties with spelling and/or written expression, or difficulties mastering number sense, calculation, or mathematical reasoning. The affected academic skills would need to be substantially below what it should be for the child's age and intellectual ability. In practice, this often means that the child's achievement test scores in academic subjects are at least 1.5 standard deviations below average for their age and sex (which translates to a standard score of 78, or below the seventh percentile).

To be classified as a disorder, the performance problems must significantly interfere with academic achievement or daily living, and to persist for more than 6 months despite efforts to improve them. (Some children and adults have found ways to compensate for their learning problems and therefore do not display a disability, despite their test findings or poor achievement.) Finally, the learning difficulties appear during the school-age years, and cannot be better accounted for by a sensory problem (such as impaired hearing or sight), intellectual disability, psychosocial adversity, or inadequate educational instruction.

Because many aspects of speaking, listening, reading, writing, and arithmetic overlap and build on the same functions of the brain, it is not surprising that a child or adult can have more than one form of SLD (Scanlon, 2013). Recall that phonological awareness facilitates the ability to speak and, later on, to read and write. A single gap in the brain's functioning can disrupt many types of cognitive activity. These disruptions, in turn, can interfere with the development of important fundamental skills and compound the learning difficulties in a short time. Moreover, as we saw with both James and Tim, numerous secondary problems can emerge, such as temper outbursts and withdrawal from social situations, as a result of frustration and lack of success.

As noted earlier in this chapter, DSM-5 integrates the frequently co-occurring problems in reading, mathematics, and written expression into one category, and uses specifiers to designate all academic domains and subskills that are impaired. Table 7.4 also describes the degrees of severity (mild, moderate, or severe) associated with each impairment. Degrees of severity reflect both the extent of the child or adolescent's learning difficulties as well as the appropriate accommodations or supports he or she requires to learn the academic skill(s) and complete activities at school, work or home as efficiently as possible. Below we take a closer look at the three core academic skill impairments specified in SLD.

SLD with Impairment in Reading

He has only half learned the art of reading who has not added to it the more refined art of skipping and skimming.

—Arthur James Balfour

Children are naturally attracted to reading, and its importance in our society is unequaled by any other academic accomplishment. We are surrounded by written signs and messages and, by about age 5 or so, most children want to know what they mean. (Capitalizing on this natural curiosity, advertisers have become expert in pairing recognizable symbols with the names of their product or establishment so that children can "read" more quickly.) By the first grade, natural interest and developmental readiness are channeled into formally learning how to read. For many children, this process is difficult and tedious; for a sizable minority, however, it can be confusing and upsetting. The role of parents in this process is critical, because children need positive feedback and need to feel satisfied with their performance, regardless of their speed and accuracy.

When you consider everything involved in learning the basics of reading, such as associating shapes of letters (graphemes) with sounds (phonemes), it is not surprising that some children have difficulty and can quickly fall behind. Read the following sentence: "I believe that abnormal child psychology is one of the most fascinating and valuable courses I have taken." As you read the sentence, did you notice that you had to simultaneously:

▶ Focus attention on the printed marks and control your eye movements across the page?

▶ Recognize the sounds associated with letters?

▶ Understand words and grammar?

▶ Build ideas and images?

▶ Compare new ideas with what you already know?

▶ Store ideas in memory?

Most of us have forgotten all the effort that goes into reading, especially in the beginning. Not surprisingly, children's initial attempts are laborious and monotonous as they wrestle with the sounds and complexities of combined letters. Such mental processing requires a complex intact network of nerve cells that connect our vision, language, and memory centers (Grigorenko, 2007). A small problem in any area can cause reading difficulties. The most common underlying feature of a reading disorder, however, is an inability to distinguish or to separate the sounds in spoken words. Phonological skills are fundamental to learning to read, and therefore this deficit is critical.

To assess a child's need for additional practice in mastering phonemes and words, it is important to understand that there are two systems that operate when one reads words, which are essential in the development of reading. The first system operates on individual units (phonemes) and is relatively slow; the second system operates on whole words more quickly. In normal readers, whole words are learned through the development of phonologically based word analysis. However, persistently poor readers seem to rely on rote memory for recognizing words (S. E. Shaywitz & Shaywitz, 2013).

Many clinical signs of reading disorders are first evident only to a trained eye. Some testing methods developed by teachers and school psychologists show how children with reading disorders function in the classroom. They often have trouble learning basic sight words, especially those that are phonetically irregular and must be memorized, such as *the, who, what, where, was, laugh, said,* and so forth. These children have developed their own unique and peculiar reading patterns, which signal the need for different teaching methods. Typical errors include *reversals (b/d; p/q), transpositions* (sequential errors such as *was/saw, scared/sacred), inversions (m/w; u/n),* and *omissions* (reading *place* for *palace* or *section* for *selection*). However, these errors are common in many younger children who are just learning to read and write and do not necessarily imply a reading disorder.

To assess a child's need for additional practice in certain areas, teachers may log the types of errors the child makes while reading out loud. In addition to decoding words, reading comprehension is assessed by having the student retell a story or suggest the next episode. Average readers rely heavily on auditory and visual modalities for gathering new information, but children with reading disorders may prefer a mode of touch or manipulation to assist them in learning. These various patterns of strengths and weaknesses, if adequately assessed, can then be used to the child's advantage in planning additional teaching methods such as computer-based learning (S. E. Shaywitz et al., 2008).

A child with a SLD with impairment in reading lacks the critical language skills required for basic reading: word reading accuracy, reading comprehension, and reading rate or fluency. **Dyslexia** is an alternative term sometimes used to describe this pattern of reading difficulties. These core deficits stem from problems in **decoding**—breaking a word into parts rapidly enough to read the whole word—coupled with difficulty reading single small words (Vellutino et al., 2007). When a child cannot detect the phonological structure of language and automatically recognize simple words, reading development will very likely be impaired (Peterson & Pennington, 2010). The slow and labored decoding of single words requires substantial effort and detracts from the child's ability to retain the meaning of a sentence, much less a paragraph or page.

SLD with Impairment in Written Expression

CARLOS

Slowly Taking Shape

Carlos, age 7, was about to finish second grade when his teacher and parents met to discuss his handwriting problems. The year had gone well in general, but his parents were bracing for bad news. Smiling and pulling out some workbooks, Carlos's teacher lined up examples of how he had gradually become able to print some letters over the course of the year. But what his parents saw was self-explanatory: His shapes were very poor and looked more like those of his 3-year-old sister. Sensing both parents' apprehension, his teacher clarified: "Carlos is having a few problems in his fine motor coordination, in activities such as artwork, putting puzzles together, and similar tasks. He goes too fast when trying to do these tasks, and he forgets to be careful or to follow the pattern. He makes a half-hearted attempt on his writing assignments and then starts talking to his classmates. I'd like him to be seen by a psychologist for testing, and hopefully next fall his new teacher can strengthen his writing and fine motor skills with some additional exercises."

During the initial interview, Carlos took an immediate interest in my computer games, exclaiming how easy it was to use the mouse to draw figures. When asked to use a pencil and paper, however, Carlos balked. I asked him to copy by hand some of the figures he drew on the computer, after first printing them for him on paper. In doing so, he switched to his preferred hand in the middle of the task. He also showed several letter reversals (b/d; p/q), and pushed down very hard on the pencil in an attempt to trace or draw the figures. Throughout these tasks he talked freely and asked a lot of questions, making me wonder at times who was assessing whom.

Carlos showed evidence on neuropsychological testing of finger *agnosia* (he could not tell which finger I touched when his hand was behind his back), especially with his left hand. He also had considerable difficulty copying a triangle, a circle, and a square based on examples shown to him (see ● Figure 7.2). On the WISC-IV he obtained a performance score of 91, in the low-average range, and a verbal IQ score of 117, in the high-average range. On performance subtests he had particular problems with block design and puzzles, such as object assembly. He had more difficulty with verbal IQ subtests that involved concentration and attention, such as math and digit-span tasks. Throughout the testing, I found Carlos to be impulsive and sometimes quite defiant: If he didn't want to do something, he simply would not do it. These observations were consistent with his parents' frustration at his immature behavior and defiance at home.

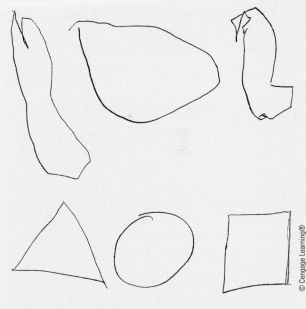

● **FIGURE 7.2** | *Top*: Drawings produced by Carlos when asked to copy a triangle, a circle, and a square. *Bottom*: Examples of a triangle, circle, and square from a typically developing 7-year-old boy.

(Based on authors' case material.)

Carlos has a specific learning disorder related to written expression. He has strong language and reasoning abilities, as well as normal problem-solving skills for his age, yet he is considerably weaker in his visual–motor abilities, as shown by his writing, figure copying, and figure rotation. Like reading and math, writing derives from several interconnected brain areas that produce vocabulary, grammar, hand movement, and memory.

SLD with impairment in written expression may manifest as problems in spelling accuracy, grammar and punctuation accuracy, and/or clarity or organization of written expression. This particular SLD is often found in combination with SLD in reading or mathematics, which also have underlying core deficits in language and neuropsychological development.

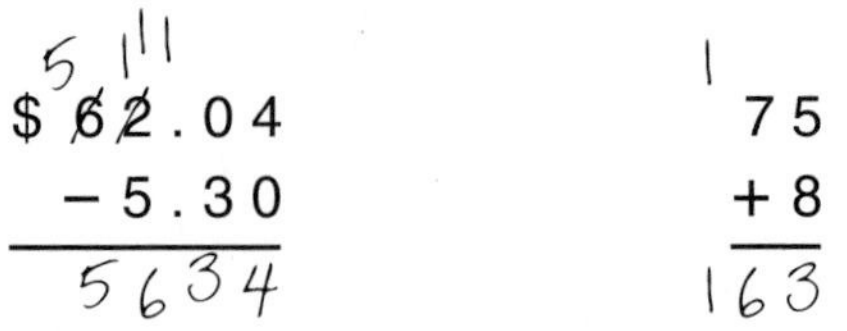

Children with impairment in written expression often have problems with tasks that require eye–hand coordination, despite their normal gross motor development. Teachers notice that, as compared with children who have normal writing skills, children with impairments in writing produce shorter, less interesting, and poorly organized essays and are less likely to review spelling, punctuation, and grammar to increase clarity (Hooper et al., 2011, 2013). However, spelling errors or poor handwriting that do not significantly interfere with daily activities or academic pursuits do not qualify a child for this diagnosis. In addition, problems in written expression signal the possibility of other learning problems because of shared metacognitive processes: planning, self-monitoring, self-evaluation, and self-modification (Heim & Benasich, 2006).

SLD with Impairment in Mathematics

During their preschool years, children are not as naturally drawn to mathematical concepts as they are to reading. This changes rapidly as they discover that they need to count and add to know how much money it takes to buy something or how many days remain until vacation. As in reading, the need to know propels children to learn new and difficult concepts, and little by little their new skills help them understand the world better.

For some children, like Francine and Tim, this curiosity about numbers is compromised by their inability to grasp the abstract concepts inherent in many forms of numerical and cognitive problem solving. Francine's difficulty with numbers and concepts began to show up well before she attended school, which is typically the case. When she encountered math concepts in second grade that required some abstract reasoning, she fell further and further behind.

The DSM-5 criteria for SLD with impairment in mathematics include difficulties in number sense, memorization of arithmetic facts, accurate or fluent calculation, and/or accurate math reasoning. *Dyscalculia* is an

● **FIGURE 7.3** | Errors in math computation by a 10-year-old girl with a mathematics disorder.

From "Learning Disabilities" by H.G. Taylor, 1988, p. 422. In E.J. Mash and L.G. Terdal (Eds.) "Behavioral Assessment of Childhood Disorders", 2nd ed.

alternative term sometimes used to describe this pattern of math difficulties. Many skills are involved in arithmetic: recognizing numbers and symbols, memorizing facts (the multiplication table), aligning numbers, and understanding abstract concepts such as place value and fractions. Any or all may be difficult for children with a mathematics disorder (Vukovic & Siegel, 2010). Children and adults with this disorder may have difficulty not only in math, but also in comprehending abstract concepts or in visual–spatial ability. Examples of calculation errors typical of children with a mathematics disorder are shown in ● Figure 7.3, an example that points out errors that suggest spatial difficulties and directional confusion.

Children with an SLD with impairment in mathematics typically have core deficits in arithmetic calculation and/or mathematics reasoning abilities, which include naming amounts or numbers; enumerating, comparing, and manipulating objects; reading and writing mathematical symbols; understanding concepts and performing calculations mentally; and performing computational operations (Andersson, 2010; Lyon et al., 2006). These deficits imply that the neuropsychological processes underlying mathematical reasoning and calculation are underdeveloped or impaired.

Prevalence and Course

Estimates of the prevalence of SLD across all three domains (reading, writing, and math) range from 5% to 15% among school-aged children (APA, 2013). Reasons for this large range focus on the notion that SLD in reading—the most common form—may be part of a continuum of reading abilities rather than a discrete, all-or-none phenomenon. Children with reading disorders are essentially those who fall at the lower end of the reading continuum (Snowling, 2008). This consideration of the range of ability is useful and important because, clearly, there are strong readers and weak readers, and no definitive cutoff point easily distinguishes the two. Estimates of the prevalence of SLD with impairment in mathematics or written expression are unclear due to the overlap among all three subtypes, although consensus is that they occur at a much lower rate than do reading difficulties (Landerl & Moll, 2010).

SLD impairments are considered lifelong, although the course varies based on severity and available supports. Recognition of SLD typically emerges during elementary school years, when a student falls significantly behind classmates in one or more of these subjects, though parents often note problems in language delays or counting in early childhood. Parents and teachers may notice specific delays in early skill development, or notice behavioral signs of the child's struggles, such as his or her unwillingness to learn to read, write, or work with numbers. In elementary school, the child shows marked difficulty in learning letter–sound correspondence and may commit reading errors by connecting sounds and letters (e.g., "big" for "got") and have difficulty sequencing numbers and letters (APA, 2013).

By the middle grades children with SLD may show poor reading comprehension and poor spelling and written work. They may be able to read and pronounce the first part of a word correctly but then guess the rest of the word. As they struggle with these difficulties throughout elementary school, being fearful of or refusing to read aloud is common. By adolescence through to adulthood, these patterns often shift from basic coding difficulties to marked problems in reading comprehension and written expression, including poor spelling and poor mathematical problem solving. Over time, teens and adults learn to manage these difficulties to the best of their ability, but may avoid situations that require reading, writing, or numerical ability. Thus, over the life span SLD is associated with many functional consequences, such as lower academic achievement, higher school dropout rates, poor overall mental health and well-being, and lower employment and income (APA, 2013).

Cultural, Class, and Gender Variations

Social and cultural factors are less relevant to SLD than other types of cognitive and behavioral problems; in fact, the diagnostic criteria state that they cannot be attributed to these factors. Nevertheless, some cultural and ethnic factors may affect how children with SLD are identified and treated (Johansson, 2006).

Many childhood disorders reflect an interaction between the child's inherent abilities and resources and the opportunities that exist in the child's local environment, as emphasized throughout this text. In the case of learning to read, some teaching approaches do not explicitly emphasize specific sound–symbol relationships that are inherent in the dialect of children from diverse ethnic backgrounds. For example, an interesting study by Wood et al. (1991) illustrated the point that deficits in phonological awareness occur more frequently among populations that use non-standard English. They followed a random sample of 485 Caucasian (55%) and African American (45%) children from first grade through third grade, and they found that although African American youngsters read at the same grade level as Caucasian children at the beginning of the first grade, they show marked declines in reading by the third grade and severe declines by the fifth grade. These findings suggest that greater attention to differences in dialect can lead to better learning opportunities.

Whereas attention to cultural and ethnic issues pertaining to SLD is a recent addition to research, sex differences have a long and contentious history. Boys are more often referred for learning difficulties than girls, perhaps because boys are more likely to show associated behavior problems such as aggression or inattention. Girls with learning problems often are quiet and withdrawn rather than loud and attention seeking, and they may be overlooked unless educators and parents are well informed. Nonetheless, when male–female ratios of SLD are derived from epidemiological estimates rather than from referrals, the ratio of boys to girls falls between 2:1 and 3:1 (APA, 2013).

Psychological and Social Adjustment

For many years, a diagnosis of learning disability or disorder required a discrepancy between IQ and performance, which hampered early identification because the assessment often was not done until the child had attempted and failed at reading, usually by the third grade. By that time, the child's achievement would be low enough to warrant a diagnosis, but the child had failed in reading for 2 to 3 years and may have developed other behavioral and emotional problems as a result.

Today's recognition of SLD as an early neurodevelopmental disorder is improving detection of children with difficulties, but they still face significant obstacles in their peer adjustment and academic progress. Children with SLD often do not know how or why they are different, but they do know how it feels to be unable to keep up with others in the classroom. Hearing themselves described as "slow," "different," or "behind," they may identify more with their disabilities rather than with their strengths. These daily experiences may cause some children to act out by either withdrawing or becoming angry and noncompliant. Like James, they may stop trying to learn. Like Francine, they may become isolated and limit their participation in activities that their peers enjoy.

Students with SLD with reading impairment feel less supported by their parents, teachers, and peers than do normal readers, and they are more likely to express poor academic or scholastic self-concepts (Heim & Benasich, 2006). Perhaps as a result of the interaction of their disorder and their environment, children and adolescents with SLD are more likely than their peers to show internalizing problems such as anxiety (Nelson & Harwood, 2011) and mood disorders (Maughan et al., 2003), as well as externalizing behaviors such as ADHD (Goldston et al., 2007). The range and types of problems are generally similar for both younger and older age groups. Accordingly, issues pertaining to both younger and older children and adolescents with SLD are considered jointly unless particular developmental differences warrant attention. Many of these issues are common to all domains of SLD unless otherwise noted.

The connection between SLD and behavioral or emotional disorders has generated considerable interest but only cautious conclusions. Common sense suggests that children with SLD encounter considerable challenges that are likely to take a toll on self-esteem and, in time, their social relationships. However, children's self-concepts in sports and appearance are usually less affected (Lyon et al., 2006).

Parents and teachers describe children with SLD as being more difficult to manage than typical children, beginning at an early age. Although overall reports of behavior problems increase considerably for all children between early and middle childhood, behavior problems among children with SLD are about three times higher than typically developing children by 8 years of age (i.e., 32% vs. 9%; Benasich, Curtiss, & Tallal, 1993) (see ● Figure 7.4). Most of these problems are not specific to SLD but cover a broad range of problems that overlap with features of conduct disorder (CD), oppositional defiant disorder (ODD), and attention-deficit/hyperactivity disorder (ADHD) across all ages (APA, 2013).

These co-occurring problems are often interpreted as individual reactions and coping styles in response to failure, frustration, and, in some instances, punishment and negative attention. However, in terms of development, it is hard to say which comes first: Behavior problems may precede, follow, or co-occur with learning problems (Hinshaw, 1992). Whereas many of these behavioral and emotional problems gradually decrease from childhood to adolescence, adolescents with SLD continue to face challenges in their social relationships (St Clair et al., 2011).

Based on a review of over 150 studies, Kavale and Forness (1996) found that about three of every four students with SLD have significant deficits in social skills. As a group, they are more isolated and less popular among peers than other children, and they tend to make negative impressions on others (Durkin & Conti-Ramsden, 2010). Like Francine, who was described by her mother as "humorless and in a bit of a fog," most children with SLD have difficulty grasping the nuances of social interaction and may not know how to greet others, make friends, or join in playground games. Subtle cues of social interaction may be missed or ignored. These children may not always interpret correctly or respond appropriately to the frequent nonverbal—but very expressive—communication of other children, such as rolling the eyes to show dislike or disinterest. When children with SLD misunderstand the situation and act inappropriately, other children turn away.

A child with SLD also can be an emotional burden for family members. Parents may experience a wide range of emotions, including denial, guilt, blame, frustration, anger, and despair. Brothers and sisters often feel annoyed, embarrassed, or jealous of the attention their sibling receives. Because behavioral problems are usually so disruptive, a child's distress and emotional needs may easily be overlooked.

Adult Outcomes

Unfortunately, the social and emotional difficulties connected to communication and learning disorders may continue into adulthood, largely because of inadequate recognition and services (Johnson et al., 2010). Adults may find ways to disguise their problems, such as watching television news rather than reading newspapers. On the other hand, many excel in nonacademic subjects such as art, music, dance, or athletics. Still others may become outstanding architects and engineers,

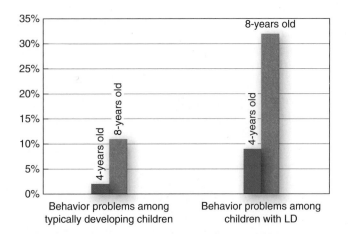

● **FIGURE 7.4** | Percentage of clinically significant behavior problems among children with and without learning disorders, at 4 years and 8 years of age.

Data from Benasich et al., 1993

or they may have extraordinary interpersonal skills (Lyon et al., 2006). Each child and adolescent has many strengths that can be developed to compensate for his or her known deficits. Thus, despite their earlier risk for academic failure and psychosocial problems, many adults with SLD lead successful and productive lives (Lovett & Lewandowski, in press).

Men with SLD with impairments in reading do not differ from their peers regarding feelings of global self-worth; symptoms of depression; feelings of competency and satisfaction with jobs, marriages, and other relationships; or frequency of antisocial behavior (Boetsch, Green, & Pennington, 1996). However, men still perceive lower levels of social support from parents and relatives—the only people still in their lives who knew of their problems as children—which confirms the indelible impressions left by early experiences.

One adult describes his own way of compensating for learning problems:

> I faked my way through school because I was very bright. I resent most that no one picked up my weaknesses. Essentially I judge myself on my failures. . . . [I] have always had low self-esteem. . . . A blow to my self-esteem when I was in school was that I could not write a poem or a story. . . . I could not write with a pen or pencil. The computer has changed my life. I do everything on my computer. It acts as my memory. I use it to structure my life and for all of my writing since my handwriting and written expression has always been so poor. (Polloway, Schewel, & Patton, 1992, p. 521)

Whereas the long-term outlook for men with SLD is generally positive, the troublesome issue of sexism arises when considering how adult women with SLD fare over time. As a group, women with SLD have more adjustment problems than men as they leave school and face the demands of adult life. Similar to other adults with disabilities, they also face greater risk of sexual assault and related forms of abuse (Brownlie et al., 2007). Problems and breakdowns in relationships are common, which may reflect the lack of opportunity available to these women to achieve in areas that capitalize on their strengths.

Reading problems often cause poorly qualified graduates to take relatively undemanding and unrewarding jobs. Women who lack competitive skills and strong career options because of school failure tend to get involved at an early age in intimate relationships that are generally unsupportive (Fairchild, 2002). Young men, in contrast, have more wide-ranging options once they leave school, which facilitates more positive social functioning in adulthood. Thus, if they are able to select their own environments in adulthood

Factors That Increase Resilience and Adaptation

Several personal characteristics and circumstances aid those with learning disorders in their successful adaptation from childhood, through adolescence, to young adulthood. As part of a longitudinal study of all children born in 1955 on the island of Kauai, Hawaii, E. E. Werner (1993) followed 22 children with learning disabilities and 22 matched controls. She found that most children with learning disabilities adapted successfully to adult life. Those who showed the greatest resilience and flexibility over time had: (1) a basic temperament that elicited positive responses from others; (2) a well-developed sense of efficacy, preparedness, and self-esteem that guided their lives; (3) competent caregivers and supportive adults; and (4) opportunities for a second chance if they made mistakes or got into trouble with the law. Although some of these characteristics are present from birth (e.g., temperament), many of the other supportive factors can be increased through the efforts of family members, schools, and communities. (Based on authors' case material.)

(and women have more obstacles in this regard than men), both men and women with SLD can build on their existing strengths, skills, and talents (Hatch, Harvey, & Maughan, 2010).

It is safe to say that even though aspects of SLD may remain, people who are given proper educational experiences have a remarkable ability to learn throughout their life spans (Gregg, 2011). A Closer Look 7.1 describes some of these important opportunities that increase resilience. Adults can learn to read, although it is difficult because brain development slows down after puberty. Current gains in knowledge of the causes and early signs of SLD are likely to have a positive impact on early recognition and proper instruction. Nonintrusive electrophysiological measurements of brain reactivity may permit an early diagnosis based on underlying deficits in phonological processing rather than on performance alone. Thus, early identification and intervention may be the key to preventing the long-term consequences of these disorders (S. E. Shaywitz & Shaywitz, 2013).

Causes

Most learning disorders do not stem from problems in a single area of the brain, but from difficulties in bringing information from various brain regions together so that information can be integrated and understood

(Damasio et al., 2004; Meyer & Damasio, 2009). Minute disturbances may underlie phonological processing deficits. Emerging evidence suggests that in many cases these subtle disturbances begin very early during development, perhaps prenatally (McGrath et al., 2007; Raschle, Chang, & Gaab, 2011).

Recent findings suggest two distinguishable types of children with reading disorders—children who are persistently poor readers and those who are accuracy-improved (i.e., they learn ways to compensate for their reading difficulties and improve over time) (S. E. Shaywitz, Mody, & Shaywitz, 2006). Persistently poor readers and accuracy-improved readers have comparable reading skills and socioeconomic status when they begin school, but by the time they are young adults, the accuracy-improved readers show better cognitive ability. The presence of compensatory factors, such as stronger cognitive ability, may allow the accuracy-improved individuals to minimize the consequences of their phonological defect over time (Ferrer et al., 2010). These compensatory factors may be genetically based, and thus the child's ability improves with maturity, whereas the persistently poor readers may face greater environmental challenges, often associated with poverty and inequality, that reduce reading opportunities.

Genetic and Constitutional Factors

Children who lack some of the skills needed for reading, such as hearing the separate sounds of words, are more likely to have a parent with a related problem. Around the turn of the twentieth century this problem was studied largely by physicians, who considered reading disorders to be an inherited condition called *congenital word blindness* (W. P. Morgan, 1896). Today, estimates based on behavioral genetic studies indicate that heritability accounts for over 60% of the variance in reading disorders (V. M. Bishop, 2006; Plomin et al., 2010), although the exact mode of transmission remains undetermined.

Most attention paid to heritability is aimed at genetic transmission of critical brain processes underlying phonetic processing (Scerri & Schulte-Körne, 2010; Vellutino et al., 2004). Because a parent's learning disorder may take a slightly different form in the child—the father may have a writing disorder and his child an expressive language disorder—it seems unlikely that subtypes of specific learning disorders are inherited directly. More likely, what is inherited is a subtle brain dysfunction that, in turn, can lead to a learning disorder (Newbury et al., 2011; Richlan et al., 2011; Scerri & Schulte-Körne, 2010). For example, on chromosome 6 an area has been identified that predisposes children to reading disorders (Grigorenko, 2007). Genetic

transmission provides a plausible explanation for the relative risk of SLD in reading or mathematics being 4 to 8 times and 5 to 10 times higher, respectively, in first-degree relatives of persons with SLD as compared to those without it (APA, 2013; Shalev, 2007). Keep in mind that environmental factors also play a role in moderating genetic influences on SLD outcomes (i.e., gene–environment interaction; Petrill, 2013).

Neurobiological Factors

Our understanding of learning disorders, particularly reading-based and language-based problems, took an important new direction in the mid-1980s with the discovery that the brains of people with these problems were characterized by cellular abnormalities in the left hemisphere, which contains important language centers (Galaburda et al., 1985). The fact that these cellular abnormalities could occur only during the fifth to seventh months of fetal development strengthened the view that learning disorders evolve from subtle brain deficits present at birth (Lyon et al., 2003). Initial autopsy findings were confirmed by sophisticated brain imaging technology that reveals the brain directly at work and makes it possible to detect subtle malfunctions that never could be seen before.

The suspected deficits, which likely are genetically based, involve specific discrimination tasks, such as detecting visual and auditory stimuli, as well as more pervasive visual–organizational deficits associated with reasoning and mathematical ability (Benassi et al., 2010; Pennington, 2006). A probable location of these deficits is a structure called the "planum temporale," a language-related area in both sides of the brain. In a normal brain, the left side of the planum temporale is usually larger than the right side; however, in the brain of an individual with a reading disorder, the two sides are equal (Tallal, 2003).

B. A. Shaywitz et al. (2002) found lower activation in numerous sites—primarily the left hemisphere of the brains of dyslexic children as compared with nonimpaired children—including the inferior frontal, parietotemporal, and occipitotemporal gyri. These three areas of the brain are responsible for understanding phonemes, analyzing words, and automatically detecting words, respectively. Once a word is learned, this three-part center recognizes it automatically, without first having to decipher it phonetically (S. E. Shaywitz & Shaywitz, 2013).

From a cognitive standpoint, these neurological findings suggest that children with learning disorders are distinctively disadvantaged as compared with average readers in terms of the processing underlying their short-term and working memory. Impairments in short-term memory affect the recall of phonemes

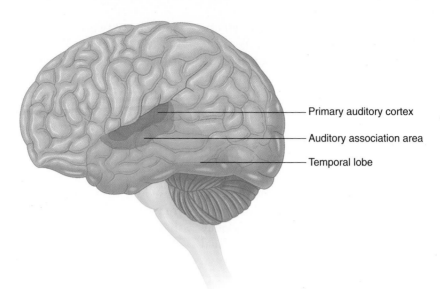

Primary auditory cortex

Auditory association area

Temporal lobe

How the brain processes speech

1 The primary auditory cortex (shown in red), which is located on the top edge of each temporal lobe, receives electrical signals from receptors in the ears and transforms these signals into meaningless sound sensations, such as vowels and the consonants in *ba* and *ga*.

2 The meaningless sound sensations are sent from the primary auditory cortex to another area in the temporal lobe, called the auditory association area.

3 The auditory association area (shown in blue), which is located directly below the primary auditory cortex, transforms basic sensory information, such as noises or sounds, into recognizable auditory information, such as words or music. Here, sounds are matched with existing patterns that have been previously formed and stored.

● **FIGURE 7.5** | How the brain processes speech.

From Plotnik/Kouyoumdjian. *Introduction to Psychology,* 9E. © 2011 Wadsworth, a part of Cengage Learning, Inc. Reproduced by permission. www.cengage.com/permissions.

and numbers; similarly, impairments in working memory affect how such information is processed and stored so that it can be rapidly accessed. Considerable support now exists concerning how memory deficits explain the performance difficulties of children with a learning disorder (Carretti et al., 2009; Maehler & Schuchardt, 2011; Swanson, Zheng, & Jerman, 2009).

We have stressed that most children with reading and writing disorders have difficulty distinguishing phonemes that occur rapidly in speech. But why is this so? Consider what is involved, as shown in ● Figure 7.5. The sound must be processed by various brain areas as it is carried by nerve impulses from the ear to the thalamus to the nerve cells within the auditory cortex, where it is matched to existing patterns, or phonic bins, that have been previously formed and stored.

Compare this process to listening to music. When you first hear a new song, do you recognize aspects that resemble other recordings by that group or another group? Can you distinguish the music of one group from another? As we listen, we tend to cluster sounds into various categories, acquiring our taste for music as we store more collections and melodies into memory. Each time we hear new music, we match it to what we already know and appreciate. Young people are particularly adept at assimilating new sounds, thereby broadening their tastes. In contrast, people who have already formed specific musical tastes tend to stick to what they know, rejecting unrecognizable sounds. This gap in music appreciation is analogous to the gap researchers describe in the phonic abilities of children with learning disorders—they lack certain auditory sites that allow certain sounds to be recognized, so their appreciation of certain words is compromised.

Each neuron in the language-processing areas of the brain has immense specificity. Some neurons fire when you silently name an object but not when you read the object's name out loud, and vice versa. Certain neurons are activated when bilingual people speak one language, but not when they speak the other (Ojemann, 1991). Someone can have an expressive language problem despite full comprehension, because the same neurons that are active when a person hears a word are not active when that person speaks it.

In the visual system, different aspects of what you see, such as form, color, and motion, are routed to different regions of the visual cortex. When something moves in your visual field, the region of the cortex that responds to visual motion is activated. Eden et al. (1996) first discovered that adults with reading disorders show no activation in visual motion when asked to view randomly moving dots. A specific defect in the perception of visual motion may interfere with many different brain functions, and it has been noted among children with autism as well as those with learning disorders (Benassi et al., 2010; Skottun & Skoyles, 2008). To detect differences between consonant sounds—such as *b* and *t*—we must be able to distinguish between very rapid changes in sound frequency. A subtle neurological deficit in sensitivity could prohibit this distinction, which would then show up clinically as problems in reading and phonological processing (Raschle et al., 2011).

Thus, two major findings implicate specific biological underpinnings of reading disorders: (1) language difficulties for people with reading disorders are specifically associated with the neurological processing of phonology and storage of such information into memory; and (2) behavioral and physiological abnormalities are found in the processing of visual information. It is not surprising, therefore, that phonological and visual processing problems often coexist among people with reading disorders (Skottun & Skoyles, 2008).

Studies of the causes of SLD mostly involve children with reading disorders, but the findings apply to disorders in written expression and mathematics as well. Many—but not all—disabled writers show deficits in reading (Lyon et al., 2003), and some mathematical concepts require reading and writing as well as mathematics skills. Similar to how deficits in phonological awareness underlie SLD with reading impairment, certain cognitive deficits involving concepts of numbers appear to underlie SLD with impairment in mathematics (Geary, 2013). For instance, if you show small sets of dots, usually up to four dots per set, to typically developing children they can tell you instantly (i.e., without counting the items) how many items are in each set, a process known as *subitizing*. But children with SLD with impairments in mathematics appear to have trouble subitizing even three items, suggesting a deficit in their rapid visual processing of enumeration concepts (Ashkenazi, Mark-Zigdon, & Henik, 2013). Similarly, most children can

quickly say which of two numbers is larger (e.g., "13" vs. "31"), but students with mathematics disorder are slower and less accurate than their peers at doing so (Rousselle & Noël, 2007).

Recall that Francine had well-developed word recognition and spelling abilities, but significantly worse mechanical–arithmetic skills. SLD with impairment in mathematics, and perhaps SLD with impairment in written expression as well, are associated with brain deficits that differ from those described for language-based learning disorders. These deficits are largely found in areas not related to verbal ability, which has led to the term nonverbal learning disability. **Nonverbal learning disability (NLD)** is associated with deficits related to right-hemisphere brain functioning, which are characteristic of children who perform considerably worse at math than reading. These deficits involve social/emotional skills, spatial orientation, problem solving, and the recognition of nonverbal cues such as body language (Hulme & Snowling, 2009). In addition to math deficiencies, NLD may be accompanied by neuropsychological problems such as poor coordination, poor judgment, and difficulties adapting to novel and complex situations (Lyon et al., 2003; Semrud-Clikeman et al., 2010). To date, the unique aspects of NLD remain unconfirmed. Critics argue that it may simply be a form of SLD with impairment in mathematics (Fine et al., 2013; Spreen, 2011).

Social and Psychological Factors

Emotional and behavioral disturbances and other signs of poor adaptive ability often accompany SLD. This is no surprise, because children with one neurodevelopmental disorder (i.e., communication disorder, SLD, ADHD, or intellectual disability) are about 40% more likely to have another neurodevelopmental disorder, most likely because of shared etiological factors (Gooch et al., 2013). The overlap between SLD with impairment in reading and ADHD, for example, ranges from 30% to 70% depending on how ADHD is defined (Del'Homme et al., 2007; Fletcher, Shaywitz, & Shaywitz, 1999). Although this degree of overlap suggests that behavioral and learning problems have certain common aspects, they are still distinct and separate disorders (Lyon et al., 2006). SLD is commonly associated with deficits in phonological awareness, whereas ADHD has more variable effects on cognitive functioning, especially in areas of rote verbal learning and memory (Jakobson & Kikas, 2007). ADHD, moreover, is relatively unrelated to phonological awareness tasks. However, some children with SLD show symptoms similar to those of ADHD, including inattention, restlessness, and hyperactivity (Del'Homme et al., 2007).

Prevention and Treatment

What can be expected of Francine, James, Tim, and Carlos during their school years and beyond? Proper planning and goal setting are the cornerstones of the helping strategies for home and for school. Specific learning disorders are not usually outgrown, but there is reason for optimism if educational planning and accommodations are ongoing (Beitchman & Brownlie, 2014).

Although SLD has strong biological underpinnings, intervention methods rely primarily on educational and psychosocial methods. Psychosocial treatments for James, Francine, Carlos, and Tim must be comprehensive and ongoing, with each new task broken down into manageable steps, including examples, practice, and ample feedback. Combined with proper teaching strategies, children and their families may benefit from counseling aimed at helping the children develop greater self-control and a more positive attitude toward their own abilities. Support groups for parents also can fill an important gap between the school and the home by providing information, practical suggestions, and mutual understanding.

Someday, breakthroughs in brain research may lead to new medical interventions, but at present no biological treatments exist for speech, language, and academic disabilities. In cases in which significant problems coexist in concentration and attention, some children respond favorably to stimulant medications that may temporarily improve attention, concentration, and the ability to control their impulsivity, albeit with little or no improvement in learning. Typically, the medication schedule ensures that the drug is active during peak school hours, when reading and math are taught.

Francine's problems in making friends were a major concern to everyone, and we believed that they were directly linked to her learning disability. A cognitive–behavioral intervention plan was developed in conjunction with her educational program. Because of Francine's strong verbal skills, we taught her to problem solve through role playing, and encouraged her mother to invite one child at a time for her to play with so that she could practice her skills. Francine had drifted into being a loner and seemed disinterested in looking after herself, so we also discussed ways to develop better self-care at home by giving her an allowance for completing household chores. We spent considerable time explaining the nature of her problems to her parents, and this guidance led to relief and understanding.

We saw the family once again one year later; although some of Francine's problems still existed, her social abilities had improved. She still had difficulties in developing friendships and tended to prefer being alone, but the problem had clearly lessened from the previous year. (Based on authors' case material.)

Consider the coordinated planning and effort that went into the treatment programs for Francine: Francine was able to get help because her problems were detected; recall, however, that by the time she was referred, she had already begun to fail at formal schooling. The first step in solving any problem is to realize that it exists. The nature of learning disorders makes this difficult for many children and parents. Although numerous signs of language-based learning disorders are present from early childhood, sophisticated means of assessing problems are not yet available before children are old enough to be formally tested.

FRANCINE

Slowly but Surely Improving

To reduce Francine's difficulties with math and, especially, with peer relationships, we considered several factors. First, we decided that teaching should be primarily verbal, with an understanding that she would have the most difficulty in math and science. Her teachers favored allowing Francine to use a calculator and a computer to assist her in learning new concepts. An emphasis on physical education was also planned, to help her with her visual–motor coordination. Her math teacher agreed that using graph paper might help her visualize numerical relationships, which led to noticeable improvements in her schoolwork.

Treatment of specific learning disabilities usually begins with a careful assessment of a child's abilities.

Issues of identification are important because a brief window of opportunity may exist for successful treatment. If a problem is detected in early childhood—say, by kindergarten—then language-based deficits can often be remediated successfully. If the problem is not detected until age 8 or so, the rates of response to treatment are much lower (Hatcher et al., 2006). This is why prevention of reading difficulties is a hot topic: Training children in phonological awareness activities at an early age may prevent subsequent reading problems among children at risk (Duff & Clarke, 2011; Snowling & Hulme, 2012). These activities involve games of listening, rhyming, identifying sentences and words, and analyzing syllables and phonemes. For example, the child might analyze *sand* as *s-and* and then synthesize it into *sand,* or colored alphabet blocks might be used to break the word into separate phonetic sounds (*s-a-n-d*).

Knowledge of communication and learning disorders has played leapfrog with the philosophy and practice of classroom instruction during the past decade. Discoveries in neurosciences, as noted above, challenged some prevailing educational practices, leading to more systematic ways of assisting children with learning disorders, as explored in the following sections.

The Inclusion Movement

Integrating children with special needs into the regular classroom began as the *inclusion movement* during the 1950s, based on studies showing that segregated classes for students with disabilities were ineffective and possibly harmful (Baldwin, 1958). Resource rooms and specially trained teachers replaced the special classes that had been in vogue, a change that had the further advantage of removing the need to label and categorize children. The Education for All Handicapped Children Act of 1975 in the United States (currently known as Individuals with Disabilities Education Improvement Act [IDEA], 2004) and the provincial Education Acts in Canada mandate that children with special needs must be afforded access to all educational services, regardless of their handicaps. Today, children with special educational needs in the United States, Canada, and many other countries are placed in regular classrooms whenever possible.

In 2002, the No Child Left Behind Act was signed into law in the United States. This act allowed for more intensified efforts by each state to improve the academic achievement of public school students considered at risk for school failure. Today, almost 14% (about 6.6 million) of school-age children in the United States from all walks of life receive some level of support through special education, and students with specific learning disabilities account for close to half of these students (National Center for Educational Statistics (2012).

Response to Intervention Models

IDEA provides for the use of response to intervention (RTI) models to identify and assess children. RTI consists of tiered instruction, in which children who have difficulty learning to read using typical methods of instruction are provided with small-group, intensive instruction. Those who need additional intervention may receive one-on-one special education. This approach seeks to provide each child with the appropriate level of instruction required for his or her individual needs (National Institutes of Health, 2007).

Initiatives to allow children with special needs to receive services without being diagnosed or labeled as intellectually disabled, learning disabled, and so forth have become widely available and hold considerable promise. However, implementation and teacher training, as well as the question of whether such initiatives succeed in meeting the special needs of students, continue to be unresolved (Lovett & Lewandowski, in 2014).

Instructional Methods

Although controversy remains over the practical aspects of including all children in regular classrooms, most educators today favor direct instruction for children with learning disorders. **Direct instruction** is a straightforward approach to teaching based on the premise that to improve a skill, the instructional activities must approximate those of the skill being taught (see example in A Closer Look 7.2) (Hammill et al., 2002). Direct instruction in word structure is necessary because of the child's phonological deficits. Direct instruction in reading emphasizes the specific learning of word structure and word reading until the skill is learned, without concern for the full context of the sentence or story. This method is based on the premise that a child's ability to decode and recognize

---

A CLOSER LOOK 7.2

Steps in Direct Behavioral Instruction

1. Review the child's existing abilities.
2. Develop a short statement of goals at the beginning of each lesson.
3. Present new concepts and material in small steps, each followed by student practice.
4. Provide clear and detailed instructions and explanations.
5. Provide considerable practice for all students.

6. Check student understanding of concepts continually, in response to teacher questions.

7. Provide explicit guidance for each student during initial practice.

8. Provide systematic feedback and corrections.

9. Provide explicit instruction and practice for exercises completed by students at their desks.

Source: From Treatment of Learning Disabilities by G. R. Lyons and L. Cutting, 1998. In E. J. Mash and L. C. Terdal (Eds.), Treatment of Childhood Disorders.

The following example illustrates how the steps in direct behavioral instruction are applied.

Example: Direct Instruction Lesson

A typical DI lesson includes explicit and carefully sequenced instruction provided by the teacher (model) along with frequent opportunities for students to practice their skills (independent practice) over time (review). For example, if the sound /m/ appeared for the first time, the teacher might say, "You're going to learn a new sound. My turn to say it. When I move under the letter, I'll say the sound. I'll keep on saying it as long as I touch under it. Get ready. mmm" (model). "My turn again. Get ready. mmm" (model). "Your turn. When I move under the letter, you say the sound. Keep on saying it as long as I touch under it. Get ready." (independent practice). "Again. Get ready." (independent practice). If an error occurs during instruction, the teacher would model the sound ("My turn. mmm"), use guided practice ("Say it with me. Get ready. mmm"), and have students practice independently ("Your turn. Get ready"). A "starting over" would be conducted based on this error; this might include starting over at the top of a column or row of sounds so that students get increased practice on the /m/ sound. The /m/ would appear throughout the lesson and in subsequent lessons to ensure skill mastery (firm responding) over time.

Source: Marchand-Martella, Martella, & Ausdemore (2005). An Overview of Direct Instruction.

words accurately and rapidly must be acquired before reading comprehension can occur (Hammill et al., 2002; Haager, Klinger, & Vaughn, 2007).

To prevent dyslexia, it is important to provide early interventions that teach both phonological and verbal abilities. Children must be able to learn the sounds of words to decode them, but they must also understand the meaning of a word to understand the message of the text (S. E. Shaywitz & Shaywitz, 2013). The techniques that have been demonstrated to work are practicing manipulating phonemes, building vocabulary, increasing comprehension, and improving fluency, which helps strengthen the brain's ability to link letters to sounds (Nation et al., 2007).

In brief, the components of effective reading instruction are the same whether the focus is prevention or intervention—phonemic awareness and phonemic decoding skills, fluency in word recognition, construction

of meaning, vocabulary, spelling, and writing (Snowling & Hulme, 2012). Evidence-based evaluations show dramatic reductions in the incidence of reading failure when direct and explicit instruction in these components is provided by the classroom teacher (Duff & Clarke, 2011; Haager et al., 2007; Schuele & Boudreau, 2008). Empirical support for teaching phonics from an early age also is emerging from brain imaging studies. For example, instruction in phonemic awareness, phonics, and other reading skills produces more activation in the automatic recognition process, noted previously (see section on "Causes," above). After undergoing such training, brain scans of people who were once poor readers begin to resemble those of good readers (National Institutes of Health, 2007).

We now turn to some practical examples of how reading, writing, and math can be taught by applying well-established principles of learning. Behavioral and cognitive–behavioral strategies have been highly beneficial in remediating the problems of children and adolescents with communication and learning disorders (Lyon et al., 2006). In addition, new methods based on the use of technology offer some children additional ways to acquire basic and advanced academic skills.

Behavioral Strategies

Many problems that children with communication and learning disorders have stem from the fact that the material is simply presented too fast for them (Tallal & Benasich, 2002). Thus, a strategy to provide children with a set of verbal rules that can be written out and re-applied may be more beneficial than one that relies on memory or on grasping the concept all at once. Tried-and-true behavioral principles of learning are well suited to this task of teaching systematically.

In addition to academic concepts, some of the associated problems with peers can be addressed in the same fashion, as we saw with Francine. A simple, gradual approach is more beneficial than an approach that tries to solve the problem all at once. Children also need help learning to generalize new information to different situations. An individualized, skills-based approach does not have to be boring or routine; in fact, speech and language therapists are skilled at providing a stimulating but structured environment for hearing and practicing language patterns. During an engaging activity with a younger child, the therapist may talk about toys and then encourage the child to use the same sounds or words. The child may watch the therapist make the sound, feel the vibration in the therapist's throat, and then practice making the sounds himself or herself in front of a mirror.

Behavioral methods often are used in conjunction with a complete program of direct instruction, which typically proceeds in a cumulative, highly structured manner (Wright & Jacobs, 2003), as shown in A Closer Look 7.2. Because this method places a strong emphasis on the behavior of the teacher in terms of explicit correction, reinforcement, and practice opportunities, it is sometimes referred to as "faultless instruction": Each concept should be so clearly presented that only one interpretation is possible. Each lesson is structured according to field-tested scripts. Teachers work with one small group of students at a time, and shoot questions at them at a rate as high as 10 to 12 per minute.

This highly structured, repetitive method is clearly effective. Students who receive direct behavioral instruction typically outperform students who receive standard classroom instruction by almost 1 standard deviation on various learning measures (Lyon et al., 2003).

Cognitive–Behavioral Interventions

Cognitive–behavioral interventions are also highly suited for children with communication and learning disorders. Like behavioral methods, these procedures actively involve students in learning, particularly in monitoring their own thought processes. Considerable emphasis is placed on self-control by using strategies such as self-monitoring, self-assessment, self-recording, self-management of reinforcement, and so on (Alwell & Cobb, 2009; Cobb et al., 2006). Essentially, children are taught to ask themselves several questions as they progress, to make themselves more aware of the material. Try it yourself: "Why am I reading this? What's the main idea the authors are trying to get across? Where can I find the answer to this question? How does this follow from what I learned a minute ago?"

Carlos's treatment program shows how some of these procedures were applied to his particular writing problems:

CARLOS

Plans

In third grade, Carlos's treatment plan was to integrate a cognitive–behavioral approach into regular teaching methods. Rather than using one-to-one instruction, I discussed with his teacher ways of blending some behavioral methods into the classroom. For example, his strengths are in the areas of thinking and speaking, so I discussed using computers and tape recorders to help him learn the materials. He seemed to like these

methods, and they helped him bypass some aspects of his writing disability. I discussed practice strategies for visual–motor integration, such as drawing and tracing and gradually made the task more complex. Because cursive writing is often easier for children than printing, I suggested that Carlos bypass learning to print. A continuous pattern of output is easier for Carlos to plan and produce than a discrete form of output, such as printing.

To help Carlos write a paper, I adopted a basic planning strategy from Graham, MacArthur, Schwatz, and Voth (1992), which helped him structure the tasks into related subproblems. The acronym PLANS helps him to remember to:

Pick goals (related to length, structure, and purpose of the paper)
List ways to meet goals
And
make Notes
Sequence notes

This mnemonic was used in a three-step writing strategy to assist Carlos to: (1) do PLANS, (2) write and say more, and (3) evaluate whether he is successful in achieving his goals. (Based on authors' case material.)

Computer-Assisted Learning

Studies have shown that a similar level of efficacy in phonetic ability can be achieved by teachers as by clinicians (Duff & Clarke, 2011), which has led to a growing number of computer and Internet training programs. One problem in reading instruction is maintaining a balance between the basic, but dull, word decoding and the complex, but engaging, text comprehension. Not all the issues have been resolved, but computer-assisted methods for spelling, reading, and math provide more academic engagement and achievement than traditional pencil-and-paper methods.

Computers have been used as simple instructional tools to deliver questions and answers since the 1970s. Since discovering phonological awareness and timing problems in the brain, researchers are now testing whether computers can remedy some basic auditory problems. Some children with communication and learning disorders are unable to process information that flashes by too quickly, such as the consonant sounds *ba* and *da*, and this deficit interferes with vital speech processes. Computer programs are able to slow down these grammatical sounds, allowing young children to process them more slowly and carefully (Loo et al., 2010; Gaab et al., 2007; Palmer, Enderby, & Hawley, 2007).

New research raises cautious hope that computer games and exercises can help children with learning disabilities develop key mental skills.

to ensure competency. As they progress, they should practice more and more reading that is contextualized. Reading materials should have controlled vocabularies that contain mostly words the children can decode. As children develop a core sight vocabulary, introduce only those irregular words that can be read with high accuracy. Guessing is counterproductive.

5. *Teach for automaticity*. Once basic decoding is mastered, children must be exposed to words often enough that they become automatically accessible. This usually requires a great deal of practice, which should be as pleasant and rewarding as possible.

Source: From Rebecca H. Felton, Effects of Instruction on the Decoding Skills of Children with Phonological-Processing Problems, Journal of Learning Disabilities, 26, 583–589

Whether taught by computers, teachers, or both, studies of interventions for learning disorders indicate that successful approaches typically include explicit instruction in phonemic awareness and phonemic decoding. These interventions also provide students with practice reading text and comprehending what they read, with ample assistance and almost daily sessions (Torgesen et al., 2010).

In summary, treatment methods for communication and learning disorders are varied and beneficial. A Closer Look 7.3 reviews some of the basic elements of a successful beginning reading program, elements that apply to other disabilities as well. For children with reading disorders to learn how to read, they must receive a balanced intervention program composed of direct and explicit instruction in phonemic awareness, a systematic way to generalize this learning to the learning of sound–symbol relationships (phonics), and many opportunities to practice these coding skills by reading meaningful, interesting, and controlled texts. The sooner this intervention occurs in schools, the better (Haager et al., 2007).

A CLOSER **LOOK** 7.3

Critical Elements for a Successful Beginning Reading Program

1. *Provide direct instruction in language analysis.* Identify at-risk children early in their school careers—preferably in kindergarten—and teach phonological awareness skills directly.

2. *Provide direct teaching of the alphabetic code.* Code instruction should be structured and systematic, in a sequence that goes from simple to more complex. Teach the regularities of the English language before introducing the irregularities. Nothing should be left to guesswork—be as explicit as possible. Teach a child who is overly reliant on letter-by-letter decoding to process larger and larger chunks of words.

3. *Teach reading and spelling in coordination.* Children should learn to spell the words they are reading correctly.

4. *Provide intensive reading instruction.* Children may need 3 or more years of direct instruction in basic reading skills

Section Summary

Specific Learning Disorder

- Specific learning disorder (SLD) includes problems in reading, mathematics, or writing ability, with reading disorders being the most common. Mathematics and writing disorders overlap considerably with reading disorders.

- Although SLD overlaps with behavioral disorders, they are distinct problems. Opportunities to develop and use particular strengths lead to more successful adult outcomes.

- SLD in reading may be caused by phonological problems that arise from physiological abnormalities in the processing of visual information in the brain. These deficits are believed to be largely inherited.

- Treatments for children with communication and learning disorders involve educational strategies that capitalize on existing strengths, and behavioral strategies involving direct instruction.

- Cognitive–behavioral techniques and computer-assisted instruction are also used successfully.

DESCRIPTION AND HISTORY

WE BEGIN OUR DISCUSSION of attention-deficit/hyperactivity disorder (ADHD) with a description of the primary symptoms and behaviors of children with this disorder. We then consider the different views of ADHD that have been presented since it was first described as a disorder more than 200 years ago.

JOHN

Inattentive, Hyperactive, Impulsive

John is a 7-year-old whose mother is desperate for help. "He walked at 10 months and has kept me running ever since. As a child he was always bouncing around the house and crashing into things. He's in constant motion, impulsive, and never listens. When I ask him to put his shirt in the hamper, I find him playing, his shirt still on the floor. John has no routines and seldom sleeps. Discipline doesn't work, nor do the techniques that work for my other boys. He's oblivious to his behavior. He never finishes anything, and except for sitting down to play a video game, rarely watches TV except on the run."

John's teacher says his main problems in school are staying on task and keeping track of what's happening. "He blurts things out in class and is constantly fidgeting or out of his chair," she says. Although John can complete his assignments, he forgets to bring home the book he needs to do his homework. When he does complete his homework, he forgets to put it in his backpack or to hand it in. John has great difficulty waiting his turn or following rules with other children. Other kids think he's weird and don't want to play with him. John's parents are demoralized and don't know what to do.

From *The Hyperactive Child Book*, by Patricia Kennedy, Leif Terdal, and Lydia Fusetti, pp. 8–9. New York: St. Martin's Press.

Fidgety Phil, 1845, and Dusty N., 1994: Mealtimes are an especially trying time for children with ADHD and their parents

Description

Attention-deficit/hyperactivity disorder (ADHD) describes children who, like John, display persistent age-inappropriate symptoms of inattention, hyperactivity, and impulsivity that are sufficient to cause impairment in major life activities (APA, 2013).

The term *ADHD* may be new, but children who display overactive and unrestrained behaviors have been around for some time. In 1845, Heinrich Hoffmann, a German neurologist, wrote in a child's storybook one of the first known accounts of hyperactivity. His humorous poem described the mealtime antics of a child aptly named "Fidgety Phil," who "won't sit still; / He wriggles, / And jiggles," and "swings backwards and forwards, / And tilts up his chair." When his chair falls, Philip screams and grabs the tablecloth, and "Down upon the ground they fall, / Glasses, plates, knives, forks, and all" (Hoffmann, 1845).

More recently, a compelling article about ADHD titled "Life in Overdrive" described the behavior of 7-year old Dusty N.:

Dusty awoke at 5:00 one recent morning in his Chicago home. Every muscle in his 50-pound body flew in furious motion as he headed downstairs for breakfast. After pulling a box of cereal from the cupboard, Dusty started grabbing cereal with his hands and kicking the box, scattering the cereal across the room. Next he began peeling the decorative paper covering off the TV table. Then he started stomping the spilled cereal to bits. After dismantling the plastic dustpan he had gotten to clean up the cereal, he moved on to his next project: grabbing three rolls of toilet paper from the bathroom and unraveling them around the house. (Adapted from *Time*, July 18, 1994, p. 43)

Although the accounts of Phil and Dusty N. are separated by almost 150 years, the mealtime behaviors of both boys typify the primary symptoms of ADHD. The boys are **inattentive**, not focusing on mealtime demands and behaving carelessly; **hyperactive**, constantly in motion; and **impulsive**, acting without thinking.

ADHD has no distinct physical symptoms that can be seen in an x-ray or a lab test. It can only be identified by characteristic behaviors that vary considerably from child to child. As we shall discuss, ADHD has become a blanket term used to describe several different patterns of behavior that likely have different causes.

The behavior of children with ADHD is puzzling and full of contradictions. Rash and disorganized behaviors are a constant source of stress for the child and for parents, siblings, teachers, and classmates. Why can't he sit still? Why can't she ever get anything done? Why does he make so many careless mistakes? Nothing seems physically wrong with the child, and at certain times or in some situations the child with ADHD seems fine. Such inconsistencies may cause others to think the child could do better if only she tried harder or if her parents or teachers would set firmer limits. However, increased effort and stricter rules usually don't help, because most children with ADHD are already trying hard. They want to do well but are constantly thwarted by their limited self-control. As a result, they experience the hurt, confusion, and sadness of being blamed for not paying attention or being called names like "space cadet." They may be scolded, put down, or even spanked for failing to complete homework or chores. Unfortunately, they may not know why things went wrong or how they might have done things differently.

Feelings of frustration, being different, not fitting in, and hopelessness may overwhelm a child with ADHD (Young et al., 2008). For example, David says: "I got no friends cause I don't play good and when they call me Dope Freak and David Dopey I cry, I just can't help it" (Ross & Ross, 1982). Such comments leave little doubt that ADHD can severely disrupt an individual's life, consume vast amounts of energy, produce emotional pain, damage self-esteem, and seriously disrupt relationships. In addition to the individual's personal suffering and exposure to stigmatizing attitudes by others (Lebowitz, 2013), the societal costs of ADHD in youth are also high, with an estimated cost of $38 billion to $72 billion a year in the United States, the highest costs related to health care and education. Estimated costs for adults with

ADHD, which take productivity and income losses into account, are nearly two to three times higher than for young people. These estimates, along with the additional billions in spillover costs borne by family members of individuals with ADHD, indicate that the economic impact of ADHD across the lifespan for individuals with ADHD in the United States is considerable (Doshi et al., 2012).

History

The symptoms of ADHD were first described in a 1775 medical textbook by the German physician, Melchior Adam Weikard (Barkley & Peters, 2012). Since then there have been numerous explanations for the troublesome behaviors of ADHD (Barkley, 2014e). In 1798, a Scottish-born physician, Sir Alexander Crichton described a syndrome similar to ADHD that included early onset, restlessness, inattention, and poor school performance. These individuals described themselves as having "the fidgets," and displayed a severe problem attending no matter how hard they tried (Palmer & Finger, 2001). Symptoms of overactivity and inattention were described as a disorder in 1902 by the English physician George Still (what a coincidence!), who believed that the symptoms arose out of poor "inhibitory volition" and "defective moral control" (see ● Figure 8.1). In the early 1900s, the onset of widespread compulsory education demanded self-controlled behavior in a group setting, which further focused attention on children with the symptoms of ADHD.

Another view of ADHD arose from the worldwide influenza epidemic from 1917 to 1926. A number of children who had developed encephalitis (brain inflammation) and survived experienced multiple behavior problems, including irritability, impaired attention, and hyperactivity. These children and others who had suffered birth trauma, head injury, or exposure to toxins displayed behavior problems that were labeled *brain-injured child syndrome*, which was associated with intellectual disability. In the 1940s and 1950s, this label was then erroneously applied to children displaying similar behaviors, but with no evidence of brain damage or intellectual disability, and led to the terms *minimal brain damage* and *minimal brain dysfunction (MBD)* (Strauss & Lehtinen, 1947). These terms provided a convenient way to attribute behavior problems to a physical cause. Although certain head injuries can explain some cases of ADHD, the brain damage theory was eventually rejected because it did not explain the majority of cases (Rie, 1980).

In the late 1950s, ADHD was referred to as *hyperkinesis*, which was attributed to poor filtering of stimuli

THE LANCET, APRIL 19, 1902.

𝕿𝖍𝖊 𝕲𝖔𝖚𝖑𝖘𝖙𝖔𝖓𝖎𝖆𝖓 𝕷𝖊𝖈𝖙𝖚𝖗𝖊𝖘

ON

SOME ABNORMAL PSYCHICAL CONDITIONS IN CHILDREN.

Delivered before the Royal College of Physicians of London on March 4th, 6th, and 11th, 1902,

BY GEORGE F. STILL, M.A., M.D. CANTAB., F.R.C.P. LOND.,

ASSISTANT PHYSICIAN FOR DISEASES OF CHILDREN, KING'S COLLEGE HOSPITAL; ASSISTANT PHYSICIAN TO THE HOSPITAL FOR SICK CHILDREN, GREAT ORMOND-STREET.

LECTURE II.

Delivered on March 6th.

MR. PRESIDENT AND GENTLEMEN,—In my first lecture I drew your attention to some points in the psychology and development of moral control in the normal child and then considered the occurrence of defective moral control in association with general impairment of intellect; before going further it may be well to review briefly the points which have been raised. Moral control, we saw, is dependent upon three psychical factors, a cognitive relation to environment, moral consciousness, and volition, which in this connexion might be regarded as inhibitory volition. Moral control, therefore, is not present at birth, but under normal psychical conditions is gradually developed as the child grows older. The variation in the degree of moral control which is shown by different children at the same age and under apparently similar conditions of training and environment suggested that the innate capacity for the development of such control might also vary in different individuals.

Courtesy of The Lancet, April 19, 1902.

● **FIGURE 8.1** | English physician George Still was one of the first to describe the symptoms of ADHD.

entering the brain (Laufer, Denhoff, & Solomons, 1957). This view led to the definition of the *hyperactive child syndrome*, in which motor overactivity was considered the main feature of ADHD (Chess, 1960). However, it was soon realized that hyperactivity was not the only problem; there was also the child's failure to regulate motor activity in relation to situational demands.

In the 1970s, it was argued that in addition to hyperactivity, deficits in attention and impulse control were also primary symptoms of ADHD (Douglas, 1972). This view was widely accepted and has had a lasting impact on the criteria of the *Diagnostic and Statistical Manual of Mental Disorders* (DSM) for defining ADHD. In the 1980s, interest in children with ADHD increased dramatically, and the sharp rise in the use of stimulants generated controversy

that continues to this day (Mayes & Rafalovich, 2007).

More recently, in addition to inattention and hyperactivity–impulsivity, the problems of poor self-regulation, difficulty in inhibiting behavior, and reward and motivational deficits have been emphasized as central impairments of the disorder (Nigg, Hinshaw, & Huang-Pollack, 2006). Increasingly, "multipathway models" have emerged that include both attention-related and motivation-related theories. These models propose different pathways to ADHD with different neural substrates, meaning that different children with ADHD may have different reasons for their behavior (Nigg & Barkley, 2014). Although there is growing agreement about the nature of ADHD, views continue to evolve as a result of new findings and discoveries. As you will learn, despite the label for this disorder, the main difficulties in ADHD are far more complex than simply a deficit in attention (Nigg & Barkley, 2014).

Section Summary

Description and History

- Attention-deficit/hyperactivity disorder (ADHD) is manifested in children who display persistent age-inappropriate symptoms of inattention, hyperactivity, and impulsivity that cause impairment in major life activities.

- ADHD can only be identified by characteristic patterns of behavior, which vary quite a bit from child to child.

- The behavior of children with ADHD is a constant source of stress and frustration for the child and for parents, siblings, teachers, and classmates; it also has high costs to society.

- The disorder that we now call ADHD has had many different names, primary symptoms, and presumed causes, and views of the disorder are still evolving.

CORE CHARACTERISTICS

ADHD is included in DSM-5 as a *neurodevelopmental disorder* because it has an early onset and persistent course, is associated with lasting alterations in neural development, and is often accompanied by subtle delays and problems in language, motor, and social development that overlap with other neurodevelopmental disorders such as autism spectrum disorder (ASD) and specific learning disorder (APA, 2013). Experts developed the DSM-5 criteria for ADHD after reviewing research, re-analyzing data, conducting field trials with children throughout North America, and receiving several rounds of public feedback (APA, 2013). Table 8.1

TABLE 8.1 | Diagnostic Criteria for Attention-Deficit/Hyperactivity Disorder

(A) A persistent pattern of inattention and/or hyperactivity-impulsivity that interferes with functioning or development, as characterized by (1) and/or (2):

DSM-5

(1) Inattention: Six (or more) of the following symptoms have persisted for at least 6 months to a degree that is inconsistent with developmental level and that negatively impacts directly on social and academic/occupational activities:

Note: The symptoms are not solely the manifestation of oppositional behavior, defiance, hostility, or failure to understand tasks or instructions. For older adolescents and adults (age 17 and older), at least five symptoms are required.

(a) Often fails to give close attention to details or makes careless mistakes in schoolwork, at work, or during other activities (e.g., overlooks of misses details, work is inaccurate).

(b) Often has difficulty sustaining attention in tasks or play activities (e.g., has difficulty remaining focused during lectures, conversations, or lengthy reading).

(c) Often does not seem to listen when spoken to directly (e.g., mind seems elsewhere, even in the absence of any obvious distraction).

(d) Often does not follow through on instructions and fails to finish schoolwork, chores, or duties in the workplace (e.g., starts tasks but quickly loses focus and is easily sidetracked).

(e) Often has difficulty organizing tasks and activities (e.g., difficulty managing sequential tasks: difficulty keeping materials and belongings in order; messy, disorganized work; has poor time management; fails to meet deadlines).

(f) Often avoids, dislikes, or is reluctant to engage in tasks that require sustained mental effort (e.g., schoolwork or homework; for older adolescents and adults, preparing reports, completing forms, reviewing lengthy papers).

(g) Often loses things necessary for tasks or activities (e.g., school materials, pencils, books, tools, wallets, keys, paperwork, eyeglasses, mobile telephones).

(h) Is often easily distracted by extraneous stimuli (for older adolescents and adults, may include unrelated thoughts).

(i) Is often forgetful in daily activities (e.g., doing chores, running errands; for older adolescents and adults, returning calls, paying bills, keeping appointments).

(2) Hyperactivity and Impulsivity: Six (or more) of the following symptoms have persisted for at least 6 months to a degree that is inconsistent with developmental level and that negatively impacts directly on social and academic/occupational activities:

Note: The symptoms are not solely a manifestation of oppositional behavior, defiance, hostility, or a failure to understand tasks or instructions. For older adolescents and adults (age 17 or older), at least five symptoms are required.

(a) Often fidgets with or taps hands or feet or squirms in seat.

(b) Often leaves seat in situations when remaining seated is expected (e.g., leaves his or her place in the classroom, in the office or other workplace, or in other situations that require remaining in place).

(c) Often runs about or climbs in situations where it is inappropriate

Note: In adolescents or adults, may be limited to feeling restless.

(d) Often unable to play or engage in leisure activities quietly.

(e) Is often "on the go," acting as if "driven by a motor" (e.g., is unable to be or is uncomfortable being still for extended time, as in restaurants, meetings; may be seen by others as being restless or difficult to keep up with).

(f) Often talks excessively.

(g) Often blurts out answers before a question has been completed (e.g., completes people's sentences; cannot wait for a turn in conversation).

(h) Often has difficulty waiting his or her turn (e.g., while waiting in line).

(i) Often interrupts or intrudes on others (e.g., butts into conversations, games or activities; may start using other people's things without asking or receiving permission; for adolescents and adults, may intrude into or take over what others are doing).

(B) Several inattentive or hyperactive–impulsive symptoms were present before age 12 years.

(C) Several inattentive or hyperactive-impulse symptoms are present in two or more settings (e.g., at home, school, or work; with friends or relatives; in other activities).

(D) There must be clear evidence that the symptoms interfere with, or reduce the quality of, social academic, or occupational functioning.

(E) The symptoms do not occur exclusively during the course of schizophrenia or another psychotic disorder and are not better explained by another mental disorder (e.g., mood disorder, anxiety disorder, dissociative disorder, personality disorder, substance intoxication or withdrawal).

(continues)

TABLE 8.1 | **Diagnostic Criteria for Attention-Deficit/Hyperactivity Disorder** (*continued*)

Specify whether:

Combined presentation: If both Criterion A1 (inattention) and Criterion A2 (hyperactivity–impulsivity) are met for the past 6 months.

Predominantly inattentive presentation: If Criterion A1 (inattention) is met but Criterion A2 (hyperactivity–impulsivity) is not met for the past 6 months.

Predominantly hyperactive–impulsive presentation: if Criterion A2 (hyperactivity–impulsivity) is met but Criterion A1 (inattention) is not met for the past 6 months.

Specify if:

In partial remission: When full criteria were previously met, fewer than the full criteria have been met for the past 6 months, and the symptoms still result in impairment in social, academic, or occupational functioning.

Specify current severity:

Mild: Few, if any, symptoms in excess of those required to make the diagnosis are present, and symptoms result in no more than minor impairments in social or occupational functioning.

Moderate: Symptoms or functional impairment between "mild" and "severe" are present.

Severe: Many symptoms in excess of those required to make the diagnosis, or several symptoms that are particularly severe, are present, or the symptoms result in marked impairment in social or occupational functioning.

Source: Diagnostic and Statistical Manual of Mental Disorders, Fifth Edition. American Psychiatric Association.

shows the two lists of key symptoms that were identified for defining ADHD and distinguishing it from related problems. The first list includes symptoms of *inattention*; the second list includes symptoms of *hyperactivity–impulsivity*.

Quantitative studies support a model of ADHD consisting of a unitary ADHD component with two separable specific dimensions of inattention and hyperactivity–impulsivity (Burns et al., 2013). These two dimensions are well documented in research with thousands of individuals across various age, ethnic, and cultural groups throughout the world (Toplak et al., 2012). The two dimensions are highly correlated but they do predict different behavioral and cognitive impairments and likely have different neural correlates (Kuntsi et al., 2013; Willcutt et al., 2012). For example, symptoms of inattention tend to predict academic problems and peer neglect, whereas those of hyperactivity–impulsivity tend to predict aggressive behavior and peer rejection, among other problems.

To define the two core dimensions of ADHD as inattention and hyperactivity–impulsivity oversimplifies the disorder. First, each dimension includes many distinct processes that have been defined and measured in various ways. Second, although we discuss attention and impulse control separately, the two are closely connected developmentally—attention helps the child regulate behavior, emotions, and impulses (Nigg et al., 2006).

Inattention

LISA

Just Can't Focus

At age 17, Lisa struggles to pay attention and act appropriately. But this has always been hard for her. She still gets embarrassed thinking about the time that her parents took her to a restaurant to celebrate her 10th birthday. She was so distracted by the waitress's bright red hair that her father had to call her name three times before she remembered to order. Then, before she could stop herself, she blurted, "Your hair dye looks awful!"

In school, Lisa was quiet and cooperative but often seemed to be daydreaming. She was smart, yet couldn't improve her grades no matter how hard she tried.

Several times she failed exams. She knew the answers, but couldn't keep her mind on the test. Her parents responded to her low grades by taking away privileges and scolding her, "You're just lazy, Lisa. You could get better grades if you only tried."

Lisa found it agonizing to do homework. Often, she forgot to plan ahead by writing down the assignment or bringing home the right books. And when trying to work, every few minutes she found her mind drifting to something else. As a result, she rarely finished and her work was full of errors. One day, after Lisa had failed yet another exam, her teacher found her sobbing, "What's wrong with me?"

Adapted from National Institute of Mental Health [NIMH], 1994a.

Inattention refers to an inability to sustain attention or stick to tasks or play activities, to remember and follow through on instructions or rules, and to resist distractions. It also involves difficulties in planning and organization and in timeliness and problems in staying alert (Nigg & Barkley, 2014). Children who are inattentive find it difficult, during work or play, to focus on one task. While playing soccer, as the rest of the team heads downfield with the ball, the child with ADHD may get sidetracked by playing in a mud puddle. The child may attend automatically to enjoyable things, but have great difficulty focusing on less enjoyable tasks. Common complaints about inattention are that the child doesn't or won't listen, follow instructions, or finish chores or assignments. Since inattention can result from a failure in one or more cognitive processes that control attention (Petersen & Posner, 2012), it is not sufficient to say that a child has an attention deficit. The child could have a deficit in only one type or in more than one type.

Attentional capacity is the amount of information we can remember and attend to for a short time. When someone gives you directions or a phone number, how much information can you attend to and remember briefly? Children with ADHD do not have a deficit in their attentional capacity. They can remember the same amount of information for a short time as do other children (Taylor, 1995).

Selective attention is the ability to concentrate on relevant stimuli and ignore task-irrelevant stimuli in the environment. When you're studying for a test (relevant stimuli), how easily are you distracted by voices in another room?

Distractibility is a term commonly used to indicate a deficit in selective attention. Distractions can be disruptive to all children, including those with ADHD. However, children with ADHD are much more likely than others to be distracted by stimuli that are *highly salient and appealing* (Milich & Lorch, 1994).

Sustained attention, or *vigilance*, is the ability to maintain a persistent focus over time on unchallenging, uninteresting tasks or activities or when fatigued (Langner & Eickhoff, 2013). When you're tired and have to study for a test, can you still pay attention until you've reviewed all the required material? A primary attention deficit in ADHD seems to be sustained attention. When children with ADHD are assigned an uninteresting or repetitive task, their performance is poor as compared with that of other children. Although no one

likes to work on uninteresting tasks, most of us will when we have to. Children with ADHD may not be able to persist at such tasks even when they want to. They work best on self-paced tasks that they themselves have chosen—playing a computer game or building a model airplane—and on tasks they find especially interesting that do not require sustained attention. Most tasks, though, require sustained attention for successful performance, and many tasks are not particularly interesting.

Deficits in sustained attention are one of the core features of ADHD. However, children with ADHD may show performance deficits from the very beginning of a task or response, not just a decline over time. This suggests that their attentional problems may also be in alerting and preparing for the task from the outset, and not only in sustaining attention during the task. **Alerting** refers to an initial reaction to a stimulus; it involves the ability to prepare for what is about to happen. It helps the child achieve and maintain an optimally alert attentional state. A child with an alerting deficit (such as the lack of alertness you may experience when you are very tired) may respond too quickly in situations requiring a slow and careful approach and too slowly in situations requiring a quick response. This pattern of responding is often seen in children with ADHD. Thus, one view is that the deficit in sustaining attention may be partly related to the difficulty in alerting (Mullane et al., 2011).

"I need you to line up by attention span."

may perceive their relationships with their parents, teachers, or peers no differently than do control children, even though their parents, teachers, or peers see things in a more negative light (Gerdes, Hoza, & Pelham, 2003; Normand et al., 2013). This exaggeration of one's competence is referred to as a **positive bias**. Positive bias can occur in relation to social competence, where it may be particularly problematic, or in other areas such as academic performance or behavioral conduct (Hoza et al., 2012). Some findings suggest that self-esteem in children with ADHD may vary with the type of ADHD presentation, the accompanying disorders, and the area of performance being assessed (e.g., conduct, scholastic achievement). Children with ADHD who display inattentive and depressive/anxious symptoms tend to report lower self-esteem, whereas those with symptoms of hyperactivity–impulsivity and conduct problems appear to exaggerate their self-worth (Owens et al., 2007). The bias in the latter group is most dramatic in the areas of performance in which the child is most severely impaired. Increases in positively biased self-perceptions of behavior in children with ADHD have also been found to predict greater aggression over time (Hoza et al., 2010). In general, research has found that children with ADHD and a positive social or behavioral bias are more likely to display persistent social impairments and more negative behaviors than those with ADHD without this bias (McQuade & Hoza, 2014).

Several explanations for the positive bias in children with hyperactivity–impulsivity have been proposed—it serves a self-protective function that allows the child to cope every day despite frequent failures; it reflects a diminished self-awareness as a result of impairments in executive functions (McQuade et al., 2011); or it is a result of not knowing what constitutes successful or unsuccessful performance (Ohan & Johnston, 2002). To date, there is some support for the self-protective function of positive bias (Hoza et al., 2010), although other explanations may also apply.

Children with ADHD also display distortions in their perceptions of **quality of life**, which refers to a person's subjective perception of their position in life as evidenced by their physical, psychological, and social functioning. According to parents, the impact of their child's ADHD on the child's quality of life is substantial, particularly when the child has co-existing emotional and conduct problems (Schei et al., 2013). However, despite experiencing many life difficulties, children with ADHD rate their own quality of life more positively than others rate it (Danckaerts et al., 2010).

Speech and Language Impairments

About 30% to 60% of children with ADHD also have impairments in their speech and language (Helland et al., 2012). Interestingly, the type of speech and language impairment may be related to the child's specific ADHD symptoms. For example, one study with preschoolers found that symptoms of hyperactivity–impulsivity were related to poor language skills, whereas those of inattention were more highly correlated with weaker receptive and expressive vocabulary skills (Gremillion & Martel, 2013). In addition to showing a higher prevalence of formal speech and language disorders (see Chapter 7), children with ADHD may have difficulty in understanding others' speech and in using appropriate language in everyday situations (McInnes et al., 2003; Wassenberg et al., 2010). The pragmatic aspects of speech, along with impaired verbal working memory and discourse analysis, are primary difficulties (Bellani et al., 2011). Impairment in pragmatic language skills has been related to these children's social difficulties, and may, in part account for these difficulties (Staikova et al., 2013). Excessive and loud talking, frequent shifts and interruptions in conversation, inability to listen, and inappropriate conversation are a few common examples of impairments.

Children with ADHD not only ramble on, but also their conversation is characterized by speech production errors, fewer pronouns and conjunctions, tangential and unrelated comments, abandoned utterances, and unclear links (Mathers, 2006; McGrath et al., 2008). Can you understand the following statement by a boy with ADHD?

> And all of a sudden the soldiers—and all of a sudden he gets faint and you know when he says "Good doctors, I want to talk with you" and all of a sudden he goes in the door and inside they come off it from the thing. So he puts—I think this something on the doorknob. (Tannock et al., 1995)

When speech is unclear, as in this example, it is difficult for the listener to understand who and what the child is talking about. Unfortunately, miscommunication is all too common in children with ADHD.

Medical and Physical Concerns

In addition to the difficulties we have discussed, children and adolescents with ADHD also experience a number of medical and physical concerns, including having health-related problems, being accident-prone, and demonstrating risk-taking behaviors (Barkley, 2014d; Nigg, 2013).

Health-Related Problems

In terms of specific problems, some studies have reported higher rates of enuresis and encopresis (Shreeram et al., 2009) and asthma (Fasmer et al., 2011). One prospective study found that asthma in early life increased the risk of developing ADHD during the school years (Chen et al., 2013). Other health concerns for which individuals with ADHD are at elevated risk include dental health problems, poor fitness, obesity, and eating problems and disorders (in females) (Barkley, 2014d). Sleep disturbances are also common in children with ADHD (Cortese et al., 2009, 2013; Owens et al., 2013). Resistance to going to bed, difficulty in falling asleep, fewer total hours asleep, and involuntary sleep movements such as teeth grinding or restless sleep may be the most significant disturbances (Spruyt & Gozal, 2011). Some of the sleep problems in children with ADHD may be related to their use of stimulant medications, and/or co-occurring conduct or anxiety disorders, rather than to only their ADHD (Mick, Biederman et al., 2000).

Accident-Proneness and Risk Taking

Given their problems with impulsivity, motor inhibition, and lack of planning and forethought, it is not surprising that over 50% of parents of children with ADHD describe their child as accident-prone. These children are about three times more likely to experience serious accidental injuries, such as broken bones, lacerations, severe bruises, burns, poisonings, or head injuries (Barkley, 2014d). Young adult drivers with ADHD are at higher risk than others for traffic accidents, and deviant peer associations may play an important role (Cardoos, Loya, & Hinshaw, 2013; Cox, Madaan, & Cox, 2011).

ADHD is a significant risk factor for the early initiation of cigarette smoking, substance-use disorders, Internet- and videogame-use problems and addictions, and risky sexual behaviors such as multiple partners and unprotected sex (Barkley, 2014d; Lee et al., 2011). Substance-use disorders among young people with ADHD are also more frequent, severe, and persistent than substance-use disorders in those without ADHD (Charach et al., 2011). There are a number of possible reasons that ADHD may lead to substance-use problems, a notable one being co-occurring or later conduct problems (Wilens, 2011). Overall, these findings suggest a progression of hyperactive–impulsive behaviors during childhood to a pattern of irresponsible and risky adolescent and adult behavior.

In support of this, a prospective 33-year follow-up study of 8-year-old boys with ADHD but without conduct disorder found that as adults they had relatively more risky driving behaviors, sexually transmitted diseases, head injuries, and emergency department admissions than a comparison group and that lifetime risk-taking was related to negative health outcomes and more deaths not related to specific medical conditions. Importantly, the relationship between ADHD and risk taking was accounted for by the later development of Conduct Disorder (CD)/Antisocial Personality Disorder (APD). Over their lifetime, individuals with ADHD who did not develop CD/APD did not differ from the comparison group in risk-taking behaviors (Ramos Olazagasti et al., 2013).

Impulsive behavior is the most significant childhood characteristic that predicts reduced life expectancy (an average of 8 years less), according to a longitudinal study spanning over a half century (Friedman et al., 1995). A reduced life expectancy for individuals with ADHD may also be predicted by a pattern of accident-proneness, auto accidents, and risk taking, combined with a reduced concern for health-promoting behaviors, such as exercise, proper diet, safe sex, and moderate use of tobacco, alcohol, and caffeine, especially for those with co-occurring CD/APD symptoms (Barkley, 2014d).

The need for further research into health-related problems in children and adolescents with ADHD is accentuated by findings that show they have significantly higher rates of inpatient and outpatient hospitalizations and emergency department visits. Average medical costs for children with ADHD are more than double the costs for those without ADHD (Le et al., 2013; Leibson et al., 2001) and at least comparable to the costs for children with asthma (Chan, Zhan, & Homer, 2002). The multitude of health and related problems and costs indicate that "ADHD is more than just a serious mental health problem—it is a serious *public health* problem" (Barkley, 2014d).

Social Problems

DENNIS

Nothing Sticks

With my other children, I could tell them one time, "Don't do that," and they would stop. But Dennis, my child with ADHD, I could tell him a hundred times, "Dennis, don't carve soap with my potato peeler," "Don't paint the house with used motor oil," or "Don't walk on Grandma's white sofa in your muddy shoes," but he still does it. It's like every day is a brand new day and yesterday's rules are long forgotten. … I just cannot stay one step ahead of him. He does things my other kids never thought of.

From *The Hyperactive Child Book*, by Patricia Kennedy, Leif Terdal, and Lydia Fusetti, pp. 8–9. New York: St. Martin's Press.

Social problems in family life and at school are common in children with ADHD (Johnston & Chronis-Tuscano, 2014; McQuade & Hoza, 2014). Those who experience the most severe social disability are at greatest risk for poor adolescent outcomes and other disorders, such as depression and conduct disorder (Greene et al., 1996). Children with ADHD don't listen

Infancy

ALAN

Off and Running

Our baby-sitter swears I was sitting up watching TV by 4 months. Then from a crawling position I ran, and we were off. ... I was all over the house, into everything, and Mom soon realized I could not be left alone. Darting here, there, and anywhere, I didn't like playing with my toys, preferring to explore on my own.

From R. A. Barkley and L. J. Pfiffner, "Off to School on the Right Foot: Managing Your Child's Education. In: Barkley, R. A. Taking Charge of ADHD: The Complete, Authorized Guide for Parents, 1995, p. 208.

It is likely that signs of ADHD are present at birth (one mother reported her child was so overactive in the womb that the kicking nearly knocked her over!). Home-based activity-level assessments in the home—using motion detectors—are related to mothers' ratings of ADHD symptoms in children as young as 2 years of age (Ilott et al., 2010). Similarly, when parents of an older child with ADHD describe what their child was like as a baby, they often say their baby had a difficult temperament—extremely active, unpredictable, oversensitive or undersensitive to stimulation, and irritable with erratic sleep patterns or feeding difficulties. Early markers of ADHD symptoms may be present in infancy and toddlerhood, but reliable identification of ADHD is difficult prior to age 3 (Arnett, MacDonald, & Pennington, 2013). In addition, there are issues with these reports that suggest the early presence of ADHD. First, parents' recollections may be colored by their child's later difficulties. Second, most infants with a difficult temperament do not develop ADHD. Although a difficult temperament in infancy may indicate something amiss in development—and in some cases may be a risk factor for later ADHD—it cannot by itself be taken as an early sign of ADHD. For example, one study reported an association between persistent crying during infancy and a 10-fold higher risk for hyperactivity at 8 to 10 years of age (Wolke, Rizzo, & Woods, 2002). However, most infants who cry persistently do not go on to develop ADHD.

Preschool

ALAN

Preschool Outcast

I often wondered why I wasn't in group-time in preschool. The teacher sent me in the corner to play with a toy by

myself. Because of being singled out I didn't have many friends. I was different, but I didn't know why or what it was.

From R. A. Barkley and L. J. Pfiffner, "Off to School on the Right Foot: Managing Your Child's Education. In: Barkley, R. A. Taking Charge of ADHD: The Complete, Authorized Guide for Parents, 1995, p. 208.

With the growing number of hyperactive–impulsive symptoms at 3 to 4 years of age, ADHD becomes an increasingly visible and significant problem (Greenhill et al., 2008). Preschoolers with ADHD act suddenly and without thinking, dashing from activity to activity, grabbing at immediate rewards; they are easily bored and react strongly and negatively to routine activities (Campbell, 2006). Parents find it very difficult to manage the hyperactivity and noncompliance of their child, who may also be defiant and aggressive. Preschoolers with ADHD often roam about the classroom or daycare, talking excessively and disrupting other children's activities. Those who display a persistent pattern of hyperactive–impulsive and oppositional behavior for at least 1 year are likely to continue on to difficulties into middle childhood and adolescence (Olson et al., 2000). Difficulties in resisting temptation, delaying gratification, and inhibiting behavior during the preschool years have also been found to predict ADHD symptoms in third grade (Campbell & von Stauffenberg, 2009). At this age, the combination of severe ADHD-related symptoms and disruptions in the parent–child relationship is especially predictive of continuing ADHD behavior patterns (Campbell, Shaw, & Gilliom, 2000).

Elementary School

ALAN

I Couldn't Do Anything Right

Toward the middle half of first grade, the teacher called my Mom in for a conference. She was telling my Mom, "I'm always having to call on Alan. 'Alan, be still. Please. Yes, you can sharpen your pencil for the third time. You have to go to the bathroom again?'" By the time I got to third grade things were getting off track. I felt like nothing I did was right. I would try to do good work. My teacher would write on my papers, "Needs to concentrate more on answers," "Needs to turn in all work," "Needs to follow directions." I really didn't think my teacher liked me. She was very stern, never seemed to smile, and was always watching me.

From R. A. Barkley and L. J. Pfiffner, "Off to School on the Right Foot: Managing Your Child's Education. In: Barkley, R. A. Taking Charge of ADHD: The Complete, Authorized Guide for Parents, 1995, p. 208.

Symptoms of inattention become especially evident when the child starts school. Classroom demands for sustained attention and goal-directed persistence are formidable challenges for these children (Kofler, Rapport, & Alderson, 2008). Not surprisingly, this is when children are usually identified as having ADHD and referred for special assistance. Symptoms of inattention continue through grade school, resulting in low academic productivity, distractibility, poor organization, trouble meeting deadlines, and an inability to follow through on social promises or commitments to peers. The hyperactive–impulsive behaviors that were present in preschool continue, with some decline, from 6 to 12 years of age (Barkley, 2006a).

During elementary school, oppositional defiant behaviors may increase or develop. By 8 to 12 years of age, defiance and hostility may take the form of serious problems, such as lying or aggression. During the school years, ADHD increasingly takes its toll, as children experience problems with self-care, personal responsibility, chores, trustworthiness, independence, social relationships, and academic performance (Stein et al., 1995).

Adolescence

ALAN

A Parent's Viewpoint

It wasn't until Alan was 13 that I understood that ADHD was a lifelong condition. His inability to block out the high level of activity in junior high caused him to become a frequent visitor to the principal's office. And he began to do poorly in math, the subject he had always done well at, because he couldn't concentrate on all the steps involved. I had him thoroughly evaluated for ADHD again and discovered he wasn't outgrowing it. In fact, it was causing him more trouble, not less. It was then that I realized how ADHD shapes personality, torments the victims, and fragments relationships.

From R. A. Barkley and L. J. Pfiffner, "Off to School on the Right Foot: Managing Your Child's Education. In: Barkley, R. A. Taking Charge of ADHD: The Complete, Authorized Guide for Parents, 1995, p. 208.

Many children with ADHD do not outgrow their problems when they reach adolescence, and sometimes their problems can get much worse. Although hyperactive–impulsive behaviors decline significantly by adolescence, they still occur at a higher level than in 95% of same-age peers who do not have ADHD. The disorder continues into adolescence for at least 50% or more of clinic-referred elementary school children (Spencer, Biederman, & Mick, 2007). In addition, most teens continue to display significant impairments in their emotional, behavioral, and social

functioning (Barkley, 2006b; Lee et al., 2008). Childhood symptoms of hyperactivity–impulsivity (more so thansymptoms of inattention) are generally related to poor adolescent outcomes (Barkley, 2006b).

Adulthood

ALAN

Adult Challenges

Alan is now 35 years old. He frequently feels restless, cannot sit at a desk for more than a few minutes, cannot get organized, does not follow through on plans because he forgets them, loses his keys and wallet, and fails to achieve up to his potential at work. During conversations, his mind wanders and he interrupts others, blurting out whatever comes to mind without considering the consequences. He often gets into arguments. His mood swings and periodic outbursts make life difficult for those around him. Now his marriage is in trouble. He feels helpless and frustrated. (Based on authors' case material)

Although difficult to confirm, many well-known and highly successful adults, including inventor Thomas Edison, recording star and actor Justin Timberlake, celebrity Paris Hilton, and 18-time Olympic gold medal winner in swimming Michael Phelps may have had ADHD as children. Some children with ADHD either outgrow their disorder or learn to cope with it, particularly those with mild ADHD and without conduct or oppositional problems. Better outcomes are more likely for children whose symptoms are less severe and who receive good care, supervision, and support from their parents and teachers and who have access to economic and community resources, including educational, health, and mental health services (Kessler et al., 2005).

Unfortunately, like Alan, most children with ADHD will continue to experience problems, leading to a life-long pattern of suffering and disappointment (Barkley, 2014a, b). Once thought of primarily as a disorder of childhood, ADHD is now well established as an adult disorder. Adults with ADHD are restless, easily bored, and constantly seeking novelty and excitement; they may experience work difficulties, impaired social relations, and suffer from depression, low self-concept, substance abuse, and personality disorder (Barkley, 2014a, b). Although the situation is changing, many adults with ADHD have never been diagnosed, particularly those without accompanying behavior problems. As a result, they may feel that something is wrong with them, but they don't know what it is. Since many adults with ADHD are bright and creative individuals, they often feel frustrated about not living up to their potential. Alan has some children more than that of others (McCann et al., 2007; Stevenson, 2010; Stevenson et al., 2010). In a close vote (8 to 6), a Food and Drug Administration Advisory Panel (March 31, 2011) concluded that foods that contain artificial dyes do not need warning labels, but this issue continues to be debated. Dietary research on ADHD is now focusing on micronutrients, with much interest currently in essential fatty acids—which are commonly lacking in the diet of North American children—as well as in other nutrients such as zinc and iron, which may be metabolized abnormally in some children (Arnold & DiSilvestro, 2005; Howard et al., 2011; Stevens et al., 2003).

Exposure to low levels of lead found in dust, water, soil, and flaking paint in areas where leaded gasoline and paint were once used may be associated with ADHD symptoms in the classroom (Fergusson, Horwood, & Lynskey, 1993). Although most children with ADHD do not have significantly elevated lead levels in their teeth or blood (Kahn, Kelly, & Walker, 1995), some work persistently links ADHD to slight, subclinical elevations in lead exposure (Goodlad, Marcus, & Fulton, 2013). All children have a little lead in their blood, and those with ADHD have a little more. In addition, lead exposure in combination with other risk factors, such as exposure to nicotine during pregnancy, may further increase a child's risk for ADHD (Froehlich et al., 2009). These findings suggest a possible role of lead exposure that requires further follow-up using causally informative prospective studies (Nigg et al., 2010).

Family Influences

Twin studies find that psychosocial factors in the family account for only a small amount of the variance in ADHD symptoms (Nikolas & Burt, 2010), and explanations for ADHD based exclusively on negative family influences have received little support (Barkley, 2006a). Nevertheless, family influences are important in understanding ADHD for several reasons (Johnston & Chronis-Tuscano, 2014; Mash & Johnston, 2005).

▸ *Family influences may lead to ADHD symptoms or to a greater severity of symptoms.* In some cases, ADHD symptoms may be the result of interfering and insensitive early caregiving practices (Carlson, Jacobvitz, & Sroufe, 1995), especially in children with a specific genetic risk for ADHD (Martel et al., 2011). Thus, parenting practices may interact with the child's genetic makeup to moderate risk for ADHD. In addition, for children at risk for ADHD, family conflict may raise the severity of their hyperactive–impulsive symptoms to a clinical level (Barkley, 2003). Especially important

is the **goodness of fit,** or the match between the child's early temperament and the parent's style of interaction (Chess & Thomas, 1984). An overactive child with an overstimulating parent is a seemingly poor fit. As we have seen, many parents of children with ADHD also have the disorder, which means that the parents' ADHD symptoms may disrupt early parent–child interactions (Johnston et al., 2012). For example, mothers with higher levels of ADHD symptoms have been found to show less involvement, less positive parenting, and more inconsistent discipline with their children than mothers with lower levels of ADHD symptoms (Chronis-Tuscano et al., 2008). Finally, one study found that mothers with variants in DAT1 were more like to display negative and controlling behaviors when interacting with their children, particularly when their children were highly disruptive (Lee et al., 2010). Although preliminary, these findings are fascinating, in that they suggest the possible importance of a parent-gene × child-gene interaction in families of children with ADHD, with the effects mediated by the child-rearing environment.

▸ *Family problems may result from interacting with a child who is impulsive and difficult to manage* (Mash & Johnston, 1990). The clearest support for this child-to-parent direction of effect comes from double-blind placebo-controlled drug studies in which children with ADHD who received stimulant medications showed a decrease in their symptoms. The decreases in children's ADHD symptoms produced a corresponding reduction in the negative and controlling behaviors that parents had previously displayed when their children were not medicated (Barkley, 1988).

▸ *Family conflict is likely related to the presence, persistence, or later emergence of associated oppositional and conduct disorder symptoms.* In children with an inherited biological risk for ADHD, family conflict may heighten the emergence of early ODD and later comorbid ADHD and CD (Beauchaine et al., 2010). For example, children with ADHD report observing more interparental conflict than do children without ADHD, which may worsen ADHD and related ODD and CD symptoms in those who have a genotype that makes them particularly vulnerable to the effects of the emotional stress and self-blame associated with interparental conflict (Nikolas et al., 2010). Many ADHD interventions aim to change patterns of family interaction to prevent an escalating cycle of oppositional behavior and conflict. Family influences may play a major role in determining the outcome of ADHD and its associated problems, even if the influences are not the primary cause of ADHD (Johnston, Hommersen, & Seipp, 2009; Kaiser, McBurnett, & Pfiffner, 2011).

In summary, ADHD has a strong biological basis and is an inherited condition for many children. It is likely that ADHD is a heterogeneous disorder, particularly at the level of neurobiology. Although evidence is converging on specific brain areas and circuits, findings are correlational, and we do not yet know the specific causes of the disorder. We are just beginning to understand the complex ways in which biological risk factors, brain development, early environmental experiences and events, family relationships, and broader system influences interact to shape the development and outcome of ADHD (Nigg & Barkley, 2014).

Section Summary

Theories and Causes

- Theories about possible mechanisms and causes for ADHD have emphasized deficits in cognitive functioning, reward/motivation, arousal level, and self-regulation.

- There is strong evidence that ADHD is a neurodevelopmental disorder; however, biological and environmental risk factors together shape its expression.

- Findings from family, adoption, twin, and specific gene studies suggest that ADHD is inherited, although the precise mechanisms are not yet known.

- Many factors that compromise the development of the nervous system before and after birth may be related to ADHD symptoms, such as pregnancy and birth complications, maternal smoking during pregnancy, low birth weight, malnutrition, maternal alcohol or drug use, early neurological insult or trauma, and diseases of infancy.

- ADHD appears to be related to abnormalities and developmental delays in the frontostriatal circuitry of the brain and the pathways connecting this region with the limbic system, the cerebellum, and the thalamus.

- Neuroimaging studies tell us that in children with ADHD there is a structural difference or less activity in certain regions of the brain, but they don't tell us why.

- The known action of effective medications for ADHD suggests that several neurotransmitters are involved, with most evidence suggesting a selective deficiency in the availability of both dopamine and norepinephrine.

- Psychosocial factors in the family do not typically cause ADHD, although they are important in understanding the disorder. Family problems may lead to a greater severity of symptoms and relate to the emergence of co-occurring conduct problems.

- ADHD is likely the result of a complex pattern of interacting influences, perhaps giving rise to the disorder through several nervous system pathways.

TREATMENT

MARK

Medication and Behavior Therapy

In third grade, Mark's teacher threw up her hands and said, "Enough!" In one morning, Mark had jumped out of his seat six times to sharpen his pencil, each time accidentally charging into other children's desks and toppling books and papers. He was finally sent to the principal's office when he began kicking a desk he had overturned. In sheer frustration, his teacher called a meeting with his parents and the school psychologist.

But even after they developed a plan for managing his behavior in class, Mark showed little improvement. Finally, after an extensive assessment, they found that he had ADHD with symptoms of both inattention and hyperactivity–impulsivity. He was put on Ritalin, a stimulant medication, to control the hyperactivity during school hours. With a psychologist's help, his parents learned to reward desirable behaviors and to have Mark take time out when he became too disruptive. Soon Mark was able to sit still and focus on learning.

Adapted from NIMH, 1994a.

LISA

Behavior Therapy and Counseling

Because Lisa wasn't disruptive in class, it took a long time for teachers to notice her problem. Lisa was first referred to the school evaluation team when her teacher realized that she was a bright girl with failing grades. The team ruled out a learning disability but determined that she had the inattentive subtype of ADHD. The school psychologist recognized that Lisa was also dealing with depression.

Lisa's teachers and the school psychologist developed a treatment plan that included a program to increase her attention and develop her social skills. They also recommended that Lisa receive counseling and cognitive behavior therapy to help her recognize her strengths and overcome her depression.

Adapted from NIMH, 1994.

In recent years, the number of children with ADHD receiving help has more than doubled. However, it is still the case that less than half, particularly those in greatest clinical need, actually receive specialty services for ADHD (Visser et al., 2013; Zima et al., 2010). Of those who do receive services, many do not continue their

Educational Intervention

Classroom requirements to sit still, pay attention, listen to instructions, wait your turn, complete assignments, and get along with classmates are not easily met by children with ADHD. Their inattention and hyperactivity–impulsivity make learning very difficult, at times even painful. Although some children with ADHD are placed in a special education class for all or part of the day, most remain in the regular classroom. Whenever possible, it is preferable to keep children with ADHD in classes with their peers.

Educational interventions focus on managing inattentive and hyperactive–impulsive behaviors that interfere with learning and on providing a classroom environment that capitalizes on the child's strengths (DuPaul & Stoner, 2003). Techniques for managing classroom behavior are similar to those recommended to parents. The teacher and child set realistic goals and objectives, set up a mutually agreed-upon reward system, carefully monitor performance, and reward the child for meeting goals. Disruptive or off-task classroom behaviors may be punished with **response-cost procedures** that involve the loss of privileges, activities, points, or tokens following inappropriate behavior or with brief periods of time-out. These procedures have proved to be effective in reducing disruptive classroom behavior and enhancing academic productivity (Pfiffner & DuPaul, 2014).

Many strategies for instructing children with ADHD are simply good teaching methods. Letting children know what is expected of them, using visual aids, providing cues for expected behavior, and giving written as well as oral instructions all help children focus their attention and remember important points. In addition, children with ADHD may require other accommodations to help them learn. For example, the teacher may seat the child near the teacher's desk, provide a designated area in which the child can move about, establish a clearly posted system of rules, and give the child frequent cues for expected behaviors. A card or a picture on the child's desk can provide a visual reminder for acceptable behavior such as raising a hand instead of shouting out. Repeating instructions, providing extra time, writing assignments on the board, and listing all of the books and materials needed for a task may increase the likelihood that children with ADHD will complete their work (Pfiffner & DuPaul, 2014).

School-based interventions for ADHD have received considerable support. A meta-analysis of 60 studies spanning 15 years found that school-based programs, including academic, contingency management, and self-regulation interventions, were related to moderate to large improvements in academic and behavioral functioning of students with ADHD (DuPaul, Eckert, & Vilardo, 2012). Some efforts have focused on a variety of school-based interventions for ADHD, including those for individual students in regular and special education classes, combined home and school interventions, and schoolwide interventions that incorporate both universal and targeted treatments (Pfiffner & Dupaul, 2014; Waschbusch, Pelham, & Massetti, 2005).

Intensive Interventions

There are no quick cures for ADHD. More intensive (and ongoing) treatments than previously used may be required to produce meaningful changes in long-term outcomes. As described below, the Summer Treatment Program and the Multimodal Treatment Study for Children with ADHD are two examples of programs that have provided intensive treatment to children with ADHD and their families.

Summer Treatment Program

Over the past 30 years, Dr. William Pelham and his colleagues have developed and disseminated an exemplary intensive summer treatment program (Pelham et al., 2010). In this program, treatment is provided to children with ADHD ages 5 to 15 in a camplike setting where they engage in classroom and recreational activities with other children. Summer treatment has two major advantages over other interventions: It maximizes opportunities to build effective peer relations in normal settings, and it provides continuity to academic work to ensure that gains made during the school year are not lost. These programs are coordinated with stimulant medication trials, parent management training, social skills training, and educational interventions in an all-out treatment effort.

The Summer Treatment Program packs 360 hours of day-treatment into a period of 8 weeks, the equivalent of 7 years of weekly therapy. Ratings by parents and counselors suggest that children who participate show overall improvements in behavior, decreases in problem severity, and improvements in social skills and academic performance. Children also rate themselves as doing better, and parents report higher levels of self-efficacy. Dropout rates are low and consumer satisfaction is high. The program is also cost-effective as compared with more traditional treatments. Preliminary findings from controlled studies of outcomes are promising (Chronis et al., 2004b; O'Connor et al., 2012; Pelham et al., 2000; Sibley et al., 2013); however, although growing in use, these programs are not yet widely available and it is still too early to tell whether this kind of intensive program will make a long-term difference for these children.

The MTA Study

The Multimodal Treatment Study of Children with ADHD (MTA Study) is a landmark multisite study sponsored by the U.S. National Institute of Mental Health (NIMH) and the U.S. Department of Education. It represents the first large, randomized clinical trial for children with ADHD. The study sought to answer three questions: How do long-term medication and behavioral treatments compare with one another? Are there additional benefits when they are used together? What is the effectiveness of systematic carefully delivered treatments versus routine community care? (MTA Cooperative Group, 1999a).

Children with ADHD participating in a Summer Treatment Program

Carefully diagnosed children 7 to 9 years of age with ADHD were randomly assigned to one of four treatment groups, followed by major assessments at periodic intervals during and after treatment.

▶ *Medication Management:* This group received stimulant medication 7 days a week;

▶ *Behavioral treatment:* This group received 35 sessions of parent management training, up to 10 teacher and school visits per year, and participation in an intensive 8-week summer treatment program, which taught academic and social skills and had a classroom aide who continued to reinforce strategies learned in the summer treatment program in the child's actual classroom for half a day, 5 days per week, for 12 weeks;

▶ *Combined behavioral treatment and medication:* This group received both medication and behavioral treatment; or

▶ *Routine community treatment:* This group received treatment as it was routinely delivered in community care. In fact, 66% of children in this group received stimulant medication.

The major finding from the MTA Study after 14 months of active treatment was that all groups showed reductions in ADHD symptoms over time, but there were significant variations in the amount of change. First, stimulant medication was superior to behavioral treatment and to routine community care in treating the symptoms of ADHD. Second, combining behavioral treatments with medication resulted in no additional benefits for the core symptoms of ADHD over medication alone, but it did provide modest benefits for non-ADHD symptoms and other outcomes related to positive functioning (MTA

Cooperative Group, 1999a). Composite outcome measures showed that combined treatment was best, followed by medication, then behavior therapy, and finally, community treatment (Conners et al., 2001; Swanson et al., 2001).

The benefits of combined treatment were also found at 24 months of follow-up (MTA Cooperative Group, 2004a, b). However, by 36 months there were no significant treatment group differences, with all groups showing equal benefits for ADHD symptoms (Jensen et al., 2007). Consistent with this result, findings from the MTA Study at 6 and 8 years after enrollment in the program indicate that the effects of both medication and behavioral treatments either decline or cease entirely when the treatment stops (Molina et al., 2009). Thus, the efficacy of treatment for children with ADHD will require that these treatments continue to be provided in a comprehensive, carefully monitored, and ongoing fashion. The interventions in the MTA Study were more intensive and monitored more closely than is typically the case in real-world clinical practice. Further research will be needed to determine the intensity of intervention and frequency of monitoring needed to maintain treatment gains and optimal functioning over time and across contexts in light of available treatment resources (Abikoff, 2009).

Other questions from the MTA Study that continue to be addressed concern which treatments work best for which children, for which outcomes, and why? (Hinshaw, 2007b). For example, children with ADHD and comorbid anxiety and children from families on social assistance may benefit more from behavioral treatments than those without these difficulties (MTA Cooperative Group, 1999b), and behavioral treatments may be associated with less substance use at a later age (Molina et al., 2007). In general, the long-term findings from the MTA study indicate that the initial clinical presentation in childhood (e.g., severity, co-occurring conduct problems, social disadvantage) and the strength of ADHD symptom response to *any* treatment are better predictors of adolescent outcomes than the type of treatment received in childhood (Molina et al., 2009).

The MTA Study findings can be interpreted in different ways and are likely to be debated for some time to come. It seems that for children who have uncomplicated ADHD with no co-occurring disorders, adequate social functioning, and good academic performance, medication management may be the best treatment option. However, for those who have ADHD complicated by oppositional symptoms, poor social functioning, and ineffective parenting, combining medication and behavioral treatment may be the best option. In both cases, ongoing interventions will likely be needed. Whatever the final verdict, findings from the MTA study continue to raise numerous questions of clinical importance for children with ADHD and their families.

Additional Interventions

Other interventions have been used to provide support to children with ADHD and their families. Among these interventions are family counseling and support groups and individual counseling for the child. (A brief overview of these interventions can be found in Table 8.3.)

Family Counseling and Support Groups

Many families of children with ADHD experience frustration, blame, and anger for some time. As we have discussed, siblings may feel neglected or resent the time their parents spend with the child with ADHD. Family members may require special assistance not only in managing behavior but also in dealing with their own thoughts and feelings. Counseling the family helps everyone develop new skills, attitudes, and an ability to relate more effectively.

Support groups for people who are coping with ADHD in various ways can be very helpful to members. There are many local and national support groups for parents of children with ADHD. Members share information, emotional support, personal frustrations and successes, referrals to qualified professionals, discoveries about what works, and their aspirations for their children and themselves. There are also online bulletin boards and discussion groups. Sharing experiences with others that have similar concerns helps parents feel that they are not alone.

Individual Counseling

Life can be very hard for children with ADHD. They have few successes on which to build their sense of self-competence. Perhaps as a result, even when they succeed, they may attribute their success to uncontrollable factors such as task ease or luck (Hoza et al., 2000). Being punished or told they are stupid or bad is often their main form of attention. They have few friends and are constantly in trouble. The cumulative impact can leave them feeling isolated and believing that they are abnormal, stupid, or doomed to failure. Individual counseling attempts to address these concerns, although evidence for its effectiveness in treating children with ADHD is limited. Children usually come into counseling with many questions about ADHD and treatment that are addressed at the outset and in later sessions (see A Closer Look 8.4. How would you answer these questions?).

A Comment on Controversial Treatments

Understandably, parents want to explore all possible ways to help their children with ADHD. Over the years, many treatments that sound plausible have been proposed. Some are enthusiastically endorsed by professionals, and individual patient reports claim dramatic success; others are pure charlatanism. Treatments proposed for children with ADHD that have not been scientifically substantiated include allergy treatments, homeopathic treatments, medication to correct inner ear problems, vestibular stimulation, running, walks in the park, treatment for yeast infection, megavitamins, sensory integration training, chiropractic adjustment, eye training, special colored glasses, metronome therapy, and applied kinesiology (realigning bones in the skull). Untested or fad treatments may prove to be expensive, provide false hope for a quick cure, delay the use of evidence-based treatments that are known to be of some benefit, and in some cases may even be harmful (AACAP, 2013; Waschbusch & Hill, 2003).

Keeping Things in Perspective

MARK

Good Support System

Through my years so far, I've been through a lot. My Mom says I have a good heart; I care about those in need. I'm not dumb. You can't always measure smartness by tests. I feel I'm doing better now. It helps to talk to people who understand. What I'm trying to say is: no matter what comes my way, I can survive. I have those who really care, and from that I draw my strength.

From R. A. Barkley and L. J. Pfiffner, "Off to School on the Right Foot: Managing Your Child's Education. In: Barkley, R. A. Taking Charge of ADHD: The Complete, Authorized Guide for Parents, 1995, p. 208.

Young people with ADHD have problems that should not be minimized, especially if doing so prevents children and adolescents with ADHD and their families from receiving help. However, as Mark's comments illustrate, in helping those with ADHD and their families, it is important not to lose sight of the fact that each child is unique and has assets and resources that need to be recognized and supported. These assets can serve as a buffer in reducing the child's behavior problems and referral concerns (Short et al., 2007).

In closing, many of our current treatments for ADHD developed prior to advances in our theory and knowledge about the possible causes of ADHD. Efforts are now underway to design more effective treatments that are sensitive to the different types of ADHD and to specific cognitive and behavioral deficits of individual children (Casey, Nigg, & Durston, 2007).

Section Summary

Treatment

- There is no cure for ADHD, but a variety of treatments can be used to help children cope with their symptoms and any secondary problems that may arise over the years.

- The primary approach to treatment combines stimulant medication, parent management training, and educational intervention.

- Stimulants are the most effective treatment for managing symptoms of ADHD; however, their limited long-term benefit raises important issues about their clinical use that are yet to be resolved.

- Parent management training (PMT) provides parents with a variety of skills to help them manage their child's oppositional and defiant behaviors and cope with the difficulties of raising a child with ADHD.

- Educational interventions focus on managing inattentive and hyperactive–impulsive behaviors that interfere with learning and on providing a classroom environment that capitalizes on the child's strengths.

- Findings from the MTA Study, a landmark controlled comparison of intensive treatments for ADHD, suggest that for children with uncomplicated ADHD, medication may be the best treatment option; however, for those with ADHD and oppositional symptoms, poor social functioning and ineffective parenting, combining medication and behavioral treatment may be the best option.
- Additional interventions for ADHD include family counseling and support groups, and individual counseling for the child.

Study Resources

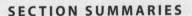

SECTION SUMMARIES

Description and History 228
Core Characteristics 230
Associated Characteristics 237
Accompanying Psychological Disorders and Symptoms 243
Prevalence and Course 245
Theories and Causes 250
Treatment 257

KEY TERMS

alerting 233
attentional capacity 233
attention-deficit/hyperactivity disorder (ADHD) 228
combined presentation (ADHD-C) 235
developmental coordination disorder (DCD) 245
distractibility 233
executive functions (EFs) 237
frontostriatal circuitry of the brain 253
goodness of fit 256

hyperactive 229
hyperactivity–impulsivity 234
impulsive 229
inattentive 229
inattention 233
methylphenidate 259
parent management training (PMT) 261
positive bias 240
predominantly hyperactive–impulsive presentation (ADHD-HI) 235
predominantly inattentive presentation (ADHD-PI) 235
presentation type 235
quality of life 240
response-cost procedures 262
sluggish cognitive tempo (SCT) 235
selective attention 233
stimulant medications 259
sustained attention 233
tic disorders 245

9

Conduct Problems

Our youth now love luxury. They have bad manners, contempt for authority and disrespect for their elders. Children nowadays are tyrants.

—Socrates, 470–399 B.C.E.

CHAPTER PREVIEW

TABLE 9.2 | **Diagnostic Criteria for** Conduct Disorder (*continued*)

Specify severity:

Mild: Few if any conduct problems in excess of those required to make the diagnosis are present, and conduct problems cause relatively minor harm to others (e.g., lying, truancy, staying out after dark without permission, other rule breaking).

Moderate: The number of conduct problems and the effect on others are intermediate between those specified in "mild" and those in "severe" (e.g., stealing without confronting a victim, vandalism).

Severe: Many conduct problems in excess of those required to make the diagnosis are present, or conduct problems cause considerable harm to others (e.g., forced sex, physical cruelty, use of a weapon, stealing while confronting a victim, breaking and entering).

Source: Diagnostic and Statistical Manual of Mental Disorders, 5th ed. American Psychiatric Association.

illegal activity, and persist in their antisocial behavior over time (Lahey, Goodman, et al., 1999). In contrast, youths diagnosed with adolescent-onset CD are as likely to be girls as boys and do not display the severity or psychopathology that characterizes the childhood-onset group. They are also less likely to commit violent offenses or to persist in their antisocial behavior as they get older. Age at onset does make a difference.

The ODD and CD Connection

There is much overlap between the symptoms of ODD and CD. This raises the question of whether ODD is a separate disorder from CD; a milder, earlier version; or a reflection of the same underlying temperament and deficits (Waldman & Lahey, 2013). Symptoms of ODD typically emerge 2 to 3 years before CD symptoms, at about 6 years of age for ODD versus 9 years for CD (Nock et al., 2007). Since ODD symptoms emerge first, it is possible that they are precursors of CD for some children. However, nearly half of all children with CD have no prior ODD diagnosis (Rowe et al., 2010), and most children who display ODD do not progress to more severe CD—at least 50% maintain their ODD diagnosis without progressing, and another 25% cease to display ODD problems entirely (Burke et al., 2010). Thus, for most children, ODD is an extreme developmental variation and a strong risk factor for later ODD and other problems, but not one that necessarily signals an escalation to more serious conduct problems (Keenan et al., 2011). Thus, ODD and CD appear to be distinguishable yet highly correlated aspects of child psychopathology.

Antisocial Personality Disorder (APD) and Psychopathic Features

Persistent aggressive behavior and CD in childhood may be a precursor of adult **antisocial personality disorder (APD)**, a pervasive pattern of disregard for, and violation of, the rights of others, including repeated illegal behaviors, deceitfulness, failure to plan ahead, repeated physical fights or assaults, reckless disregard for the safety of self or others, repeated failure to sustain work behavior or honor financial obligations, and a lack of remorse (APA, 2013). Research has found that as many as 40% of children with CD develop APD as young adults (Lahey et al., 2005). In addition to their early CD, adolescents with APD may also display **psychopathic features**, which are defined as a pattern of callous, manipulative, deceitful, and remorseless behavior—the more menacing side of human nature (Blair et al., 2006). Consider these chilling comments by Jason.

JASON

No Conscience

Jason, age 13, had been involved in serious crime—including breaking and entering, thefts, and assaults on younger children—by age 6. Listening to Jason talk was frightening. Asked why he committed crimes, this product of a stable, professional family replied, "I like it. My f___ parents really freak out when I get in trouble, but I don't give a sh ___ as long as I'm having a good time. Yeah, I've always been wild." About other people, including his victims, Jason had this to say: "You want the truth? They'd screw me if they could, only I get my shots in first." He liked to rob homeless people, especially "f_gots," "bag ladies," and street kids, because, "They're used to it. They don't whine to the police. ... One guy I got into a fight with pulled a knife and I took it and rammed it in his eye. He ran around screaming like a baby. What a jerk!"

Adapted from Hare, 1993, p. 162.

Like Jason, youths who display psychopathic features appear to be aware that their aggressive behavior will cause others to suffer—but they don't care. Rather, their goals in conflict situations involve revenge, dominance, and forced respect (Pardini, 2011). Although less is known about psychopathic features in children than in adults this situation is changing. Signs of a lack of conscience occur in some children as young as 3 to 5 years (Kochanska et al., 1994). Other children, like Jason, began committing brutal acts of violence at age 6 with little remorse. A subgroup of preschoolers with behavior problems show a worrisome increase in their lack of concern for others as they begin to enter middle childhood (Hastings et al., 2000). Finally, adolescents with CD are less likely than peers to show affective empathy or embarrassment, which suggests a failure to inhibit emotions and actions in accordance with social conventions (Lovett & Sheffield, 2007).

These and many other findings point to a subgroup of children with CD whose lack of concern for others may place them at especially high risk for extreme antisocial and aggressive acts and for poor long-term outcomes. They display a **callous and unemotional (CU) interpersonal style** characterized by an absence of guilt, lack of empathy, uncaring attitudes, shallow or deficient emotional responses, and related traits of narcissism and impulsivity (Frick et al., 2014; Kahn et al., 2012). Children with CU traits display a greater number and variety of conduct problems, and they have more frequent contact with police and a stronger parental history of APD than other children with conduct problems (Frick & White, 2008). Research with children and adolescents has found that CU interpersonal and affective traits predict persistent delinquency, future recidivism, and symptoms of APD in early adulthood (Byrd, Loeber, and Pardini, 2012; McMahon et al., 2010; Pardini & Loeber, 2008). CU symptoms in childhood are about as stable as ODD and CD symptoms over time, but developmental changes have also been noted, suggesting that these are not unchanging characteristics of the child. For example, some children display stable high levels of CU traits, others show increasing or decreasing levels, and others show stable low levels (Fontaine et al., 2011). CU traits in childhood and early adolescence are likely precursors of adult forms of psychopathy, although further research is needed to confirm this (Lynam et al., 2007).

Given the evidence in support of CU traits in identifying an important characteristic of children with conduct problems, DSM-5 uses the specifier **"with limited prosocial emotions"** to describe youth with CD who display a persistent and typical pattern of interpersonal and emotional functioning involving at least two of the following three characteristics: lack of remorse or guilt; callous–lack of empathy; and unconcerned about performance. The term "limited prosocial emotions" was used, in part, in DSM-5 to avoid the possible negative connotations associated with the term "callous-unemotional" (Frick & Nigg, 2012).

At this point you might want to consider A Closer Look 9.2 to sharpen your knowledge of DSM-5 criteria for ODD and CD by considering whether or not TV cartoon personality Bart Simpson qualifies for a diagnosis of one, both, or neither of these disorders.

Section Summary

DSM-5: Defining Features

- Children with oppositional defiant disorder (ODD) display an age-inappropriate pattern of stubborn, hostile, and defiant behaviors that reflect symptoms of emotionality

---

A CLOSER **LOOK** 9.2

Bart Simpson: What's the Diagnosis?

Sharpen your knowledge of DSM-5 criteria for ODD and CD by considering whether TV cartoon personality Bart Simpson qualifies for a diagnosis of one, both, or neither of these disorders. Here is a list of antisocial acts displayed by Bart:

- Flushes a cherry bomb down the toilet
- Rearranges party snacks to say "Boy our party sucks"
- Loosens the top on Milhouse's salt shaker
- Lights Homer's tie on fire
- Tricks Flanders kids into giving cookies away
- Pretends to be Timmy (trapped in a well)
- Blames Lisa for making long distance calls
- Pulls carpet up, writes "Bart" on carpet
- Plays with and later breaks grandpa Abe's false teeth
- Flushes Homer's wallet and keys down toilet
- Cuts all of baby Maggie's hair off
- Paints extra lines on parking lot
- Leaves box factory tour
- Pops heads off Mr. Burns's statues/floods his car
- Smashes Mr. Burns's windows
- Recounts throwing mail in sewer with Milhouse
- Phones 911 to get babysitter into trouble

Comment: Based on Bart's symptoms of aggression, destruction of property, deceitfulness, and serious violation of rules, he easily qualifies for a DSM diagnosis of CD. Like most children with CD, Bart also displays symptoms of ODD (e.g., not complying with rules, deliberately annoying others, blaming others for his misbehavior, engaging in spiteful behavior) and qualifies for this diagnosis as well. (Based on authors' case material.)

and temperamental activity. ODD symptoms can be grouped into three dimensions: negative affect, defiance, and vindictiveness.

- Conduct disorder (CD) describes children who display severe aggressive and antisocial acts involving inflicting pain upon others or interfering with the rights of others through physical and verbal aggression, stealing, or committing acts of vandalism.
- Children who display childhood-onset CD (before age 10) are more likely to be boys, show more aggressive symptoms, account for a disproportionate amount of illegal activity, and persist in their antisocial behavior over time.
- Children with adolescent-onset CD are as likely to be girls as boys and do not display the severity or psychopathology that characterizes the childhood-onset group.
- There is much overlap between CD and ODD. However, most children who display ODD do not progress to more severe CD.
- Persistent aggressive behavior and conduct problems in childhood may be a precursor of adult antisocial personality disorder (APD), a pervasive pattern of disregard for, and violation of, the rights of others.
- A subgroup of children with conduct problems display psychopathic features, including callous–unemotional (CU) traits such as lacking in guilt, not showing empathy, and not displaying feelings or emotions. These children also display a preference for novel and perilous activities and a diminished sensitivity to cues for danger and punishment when seeking rewards.
- DSM-5 uses the specifier "with limited prosocial emotions" to describe youth with CD who display a pattern of interpersonal and emotional functioning involving a lack of remorse or guilt, empathy, or concern about performance.

ASSOCIATED CHARACTERISTICS

Many child, family, peer, school, and community factors are associated with conduct problems in youths. Some factors co-occur with conduct problems, others increase their likelihood, and still others are the result of these problems. To fully understand conduct problems, we must examine these various factors and how they interact over time.

Cognitive and Verbal Deficits

Although most children with conduct problems have normal intelligence, they score nearly 8 points lower than their peers on IQ tests (Pajer et al., 2008). This IQ deficit may be greater (more than 15 points) for children with childhood-onset CD, and cannot be accounted for solely by socioeconomic disadvantage, race, or detection by the police (Lynam, Moffitt, &

Stouthamer-Loeber, 1993). Lower IQ scores in children with CD may be related to the co-occurrence of ADHD (Waschbusch, 2002). When ADHD is also present, the association between a lower IQ and an increased risk for CD is clear. It is less clear how a lower IQ mediates this risk (Rutter, 2003b).

Verbal IQ is consistently lower than performance IQ in children with CD, suggesting a specific and pervasive deficit in language (Zadeh, Im-Bolter, & Cohen, 2007). This deficit may affect the child's receptive listening, reading, problem solving, pragmatic language, expressive speech and writing, and memory for verbal material (Brennan et al., 2003; Gremillion & Martel, 2013; Jaffee & D'Zurilla, 2003). Some suggest that verbal and language deficits may contribute to conduct problems by interfering with the development of self-control, emotion regulation, or the labeling of emotions in others, which may lead to a lack of empathy (Hastings et al., 2000). One study found that poor language ability predicted the development of later conduct problems, suggesting that targeting language deficits may be useful in preventing or treating conduct problems (Peterson et al., 2013).

Verbal deficits are present early in a child's development, long before the emergence of conduct problems. However, their presence alone does not predict future aggression—family factors are also important. Children with both verbal deficits and family adversity display four times as much aggressive behavior as children with only one factor (Moffitt, 1990). Thus, verbal deficits may increase the child's vulnerability to the effects of a hostile family environment. How this occurs is not known, but one possibility is that a child's verbal deficits may make it more difficult for parents to understand their child's needs, which leads to parents' frustration, fewer positive interactions, more punishment, and greater difficulties in teaching social skills (Patterson, 1996). Verbal deficits, such as poor receptive language skills, may also lead to rejection by mainstream peers, adding to the development of conduct problems (Menting, van Lier, & Koot, 2011).

It is important to keep in mind that the relationship between different cognitive/verbal deficits and antisocial behavior may vary for specific types of antisocial behaviors. For example, one study found that verbal abilities were negatively related to physical aggression but positively associated with theft, and that inductive reasoning was negatively associated with increases in theft across adolescence (Barker et al., 2011). These findings highlight the importance of studying specific types of conduct problem behaviors in order to better understand their possible underlying mechanisms.

Children with conduct problems rarely consider the future consequences of their behavior or its impact

"How am I supposed to think about consequences before they happen?"

David Sipress/Cartoon Bank.com

on others. They fail to inhibit their impulsive behavior, keep social values or future rewards in mind, or adapt their actions to changing circumstances. This pattern suggests deficits in executive functions similar to those of children with ADHD (Raine et al., 2005). Because ODD/CD and ADHD frequently co-occur, the observed deficits in executive functions in these children could be due to the presence of co-occurring ADHD (Pennington & Ozonoff, 1996).

It is also possible that the types of executive functioning deficits experienced by children with ODD and CD may differ from those experienced by children with ADHD (Nigg et al., 2006). For example, Rubia (2010) has made the distinction between *cool* (as in temperature, not as in Lady Gaga) cognitive executive functions, such as attention, working memory, planning, and inhibition, and *hot* executive functions that involve incentives and motivation. Both cool and hot executive functions are associated with distinct but interconnected brain networks. Cool executive function deficits are thought to be more characteristic of children with ADHD, whereas hot executive function deficits are more characteristic of children with conduct problems. Children with both ADHD and conduct problems, which is common, likely display a combination of the two types of executive function deficits.

School and Learning Problems

Every time you stop a school, you will have to build a jail.

—Mark Twain (November 23, 1900)

Children with conduct problems display many school difficulties, including academic underachievement, grade retention, special education placement, dropout,

suspension, and expulsion (Roeser & Eccles, 2000). Although the frustration and demoralization associated with school failure can lead to antisocial behavior in some children (Maughan, Gray, & Rutter, 1985), there is little evidence that academic failure is the primary cause of conduct problems, particularly in early childhood. Since many young children display patterns of disruptive behavior long before they enter school, it is more likely that a common factor, such as a neuropsychological or language deficit, lack of self-control, or socioeconomic disadvantage, underlies both conduct problems and school difficulties (Lahey & Waldman, 2003).

Over time, underachievement and conduct problems influence each other. Subtle early language deficits may lead to reading and communication difficulties, which in turn may heighten conduct problems in elementary school. Children with poor academic skills are increasingly likely to lose interest in school and to associate with delinquent peers. By adolescence, the relationship between conduct problems and underachievement is firmly established, which, in one pathway, may lead to anxiety or depression in young adulthood (Masten et al., 2005).

Family Problems

He is so violent with his sister. He split her lip a couple of times. And he almost knocked her out once when he hit her over the head with a 5-pound brass pitcher. He's put plastic bags over her head.

—Webster-Stratton and Herbert (1994)

Family problems are among the strongest and most consistent correlates of conduct problems (Dishion & Patterson, 2006). Two types of family disturbances are related to these problems in children. *General family disturbances* include parental mental health problems, a family history of antisocial behavior, marital discord, family instability, limited resources, and antisocial family values. *Specific disturbances in parenting practices and family functioning* include excessive use of harsh discipline, lack of supervision, lack of emotional support and involvement, and parental disagreement about discipline.

The two types are interrelated, since general family disturbances such as maternal depression often lead to poor parenting practices that can lead to antisocial behavior and feelings of parental incompetence that may lead to increased maternal depression, which completes the circle.

High levels of conflict are common in families of children with conduct problems. So, too, are poor parenting practices such as ineffective discipline, negative control, inappropriate use of punishment and rewards, failure to follow through on commands, and a lack

- ADHD may be a catalyst for CD by contributing to its persistence and escalation to more severe forms, particularly when shaped by ineffective parenting emotional reactions and behaviors.
- ADHD may lead to childhood onset of CD, which is a strong predictor of continuing problems.

Despite the large overlap, two lines of research suggest that CD and ADHD are distinct disorders. First, a model that includes both CD and ADHD consistently provides a better fit to the data than a model based on only a single disorder (Waschbusch, 2002). Second, CD is less likely than ADHD to be associated with cognitive impairments, neurodevelopmental abnormalities, inattentiveness in the classroom, and higher rates of accidental injuries (Hinshaw & Lee, 2003).

Depression and Anxiety

About 50% of youths with conduct problems also receive a diagnosis of depression or anxiety (Wolff & Ollendick, 2006). Some evidence suggests that it is ODD and not CD that best accounts for the connection between conduct problems and depression and that this relationship is driven by the negative mood symptoms of ODD (e.g., anger/irritability) rather than by its behavioral symptoms of defiance (Burke & Loeber, 2010). Boys with combined conduct and internalizing problems have poor outcomes in early adulthood, including having the highest risk of later psychiatric disorders and criminal offenses (Sourander et al., 2007). Most girls with CD develop a depressive or anxiety disorder by early adulthood, and for both sexes, increasing severity of antisocial behavior is associated with increasing severity of depression and anxiety (Zoccolillo et al., 1992). Adolescent CD is also a risk factor for completed suicide in young people with a family history of depression (Renaud et al., 1999).

Findings regarding the relation between anxiety disorders and antisocial outcomes for children with conduct problems are puzzling but quite interesting (Drabick, Ollendick, & Bubier, 2010). In some studies, co-occurring anxiety has been identified as a protective factor that inhibits aggressive behavior (Pine et al., 2000). However, other studies have found that anxiety increases the risk for later antisocial behavior (Rutter, Giller, & Hagell, 1998). Boys with CD and anxiety disorder show a higher level of salivary cortisol associated with a greater degree of behavioral inhibition, which supports the theory of anxiety as a protective factor (McBurnett et al., 1991). In boys with CD only, lower levels of salivary cortisol are directly associated with more aggressive and disruptive behaviors (McBurnett et al., 2000). It has been hypothesized that the relation between anxiety and antisocial outcomes may depend on the type of anxiety. In this formulation, anxiety related to shyness, inhibition, and fear may protect against conduct problems, whereas anxiety associated with negative emotionality and social avoidance/withdrawal based on a lack of caring about others may increase the child's risk for conduct problems (Lahey & Waldman, 2003). Consistent with this view, children with callous–unemotional traits show less anxiety than other children with conduct problems (Frick et al., 1999). It has been proposed that different pathways underlie the relationship between conduct problems and anxiety, such that anxiety may serve as a buffer or facilitator of conduct problems, depending on the underlying conditions (Drabick et al., 2010).

Section Summary

Accompanying Disorders and Symptoms

- About 50% of children with CD also have ADHD. Despite the overlap, CD and ADHD appear to be distinct disorders.
- About 50% of children with conduct problems are diagnosed with depression or a co-occurring anxiety disorder. Symptoms of negative mood associated with ODD best account for the relationship between conduct problems and depression.
- Anxiety related to shyness, inhibition, and fear may protect against conduct problems, whereas anxiety associated with negative emotionality and social avoidance/withdrawal based on a lack of caring about others may increase the child's risk for conduct problems.

PREVALENCE, GENDER, AND COURSE

In the sections that follow we consider the prevalence of conduct problems, the important role that gender plays in the expression of antisocial behavior, and the different ways that conduct problems emerge over the course of development.

Prevalence

ODD is more prevalent than CD during childhood, but by adolescence they occur equally often. *Lifetime prevalence estimates* are 12% for ODD (13% for males, and 11% for females), and 8% for CD (9% for males and 6% for females) (Merikangas et al., 2010). The reason overall lifetime prevalence rates are comparable is that ODD either declines or stays constant from early childhood to adolescence, whereas CD increases over the same time period. Prevalence estimates for CD and ODD are similar across cultures, although most comparisons to date have been made between Western countries rather than between Western and non-Western countries (Canino et al., 2010; Erskine et al., 2013).

Gender

In all of the recorded history of the more than ten million animal species, including four thousand mammals which populate the planet, only two species have been documented to engage in warfare... male chimpanzees and male humans.

—From Eme (2007)

ANN

Runaway

Until recently, Ann, age 13, lived with her mother, stepfather, and younger brother. For the past 6 months, she has been living in a youth shelter under the custody of the courts, because she repeatedly ran away from home. Ann was described by her parents as defiant and argumentative, and she frequently lied and stole. She often stole clothes and jewelry from the homes of relatives and friends, as well as from her parents. ... Over the past 3 years, Ann had run away from home on four occasions. Each time, the police had to be called. Running away was precipitated by being grounded for stealing or smoking cigarettes. ... One time, Ann was gone for 3 nights. The police found her wandering the streets late at night on the other side of town (about 10 miles from her home). Ann would not tell them who she was or where she lived.

Based on Conduct Disorders in Childhood and Adolescence by A. E. Kazdin, p. 17.

Clear gender differences in the frequency and severity of antisocial behavior are evident by 2 to 3 years of age (Dodge, Coie, & Lynam, 2006). During childhood, rates of conduct problems are about 2 to 4 times higher for boys than for girls, with boys showing an earlier age at onset and greater persistence (Eme, 2007; Lahey et al., 2006). Boys also display more conduct problems and report using more physical aggression than girls across countries throughout the world (Erskine et al., 2013; Lansford et al., 2012). This gender difference does not imply that girls do not display severe conduct problems, including physically aggressive behavior, they just do so much less often than boys.

The gender disparity in conduct problems increases through middle childhood, narrows greatly in early adolescence—due mainly to a rise in covert nonaggressive antisocial behavior in girls (McDermott, 1996)—and then increases again in late adolescence when boys are at the peak of their delinquent behavior (Lahey

et al., 2006). Ann steals, lies, and runs away from home, but she is not physically aggressive. In contrast to boys, whose early symptoms of CD are aggression and theft, early symptoms for girls are usually sexual misbehaviors (Offord, Alder, & Boyle, 1986). Antisocial girls are more likely than others to develop relationships with antisocial boys, then become pregnant at an earlier age and display a wide spectrum of later problems, including anxiety, depression, and poor parenting (Foster, 2005).

Although gender differences in the overall amount of antisocial behavior decrease in early adolescence, boys remain more violence-prone than girls throughout their life span, and are more likely to engage in repeated acts of physical violence (Odgers & Moretti, 2002). For conduct problems that are chronic from early childhood to adulthood, the male-to-female ratio is marked, about 10:1. In contrast, more transient forms of antisocial behavior in adolescence show a male-to-female ratio of about 2:1 (Moffitt et al., 2001).

In addition, physical aggression by girls during childhood, when it does occur, does not seem to forecast continued physical violence and other forms of delinquency in adolescence, as it does for boys (Broidy et al., 2003). This does not mean that girls are nonviolent—about 25% of teenage girls commit at least one violent act such as getting into a serious fight at school or work, taking part in a group-against-group fight, or attacking others with the intent to seriously harm them (compared with about 50% of teenage boys) (Substance Abuse and Mental Health Services Administration [SAMHSA], 2009). Interestingly, the sex difference in antisocial behavior has decreased by more than 50% over the past 60 years, suggesting that females may be more susceptible to or more affected by contemporary risk factors, such as family discord or media influences and/or that there is a growing recognition of these problems in girls (Rutter et al., 1998). Unfortunately, antisocial behavior is increasingly becoming an equal

Girls will be girls.

and for those with callous–unemotional traits (Viding et al., 2008). However, all externalizing disorders appear to share substantial genetic influences, suggesting at least some common causal factors among them(Lahey et al., 2011). Overall, adoption and twin studies suggest that both genetic and environmental factors contribute to antisocial behavior across

TABLE 9.3 | **Summary of Risk Factors for Antisocial Behaviors**

Child
Genetic risk, prenatal and birth complications, exposure to lead and other toxins, low arousal and reactivity, anterior and posterior cingulate cortex development, functional and structural deficits in prefrontal cortex, reduced amygdala activity, blunted emotional and cortisol reactivity (CU -type), insensitivity to stress (CU-type), fearlessness/low anxiety (CU-type), difficult temperament, emotion dysregulation, attention-deficit/hyperactivity disorder (ADHD), insecure/disorganized attachments, childhood onset of aggression, social avoidance and withdrawal, social–cognitive deficits (hostile attributional bias), lowered verbal intelligence and verbal deficits, executive functioning deficits

Family
Antisocial family values, parental antisocial or criminal behavior, paternal antisocial personality disorder, maternal depression, parental substance abuse, marital discord, teen motherhood, single parenthood, family stress/conflict/instability, chaotic household, large family, low socioeconomic status, low education of mother, family carelessness in permitting access to weapons

Ineffective Parenting
Poor supervision and monitoring, inconsistent discipline, avoidance of discipline due to concerns about the child's reaction, harsh discipline and maltreatment, discordant parent–child interactions, poor communication and problem solving, low parental involvement, parental neglect, low parental warmth, parental hostile attributional bias

Peers
Early peer aggression, rejection by peers, association with deviant siblings, association with deviant peers, bullying

School
Poor academic performance, weak bonding to school, low educational aspirations, low school motivation, poorly organized and functioning schools

Neighborhood and Community
Neighborhood disadvantage and poverty, disorganized neighborhoods, gang membership, availability of weapons

Sociocultural
Media portrayal of violence, cultural attitudes encouraging use of aggression, socialization of children for aggression

Adapted from Loeber and Farrington, 2000, p. 749.

development. The studies do not, however, specify the mechanisms by which the factors operate.

It is likely that genetic risks for antisocial behavior operate via several pathways (Rutter, 2003b). First, genetic factors may be related to a difficult temperament, lack of response to distress in others, impulsivity, a tendency to seek rewards, or an insensitivity to punishment that combine to create an antisocial "propensity" or "personality" (Waldman et al., 2011). Second, genetic factors may increase the likelihood that a child will be exposed to environmental risk factors, such as prenatal stress, parental maltreatment, divorce, or other negative life events that are associated with an increased risk of antisocial behavior. Third, children's genotype and neurobiology may moderate their susceptibility to these environmental insults in determining whether they later develop antisocial behavior (Ellis & Boyce, 2011; Zohsel et al., 2014). These and other pathways will need to be addressed if the causes of antisocial behavior are to be understood (Rutter, 2006a).

Exciting new studies into gene variants have identified possible gene–environment (G×E) interactions in the development of conduct problems (Dodge, 2009). A variant of the gene that encodes the neurotransmitter-metabolizing enzyme monoamine oxidase A (MAOA) has been of particular interest because this gene is related to neural systems involved in aggression. When threatened or provoked, humans naturally feel rage and an impulse to react aggressively. Activation of the MAOA enzyme helps us inhibit that response; thus, it plays a key role in regulating behavior following threatening events. Research has found that maltreated children with a low-active MAOA genotype are much more likely to develop antisocial behavior than maltreated children who do not have this genotype (Kim-Cohen et al., 2006). An interaction between the low-active MAOA genotype and physical discipline before age 5 has also been found to be related to adolescent delinquent behavior (Edwards et al., 2010). Brain imaging studies have also found that individuals with the low-active MAOA genotype show patterns of arousal in areas of the brain that are associated with aggression in response to emotion-provoking stimuli (Buckholtz & Meyer-Lindenberg, 2008).

In addition to MAOA, other genes and G×E interactions have been implicated in the association between negative parenting and childhood conduct problems (Albaugh et al., 2010; Lahey et al., 2011). Findings to date suggest that some of these genes may not be specific to any one type of externalizing disorder but will predispose individuals to a broad spectrum of conduct problems (Dick, 2007). G×E interaction effects in conduct disorders are fascinating. However, research into these effects is just beginning, and replication studies are needed (Hebebrand et al., 2010). Similarly, research into how G×E interaction effects develop over time is still in its infancy (Dodge, 2009).

Prenatal Factors and Birth Complications

A number of pregnancy and birth factors (e.g., low birth weight) are related to the development of serious conduct problems (Brennan, Grekin, & Mednick, 2003). Malnutrition during pregnancy is associated with later antisocial behavior, which may be mediated by protein deficiency (Raine, 2002). Exposure to lead before and after birth and the mother's use of nicotine, marijuana, and other substances during pregnancy may also be associated with later conduct problems (Carpenter & Nevin, 2010; Gaysina et al., 2013; Murray et al., 2010; Nigg & Breslau, 2007). There is also support for maternal alcohol use during pregnancy playing a role in conduct problems—the greater the amount of alcohol consumed, the greater the risk of child conduct problems (D'Onofrio et al., 2007; Larkby et al., 2011). Although pregnancy and birth factors are correlated with conduct problems, strong evidence of direct biological causation is lacking (Hodgins, Kratzer, & McNeil, 2001). For example, it is likely that the relation between mothers' smoking during pregnancy and adolescent conduct problems and criminality is best accounted for by the transmission of an underlying antisocial tendency from mother to child and other family background variables, rather than by exposure to cigarette by-products during pregnancy (D'Onofrio et al., 2008, 2010b; Gatzke-Kopp & Beauchaine, 2007).

Neurobiological Factors

Gray (1987) proposed that people's behavioral patterns are related to two subsystems of the brain, each having distinct neuroanatomical regions and neurotransmitter pathways. The **behavioral activation system (BAS)** stimulates behavior in response to signals of reward or nonpunishment. In contrast, the **behavioral inhibition system (BIS)** produces anxiety and inhibits ongoing behavior in the presence of novel events, innate fear stimuli, and signals of nonreward or punishment. Other behavioral patterns may result from the relative balance or imbalance of activity in these two neural systems. Think of the BAS as similar to the gas pedal and the BIS as similar to the brake pedal—some individuals ride one more heavily than the other.

It has been proposed that antisocial patterns of behavior result from an overactive BAS *and* an underactive BIS—a pattern determined primarily by genetic predisposition. Consistent with an overactive BAS,

children with conduct problems show a heightened sensitivity to rewards (Frick et al., 2003). In addition, they fail to respond to punishment and continue to respond under conditions of no reward—patterns that are consistent with an underactive BIS (Fowles, 2001). Strikingly, a lack of fear conditioning at age 3 has been found to predict criminal offending 20 years later (Gao et al., 2010).

Individual differences in antisocial behavior have been related to variations in stress-regulating mechanisms, including the hypothalamic–pituitary–adrenal (HPA) axis and the autonomic nervous system (ANS), serotonergic functioning, and structural and functional deficits in the prefrontal cortex of the brain (van Goozen et al., 2007). Children with CD who show an early onset of aggressive symptoms display low psychophysiological/cortical arousal and low reactivity of the autonomic nervous system (e.g., a lower resting heart rate) (Lorber, 2004; Raine, 2002). Low arousal and autonomic reactivity may lead to diminished avoidance learning in response to warnings or reprimands, a poor response to punishment, and a fearless, stimulus-seeking temperament. In turn, this may lead to antisocial behavior, a failure to develop the anticipatory fear needed to avoid such behavior, and a lack of conscience. Most children respond to discipline and punishment by reducing their antisocial behavior. Often, the opposite occurs with children with conduct problems—when disciplined or punished they may increase their antisocial behavior and become even more defiant (Briggs-Gowan et al., 2014).

Neuroimaging studies have identified structural and functional brain abnormalities in several brain regions in youths with conduct disorders, including in those with high levels of psychopathic features (Pardini et al., 2013). These brain regions include the amygdala, prefrontal cortex, posterior and anterior cingulate, and insula, as well as interconnected regions. Imaging studies also show reduced activation in some of these areas (e.g., the amygdala) when viewing emotional stimuli such as angry or sad faces, or during tasks that require learning not to respond to punishing stimuli (Finger et al., 2011; Huebner et al., 2008; Passamonti et al., 2010). These brain regions are involved in processing social and emotional information. Therefore, abnormalities in these regions likely underlie the social–cognitive and emotional deficits that characterize youths with conduct problems. Interestingly, as described in A Closer Look 9.5, similar brain abnormalities may be present both in youths with early-onset and those with adolescent-onset conduct disorders (Fairchild et al., 2011).

Although much additional work is needed, early findings from neuroimaging and other studies suggest three neural systems underlying cognitive, social, and emotional differences across different types of conduct problems. The first includes subcortical neural systems that lead to

Do the Brains of Children with Early-Onset Conduct Disorders Differ from Those of Children with Adolescent-Onset Conduct Disorders?

Despite the many differences between children with early-onset and those with adolescent-onset CD, brain-imaging findings suggest that the two groups may display similar brain abnormalities as compared with children without CD. Using magnetic resonance imaging (MRI), neuroscientists in England measured the size of specific brain regions of 65 teenage boys with CD and 27 teenage boys without CD (Fairchild et al., 2011). They found that the amygdala, a region of the brain involved in reading others' emotions, empathy, and recognizing when others are distressed, was markedly smaller in teens with CD than in the healthy comparison group. However, no differences were found between teens with early-onset and those with adolescent-onset conduct disorders. The image to the right, shows the amygdala (for each side of the brain), the region of the brain for which the reduction in volume was largest for teens with CD versus healthy comparison children.

These preliminary findings are important, since it has been argued that early-onset CD is a neurodevelopmental condition, whereas adolescent-onset CD is mostly the result of teens associating with and mimicking other teens who are getting into trouble. However, this study shows that abnormalities in

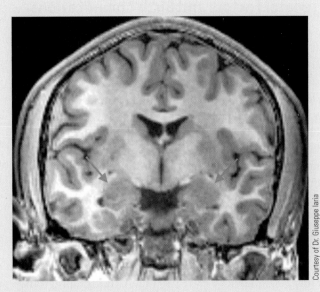

Courtesy of Dr. Giuseppe Iaria

brain structures underlying social-information processing may contribute to the emergence of both adolescent-onset as well as early-onset CD (Fairchild et al., 2011).

aggressive behavior. In this context, dysfunction in the integrated functioning of brain circuits involving the amygdala has been implicated (Blair, 2011). The second neural circuit includes prefrontal cortex decision-making circuits and socioemotional information-processing circuits that assess social cues and evaluate the consequences of aggressing or not aggressing; the third neural circuit includes frontoparietal regions involved in regulating emotions and impulsive motivational urges (Coccaro et al., 2011). In the future, further research into these neural circuits may help to reveal mechanisms through which inborn dispositions may place a child at risk for later conduct problems (Viding & Jones, 2008).

Social–Cognitive Factors

Social–cognitive abilities refer to the skills involved in attending to, interpreting, and responding to social cues. There is a strong relationship between social–cognitive deficits and antisocial behavior across all types of conduct-problem trajectories (e.g., childhood limited, adolescent-onset, early-onset persistent), especially for children showing early-onset persistent conduct problems. As many as 40% of boys and 25% of girls with persistent conduct problems display significant social–cognitive impairments (Oliver et al., 2011).

The connection between children's thinking in social situations and their aggressive behavior has been looked at in several ways. Some approaches focus on immature forms of thinking, such as egocentrism, a lack of social perspective taking, theory of mind deficits, or deficits in moral reasoning (Blair, 2010; Olson et al., 2011). Others emphasize cognitive deficiencies, such as a child's failure to use verbal mediators to regulate his or her behavior (Meichenbaum, 1977), or cognitive distortions, such as interpreting a neutral event as an intentionally hostile act (Crick & Dodge, 1994). Other approaches focus more broadly on the social–cognitive processes involved in antisocial decision making (Fontaine et al., 2010). Some research has also found deficits in facial expression recognition and eye contact in children with conduct problems, which may further contribute to their antisocial behavior and social difficulties (Dadds et al., 2011; Fairchild et al., 2009).

Dodge and Pettit (2003) have presented a comprehensive social–cognitive framework to account for aggressive behavior and antisocial behavior in children. In their model, cognitive and emotional processes play a central mediating role. Children are presumed to develop social knowledge about their world based on a unique set of predispositions, life experiences, and sociocultural contexts. In specific social situations, children

TABLE 9.4	Steps in the Thinking and Behavior of Aggressive Children in Social Situations

Step 1: Encoding. Socially aggressive children use fewer cues before making a decision. When defining and resolving an interpersonal situation, they seek less information about the event before acting.

Step 2: Interpretation. Socially aggressive children attribute hostile intentions to ambiguous events.

Step 3: Response Search. Socially aggressive children generate fewer and more aggressive responses and have less knowledge about social problem solving.

Step 4: Response Decision. Socially aggressive children are more likely to choose aggressive solutions.

Step 5: Enactment. Socially aggressive children use poor verbal communication and strike out physically.

Source: From A Review and Reformulation of Social information Processing Mechanism in Children's Social Adjustment by N. R. Crick and K. A. Dodge, 1994, Psychological Bulletin, 115, 74–101.

then use this social knowledge to guide their processing of social information in ways that lead directly to certain behaviors. For example, when teased in the schoolyard by peers, does the child laugh with the crowd, walk away, or strike back aggressively? A set of emotional and thought processes are presumed to occur between the social stimulus of being teased and the child's reaction. The thinking and behavior of antisocial/aggressive children in social situations are often characterized by deficits in one or more of these steps, as outlined in Table 9.4.

Family Factors

I am convinced that increasing rates of delinquency are due to parents who are either too careless or too busy with their own pleasure to give sufficient time, companionship, and interest to their children.

—Former FBI director J. Edgar Hoover, *The New York Times*,
December 6, 1947

Many family factors have been implicated as possible causes of children's antisocial behavior—early maternal age at childbearing, poor disciplinary practices, harsh discipline, a lack of parental supervision, a lack of affection, marital conflict, family isolation, and violence in the home (D'Onofrio et al., 2009; Hoeve et al., 2008; Lansford et al., 2011). For children who are at genetic risk for antisocial behavior, positive parenting practices may reduce the influence of the child's genotype on later antisocial behavior, whereas negative parenting practices can have the opposite effect (Feinberg et al., 2007). Although the association between family

factors and conduct problems is well established, the nature of this association and the possible causal role of family factors continue to be debated.

Family difficulties are related to the development of both ODD and CD, with a stronger association for children on the LCP as compared with those on the AL path (Lahey et al., 1992). A combination of individual child risk factors (e.g., difficult temperament) and extreme deficits in family management skills most likely accounts for the more persistent and severe forms of antisocial behavior (Caspi & Moffitt, 1995).

Family factors are related to children's antisocial behavior in complex ways. For example, physical abuse is a strong risk factor for later aggressive behavior. One reason for this link between factors appears to be deficits in the child's social information processing that result from the physical abuse (Dodge & Pettit, 2003). As we have seen, the child's genotype can also moderate the link between maltreatment and later antisocial behavior, a possible reason that not all children who have been abused grow up to victimize others (Caspi et al., 2002).

Several factors may affect the consequences of marital conflict on children's aggressive behavior; these include the parents' unavailability, the use of

Physical abuse is a strong risk factor for later aggressive behavior.

Bob Kalman / The Image Works

inconsistent or harsh discipline, lax monitoring, and how the child interprets conflict between parents (Cummings & Davies, 2002). Other conditions associated with marital conflict or divorce such as stress, depression, loss of contact with one parent, financial hardship, and greater responsibility at home may also contribute to antisocial behavior (Emery, 1999). Interestingly, contact with an absent father after the breakup of the parents' marriage can be either a risk or a protective factor for antisocial behavior, depending on whether or not the father is antisocial (Jaffee et al., 2003).

Nick's mother says:

Nick hit a neighborhood kid on the head with a two-by-four; the injured child required 16 stitches. Then he killed another kitten by jumping on it from his bunk bed. I lost control. I told him I hated him, I grabbed him by the cheek, I pinched it a little too hard. I didn't know what to do. (Colapinto, 1993, p. 150)

Cruel and aggressive child behaviors can evoke strong reactions, like the anger and overly harsh response by Nick's mother. An important concept for understanding family influences on antisocial behavior is **reciprocal influence**, which means that the child's behavior is both influenced by and influences the behavior of others. Negative parenting practices and parent–child conflict may lead to antisocial behavior, but they may also be a reaction to the oppositional and aggressive behaviors of their children (Klahr et al., 2011).

For example, in an interesting study of reciprocal influence, mothers of boys with and without CD were asked to interact with three boys—their own son, a boy with CD, and a boy without CD (Anderson, Lytton, & Romney, 1986). All mothers were more demanding and negative when interacting with a child with CD, which supports a child-to-parent effect. However, mothers of boys with CD responded most negatively to their own sons, suggesting that previous negative interactions with their child also had an effect. Reciprocal influence is a useful way to think of the interplay between family influences and antisocial behavior over the course of development. However, it is also possible that some aspects of the family environment are related to antisocial behavior as a result of a shared genetic predisposition that leads parent and child to display similar behavior patterns.

Some studies generally support the view that child behaviors exert greater influence on parenting behaviors than the reverse, perhaps more so for mothers than fathers (Narusyte et al., 2011). This suggests that the inborn level of emotional dysregulation that children bring to their interactions with parents may have a greater influence on outcomes than ineffective parenting behaviors (Loeber et al., 2009). Nevertheless, as we will

A child's oppositional behavior may also lead to negative parenting behavior.

discuss, interventions directed at changing ineffective parenting behaviors are among the most effective methods for reducing children's conduct problems.

Coercion Theory

Gerald Patterson's **coercion theory** contends that parent–child interactions provide a training ground for the development of antisocial behavior (Patterson, Reid, & Dishion, 1992). This occurs through a four-step, escape-conditioning sequence in which the child learns to use increasingly intense forms of noxious behavior to escape and avoid unwanted parental demands. The *coercive parent–child interaction* described in A Closer Look 9.6 begins when a mother finds her son Paul, who is failing in school, watching TV rather than doing his homework. Coercive parent–child interactions are made up of well-practiced actions and reactions, which may occur with little awareness. This process is called a "reinforcement trap" because, over time, all family members become trapped by the consequences of their own behaviors. For example, mothers of antisocial children are eight times *less* likely to enforce demands than are mothers of nonproblem children (Patterson et al., 1992).

The relationship between parenting and conduct problems also appears to be affected by a child's callous–unemotional traits. In one report, ineffective parenting was related to conduct problems, but only in children who were rated low on CU traits (Wootton et al., 1997). Children with CU traits displayed significant conduct problems regardless of the quality of parenting they received. The relationship between parental discipline and conduct problems may also be affected by the amount of discipline—too much or too little can both have adverse effects. The relationship between parental discipline and antisocial behavior may

Coercive Parent–Child Interaction: Four-Step Escape Conditioning Sequence

Step 1

Raising her voice, Paul's mother scolds, "Why are you sitting in front of the TV when you should be doing your homework?"

Step 2

Paul snaps back, "School is boring, my teachers are stupid, and I don't have any homework to do." Paul's arguing has the immediate effect of punishing his mother for her scolding and, over time, may reduce her efforts to do something about his homework and school problems.

Step 3

Paul's mother withdraws her demand for him to complete his homework, allowing herself to be satisfied that he does not have any homework to do. She lowers her voice and says, "Does Mrs. Smith still put everyone to sleep in her English class?" The mother's withdrawal of her demand for homework reinforces Paul's arguing and increases the chances that the next time she makes an issue of homework, he will argue with her. Over time, Paul may also turn up the volume of his negative reactions by shouting or throwing things.

Step 4

As soon as Paul's mother withdraws her demand, Paul stops arguing and engages in neutral or even positive behavior. He says "You're sure right about Mrs. Smith, Mom. It's tough to keep your eyes open in her class." Paul, by ceasing his noxious behavior, reinforces his mother for giving in and increases the likelihood that she will do so again in response to his arguing and protests.

Based on Antisocial Boys, by G. R. Patterson, J. B. Reid, and T. J. Dishion, 1992, p. 41.

---

also vary with the family's cultural background, the emotional climate in which discipline is used, and the gender of the parent–child pair. For example, discipline may be most effective in same-gender parent–child pairs: discipline of daughters by mothers and sons by fathers (Deater-Deckard & Dodge, 1997).

Attachment Theories

Attachment theories emphasize that the quality of children's attachment to parents will determine their eventual identification with parental values, beliefs, and standards. Secure bonds with parents promote a sense of closeness, shared values, and identification with the social world. Attachment theories contend that children refrain from antisocial behavior because they have a stake in conformity.

Children with conduct problems often show little internalization of parent and societal standards. Even when they comply with parental requests, they may do so because of perceived threats to their freedom or physical safety (Shaw & Bell, 1993). When these threats are not present, such as when the child is unsupervised, antisocial behavior is likely to occur. Weak bonds with parents may lead the child to associate with deviant peers, which in turn may lead to delinquency and substance abuse (Elliott, Huizinga, & Menard, 1989).

Research findings support a relationship between insecure attachments, particularly for children with disorganized attachments, and the development of antisocial behavior during childhood and adolescence (Pasco Fearon et al., 2010). However, it is unclear whether attachment quality by itself can predict current or future variation in the severity of conduct problems. It is likely that the relationship between attachment and antisocial behavior is affected by many factors, including the child's gender, clinical status, temperament, and family management practices (Pasco Fearon et al., 2010).

Other Family Problems

In addition to the negative parenting practices and attachment problems that we have discussed, other family factors such as family instability and stress, and parental criminality and psychopathology may also contribute to children's conduct problems.

JAKE AND REGGIE

All Odds Against Them

Linda M., single mother of 2-year-old Jake and 4-year-old Reggie, sought treatment because Reggie was engaging in severe and uncontrollable aggressive behaviors, including hitting, kicking, and biting Jake. She was depressed and at risk for suicide. Her boyfriend Hank is the father of the two children. He lives nearby and demands that she come over so he can see the children. During these visits, he engages her in what she refers to as "forced sex" (i.e., rape), and he demands that Jake and Reggie remain with them and watch. In principle, Linda could have refused the visits. However, Hank threatened that if she did not comply, he would stop paying child support, take Jake and Reggie away in a custody battle, kill himself, or come over to the house and kill her and the two boys. These threats of violence were to be taken seriously because Hank had a prior arrest record for assault and brandished a gun.

Based on Conduct Disorders in Childhood and Adolescence by A. E. Kazdin, p. 17.

system (i.e., "the world is a hostile place," "aggression is acceptable," "aggression can be used to solve social problems") (Huesmann et al., 2003).

Exposure to media violence may reinforce pre-existing antisocial tendencies in some children. For example, in a series of studies spanning more than a decade, children with conduct problems were found to view relatively large amounts of violent material, prefer aggressive characters, and believe fictional content to be true (Gadow & Sprafkin, 1993). However, it is not only children with preexisting violent tendencies who are likely to be affected. Long-term studies have found that childhood exposure to media violence between ages 6 and 9, identification with aggressive TV characters, and perceived realism of TV violence predict serious aggressive and criminal behavior 15 years later (Huesmann et al., 2003).

The correlation between TV violence and aggression is indisputable—but does TV violence cause aggression, and if so, how? Although research suggests a causal relation (Anderson & Bushman, 2002; Johnson et al., 2002), answers to these questions remain elusive despite decades of research and a pressing urge to act on research findings through social policies to filter violent content and inform users. It is unlikely that media influences (TV or other forms) alone can account for the substantial amount of antisocial behavior in young people (Rutter & Smith, 1995). Like other risk factors, media influences interact with child, family, community, and cultural factors in contributing to conduct problems. But clearly they are an important and unique contributing factor. Exposure to media violence will not turn an otherwise well-adjusted child into a violent criminal. However, "just as every cigarette one smokes increases a little bit the likelihood of a lung tumor some day … every violent TV show increases a little bit the likelihood of a child growing up to behave more aggressively in some situation" (Huesmann et al., 2003, p. 218).

Cultural Factors

Cultural differences in the expression of aggressive behavior are dramatic. Across cultures, socialization of children for aggression has been found to be one of the strongest predictors of aggressive acts such as homicide and assault. As the following examples of contrasting socialization practices illustrate, aggression may be an inadvertent consequence of a culture's emphasis on training "warriors":

The Kapauku of Western New Guinea:

At about 7 years of age, a Kapauku boy begins to be under the father's control, gradually sleeping and eating only with the men and away from his mother. … His training [to be a brave warrior] begins when the father engages his son in mock stick fights. Gradually the fights become more serious and possibly lethal when the father and son shoot real war arrows at each other. Groups of boys play at target shooting; they also play at hitting each other over the head with sticks. (Ember & Ember, 1994, p. 639–640)

The homicide rate among the Kapauku from 1953 to 1954 was estimated at 200 per 100,000, approximately 40 times the current murder rate in the United States.

The Lepcha of the Indian Himalayas:

The Lepcha are very clear about what they expect from their children. "Good children help out with the work, tell the truth, listen to teaching from elders, help old people, and are peaceable. Bad children quarrel with and insult people, tell lies, draw their

Calvin and Hobbes   by Bill Watterson

knives in anger when reprimanded, and do not do their share of the work." (Ember & Ember, 1994, p. 641)

Interviews with the Lepcha people revealed that the only authenticated murder in their culture had occurred about 200 years ago (Ember & Ember, 1994).

Rates of antisocial behavior vary widely across and within cultures, and not necessarily in relation to technological gains, material wealth, or population density. For example, some third world countries that value interdependence are characterized by high rates of prosocial behavior, and some places with high population density have very low rates of violence. The United States is by far the most violent of all industrialized nations, with homicide rates about 5 times higher than those in Europe and 10 times higher than those in Japan (OECD, 2013).

Minority status is related to antisocial behavior in the United States, with elevated rates of antisocial behavior in African American, Hispanic American, and Native American youths (Elliott, Huizinga, & Ageton, 1985). However, studies of national samples have reported either no or very small differences in antisocial behavior related to race or ethnicity when SES, gender, age, and referral status are controlled for (Lahey et al., 1995). Thus, although externalizing problems are reported to be more frequent among minority-status youths, this finding is likely related to disparities that include economic hardship, limited employment opportunities, residence in high-risk urban neighborhoods, and membership in antisocial gangs (Children's Defense Fund, 2007; Egley & Howell, 2013). Importantly, both Mexican American and African American children who live in dangerous or disadvantaged neighborhoods and who have high levels of family support show fewer antisocial behaviors than children who have low or no family support (Schofield et al., 2012). For immigrant groups in the United States, the risk for CD also seems to vary according to migration status and amount of exposure to American culture. For example, one study found that the risk for CD was highest among Mexican American children of U.S.-born parents as compared with children of Mexican-born immigrants raised in the United States or the general population of Mexico (Breslau et al., 2012).

Section Summary

Causes

- Conduct problems in children are best accounted for by multiple causes or risk and protective factors that operate in a transactional fashion over time.
- Adoption and twin studies indicate that genetic influences account for about 50% of the variance in antisocial behavior.

- Genetic contributions to overt forms of antisocial behavior, such as aggression, are stronger than for covert acts, such as stealing or lying.
- Antisocial behavior may result from an overactive behavioral activation system (BAS) and an underactive behavioral inhibition system (BIS). Low levels of cortical arousal and autonomic reactivity and deficits in the amygdala, prefrontal cortex, and other brain regions play an important role, particularly for childhood-onset/persistent CD.
- Many family factors have been implicated as possible causes of children's antisocial behavior, including marital conflict, family isolation, violence in the home, poor disciplinary practices, a lack of parental supervision, and insecure attachments.
- Family instability and stress, parental criminality and antisocial personality, and antisocial family values are risk factors for conduct problems.
- The structural characteristics of the community provide a backdrop for the emergence of conduct problems by giving rise to community conditions that interfere with the adoption of social norms and the development of productive social relations.
- School, neighborhood, and media influences are all potential risk factors for antisocial behavior, as are cultural factors, such as minority group status and ethnicity.

TREATMENT AND PREVENTION

SCOTT

Salvageable?

Scott, age 10, was referred after setting a fire in the schoolyard. While his therapist saw Scott as "potentially salvageable," his parents were not willing to pursue therapy. As a result, Scott was placed in a boarding school for "troubled boys." ... After 3 weeks at this school, he was expelled for burning down the dorm. ... Charges were pressed and he was sent to a group home for delinquent boys. He remained there for 3 months before he and two older boys ran away. They were caught a few days later when they attacked a homeless man, stealing his money ($4.85) and beating him. As a result of this crime, Scott was sent to a detention facility until he turned 18. His therapist heard nothing further.

Based on Morgan, 1999.

Many forms of treatment will be tried throughout the life of a child with severe conduct problems. Treatment may begin during the preschool years or, more typically, as was the case with Scott, when severe antisocial behavior at school leads to referral. Ongoing contacts with the educational, mental health, and judicial systems may result in referral for one or more of a wide range of treatments. The most promising treatments use a combination of approaches that are applied across individual, family, school, and community settings (Kazdin, 2007; Lochman et al., 2011; Sanders, 2012). In addition, treatment frequently requires that related family problems, such as maternal depression, marital discord, abuse, and other stressors be addressed if gains are to be generalized and maintained (McMahon, Wells, & Kotler, 2006).

Most people understand that family dysfunction, abuse, school expulsion, association with drug-using peers, residence in a high-crime area, and minimal parental supervision contribute to serious conduct problems (Henggeler, 1996). However, despite this recognition, typical and often court-mandated treatments such as psychotherapy, group therapy, tutoring, punishment, wilderness programs, and boot camps fail to meaningfully address these determinants, and thus are among the least effective approaches (Lipsey, 1995). Despite their lack of effectiveness in treating serious antisocial behavior, office-based individual counseling and family therapy are often provided because they can be relatively inexpensive (Tate, Reppucci, & Mulvey, 1995). Group treatments that bring together antisocial youth may only make the problem worse, since associating with like-minded individuals often encourages antisocial behavior (Dishion & Dodge, 2005).

As we saw for Scott, restrictive approaches such as residential treatment, inpatient psychiatric hospitalization, and incarceration also show little effectiveness and have the additional disadvantage of being extremely expensive (Henggeler & Santos, 1997). Unfortunately, a significant proportion of mental health dollars for youths continues to be spent on restrictive out-of-home placements that may cause more harm than good (Sondheimer, Schoenwald, & Rowland, 1994). Incarceration may not even serve a community protection function, since youths who are incarcerated and then released often commit more crimes than youths kept at home and given treatment (Henggeler, 1996).

Since youth conduct problems are known to show a developmental progression, diversification, and escalation over time, treatments must be sensitive to where a youth is in this trajectory. Treatment methods and goals will differ for preschoolers, school-age children, and adolescents and will differ according to the type and severity of the child's conduct problems. In general, the more progressed the antisocial behavior, the greater is the need for intensive interventions and, unfortunately, for children like Scott, the poorer is the prognosis. In fact, if early-onset antisocial behavior is not changed by the end of grade 3, it might best be treated as a chronic condition, much like diabetes, which cannot be cured but can be managed or contained through ongoing interventions and supports (Kazdin, 1995). This troubling situation of high treatment effort and cost with less return for older children has led to a reevaluation of priorities and a growing emphasis on early intervention and prevention (Powell, Lochman, & Boxmeyer, 2007). A comprehensive, two-pronged approach to the treatment of conduct problems is needed that includes (Frick, 2000):

▸ *Early intervention/prevention* programs for young children at risk for or just starting to display problem behaviors

▸ *Ongoing interventions* to help older youths and their families cope with the many associated social, emotional, and academic problems

To illustrate the many treatments for children and adolescents with conduct problems, we next highlight three representative treatment approaches that have had some proven success (Eyberg, Nelson, & Boggs, 2008)—parent management training (PMT), problem-solving skills training (PSST), and multisystemic therapy (MST) (see Table 9.5). We also discuss promising new

TABLE 9.5 | Effective Treatments for Children with Conduct Problems

Treatment	Overview
Parent Management Training (PMT)	Teaches parents to change their child's behavior in the home and in other settings using contingency management techniques. The focus is on improving parent–child interactions and enhancing other parenting skills (e.g., parent–child communication, monitoring, and supervision).
Problem-Solving Skills Training (PSST)	Identifies the child's cognitive deficiencies and distortions in social situations and provides instruction, practice, and feedback to teach new ways of handling social situations. The child learns to appraise the situation, change his or her attributions about other children's motivations, be more sensitive to how other children feel, and generate alternative and more appropriate solutions.
Multisystemic Therapy (MST)	An intensive approach that draws on other techniques such as PMT, PSST, and marital therapy, as well as specialized interventions such as special education, and referral to substance abuse treatment programs or legal services.

preventive interventions for young children. Almost all forms of treatment provide corrective interpersonal experiences with parents, siblings, and peers because most antisocial acts, including violence, occur between the child and family members or peers. In addition, given the pervasiveness of conduct problems across settings, nearly all treatments include components designed to change the child's behavior at home, in the community, and at school (Liber et al., 2013).

Parent Management Training (PMT)

Parent management training (PMT) teaches parents to change their child's behavior at home and in other settings (Brinkmeyer & Eyberg, 2003; McMahon & Forehand, 2003). Its underlying assumption is that maladaptive parent–child interactions are at least partly responsible for producing and sustaining the child's antisocial behavior. Changing the way parents interact with their child will lead to improvements in the child's behavior. Although both child and parent behavior jointly contribute to negative parent–child interactions, the easiest and most desirable point of entry in modifying these interactions is changing parent behavior. The goal of PMT is for the parent to learn specific new skills (Forgatch & Patterson, 2010). To achieve this goal, many of the same procedures that we have discussed for working with children with ADHD and their families are used (see Chapter 8). These include teaching parents to monitor their children's behavior, to present clear commands and rules, and to systematically provide rewards and minor forms of punishment such as time out from positive reinforcement. Many variations of PMT can be individual versus group training, training in the clinic versus in the home, or the use of live versus videotaped training materials.

PMT has a number of strengths and some limitations (McMahon et al., 2006). Many excellent treatment manuals and training materials have been developed that facilitate its widespread use (e.g., Barkley, 2013a; McMahon & Forehand, 2003). In addition, PMT has been evaluated more than any other treatment for conduct problems (Eyberg et al., 2008). These evaluations have repeatedly demonstrated short-term effectiveness in producing changes in parent and child behavior. The average child whose parents participate in PMT shows better adjustment after treatment than 80% of referred children whose parents do not participate (Serketich & Dumas, 1996). In addition to changes in the referred child, PMT has also been associated with reductions in the problem behaviors of siblings and reduced stress and depression in the parents.

PMT has been most effective with parents of children younger than 12 years of age and less so with adolescents (Dishion & Patterson, 1992). In light of this, promising adaptations of these interventions have also been developed for working with older adolescents and their families (Dishion & Kavanagh, 2003). Although PMT can produce short-term gains, its long-term effectiveness is less clear (McMahon et al., 2006). In addition, PMT makes numerous demands on parents to master and implement procedures in the home, attend meetings, and maintain phone contact with the therapist. For families under stress and with few resources, these demands may be too great to allow the family to continue in treatment (Lundahl, Risser, & Lovejoy, 2006). In order to increase engagement of low-income families, smart phone–enhanced versions of PMT have been developed to include series of skills videos, brief daily surveys, text message reminders, video recording of home practice, and midweek video calls (Jones et al., 2014). There is also growing recognition of the importance of identifying barriers to, and facilitators of, access/engagement of parents in PMT programs (Koerting et al., 2013).

The application of PMT is rarely straightforward. The need to change their own parenting practices may not be recognized by parents who believe that difficulties occur because their child is stubborn, their marriage is bad, work is interfering with the time they spend together, or school personnel are unfair. In fact, parents of children with conduct problems frequently believe they use good parenting practices but their child fails to respond. It is important to address these parental beliefs and concerns if treatment is to be successful (Morrisey-Kane & Prinz, 1999). In addition, PMT practitioners have increasingly come to recognize the importance of marital and social support, therapy style and engagement, and ethnic and cultural factors in treatment (Scott et al., 2010; Yasui & Dishion, 2007).

Problem-Solving Skills Training (PSST)

Problem-solving skills training (PSST) is a form of cognitive behavioral therapy that focuses on the cognitive deficiencies and distortions displayed by children and adolescents with conduct problems in interpersonal situations (Kazdin, 2010). PSST is used both alone and in combination with PMT, as required by the family's circumstances. The underlying assumption of PSST is that the child's perceptions and appraisals of environmental events will trigger aggressive and antisocial responses, and that correcting faulty thinking will lead to changes in behavior. As described in A Closer Look 9.7, the child is taught to use five problem-solving steps to identify thoughts, feelings, and behaviors in problem social situations.

During PSST, the therapist uses instruction, practice, and feedback to help the child discover different ways to handle social situations. To accomplish this, children learn to appraise the situation, identify self-statements and reactions, and alter their attributions about other children's motivations. They also learn to be more sensitive to how other children feel, to anticipate others' reactions, and to generate appropriate solutions to social problems.

PSST is effective with children and youths who are clinically referred for conduct problems, with benefits extending to parent and family functioning (Kazdin, 2010). Research supports the emphasis on the relationship between maladaptive cognitions and aggressive behavior on which PSST is based, and PSST procedures are carefully specified in treatment manuals. Until relatively recently it was not clear whether changes in maladaptive cognitions were responsible for behavioral improvements. Indeed, the alteration of social–cognitive processes may not necessarily lead to changes in behavior. However, in one major study using a multifaceted intervention (Fast Track) it was found that 27% of the intervention's impact on antisocial behavior was mediated by its effect on three social–cognitive processes: reducing hostile-attribution biases, increasing competent response generation to social problems, and devaluing aggression (Dodge, Godwin, & The Conduct Problems Prevention Research Group, 2013). Finally, although most children improve as a result of PSST, some may continue to display more problems than their nondeviant peers. Thus, more enduring PSST and other interventions are being developed to meet the needs of families of children with conduct problems whose problems are particularly severe.

Multisystemic Therapy (MST)

Multisystemic therapy (MST) is an intensive empirically supported family and community-based treatment for adolescents with severe conduct problems that make out-of-home placement highly likely (Henggeler & Schaeffer, 2010). MST views the adolescent with conduct problems as functioning within interconnected social systems, including the family, school, neighborhood, and court and juvenile services (Henggeler et al., 2009). Antisocial behavior results from, or can be maintained by, transactions within or between any of these systems. MST seeks to empower caregivers to improve youth and family functioning (Cunningham et al., 1999). Thus, treatment is carried out with all family members, school personnel, peers, juvenile justice staff, and other individuals in the child's life. MST is an intensive approach that also draws on PMT, PSST, and marital therapy, as well as specialized interventions such as special education and referral to substance-abuse treatment programs or legal services. In effect, MST attempts to address the many determinants of severe antisocial behavior (Wells et al., 2010). The guiding principles of MST are outlined in Table 9.6.

Outcome studies of MST with extremely antisocial and violent youths have found this approach to be superior to usual services, individual counseling, community services, and psychiatric hospitalization. In addition, studies have found decreases in delinquency and aggression with peers, improved family relations, and reductions in out-of-home placements (Weiss et al., 2013). Importantly, MST has been found to reduce long-term rates of criminal behavior for as long as 5 years after treatment. MST is also cost-effective; its costs are 10 times less than conventional interventions and its estimated savings over the years are about $10 to $20 for each dollar spent on MST (Klietz, Borduin, & Schaeffer, 2010).

Since studies of MST have not yet differentiated between adolescents who show life-course–persistent and those with adolescence-limited patterns of antisocial behavior, it is difficult to know whether successful outcomes reported for this approach apply

TABLE 9.6	The Nine Principles of Multisystemic Therapy (MST)

1. **Finding the fit** The primary purpose of assessment is to understand the "fit" between the identified problems and their broader systemic context.

2. **Positive and strength-focused** Therapeutic contacts emphasize the positive and use systemic strengths as levers for change.

3. **Increasing responsibility** Interventions are designed to promote responsible behavior and decrease irresponsible behavior among family members.

4. **Present-focused, action-oriented, and well defined** Interventions are present-focused and action-oriented, targeting specific and well-defined problems.

5. **Targeting sequences** Interventions target sequences of behavior within and between multiple systems that maintain identified problems.

6. **Developmentally appropriate** Interventions are developmentally appropriate and fit the developmental needs of the youth.

7. **Continuous effort** Interventions are designed to require daily or weekly effort by family members.

8. **Evaluation and accountability** Intervention efficacy is evaluated continuously from multiple perspectives, with providers assuming accountability for overcoming barriers to successful outcomes.

9. **Generalization** Interventions are designed to promote treatment generalization and long-term maintenance of therapeutic change by empowering caregivers to address family members' needs across multiple systemic contexts.

Based on Table 2.1 in Multisystemic Therapy for Antisocial Behavior in Children and Adolescents (2nd ed.), by S. W. Henggeler, S. K. Schoenwald, C. M. Borduin, M. D. Rowland, & P. B. Cunningham. New York: Guilford Press.

equally to both groups. It is possible that part of the success of MST may be in helping youths on the adolescent-limited path decrease their association with deviant peers and, by doing so, lowering the age at which they cease delinquent behavior.

Preventive Interventions

Until recently, treatments for older children with conduct problems were given far greater attention than programs for early intervention and prevention. Fortunately, this situation is changing, with a growing recognition of the need for intensive home and school-based interventions that can compete with the child's negative developmental history, poor family and community environment, and deviant peer associations (Prinz & Sanders, 2007; Wilson & Lipsey, 2007). Annual family

checkups that provide tailored PMT to preschool-age children within the context of early childhood social, health, and educational services have also been developed to prevent early-onset pathways of antisocial behavior (Dishion et al., 2013). The main assumptions of preventive interventions are (Webster-Stratton, 1996):

▶ Conduct problems can be treated more easily and more effectively in younger than in older children.

▶ By counteracting risk factors and strengthening promotive factors at a young age, it is possible to limit or prevent the escalating developmental trajectory of increased aggression, peer rejection, self-esteem deficits, conduct disorder, and academic failure that is commonly observed in children with childhood-onset conduct problems.

▶ In the long run, preventive interventions will reduce the substantial costs to the educational, criminal justice, health, and mental health systems that are associated with conduct problems.

Carolyn Webster-Stratton has developed an intensive and multifaceted early-intervention program for parents and teachers of 2- to 10-year-old children with or at risk for conduct problems (Incredible Years; Webster-Stratton & Reid, 2010). This program uses interactive videotapes as a foundation for training, which permits widespread use at a relatively low cost. In addition to teaching child management skills, the program also addresses the associated individual, family, and school difficulties that accompany conduct problems. Parents are taught personal self-control strategies for managing anger, depression, and blame. As a result, they learn effective communication skills, strategies for coping with conflict at home and at work, and ways to strengthen social supports. Teachers are taught ways to strengthen positive relationships with students, effective classroom discipline, strategies for teaching social skills, anger management, problem-solving skills, and how to increase collaboration with parents (Webster-Stratton & Herman, 2010). In addition to the parent and teacher training programs, there is also an Incredible Years Child Training program for 3- to 8-year-olds, who meet with a therapist in groups of six for 2 hours a week. Children view videotapes of conflict situations at school and home that illustrate problem-solving and social skills. Following this, children discuss feelings, generate ideas for more effective responses, and role-play alternative behaviors.

A number of studies have provided support for the effectiveness of these early interventions in reducing later conduct problems and maintaining positive outcomes in adolescence for two-thirds or more of children whose parents are involved (Webster-Stratton, Reid, & Hammond, 2004; Webster-Stratton, Rinaldi, & Reid, 2010). This early intervention/prevention program is

10

Depressive and Bipolar Disorders

This is my depressed stance. When you're depressed, it makes a lot of difference how you stand. The worst thing you can do is straighten up and hold your head high because then you'll start to feel better. If you're going to get any joy out of being depressed, you've got to stand like this.

—Charlie Brown (Charles M. Schulz, 1922–2000)

CHAPTER PREVIEW

DONNA

Desperate Despair

Donna, age 12, says, "Sometimes I feel like jumping off the roof or finding some other way to hurt myself." Over the past 3 months, Donna has become more and more withdrawn, and her feelings of sadness, worthlessness, and self-hatred scare her. Her teacher describes Donna as "a loner who seems very troubled and unhappy." She's always been a good student, but she is now having difficulty concentrating, is failing tests, and feels totally unmotivated. At home, Donna is having trouble sleeping, has no appetite, and frequently complains of headaches. Most days she stays in her room and does nothing. When her mother asks her to do something, Donna becomes extremely upset. Her mother says Donna is "moody and irritable most of the time." (Based on authors' case material)

MICK

Up and Down

Mick, age 16, is moody all of the time. Sometimes he is sad, sullen, and apathetic. At other times he is full of life and energy, or intensely angry. When full of energy, he can go with little or no sleep for days without feeling tired. He moves constantly, talks incessantly, and cannot be interrupted. These extreme changes in mood make Mick feel out of control, and sometimes he thinks about hurting himself. He is frightened by his thoughts and drinks or uses drugs when they are available to reduce the pain. (Based on authors' case material)

PERHAPS YOU KNOW A child or teen who seems constantly unhappy, shows little enthusiasm for anything, is moody, or—at worst—thinks life just isn't worth living. This child may have a **mood disorder** (also called an *affective disorder*), in which a disturbance in mood is the central feature. Mood is broadly defined as a feeling or emotion—for example, sadness, happiness, anger, elation, or crankiness. Children with mood disorders suffer from extreme, persistent, or poorly regulated emotional states, such as excessive unhappiness, ongoing irritability or anger, or swings in mood from deep sadness to high elation. Mood disorders are one of the most common, chronic, and disabling illnesses in young people (Kessler et al., 2012a, b).

OVERVIEW OF MOOD DISORDERS

Mood disorders come in several types. At one end of the spectrum is severe depression. Like Donna, children who have severe depression suffer from **dysphoria**, a state of prolonged bouts of sadness (Kovacs & Yaroslavsky, 2014). They feel little joy in anything they do and lose interest in nearly all activities, a state known as **anhedonia**. In the words of one depressed teen:

> Depression makes you lose interest in all the stuff you used to think was fun. You might quit playing guitar or drop out of yearbook, and claim that you just don't have the energy or desire to pursue extracurricular activities—or curricular activities, for that matter. From Solin, 1995.

Many young people with depression express these combined feelings of sadness and loss of interest or pleasure. However, some may never report feeling sad. Rather, they express their depression through their irritable mood. **Irritability** refers to easy annoyance and touchiness, characterized by an angry mood and temper outbursts (Stringaris, 2011). Others may describe these children as cranky, grouchy, moody, short-fused, or easily upset. Being around them is difficult because any little thing can set them off. Irritability is one of the most common co-occurring symptoms of depression, present in as many as 80% of clinic-referred and 36% of community samples of youngsters with depression (Stringaris et al., 2013).

At the other end of the mood spectrum are a smaller number of youths, those like Mick, who also experience episodes of **mania**, an abnormally elevated or expansive mood, increased goal-directed activity and energy, and feelings of **euphoria**, which is an exaggerated sense of well-being. They suffer from an ongoing combination of extreme highs and extreme lows, a condition known as **bipolar disorder** (BP) or *manic–depressive illness*. Their highs may alternate with lows, or they may feel both extremes at about the same time.

The two major types of mood disorders in the *Diagnostic and Statistical Manual of Mental Disorders*, 5th edition (DSM-5) are depressive disorders and bipolar disorders. We discuss each of these in the sections that follow.

Section Summary

Overview of Mood Disorders

- Children with mood disorders suffer from extreme, persistent, or poorly regulated emotional states—for example, excessive unhappiness, irritability, or swings in mood from deep sadness to high elation.

(continues)

- Mood disorders are common and are among the most persistent and disabling illnesses in young people.
- There are two major types of mood disorders: depressive disorders and bipolar disorders.

DEPRESSIVE DISORDERS

"And how are you?" said Winnie-the-Pooh.

Eeyore shook his head from side to side.

"Not very how," he said. "I don't seem to have felt at all how for a long time."

—A. A. Milne, *Winnie-the-Pooh* (1926)

Depression refers to a pervasive unhappy mood, the kind of gloomy feeling displayed by Eeyore, the sad and indecisive old gray donkey in *Winnie-the-Pooh*. The symptoms of depression are so universal that depression is sometimes called "the common cold of psychopathology." Everyone feels sad, blue, out of sorts, or "down in the dumps" at times. (Even reading or writing about depression can be a real downer—can anyone think of a way to put a positive spin on feelings of dejection, hopelessness, irritability, loneliness, or self-blame?) Sometimes our sadness is a normal reaction to an unfortunate event in our lives like losing a friend or a job. At other times, we may feel depressed without really knowing why. These feelings soon pass, however, and we resume our normal activities. Clinical depression, in contrast, is more severe than the occasional blues or mood swings that everyone gets from time to time.

Childhood is usually thought of as a happy and carefree time, a period unfettered by the worries, burdens, and responsibilities of adulthood. We tend to think of young people as positive and upbeat, not depressed. In fact, a common reaction to hearing that a child is depressed is "What does she have to be depressed about?" Even when children experience disappointment, disapproval, or other inevitable negative events in their lives, their sadness, frustration, and anger are expected to be short-lived. When children become sad, irritable, or upset, parents often attribute the negative moods to temporary factors—such as a lack of sleep or not feeling well—and expect the moods to pass. Thus, for a long time it was thought that children did not get depressed, and when they did, the depression would be short-lived. We now know this is not true. Current estimates indicate that more than 3 million children and adolescents in the United States suffer from significant depression each year (Kessler et al., 2012a).

Depression in children goes well beyond normal mood swings.

Unlike most children, who bounce back quickly when they are sad, children who are depressed cannot seem to shake their sadness, and it begins to interfere with their daily routines, social relationships, school performance, and overall functioning. Depressed youths often have accompanying problems such as anxiety or oppositional/conduct disorders. Although clinical depression may resemble the normal emotional dips of childhood, for many young people it is pervasive, disabling, long-lasting, and life-threatening (Abela & Hankin, 2008b; Hammen, Rudolph, & Abaied, 2014). Unfortunately, depression often goes unrecognized and untreated because parents and, in some cases, teachers may not recognize the child's underlying subjective negative mood.

History

Not long ago, people doubted the existence of depression in children. This mistaken belief was rooted in traditional psychoanalytic theories, which viewed depression as hostility or anger turned inward. Because children lacked sufficient superego development to permit aggression to be directed against the self, it was believed that they were incapable of experiencing depression (Rochlin, 1959). In another mistaken view, symptoms of depression were considered normal and passing expressions of certain stages of development, a belief that also has proved false. Depression in young people is a recurrent problem, as it is for adults.

As depression in children was acknowledged, a popular view emerged that children express depression in a much different way than adults, ways that are often indirect and hidden. This idea came to be known as *masked depression*. It was thought that any known clinical symptom in children, including hyperactivity, learning problems, aggression, bed-wetting, separation anxiety, sleep problems, and running away, could be a sign of an underlying but masked depression (Cytryn & McKnew, 1974). Because this concept is too encompassing to be useful, the once popular notion of masked depression has been rejected. Depression in children is not masked, but it may simply be overlooked because it frequently co-occurs with more visible disorders, such as conduct problems.

Depression in Young People

Almost all young people experience some symptoms of depression, and many experience significant depression at some time (Avenevoli et al., 2008). These youngsters display lasting depressed mood while facing real or perceived distress and experience disturbances in their thinking, physical functioning, and social behavior. Suicidal behavior among teens, which is frequently associated with depression, is also a very serious concern (Cha & Nock, 2014).

As many as 90% of youngsters with depression show significant impairment in their daily functions, and, even when they recover from their depression, they are likely to experience recurrent bouts of depression and continued impairments (Simonoff et al., 1997). The long-lasting emotional suffering, problems in everyday living, and heightened risk of these youths for suicide, substance use, other mental health problems, poorer health outcomes, and higher health care costs make depression in young people a significant concern (Fombonne et al., 2001a; Keenan-Miller, Hammen, & Brennan, 2007).

Depression and Development

Children express and experience depression differently at different ages (Weiss & Garber, 2003). An infant may show sadness by being passive and unresponsive; a preschooler may appear withdrawn and inhibited; a school-age child may be argumentative and combative or complain of feeling sick; a teenager may express feelings of guilt and hopelessness, sulk, or feel misunderstood. These examples are not various types of depressions, but likely represent different stages in the developmental course of the same process.

No one pattern fits all children within a particular age group or developmental period, and depression is not clearly recognizable as a clinical disorder using DSM criteria until children are older. Depression in children under the age of 7 is diffuse and less easily identified. However, some studies have found that age-adjusted diagnostic criteria can be used to identify and treat depression in children as young as 3 to 5 years (Luby, 2013). It is important to recognize depressive symptoms in preschool children, since their symptoms can persist or reoccur and develop into depressive disorders during late childhood or early adolescence (Luby, Si et al., 2009).

We know the least about depression in infants (Guedeney, 2007). In the 1940s, American psychoanalyst René Spitz described a condition he called *anaclitic depression,* in which infants raised in a clean but emotionally cold institutional environment displayed reactions that resembled depression (Spitz & Wolf, 1946). These infants displayed weeping, withdrawal, apathy, weight loss, and sleep disturbance. They also showed an overall decline in development, and in some cases, death. Although Spitz attributed this depression to an absence of mothering and the lack of opportunity to form an attachment, other factors, such as physical illness and sensory deprivation, may also have played a role. Nevertheless, even young children exposed to institutional neglect and later adopted may display emotional and behavioral disturbances that place them at heightened risk for depression and other internalizing disorders (Stellern et al., 2014).

Depression in institutionalized infants: When observed over time, these infants display a physical appearance that in an adult might be described as depression.

It also became clear that similar symptoms could occur even in noninstitutionalized infants raised in severely disturbed families in which the mother was depressed, psychologically unavailable, or physically abusive. These infants may experience sleep disturbances, loss of appetite, increased clinging, apprehension, social withdrawal, crying, and sadness (Goodman & Brand, 2009).

Preschool children who are depressed may appear extremely somber and tearful. They generally lack the exuberance, bounce, and enthusiasm in their play that characterize most preschoolers. They may display excessive clinging and whiny behavior around their mothers, as well as fears of separation or abandonment. In addition to getting upset when things do not go their way, many are irritable for no apparent reason. Negative and self-destructive verbalizations may occur, and physical complaints such as stomachaches are common (Luby et al., 2003).

School-age children with depression display many of the symptoms of preschoolers in addition to increased irritability, disruptive behavior, temper tantrums, and combativeness. A parent may say, "Nothing ever pleases my child—she hates herself and everything around her." School-age children may look sad, but are often unwilling to talk about their sad feelings. Physical symptoms may include weight loss, headaches, and sleep disturbances. Academic difficulties and peer problems are also common, and may include frequent fighting and complaints of not having friends or being picked on. Suicide threats may also begin to occur at this age.

Preteens and teens with depression display many of the symptoms of younger children, in addition to increasing self-blame and expressions of low self-esteem, persistent sadness, and social inhibition. A child may say, "I'm stupid" or "Nobody likes me." Feelings of isolation from family are also common. The preteen may also experience an inability to sleep or may sleep excessively. Disturbances in eating are also common. Teens show increased irritability, loss of feelings of pleasure or interest, and worsening school performance. Angry discussions with parents regarding normal parent–teen issues, such as choice of friends or curfew, are also more common. Other symptoms at this age include a negative body image and self-consciousness, physical symptoms such as excessive fatigue and energy loss, feelings of loneliness, guilt, and worthlessness, and suicidal thoughts, plans, and attempts.

Many of these symptoms and behaviors may also occur in children and teens who are developing normally or in those with other disorders or conditions. Therefore, the presence of sad mood, diminished interest or pleasure, or irritability is essential for diagnosing depression. In addition, regardless of the child's age, the symptoms must reflect a change in behavior, persist over time, and cause significant impairment in functioning (Rudolph & Lambert, 2007).

Anatomy of Depression

The term *depression* has been used in various ways. It is important to distinguish between depression as a symptom, depression as a syndrome, and depression as a disorder.

As a *symptom*, depression refers to feeling sad or miserable. Depressive symptoms often occur without the existence of a serious problem, and they are relatively common at all ages. For most children, symptoms of depression are temporary, related to events in the environment, and not part of any disorder.

As a *syndrome*, depression is more than a sad mood. A syndrome refers to a group of symptoms that occur together more often than by chance. Along with sadness, the child may display a reduced interest or pleasure in activities, cognitive and motivational changes, and somatic and psychomotor changes. As a syndrome, depression represents an extreme on a dimension reflecting the number or severity of co-occurring symptoms that the child displays. The occurrence of depression as a syndrome is far less common than isolated depressive symptoms, and it often includes mixed symptoms of anxiety and depression, which tend to cluster on a single dimension of *negative affect* (Ollendick et al., 2003).

As a *disorder*, depression comes in several forms. We will consider three types. The first, **major depressive disorder (MDD)**, has a minimum duration of 2 weeks and is associated with depressed or irritable mood, loss of interest or pleasure, other symptoms (e.g., sleep disturbances, difficulty concentrating, feelings of worthlessness), and significant distress or impairment in functioning. The second, **persistent depressive disorder [P-DD]**, or **dysthymia**, is associated with depressed or irritable mood, generally fewer, less severe, but longer-lasting symptoms (a year or more in children) than MDD, and significant impairment in functioning. The third, **disruptive mood dysregulation disorder (DMDD)**, is a recently introduced depressive disorder characterized by: (1) frequent and *severe temper outbursts* that are extreme overreactions to the situation or provocation; and (2) chronic, persistently *irritable or angry mood* that is present between the severe temper outbursts.

The common characteristic of all depressive disorders is the presence of sad, empty, or irritable mood, along with somatic and cognitive symptoms that interfere with the individual's functioning. The differences among depressive disorders are related to their duration, timing, associated features, or presumed causes. As we discuss next, these disorders are defined using DSM-5 criteria.

Depressive Disorders

- Depression in young people involves numerous and persistent symptoms, including impairments in mood, behavior, attitudes, thinking, and physical functioning.

- For a long time it was mistakenly believed that depression did not exist in children in a form comparable to depression in adults.

- It is now known that depression in young people is prevalent, disabling, and often under-referred.

- The way in which children express and experience depression changes with age.

- It is important to distinguish between depression as a symptom, a syndrome, and a disorder.

- Three types of DSM-5 depressive disorders are major depressive disorder (MDD), persistent depressive disorder [P-DD], or dysthymia, and disruptive mood dysregulation disorder (DMDD).

MAJOR DEPRESSIVE DISORDER (MDD)

JOEY

Feeling Worthless and Hopeless

Ten-year-old Joey's mother and teacher are concerned about his irritability and temper tantrums at home and at school. With little provocation, he bursts into tears, yells, and throws objects. In class he seems to have difficulty concentrating and seems easily distracted. Increasingly shunned by his peers, he plays by himself at recess, and at home spends most of his time in his room watching TV. His mother notes that he has been sleeping poorly and has gained 10 pounds over the past couple of months from constant snacking. The school psychologist has ruled out learning disabilities or ADHD; instead, she says Joey is a deeply unhappy child who expresses feelings of worthlessness and hopelessness, and even a wish that he would die. These feelings began about 6 months ago when Joey's father, divorced from his mother for several years, remarried and moved to another town, and now spends far less time with Joey.

Adapted from Hammen & Rudolph, 2003.

ALISON

"I Couldn't Take It Any More"

Alison, age 17, gets high grades, is a talented musician, and is attractive. However, for the past 3 years, she has been fighting to stay alive. "There are times when I was in school and I would start to cry—I had no idea why. My friends would say, 'What have you got to be depressed about, Alison? You're smart, talented, and can have any boy you want.' When my closest friend moved away 3 years ago, I was really lonely," says Alison. "I'd write notes about suicide and talk about killing myself. I couldn't eat and was tired most of the time. Even the smallest decision was overwhelming. Some days I'd never get out of bed I was so depressed. I couldn't stand school and hated everyone." Alison's feelings of hopelessness lasted for days, then weeks, then months. Finally, "I couldn't take it anymore," says Alison. "I wanted to die—so I tried to kill myself." (Based on authors' case material)

Although Joey and Alison differ in age and symptoms, both display the key features of MDD: sadness, loss of interest or pleasure in nearly all activities, irritability, plus a number of additional specific symptoms that are present during the same 2-week period. These symptoms must also represent a change from previous functioning. DSM-5 criteria for MDD are presented in Table 10.1.

A diagnosis of MDD depends on the presence of a major depressive episode plus the exclusion of other conditions, such as the prior occurrence of a manic episode (in this case, a diagnosis of bipolar disorder would be made). It also requires ruling out physical factors such as the physiological effects of a substance, another medical condition that may have caused or prolonged the depression, depression that is part of normal bereavement, and underlying thought disorders. Finally, the symptoms must cause clinically significant distress or impairment in important areas of life functioning (e.g., social, academic).

If full criteria are currently met for MDD, DSM-5 also provides for severity ratings of "mild," "moderate," or "severe" based on the number of symptoms in excess of those required to make the diagnosis, the amount of symptom distress and its manageability, and the extent of impairment in life functioning caused by the symptoms. In addition to severity, other specifiers are used to designate whether this is a single or recurrent depressive episode; whether a previous episode is in partial or full remission; whether the episode includes psychotic features (presence of delusions and/or hallucinations); or, whether the episode is accompanied by other features, for example, anxious distress (e.g., feeling tense, restless, or that something awful may happen).

The cases of Joey and Alison highlight three important points about the diagnosis of MDD in children and adolescents (Hammen et al., 2014):

roles, interpersonal changes and expectations may result in heightened exposure to stressful life events, and non-normative changes such as early maturation may lead to isolation from one's peer group (Hankin et al., 2008).

These changes may diminish self-worth, lead to depressed mood, and evoke self-focused attention. It is also thought that girls may be at higher risk than boys because they have a greater orientation toward cooperation and sociality. They also use ruminative coping styles to deal with stress (focusing on the symptoms of distress and its causes rather than on solutions)—especially stress involving interpersonal loss and disruptions. These two characteristics may put girls at a disadvantage during adolescence, when they face somewhat greater biological and stressful role-related challenges than boys (Zahn-Waxler et al., 2005). Interpersonal stress and a lack of social support are particularly salient aspects of depression for adolescent girls (Rudolph & Flynn, 2007).

Low birth weight has been found to predict depression in adolescent girls but not in adolescent boys, and girls born at a low birth weight are especially vulnerable to adversity after puberty (Costello et al., 2007; Van Lieshout & Boylan, 2010). This suggests that low birth weight may be a marker for poor intrauterine conditions that lead to adjustments in fetal development, which in turn have long-term consequences for girls' response to stress in adolescence. Research also suggests that increased levels of testosterone and estrogen at puberty, particularly when they occur in combination with social stress, increase the risk for depression in girls (Angold, Worthman, & Costello, 2003). Hormones and sleep cycles, which can alter mood, differ dramatically between boys and girls. One study of blood flow in regions of the brain during periods of sadness in men and in women found that although men and women considered themselves to be equally sad, their brain activity differed. When asked to feel sad on cue, both sexes activated regions of the prefrontal cortex, but women showed a much wider activation of the limbic system (George et al., 1996). These and other findings suggest that sex differences in depression may be partly rooted in biological differences in the brain processes that regulate emotions (Martel, 2013).

Ethnicity and Culture

The incidence of depression has been found to vary across regions worldwide (Culbertson, 1997); however, few studies have examined ethnic, racial, or cultural differences in clinically depressed youths, and findings have been inconsistent (Anderson & Mayes, 2009). One study compared the prevalence of MDD across nine ethnic groups in a large community sample of children in grades 6 to 8 (Roberts, Roberts, & Chen, 1997). Of these groups, African American and Hispanic youths both had significantly higher rates of depression. However, only Hispanic youths with depression showed an elevated risk for impaired functioning. In another study, pubertal status was found to be a better predictor of depressive symptoms than chronological age in Caucasian girls, but not in African American or Hispanic girls (Hayward et al., 1999). Similarly, obesity in the sixth grade was found to be associated with a greater likelihood of depressed mood in the eighth grade for Caucasian girls but not for African American or Hispanic girls (Anderson et al., 2011).

A large community study of high school students found that nonwhite (African American, Hispanic, and Asian) adolescents reported more symptoms of depression than white adolescents (Rushton, Forcier, & Schectman, 2002). However, these differences likely reflect differences in socioeconomic status (SES), since depression and lower SES are related. Race and ethnicity are known sources of varying levels of exposure to stress and availability of resources. As a result, low SES may increase vulnerability to stress, and by doing so it may increase the likelihood of depression. In a longitudinal study of four race–ethnic groups (whites, African Americans, Hispanics, and Asians) during the transition from adolescence to young adulthood, it was found that race and ethnicity were important in understanding depressive symptoms during this period (Brown, Meadows, & Elder, 2007). In females, initial rates of depressive symptoms were highest for Hispanic and Asian teens and lowest for whites, with African American youths falling in between. As expected, males displayed lower levels of symptoms, but the findings for race–ethnic group differences were similar to those for females. Within gender, all groups showed decreases in symptoms over time; however, whites continued to display fewer depressive symptoms than the other three groups, particularly as compared with African Americans. This lasting race–ethnic inequality in depressive symptoms creates a risk for emotional and physical health in later life, as stress may accumulate in the context of a lack of resources.

Section Summary

Major Depressive Disorder (MDD)

- The key features of MDD are sadness, loss of interest or pleasure in nearly all activities, and irritability, plus many specific symptoms that are present for at least 2 weeks.
- The overall prevalence of MDD annually for youths 4 to 18 years of age is between 2% and 8%, with rates that are low during childhood but increase dramatically during adolescence. The likelihood that a youth has ever had MDD is higher, from 10% to 20% or more.

- The most frequent accompanying disorders in young people with MDD are anxiety disorders, persistent depressive disorder, conduct problems, ADHD, and substance-use disorder.
- Almost all young people recover from their initial depressive episode, but about 70% have another episode within 5 years and many develop bipolar disorder.
- Depression in preadolescent children is equally common in boys and girls, but the ratio of girls to boys is about 2:1 to 3:1 after puberty.
- The relationship between depression and race/ethnicity during childhood and adolescence is an understudied area.

In the next section, we discuss persistent depressive disorder, a milder but more chronic form of depression, about which we know relatively little as compared with MDD. Many children with persistent depressive disorder eventually develop MDD; therefore, the two disorders are related.

PERSISTENT DEPRESSIVE DISORDER [P-DD] (DYSTHYMIA)

DEBORAH

A Childhood without Laughter

A few months ago, my mother unearthed some pictures of me as a baby that I had never seen before. One showed me at about 9 months old, crawling on the grass of Golden Gate Park. I was looking directly at the camera, my tongue sticking out of the corner of my mouth, and I was laughing happily. My face was lit from within and looked more than a little mischievous. I was absolutely transfixed by that photo for days. I would continually take it out of my wallet and stare at it, torn between laughter and tears. For a while I couldn't figure out what it was about the picture that drew me. Finally it hit me; this was the only picture of myself as a child that I had seen that showed me laughing. All the photos I had ever seen depicted a child staring solemnly or smiling diffidently, but never laughing. I looked at the Golden Gate Park picture and wished that I had remained that happy and that depression had not taken away my childhood. When I first was diagnosed with depression at age 24, I discussed my childhood with my doctor. Although it is hard to diagnose a child from 20 years in the past, it seemed clear to both of us that I had suffered from dysthymia (mild, long-term depression) probably from the time I was a small child.

Based on A Childhood Without Laughter by D. M. Deren.

Like Deborah, young people who suffer from **persistent depressive disorder (P-DD)** experience symptoms of depressed mood that occur for most of the day, on most days, and persist for at least 1 year. They are unhappy or irritable most of the time. (The sad and gloomy life of Eeyore the donkey in the 100 Acre Wood likely qualifies for a diagnosis of P-DD.) Combined with their chronic depressed (or irritable) mood, these children also display at least two somatic (e.g., eating problems, sleep disturbances, low energy) or cognitive symptoms (e.g., lack of concentration, low self-esteem, feelings of hopelessness) that are present while they are depressed. Although the symptoms of P-DD are chronic, they are less severe than those for children with MDD.

P-DD is a "new" category in DSM-5; it combines the previous DSM-IV categories of Dysthymic Disorder and MDD—Chronic. This was done because of the lack of differences between youths with a dysthymic disorder and those with a chronic type of major depression. In comparison to nonchronic MDD, chronic forms of depression, whether referred to as dysthymic disorder, chronic major depression, or P-DD are associated with a poorer response to treatment, greater long-term morbidity at follow-up, and greater familial loading for affective disorders (McCullough et al., 2003).

Children with P-DD are characterized by poor emotion regulation, which includes constant feelings of sadness, feelings of being unloved and forlorn, self-deprecation, low self-esteem, anxiety, anger, and temper tantrums (Masi et al., 2003). Some may experience **double depression**, in which MDD is superimposed on the child's previous P-DD, causing the child to present with both disorders (Klein, Shankman, & Rose, 2008).

The chronic nature of P-DD raises the issue of whether it is a mood disorder or a general personality style (Daley et al., 1999). For example, we all know people we would describe as "sad sacks"—nothing ever seems to make them happy. However, P-DD seems to follow a chronic course that is typical of mood disorders, and the similarities between P-DD and MDD in young people suggest that it is a mood disorder, not a personality style (Renouf & Kovacs, 1995). One study found that children with either MDD or P-DD alone did not differ in their clinical features, demographics, or associated characteristics, leading to unanswered questions about the validity of this distinction. However, those with both disorders were more severely impaired than children with just one of them (Goodman et al., 2000).

Prevalence and Comorbidity

Rates of P-DD are lower than those of MDD, with approximately 1% of children and 5% of adolescents

(Jordan & Cole, 1996). Self-views are constructed from this feedback, and the outcome may be a varied and positive self-view leading to optimism, energy, and enthusiasm. Or it may be a narrow and negative self-view leading to pessimism, a sense of helplessness, and possibly, depression (Seroczynski, Cole, & Maxwell, 1997). Children whose self-views are negative and narrowly focused in one domain—for example, in academics—may show instability in their self-esteem because they lack alternative compensatory areas of functioning, such as sports or social relations. This may make them vulnerable to developing depression when faced with stress in their primary domain.

Social and Peer Problems

Young people who are depressed experience significant disruptions in their relationships. They have few friends or close relationships, feel lonely and isolated, feel that others do not like them (which, unfortunately, often becomes a reality), and display extensive impairments in their social skills (Rudolph, Flynn, & Abaied, 2008). The low social status of youngsters with depression has been found to emerge via two pathways (Agoston & Rudolph, 2013). In the first pathway, depressive symptoms promote socially helpless behavior and subsequent neglect by peers. In the second pathway, depressive symptoms promote aggressive behavior and subsequent rejection by peers. Chronic peer-related loneliness during childhood has also been found to predict depressive symptoms in early adolescence (Qualter et al., 2010). In addition, children with depression who report poor friendships at the time of referral have a reduced likelihood of recovery from depression (Goodyer et al., 1997). Even when children recover from their depression, they continue to experience some social impairment.

Social withdrawal is common in youngsters with depression. They often spend significant amounts of time alone, show little interest in seeing friends, and engage in few activities. Their social withdrawal may reflect an inability to maintain social interactions—possibly related to negative, irritable, and aggressive behavior toward others—and deficits in initiating conversations or making friends (Rockhill et al., 2007). These factors can seriously interfere with social development, depriving youngsters with depression of the social exchanges that lead to healthy interpersonal relationships.

Youngsters who are depressed use ineffective styles of coping in social situations. For example, they use less active and problem-focused coping and more passive, avoidant, ruminative, or emotion-focused coping (Hammen et al., 2014). A strong risk factor for the onset of depression in adolescent females is **co-rumination**, a

negative form of self-disclosure and discussion between peers focused narrowly on problems or emotions to the exclusion of other activities or dialogue (Stone et al., 2011). Co-rumination seems to be one mechanism underlying adolescent females' heightened risk for depression. Ironically, co-rumination between peers is associated with higher ratings of friendship quality and closeness, which in turn, have been found to predict increases in co-rumination. Thus, what appear to be socially rewarding and supportive relationships with peers not only fail to protect female teens from distress, but also may increase their risk for depression when based on maladaptive styles of interaction (Stone et al., 2011).

Depressed teens may also make poor choices in dealing with social problems, such as turning to alcohol or drugs in response to a break-up with a boyfriend or girlfriend. In the words of Page, age 17:

> I was so unhappy that I didn't care about myself—even about being safe. I was out drinking a lot, doing a lot of pot. Sometimes I would just black out and not know what was happening. One night I think a bunch of guys had sex with me when I passed out, I don't know. I never remembered anything, it was all hearsay the next day. I made some really bad boyfriend choices. I would date guys who reinforced my view of myself as ugly, stupid, and uncool. I dropped my preppy boyfriend and started dating a 20-year-old guy who was living in his own apartment and playing in a band. He had tattoos on his arms and stomach. I would date guys just so I could get a ride, even though I didn't like them. I would pick boyfriends who were depressed or ones that my parents really didn't like. (From "I Did Not Want to Live," by Sabrina Solin Weill, 1995. *Seventeen*, April 1, 1995, pp. 154–156, 176.)

Interestingly, the basic understanding required for appropriate social relations appears to be relatively intact in youngsters with depression. They are generally capable of providing cognitive solutions to interpersonal problems (Kovacs & Goldston, 1991). However, as with Page, their deficits in social problem solving and behavior in real-life situations, particularly when they are under stress, are in sharp contrast to their social understanding (Calhoun et al., 2012). Adolescents with depression and poor social problem-solving skills are likely to show increases in the severity of their depression over time (Becker-Weidman et al., 2010).

Family Problems

Youngsters with depression experience less supportive and more conflictual relationships with their mothers, fathers, and siblings than do children who do not have depression. They report feeling socially isolated from

"It's my youth, and I don't have to enjoy it if I don't want to."

their families and prefer to be alone rather than with them. In family situations, the child's social isolation may not be a social skill deficit, but rather a reflection of the child's desire to avoid conflict. Family relationship difficulties have been found to persist even when children are no longer clinically depressed (Sheeber et al., 2007).

During interactions, these youngsters may be quite negative toward their parents, and their parents in turn may respond in a negative, dismissing, or harsh manner. When repeated over time, these interactions may adversely affect family relationships. Children with depression who are irritable, unresponsive, and unaffectionate provide little positive reinforcement for their parents, and they frustrate their parents' desire for satisfaction in the parenting role (Kovacs, 1997).

Depression and Suicide

CARLA

"It Became Too Much"

Carla, age 12, was admitted to the intensive care unit unconscious and unstable after ingesting eight of her mother's 50-mg Elavil tablets, an unknown quantity of antidepressants, and approximately 20 tablets of Tylenol 3. This suicide attempt, her first, came after arguing with her father over chores and restrictions imposed because her grades were so bad. Carla said she went to the medicine cabinet and ingested everything she could find because "it became too much" and she "did not want to live." For the previous month, she had

displayed a noticeable change of mood, behaving with more instability and depression, feeling worthless and hopeless. During this period she had lost her appetite and had dropped two dress sizes. She had increasingly isolated herself, staying alone in her room. Her school performance, for which her father had restricted her, had declined from B's the previous term to D's.

From Adolescent Suicide: Assessment and Intervention by A. L. Berman and D. A. Jobes, 1991, p. 144.

Carla's case illustrates the profound feelings of hopelessness, helplessness, and despair that often lead a youngster with depression to attempt suicide. Most youngsters with depression report suicidal thinking, and as many as one-third who think about killing themselves actually attempt it (Goldston, Daniel, & Arnold, 2006). Drug overdose and wrist cutting are among the most common methods for adolescents who attempt suicide. In one long-term follow-up study, adolescents with MDD had a fivefold increased risk of a first suicide attempt as compared with controls without MDD, and nearly 8% of them committed suicide within 15 years of their first episode of MDD (Weissman et al., 1999b). For adolescents who complete suicide, the most common methods are firearms (45%), suffocation (40%), and poisoning (8%) (CDC, 2013).

The link between depression, suicidal behavior, and completed suicide is undeniable, strong, and sobering (Dervic, Brent, & Oquendo, 2008). Suicidal ideation (e.g., thinking about killing oneself) is common across many different types of psychological disorders, but actual suicide attempts are much more common during depression (Nock et al., 2013) (see A Closer Look 10.1). In one 7-to 9-year follow-up of youngsters with psychiatric disorders, 84% of all suicide attempts were found to occur because of depressive disorders (Shaffer et al., 1996).

About 60% of youngsters who are clinically depressed report having thoughts about suicide, and 30% attempt suicide by 17 years of age, with most attempts coming within the first year after the onset of suicidal thoughts. Unfortunately, about half of them eventually make further attempts (AACAP, 2001). The suicide attempts of youngsters with depression almost never occur during times when they are symptom-free—90% or more have depressive features at the time of their suicidal episode. Finally, among youngsters who kill themselves, the odds of having major depression are 27 times higher than among controls (Brent et al., 1993; Shaffer et al., 1996).

Although rates of suicidal behavior vary across countries, the two strongest risk factors for suicidal behavior are consistent worldwide—having a mood disorder and

Depressive Disorder Is Associated with Suicide Thoughts and Suicide Attempts

What's the use?

I look ~~erott~~ around here and all I see,
Is a school and a world that could do without me.
I've gotten here but only by fate.
My death, I'm sure, will not come late.
I try each day to see the use of being here.
There is none.
I try to find a meaning,
But the wars have been fought, my battle is yet to come.
When I close my eyes the pain goes.
When I open them again the pain. snows.
I try to not cry aloud,
Wouldn't matter anyway I'm lost in this crowd.
You can pretend I don't live,
But I'll keep living 'till my life gives.

Teri's note

Teri: What's the Use?

Teri, age 15, had been depressed since her father died when she was 11. According to her mother, over the past 14 months her behavior had gone from moody to sullen. She had disobeyed restrictions imposed as punishments and had run away from home on several occasions. She labeled herself as "stupid," spoke and wrote often of death and suicide (see accompanying note). On three occasions she had cut her wrists, albeit only superficially. Her school performance had declined and she spoke now of hating school. Her peer associations were almost exclusively with other alienated teens, described by her as "punks and other anarchists."

Source: Adolescent Suicide: Assessment and Intervention by A. L. Berman and D. A. Jobes, 1991, p. 144.

being a young female (Cha & Nock, 2014; Nock et al., 2008). In general, young females with depression show more suicidal ideation and attempt suicide more often than young males (Nock et al., 2013). The risk factors for nonfatal suicide attempts are similar for males and females (Thompson & Light, 2010). However, since girls typically do not use guns, they are usually less successful in completing suicide than boys (Goldston et al., 2006). Ages 13 and 14 are peak periods for a first suicide attempt by youngsters with depression. Suicide prior to puberty is rare, most likely because depression and substance abuse before puberty are also rare. In adolescents with depression, suicide attempts double during the teen years but show an abrupt decline after age 17 or 18. It is possible that as young people mature, they are better able to tolerate their negative mood states and acquire more resources for coping, thus making it less likely that they will attempt suicide during periods of sadness (Borowsky, Ireland, & Resnick, 2001).

In light of the strong connection between symptoms of depression and suicidal ideation and behavior, a primary strategy for reducing suicide in young people is to increase the availability of effective treatments for depression (Brown et al., 2007). We discuss these treatments later in this chapter. Prevention and treatment programs for suicidal behavior generally focus on family involvement and support, and they emphasize intervening early after the suicidal crisis (Brent et al., 2013; Pineda & Dadds, 2013). Since racial and ethnic groups are known to differ in rates of suicidal behaviors and the circumstances under which they occur (e.g., precipitants, risk and protective factors, and patterns of seeking help), it is also important that suicide prevention and treatment programs are sensitive to these cultural differences (Goldston et al., 2008).

Our discussion of suicidal behavior in this chapter has focused primarily on its relationship with depressive disorders. However, it is important to recognize that self-injurious thoughts and behaviors in young people is a significant topic in its own right, and one that is just beginning to receive the attention it deserves (Cha & Nock, 2014). Self-injurious thoughts and behaviors range from nonsuicidal self-injury such as self-cutting, to suicidal ideation, suicide attempts, and completed suicide. Suicide is especially worrisome, as it is the second leading cause of death among adolescents and young adults in the United States, resulting in about 4,600 deaths per year (CDC, 2013). DSM-5 includes two newly proposed disorders in its section on conditions for further study: Suicidal Behavior Disorder describes individuals who have made a suicide attempt within the past 24 months, and Nonsuicidal Self Injury describes individuals who engage in intentional self-inflicted damage to the surface of the body (e.g., cutting, burning, stabbing, excessive rubbing) without suicidal intent. These proposed diagnoses and other efforts will hopefully bring further attention and understanding to self-injurious behaviors in young people so we can learn how to best predict and prevent these behaviors (Cha & Nock, 2014).

Section Summary

Associated Characteristics of Depressive Disorders

- Youngsters with depression have normal intelligence, although certain symptoms such as difficulty concentrating, loss of interest, and slowness of thought may negatively affect intellectual functioning.
- They perform more poorly than others in school, score lower on standard achievement tests, and have lower levels of grade attainment.
- They often experience deficits and distortions in their thinking, including negative beliefs, attributions of failure, and self-critical automatic negative thoughts.
- Almost all youngsters with depression experience low or unstable self-esteem.
- Youngsters with depression have few friends and close relationships, feel lonely and isolated, and feel that others do not like them.
- They experience poor relationships and conflict with their parents and siblings, who in turn may respond in a negative, dismissing, or harsh manner.
- Most youngsters with depression report suicidal thinking, and about 30% who think about killing themselves actually attempt it.

THEORIES OF DEPRESSION

Many theories have been proposed to explain the onset and course of depression. Until recently, however, most were developed to explain depression in adults, then directly applied to children with minimal regard for developmental differences (Garber & Horowitz, 2002). In the sections that follow, we consider several of these theories. Keep in mind, however, that depression is likely a final, common pathway for interacting influences that predispose a child to develop the disorder (Hammen et al., 2014). No one theory can explain all forms of depressive disorder and differences in symptoms and severity within the same disorder. An overview of the primary theories of depression is presented in Table 10.2.

Psychodynamic

Early psychodynamic theories viewed depression as the conversion of aggressive instinct into depressive

TABLE 10.2 | **Overview of Theories of Depression**

Psychodynamic	Actual or symbolic loss of love object (e.g., caregiver) that is loved ambivalently; anger toward love object turned inward; excessive severity of the superego; loss of self-esteem
Attachment	Insecure early attachments; distorted internal working models of self and others
Behavioral	Lack or loss of reinforcement or quality of reinforcement; deficits in skills needed to obtain reinforcement
Cognitive	Depressive mindset; distorted or maladaptive cognitive structures, processes, and products; negative view of self, world, and future; poor problem-solving ability; hopelessness
Self-Control	Problems in organizing behavior toward long-term goals; deficits in self-monitoring, self-evaluation, and self-reinforcement
Interpersonal	Impaired interpersonal functioning related to grief over loss; role dispute and conflict; role transition; interpersonal deficit; single parenting; social withdrawal; interaction between mood and interpersonal events
Socio-environmental	Stressful life circumstances and daily hassles as vulnerability factors; social support, coping, and appraisal as protective factors
Neurobiological	Neurochemical and receptor abnormalities; neurophysiological abnormalities; neuroendocrine abnormalities; genetic variants; abnormalities in brain structure and function; effects of early experience on the developing brain

Based on A Developmental Cognitive Model of Unipolar Major Depression, by D. J. A. Dozois, unpublished manuscript.

affect. Depression is presumed to result from the loss of a love object (e.g., mother). This loss can be actual, as in the case of the death of a parent, or symbolic, as a result of emotional deprivation, rejection, or inadequate parenting. The individual's subsequent rage toward the love object is then turned against the self. Since children variants in the hippocampus, individuals with depression may experience a constant state of anxiety and have difficulty recognizing situations that are safe (Davidson, Pizzagalli, & Nitschke, 2002). Studies of other brain regions have found that healthy adolescents who respond to peer rejection with greater activation of the anterior cingulate cortex are more likely to show an increase in depressive symptoms over the following year (Masten et al., 2011). These findings suggest that activity in brain regions involved in affective processing of socioemotional stimuli may provide a possible neurobiological marker for predicting healthy youngsters' future risk for depression.

Other studies into the neurobiological correlates of depression in young people have focused on hypothalamic–pituitary–adrenal (HPA)-axis dysregulation; sleep abnormalities suggestive of reduced neuroplasticity; variants in BDNF, which is involved in nerve growth and development; and the brain neurotransmitters serotonin, dopamine, and norepinephrine, which are widely spread throughout brain circuits thought to underlie mood disorders (Miller, 2007). Although findings related to these neurobiological correlates are suggestive, keep in mind that studies of children are few in number, and the findings are far less consistent than those for adults (Kaufman et al., 2001).

HPA-axis dysregulation is evidenced by abnormal cortisol responses in children and adolescents with depression, including higher baseline levels and atypical or overactive responses to stressors (Lopez-Duran, Kovacs, & George, 2009). HPA-axis and other neurobiological findings have led to a strong interest in the impact of early exposure to stress on later negative moods. Mounting evidence suggests that early adversity (e.g., prenatal stress, harsh or neglectful parenting) may produce HPA-axis abnormalities (e.g., alterations in corticotropin-releasing hormone [CRH] circuits), which sensitize the child to later stress, thus increasing the risk for developing depression (Heim & Nemeroff, 2001; Huizink, Mulder, & Buitelaar, 2004).

Infants of depressed mothers show higher levels of salivary cortisol (the stress hormone) and less relative left frontal lobe electrical activity than infants of mothers without depression (Dawson et al., 1997). Like higher levels of cortisol, decreased relative left frontal lobe activity may be a vulnerability factor for negative emotional states and later onset of depression (Nusslock et al., 2011; Forbes et al., 2008), although not all studies support this finding (e.g., Shankman et al., 2011). Nevertheless, research suggests that interactions between depressed mothers and their infants may produce biochemical and neurological changes that form and perpetuate a lasting basis for depressive disorder (Cytryn & McKnew, 1996; Post et al., 1996).

In summary, findings from studies of neurobiological correlates suggest that youngsters with depression may have a heightened sensitivity to stress. Repeated neuroendocrine activation related to stress might increase youngsters' susceptibility to chronic depressive symptoms, which in turn may lead to further extreme biological activation and psychosocial stress. Neurobiological findings over a wide age range of children are suggestive of widespread abnormalities in executive, affective, and motor networks of the brain, and in brain areas supporting emotional regulation (Ho et al., 2013). However, further research will be needed to clarify the specific neural circuits underlying depression in young people. The characteristics, severity, course, and outcome of a depressive episode may depend on the extent to which different neural circuits and processes are involved in response to environment demands and on when during development these networks are formed (Gabbay et al., 2013; Goodyer, 2008).

Family Influences

"I was always able to explain away my daughter's symptoms," says the mother of a 12-year-old. *"When she was 10 and fought with me about everything, I just wrote it off as preadolescent hissy fits. When she dropped out of gymnastics—which had been her raison d'être—and started losing weight, I told myself she was just searching for a new identity. But when her best friend came to me and told me that my daughter was talking about suicide, I was forced to face the truth. I keep blaming myself. What did I do to cause this depression? What could I have done to prevent it?"*

—From "Childhood Depression," by K. Levine, pp. 42–45, *Parents*, October 1995.

Family influences play an important role in the development, onset, maintenance, and course of depression in young people (Schwartz et al., 2013; Restifo & Bögels, 2009). One approach to examining these influences looks at families of children and adolescents with depression; the second approach considers families in which parents, particularly mothers, are depressed.

When Children Are Depressed

Families of children with depression display more critical and punitive behavior toward their depressed child than toward other children in the family. As compared with families of youngsters without depression, these families display more anger and conflict, greater use of control, poorer communication, more overinvolvement, and less warmth and support (Sheeber et al., 2007; Stein et al., 2000). They often experience high levels of stress, disorganization, marital discord, and a lack of social support (Messer & Gross, 1995; Slavin & Rainer, 1990). Youngsters with depression describe their families as less cohesive and more disengaged than do youngsters without depression (Kashani et al., 1995).

Research points strongly to the link between childhood depression and family dysfunction. One longitudinal study found that less support and more conflict in the family were associated with more depressive symptoms in adolescents both concurrently and prospectively over a 1-year period. In contrast, more depressive symptoms did not predict a worsening of family relationships over the same time period. Thus, family problems precede and may be directly related to the development of depressive symptoms (Sheeber et al., 1997).

When Parents Are Depressed

To mother appropriately requires the action of systems that regulate sensation, perception, affect, reward, executive function, motor output and learning. When a mother is at risk to engage in less than optimal mothering, such as when she is depressed … the function of many or all of maternal and related systems may be affected.

— Barrett & Fleming, 2011, p. 368

MRS. D.

Not Up to Mothering

Mrs. D. is depressed and has been helpless and needy for most of her 5-year-old daughter Maria's life. She moves ever so slowly to prepare breakfast for Maria and herself. Wringing her hands, she pays little attention to events around her. Maria has been tugging at her mother for some time, apparently wanting food. Mrs. D. mumbles something, sobs continuously, and wipes tears from her cheek as she moves between the cupboard and kitchen table. Maria persists in trying to gain her mother's attention, and finally Mrs. D. hugs her and strokes her hair. At first Maria pulls back; then she snuggles against her mother's legs. Finally, Mrs. D. fills a bowl with cereal, and she and Maria sit down to eat in total silence, during which Mrs. D. looks sadly at her daughter. Deep bouts of depression periodically incapacitate Mrs. D., and any problem that Maria has sends her to bed. Mostly, Maria is left on her own to handle problems.

Adapted from Radke-Yarrow & Zahn-Waxler, 1990.

Depression interferes with a parent's ability to meet the basic physical and emotional needs of a child, including feeding, bedtime routines, medical care, and safety practices. Mothers who suffer from depression, like Mrs. D.,

also create a child-rearing environment teeming with negative mood, irritability, helplessness, less emotional flexibility, and unpredictable displays of affection. When their children display negative emotions and distress, mothers with a history of depression are less likely to respond supportively with comfort, empathy, or assistance and are more likely to disapprove, dismiss, punish, or ignore their child's negative emotions (Silk et al., 2011). Depressed mothers also display less energy in stimulating play, less consistent discipline, less involvement, poor communication, lack of affection, and more criticism and resentment of their children than mothers without depression (Goodman, 2007). High levels of marital conflict, family discord, and stress may also be present in the home when a parent is depressed (Hammen, 2002). Critically, this type of negative family environment in combination with a child's genetic predispositions can adversely affect the development of stress regulatory systems and predispose the child to a lifetime of depressive illness and other negative health outcomes (Taylor, Way, & Seeman, 2011).

Maternal depressions during and shortly after pregnancy have been found to be independent risk factors for major depression in the offspring at age 18 years (O'Connor, Monk, & Fitelson, 2014; Pearson et al., 2013). The first year of a child's life seems to be a particularly sensitive period for the effects of maternal depression on the child's later behavior and other adverse outcomes (Bagner et al., 2011). Depressed mothers may differ from one another in their styles of interaction; some are more intrusive and others are more withdrawn. These differences are important because they may be associated with different child outcomes. For example, children of depressed mothers with an intrusive maternal style display avoidance and "tuning out," whereas children of depressed mothers with a withdrawn maternal style display heightened

Maternal depression interferes with the mother's ability to meet the needs of her children

the use of homework to practice these skills between sessions (Young & Mufson, 2008).

The *termination phase* (3 sessions) reviews progress in the identified problem area, links changes in interpersonal functioning and relationships to improved mood and decreased depressive symptoms, and identifies strategies that have been most helpful. It also addresses the importance of continuing to use the learned strategies following treatment, highlights areas that still need improvement, and considers what to do if symptoms of depression return.

IPT-A has been shown to be an effective treatment for adolescent depression in a number of controlled studies in clinic, school, and community settings, using both individual and group formats (Mufson, 2010; Mufson et al., 2012). In an effort to reach more youngsters, IPT-A is also being developed as a preventive intervention ("Teen Talk") for adolescents in grades 7 to 10 who display elevated levels of depressive symptoms. Preliminary findings suggest that IPT-A and Teen Talk may useful approaches to preventing more severe forms of depression and reducing symptoms of anxiety (Young et al., 2012; Young, Mufson, & Davies, 2006).

In concluding our discussion of psychosocial treatments, the good news is that a wide variety of treatments for young people with depression have been shown to be effective for most youths who receive them (March & Vitiello, 2009; TADS Team, 2009). However, nearly half of those who recover, especially girls, have a relapse of their depression (Curry et al., 2011), and effect sizes have been moderate and smaller than those reported for adults (Weisz, McCarty, & Valeri, 2006). Hence, there is a need to explore more effective treatments that build on our growing understanding of childhood depression; reduce the rate of depression relapse or deterioration; personalize treatment to meet the child's cognitive, emotional, and developmental profile; and are likely to be used in clinical practice settings (Brent & Maalouf, 2009; Weisz et al., 2013). There is also a need to study treatments of longer duration and the use of booster sessions following treatment and to evaluate outcomes over longer follow-up periods.

Medications

"I kept hearing about Prozac in the news," says one father, "and when we finally brought my 9-year-old to a psychiatrist, I thought he could just give her this pill and change our lives. After a year, I can say that things are a bit better. But it took lots of trials with lots of different pills."

—From "Childhood Depression," by K. Levine, pp. 42–45, *Parents*, October 1995. Reprinted by permission of the author/

Antidepressant medications are commonly used to treat youngsters with depression. An estimated 1.4 million youngsters in the United States received antidepressant medication in 2002 (Vitiello, Zuvekas, & Norquist, 2006), with over 60% of those treated in outpatient settings filling prescriptions for these drugs (Olfson et al., 2014). For many youngsters, antidepressant medications can shorten a depressive episode and return them to the important developmental tasks of childhood and adolescence. As we have noted, although tricyclic antidepressants are effective with adults, they have consistently failed to demonstrate any advantage over placebo in treating depression in young people, and may have some potentially serious cardiovascular side effects (Fombonne & Zinck, 2008). As a result they are no longer regarded as primary drugs for the management of depressive symptoms in young people.

SSRIs have clearly become the first line of antidepressant medication treatment for youngsters with depression, with one national survey reporting that over 90% of prescriptions written for these youngsters were for SSRIs (Olfson et al., 2003). Among the most commonly used SSRIs are fluoxetine (Prozac), sertraline (Zoloft), and citalopram (Celexa). SSRIs achieve their antidepressant effects by blocking the reuptake of serotonin, thereby increasing its availability in the synapse and stimulating the postsynaptic neuron. At present, the only SSRI that is approved by the Food and Drug Administration (FDA) for use with children and adolescents with MDD is fluoxetine.

A number of controlled investigations have demonstrated that some SSRIs are moderately effective in reducing symptoms of depression in children and adolescents. One meta-analysis found that 40% to 60% of children responded to Prozac versus 20% to 35% of those on placebo (Hetrick, McKenzie, & Merry, 2010). Support for the effectiveness of other SSRIs was limited. There was also little evidence that children and adolescents who took SSRIs showed improvement in their school performance, interpersonal relations, or social functioning on a day-to-day basis (Hetrick et al., 2010). Others have argued that research supports the use of SSRIs, that combined treatments using medication and CBT in combination are likely to be the most effective, and that greater treatment effects are obtained for children with more severe depressions (March, 2010).

After they were first marketed in the late 1980s, the use of Prozac and other SSRIs increased dramatically. For example, nearly three-quarters of a million prescriptions for SSRIs for children ages 6 to 18 were written in 1996—an 80% increase in only 2 years (*APA Monitor*, December 1997). However, despite some support for their efficacy, both professional and public concerns have been voiced about their use with children and adolescents. The main concerns are possible serious side effects such as suicidal thoughts and self-harm and a lack of information about the long-term effects of these medications on the developing brain. Related to these concerns and warnings by the FDA, the use of SSRIs with young people has decreased by about 20% in more recent years (Gibbons et al., 2007; Libby et al., 2007). In 2004, the FDA asked all manufacturers of antidepressant medications to include in their labeling a boxed warning (black box) and Patient Education Guide to alert consumers about the increased risk of suicidal thinking and behavior in youngsters treated with these medications. A summary of the main points included in these black box warnings is presented in A Closer Look 10.2.

The FDA warnings were based on a pooling of findings from 24 short-term, placebo-controlled studies of antidepressant trials with more than 4,400 youngsters with MDD and other disorders. The overall findings indicated an increased risk of suicidal thinking or behavior in youngsters with depression (4% on active medication vs. 2% on placebo) (Hammad, Laughren, & Racoosin, 2006). The risk for untreated youths with depression, the long-term effects of medication, and the combination of medication and psychosocial interventions were not evaluated, and there were no completed suicides in any of the studies. In addition, findings regarding increases in suicidality from other

studies have been inconsistent (Gibbons et al., 2012). Also inconsistent are findings regarding the use of medications either alone or in combination with psychosocial interventions. Some studies have found a benefit of combined treatment versus medication alone, with an enhancement of the safety of medications when used in combination with CBT (e.g., Treatment of Adolescents with Depression Study [TADS] Team, 2004, 2007), whereas others have not (e.g., Goodyer et al., 2007).

Thus, despite much research, the risks, long-term safety, and benefits associated with the use of antidepressant medications with young people remain uncertain (Moreno et al., 2007a). In light of the potential effectiveness of the psychosocial treatments for depression in youths that we have discussed, careful consideration must be given to determining which youngsters are most or least likely to benefit from antidepressant medication (AACAP, 2007d).

Notwithstanding these concerns, untreated depression has profound long-term consequences, including a high risk for suicide, and there is some evidence that a higher use of antidepressant medications across counties in the United States is associated with lower rates of suicide in young people (Gibbons et al., 2006). Thus, there may be possible risks that go along with not using medications relative to the risks from suicidal ideation and suicide attempts, especially when numerous research and clinical studies indicate that many young people benefit from drug treatment (Bridge et al., 2007).

In the absence of better data regarding drug effects, side effects, and long-term safety of medication use with depressed children, there are currently no easy answers to this dilemma. Some say it is unethical to treat depressed children using medications in light of the potential dangers. Others say that the risks associated with drug treatment are no greater than risks for other treatments and that it is unethical to withhold treatment in light of the known benefits. Given the many social, political, and economic implications surrounding the use of medications to treat depression in young people, we may hear a lot more about this issue for some time to come (e.g., Riddle, 2004).

In concluding our discussion of the treatment of depression, we note that controlled studies of psychological treatments and medication have found that up to 60% of youngsters with depression respond to placebo (Bridge et al., 2007) and about 15% to 30% respond to brief treatment (Goodyer et al., 2007). Thus, in youngsters with mild or brief depression, an absence of suicidality, and minor impairment in functioning, the use of education, support, and case management related to school and family stressors may be effective. However, for those who are more severely depressed, display suicidal ideation and behavior, and show significant impairment in functioning, the specific types of

---

A CLOSER LOOK 10.2

Summary of Food and Drug Administration (FDA) Black Box Warnings for the Use of Antidepressants with Children and Adolescents

- Youths with MDD are at an increased risk for suicidal thinking or behavior.
- When considering an antidepressant for a child or adolescent, it is important to weigh the increased risk of suicidality with the possible benefits of the medication.
- When starting young people on antidepressants, they must be very closely monitored for worsening of symptoms, suicidality, or unusual changes in behavior.
- Family members must closely observe the youngster for increases in symptoms or worsening of functioning, and immediately communicate any such observations to their provider.
- A statement needs to be included regarding whether the medication is approved for use with children and adolescents.

© Cengage Learning®

as young as 6 months of age; this is a possible early vulnerability factor for later mood disorders (Johnson et al., 2014). If one or both parents have BP, the chances are about 5 times greater that their children will also develop BP or often, like Jessi, another recurrent mood disorder (Hodgins et al., 2002; Mesman et al., 2013).

Besides mood disorder, children at risk for BP by virtue of having parents with the disorder also display a wide range of psychopathology, particularly conduct problems and ADHD, as well as social and academic difficulties (Singh et al., 2007). Relatives of youngsters with BP also have a higher incidence of the disorder. Family incidence and risk for a broad range of psychiatric problems are highest in cases of early-onset BP, with lifetime prevalence rates of about 15% in first-degree relatives (AACAP, 2007c; Rende et al., 2007). This rate is 15 times greater than the prevalence of the disorder in the general population.

Increasing evidence suggests that BP arises from multiple genes, and some studies have identified several chromosomal regions and susceptibility genes (Alsabban, Rivera, & McGuffin, 2011; McInnis et al., 2003). As we have found for other disorders, specific genes that have been identified contribute only a small amount to the risk for BP. In addition, several of these genes have also been identified for youths with depression, anxiety, ADHD, or psychosis. There is likely a complex mode of inheritance rather than a single dominant gene. Individuals with a genetic predisposition do not necessarily develop BP, since environmental factors also play an important role in determining how genes are expressed (Geller & Luby, 1997).

A number of nonspecific risk factors that raise the risk for BP include poor maternal health or nutrition during pregnancy, substance use during pregnancy, a stressful early environment, exposure to traumatic events, and parental mood disorders (Youngstrom & Algorta, 2014). The ways in which environmental factors play a role are not well understood. However, one study suggests that parental BP may create a negative family climate, including problem-solving and communication deficits, which predict family conflict, which in turn predicts childhood BP (Du Rocher et al., 2008).

Brain scans of children identified as being at risk for BP that were taken before and after the onset of a manic episode have shown changes in the brain that reflect a pattern of emotion dysregulation in general, rather than one that is specific to BP onset (Gogtay et al., 2007). Generally, mood fluctuations in BP have been related to abnormalities in the structure and function of the amygdala, prefrontal and anterior cingulate cortex, hippocampus, thalamus, and basal ganglia, but findings have not always been consistent with respect to the types of abnormalities (Garrett & Chang,

2008; Gogtay et al., 2007). Such inconsistencies may be related to ongoing brain changes that are occurring in young people and the point in development at which brain structure and function are assessed.

Some studies have found that BP in adolescents is related to reduced volumes of the amygdala and hippocampus (Beardon et al., 2007; Blumberg et al., 2003). As you may recall, we discussed the importance of the amygdala for recognizing and regulating emotions in relation to depression. Research has found that youngsters with BP misread neutral facial expressions as hostile and in doing so show heightened activation of the amygdala and its connectivity to other parts of the brain involved in processing facial information (Perlman et al., 2013; Rich et al., 2008). These and other findings suggest that youths at risk for and those with BP may display unique neural correlates and deficits in facial emotion processing and dysregulation in brain regions associated with emotion regulation (Brotman et al., 2010; Garrett et al., 2012). Such deficits may be related to the poor social skills, aggression, and irritability that characterize youngsters with BP. In addition, adolescents with BP also show abnormal activation of prefrontal and subcortical areas of the brain during the anticipation of and response to monetary gains and loss, which suggest problems in reward processing, motivation, and goal pursuit (Singh et al., 2012).

Treatment

Treatment of BP in children and adolescents is receiving increasing attention. Although there is currently no cure for BP, in most cases treatment can stabilize mood and allow for management and control of symptoms. Treatment of BP generally requires a multimodal plan that includes close monitoring of symptoms, educating the patient and the family about the illness, matching treatments to individuals, administering medications such as lithium or atypical antipsychotics to stabilize mood, and performing psychotherapeutic interventions to address the youngster's symptoms and related psychosocial impairments (AACAP, 2007c; Kowatch et al., 2005). The general goals of treatment are to decrease the child's symptoms and to prevent relapse, while also reducing long-term illness and enhancing the youngster's normal health and development (Geller & Delbello, 2008).

Medications

Multiple medications have been used to treat youngsters with BP (Goldstein, Sassi, & Diler, 2012). The FDA has approved lithium for use in children as young as 12 years of age. However, there are currently no drugs that are FDA-approved for the treatment of BP in children younger than this (AACAP, 2007c). Medications are typically used to address manic or mixed symptoms and depressive symptoms or to prevent relapse. Clinical trials of medication have had some success, and controlled studies of medication treatment for adolescents with BP are rapidly increasing in number, although few studies have evaluated effects in children younger than age 10 years of age (Goldstein et al., 2012; Liu et al., 2011). Until very recently, recommended treatments were based on findings with adults; however, as we saw with tricyclic antidepressants, such an extrapolation may not be warranted (Geller et al., 1998). Hence, mood-stabilizing medications need to be used with caution and conservatively with young people with BP, particularly in those who do not fit the classic presentation of symptoms seen in adults with bipolar I disorder; these youngsters may constitute as many as 75% of cases of BP (Horst, 2009; Merikangas & Pato, 2009).

Based on its use with adults with BP, lithium has been the agent of first choice in the treatment of youths with BP, and its efficacy has been demonstrated in a number of controlled studies (Goldstein et al., 2012). Lithium is a common salt that is widely present in the natural environment—for example, in drinking water—usually in amounts too small to have any effects. However, the side effects of therapeutic doses of lithium can be serious, especially when used in combination with other medications; side effects may include toxicity (poisoning), renal and thyroid problems, and substantial weight gain (Gracious et al., 2004). It can be given to young people when used with the same safety precautions and similar careful monitoring used for adults. However, lithium cannot be given to children in chaotic families or to children who are unable to keep the multiple appointments needed for monitoring potentially dangerous side effects (Carlson, 1994; Geller & Luby, 1997). In addition, one study found that only 35% of adolescents with BP reported full adherence with the medication regimen (DelBello et al., 2007). Some studies have found atypical antipsychotic agents to be more efficacious than lithium in treating acute manic and mixed episodes in young people with BP, suggesting that these medications may be a preferred option for many youths with BP (Goldstein et al., 2012). However, they too have many metabolic side effects. In addition, adjunctive medications to treat secondary symptoms such as ADHD, depression, and anxiety have also been used (AACAP, 2007c; Sanchez & Soares, 2011).

Psychosocial Treatments

A focus on biological causes and pharmacological interventions for BP has resulted in a relative lack of attention to psychosocial treatments, although this situation is changing (Fristad & MacPherson, 2014). There is also a pressing need for studies on prevention, targeted interventions to delay or prevent progression to full manic or depressive episodes, and approaches that focus on possible environmental moderators of risk (Youngstrom & Algorta, 2014).

Medications may decrease symptoms of BP, but they do not help with the associated functional impairments or preexisting or co-occurring substance-use disorders, learning and behavior problems, and family- and peer-related issues. Nonadherence to medication regimens has been shown to be a major contributor to relapse. Thus, the family must be educated about the negative effects of nonadherence and to recognize possible symptoms of relapse. Psychosocial interventions focus on providing information to the child and family about the disorder, symptoms and course, possible impact on family functioning, and heritability of the disorder. Youths and parents are also taught ways of coping with symptoms and preventing relapse by using problem-solving, communication, emotion regulation, and cognitive—behavioral skills (Fristad, Goldberg Arnold, & Leffler, 2011; Fristad & MacPherson, 2014). Controlled research on psychosocial treatments for youngsters with BP is beginning to appear (Fristad et al., 2009; Goldstein et al., 2007; Miklowitz et al., 2011). This has resulted in several promising new early interventions for high-risk youths using family-focused therapy, CBT, and combined treatments to reduce symptoms of BP (Fristad & MacPherson, 2014; Miklowitz et al., 2013). Further efforts to identify young children at risk for developing BP are needed to enhance opportunities for both psychosocial and pharmacological preventive interventions (Howes & Falkenberg, 2011; Luby & Navsaria, 2010).

Section Summary

Bipolar Disorder

- A recent surge in interest in the diagnosis of bipolar disorder (BP) in children and adolescents has generated considerable controversy surrounding difficulties in identifying the disorder in young people.

- Youngsters with BP show periods of abnormally and persistently elevated, expansive, and/or irritable mood.

- They may display symptoms such as an inflated self-esteem, decreased need for sleep, pressured speech, flight of ideas, distractibility, and reckless behavior.

- BP is far less common than MDD in young people, with lifetime prevalence estimates of 0.5% to 2.5% worldwide.

- BP has a peak age at onset in late adolescence and, unlike depression, affects males and females about equally.

(continues)

TABLE 11.1 | The Many Symptoms of Anxiety

Physical		
Increased heart rate	Dizziness	Blushing
Fatigue	Blurred vision	Vomiting
Increased respiration	Dry mouth	Numbness
Nausea	Muscle tension	Sweating
Stomach upset	Heart palpitation	

Cognitive		
Thoughts of being scared or hurt	Thoughts of incompetence or inadequacy	Thoughts of bodily injury
Thoughts or images of monsters or wild animals	Difficulty concentrating	Images of harm to loved ones
Self-deprecatory or self-critical thoughts	Blanking out or forgetfulness	Thoughts of going crazy
	Thoughts of appearing foolish	Thoughts of contamination

Behavioral		
Avoidance	Trembling lip	Avoidance of eye contact
Crying or screaming	Swallowing	Physical proximity
Nail biting	Immobility	Clenched jaw
Trembling voice	Twitching	Fidgeting
Stuttering	Thumb sucking	

Based on Fears and Anxieties, by B. A. Barrios and D. P. Hartmann, 1997, p. 235. In E. J. Mash and L. G. Terdal (Eds.), Assessment of Childhood Disorders, 3rd ed.

How many of these symptoms did you experience? What do these many symptoms have in common?

The symptoms of anxiety are expressed through three interrelated response systems: the *physical system*, the *cognitive system*, and the *behavioral system*. It is essential to know how the three sets of symptoms work, since more than one may be evident in different children with the same anxiety disorder. Also, as we will discuss, different response systems are more dominant in certain anxiety disorders. Let's take a closer look at how each response system works.

Physical System

When a person perceives or anticipates danger, the brain sends messages to the sympathetic nervous system, which produces the fight/flight response. The activation of this system produces many important chemical and physical effects that mobilize the body for action:

▶ *Chemical effects.* Adrenaline and noradrenaline are released from the adrenal glands.

▶ *Cardiovascular effects.* Heart rate and strength of the heart beat increase, readying the body for action by speeding up blood flow and improving delivery of oxygen to the tissues.

▶ *Respiratory effects.* Speed and depth of breathing increase, which brings oxygen to the tissues and removes waste. This may produce feelings of breathlessness, choking or smothering, or chest pains.

▶ *Sweat gland effects.* Sweating increases, which cools the body and makes the skin slippery.

▶ *Other physical effects.* The pupils widen to let in more light, which may lead to blurred vision or spots in front of the eyes. Salivation decreases, resulting in a dry mouth. Decreased activity in the digestive system may lead to nausea and a heavy feeling in the stomach. Muscles tense in readiness for fight or flight, leading to subjective feelings of tension, aches and pains, and trembling.

These physical symptoms are familiar signs of anxiety. Overall, the fight/flight response produces general activation of the entire metabolism. As a result, the individual may feel hot and flushed and, because this activation takes a lot of energy, he or she feels tired and drained afterward.

Cognitive System

Since the main purpose of the fight/flight system is to signal possible danger, its activation produces an immediate search for a potential threat. For children with anxiety disorders, it is difficult to focus on everyday tasks because their attention is consumed by a constant search for threat or danger. When these children can't find proof of danger, they may turn their search inward: "If nothing is out there to make me feel anxious, then something must be wrong with me." Or they may distort the situation: "Even though I can't find it, I know there's something to be afraid of." Or they may do both. Children with anxiety disorders will invent explanations for their anxiety: "I must be a real jerk." "Everyone will think I'm a dummy if I say something." "Even though I can't see them, there are germs all over the place." Activation of the cognitive system often leads to subjective feelings of apprehension, nervousness, difficulty concentrating, and panic.

Behavioral System

The overwhelming urges that accompany the fight/flight response are aggression and a desire to escape the threatening situation, but social constraints may prevent fulfilling either impulse. For example, just before a final exam you may feel like attacking your professor or not showing up at all, but fortunately for your professor and your need to pass the course, you are likely to inhibit these urges! However, they may show up as foot tapping, fidgeting, or irritability (consider the number of teeth marks in pencils) or as escape or avoidance by getting a doctor's note, requesting a deferral, or even faking illness. Unfortunately, avoidance perpetuates anxiety, despite the temporary feeling of relief. Avoidance behaviors are negatively reinforced; that is, they are strengthened when they are followed by a rapid reduction in anxiety. As a result, each time a child is confronted with an anxiety-producing situation, the faster she or he gets out of it, the faster the anxiety drops off—so the more the child avoids such situations. As children with anxiety disorders engage in more and more avoidance, carrying out everyday activities becomes exceedingly difficult.

CHANTELLE

The Terror of Being Home Alone

When Chantelle, age 14, realized she was at home alone, she was terrified. Her thoughts raced so fast it was impossible to think clearly. She forgot all the right things to do. Her heart pounded and she tensed up. She felt like she couldn't breathe, and she began to sob. She wanted to run but felt completely immobilized. (Based on authors' case material.)

Chantelle's reactions show how the three response systems of anxiety interact and feed off one another. Physically, Chantelle's heart pounded, she tensed, and she had difficulty breathing. Cognitively, she could not think clearly. Behaviorally, she was completely immobilized.

Anxiety versus Fear and Panic

It is important to distinguish anxiety from two closely related emotions—fear and panic. **Fear** is an immediate alarm reaction to current danger or life-threatening emergencies. Although fear and anxiety have much in common, the fear reaction differs both psychologically and biologically from the emotion of anxiety. Fear is a *present-oriented* emotional reaction to current danger marked by a strong escape tendency and an all-out surge in the sympathetic nervous system.

The overriding message is alarm: "If I don't do something right now, I might not make it at all." In contrast, anxiety is a *future-oriented* emotion characterized by feelings of apprehension and lack of control over upcoming events that might be threatening. Fear and anxiety both warn of danger or distress. However, only anxiety is frequently felt when no danger is actually present (Barlow, 2002).

Panic is a group of physical symptoms of the fight/flight response that unexpectedly occur in the absence of any obvious threat or danger. With no explanation for physical symptoms such as a pounding heart, the child may invent one: "I'm dying." The sensations themselves can feel threatening and may trigger further fear, apprehension, anxiety, and panic (Barlow, 2002).

Normal Fears, Anxieties, Worries, and Rituals

Since fear and anxiety in moderate doses are adaptive, it is not surprising that emotions and rituals that increase feelings of control are common during childhood and adolescence. It is only when the emotions and rituals become excessive, occur in a developmentally inappropriate context, or lead to impairment in functioning such as an inability to go to school, make friends, complete academic tasks, or meet other developmental goals that they are of concern.

Normal Fears

Since young people and their environments constantly change, fears that are normal at one age can be debilitating a few years later. For example, fear of strangers may serve a protective function for infants and young children, but when it persists beyond a certain age it can seriously interfere with the development of peer relations (Brooker et al., 2013). Whether or not a specific fear is normal also depends on its effect on the child and how long it lasts. If a fear has little impact on the child's daily life or lasts only a few weeks, it is likely a part of normal development.

The number and types of common childhood fears change over time, with a general age-related decline in number (Gullone, 1999). Even so, specific fears are common in older children, and many teens report that their fears cause them considerable distress and significantly interfere with daily activities (Ollendick & King, 1994). Girls tend to have more fears than boys at almost every age; they also rate themselves as more fearful and report fears that are more intense and disabling than do boys. Although fears show a general decline with age, some, such as school-related fears, remain stable; others, such as social fears, may increase (Muris, 2007). Common fears and anxieties of infants, children, and adolescents are shown in Table 11.2. Also shown are possible relevant symptoms and corresponding DSM-5 anxiety disorders that may develop in relation to these symptoms.

TABLE 11.2 | **Common Fears and Anxieties of Infancy, Childhood, and Adolescence; Possible Symptoms; and Corresponding DSM-5 Diagnoses**

Developmental Period	Age	Common Fears and Anxieties	Possible Symptoms	Corresponding DSM-5 Anxiety Disorder
Early Infancy	Within first weeks	Loss of physical support, loss of physical contact with caregiver	—	—
	0–6 months	Intense sensory stimuli (loud noises)	—	—
Late Infancy	6–8 months	Shyness/anxiety with stranger, sudden, unexpected, or looming objects	—	Separation anxiety disorder
Toddlerhood	12–18 months	Separation from parent, injury, toileting, strangers	Sleep disturbances, nocturnal panic attacks, oppositional defiant behavior	Separation anxiety disorder, panic attacks
	2–3 years	Fears of thunder and lightning, fire, water, darkness, nightmares	Crying, clinging, withdrawal, freezing, avoidance of salient stimuli (e.g., turning the light on), night terrors, enuresis	Specific phobias (natural environment), panic attacks
		Fears of animals	—	Specific phobias (animal)
Early Childhood	4–5 years	Separation from parents, fear of death or dead people	Excessive need for reassurance	Separation anxiety disorder, generalized anxiety disorder, panic attacks
Primary/Elementary School Age	5–7 years	Fear of specific objects (animals, monsters, ghosts)	—	Specific phobias
		Fear of germs or of getting a serious illness	—	Obsessive–compulsive disorder (OCD)
		Fear of natural disasters, fear of traumatic events (e.g., getting burned, being hit by a car or truck)	—	Specific phobias (natural environment), acute stress disorder, post-traumatic stress disorder, generalized anxiety disorder
	5–11 years	School anxiety, performance anxiety, physical appearance, social concerns	Withdrawal, timidity, extreme shyness with unfamiliar adults and peers, feelings of shame	Social anxiety disorder (social phobia)
Adolescence	12–18 years	Personal relations, rejection from peers, personal appearance, future, natural disasters, safety	Fear of negative evaluation	Social anxiety disorder (social phobia)

Based on Beesdo, Knappe, & Pine, 2009.

All children experience some fear, anxiety, and worry as a normal part of growing up.

Jacqueline Veissid/Photodisc/Getty Images

Normal Anxieties

Like fears, anxieties are very common during childhood and adolescence. Various types of anxiety are evident by age 4 (Eley, Lichenstein, & Moffitt, 2003), and about 25% of parents report that their child is too nervous, fearful, or anxious (Achenbach, 1991a). The most frequent symptoms in samples of children with normal anxieties are separation anxiety, test anxiety, overconcern about competence, excessive need for reassurance, and anxiety about harm to a parent (Barrios & Hartmann, 1997).

Younger children generally experience more anxiety symptoms than do older children, primarily about separation from parents. Girls display more anxiety than boys, but they generally experience similar types of symptoms. Although some specific anxieties decrease with age, such as separation anxiety and anxiety about school, nervous and anxious symptoms may not show the age-related decline observed for many specific fears (Hale et al., 2008). Anxious symptoms may reflect a stable trait that predisposes children to develop excessive fears related to their stage of development. Thus, the disposition to be anxious may remain stable over time, even though the objects of children's fears change.

Normal Worries

If worrying about the future is so unproductive, why do we do so much of it? Part of the reason seems to be that the process of worry—thinking about all possible negative outcomes—serves an extremely useful function in normal development. In moderate doses, worry can help children prepare for the future—for example, by checking their homework before they hand it in or by rehearsing for an upcoming class play. Worry is a central feature of anxiety, and anxiety is related to the number of children's worries and to their intensity (Silverman, La Greca, & Wasserstein, 1995). Children of all ages worry, but the forms and expressions change. Older children report a greater variety and complexity of worries and are better able to describe them than are younger children (Chorpita et al., 1997).

Normal Rituals and Repetitive Behavior

Ritualistic, repetitive activity is extremely common in young children (Peleg-Popko & Dar, 2003). A familiar example is the bedtime ritual of saying good night—addressing people in a certain order or giving a certain number of hugs and kisses. Normal ritualistic behaviors in young children include preferences for sameness in the environment (e.g., watching the same DVD over and over again), rigid likes and dislikes, preferences for symmetry (e.g., carrying a toy in each hand), awareness of minute details or imperfections in toys or clothes (e.g., being bothered by a minuscule thread on a jacket sleeve), and arranging things so they are "just right" (e.g., insisting that different foods not touch each other on the plate). Rituals help young children gain control and mastery over their social and physical environments and make their world more predictable and safer (Evans et al., 1997). Any parent who has violated these rituals and paid the price can appreciate how important they are to the young child.

Many common routines of young children fall into two distinct categories: repetitive behaviors and doing things "just right." These categories are strikingly similar to those found for older individuals with OCD and related disorders, which we discuss later in the chapter. It is not known whether OCD is an extreme point on a continuum of normal developmental rituals or an entirely different problem (Evans, Gray, & Leckman, 1999). However, research suggests that the neuropsychological mechanisms underlying compulsive, ritualistic behavior in normal development and those in OCD may be similar (Pietrefesa & Evans, 2007).

Anxiety Disorders According to DSM-5

Anxiety disorders in DSM-5 are divided into seven categories that closely define the focus of the child's anxiety and the types of reaction and avoidance. To give you an overall picture, these disorders are described briefly in A Closer Look 11.1. The number of youths with multiple anxiety disorders increases with age. Keep in mind that significant associations exist between nearly all anxiety disorders. These associations are best explained by a model that

Main Features of Seven DSM-5 Anxiety Disorders

Separation Anxiety Disorder (SAD)

Characterized by excessive worry regarding separation from home or parents. Youths may show signs of distress and physical symptoms on separation, experience unrealistic worries about harm to self or others when separated, and display an unwillingness to be alone.

Specific Phobia

Characterized by severe and unreasonable fears and avoidance of a specific object or situation, for example, dogs, spiders, darkness, or riding on a bus.

Social Anxiety Disorder (SOC) (Social Phobia)

Characterized by a severe and unreasonable fear of being embarrassed or humiliated when doing something in front of peers or adults.

Selective Mutism

Characterized by a consistent failure to speak in specific social situations in which there is an expectation for speaking (e.g., school), even though the child may speak loudly and frequently at home or in other settings.

Panic Disorder (PD)

Characterized by recurrent, unexpected and severe panic attacks. These attacks may consist of an accelerated heart rate, shortness of breath, sweating, upset stomach, dizziness, fear of dying, and others. The individual also experiences a persistent concern or worry about additional panic attacks or their consequences, or displays a significant maladaptive change in behavior to avoid having panic attacks (e.g., avoidance of exercise or new situations).

Agoraphobia

Characterized by fear or anxiety about two or more situations such as using public transportation, being in open spaces (e.g., parking lots, marketplaces), being in enclosed spaces (e.g., theaters), being in a crowd, or being outside of the home alone. The fear or anxiety about these situations occurs because the individual thinks that escape might be difficult or help not available if they were to develop panic-like or other incapacitating symptoms.

Generalized Anxiety Disorder (GAD)

Characterized by ongoing and excessive worry about many events and activities. Youths may worry about their grades in school, their relations with peers, and their own or others' safety. They may constantly seek comfort or approval from others to help reduce their worry.

---

specifies multiple distinct anxiety syndromes that are related to a higher-order factor (e.g., negative affect) that is common to most if not all anxiety disorders, as well as depression (Higa-McMillan et al., 2014).

Section Summary

Description of Anxiety Disorders

- Anxiety disorders are among the most common mental health problems in children and adolescents, but they often go unnoticed and untreated.

- Anxiety is an adaptive emotion that prepares youngsters to cope with potentially threatening people, objects, or events. Strong negative emotions, physical tension, and apprehensive anticipation of future danger or misfortune characterize it.

- The symptoms of anxiety are expressed through three interrelated response systems: physical, cognitive, and behavioral.

- Fear is a present-oriented emotional reaction to current danger. In contrast, anxiety is a future-oriented emotion characterized by feelings of apprehension and a lack of control over upcoming events that might be threatening.

- Fears, anxieties, worries, and rituals in children are common, change with age, and follow a predictable developmental pattern with respect to type.

- DSM-5 specifies several types of anxiety and related disorders based on types of reaction and avoidance.

SEPARATION ANXIETY DISORDER

BRAD

"Don't Leave Me!"

Brad, age 9, is unable to enter any situation that requires separation from his parents—playing in the backyard, going to other children's homes, or staying with a babysitter. When forcibly separated from his parents, Brad cries or throws a full-blown tantrum. When his mother plans to leave the house, he runs through all the horrible things that might happen to her, in an endless series of what-if questions. When she becomes frustrated and angry, Brad becomes even more anxious. The more anxious he gets, the more he argues with his mother, and the angrier she gets. Brad has also threatened to hurt himself if forced to go to school.

Brad's separation problems began about a year ago, when his father was drinking too much and was frequently absent for long periods. Brad's problem gradually worsened over the course of the year, until he completely refused to go to school. Help was sought, but Brad continued to get worse. He developed significant depressive symptoms, including sadness, guilt about his problems, and occasional wishes to die.

Adapted from Last, 1988.

Separation anxiety is important for the young child's survival and is normal at certain ages. From about age 7 months through the preschool years, almost all children fuss when they are separated from their parents or others to whom they are close. In fact, a lack of separation anxiety at this age may suggest insecure attachment or other problems. Unfortunately, like Brad, some children continue to display such anxiety long after the age at which it is typical or expected. When anxiety persists for at least 4 weeks and is severe enough to interfere with normal daily routines such as going to school or participating in recreational activities, the child may have a separation anxiety disorder. The DSM-5 criteria are presented in Table 11.3.

Children with **separation anxiety disorder (SAD)** display age-inappropriate, excessive, and disabling distress related to separation from their parents or other major attachment figures and fear of being alone (Cooper-Vince et al., 2014). Young children with SAD may have vague feelings of anxiety or repeated nightmares about being kidnapped or killed or about the death of a parent. They frequently display excessive demands for parental attention by clinging to their parents and shadowing their every move. Often, they are reluctant to sleep separated from their parents, and they try to climb into their parents' bed at night or sleep on the floor just outside their parents' bedroom door (Allen et al., 2010). Older children with SAD may have difficulty being alone in a room during the day, sleeping alone even at home, running errands, going to school, or going to camp. They may also have specific fantasies of illness, accidents, kidnapping, or physical harm.

Children with SAD fear new situations and may display physical symptoms. To avoid separation, they may fuss, cry, scream, or threaten suicide if the parent leaves (although serious suicide attempts are rare);

TABLE 11.3 | **Diagnostic Criteria for** Separation Anxiety Disorder (SAD)

DSM-5

(A) Developmentally inappropriate and excessive fear or anxiety concerning separation from those to whom the individual is attached, as evidenced by at least three of the following:

(1) Recurrent excessive distress when anticipating or experiencing separation from home or from major attachment figures.

(2) Persistent or excessive worry about losing major attachment figures or about possible harm to them, such as illness, injury, disasters, or death.

(3) Persistent and excessive worry about experiencing an untoward event (e.g., getting lost, being kidnapped, having an accident, becoming ill) that causes separation from a major attachment figure.

(4) Persistent reluctance or refusal to go out, away from home, to school, to work, or elsewhere because of fear of separation.

(5) Persistent and excessive fear of or reluctance about being alone or without major attachment figures at home or in other settings.

(6) Persistent reluctance or refusal to sleep away from home or to go to sleep without being near a major attachment figure.

(7) Repeated nightmares involving the theme of separation.

(8) Repeated complaints of physical symptoms (e.g., headaches, stomachaches, nausea, vomiting) when separation from major attachment figures occurs or is anticipated.

(B) The fear, anxiety, or avoidance is persistent, lasting at least 4 weeks in children and adolescents and typically 6 months or more in adults.

(C) The disturbance causes clinically significant distress or impairment in social, academic, occupational, or other important areas of functioning.

(D) The disturbance is not better explained by another mental disorder, such as refusing to leave home because of excessive resistance to change in autism spectrum disorder; delusions or hallucinations concerning separation in psychotic disorders; refusal to go outside without a trusted companion in agoraphobia; worries about ill health or other harm befalling significant others in generalized anxiety disorder; or concerns about having an illness in illness anxiety disorder.

(E) criteria and Specify if should be deleted in their entirety. No substitutions for either.

Source: Diagnostic and Statistical Manual of Mental Disorders, Fifth Edition, American Psychiatric Association.

physical symptoms may include rapid heartbeat, dizziness, headaches, stomachaches, and nausea. Not surprisingly, parents, especially mothers, become highly distressed. Over time, as we saw with Brad, children with SAD may become increasingly withdrawn, apathetic, and depressed, and are at risk for developing a variety of other anxiety disorders during adolescence (Lewinsohn et al., 2008).

Prevalence and Comorbidity

SAD is one of the two most common anxiety disorders to occur during childhood (the other is specific phobia), and it is found in about 4% to 10% of all children (Merikangas et al., 2010). It is common in both boys and girls, although it is more prevalent in girls. About two-thirds of children with SAD have another anxiety disorder, and about half develop a depressive disorder following the onset of SAD. They may also display specific fears of getting lost or of the dark. School reluctance or refusal is also quite common in older children with SAD (Albano, Chorpita, & Barlow, 2003).

Onset, Course, and Outcome

Of children referred for anxiety disorders, SAD has the earliest reported age at onset (7 to 8 years) and the youngest age at referral (Shear et al., 2006). SAD generally progresses from mild to severe. It may begin with harmless requests or with symptoms such as restless sleep or nightmares, which progress to the child sleeping nightly in his or her parents' bed. Similarly, school mornings may evoke physical symptoms and an occasional absence from school, which escalates into daily tantrums about leaving for school and outright refusal. The child may become increasingly concerned about the parents' daily routine and whereabouts (Albano et al., 2003).

Often, SAD occurs after a child has experienced major stress, such as moving to a new neighborhood, entering a new school, death or illness in the family, or an extended vacation. Brad's SAD emerged after his father developed a problem with alcohol and subsequently left home. The symptoms of SAD may also fluctuate over the years as a function of stress and transitions in the child's life. Although they may lose friends as a result of their repeated refusal to participate in activities away from home, children with SAD are reasonably skilled socially and get along with others. However, their school performance may suffer as a result of frequent school absences. The child may require special assignments just to keep up; in extreme cases, they may have to repeat the school year (Albano et al., 2003).

SAD persists into adulthood for more than one-third of children and adolescents. As adults, these individuals are more likely than others to experience relationship difficulties (e.g., never marry or become separated or divorced), other anxiety disorders and mental health problems (particularly panic disorder and depression),

and functional impairment in their social and personal lives (Milrod et al., 2014; Shear et al., 2006).

School reluctance and refusal are quite common in youngsters with SAD.

ERIC

Won't Go to School

Eric, age 12, was referred by a school psychologist and his parents for his intense school refusal behavior. On entering seventh grade and a new school, he began to experience a variety of negative symptoms, such as hyperventilation, anxiety, sad mood, and somatic symptoms. Although attendance was not a problem at first, by mid-September Eric began to report severe headaches on school mornings. School attendance then became intermittent. By late September, his aversion to school had worsened and he was staying at home on most days.

Adapted from Kearney, 1995.

School Reluctance and Refusal

Although starting school is exciting and enjoyable for most children, many are reluctant to go to school and—for a few—school may create so much fear and anxiety that they will not go. These children can become literally sick with worry, let minor physical symptoms keep them at home, or pretend to be ill. **School refusal behavior** is defined as the refusal to attend classes or difficulty remaining in school for an entire day. It includes youngsters who resist going to school in the morning but eventually attend, those who go to school but leave at some point during the day, those who attend with great dread that leads to future pleas for nonattendance, and those who miss the entire day (Kearney, 2007).

School refusal is equally common in boys and girls, and it occurs most often between the ages of 5 and 11 years. Excessive and unreasonable fears of school usually first occur during preschool, kindergarten, or first grade and peak during the second grade. However, school refusal can occur at any time and may have a sudden onset at a later age, as happened with Eric. Children who refuse school may complain of a headache, upset stomach, or sore throat just before it's time to leave for school, then begin to "feel better" when permitted to stay at home, only to feel "sick" again the next morning. As the time for school draws near, the child may plead, cry, and refuse to leave the house and may even have a full-blown panic reaction. School refusal often follows a period at home during which the child has spent more time than usual with a parent (e.g., brief illness, holiday break, or summer vacation). At other times, school refusal may follow a stressful event such as a change of schools (as happened with Eric), an accident, or the death of a relative or family pet.

For many children, fear of school is really a fear of leaving their parents—separation anxiety. However, school reluctance and refusal can occur for many reasons (Kearney & Albano, 2004). Most children who refuse to go to school have average or above-average intelligence, suggesting that it is not a difficulty with academics that leads to this problem. A fear of school may be associated with submitting for the first time to authority and rules outside the home, being compared with unfamiliar children, and experiencing the threat of failure. Some children fear school because they are afraid of being ridiculed, teased, or bullied by other children or being criticized or disciplined by their teachers. In other cases, the child's fear may result from an excessive or irrational fear of being socially evaluated or embarrassed when having to recite in class or undress in front of unfamiliar people in a gym class. Eric was extremely anxious about meeting new people, being late for class,

moving from class to class, taking classes involving public speaking, and participating in gym class. He refused to attend school mainly to escape being socially evaluated and, to a lesser extent, to gain attention from his parents (Kearney & Silverman, 1996).

The possible long-term consequences are serious for a child who displays a persistent pattern of school refusal behavior and does not receive help. Academic or social problems may develop as a result of missed instruction and peer interaction. Treatment usually emphasizes an immediate return to school and other routines and must take into account the specific functions being served by school refusal behaviors (Kearney & Albano, 2007).

Section Summary

Separation Anxiety Disorder

- Children with SAD display age-inappropriate, excessive, and disabling distress related to separation from and fear of being alone without their parents or other major attachment figures.
- SAD is one of the most common anxiety disorders of childhood, with the earliest reported age at onset and the youngest age at referral.
- School refusal behavior is defined as the refusal to attend classes or difficulty remaining in school for an entire day.

SPECIFIC PHOBIA

CHARLOTTE

Arachnophobia

For 2 years, Charlotte, age 8, has complained of an intense fear of spiders. "Spiders are disgusting," she says. "I'm scared to death that one will crawl on me, especially when I'm sleeping. When I see a spider, even a little one, my heart pounds, my hands feel cold and sweaty, and I start to shake." Charlotte's mother says that her daughter goes completely pale when she sees a spider, even at a distance, and tries to avoid any situation where she thinks there might be one. Charlotte's fear is beginning to interfere with her daily activities. For example, she won't play in the backyard and refuses to go on class or family outings where she might encounter a spider. She is afraid to go to sleep at night because she thinks a spider might crawl on her. (Based on authors' case material.)

School reluctance and refusal are common problems related to anxiety.

© iStockphoto.com/Sean Locke

Many children have specific fears that are mildly troubling, come and go rapidly until about age 10, and rarely require special attention. However, if the child's fear occurs at an inappropriate age, persists, is irrational or exaggerated, leads to avoidance of the object or event, and causes impairment in normal routines, it is called a **specific phobia**. Like Charlotte, children with a specific phobia display a marked fear or anxiety about specific objects or situations (e.g., animals, heights) for at least 6 months. The DSM-5 criteria for specific phobia are shown in Table 11.4.

Children with a specific phobia show an extreme and disabling fear about objects or situations that in reality pose little or no danger or threat; these children go to great lengths to avoid these objects or situations. They experience extreme fear or dread, physiological arousal to the feared stimulus, and fearful anticipation and avoidance when confronted with the object of their fear. Their fear or anxiety may be expressed by crying, tantrums, freezing, or clinging. Their thinking usually focuses on threats to their personal safety, such as being stung by a bee or struck by lightning. Anticipatory anxiety is also common. For example, a child with a phobia of dogs may think: "What if a big dog is running loose on my way to school and I get attacked and bitten in the face?" These worries cause distress severe enough to disrupt everyday activities. The children are constantly on the lookout for the feared stimulus and, as we saw with Charlotte, go to great lengths to avoid contact.

Children's beliefs regarding the danger of the feared stimulus are likely to persist despite evidence that no danger exists or despite efforts to reason with them. Unlike most adults with a specific phobia, children often do not recognize that their fears are extreme and unreasonable. If the feared object is rarely encountered, the phobia may not lead to serious impairment. However, if it is encountered regularly or if the fear causes significant distress or seriously interferes with important life events, the child's phobia can become a serious problem (Albano et al., 2003).

The phobias that can develop in children and adolescents seem limitless; they include fears of telephones, water, menstruation, newspapers, mathematics, haircuts, and bowel movements, to name just a few. Although it is possible to develop a phobia about almost any object, situation, or event—ranging from A (apiphobia, a fear of bees) to Z (zemmiphobia, a fear of the great mole rat)—children are much more likely to develop certain fears than others (Depla et al., 2008).

TABLE 11.4 | Diagnostic Criteria for Specific Phobia

(A) Marked fear or anxiety about a specific object or situation (e.g., flying, heights, animals, receiving an injection, seeing blood). **DSM-5**

Note: In children, the fear or anxiety may be expressed by crying, tantrums, freezing, or clinging.

(B) The phobic object or situation almost always provokes immediate fear or anxiety.

(C) The phobic object or situation is actively avoided or endured with intense fear or anxiety.

(D) The fear or anxiety is out of proportion to the actual danger posed by the specific object or situation and to the sociocultural context.

(E) The fear, anxiety, or avoidance is persistent, typically lasting 6 months or more.

(F) The fear, anxiety or avoidance causes clinically significant distress or impairment in social, occupational, or other important areas of functioning.

(G) The disturbance is not better accounted for by another mental disorder, including fear, anxiety, and avoidance of situations associated with panic-like symptoms or other incapacitating symptoms (as in agoraphobia); objects or situations related to obsessions (as in obsessive–compulsive disorder); reminders of traumatic events (as in post-traumatic stress disorder); separation from home or attachment figures (as in separation anxiety disorder); or social situations (as in social anxiety disorder).

Specify if (code based on the phobic stimulus):

Animal (e.g., spiders, insects, dogs)

Natural environment (e.g., heights, storms, water)

Blood, injection, injury (e.g., needles, invasive medical procedures)

Situational (e.g., airplanes, elevators, enclosed places)

Other (e.g., situations that may lead to choking or vomiting; in children, loud sounds or costumed characters)

Source: Diagnostic and Statistical Manual of Mental Disorders, Fifth Edition, American Psychiatric Association.

Fear of animals is one of the most common and heritable specific phobias.

According to evolutionary theory, human infants are biologically predisposed as a result of natural selection to learn certain fears (Seligman, 1971). The sources of most children's phobias can be traced to the natural dangers encountered during human evolution—snakes, the dark, predators, heights, blood, loud noises, and unfamiliar places. For example, when listening to evolutionary fear-relevant sounds (e.g., snake hissing), infants as young as 9 months of age display heart rate slowing, an increased eye-blink startle response, and more visual orienting, as compared to when they listen to modern fear-relevant sounds (e.g., siren wailing) or pleasant sounds (e.g., crowd cheering) (Erlich, Lipp, & Slaughter, 2013). These fears are adaptive in an evolutionary sense because they alert the individual to possible sources of danger, thereby increasing the likelihood of survival. It is not only by chance that the most common and most heritable specific phobias in children are a fear of events in the natural environment (e.g., heights, thunder) and a fear of animals, particularly dogs, snakes, insects, and mice (Essau, Conradt, & Petermann, 2000). Although evolutionary theory explains a readiness to acquire specific types of fears, it does not explain why children differ in their fearfulness or why some children develop extreme and disabling anxiety.

As specified in DSM-5, common types of specific phobias in young people include fears of animals or insects (e.g., dogs or spiders); fears of natural events (e.g., heights or thunderstorms); fears of blood, injuries, or medical procedures (e.g., seeing blood or receiving an injection); and fears of specific situations (e.g., flying in airplanes, riding on a bus). Both similarities (e.g., age at onset, gender, treatment response) and differences (e.g., focus of fear, physiological reaction, neural response patterns, impairment, comorbidity) have been found across these types, with natural environment and animal phobias having the most in common with other types, and blood, injury, and injection phobias the least (LeBeau et al., 2010; Lueken et al., 2011).

Prevalence and Comorbidity

About 20% of all youngsters experience specific phobias at some time in their lives, and those with this disorder tend to have multiple phobias (Kessler et al., 2012a; Merikangas et al., 2010). However, very few of these children are referred for treatment, suggesting that most parents do not view specific phobias as significantly harmful. There does seem to be a family vulnerability for particular types of phobias—children are at increased risk for the phobic disorder exhibited by their parent (LeBeau et al., 2010). Family risk can be attributed to both genetic and environmental factors. Specific phobias, particularly blood phobia, are more common in girls than boys

(Essau et al., 2000). The most common co-occurring disorders for youngsters with a specific phobia are another anxiety disorder and depressive disorders (Leyfer et al., 2013). Although comorbidity is frequent for children with specific phobias, it tends to be lower than for other anxiety disorders (LeBeau et al., 2010).

Onset, Course, and Outcome

Phobias involving animals, darkness, insects, blood, and injury typically have their onset at 7 to 9 years of age, which is similar to normal development. However, even though fears and phobias decline with age, clinical phobias are more likely to persist over time than are normal fears. Specific phobias can occur at any age but seem to peak between 10 and 13 years of age (LeBeau et al., 2010).

Section Summary

Specific Phobia

- Children with a specific phobia exhibit an extreme and disabling fear of particular objects or situations that in reality pose little or no danger.

- Evolutionary theory contends that human infants are biologically predisposed to learn certain fears that alert them to possible sources of danger. This may explain why the most common specific phobia in children is a fear of animals, such as dogs, snakes, and insects.

- DSM-5 categorizes specific phobias into five subtypes based on the focus of the phobic reaction and avoidance: animal; natural environment; blood, injection, injury; situational; and other.

- About 4% to 10% of children experience specific phobias, but only a very few are referred for treatment. Specific phobias can occur at any age, but seem to peak between 10 and 13 years of age.

SOCIAL ANXIETY DISORDER (SOCIAL PHOBIA)

To understand the world one must not be worrying about one's self.

—Albert Einstein (1879–1955)

▶ Kaylie is terrified to use the phone because, she says, she doesn't know how to have a conversation and would be embarrassed by the long periods of silence.

▶ Eugene is too embarrassed to use a public restroom.

▶ Li-Ming is terrified of speaking in front of her class—she's afraid of being humiliated.

Each of these youngsters has a **social anxiety disorder** (SOC [for "social"]) or **social phobia**—a marked and persistent fear of social or performance requirements that expose them to scrutiny and possible embarrassment (Knappe, Beesdo-Baum, & Wittchen, 2010). They go to great lengths to avoid these situations, or they may face the challenge with great effort, wearing a mask of fearlessness. Long after the age at which a fear of strangers is considered normal, children with SOC continue to shrink from people they do not know. When in the presence of other children or adults, they may blush, fall silent, cling to their parents, or try to hide. To be classified as SOC, their anxiety must occur in peer settings, not just when interacting with adults. The DSM criteria for SOC are shown in Table 11.5.

In addition to their extreme anxiety in social situations that make many people anxious, youngsters with SOC may feel anxious about the most mundane activities—handing out papers in class, buttoning their coat in front of others, or ordering a Big Mac and fries at McDonalds. Their most common fear is doing something in front of other people. They fear that if they speak in public, they may stumble over their words; if they ask a question, they may sound stupid; if they enter a room, they may trip and look awkward. One teenage girl was so fearful of being the focus of attention during meals that she spent every lunch period during her first year in high school sitting in a bathroom stall (Albano et al., 2003, p. 287).

Youngsters with SOC are more likely than other children to be highly emotional, socially fearful, and inhibited, sad, and lonely. They frequently experience socially distressing events with which they are unable to cope effectively, in part related to a lack of social skills (Beidel, Turner, & Morris, 1999). These children want to be liked by other people. However, their fear of acting in a way that may invite humiliation is so intense and pervasive that it often leads to loneliness and suffering because they cannot form the relationships they desire (La Greca & Lopez, 1998). If other people attempt to push them into social situations they may cry, have a tantrum, freeze, or withdraw even further. They fear most social situations, are afraid to meet or talk with new people, avoid contact with anyone outside their family, and find it extremely difficult to attend school, participate in recreational activities, or socialize (Beidel et al., 2007; Bernstein et al., 2008). Current evidence supports the view of SOC as existing on a continuum of severity from lesser to greater as a function of the number of social situations that are feared and/or avoided (Bögels et al., 2010).

The anxiety associated with SOC can be so severe that it produces stammering, sweating, upset stomach, rapid heartbeat, or a full-scale panic attack. Adolescents with SOC frequently believe that their visible physical reactions will expose their hidden feelings of

TABLE 11.5 | **Diagnostic Criteria for** Social Anxiety Disorder (Social Phobia)

(A) Marked fear or anxiety about one or more social situations in which the individual is exposed to possible scrutiny by others. Examples include social interactions (e.g., having a conversation, meeting unfamiliar people), being observed (e.g., eating or drinking), or performing in front of others (e.g., giving a speech).   **DSM-5**

Note: In children, the anxiety must occur in peer settings and not just during interactions with adults.

(B) The individual fears that he or she will act in a way or show anxiety symptoms that will be negatively evaluated (i.e., will be humiliating or embarrassing; will lead to rejection or offend others).

(C) The social situations almost always provoke fear or anxiety.

Note: In children, the fear or anxiety may be expressed by crying, tantrums, freezing, clinging, shrinking away, or failing to speak in social situations.

(D) The social situations are avoided or endured with intense fear or anxiety.

(E) The fear or anxiety is out of proportion to the actual danger posed by the social situation and to the sociocultural context.

(F) The fear, anxiety, or avoidance is persistent, typically lasting for 6 months or more.

(G) The fear, anxiety, and avoidance causes clinically significant distress or impairment in social, occupational, or other important areas of functioning.

(H) The fear, anxiety, and avoidance is not attributable to the direct physiological effects of a substance (e.g., a drug of abuse, a medication) or another medical condition.

(I) The fear, anxiety, or avoidance is not better explained by the symptoms of another mental disorder, such as panic disorder, body dysmorphic disorder, or autism spectrum disorder.

(J) If another medical condition (e.g., Parkinson's disease, obesity, disfigurement from burns or injury) is present, the fear, anxiety, or avoidance is clearly unrelated or is excessive.

Specify if:

Performance only: If the fear is restricted to speaking or performing in public.

Source: Diagnostic and Statistical Manual of Mental Disorders, Fifth Edition, American Psychiatric Association.

inadequacy, which makes them even more anxious. In a repeating cycle, children with SOC anticipate their awkwardness and poor performance, which triggers further anxiety as they approach the feared situation, and further increases their nervousness and physical symptoms. As a result, they avoid social activities such as calling a classmate for missed homework, asking the teacher to explain something, answering the telephone, going to parties, and dating (Albano, 1995).

SOC encompasses a variety of social fears, including fear of performance situations, such as speaking in front of others, and fear of interaction situations, such as talking to others at a party. Some research has suggested that performance- and interaction-related social fears may differ from one another in their risk factors and clinical characteristics and that identifying children with SOC who differ in their types of social fears may help to further our understanding of this disorder (Knappe et al., 2011). To this end, DSM-5 provides a "performance only" specifier to identify youngsters with SOC whose anxiety is restricted to performance situations such as speaking in front of others or performing in public (e.g., at a sporting event or musical recital).

Prevalence, Comorbidity, and Course

SOC is common; it has a lifetime prevalence of 6% to 12% and affects nearly twice as many girls as boys (Knappe et al., 2010). Girls may experience greater social anxiety because they are more concerned with social competence than are boys and attach greater importance to interpersonal relationships and evaluation by peers (Inderbitzen-Nolan & Walters, 2000). Some support for this hypothesis comes from a brain functional magnetic resonance imaging study into the neural correlates of anticipated evaluation by peers in 9- to 17-year-old male and female adolescents (Guyer et al., 2009). Females who thought that a peer they wished to interact with was evaluating them showed age-related increases in activation of brain regions (e.g., hippocampus) associated with processing emotional information. These increases did not occur in males. Representative findings from this study are shown in ● Figure 11.1 and suggest that, relative to males, adolescent females may have an increasing biological sensitivity to being evaluated by peers, which may, over time, increase their vulnerability to developing SOC.

Among children and adolescents referred for treatment for anxiety disorders, about one-third have SOC as their primary diagnosis. It is also the most common secondary diagnosis for children referred for other anxiety disorders (Leyfer et al., 2013). Even so, many cases of SOC are overlooked because shyness is common and because these children are not likely to call attention to their problem even when they are severely distressed (Essau, Conradt, & Petermann, 1999).

Two-thirds of children and adolescents with SOC have another anxiety disorder—most commonly, generalized anxiety disorder (Bernstein et al., 2008; Leyfer et al., 2013). Other common comorbid anxiety disorders are SAD and specific phobias (Beidel et al., 2007). About 20% of adolescents with SOC also suffer from major depression. They may also use alcohol and other drugs as a

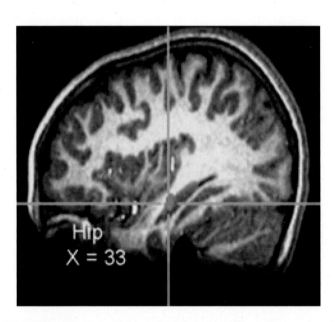

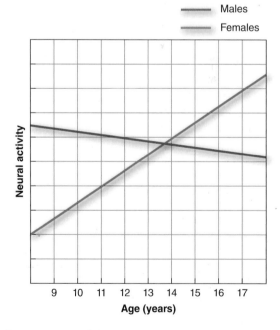

● **FIGURE 11.1** | (a) Increased neural activity as detected in the hippocampus while participants appraised how they thought preferred peers would evaluate them. (b) As age increased, neural activity in the hippocampus increased in females but did not change in males.

(a) © 2009, Amanda E. Guyer, Erin B. McClure-Tone, Nina D. Shiffrin, Daniel S. Pine, Eric E. Nelson; "Probing the Neural Correlates of Anticipated Peer Evaluation in Adolescence" *Child Development*, © 2009, Society for Research in Child Development, Inc. (b) From Probing the neural correlates of anticipated peer evaluation in adolescence by Guyer et al. *Child Development*, *80*, 1000–1015. Journal Compilation © 2009, Society for Research in Child Development, Inc. John Wiley and Sons.

form of self-medication to reduce their anxiety in social situations and are at risk for later substance-use problems (Albano et al., 2003; Buckner et al., 2008).

SOC is extremely rare in children under the age of 10, and it generally develops after puberty, with the most common age at onset in early- to mid-adolescence (Wittchen, Stein, & Kessler, 1999). However, given the nature of the disorder, individuals with SOC are often the most reluctant to seek treatment following the onset of their problem. The prevalence of SOC appears to increase with age, with considerable persistence and fluctuations in symptom severity over time (Beesdo-Baum et al., 2012). As adults, individuals with SOC may experience significant impairment in role functioning, including relationship problems, educational difficulties, and poorer overall quality of life. The average duration of symptoms of social anxiety is about 20 to 25 years—thus, it is not a short-lived condition of adolescence and young adulthood. In the absence of effective treatment, the likelihood of a complete and long-lasting remission for SOC is the lowest for all anxiety disorders (Knappe et al., 2010).

Section Summary

Social Anxiety Disorder (SOC) (Social Phobia)

- Children with SOC fear being the focus of attention or scrutiny or of doing something in public that will be intensely humiliating.

- SOC is common, with a lifetime prevalence of 6% to 12%, and affecting nearly twice as many girls as boys.

- SOC generally develops after puberty, at a time when most teens experience heightened self-consciousness and worries about what others think of them.

SELECTIVE MUTISM

KEISHA

Mum's the Word

Keisha, age 6, doesn't speak at kindergarten to teachers or peers and did not do so during her 2 years in preschool. Two years ago she had difficulties being left at preschool and it took about 2 months before she could be left without crying. Although she doesn't talk to other children, she interacts with them and participates in school activities. Keisha speaks openly to all family members at home but does not speak to them in public if others might hear her. She says that she does not know why she doesn't talk, but has told her mother that she feels scared. Her mother says Keisha is shy and is a worrier.

Adapted from Leonard & Dow, 1995.

Children with **selective mutism** fail to speak in specific social situations in which there is an expectation to speak (e.g., at school), even though they may speak loudly and frequently at home or in other settings (Viana, Beidel, & Rabian, 2009). The DSM-5 criteria also require that the child's disturbance interferes with educational or work achievement or with social communication, that it is present for at least 1 month, that it is not limited to a lack of knowledge or discomfort with the spoken language required in the social situation, that it is not better explained by a communication disorder, and that it does not occur only during the course of autism spectrum disorder, schizophrenia, or another psychotic disorder (APA, 2013).

Prevalence, Comorbidity, and Course

Selective mutism is rare, estimated to occur in about 0.7% of all children in community samples (Bergman, Piacentini, & McKracken, 2002). Prevalence does not seem to vary by sex or race/ethnicity. The most common co-occurring disorders are other anxiety disorders, particularly SOC and specific phobia. Oppositional behaviors may also occur, but these may be limited to situations in which the child is required to speak (Cunningham, McHolm, & Boyle, 2006). The average age at onset is about 3 to 4 years; however, there is often a considerable lag between onset and referral, possibly because the child's mutism may not occur at home. With school entry and the associated increase in social interaction and tasks (e.g., reading aloud), the child is more likely to be identified and referred. The persistence of selective mutism is variable, although many children seem to "outgrow" the disorder. However, research in this area is limited, and the long-term course of the disorder is not known (APA, 2013).

Although it was not previously included as a diagnosable disorder in DSM-IV, selective mutism has many features in common with the anxiety disorders (Leonard & Dow, 1995), which resulted in its inclusion as an anxiety disorder in DSM-5. For example, about 45% to 75% of children with selective mutism meet diagnostic criteria for SOC in ways other than their reluctance to speak (Viana et al., 2009), and nearly 40% of their parents have also been diagnosed with SOC during their lifetime (Chavira et al., 2007). Other common comorbidities include communication, elimination, and oppositional disorders (Cohan et al., 2008).

Based on the similarities between selective mutism and SOC, it has been suggested that selective mutism may be a developmentally specific variant of SOC in young children or an early precursor to SOC, rather than a unique disorder (Bergman et al., 2002; Dummit et al., 1997). However, there are also differences between the two disorders—for example, nonverbal social engagement and oppositional features occur in selective mutism, but less so in SOC (Yaganeh, Beidel, & Turner, 2006). Relatedly, one study identified three subgroups of children with selective mutism: anxious—mildly oppositional; (2) anxious—communication delayed; and (3) exclusively anxious (Cohan & Chavira, 2008). Anecdotal accounts from adults who suffered from selective mutism as children also suggest that in some cases trauma played a role and not talking was a self-protective response (Omdal, 2007). For example, Dr. Maya Angelou, a celebrated African-American poet and writer who captivated audiences with her words, was mute for nearly 5 years after suffering the trauma of being raped at 8 years old.

Section Summary

Selective Mutism

- Children with selective mutism fail to talk in specific social situations where there is an expectation to do so, even though they may speak in other settings.

- Selective mutism is a rare disorder occurring in about 0.7% of all children. Its prevalence does not seem to vary by sex or race/ethnicity.

- The most common co-occurring disorders are other anxiety disorders, particularly SOC and specific phobia.

- The average age at onset is about 3 to 4 years, but there is often a considerable lag between onset and referral.

- Selective mutism and SOC are currently viewed as distinct but strongly related disorders.

PANIC DISORDER AND AGORAPHOBIA

CLAUDIA

An Attack Out of Nowhere

Claudia, age 16, was watching TV after a noneventful day at school. She suddenly felt overwhelmed by an intense feeling of light-headedness and a smothering sensation, as if she couldn't get any air to breathe. Her heart started to pound rapidly, as if it would explode. The attack came on so fast and was so intense that Claudia panicked and thought she was having a heart attack that would kill her. She began to sweat and tremble, and she felt the room was spinning. These feelings reached a peak within 2 minutes ... but this was the seventh attack that Claudia had experienced this month. She frantically ran to her mother and pleaded to be taken to the hospital emergency room—again. (Based on authors' case material.)

Prior to DSM-5, panic disorder and agoraphobia were connected because diagnosing panic disorder included the designation "with" or "without" agoraphobia (i.e., a marked fear or avoidance of certain situations in which the individual thinks that escape may be difficult, or help not available, if they were to experience panic-like or other incapacitating symptoms). However, in DSM-5, panic disorder and agoraphobia are now separate disorders with different diagnostic criteria. This change was based on research suggesting that a number of adolescents and adults experience agoraphobia without panic symptoms. However, to date, most studies of young people have considered the two conditions together (Higa-McMillan et al., 2014). Therefore, we discuss both disorders in this section.

Adolescents like Claudia with a **panic disorder** (PD) display recurrent unexpected panic attacks followed by at least 1 month of persistent concern or worry about having another attack and its consequences or a significant change in their behavior related to the attacks in order to avoid having them. The DSM-5 diagnostic criteria for Panic Disorder are presented in Table 11.6.

A **panic attack** is a sudden and overwhelming period of intense fear or discomfort that is accompanied by four or more physical and cognitive symptoms characteristic of the fight/flight response (see Table 11.6). Usually, a panic attack is short, with symptoms reaching maximal intensity in 10 minutes or less and then diminishing slowly over the next 30 minutes or the next few hours. Panic attacks are accompanied by an overwhelming sense of imminent danger or impending doom, and

Chris Collins/Cusp/Corbis

Panic

TABLE 11.6 | Diagnostic Criteria for Panic Disorder

DSM-5

(A) Recurrent unexpected panic attacks. A panic attack is an abrupt surge of intense fear or intense discomfort that reaches a peak within minutes and during which time four (or more) of the following symptoms occur:

Note: The abrupt surge can occur from a calm state or an anxious state.

(1) Palpitations, pounding heart, or accelerated heart rate.

(2) Sweating.

(3) Trembling or shaking.

(4) Sensations or shortness of break or smothering.

(5) Feelings of choking.

(6) Chest pain or discomfort.

(7) Nausea or abdominal distress.

(8) Feeling dizzy, unsteady, light-headed, or faint.

(9) Chills or heat sensations.

(10) Paresthesias (numbness or tingling sensations).

(11) Derealization (feelings of unreality) or depersonalization (being detached from oneself).

(12) Fear of losing control or "going crazy."

(13) Fear of dying.

Note: Culture-specific symptoms (e.g., tinnitus, neck soreness, headache, uncontrollable screaming or crying) may be seen. Such symptoms should not count as one of the four required symptoms.

(B) At least one of the attacks has been followed by 1 month (or more) of one or both of the following:

(1) Persistent concern or worry about additional panic attacks or their consequences (e.g., losing control, having a heart attack, "going crazy")

(2) Significant maladaptive change in behavior related to the attacks (e.g., behaviors designed to avoid having panic attacks, such as avoidance of exercise or unfamiliar situations).

(C) The disturbance is not attributable to the physiological effects of a substance (e.g., a drug of abuse, a medication) or another medical condition (e.g., hyperthyroidism, cardiopulmonary disorders).

(D) The disturbance is not better accounted for by another mental disorder.

Source: Diagnostic and Statistical Manual of Mental Disorders, Fifth Edition, American Psychiatric Association.

by an urge to escape. Although they are brief, they can occur several times a week or month. It is important to remember that although the symptoms are dramatic, they are not physically harmful or dangerous.

Panic attacks are easily identified in adults, but some controversy exists over how often they occur in children and adolescents. Although panic attacks are extremely rare in young children, they are common in adolescents (Mattis & Ollendick, 2002). One explanation is that young children lack the cognitive ability to make the catastrophic misinterpretations (e.g., "my heart is beating rapidly and I'm sitting here watching TV like I always do—I must be going crazy") that usually accompany panic attacks (Nelles & Barlow, 1988). However, research suggests that young children may in fact be capable of such misinterpretations (Mattis & Ollendick, 1997).

If limited cognitive capacity is not the primary reason that panic attacks are so rare in young children, what is? In a revealing study, the relationship between the occurrence of panic attacks and pubertal stage was assessed in 754 girls in the sixth and seventh grades. Importantly, increasing rates of panic were related to pubertal development, not to increasing age (Hayward et al., 1992). The significance of pubertal development and anxiety disorders in females has received general support (Reardon, Leen-Feldner, & Hayward, 2009). For example, in one study, sixth- to eighth-grade females who developed internalizing symptoms were on average 5 months earlier in their pubertal development than females who did not develop symptoms (Hayward et al., 1997). Given that spontaneous panic attacks are rare before puberty and are related to pubertal stage, and that adolescence is the peak time for the onset of the disorder, the physical changes that take place around puberty seem critical to the occurrence of panic.

Why do the physical symptoms of the fight/flight response occur if an adolescent is not initially frightened? One possibility is that things other than fear can produce these symptoms. A youngster may be distressed for a particular reason and that stress may increase production of adrenaline and other chemicals that produce physical symptoms of panic. Increased adrenaline may be chemically maintained in the body even after the stress is no longer present. Another possibility is that the youngster may breathe a little too fast (subtle hyperventilation), which also can produce symptoms. Because the over-breathing is very slight, the child gets used to it and does not realize that he or she is hyperventilating. A third possibility is that some youngsters are experiencing normal bodily changes but, because they are constantly monitoring their bodies (as adolescents are prone to do), they notice these sensations far more readily (Barlow, 2002).

Adolescents with PD may avoid locations where they've had a previous panic attack or situations or activities in which they fear an attack might occur. An adolescent with PD might think: "It would be bad enough to have an attack at all, but it would be really dangerous if I had one while riding my bike to school. I'd be totally preoccupied with the attack and would have an accident. I'd probably destroy my bike and wind up seriously hurting myself or someone else in the process!" The youth's avoidance of riding a bike to school could be misinterpreted as a fear of bike riding, when it is actually a fear of having a panic attack while riding the bike.

If not recognized and treated, PD and its complications can seriously interfere with relationships at home and at school and with school performance. Some adolescents with PD may be reluctant to go to school or be separated from their parents. In severe cases, the tendency to avoid everyday life circumstances may increase and generalize, to the point at which the older adolescent with PD becomes terrified to leave the house at all.

Agoraphobia is characterized by marked fear or anxiety in certain places or situations (i.e., being in a crowd, being outside the home alone; see Table 11.7). The individual fears or avoids these situations because of thoughts that escape might be difficult, or help might not be available, if they were to experience panic-like or other incapacitating symptoms (e.g., fear of falling in an elderly person) (Craske et al., 2010; Wittchen et al., 2010). An older adolescent with agoraphobia who dares to venture into a feared situation does so only with great distress or when accompanied by a family member or a friend.

Agoraphobia is a distinct disorder that can be conceptualized independently from both panic attacks and panic disorder. Support for this comes from a 10-year longitudinal follow-up study of a normative sample of 3,000 individuals 14 to 24 years of age at the outset of the study (Wittchen et al., 2008). Sex and age differences in incidence and age at onset were observed between those with agoraphobia and those with panic attacks and panic disorder. The course and stability of agoraphobia also differed from that of panic disorder, and panic attacks did not reliably predict the onset of agoraphobia. Thus, rather than being an outcome of panic disorder, consistent with DSM-5, agoraphobia appears to be an anxiety disorder in its own right (Higa-McMillan et al., 2014).

Prevalence and Comorbidity

Panic attacks are common among nonreferred adolescents, affecting about 16% of teens (Mattis & Ollendick, 2002). PD and agoraphobia are much less common, with an estimated lifetime prevalence for both of about 2.5% for youths 13 to 17 years of age (Merikangas et al., 2010). Adolescent females are about twice as likely as adolescent males to experience panic attacks, and a fairly consistent association has been found between panic attacks and stressful life

TABLE 11.7 | Diagnostic Criteria for Agoraphobia

DSM-5

(A) Marked fear or anxiety about two (or more) of the following five situations:

   (1) Using public transportation (e.g., automobiles, buses, trains, ships, planes).

   (2) Being in open spaces (e.g., parking lots, marketplaces, bridges).

   (3) Being in enclosed spaces (e.g., shops, theatres, cinemas).

   (4) Standing in line or being in a crowd.

   (5) Being outside of the home alone.

(B) The individual fears or avoids these situations because of thoughts that escape might be difficult or help might not be available in the event of developing panic-like symptoms or other incapacitating or embarrassing symptoms (e.g., fear of falling in the elderly; fear of incontinence).

(C) The agoraphobic situations almost always provoke fear or anxiety.

(D) The agoraphobic situations are actively avoided, require the presence of a companion, or are endured with intense fear or anxiety.

(E) The fear or anxiety is out of proportion to the actual danger posed by the agoraphobic situations and to the sociocultural context.

(F) The fear, anxiety, or avoidance is persistent, typically lasting for 6 months or more.

(G) The fear, anxiety, or avoidance causes clinically significant distress or impairment in social, occupational, or other important areas of functioning.

(H) If another medical condition (e.g., inflammatory bowel disease, Parkinson's disease) is present, the fear, anxiety, or avoidance is clearly excessive.

(I) The fear, anxiety, or avoidance is not better explained by the symptoms of another mental disorder.

Note: Agoraphobia is diagnosed irrespective of the presence of panic disorder. If an individual's presentation meets criteria for panic disorder and agoraphobia, both diagnoses should be assigned.

Source: Diagnostic and Statistical Manual of Mental Disorders, Fifth Edition. American Psychiatric Association.

events (King, Ollendick, & Mattis, 1994). Most referred adolescents with PD have one or more other disorders, most commonly an additional anxiety disorder (particularly generalized anxiety disorder or SAD) and major depressive disorder. Other comorbid conditions include mania and hypomania, attention-deficit/hyperactivity disorder (ADHD), and oppositional defiant disorder (ODD) (Doerfler et al., 2007). The most common comorbidities for agoraphobia are other anxiety disorders (e.g., PD, specific phobias, and SOC), major depressive disorder, post-traumatic stress disorder, and alcohol-use disorder (APA, 2013).

Did Darwin Have a Panic Disorder?

Charles Darwin (1809–1882) was a gregarious and daring traveler and outdoorsman in his college days. However, in his late 20s—just a year after returning to England after a 5-year voyage to South America and the Pacific aboard the HMS *Beagle*—he started to have an "uncomfortable palpitation of the heart." The symptoms arose shortly after he began keeping a secret notebook that, 22 years later, would become his book-length elaboration of the theory of evolution, *On the Origin of Species*. Over the years, his affliction was described as a case of bad nerves, a tropical disease, intellectual exhaustion, arsenic poisoning, suppressed gout, and a host of other symptoms. However, in his journal Darwin described his malady as a "sensation of fear ... accompanied by troubled beating of the heart, sweat, trembling of muscles."

From Desmond & Moore, 1991.

Bettmann/Corbis

The relation between SAD and PD has received considerable attention, to see whether separation experiences during childhood contribute to the development of later PD or whether SAD is a childhood form of adult panic disorder (Craske et al., 2010). Findings generally support SAD as a strong predictor of PD. However, since SAD also predicts other anxiety disorders (but not depressive or substance-use disorders), it may be an early marker for anxiety disorders in general, rather than a specific risk factor for PD (Kossowsky et al., 2013).

After months or years of unrelenting panic attacks and the restricted lifestyle that results from avoidance behavior, adolescents and young adults with PD and agoraphobia may develop severe depression and may be at risk for suicidal behavior. Others may begin to use alcohol or drugs as a way of alleviating their anxiety (Higa-McMillan et al., 2014).

Onset, Course, and Outcome

Although PD has been found to occur in young children, few cases have been reported (Higa-McMillan et al., 2014). The average age at onset for a first panic attack in adolescents with PD is 15 to 19 years, and 95% of adolescents with the disorder are postpubertal (Bernstein, Borchardt, & Perwien, 1996). PD occurs in otherwise emotionally healthy youngsters about half the time. The most frequent prior disturbance, if one exists, is a depressive disorder (Last & Strauss, 1989). Unfortunately, PD and agoraphobia are stable over time and have one of the lowest complete remission rates for any of the anxiety disorders (Wittchen et al., 2000). Individuals with PD and those with PD and agoraphobia with an

early onset are more likely to experience comorbid disorders and a recurrence of symptoms following a period of remission than those with a later onset, indicating that early onset PD and agoraphobia are particularly serious disorders (Ramsawh et al., 2011). In the absence of treatment, these disorders are likely to have a persistent and chronic course.

Section Summary

Panic Disorder and Agoraphobia

- A panic attack is a sudden and overwhelming period of intense fear or discomfort accompanied by physical and cognitive symptoms.

- Adolescents with PD display recurrent unexpected panic attacks followed by persistent concern about having another attack, constant worry about the consequences, or a significant maladaptive change in their behavior related to the attacks, designed to avoid having additional attacks.

- Agoraphobia is characterized by marked fear or anxiety in certain situations. The individual fears or avoids these situations because of thoughts that escape might be difficult or help might not be available if they were to experience panic-like or other incapacitating symptoms.

- Many postpubertal adolescents experience panic attacks, but PD and agoraphobia are much less common, affecting about 2.5% of teens, and females about twice as often as males. Average age at onset for a first panic attack in adolescents with PD is 15 to 19 years.

- PD and agoraphobia are associated with many other disorders, most commonly other anxiety disorders.

- PD and agoraphobia are stable and over time and have one of the lowest rates of complete remission for any of the anxiety disorders.

GENERALIZED ANXIETY DISORDER

JARED

Perpetual Worrywart

Jared, age 13, was referred because of his excessive anxiety, worry, and somatic symptoms—his mother describes him as overly concerned about everything. Jared says he worries about most things, but especially about not being good enough for his parents, being teased by other kids, not doing well at school, making mistakes, and being in an accident in which he or his parents are injured. Jared ruminates for days about things that have already occurred, such as what he said in class the previous day or how he did on last week's test. Once he begins to worry, he says, "I just can't stop, no matter how hard I try." Jared reports that when he is worrying about the past or anticipating an upcoming event he has headaches, stomachaches, and a rapid heartbeat. His mother (who also worries a lot, but not nearly as much as Jared) says that Jared is extremely self-critical and needs constant reassurance. (Based on authors' case material.)

Some worrying is a part of normal development. However, children like Jared with a **generalized anxiety disorder (GAD)** experience excessive and uncontrollable anxiety and worry about many events or activities on most days. They worry when there is nothing obvious to provoke the worry. For children with GAD, worrying can be episodic or almost continuous. The worrier is unable to relax and may experience physical symptoms such as muscle tension, headaches, or nausea. Common symptoms of GAD include irritability, difficulty concentrating, and a lack of energy, difficulty falling asleep, and restless sleep (Comer et al., 2012; Layne et al., 2009). The DSM-5 criteria for GAD are presented in Table 11.8.

In other anxiety disorders, anxiety converges on specific situations or objects, such as separation, social performance, animals or insects, or bodily sensations. In contrast, the anxiety experienced by individuals with GAD is widespread and focuses on a variety of everyday life events (Andrews et al., 2010). It was once thought that children who were generally anxious did not focus their anxiety on one specific thing, which is referred to as "free-floating anxiety." However, these youngsters do, in fact, focus their anxiety, but they focus it on many different things. Hence, the term *generalized anxiety* is more accurate.

TABLE 11.8 | Diagnostic Criteria for Generalized Anxiety Disorder (GAD)

DSM-5

(A) Excessive anxiety and worry (apprehensive expectation) occurring more days than not for at least 6 months, about a number of events or activities (such as work or school performance).

(B) The individual finds it difficult to control the worry.

(C) The anxiety and worry are associated with three (or more) of the following six symptoms (with at least some symptoms present for more days than not for the past 6 months).

Note: Only one item is required for children.

(1) Restlessness or feeling keyed up or on edge.

(2) Being easily fatigued.

(3) Difficulty concentrating or mind going blank.

(4) Irritability.

(5) Muscle tension.

(6) Sleep disturbance (difficulty falling or staying asleep, or restless unsatisfying sleep).

(D) The anxiety, worry, or physical symptoms cause clinically significant distress or impairment in social, occupational, or other important areas of functioning.

(E) The disturbance is not due to the general physiological effects of a substance (e.g., a drug of abuse, a medication) or a another medical condition (e.g., hyperthyroidism).

(F) The disturbance is not better explained by another mental disorder.

Source: Diagnostic and Statistical Manual of Mental Disorders, Fifth Edition, American Psychiatric Association.

Children with GAD are likely to pick up on every frightening event in a movie, on the Internet, or on TV and relate it to themselves. If they see a news report on TV about a car accident, they may begin to worry about being in a car accident themselves. They always expect the worst possible outcome and underestimate their ability to cope with situations or events that are less than ideal. They do not seem to realize that the events they worry about have an extremely low likelihood of actually happening. Thus, their thinking often consists of what-if statements: "What if the school bus breaks down?" "What if I get hit by lightning?" Children with GAD do not restrict their worries to frightening or catastrophic events; they also worry excessively about minor everyday occurrences, such as what to wear or what to watch on TV. This generalized worry about minor events distinguishes children with GAD from those with other anxiety disorders (Albano et al., 2003).

Like Jared, children with GAD are often self-conscious, self-doubting, and worried about meeting others' expectations. Their worry may lead to significant interpersonal problems, especially those involving a tendency to be overly nurturing to others. Children with GAD seek constant approval and reassurance from adults and fear people whom they perceive as unpleasant, critical, or unfair. They tend to set extremely high standards for their own performance and are highly self-critical when they fall short. Moreover, they continue to worry even when evidence contradicts their concern. For example, a child with GAD who received a grade of A on every previous class assignment may worry about failing on the next assignment (Silverman & Ginsburg, 1995). Children with GAD also show an intolerance of uncertainty, which may be a cognitive disposition for GAD that may result in impaired decision making under conditions of uncertainty, as well as other cognitive processes that serve to maintain worry (Fialko, Bolton, & Perrin, 2012; Krain et al., 2006).

Children with GAD cannot seem to stop worrying even when they recognize how unhappy they are making themselves and others. This characteristic is what makes their anxiety abnormal. A normal child who is worried about an upcoming sports competition can still concentrate on other tasks and will stop worrying once the competition is over. However, for children with GAD one "crisis" is followed by another in a never-ending cycle. The intensity of the child's worries is one of the best predictors of impairment in children with GAD (Layne et al., 2009). It may also lead to a sense that the worry is uncontrollable, which is an important clinical feature of GAD (Kertz & Woodruff-Borden, 2011). The cognitive beliefs that children with GAD hold about worry may also play a role. *Meta-worry*, or worrying about worry, involves the development of beliefs such as worrying is uncontrollable or that it can lead to negative consequences for the worrier. For children with GAD, these negative beliefs about worry may lead to even higher levels of anxiety and more widespread anxiety (Ellis & Hudson, 2010; Esbjørn et al., 2014).

Prevalence and Comorbidity

GAD was the least common anxiety disorder reported in a large national survey of more than 10,000 teens (13 to 18 years of age) in the United States, with a lifetime prevalence rate of 2.2% (Merikangas et al., 2010). In contrast, a more recent study found that it was the most common anxiety disorder diagnosis (37%) among children referred to an anxiety specialty clinic (Leyfer et al., 2013). In general, the disorder is equally common in boys and girls, with a slightly higher prevalence in older adolescent females. Children with GAD have a high rate of other anxiety disorders. For younger children, co-occurring SAD and conduct problems are most common; older children with GAD tend to have specific phobias, SOC, panic disorder, and MDD, as well as impaired social adjustment, low self-esteem, and an increased risk for suicide (Keller et al., 1992; Leyfer et al., 2013; Masi et al., 2004). Rates of co-occurring MDD for GAD are especially high, in some cases, even higher than for other anxiety disorders (Higa-McMillan et al., 2014).

Onset, Course, and Outcome

The average age at onset for GAD is in early adolescence (Beesdo et al., 2010). Older children present with a higher total number of symptoms and report higher levels of anxiety and depression than younger children, but these symptoms may diminish with age (Strauss et al., 1988). In a community sample of adolescents with GAD, the likelihood of their having GAD at follow-up was higher if symptoms at the time of initial assessment were severe (Cohen, Cohen, & Brook, 1993). Nearly half of severe cases were rediagnosed after 2 years, suggesting that severe GAD symptoms persist over time, even in youngsters who have not been referred for treatment.

Youngsters with a generalized anxiety disorder worry about almost everything.

Generalized Anxiety Disorder

- Youngsters with a GAD experience chronic or exaggerated worry and tension, often accompanied by physical symptoms.
- GAD occurs in about 2% of children in community samples, but it is one of the most common anxiety disorders in children who are referred to specialty clinics for treatment of anxiety.

OBSESSIVE—COMPULSIVE AND RELATED DISORDERS

Insanity: doing the same thing over and over again and expecting different results.

—Attributed to Albert Einstein

OCD was previously included as an anxiety disorder in the DSM. While recognizing its close relationship with the anxiety disorders, the DSM-5 includes OCD in a separate chapter with a number of related disorders that are distinct from OCD but contain overlapping diagnostic features such as preoccupations and repetitive behaviors or mental acts in response to the preoccupations (Piacentini, Chang, et al., 2014). This grouping was based on similarities that have been found between OCD and these related conditions in terms of their features, comorbidity, familial and genetic factors, brain circuitry, and response to treatment (Bienvenu et al., 2012). To give you a brief overview of the OCD-related disorders, the main features of each are described in A Closer Look 11.3. We will focus our discussion on OCD since it is the disorder that is most closely connected to the anxiety disorders and the one we know the most about.

Obsessive–Compulsive Disorder

ETHAN

Counting and Cleaning

Ethan, age 15, is continually distracted by powerful and peculiar thoughts, such as counting how many times he blinks and how many steps it takes to get to the kitchen. He avoids stepping on any floor tiles with dirt on them because he doesn't want to get germs on his feet. He is obsessed with germs on door handles and feels compelled to avoid touching them unless he first uses a cloth (which he always has with him) to clean the handle off. On those rare occasions that he misplaces or forgets to bring a clean cloth with him, he gets extremely anxious, freezes, and feels sick to his stomach. (Based on authors' case material.)

A CLOSER **LOOK** 11.3

Main Features of DSM-5 OCD-Related Disorders

Body Dysmorphic Disorder
Body dysmorphic disorder is characterized by a preoccupation with defects or flaws in physical appearance that are not observable or appear slight to others. During the course of the disorder, the individual engages in repetitive behaviors (e.g., mirror checking, excessive grooming, seeking reassurance) or mental acts (comparing her or his appearance to others) in response to appearance concerns. This preoccupation causes significant distress or impairment in important areas of life functioning (e.g., social, occupational).

Hoarding Disorder
Hoarding disorder is characterized by persistent difficulty discarding or parting with possessions, regardless of their actual value. This difficulty is due to a perceived need to save the items and to distress associated with discarding them. The difficulty discarding possessions results in an accumulation of possessions that congest and clutter active living areas and substantially compromises their intended use. The hoarding causes significant distress or impairment in important areas of life functioning (e.g., social, occupational, maintaining a safe environment).

Trichotillomania (Hair-Pulling Disorder)
Trichotillomania is characterized by recurrent pulling out of one's hair, resulting in hair loss (not attributable to another medical condition), repeated attempts to decrease or stop hair pulling, and significant distress or impairment in important areas of life functioning.

Excoriation Disorder (Skin-Picking Disorder)
Excoriation disorder (skin-picking disorder) is characterized by recurrent skin picking resulting in skin lesions, repeated attempts to stop skin picking, and significant distress or impairment in important areas of life functioning.

Source: Diagnostic and Statistical Manual of Mental Disorders, Fifth Edition, American Psychiatric Association.

that female vulnerability to anxiety may also be related to genetic influences and related neurobiological differences, as well as to varying social roles and experiences (Lewinsohn et al., 1998).

One study of gender-role orientation in boys and girls with anxiety disorders found that self-reported masculinity was related to lower overall levels of fearfulness and fewer specific fears of failure and criticism, medical fears, and fears of the unknown (Ginsburg & Silverman, 2000). In contrast, no relation was found between self-reported femininity and fearfulness. This suggests that gender-role orientation, especially masculinity, may play a role in the development and persistence of fearfulness in children.

There is general support for a higher prevalence of anxiety in ethnic minority groups in the United States. However, symptom expression, biological factors, and family processes may differ somewhat by ethnic group (Anderson & Mayes, 2010). Studies comparing the number and nature of fears in African American and white youngsters have found the two groups to be quite similar (Ginsburg & Silverman, 1996). However, African American children generally report more symptoms of anxiety than do white children (Cole et al., 1998), although white children report more symptoms of SOC and fewer symptoms of SAD than do African American children (Compton, Nelson, & March, 2000). Among children who are referred for anxiety or related disorders, whites are more likely to present with school refusal and with higher severity ratings than African Americans. It has been found that symptoms of anxiety are higher in children of parents with fewer years of formal education, suggesting that variations in child anxiety across racial/ethnic groups may also be accounted for by group differences in parental education (Wren et al., 2007).

Patterns of referral, help-seeking behaviors, diagnoses, and treatment processes are also likely to differ across racial/ethnic groups. For example, African American parents who need help with their child's OCD symptoms may be more likely to turn to members of their informal social network, such as clergy or medical personnel, than to mental health professionals (Hatch, Friedman, & Paradis, 1996). Their family members are also less likely to be drawn into the child's OCD symptoms. Although ethnicity is not related to outcomes in the treatment of anxiety disorders, it may be related to premature termination of treatment (Kendall & Flannery-Schroeder, 1998).

Research comparing anxiety disorders in Hispanic and white children has found marked similarities in age at presentation, gender, primary diagnosis, proportion with school refusal, and proportion with more than one diagnosis. Hispanic children are more likely to have a primary diagnosis of SAD. Hispanic parents also rate their children as more fearful than do white parents (Ginsburg & Silverman, 1996). Few studies have examined anxiety disorders in Native American children. Prevalence estimates from one study of Native American youths in Appalachia (mostly Cherokee) indicate rates of anxiety disorders similar to those for white youths, with the most common disorder for both groups being SAD. Rates of SAD were slightly higher for Native American youths, especially girls (Costello et al., 1997). Native Hawaiian adolescents display rates of OCD that are twice as high as those of other ethnic groups (Guerrero et al., 2003). When attempting to explain such differences, it is important to keep in mind that genetic and/or environmental risk factors may play a role.

The experience of anxiety is pervasive across cultures. Although cross-cultural research into anxiety disorders in children is limited (Lewis-Fernández et al., 2010), specific fears in children have been studied and documented in virtually every culture. Developmental fears (e.g., a fear of loud noises or of separation from the primary caregiver) occur in children of all cultures at about the same age. The details may vary from culture to culture, but the number of fears in children tends to be highly similar across cultures, as does the presence of gender differences in pattern and content.

Nevertheless, the expression, developmental course, and interpretation of symptoms of anxiety are affected by culture (Higa-McMillan et al., 2014; Ingman, Ollendick, & Akande, 1999). For example, in relation to panic-like symptoms, higher rates are found for paresthesias (feelings of tingling or numbing of the skin) among African Americans, trembling among Caribbean Latinos, dizziness among several East Asian Groups, and fear of dying among Arabs and African Americans (Craske et al., 2010).

Cultural differences in traditions, beliefs, and practices about children can affect the occurrence of anxiety and related symptoms and how they are perceived by others and experienced by the child (Wang & Ollendick, 2001). For example, James, a 16-year-old Chinese American boy, had been to multiple doctors throughout his life for treatment for stomach cramps, nausea, and hot flushes in the morning before going to school and also in anticipation of social interactions. James had a social anxiety disorder but both he and his family felt his problem was physical and wanted to focus only on his physical symptoms in therapy and not his subjective feelings of anxiety.

Increased levels of fear in children are found in cultures that favor inhibition, compliance, and obedience (Ollendick et al., 1996). Chinese cultural values such as human malleability and self-cultivation may heighten levels of general distress and specific fears (e.g., social evaluative) (Dong, Yang, & Ollendick, 1994). In addition, Chinese adolescents report higher levels of social anxiety than do American youths, including anxiety about humiliation and rejection and public performance fears (Yao et al., 2007). This is likely related to their collectivistic versus individualistic value orientation. Children in Thailand display more symptoms of anxiety, such as shyness and somatic symptoms, than children in the United States (Weisz et al., 2003). Perhaps the most accurate way to analyze cultural differences in anxiety is using Weisz and colleagues' (2003, p. 384) **behavior lens principle**, which states that child psychopathology reflects a mix of actual child behavior and the lens through which it is viewed by others in a child's culture.

Section Summary

Gender, Ethnicity, and Culture

- About twice as many girls as boys experience symptoms of anxiety, and this difference is present in children as young as 6 years of age.
- Children's ethnicity and culture may affect the expression and developmental course of fear and anxiety, how anxiety is perceived by others, and expectations for treatment.

THEORIES AND CAUSES

Over the years, numerous theories and causes have been proposed to explain the origins of fear and anxiety in children, including brain disease, mental strain, parenting practices, conditioning, and instinct (Treffers & Silverman, 2011). The study of fear and anxiety in children dates back to Freud's (1909/1953) classic account of the case of Little Hans; Watson and Rayner's (1920) conditioning of a fear in Little Albert; and Bowlby's (1973) monumental works on early attachment and loss. Although each early theory has been debated since it was introduced, all have had a lasting impact on how we think about anxiety in children.

Early Theories

Classical psychoanalytic theory views anxieties and phobias as defenses against unconscious conflicts rooted in the child's early upbringing. Certain drives, memories, and feelings are so painful that they must be repressed and displaced onto an external object or symbolically associated with the real source of anxiety. Thus, anxiety and phobias will protect the child against unconscious wishes and drives. Freud's most famous case of a phobia was Little Hans, a 5-year-old who feared horses. According to Freud, Little Hans unconsciously felt that he was in competition with his father for his mother's love and feared his father's revenge (the Oedipus complex). Hans's fear was repressed and displaced onto horses, a symbol of his castrating father. Having something specific to fear was less stressful for Hans than suffering from anxiety without apparent cause.

Behavioral and learning theories held that fears and anxieties were learned through classical conditioning. In the case of Little Albert, Watson and Rayner (1920) created what looked very much like a rat phobia (see A Closer Look 1.3), and claimed that fears were learned by association. Operant conditioning has been cited in explaining why fears persist once they are established. The principle is that behavior will continue if it is reinforced or rewarded. Once something has become frightening, there is the automatic reward of instant relief whenever the child avoids the feared object or situation. Thus, through negative reinforcement, avoidance of a feared stimulus becomes a learned response, which serves to maintain the child's fear even when not exposed to it. The combination of classical and operant conditioning in the learning and maintenance of fears is called the **two-factor theory** (Mowrer, 1947). Social learning theories also showed that children could learn fears through observation of others, without experiencing the feared stimulus directly (Bandura & Walters, 1963).

Bowlby's *theory of attachment* (1973) presents a very different explanation for children's fears. According to attachment theory, fearfulness in children is biologically rooted in the emotional attachment needed for survival. Infants must be close to their caregivers if their physical and emotional needs are to be met. Attachment behaviors, such as crying, fear of strangers, and distress, represent active efforts by the infant to maintain or restore proximity to the caregiver. Separation gradually becomes more tolerable as the child gets older. However, children who are separated from their mothers too early, who are treated harshly, or who fail to have their needs met consistently show atypical reactions to separation and reunion. Early insecure attachments become internalized and determine how children see the world and other people. Children who view the environment as undependable, unavailable, hostile, or threatening may later develop anxiety and avoidance behavior.

No single theory is sufficient to explain the various anxiety disorders in children, the differences among children in the expression of these disorders, or the variations in outcomes over time. It is important to for anxiety are needed (Gregory & Eley, 2007). For example, one study found a significant G×E interaction in which stressful life events presented a greater risk for anxiety/depressive symptoms when a specific serotonin-related genotype was present (Petersen et al., 2012). Future research examining the ways in which multiple genetic factors interact with multiple sources of environmental adversity, may help to overcome the unreliability of findings in studies that attempt to identify interactions between a single gene and a single measure of environmental adversity (Fergusson et al., 2011).

Neurobiological Factors

No single structure or neurotransmitter controls the entire anxiety response system. Rather, several interrelated systems operate together in complex ways to produce anxiety. The parts of the brain most often connected with anxiety involve neural circuits related to potential threat and fear conditioning—the hypothalamic–pituitary–adrenal (HPA) axis; the limbic system (amygdala, hippocampus), which acts as a mediator between the brain stem and the cortex; the ventrolateral and dorsolateral prefrontal cortex; and other cortical and subcortical structures (Fitzgerald et al., 2013; Monk, 2008; Pine, 2011). Potential danger signals are monitored and sensed by the more primitive brain stem, which then relays the signals to the higher cortical centers through the limbic system. As noted in Chapter 9, this brain system is referred to as the *behavioral inhibition system*, and it is believed to be overactive in children with anxiety disorders. As we have discussed, anxious individuals display threat biases at multiple levels of information processing (e.g., attention to threat, fear learning). It has been proposed that abnormalities in learning safety cues in childhood may establish threat-related appraisal biases early in development, which may then lead to chronic anxiety disorders in adulthood (Britton et al., 2011). Consistent with this, healthy teens have greater difficulty distinguishing between threat and safety cues than adults, relying more on areas of the brain involved in basic fear responses (hippocampus, right amygdala) than on areas involved in more reasoned judgment about what is safe or not (prefrontal cortex) (Lau et al., 2011). This may be one reason why teens (and youths with anxiety disorders) generally report more pervasive worries and are more vulnerable to stress-related problems.

Particularly noteworthy are findings that the regulation of the brain circuits underlying threat and fear conditioning can be shaped by early life stress, thus providing a possible biological basis for an increased vulnerability to later stress and the development of fearfulness and anxiety disorders (Heim et al., 2010).

As we discussed in A Closer Look 2.2, activation of the HPA axis is closely related to the regulation of stress and fear and involves the release of cortisol needed to meet a challenging situation. Pathological anxiety has been related to elevations of cortisol secretion, reflected in an exaggeration of normal HPA reactions or a failure of the HPA axis response to habituate to repeated exposure to the same stressor (van der Vegt et al., 2010). Prolonged exposure to elevated levels of cortisol as a result of early stress or trauma may have neurotoxic effects on the developing brain—for example, reduced cerebral volume or changes in the volume of the hippocampus (Weems & Silverman, 2013). Early life stress may also produce lasting hyperreactivity of corticotropin-releasing factor (CRF) systems, which are closely related to the HPA axis, as well as alterations in other neurotransmitter systems that create a heightened response to stress (Pine, 2003).

Brain scans of children with GAD suggest abnormalities (larger volume) in brain regions and circuits associated with social–emotional information processing and fear conditioning (amygdala and superior temporal gyrus) (De Bellis, Keshavan, Frustaci, et al., 2002; De Bellis, Keshavan, Shifflett et al., 2002; Roy et al., 2013). These studies also report more pronounced right–left hemisphere brain asymmetries in children with GAD, which have also been reported in children who are behaviorally inhibited or anxious/depressed (Kagan & Snidman, 1999). As we have discussed, an overexcitable amygdala has been strongly implicated in children who are behaviorally inhibited and in youngsters with anxiety disorders (McClure et al., 2007b; Schwartz et al., 2003). The amygdala detects and organizes reactions to natural dangers by quickly scanning incoming stimuli that are novel and/or potentially threatening. Interestingly, children with anxiety disorders who have higher levels of pretreatment amygdala activation in response to emotional information show a better response to both cognitive–behavioral therapy and drug treatment (McClure et al., 2007a). In addition to the brain regions we have discussed, neuroimaging studies have also suggested the importance of other brain regions for specific anxiety-related disorders such as OCD (Friedlander & Desrocher, 2006; Hajcak et al., 2008).

The neurotransmitter system that has been implicated most often in anxiety disorders is the γ-aminobutyric acid–ergic (GABA-ergic) system. Neuropeptides are generally viewed as anticipatory stress modulators whose abnormal regulation may play a role in anxiety disorders (Sallee & Greenawald, 1995). A group of neurons known as the locus ceruleus ("deep blue place") is a major brain source for norepinephrine, an inhibitory neurotransmitter. Overactivation of this region is presumed to lead to a fear response, and underactivity to inattention, impulsivity, and risk-taking. Abnormalities of these systems may be related to anxiety states in children (Sallee & Greenawald, 1995).

New findings using brain scans have increased our understanding of the neurobiological mechanisms in anxiety disorders. The brain regions we have described have been consistently implicated in fear and anxiety. While acknowledging that pathways are likely to be complex, the plasticity of these neural systems during early development makes research into possible mechanisms a priority for both understanding and preventing future anxiety disorders in children.

Family Factors

As we have discussed, anxiety runs in families, and the relationship between family factors and childhood anxiety disorders has generated considerable attention (Knappe et al., 2010). Among the many family factors of interest are specific parenting practices, including the parent's use of discipline and modeling of anxious behaviors; broader family dimensions such as family functioning as a whole, parenting stress, and the marital relationship; the parent–child attachment relationship; and the beliefs that parents hold about their child's anxious behavior (Bögels & Brechman-Toussaint, 2006; Creswell et al., 2011; Manassis, 2011).

Parenting practices such as rejection, overcontrol, overprotection, and modeling of anxious behaviors have all been identified as contributors to childhood anxiety symptoms and disorders (Edwards, Rapee, & Kennedy, 2010; McLeod, Wood, & Weisz, 2007). Although most research has focused on mothers, fathers also play a role, and both parents may contribute to their child's anxiety in ways that are specific to their different parenting roles (Bögels & Phares, 2008). Parents of anxious children are often described as overinvolved, intrusive, or limiting of their child's independence.

Observations of interactions between 9- to 12-year-old children with anxiety disorders and their parents found that parents of children with anxiety disorders were found to grant less autonomy to their children than other parents; the children found their mothers and fathers to be less accepting than other parents (Siqueland, Kendall, & Steinberg, 1996). Other studies have found that mothers of children previously identified as behaviorally inhibited or anxious are more likely to be critical and to be less positive when interacting with their children (Whaley, Pinto, & Sigman, 1999). Emotional overinvolvement by parents is also associated with an increased occurrence of SAD in their children (Hirshfeld, Biederman, & Rosenbaum, 1997). These findings generally support the association between excessive parental control and anxiety disorders in children, although the

strength of this association appears to be small and the causal mechanisms and directionality of effect are not yet known (McLeod et al., 2007). One study found a relationship between mothers' use of extreme control and higher levels of child anxiety. However, the overlap between high child anxiety and maternal control was mainly due to shared genetic factors. This suggests that mothers not only influence their children's anxiety, but also that children with high levels of anxiety may elicit extreme maternal control (Eley et al., 2010).

Another study looked at the broader relationship between family functioning and child anxiety (Pagani et al., 2008). The dimensions of family functioning that were of interest included problem solving, communication, family roles, affective involvement, and emotional responsiveness. It was found that prolonged exposure to high levels of family dysfunction was associated with the most extreme trajectories of anxious behavior during middle childhood. This association was found to exist over and above the influence of other aspects of family dysfunction, such as marital transitions, socioeconomic status (SES), family size, and a parent's depressive symptoms. In general, findings in support of an association between family functioning and anxiety disorders are suggestive, but it is unclear whether family dysfunction relates specifically to anxiety disorders (Bögels & Brechman-Toussaint, 2006).

Not only are parents of children with anxiety disorders more controlling than other parents, they also have different expectations. For example, when they thought the child was being asked to give a videotaped speech, mothers of children with anxiety disorders expected their children to become upset and had low expectations for their children's coping (Kortlander, Kendall, & Panichelli-Mindel, 1997). It is likely that parental attitudes shape—and are shaped by—interactions with the child, during which parent and child revise their expectations and behavior as a result of feedback from each other (Barrett, Rapee, et al., 1996). This process may not only impact on the child's behavior, but may also play a role in the development of information-processing biases in the child (Hadwin, Garner, & Perez-Olivas, 2006).

Parental anxiety disorder alone may not lead to an elevated risk of anxiety disorders in children of high- or middle-SES parents, but it may increase risk in children of low-SES parents (Beidel & Turner, 1997). These findings are consistent with the idea that some children have a genetic vulnerability to anxiety, which may be actualized in the context of specific life circumstances, such as the stressful conditions that are often present in low-SES families. Children with an initial disposition to develop high levels of fear may be especially vulnerable to the type of power-assertive parenting often used by low-SES parents. These children may be particularly sensitive to punishment and, when exposed to physical discipline, may become hypervigilant to hostile cues and develop a tendency to react defensively or aggressively (Colder, Lochman, & Wells, 1997).

Insecure attachments may be a risk factor for the development of later anxiety disorders (Brumariu & Kerns, 2010; Kerns & Brumariu, 2014) and are associated with anxiety disorder symptoms in early adolescence (Muris & Meesters, 2002). Mothers with anxiety disorders have been found to have insecure attachments, and 80% of their children are also insecurely attached (Manassis et al., 1994). This relationship may be mediated by the impact of the mother's anxiety on her sensitivity to her child (Stevenson-Hinde et al., 2014).

Infants who are ambivalently attached have more anxiety diagnoses during childhood and adolescence than infants who are securely attached (Bernstein et al., 1996), although a clear link between specific types of insecure attachments and specific anxiety disorders has not been established. It may be a risk factor, but insecure attachment may be a nonspecific factor because many infants with insecure attachments develop disorders other than anxiety (e.g., depression, disruptive behavior disorder), and many do not develop disorders.

Clearly articulated causal models for anxiety disorders in children are just beginning to emerge (Muris, 2007). In the absence of an integrative model, we present the possible developmental pathway shown in ● Figure 11.3. Children with an inborn predisposition

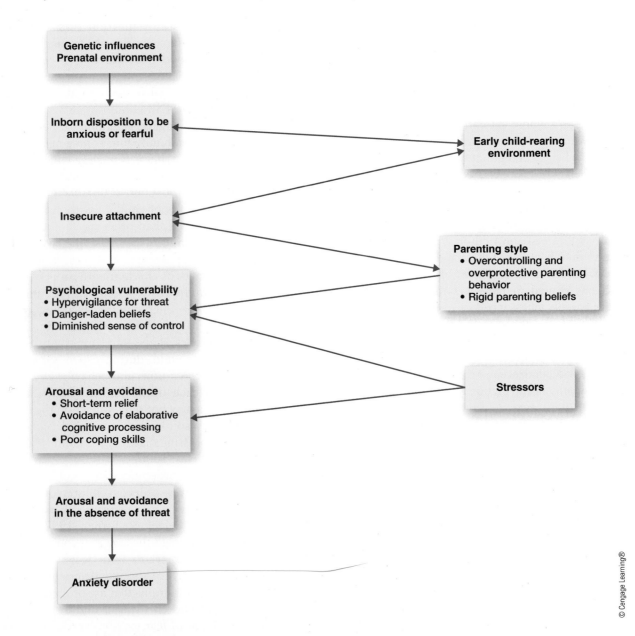

● **FIGURE 11.3** | A possible developmental pathway for anxiety disorders.

to be anxious or fearful who sense that the world is not a safe place may develop a psychological vulnerability to anxiety. Once anxiety occurs, it feeds on itself. The anxiety and avoidance continue long after the stressors that provoked them are gone. Keep in mind that many children with anxiety disorders do not continue to experience problems as adults. Therefore, it will be important to identify risk and protective factors that would explain these differences in outcomes (Pine & Grun, 1999). In addition, it is also important to keep in mind that different developmental pathways may occur for children with different anxiety disorders, or even for those with the same disorder.

Section Summary

Theories and Causes

- No single theory can explain the many different forms of anxiety disorder in children.
- Early theories viewed anxiety as a defense against unconscious conflicts, a learned response, or an adaptive mechanism needed for survival.
- Some children are born with a tendency to become overexcited and to withdraw in response to novel stimulation (behavioral inhibition)—an enduring trait for some, and a possible risk factor for later anxiety disorders.
- Family and twin studies suggest a moderate biological vulnerability to anxiety disorders.
- Anxiety is associated with specific neurobiological processes. The potential underlying vulnerability of children at risk for anxiety is most likely localized to brain circuits involving the brain stem, the limbic system, the HPA axis, and the frontal cortex.
- Anxiety is associated with a number of family factors, including specific parenting practices, family functioning, the parent–child attachment, and parents' beliefs about their children's anxious behavior.
- Children with anxiety disorders will likely display features that are shared across the various disorders, as well as other features that are unique to their particular disorder.

TREATMENT AND PREVENTION

CANDY

Afraid to Swallow

Candy, age 11, was hospitalized for dehydration. Her voice trembled and her eyes widened with fear as she described being rushed to the emergency room in an ambulance after she fainted. She was embarrassed that something as simple as eating was so hard for her, but it terrified her to even think about trying. Candy detested being thin, and desperately wanted to be "just like other kids." After talking with Candy, it was clear that she dreaded eating because she was afraid of vomiting in public. Her fear began when she couldn't eat in front of other kids in the school cafeteria, but advanced quickly to her not being able to eat at all. Candy doesn't have an eating disorder—she has a severe social anxiety disorder. (Based on authors' case material.)

Since many fears and anxieties are not associated with serious disturbances, deciding whether a child's anxiety is serious enough to warrant treatment is seldom easy. Although anxiety disorders are extremely disabling for the child and family, they are rarely life threatening. Children with anxiety disorders can be exceedingly quiet, shy, compliant, eager to please, or secretive, and their distress may go unnoticed. Sometimes a severe disruption to a normal routine may be needed before a parent seeks help. If a child is so afraid of spiders or dogs that she is terror-stricken when going outside regardless of whether a spider or dog is nearby, then treatment may be needed. Treatment may also be required when parents repeatedly make important decisions that interfere with family life to accommodate a child's fears, such as not going camping or not driving on holidays. Unlike children who provoke or offend others, children with anxiety disorders typically do not cause trouble, and as a result they receive far less professional attention than children with conduct problems. This situation is unfortunate, because many of these children can be helped with treatment (AACAP, 2007b; Shin-ichi et al., 2007).

In 1924, Mary Cover Jones worked with 3-year-old Peter, who was afraid of a rabbit. She eliminated Peter's fear by gradually exposing him to the rabbit when he was relaxed, by having him watch other children play with a rabbit, and by rewarding him for approaching the rabbit. These treatment techniques are still used today. Teaching children to use behavioral and cognitive coping skills to reduce anxious avoidance also increases the child's options and opportunities. In this regard, in addition to reducing or preventing symptoms of anxiety, early intervention may prevent future problems, such as loss of friends, failure to reach social and academic potential, low self-esteem, and depression (Rapee, 2002).

Overview

Timidity will always diminish if the occasions that produce it be skillfully repeated, until they cease to cause surprize, for the timid apprehend the unexpected.

—Yoritomo-Tashi (1916)

Decades of research from almost every perspective imaginable corroborate the popular adage that the best way to defeat your fears is to face them. Although specific procedures may vary, exposing children and adolescents to the situations, objects, and occasions that produce anxiety is the main line of attack in any treatment for anxiety disorders (Chorpita & Southam-Gerow, 2006). As described in A Closer Look 11.4, when former three-time world heavyweight boxing champion Evander Holyfield was only 17 years old, he faced his fears—and was never afraid again.

Treatments for anxiety are directed at modifying four primary problems (Barlow, 2002):

▸ Distorted information processing
▸ Physiological reactions to perceived threat
▸ Sense of a lack of control
▸ Excessive escape and avoidance behaviors

These central problems are addressed using a variety of treatment strategies that are matched to the types of anxiety symptoms the child is experiencing (Muris, 2007). In the following sections, we describe the most commonly used treatments for anxiety disorders, including behavior therapy, cognitive–behavioral therapy (CBT), family interventions, and medications. These treatments have been shown to be highly effective in treating anxiety disorders in young people (Piacentini, Bennett et al., 2014). Typically, combined forms of treatment that involve multiple components and target multiple symptoms and problems are used (Chorpita, 2007; Hannesdottir & Ollendick, 2007). It is also important that treatments for children with anxiety disorders are sensitive to the ethnic and cultural factors that we discussed earlier in the chapter (Harmon, Langley, & Ginsburg, 2006). We conclude by highlighting recent efforts directed at the prevention of anxiety.

Behavior Therapy

The main technique of behavior therapy for phobias and anxiety and related disorders is **exposure**, having children face what frightens them, while providing ways of coping other than escape and avoidance. Exposure procedures have been used successfully with boys and girls of all ages from a variety of ethnic backgrounds. About 75% of children with anxiety disorders

---

A CLOSER LOOK 11.4

Evander Holyfield: The Best Way to Defeat Fear Is to Face It

Evander Holyfield, a former three-time world heavyweight boxing champion, has the reputation of having no fear of failure or injury. In fact, Holyfield is amazed by his courage, since he used to be paralyzed by fear. From age 8, when he began boxing, until he was 17, he knew nothing but the constant anxiety of being bullied. "I was scared at everything I did, but especially boxing," he says. "I don't know how I ever got started, but I was scared. I don't know why I stayed. But I won a lot of fights, never got hurt, and as much torment as I was living in, I just assumed I would quit before I got to, say, 18. From watching the older kids box, I knew there came a time when you could get hurt, your nose would be bloody, your eye cut. I'd quit before that happened to me."

However, at 17, he suddenly found himself looking at a left hook from nowhere. Holyfield, then a slim 147 pounds of quivering nerves, was knocked unconscious, more or less, but he rose from the deck and charged his opponent. It was quite a little amateur fight.

The fight came back to him in a dream that night, after his head had cleared. He had been knocked down, yes, but he had

gotten up and fought, after a fashion. Amazingly, he remembered nothing from the experience except numbness; it hadn't hurt at all. "I was never afraid again" he says.

Adapted from "Lovestruck" by Richard Hoffer, *Sports Illustrated*, June 30, 1997.

are helped by this treatment (Chorpita & Southam-Gerow, 2006).

Usually the process is gradual and is referred to as **graded exposure**. The child and therapist make a list of feared situations, from least to most anxiety-producing, and the child is asked to rate the distress caused by each situation on a scale from 1 to 10; this is called a Subjective Units of Distress Scale (SUDS) or fear thermometer. The child is then exposed to each situation, beginning with the least distressing and moving up the hierarchy as the level of anxiety permits.

For Wayman, an 8-year-old-boy with OCD, leaving his bedroom closet door open was an anxiety-provoking situation with a SUDS rating of 8. Exposure was achieved by asking him to imagine being in this bedtime situation:

> THERAPIST: It is nighttime. Your parents have tucked you in and have gone to bed themselves. You reach over to shut off the light on the nightstand, and you notice that your bedroom closet door is open just a bit, just enough for something to crawl out and into your room. It's dark in that corner and you think you see something. You shut off the light and lie down. You hear a strange, scratching noise coming from the closet. It sounds like something is moving. What's your SUDS rating?

> WAYMAN: (Points to fear thermometer.) It's a seven.

> THERAPIST: Stay with it. Tell me about what happens next.

> WAYMAN: The closet door creaks open a bit more, and now I know that something is there. It can come get me. It's a monster.

> THERAPIST: You begin to sweat. You want so badly to go and shut that door, but you stay in bed. You close your eyes, but the sound doesn't stop. It seems to be getting closer. You look over and see a horrible face, with red eyes staring at you. You want to scream, but you know you can't. What's your SUDS rating now?

> WAYMAN: Eight. This is the worst part.

> THERAPIST: Okay, good, stay with the image. Stay with it. What's your SUDS rating now?

> WAYMAN: Five.

With repeated exposure to the fear, Wayman's SUDS ratings continued to decrease, and he was able to leave his bedroom closet door open without feeling anxious. (Adapted from Albano, Knox, & Barlow, 1995)

A second behavior therapy technique for treating children's fears and anxiety is **systematic desensitization**, which consists of three steps: (1) teaching the child to relax; (2) constructing an anxiety hierarchy; and (3) presenting the anxiety-provoking stimuli sequentially while the child remains relaxed. With repeated presentation, the child feels relaxed in the presence of stimuli that previously provoked anxiety.

In a third technique, known as **flooding**, exposure is carried out in prolonged and repeated doses (massed exposure). Throughout the process, the child remains in the anxiety-provoking situation and provides anxiety ratings until the levels diminish. Flooding is typically used in combination with **response prevention**, which prevents the child from engaging in escape or avoidance behaviors. More than other approaches, flooding may create distress, especially during the early stages of treatment. This procedure must be used carefully, especially with young children who may not understand the rationale. More recently, modified flooding procedures have been used in controlled settings to effectively treat a variety of specific phobias. For example, *one-session treatment* (OST) begins with pre-session meeting(s) with the child and family to build rapport and provide information about anxiety and therapy. This is followed by a 2.5- to 3-hour long, single-session of massed exposure therapy that, in addition to exposure, uses a variety of CBT techniques, such as reinforcement, participant modeling (see below), psychoeducation, skills training, and cognitive challenges (Ollendick & Davis, 2013). This approach has shown promising results but requires further evaluation with children in clinical practice settings.

In exposure-based therapies, the feared object can be confronted in many ways, including real-life, role playing, and imagining or observing others in contact with the feared object or situation (modeling). There is also evidence that exposure through virtual environments can be effective (Krijn et al., 2004; Sarver, Beidel, & Spitalnick, 2014).

One of the most effective procedures for treating specific phobias involves *participant modeling and reinforced practice*. Using this procedure, the therapist models the desired behavior (e.g., approaching the feared object), encourages and guides the child in practicing this behavior, and reinforces the child's efforts. Although all exposure procedures are effective, real-life, or in vivo exposure, works best—but it is not always easy to implement. Once the child faces her fear in a real-life situation with no adverse consequences, she is more confident about doing it again.

Other useful behavior therapies are directed at reducing the physical symptoms of anxiety. These include muscle relaxation and special breathing exercises. Children who are anxious often take rapid shallow breaths (hyperventilation) that can produce increased heartbeat, dizziness, and other symptoms. Relaxation procedures are often used with gradual exposure.

A 5-year-old girl with a fear of water is being encouraged and guided to enter a swimming pool.

Purestock/Jupiterimages

Cognitive–Behavioral Therapy (CBT)

The most effective procedure for treating most anxiety disorders in young people is CBT (Chorpita et al., 2011; Silverman, Pina, & Viswesvaran, 2008). In addition to using behavior therapy procedures, CBT teaches children to understand how thinking contributes to anxiety and how to modify their maladaptive thoughts to decrease their symptoms (Kendall & Suveg, 2006). For example, as part of comprehensive CBT for panic disorder, a teen who becomes light-headed during a panic attack and fears she is going to die may be helped by a clinical strategy in which the therapist asks her to spin in a circle until she becomes dizzy. When she becomes alarmed and thinks, "I'm gonna die," she learns to replace this thought with one that is more appropriate; for example, "It's just a little dizziness—I can handle it" (Hoffman & Mattis, 2000). Making the youngster aware of thought patterns and ways to change them complements exposure and other behavioral therapy procedures, such as positive reinforcement and relaxation. CBT and exposure-based treatments are almost always used in combination. An example of a combined approach for treating adolescents with social anxiety disorder

is presented in A Closer Look 11.5 (Albano & DiBartolo, 2007). Similar programs for treating teens with social anxiety in the school setting have also proven effective (Warner et al., 2007).

The CBT treatment program *Coping Cat,* developed by Philip Kendall and his colleagues, is one of the most carefully evaluated treatments for youngsters 7 to 13 years old who have GAD, SAD, and SOC (Kendall, Furr, & Podell, 2010). A teen version is available, as is an Australian adaptation (*Coping Koala*). This approach emphasizes learning processes and the influence of contingencies and models, as well as the pivotal role of information processing. Treatment is directed at decreasing negative thinking, increasing active problem solving, and providing the child with a functional coping outlook. The intervention creates behavioral experiences with emotional involvement, while simultaneously addressing thought processes (Kendall et al., 2010).

Skills training and exposure are used to combat the problematic thinking that contributes to anxious distress and the behavioral avoidance that serves to maintain it. A variety of effective techniques are used, including modeling, role play, exposure, and relaxation training. Therapists use social reinforcement to encourage and reward the children, who are also taught to reward themselves for successful coping. Children first learn to use the following four steps of a "FEAR" plan:

F = Feeling frightened? (recognizing physical symptoms of anxiety)

E = Expecting bad things to happen? (recognizing anxious cognitions)

A = Attitudes and actions that will help (coping self-talk and behavior to use when anxious)

R = Results and rewards (evaluating performance and administering self-reward for effort)

After children learn the FEAR plan, the second part of the program is devoted to exposure and practice. Children attend 16 to 20 sessions over a period of 8 weeks. To enhance the skills learned in therapy, they must practice using them in anxiety-producing situations at home and school. Controlled evaluations of this approach have found it to be extremely effective. Most children show reductions in anxiety, with 71% of children freed of their primary diagnosis at the end of treatment and 54% not meeting the criteria for any anxiety disorder. For many children, these gains have been maintained for 7 to 19 years after treatment (Benjamin et al., 2013; Kendall et al., 2004). Compared to children who were responsive to the initial treatment, those who were not responsive had higher rates of panic disorder, alcohol dependence and drug abuse as adults

Cognitive–Behavioral Therapy for Adolescent Social Anxiety Disorder

Ann Marie Albano and her colleagues have developed a comprehensive group CBT treatment program for adolescents with a social anxiety disorder (Albano, 2003). Treatment is carried out in small groups of four to six teens and involves sixteen 90-minute sessions. The treatment includes a number of important elements (Albano, Detweiler, & Logsdon-Conradsen, 1999).

Psychoeducational

In this phase, teens are informed about the nature of anxiety. A model emphasizing the cognitive, physiological, and behavioral symptoms increases their awareness and understanding of what provokes and maintains their symptoms. They are taught self-monitoring to help them identify anxiety triggers and reactions. To help the teens identify their symptoms, they are placed in anxiety-provoking situations, such as entering a classroom late, and asked to describe their physical, cognitive, and behavioral reactions:

> THERAPIST: What would you be feeling? (physical)
>
> TEEN: Butterflies, dizziness, shortness of breath.
>
> THERAPIST: What would you be thinking? (cognitive)
>
> TEEN: Everyone will be looking at me. What if the teacher yells at me? My face will be all red; they'll see it.
>
> THERAPIST: What would you do? (behavioral)
>
> TEEN: Skip the class. Not look up at anyone. Go to the nurse's office instead.

(Adapted from Marten et al., 1991)

Skill Building

In this phase, teens learn cognitive restructuring, social skills, and problem-solving skills. Adolescents are taught to identify cognitive distortions—errors in thinking that perpetuate anxiety. Systematic rational responses are developed to replace these cognitions. Modeling, role-playing, and systematic-exposure exercises are used.

Specific social skills for interpersonal interactions, maintenance of relationships, and assertiveness are identified and taught. Adolescents first identify behaviors that negatively influence social interactions, such as not smiling, making nervous gestures, not showing interest, speaking too softly, or criticizing or ignoring others. They then practice better forms of social interaction (Marten et al., 1991).

Problem Solving

In this phase, a model for identifying problems and developing realistic goals is presented and rehearsed. The teen is taught how to cope by using a proactive approach rather than avoidance. Two therapists role-play a situation that produces social anxiety. They verbalize their automatic thoughts and rational coping responses to model stages of cognitive restructuring. One therapist (T1) verbalizes the automatic thoughts, and the other therapist (T2) acts as the "rational responder," as illustrated in the following example:

Scene: You Have Been Called on to Give a Brief Talk in Front of Your Class

> T1: "Oh no, I can't do this!"
>
> T2: "Okay, calm down, stay cool. Don't think so negatively."
>
> T1: "Everyone will be looking at me. I'll mess up."
>
> T2: "They have to do this too. We're all a little nervous."
>
> T1: "What will I say? I can't think!"
>
> T2: "Okay, I can say things clearly, I know this stuff."
>
> T1: "My heart is beating so fast, I'm gonna be sick."
>
> T2: "I feel nervous, but it will pass. I'll be fine."
>
> T1: "Boy, I'm glad that's over, I'll never do this again."
>
> T2: "Alright! I did it! That was okay. I made it!" (Adapted from Marten et al., 1991.)

Therapists then discuss the role play with the group, drawing on the members' experiences in similar situations.

Exposure

In this phase, teens develop a fear and avoidance hierarchy of social situations, which serves as the focus of in-session exposures. Group members and therapists simulate the situations. Exposures target the behavioral avoidance and cognitive component of anxiety, showing that anxiety will dissipate with habituation.

Generalization and Maintenance

To enhance generalization and maintenance of treatment effects, the prosocial and coping behaviors that the teen learns in the group are modeled and practiced during snack-time sessions. In addition, to increase generalization to the home setting, the program also includes a component for active parent participation (Marten et al., 1991).

When asked how she had changed following treatment for her social anxiety disorder, here's what one girl said:

> "Well, my friends told me that when they used to ask my opinion about something, I would always say, 'I don't care' or 'I don't know.' Now when they ask me, I give them my opinion. They said they like me much better now because I say what I think." (Beidel & Turner, 1998, p. 223)

Used by permission of Ann Marie Albano.

(Benjamin et al., 2013). Replication studies using CBT have found gains to be maintained for 8 to 13 years after treatment (Saavedra et al., 2010). In general, children who are younger and have fewer internalizing symptoms, and whose mothers do not display depressive symptoms, generally show more favorable outcomes (Southam-Gerow, Kendall, & Weersing, 2001).

Computer-based, computer-assisted, and online CBT have also been shown to be effective in treating anxiety disorders and OCD in children and adolescents (Comer et al., 2014; Khanna & Kendall, 2010; Spence et al., 2011). These approaches have the added benefit of using less therapist time and/or providing greater access for families who have difficulty accessing clinic-based treatment, making it a viable and cost-effective option for many youngsters with anxiety disorders. Although CBT is effective in a variety of formats in treating childhood anxiety disorders, studies have not tested whether its effectiveness is through changes in the hypothesized key components—the child's cognitions and coping skills. Thus, CBT in a variety of formats works, but we do not yet know why. In addition, the treatment response to CBT may not be consistent across anxiety disorders. Evidence suggests that children with SAD and GAD may show more favorable outcomes than those with SOC (Rapp et al., 2013). One study found that youngsters with anxiety disorders who had more severe and impairing anxiety, greater caregiver strain, and a main diagnosis of SOC had less favorable treatment outcomes (Compton et al., 2014).

Family Interventions

Anxiety disorders often occur in a context of parental anxiety and problematic family relationships, which may influence the effectiveness of any of the treatment approaches. In some cases, child-focused treatment may have spillover effects into the family. For example, as children come to view themselves as more competent and less avoidant, parents' perceptions about what their child can and cannot do change as well. As a result, parents may begin to respond differently to their child, and their own feelings and functioning improve (Kendall & Flannery-Schroeder, 1998). Greater parental involvement in modeling and reinforcing coping techniques, inclusion of parental anxiety-management strategies, and inclusion of parent skills training may be especially important in treating younger children with anxiety. Some studies have found these types of modified CBT approaches for younger children and their families to be effective in reducing anxiety and improving coping skills in children in the 4-to-9-year age range,

with outcomes comparable to those for treatments for CBT with older children (Cartwright-Hatton et al., 2011; Hirshfeld-Becker et al., 2010). Several age-adapted forms of CBT have also been developed for preschool-age children with anxiety disorders. These adaptations mainly involve including the child's primary caregivers in treatment and the use of age-appropriate materials such as cartoons, drawings, and narratives (Luby, 2013).

Addressing children's anxiety disorders in a family context may result in more dramatic and lasting effects than focusing only on the child, particularly for children of anxious parents (Creswell & Cartwright-Hatton, 2007; Suveg et al., 2006). In one study, it was found that nearly 70% of the children with anxiety disorders who completed individual or family treatment did not meet criteria for any anxiety disorder at posttreatment. The addition of a family component that focused on interactions, managing emotion, communication, and problem solving significantly enhanced short-term outcomes and long-term maintenance (Barrett, Dadds, & Rapee, 1996).

Given the important role of the family in childhood OCD, treatments for OCD have increasingly emphasized family involvement (Waters & Barrett, 2000). The primary treatment for children with OCD involves CBT that helps them learn to confront their worst fears gradually (graded exposure) while being prevented from engaging in their rituals (response prevention) (Freeman et al., 2008; March & Mulle, 1998; Piacentini et al., 2012). Family treatment for OCD provides education about the disorder and helps families cope with their feelings, such as helplessness in not being able to relieve the child's pain, frustration that the child cannot "just stop," jealousy from siblings, and disappointment that the child is not "normal" (Piacentini, Jacobs, & Maidment, 1997). Both individual child CBT and family-based interventions have proven to be effective in treating children with OCD (Barrett et al., 2008; Freeman et al., 2014; Geller et al., 2012). A number of excellent CBT manuals and self-help books are also available for treating OCD and related disorders (see www.ocfoundation.org). Generally, CBT has been found to be most effective for less severe cases of OCD, in which children display less severe symptoms, less impairment, greater insight, and fewer externalizing symptoms (Garcia et al., 2010).

Medications

A variety of medications have been used to treat the symptoms of anxiety in children and adolescents; the most common and effective ones are selective serotonin reuptake inhibitors (SSRIs) (Reinblatt & Riddle, 2007; Rynn et al., 2011). Although used to treat all types of anxiety and related disorders, the strongest evidence of their effectiveness is in treatment of OCD (Garcia et al., 2010). Findings regarding the effectiveness of medications for treating anxiety and related disorders other than OCD have been less consistent (Huemer, Erhart, & Steiner, 2010). Nevertheless, a number of controlled studies have found SSRIs to be effective in managing the symptoms of anxiety for youngsters with SOC, SAD, and GAD, with effects comparable to those in CBT in some studies (Reinblatt & Riddle, 2007; Piacentini, Bennett et al., 2014).

Given the lack of controlled studies and possible adverse side effects associated with the use of SSRIs for children with anxiety disorders, CBT is generally considered the first line of treatment; medication is used for children with severe symptoms or comorbid disorders or when CBT is not available or proves unsuccessful (AACAP, 2007b). Some children who are severely anxious may require medication before they are able to participate in CBT. To date, there have been relatively few studies of the effectiveness of medications for the treatment of anxiety disorders in children, particularly for specific phobias; however, clinical trials and a growing number of controlled studies provide some knowledge about the use of these compounds (Geller et al., 2012; Reinblatt & Riddle, 2007).

Prevention

Given their frequency, early onset, and chronicity and the personal suffering and public health costs associated with anxiety disorders, early identification and prevention efforts need to be a priority. In an innovative prevention study, researchers first identified very young children (mean age, <4 years) who were at risk for later anxiety disorders (Rapee et al., 2010). As described in the case of Jack (see A Closer Look 11.6), children were selected based on both a

---

A CLOSER LOOK 11.6

Early Intervention and Prevention of Anxiety Disorders

Jack: "Participating with Confidence"

Background

"Jack," 3 years 11 months of age, was referred by his parents, who were concerned about his difficulty interacting with people outside the immediate family and participating in new activities. Despite attending the same preschool for 6 months, Jack was unable to initiate or reciprocate play with other children and spoke only to his main teacher. He tended to watch rather than participate in group activities. Jack's parents had withdrawn him from group swimming classes because he cried if he thought anyone was looking at him. His parents also avoided most social engagements because Jack constantly clung to them and demanded to go home. Both parents described themselves as having been very shy as children and were keen for Jack to avoid this experience.

Behavioral Inhibition Assessment

When Jack arrived at the laboratory for the behavioral inhibition assessment, he hid behind his mother when greeted and sat on his mother's lap rather than at the table with the assessor. He did not respond verbally to the assessor for over 30 minutes, and when he did, his speech was soft and monosyllabic and he avoided eye contact. He reacted fearfully in the cloaked stranger interaction and returned to his mother's lap. Jack did not approach the novel toy or interact with the other child in the peer interaction component. Jack's assessment showed that he met all criteria for behavioral inhibition, and he also met DSM-5 criteria for social anxiety disorder.

Intervention

Jack's parents were randomly allocated to the 6-week parent education program. In the program, Jack's parents were encouraged to reduce their overprotective parenting style by not allowing Jack to avoid situations that made him anxious, such as attending parties and new activities. They were also encouraged to give Jack the opportunity to speak for himself rather than answering for him. Jack's parents were assisted in developing a graded-exposure hierarchy to previously feared situations. They began with reinforcing Jack's efforts to reply when familiar people greeted him and gradually worked up to helping him to join in small group activities.

Outcome

At his final follow-up assessment, at 6 years 10 months of age, Jack no longer met the criteria for social anxiety disorder and was no longer as strongly inhibited. Jack's mother reported that he was still reserved when he first met unfamiliar people and that she would still describe him as "shy." However, he was participating with confidence in most school and extracurricular activities, and he had a small group of close friends.

Excerpt from Altering the Trajectory of Anxiety in At-Risk Young Children. Ronald M. Rapee, Ph.D.; Susan J. Kennedy, Ph.D.; Michelle Ingram, M.Clin.Psych.; Susan L. Edwards, Ph.D.; Lynne Sweeney, Ph.D. From the Centre for Emotional Health, Department of Psychology, Macquarie University. *Am J Psychiatry* 2010;167: 1518–1525. Adapted with permission from the *American Journal of Psychiatry* (Copyright © 2010). American Psychiatric Association.

high *withdrawal* score on a temperament questionnaire and high scores on a laboratory test of *behavioral inhibition*. A relatively brief intervention consisting of six 90-minute group sessions with parents was then carried out. The sessions provided an overview of the developmental aspects of anxiety, principles of parenting techniques (particularly the role that parental overprotection plays as a risk factor for anxiety), cognitive restructuring for parental worries about their child, and—for the children as they matured—the use of exposure hierarchies for the child, and the importance of ongoing use of these techniques, especially during high risk periods such as school entry. A no treatment control group was simply monitored in the clinic at 12-month intervals, on the same schedule as the parents who received intervention.

As shown in ● Figure 11.4, the overall number and the severity of diagnosed anxiety disorders decreased for both groups following the start of the study. Importantly, like Jack, children in the intervention group showed significantly fewer anxiety disorders and lower symptom severity at the last two follow-up visits

relative to controls. Mothers also reported that their children showed lower levels of anxiety 3 years after treatment, with a similar trend for children's reports of their own anxiety at the 3-year follow-up. Particularly interesting was that the intervention effects were modest at 1 year but stronger at 2 and 3 years. Also, the severity differences between treated and untreated children seem to be mainly due to an increase in symptoms for the control group, suggesting that untreated children may be on a worsening developmental trajectory (Cuthbert, 2010). Follow-up studies are needed to explore possible reasons for these outcomes. Universal programs of primary prevention have also proven to be a promising approach to preventing anxiety in older children (Barrett et al., 2006). With further research, these and other innovative programs of early intervention and prevention offer hope for the many children and families who suffer from anxiety disorders.

Section Summary

Treatment and Prevention

- Exposing youngsters to the situations, objects, and occasions that produce their anxiety is the main line of attack in treating fears and anxieties.

- The most effective procedures for treating specific phobias involve participant modeling and reinforced practice.

- Cognitive–behavioral therapy (CBT) teaches children to understand how their thinking contributes to anxiety, how to change maladaptive thoughts to decrease their symptoms, and how to cope with their fears and anxieties other than by escape and avoidance.

- Medications such as SSRIs are effective in treating children with anxiety disorders. CBT is generally considered the first line of treatment, with medication reserved for those with severe symptoms or comorbid disorders or when CBT is not available or proves unsuccessful.

- Family interventions for anxiety disorders may result in more dramatic and lasting effects than focusing only on the child.

- Prevention programs have had some success in decreasing symptoms of anxiety, although further research is needed to evaluate their long-term benefits.

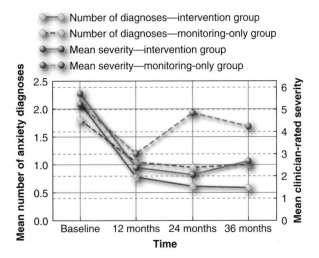

Number of diagnoses—intervention group
Number of diagnoses—monitoring-only group
Mean severity—intervention group
Mean severity—monitoring-only group

● **FIGURE 11.4** | Number and severity of diagnosed anxiety disorders over 3 years in children whose parents received an intervention or who received only monitoring.

Reprinted with permission from the *American Journal of Psychiatry* (Copyright © 2010). American Psychiatric Association.

Study Resources

12

Trauma- and Stressor-Related Disorders

*I think the thumbprint on the throat of many people is childhood trauma
that goes unprocessed and unrecognized.*

—Tom Hooper (British film and television director)

CHAPTER PREVIEW

ALTHOUGH STRESS AND TRAUMA in childhood or adolescence have always existed, only recently have these events been receiving the attention they duly deserve. Considerable evidence supports the significant link between childhood trauma and immediate and long-term mental health consequences, leading some to call childhood trauma "the hidden epidemic" (Lanius, Vermetten, & Pain, 2010). Childhood trauma has the potential to undermine healthy child development and cause many of the forms of abnormal child development described in this text, such as anxiety, depression, eating disorders, and many others (Chapman, Dube, & Anda, 2007).

It is now known that trauma occurring during childhood or adolescence is common, with about one in four youths reporting some form of major trauma before age 16 (Costello et al., 2002). **Traumatic events** are defined as exposure to actual or threatened harm or fear of death or injury and are considered uncommon or extreme stressors. Such terrifying or life-threatening events are wide-ranging. They include careless or intentional acts such as physical and sexual abuse, neglect, and exposure to domestic and community violence, as well as unintended medical traumas, accidents, natural disasters, war, terrorism, refugee trauma, and traumatic loss (Gerson & Rappaport, 2013). **Stressful events** are typically more common and less extreme than traumatic events. Stressors may be a single event, such as parental separation or romantic breakups, or may involve multiple or ongoing stressful situations or events. Some stressful events are developmentally connected—for example, going to school or leaving home for the first time. Even childhood bullying, once considered a common rite of passage, is now recognized as a major stressor that contributes to adult mental health problems for some individuals (Copeland et al., 2013). Although many traumatic and stressful events do not lead to a mental health disorder, they can affect ongoing developmental processes in insidious and disruptive ways.

Trauma- and stressor-related disorders is a new category in the *Diagnostic and Statistical Manual of Mental Disorders*, 5th edition (DSM-5); it includes Acute Stress Disorder, Adjustment Disorder, and Posttraumatic Stress Disorder (PTSD), which were classified as anxiety disorders in previous editions of the DSM. This category also includes two other stressor-related disorders previously listed as "Disorders usually first diagnosed in infancy, childhood, or adolescence": Reactive Attachment Disorder and Disinhibited Social Engagement Disorder. These changes were made to create the more specific category of trauma- and stressor-related disorders. These disorders have in common direct or indirect exposure to acute or chronic stressors or catastrophic events, which may consist of multiple events over time, such as child maltreatment.

Considerable research concerning child maltreatment has been done, so we refer to this literature throughout this chapter to illustrate the nature and scope of childhood trauma- and stressor-related disorders. **Child maltreatment** is a generic term that refers to four primary acts: physical abuse, neglect, sexual abuse, and **psychological abuse**. Maltreatment can take many forms, including acts experienced by many children, such as harsh corporal punishment, sibling violence, and peer assault, as well as acts experienced by a significant minority, such as beatings or abandonment (Centers for Disease Control [CDC], 2011d). Child maltreatment cuts across all lines of gender, national origin, language, religion, age, ethnicity, disability, and sexual orientation.

MARY ELLEN

Her Legacy

She is a bright little girl, with features indicating unusual mental capacity, but with a careworn, stunted, and prematurely old look. Her apparent condition of health, as well as her scanty wardrobe, indicated that no change of custody or condition could be much for the worse.

. . . On her examination [in court] the child made a statement as follows: "I don't know how old I am. . . . I have never had but one pair of shoes, but I cannot recollect when that was. I have had no shoes or stockings on this winter. . . . I am never allowed to play with any children, or to have any company whatever. Mamma has been in the habit of whipping and beating me almost every day. She used to whip me with a twisted whip—a raw hide. The whip always left a black and blue mark on my body. I have now the black and blue marks on my head which were made by mamma, and also a cut on the left side of my forehead which was made by a pair of scissors. She struck me with the scissors and cut me; I have no recollection of ever having been kissed by any one. . . . I have never been taken on my mamma's lap and caressed or petted. . . . I do not know for what I was whipped—mamma never said anything to me when she whipped me."

New York Times, April 10, 1874.

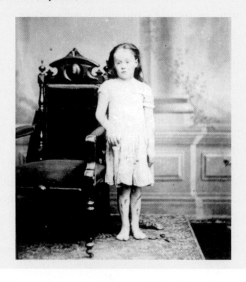

This heartbreaking and tragic report of Mary Ellen's abuse led to the formation in the winter of 1874 of the New York Society for the Prevention of Cruelty to Children, as citizens discovered that animals were protected from mistreatment but children were not. It took another 100 years to pass legislation that clearly defined and mandated the reporting of child abuse and neglect, finally launching new efforts to identify and assist abused and neglected children in North America. Despite these efforts, child abuse and neglect remain one of the most common causes of trauma- and stressor-related disorders across the lifespan (Wekerle & Wolfe, 2014).

In North America, before they reach adulthood, 1 in 10 children experiences some form of sexual victimization by an adult or peer (Finkelhor et al., 2009). Each year, about 1 in 10 children receives physical punishment by a parent or other caregiver harsh enough to put the child at risk of injury or harm (Straus & Stewart, 1999). Sadly, each day in the United States more than five children—most of whom are under 4 years old—die at the hands of their parents or caregivers (U.S. Department of Health and Human Services, Administration on Children, Youth, and Families [USDHHS], 2010). Countless other children suffer the effects of psychological abuse and neglect or are exposed to catastrophic events or accidents. Most show profound changes in mood, arousal, or behavior immediately after these events. Although many recover or manage to cope effectively, about one-third go on to develop symptoms of post-traumatic stress disorder (PTSD) or other mental disorders that affect their daily lives (Gerson & Rappaport, 2013).

For many generations, violence against children and other family members was viewed as a private matter, and its significant negative effects continue to be poorly acknowledged. Until very recently, violence between family members was considered, in the eyes of the law, to be less consequential, less damaging, and less worthy of society's serious attention than violence between strangers. Today we know better: violence against children occurs in numerous forms, from mild acts of frightening or yelling at children, to severe acts of assaulting them with fists and weapons. Moreover, violence and abuse wax and wane in a cyclical manner that creates tension, uncertainty, and fear in children, forcing them to cope with harsh realities and fearful demands (Wekerle et al., 2006).

Many forms of childhood trauma, especially child abuse and neglect, have considerable psychological importance because they often occur within ongoing relationships that are expected to be protective, supportive, and nurturing. Children from abusive and neglectful families grow up in environments that fail to provide consistent and appropriate opportunities to guide their development; instead, these children are placed in jeopardy of physical and emotional harm (Jaffe, Wolfe, & Campbell, 2011). Yet, their ties to their families—even to the abuser—are very important, so child victims may feel torn between a sense of belonging and a sense of fear and apprehension. Because children are dependent on the people who harm or neglect them, they face other paradoxical dilemmas as well (American Psychological Association, 1996/2007):

▸ *The victim not only wants to stop the violence but also longs to belong to a family.* Loyalty and strong emotional ties to the abuser are powerful opponents to the victim's desire to be safe and protected.

▸ *Affection and attention may coexist with violence and abuse.* A recurring cycle may begin, whereby mounting tension, characterized by fear and anticipation, ultimately gives way to more abusive behavior. A period of reconciliation may follow, with increased affection and attention. Children are always hopeful that the abuse will not recur.

▸ *The intensity of the violence tends to increase over time, although in some cases physical violence may decrease or even stop altogether.* Abusive behavior may vary throughout the relationship, taking verbal, sexual, emotional, or physical forms, but the adult's abuse of power and control remains the central issue.

We begin our discussion of child trauma and stress with some significant historical issues, followed by consideration of the family's role in children's healthy socialization and safety.

HISTORY AND FAMILY CONTEXT

Because the most severe and long-lasting forms of childhood trauma occur at the hands of caregivers, we begin this discussion with a look at how society's view of child-rearing and intolerance of child abuse and neglect have evolved over a relatively short period. Intentional and unintentional forms of trauma have always existed, and most likely were even more common place in previous generations (Radbill, 1987), but these events were seldom identified as problematic. For generations, children were viewed as the exclusive property and responsibility of their fathers, who had full discretion as to how punishment could be administered. This right was unchallenged by any countermovement to seek more humane treatment for children up until the recognition of the abuse Mary Ellen experienced, just 140 years ago.

Ironically, the same legal system that was designed to support and assist the family has tolerated, and in some respects condoned, the abuse of family members, including children, women, and the elderly (Jaffe et al., 1996). Two major cultural traditions have influenced this position until recently: absolute authority over the family by the husband and the right to family privacy. The Roman Law of Chastisement (753 B.C.), for example, made women the possessions of men, who they were required to obey. English common law similarly allowed parents and others to punish their children using "moderate and reasonable" chastisement. For centuries since, it has been up to the courts in various countries to determine what is moderate and reasonable. Sadly, many developed and developing societies still adhere to this view of children as personal property to be managed however the parent wishes (Wolfe & Nayak, 2003).

Fortunately, over the past century and a half, particularly the past 30 years, the legal system's response has shifted to condemn such behavior throughout much of the Western world (albeit with considerable resistance). The UN Convention on the Rights of the Child (1989) spurred efforts to value the rights and needs of children, and to recognize their exploitation and abuse in many developed countries. Today, 42 countries have established an official government policy regarding child abuse and neglect, and about one-third of the world's population is included in the various countries that conduct an annual count of child abuse and neglect cases (International Society for Prevention of Child Abuse and Neglect, 2010). These efforts provide the critical first steps to identifying the scope of the problem, and justify the implementation of important societal, community, and cultural changes to combat child abuse and related forms of stress and trauma.

Healthy Families

You know the only people who are always sure about the proper way to raise children? Those who've never had any.

—Bill Cosby

It is difficult to talk about childhood trauma and maltreatment without talking about the importance of healthy families. Family relations are the earliest and most enduring social relationships that significantly affect a child's competence, resilience, and sense of well-being. For most of us, family influences are positive and beneficial, offering a primary source of support and nurturance that sets the stage for lifetime patterns of secure relationships and well-being. For others, however, family events and experiences are profoundly negative and harmful, providing the context for some of the most severe violence in society (Straus, Gelles, & Steinmetz, 2003).

As parents, we recognize that children require considerable direction and control and that they sometimes behave in ways that challenge our decisions and interfere with our plans. If you have not experienced this yourself, ask a parent you know if you can take their young child grocery shopping! Individuals who are ill-prepared for the vital and challenging role of being parents may rely heavily on child-rearing methods from their own childhood, without questioning or modifying those methods. Although this approach to parenting is natural and often appropriate, in some cases it can perpetuate undesirable child-rearing methods, such as physical coercion, verbal threats, and neglect of the child's needs (Gershoff, 2013; Wolfe, 1999).

Understanding the dire effects of trauma and abuse on the mental health of children and adults must begin with a discussion of what children should expect from a healthy family environment. For healthy development, children need a caregiving environment that balances their need for control and direction, or "demandingness," with their need for stimulation and sensitivity, or "responsiveness" (Maccoby & Martin, 1983). Determinants of healthy parent–child relationships and family roles derived from these two primary developmental needs include:

▸ Adequate knowledge of child development and expectations, including knowledge of children's normal sexual development and experimentation;

▸ Adequate skill in coping with the stress related to caring for small children, and knowledge of ways to enhance child development through proper stimulation and attention;

▸ Opportunities to develop normal parent–child attachment and early patterns of communication;

▸ Adequate parental knowledge of home management, including basic financial planning, proper shelter, and meal planning;

▸ Opportunities and willingness to share the duties of child care between two parents, when applicable;

▸ Provision of necessary social and health services.

These healthy patterns depend not only on parental competence and developmental sensitivity, but also on family circumstances and the availability of community resources, such as education and child-rearing information, as well as social networks and supports. The family situation itself, including the parents' marital relationship and the child's characteristics, such as temperament, health, and developmental limitations, provides the basic context for child-rearing.

Although we would expect a considerable range in ability and resources among North American families, certain features of a child's environment should be fundamental and expectable. For young children, an **expectable environment** requires protective and nurturing adults, as well as opportunities for socialization

Young Jason never goes unarmed. Grabbing his plastic gun and rubber knife, he tells his mother, "If daddy comes, I'll be able to stop him."

been exposed to bombing, shelling, sniper fire, and terrorist attacks resulting in untold loss of family, friends, and community support (Bellamy, 2002). The tragedy of these events underscores the need to understand how they affect children's mental health, and, more importantly, to find effective ways of helping the child victims of such atrocities (Ehntholt & Yule, 2006).

Estimates based on a nationally representative sample of dual-parent U.S. households indicate that over 15 million American children live in families in which partner violence occurred at least once in the previous year (McDonald et al., 2006). Child witnesses of abuse and violence in the home or in their community are exposed to traumatic events that pose a high risk to development (Jaffe et al., 2011; Wolfe et al., 2003). Younger children exposed to violence are fearful and often show regressive and somatic signs of distress, such as sleep problems, bed-wetting, headaches, stomachaches, diarrhea, ulcers, and enuresis. Older boys tend to be more aggressive with peers and dating partners; girls tend to be more passive and withdrawn and to have low self-esteem (Crooks & Wolfe, 2007). All of these symptoms can be directly or indirectly linked to a stressful family environment, as well as threats to the child's safety and the safety of one or more caregivers.

Less extreme, non-life-threatening forms of stressful experiences in childhood or adolescence are common, and most do not lead to enduring harm or disorders. Changing schools, parental separation, medical problems, and peer conflict are just a few of the myriad forms of stress that are a part of life, which some adults reflect back on as building character while others fear to discuss. However, teens today are reporting levels of stress that rival those of adults, which poses risks to their physical and emotional health (Bethune, 2014) (see A Closer Look 12.1).

How Stress Affects Children

To cope with everyday forms of stress, children and youths need a basic expectable environment to adapt successfully or their development may be compromised. All children must cope with various degrees of stress, and these experiences can be strengthening if they do not exceed the child's coping ability—that is, the nature and amount of stress is *manageable* (Masten & Wright, 2010). Stressful experiences that are mild, predictable, and brief are usually manageable and can actually enhance a child's biological and psychological competence (Thompson, 2014). However, a child's method of adapting to or coping with immediate environmental demands (such as avoiding an

"If you think you're stressed out, imagine being a teenager in today's society. American teens say they experience stress in patterns similar to those for adults, and during the school year they report stress levels even higher than those reported by adults. These were the prime conclusions of APA's poll *Stress in America™: Are Teens Adopting Adults' Stress Habits?*

Teens reported that their stress levels during the school year far exceeded what they believe to be healthy (5.8 vs. 3.9 on a 10-point scale) and topped adults' average reported stress levels (5.8 for teens vs. 5.1 for adults). Even during the summer, teens reported their stress during the prior month at levels higher than what they believe is healthy (4.6 vs. 3.9 on a 10-point scale).

Many teens also reported feeling overwhelmed (31%) and depressed or sad (30%) as a result of stress. More than one-third of teens reported feeling tired (36%) and nearly one-quarter of teens (23%) reported skipping a meal due to stress."

Source: Bethune, S. (2014, April). Teen stress rivals that of adults. *Monitor on Psychology, 45*(4), pp. 20–22. Retrieved from http://www.apa.org/monitor/2014/04/teen-stress.aspx

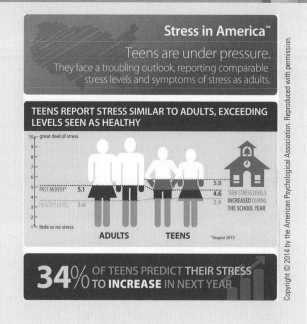

abusive caregiver) may later compromise his or her ability to form relationships with others. A child's successful methods of adapting to outbursts of anger and aggression between family members are constantly challenged. Signs of stress appear, such as increased illness, symptoms of fear and anxiety, and problems with peers or school (El-Sheikh et al., 2013; Kim & Cicchetti, 2010).

Stressful events in the child's family or immediate environment affect each child in different and unique ways. However, certain situations trigger more intense or more chronic stress reactions and carry more severe consequences than others. (Consider, for example, the difference between the stress of moving to a new school and the stress of being bullied by an older child.) Early, chronic stress challenges the child's developing biological and social development, influencing multiple neurobiological changes in an effort to adapt (described later in this chapter). However, such adaptation to threat and chronic stress carries trade-offs in children's abilities to perform at school, to interact with peers, and to control their impulses. Stress provokes strong biological responses (e.g., elevated blood pressure, activation of immunological and hormonal systems) that are designed for short-term reactions, such as fight or flight. Children who are chronically aroused by a stressful environment mobilize these biological responses repeatedly, often to the point of overload. Over time, some of these children may show signs of being *hyperresponsive* to stress: excessive threat vigilance, mistrust, poor social relationships, impaired self-regulation, and unhealthy lifestyle choices

(Miller, Chen, & Parker, 2011). Paradoxically, some children may become *hyporesponsive* to stressful events—underreacting to signs of danger or threat—indicating that their stress system is overtaxed and may be shutting down. **Allostatic load** is a concept used to describe this progressive "wear and tear" on biological systems due to the effects of chronic stress (Thompson, 2014).

Child maltreatment, exposure to domestic violence, and chronic child poverty are among the worst and most intrusive forms of childhood stress and trauma (Graham-Bermann et al., 2012; Yoshikawa, Aber, & Beardslee, 2012). These circumstances impinge directly on the child's daily life, may be ongoing and unpredictable, and are often the result of actions or inactions of people the child is supposed to trust and depend on. However, keep in mind that even events such as abuse, neglect, family violence, and poverty do not affect each child in a predictable, characteristic fashion. Rather, their impact depends on the child's makeup and available supports (El-Sheikh & Erath, 2011).

A prime factor in how children respond to various forms of stress is the degree of parental support and assistance they receive to help them cope and adapt. Parents provide a model that teaches the child how to exert some control even in the midst of confusion and upheaval. Understandably, a warm relationship with an adult who provides a predictable routine and consistent, moderate discipline, and who buffers the child from unnecessary sources of stress, is a valuable asset. Maltreated children may have the hardest time adapting appropriately to any form of stress when they are deprived of positive adult relationships, effective models of problem solving, and a sense of personal control or predictability (Luthar, 2006; Wekerle & Wolfe, 2014).

Maltreatment

Peace in society depends upon peace in the family.

—Augustine

Have you ever babysat a young child or been in charge of a group of children at a camp or school? If you saw bruises on a child, what would you do? First, you would consider that bruises on a child can be caused by any number of factors, so you would need to obtain more information, if possible, to see whether the bruises were accidental. You should be aware that all states and provinces in North America have civil laws, or statutes, that obligate persons who come in contact with children as part of their job or volunteer work (bus drivers, day-care workers, teachers, babysitters, and so forth) to report known or suspected cases of abuse to the police or child welfare authorities. These statutes also provide criteria for removing children from their homes if it is suspected that they are being maltreated. Criminal statutes further specify the forms of maltreatment that are criminally punishable. We all have a role to play in keeping children safe from harm, and it begins with being attentive to signs of possible abuse; professional or police involvement should be sought if you are concerned or uncertain.

Child maltreatment is broadly defined as "Any recent act or failure to act on the part of a parent or caretaker, which results in death, serious physical or emotional harm, sexual abuse, or exploitation, or an act or failure to act which presents an imminent risk of serious harm" (Child Welfare Information Gateway, 2011). Each year, over a million children in the United States experience maltreatment that results in some degree of harm, resulting in a rate of 17 per 1,000 children in the population (Sedlak et al, 2010). Incidence rates of maltreatment resulting in harm in Canada and the United Kingdom are similar, about 14 per 1,000 children (Public Health Agency of Canada, 2010; National Society for the Prevention of Cruelty to Children, 2011).

● Figure 12.2 shows the percentages of each subtype of abuse and neglect, based on U.S. data. As shown, child neglect (including medical neglect) continues to be a worrisome problem, accounting for four out of five documented cases of maltreatment in the United States. Physical abuse (10.9%), sexual abuse (7.6%), psychological maltreatment (7.6%), and other forms of maltreatment (e.g., abandonment or threats of harm, 9.6%) make up the remaining substantiated

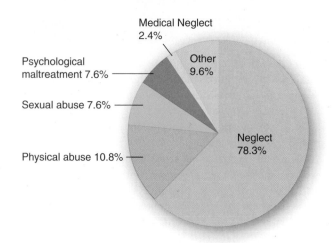

● **FIGURE 12.2** | Types of child maltreatment by percentage. "Other" forms of maltreatment include abandonment, threats of harm to the child, and congenital drug addiction. (Note that the percentages total more than 100% because children may have suffered from more than one type of maltreatment.)

Data from USDHHS (2010).

cases. In addition, about one in four of these children suffered more than one form of maltreatment.

Neglect

JANE AND MATT

Used to Neglect

Although Janet had worked for child protective services for over 10 years, she still cringed when she described the conditions of the home from which she had just removed two young siblings. "Neighbors and relatives have complained about the parents' never being around much, and how they often hear children crying," Janet explained during our interview. "I've been to the home before, and usually it stays clean for a few days after my visit. But this time the children were left with a teenaged babysitter, who went off to play in an arcade. They walked out of the home and had to be returned by the police. What I saw this time was worse than before. Little Matt, who's almost 3 years old, was running around in soiled diapers, crawling across broken dishes and spilled food, putting things in his mouth. His sister Jane, who turns 6 next month, was dressed in dirty clothes and looked like she hadn't eaten in a week. The odor from the house forced me to step outside for air. The children seemed used to it—they just moved things out of their way and didn't seem to care."

I met with both children once they were settled into a foster home, and offered ways for the foster parents to manage Jane's strong-willed behavior and Matt's delay in speech and toileting. The foster mother noted how both children seemed to need "constant attention and control" and how neither had knowledge of typical routines such as sitting down together for dinner, cleaning up, bed times, basic hygiene, and the need to wear clean clothing. (Based on authors' case material.)

These two children suffered the effects of physical and emotional neglect, characterized by a failure to provide for their basic physical, educational, and emotional needs. **Physical neglect** includes refusal or delay in seeking health care, expulsion from the home or refusal to allow a runaway to return home, abandonment, and inadequate supervision. **Educational neglect** involves actions such as allowing chronic truancy, failing to enroll in school a child who is of mandatory school age, and failing to attend to a child's special educational needs. **Emotional neglect**, one of the most difficult categories to define, includes actions such as marked inattention to the child's needs for affection, refusal or failure to provide needed psychological care, spousal abuse in the child's presence, and permission for drug or alcohol use by the child.

The determination of child neglect requires consideration of cultural values and standards of care, as well as recognition that the failure to provide the necessities of life may be related to poverty. The examples shown in Table 12.1 are actual cases of the three forms of neglect (Sedlak & Broadhurst, 1996).

Neglected children may suffer physical health problems, limited growth, and increased complications in other health conditions, such as diabetes, allergies, and failure to thrive (Lyons-Ruth et al., 2014; van Tilburg et al., 2010). They also may show behavior patterns that vacillate between undisciplined activity and extreme passivity as a result of the ways they adapt to an unresponsive caregiver (Hildyard & Wolfe, 2002). As toddlers, they show little persistence and enthusiasm; as preschoolers, neglected children show poor impulse control and are highly dependent on teachers for support and nurturance (Erickson & Egeland, 2002).

Child neglect, the most common form of maltreatment, is tied to poverty, substance abuse, and parental indifference.

TABLE 12.1 | **The Three Forms of Child Neglect**

Physical Neglect	Educational Neglect	Emotional Neglect
• A 2-year-old who was found wandering in the street late at night, naked and alone	• An 11-year-old and a 13-year-old who were chronically truant	• Siblings who were subjected to repeated incidents of family violence between their mother and father
• An infant who had to be hospitalized for near-drowning after being left alone in a bathtub	• A 12-year-old whose parents permitted him to decide whether to go to school, how long to stay there, and in which activities to participate	• A 12-year-old whose parents permitted him to drink and use drugs
• Children who were living in a home contaminated with animal feces and rotting food	• A special education student whose mother refused to believe he needed help in school	• A child whose mother helped him shoot out the windows of a neighbor's house

© Cengage Learning®

Abuse

MILTON

Abused and Abusive

Four-year-old Milton's rambunctious nature and his mother's hair-trigger temper were an explosive mix. He was constantly in trouble at home and often was spanked, yelled at, and locked in his room. One evening his babysitter took him to the emergency department because she thought he had a bad cold. During the examination, the doctor discovered that Milton had a fracture to his left forearm that was a couple of weeks old. There was a goose egg on Milton's forehead and multiple bruises on his face at various stages of healing, as well as bruises on his back. Several people had noticed Milton's aggressive behavior—pushing other children or hitting them with something at preschool—but no one had realized that he was being abused. His preschool teacher told investigators, "I'm never sure from one minute to the next how Milton will react to the other children. He could be playing and suddenly become angry at something and start to destroy things or hit someone. I've also seen him become frightened—at what I don't know—and withdraw into a corner. I've tried several times to discuss these things with his mother, but she says he's just trying to get his way all the time." (Based on authors' case material.)

Milton has been physically abused. His behavior indicates growing up in an environment with punitive disciplinary methods that are the norm and are detrimental to child-centered stimulation and appropriate limit setting. **Physical abuse** is multiple acts of aggression that include punching, beating, kicking, biting, burning, shaking, or otherwise physically harming a child. In most cases, the injuries from physical abuse are not intentional, but they occur as a result of overdiscipline or severe physical punishment. The severity and nature of the injuries vary considerably, as shown by these sobering examples of physical abuse (Sedlak & Broadhurst, 1996):

▸ A 1-year-old child died of a cerebral hemorrhage after being shaken by her father.

▸ A teen's mother punched her and pulled out her hair.

▸ A child sustained second- and third-degree "stocking" burns to the feet after being held in hot water.

As a result of their harsh and insensitive treatment, physically abused children like Milton often are described as more disruptive and aggressive than their age-mates, with disturbances that reach across a broad spectrum of emotional and cognitive functioning (Teisl

& Cicchetti, 2008). Physical injuries may range from minor (bruises, lacerations), to moderate (scars, abrasions), to severe (burns, sprains, broken bones). These physical signs represent only the visible injuries; we will see later in this chapter that the psychological development of physically abused children often is impaired in less visible—but very serious—ways as well. We ask you to keep Milton's case in mind, since we refer to him several times throughout the chapter.

Some forms of abuse are psychological rather than physical, but carry a similar blow to a child's health and well-being. Harsh, emotionally abusive threats and put-downs from one's parents or caregivers can be as harmful to a child's development as physical abuse or neglect. **Psychological abuse** (also known as emotional abuse) includes repeated acts or omissions by the parents or caregivers that have caused, or could cause, serious behavioral, cognitive, emotional, or mental disorders. For example, parents or caregivers may use extreme or bizarre forms of punishment, such as confinement of a child in a dark closet. Psychological abuse also includes verbal threats and put-downs, habitual scapegoating, belittling, and name-calling. Psychological abuse exists, to some degree, in all forms of maltreatment, so the specific consequences of this form of maltreatment are less well understood than those of other forms of maltreatment (Glaser, 2011; Wolfe & McIsaac, 2011).

Sexual Abuse and Exploitation

ROSITA

No Haven at Home

Rosita was not quite 4 years old when her family doctor suspected that something was going on that troubled her. He expressed his concerns to child welfare, and Rosita reenacted several sexual acts for them, using dolls depicting her father and herself. "Daddy said I can play a game, and it's OK 'cause grownups do it," she hesitantly explained. Rosita made the dolls kiss, then the male doll rubbed the female doll's vagina. "But he hurt me, and it made me scared. I didn't want to get in trouble." To make matters worse, her mother became furious with Rosita and the agency when she heard the accusations, and was unwilling to ensure her daughter's protection and safety at home. "Rosita just wants a lot of attention—she's said this stuff before and I don't believe her one minute," was her mother's only comment. (Based on authors' case material.)

Rosita was sexually abused by her father and disbelieved by her mother; as a result, she faces many ongoing psychological complications. Because Rosita was seen several times throughout the course of her childhood and adolescent development, her case is discussed further in a later section of this chapter on the course of development of children and adolescents who have been sexually abused.

Sexual abuse includes fondling a child's genitals, intercourse with the child, incest, rape, sodomy, exhibitionism, and commercial exploitation through prostitution or the production of pornographic materials. The actual number of sexual abuse cases may be underreported because of the secrecy or "conspiracy of silence" that so often characterizes these cases, making determination of abuse difficult (Mitchell, Wolak, & Finkelhor, 2007). The following are actual reported cases of sexual abuse (Sedlak & Broadhurst, 1996):

▸ A 10-year-old girl who was raped by her father;

▸ Two sisters and a brother who were sexually molested by their mother's live-in boyfriend;

▸ A 4-year-old who was fondled by his father during weekend visitations.

The behavior and development of sexually abused children may be affected significantly, especially in relation to the duration or frequency of abuse, the use of force, the use of penetration, and a close relationship to the perpetrator (Berliner & Elliott, 2002). The physical health of these children may be compromised by urinary tract problems, gynecological problems, sexually transmitted diseases (including AIDS), and pregnancy (Maniglio, 2009).

About one-third of sexually abused children neither report nor exhibit visible symptoms, and about two-thirds of those who do show symptoms recover significantly during the first 12 to 18 months after the abuse (Kendall-Tackett, Williams, & Finkelhor, 2001). Nonetheless, the possibility of delayed emergence of symptoms, especially PTSD, is becoming more widely recognized (Fergusson, McLeod, & Horwood, 2013; Trickett, Noll, & Putnam, 2011). Children's reports of sexual abuse and their reactions and recovery vary depending on the nature of the sexual assault and the response of their important others, especially the mother (London et al., 2008). Many acute symptoms of sexual abuse resemble children's common reactions to stress, such as fears, increased anger, anxiety, fatigue, depression, passivity, difficulties focusing and sustaining attention, and withdrawal from usual activities.

In reaction to an abusive incident, it is common for younger children to regress temporarily, such as by becoming enuretic or easily upset or by having problems sleeping. In later childhood and early adolescence, these signs of distress may take the form of acting-out behaviors (such as delinquency, drug use, and promiscuity) or unhealthy relationships and self-destructive behavior (Trickett et al., 2011). Some sexually abused children may exhibit sexualized behaviors with other children or toys that may include excessive masturbation, age-inappropriate knowledge of sexual activity, and/or pronounced seductive or promiscuous behavior. Any of these symptoms of distress may be associated with a decline or sudden change in school performance, behavior, and peer relations.

Unlike physical abuse and neglect, sexual abuse rarely has any connection to child-rearing, discipline, or inattention to developmental needs. Rather, it constitutes a breach of trust, deception, intrusion, and exploitation of a child's innocence and status. Whereas all types of maltreatment share a common ground in relation to the abuse of power by an adult over a child, sexual abuse stands out from physical abuse and neglect in terms of these specific dynamics.

Children may also suffer trauma from commercial or sexual exploitation, such as child labor and child prostitution. Globally, as many as 10 million children may be victims of child prostitution, the sex industry, sex tourism, and pornography, although accurate statistics are not available (United Nations, 2006). Sadly, many exploited children began as victims of abuse and rape in their homes and are forced into commercial sexual activity at a young age (Cooper et al., 2005). Rates of child prostitution tend to be higher in Asia and Latin America, but an alarming growth has been recorded in Africa, North America, and Europe (Wolfe & Nayak, 2003). Poverty is the greatest factor in the child prostitution explosion, as migration of families from rural areas into cities creates unemployment, the breakdown of family structures, homelessness, and inevitably, an increase in child prostitution.

Characteristics of Children Who Suffer Maltreatment

Improvements in data-collection methods over the past decade indicate that trauma and maltreatment affect vulnerable or disadvantaged children disproportionately, as indicated by age, sex, and racial differences. For example, there is correspondence between certain types of maltreatment and children's ages. Younger children, who have the greatest need for care and supervision, are the most common victims of abuse and neglect, which corresponds to the emergence of their greater independence and to parental conflict during this developmental period. Sexual abuse, in contrast, is more common among the older age groups (>12 years). Other than for sexual abuse, the rate of victimization is inversely related to the age of the child (USDHHS, 2010).

Child maltreatment affects boys and girls almost equally except for sexual abuse, for which girls account for about 80% of the reported victims (USDHHS,

I tried to quiet my kids down, I would start shouting. When I tried to run away, everything followed me like a trail of debris. I just wanted the craziness to stop.

Like a chain reaction, a tragic combination of events can cause some predisposed individuals to maltreat a child in their care. Most of these events have one factor in common: They pose added stress for an individual who has already reached his or her limit.

Because child maltreatment usually occurs in relation to child-rearing demands, it is not surprising that maltreating parents interact with their children less often than other parents during everyday activities involving their children. In general, neglectful parents actively avoid interacting with their children, even when the child appropriately seeks attention, most likely because social interaction is unfamiliar and even unpleasant. Physically abusive parents, in contrast, tend to deliver a lot of threats or angry commands that exceed the demands of the situation when interacting with their children, rather than offer their children positive forms of guidance and praise (Azar & Wolfe, 2006; Wolfe, 1985).

Let's return to Brenda's situation and consider how her learning history, combined with her situational events, became a recipe for disaster. When her son misbehaved, she responded with a harsh combination of emotional and physical threats—the methods most familiar to her. At first, the physical punishment would stop Milton's misbehavior, but over time it led to a standoff, forcing her to increase the severity of her punishment, and the child to escalate his aversiveness to the punishment.

Brenda's cognitive perceptions and distortion of events also played a significant role in this coercive process. **Information-processing disturbances** cause maltreating parents to misperceive or mislabel typical child behavior in ways that lead to inappropriate responses and increased aggression (Berlin et al., 2011; Francis & Wolfe, 2008). They are unfamiliar with their roles as parents and with what is developmentally appropriate behavior for a child at a given age. Brenda believed not only that her son was able to understand—at age 4— what she was thinking and feeling, but also that he was able to put her needs ahead of his own.

Over time, Brenda thought Milton was misbehaving intentionally, presumably because, in her mind, he should have known better. ("I can never get him to listen—he's a troublemaker, and he knows how to push my buttons.") Some parents apply the same faulty reasoning to their own behavior as well, which results in lowered self-efficacy. ("I'm not a good mother; other mothers can get their children to do these things.") These unrealistic expectations and attributions of negative intent can lead to greater punishment for child misbehavior and less reliance on explanation and positive teaching methods (Azar & Wolfe, 2006).

Children are seen as deserving harsh punishment, and its use is rationalized as a way to maintain control. By now you can see where this process might end up.

Like a tropical storm with an unpredictable course, a conflict between the parent and child suddenly can increase in intensity and turn into a damaging hurricane, or it simply can blow over. Negative arousal and emotions are highly "conditionable," so that salient events later can trigger the same feelings. This conditioning may occur gradually and build into uncontrollable outbursts, or it may occur suddenly during highly stressful, provocative episodes of conflict (Averill, 2001).

To illustrate, imagine yourself trying to get your child ready for school each day, and going through the same frustrating chain of events: You're late for work and under pressure to get to a meeting, when your preschooler starts to fuss about wearing boots or combing hair. For all but a hearty few, this combination of stress and all-too-familiar child demands spells anger and frustration. While most of us manage to control our emotions to deal with the situation in the best possible way, parents who have deficits in child-rearing and information-processing skills may see the child as intentionally causing them to be late. Anger and arousal are powerful emotions, so rational problem solving quickly can give way to emotional and reflexive reactions.

Anger and rage are highly dependent on situational cues that usually stem from prior emotionally arousing events. In Brenda's case, certain "looks" that her son gave led her to believe that he wasn't going to comply. We discovered this interaction by videotaping the two of them playing together and then having Brenda ask Milton to straighten up the room. We played the tape back and asked Brenda to tell us whenever she felt that Milton was doing something that bothered her. She stopped the tape at several different points, telling us, "He's giving me that look," or "I know what he's thinking—why should I have to do what she says?" At this point, Brenda's tone of voice would become more tense and frustrated and her instructions to Milton more forceful and abrupt.

Although Brenda could acknowledge she was getting very angry, at first she was not able to interrupt this process and calm herself down. This demonstrates how parental arousal can be triggered by events, including past memories and current emotional tension, that may be highly specific to a particular parent–child relationship. This may lead to an overgeneralized—more angry, more aggressive—parental response, because the parent is responding impulsively to cues that in the past were associated with frustration and anger.

Neglectful parents have received far less research attention than physically abusive ones, perhaps because omissions of proper caretaking behaviors are more difficult to describe and detect than commissions

(Dubowitz & Bennett, 2007). As groups, the personality characteristics and lifestyle choices of abusive and neglectful parents overlap considerably. However, neglectful parents have more striking personality disorders and inadequate knowledge of children's needs, and they suffer more chronic patterns of social isolation than both abusive parents and parents who do not maltreat their children. Furthermore, neglectful caregivers typically disengage when they are under stress, whereas abusive parents become emotionally and behaviorally reactive. Neglectful parents try to cope with the stress of child-rearing and related family matters through escape and avoidance, which can lead to severe consequences for the child and to higher risk of substance abuse and similar coping failures for the parents (Hildyard & Wolfe, 2007).

Those seeking explanations for child sexual abuse have looked for evidence of deviant sexual histories in the adult offender, as well as environmental and cultural risk factors that play a role in the sexual exploitation of children. Yet, similar to physical abusers of children, sexual abusers are a very mixed group who defy most personality labels or psychiatric descriptors. Some are described as timid and unassertive, whereas others show a pattern of poor impulse control and domineering interpersonal style. Their common ground is a preference for sexual exploitation of children and adolescents who, because of their age and innocence, cannot consent to the activities or readily disclose the abuse to someone.

Sexual abusers of children come from many walks of life, and they are seldom discernible based on personality traits, occupation, or age (other than the conclusion that the vast majority of offenders are male). As a group, these offenders are more likely to have significant social and relationship deficits, including social isolation; difficulty forming emotionally close, trusting relationships; and low self-esteem (Marshall et al., 2008). Comorbid psychiatric disorders and substance abuse also emerge as proximate risk factors for sexual abuse of children (Fagan et al., 2002).

Persons who engage in sexual acts with minor children or youths (pedophiles) may limit their activities to incest that involves their own children, stepchildren, or other relatives, or they may victimize children outside their families (APA, 2013; Marshall et al., 2008). Significantly, over 50% of pedophiles report an awareness of their pedophilic interests before they turn 17 years old (63% of those who target male children and 50% of those who target female children), which they begin to act out, on average, by their late teens or early 20s (Abel, Osborn, & Twigg, 1993; Seto, 2008). Emerging evidence shows deficiencies in cerebral white matter in cortical regions of the brain that respond to sexual cues, suggesting that pedophilia may result from early neurodevelopmental problems that cause a partial disconnection within that network (Cantor & Blanchard, 2012; Kruger & Schiffer, 2011).

Those who victimize children develop complicated techniques to gain access to and compliance from the child, which emphasizes the sexually opportunistic and predatory nature of this behavior. Pedophiles may win the trust of the child's mother or have a relationship with a woman with a child. They may use methods to lower a child's resistance, such as initiating a friendship, playing games or giving presents, having hobbies or interests that appeal to the child, and using peer pressure (Wekerle et al., 2006; Wolak et al., 2008). They seldom resort to violence or force to gain the child's compliance; rather, they are attentive to the child's needs in order to gain the child's affection, interest, and loyalty as well as to reduce the chances that the child will report the sexual activity. Typically, sexual behavior takes place only after a period of "grooming," with a gradual indoctrination into sexual activity, underscoring how sex offenders of children are "sophisticated, calculating, and patient" (Singer, Hussey, & Strom, 1992, p. 884). As one offender asserted, "You can spot the child who is unsure of himself and target him with compliments and positive attention" (Elliott, Browne, & Kilcoyne, 1995, p. 584).

A perpetrator's efforts to establish a relationship with the child or youth, such as spending time alone with the child or singling the child out as favored or special, also may reduce the child's internal inhibition by distorting the roles of the relationship and blurring interpersonal boundaries. Special status as a teacher, religious figure, or scout leader may cover the abuser's intentions with a sense of entitlement or privilege with a child, distorting the role into one that is a central part of the child's life (Wolfe, Jaffe, et al., 2003). Sadly, children made more than 11,000 allegations of sexual abuse by over 4,000 priests between 1950 and 2002, which represents about 4% of the 110,000 priests who served during the 52 years covered by the study (U.S. Conference of Catholic Bishops, 2004).

Two meta-analyses comparing thousands of sexual offenders who targeted children and nonoffenders confirmed a link between offenders and a history of having been sexually abused during their own childhood (Jespersen, Lalumière, & Seto, 2009; Seto & Lalumière, 2010). One possibility is that negative childhood experiences—sexual abuse, as well as other forms of stress or maltreatment—set in motion a cautious, distrustful approach to intimate relationships. A history of child sexual abuse or exposure to other stressors may lead to atypical sexual interests in early adolescence for some male victims. In turn, deviant sexual fantasies provide a way of temporarily avoiding, interrupting, or reducing painful abuse-related mental states and psychiatric symptoms (Maniglio, 2011).

For example, an adolescent male with a history of unhealthy or exploitative relationships may justify using coercive and abusive actions toward others who are smaller or weaker because his other attempts at closeness have failed (Ward & Beech, 2008). His sexual interests and arousal become fused with his need for emotional closeness, which can lead to sexual preoccupation, promiscuity, and the possibility of increasing sexual deviancy as his attempts to gain intimacy escalate through sexual contact (Seto, 2008).

Certain situational factors increase children's vulnerability to sexual abuse, a fact that offenders exploit to their advantage. Offenders see children as more vulnerable if they have family problems, spend a lot of time alone, and seem unsure of themselves; they also admit to preferring victims who are attractive, trusting, and young (Elliott et al., 1995). To gain access to the child, offenders look for circumstances that create lax supervision or opportunities for them to become involved, such as parental unavailability, illness, stress, spousal abuse, or lack of emotional closeness to the child.

Child and Family Influences

Do certain child characteristics or behaviors increase the likelihood of trauma or maltreatment? Children have an uncanny ability to figure out what their parents are going to do before they actually do it, and they become amazingly accomplished at weighing the odds for desired outcomes. However, even though children might do things that are annoying, adults are fully responsible for abuse and neglect. No child—no matter how difficult to manage or how challenging to teach—ever deserves to be mistreated. Children's behavior or developmental limitations may increase the potential for abuse, but only if they are accompanied by the other critical factors noted previously. With the important exception of girls being sexually abused more often than boys, no child characteristic, such as conduct problems, has been associated with the risk of maltreatment, once environmental and adult factors are controlled (USDHHS, 2010). Unintentionally, however, the child may still play a role in the continuation or escalation of harsh or stressful relationships.

The kind of coercive family interactions that we discussed in Chapter 9 with regard to aggressive children, frequently occur in abusive families (Stith et al., 2009; Wolfe, 1999). Physically abused or neglected children, for example, may learn from an early age that misbehaving often elicits a predictable parental reaction—even though it's negative—which gives the child some

"I hate you! Never come back to my house," screamed an 8-year-old at his father as police arrested the man for attacking his wife.

sense of control. If crying and clinging are the only ways to get a parent's attention, these behaviors may escalate in intensity over time, especially if the parent fails to provide appropriate child stimulation and control.

This type of coercive interaction explains why abusive incidents occur most often during difficult—but not uncommon—episodes of child behavior such as disobedience, fighting and arguing, accidents, and dangerous behavior, which may produce anger and tension in some adults. In contrast, circumstances surrounding incidents of neglect relate more to chronic adult inadequacy that spills over into daily family functioning (Stith et al., 2009). Neglected children's early feeding problems or irritability may place an increased strain on the parents' limited child-care abilities, again setting in motion an escalation in the child's dependency needs and demands, accompanied by further parental withdrawal (Drotar, 1999).

Family circumstances, most notably conflict and marital violence, also have a causal connection to child maltreatment. In about half of the families in which adult partners are violent toward one another, one or both parents also have been violent toward a child at some point during the previous year (Edleson, 1999). Domestic conflicts and violence against women most often arise during disagreements over child-rearing, discipline, and each partner's responsibilities in child care (Gewirtz & Edleson, 2007). Children may be caught in the cross fire between angry adults, or in some cases they may instigate a marital conflict by misbehaving or demanding attention. In either case, an escalating cycle of family turmoil and violence begins, whereby children's behavioral and emotional reactions to the violence create additional stress on the marital relationship, further aggravating an already volatile situation.

The physical and psychological consequences of violence, moreover, cause abused women to be less capable of responding to their children's needs, which again increases pressure on the family system. Tragically, not only do marital violence and family turmoil frighten and disturb children in a direct manner, but the resulting fallout from these events—ranging from changes in financial status and living quarters to loss of family unity and safety—prolongs the stress and thus the harmful impact on children's development (Jaffe et al., 2011).

In a dynamic process, parental and situational factors interact over time to either increase or decrease the risk of physical abuse or neglect (MacKenzie, Kotch, & Lee, 2011). ● Figure 12.3 depicts this dynamic process in relation to three hypothetical transitional stages. These stages suggest that maladaptive interaction patterns, like adaptive ones, do not develop simply because of the predilections of the parent or child. On the contrary, these patterns are the result of complex interactions between child characteristics, parental personality and style, the history

Stage 1: Reduced tolerance for stress and disinhibition of aggression

Destabilizing factors	Compensatory factors
• Poor child-rearing preparation • Low sense of control and predictability • Stressful life events	• Supportive spouse • Socioeconomic stability • Success at work and school • Social supports and healthy models

Stage 2: Poor management of acute crises and provocation

Destabilizing factors	Compensatory factors
• Conditioned emotional arousal to child behavior • Multiple sources of anger and aggression • Belief that child's behavior is threatening or harmful to parent	• Improvement in child behavior • Community programs for parents • Coping resources

Stage 3: Habitual patterns of arousal and aggression with family members

Destabilizing factors	Compensatory factors
• Child habituates to physical punishment • Parent is reinforced for using strict control techniques • Child increases problem behavior	• Parental dissatisfaction with physical punishment • Child responds favorably to noncoercive methods • Community restraints/services

● **FIGURE 12.3** | An integrated model of physical child abuse.

Reprinted from Wolfe, 1999.

TABLE 12.4 | Diagnostic Criteria for Post-traumatic Stress Disorder　`DSM-5`

(A) Exposure to actual or threatened death, serious injury, or sexual violence in one (or more) of the following ways:

　(1) Directly experiencing the traumatic event(s).

　(2) Witnessing, in person, the event(s) as it happened to others.

　(3) Learning that the event(s) happened to a close relative or close friend. In cases of actual or threatened death of a family member or friend, the event(s) must have been violent or accidental.

　(4) Experiencing repeated or extreme exposure to aversive details of the traumatic event(s) (e.g., first responders collecting human remains; police officers repeatedly exposed to details of child abuse).

Note: Criterion A4 does not apply to exposure through electronic media, television, movies, or pictures, unless this exposure is work-related.

(B) Presence of one (or more) of the following intrusion symptoms associated with the traumatic event(s), beginning after the traumatic event(s) occurred:

　(1) Recurrent, involuntary and intrusive distressing memories of the traumatic event(s). **Note:** In young children, repetitive play may occur in which themes or aspects of the traumatic event(s) are expressed.

　(2) Recurrent distressing dreams in which the content and/or affect of the dream are related to the traumatic event(s). **Note:** In children, there may be frightening dreams without recognizable content.

　(3) Dissociative reactions (e.g., flashbacks) in which the individual feels or acts as if the traumatic event(s) were recurring. (Such reactions occur on a continuum, with the most extreme expression being a complete loss of awareness of present surroundings). **Note:** In young children, trauma-specific reenactment may occur in play.

　(4) Intense or prolonged psychological distress at exposure to internal or external cues that symbolize or resemble an aspect of the traumatic event(s).

　(5) Marked physiological reactions to internal or external cues that symbolize or resemble an aspect of the traumatic event(s).

(C) Persistent avoidance of stimuli associated with the traumatic event(s), beginning after the traumatic event(s) occurred, as evidenced by one or both of the following:

　(1) Avoidance of or efforts to avoid distressing memories, thoughts, or feelings about or closely associated with the traumatic event(s).

　(2) Avoidance of or efforts to avoid external reminders (people, places, conversations, activities, objects, situations) that arouse distressing memories, thoughts, or feelings about or closely associated with the traumatic event(s).

(D) Negative alterations in cognitions and mood associated with the traumatic event(s), beginning or worsening after the traumatic event(s) occurred, as evidenced by two (or more) of the following:

　(1) Inability to remember an important aspect of the traumatic event(s) (typically due to dissociative amnesia and not to other factors such as head injury, alcohol, or drugs).

　(2) Persistent and exaggerated negative beliefs or expectations about oneself, others, or the world (e.g., "I am bad," "No one can be trusted," "The world is completely dangerous," "My whole nervous system is permanently ruined").

　(3) Persistent distorted cognitions about the cause or consequences of the traumatic event(s) that lead the individual to blame himself/herself or others.

　(4) Persistent negative emotional state (e.g., fear, horror, anger, guilt, or shame).

　(5) Markedly diminished interest or participation in significant activities.

　(6) Feelings of detachment or estrangement from others.

　(7) Persistent inability to experience positive emotions (e.g., inability to experience happiness, satisfaction, or loving feelings).

(E) Marked alterations in arousal and reactivity associated with the traumatic event(s), beginning or worsening after the traumatic event(s) occurred, as evidenced by two (or more) of the following:

　(1) Irritable behavior and angry outbursts (with little or no provocation) typically expressed as verbal or physical aggression toward people or objects.

　(2) Reckless or self-destructive behavior.

　(3) Hypervigilance.

　(4) Exaggerated startle response.

　(5) Problems with concentration.

　(6) Sleep disturbance (e.g., difficulty falling or staying asleep or restless sleep).

(F) Duration of the disturbance (Criteria B, C, D and E) is more than 1 month.

(G) The disturbance causes clinically significant distress or impairment in social, occupational, or other important areas of functioning.

(H) The disturbance is not attributable to the physiological effects of a substance (e.g., medication, alcohol) or another medical condition.

(continues)

Specify if:

With Dissociative Symptoms: The individual's symptoms meet the criteria for post-traumatic stress disorder, and in addition, in response to the stressor, the individual experiences persistent or recurrent symptoms of either of the following:

(1) **Depersonalization:** Persistent or recurrent experiences of feeling detached from, and as if one were an outside observer of, one's mental processes of body (e.g., feeling as though one were in a dream; feeling a sense of unreality of self or body or of time moving slowly).

(2) **Derealization:** Persistent or recurrent experiences of unreality of surroundings (e.g., the world around the individual is experienced as unreal, dreamlike, distant or distorted).

Note: To use this subtype, the dissociative symptoms must not be attributable to the physiological effects of a substance (e.g., blackouts, behavior during alcohol intoxication) or another medical condition (e.g., complex partial seizures).

Specify if:

With Delayed Expression: If the diagnostic threshold is not exceeded until at least 6 months after the event (although it is understood that onset and expression of some symptoms may be immediate).

Source: Diagnostic and Statistical Manual of Mental Disorders, Fifth Edition. American Psychiatric Association.

▶ Avoidance of distressing memories, thoughts, or feelings, as well as avoidance of any reminders that arouse such thoughts or feelings.

▶ Distortions in thoughts or feelings (i.e., alterations in cognitions and mood) associated with the traumatic event(s), such as elevated fear, inability to feel positive emotions, self-blame and guilt.

▶ Symptoms of extreme arousal and reactivity, such as angry outbursts, self-destructive behavior, sleep problems, or hypervigilance (i.e., watchfulness).

PTSD symptoms usually begin within the first three months following the trauma, although a delay of many months or even years is not uncommon, especially in cases of physical and sexual abuse (Lyons-Ruth et al., 2014). Symptoms of PTSD are both conspicuous and complex. They may include intense fear, helplessness, and horror, which children may express as agitated behavior and disorganization. Some children with PTSD or partial-PTSD show many of the same symptoms as combat soldiers exposed to the horrors of war. They may experience physiological symptoms, nightmares, fears, and panic attacks either in the short term or for many years (Kirsch, Wilhelm, & Goldbeck, 2011). They may regress developmentally and display age-inappropriate behaviors, such as a fear of strangers. Children with PTSD avoid situations that could remind them of the traumatic event, or they may reenact the event in play. They may feel sadness or shame, become socially withdrawn, and/or have problems concentrating in school (Anthony, Lonigan, & Hecht, 1999).

Some key symptoms of PTSD are expressed differently in children than in adults. For example, instead of flashbacks and waking recall of the traumatic event, young children are likely to re-experience trauma in nightmares. Initially, the nightmares reflect the traumatic event, but over time they may become less specific and vague. Similarly, daytime recall may be expressed in play or through reenactment of the event or related themes. Trauma reactions of preschool children may include repetitive drawing and play focused on trauma-related themes, regressive behavior, antisocial or aggressive behavior, and destructive behavior (Perrin, Smith, & Yule, 2000).

Given these differences in how young children express their thoughts and emotions, DSM-5 criteria include different age-related manifestations for children age 6 and under (shown in Table 12.5). This category was added in DSM-5 to reflect findings that modified (simplified) criteria can more accurately diagnose PTSD among younger children. A principle difference between criteria for younger children and those for older children reflects younger children's use of play reenactment, rather than words, to display their feelings and memories (see Criterion B). Also, criteria for younger children combine symptoms of avoidance and symptoms of negative alterations in cognition into one category, using more age-appropriate examples.

Prevalence and Course

About 14% of children 2 to 17 years of age in the United States report lifetime exposure to natural disaster and about two-thirds experience one or more potentially traumatic events by age 16 (Becker-Blease,

TABLE 12.5 Diagnostic Criteria for Post-traumatic Stress Disorder for Children 6 Years and Younger

DSM-5

(A) In children 6 years and younger, exposure to actual or threatened death, serious injury, or sexual violence in one (or more of the following ways):

    (1) Directly experiencing the traumatic event(s).

    (2) Witnessing, in person, the event(s) as it occurred to other, especially primary caregivers. **Note:** Witnessing does not include events that are witnessed only in electronic media, television, movies, or pictures.

    (3) Learning that the traumatic event(s) occurred to a parent or caregiving figure.

(B) Presence of one (or more) of the following intrusion symptoms associated with the traumatic event(s), beginning after the traumatic event(s) occurred:

    (1) Recurrent, involuntary, and intrusive distressing memories of the traumatic event(s). **Note:** Spontaneous and intrusive memories may not necessarily appear distressing and may be experienced as play reenactment.

    (2) Recurrent distressing dreams in which the content and/or affect of the dream are related to the traumatic event(s). **Note:** It may not be possible to ascertain that the frightening content is related to the traumatic event(s).

    (3) Dissociative reactions (e.g., flashbacks) in which the child feels or acts as if the traumatic event(s) were recurring. (Such reactions may occur on a continuum, with the most extreme expression being a complete loss of awareness of present surroundings). Such trauma-specific reenactment may occur in play.

    (4) Intense or prolonged psychological distress at exposure to internal or external cues that symbolize or resemble an aspect of the traumatic event(s).

    (5) Marked physiological reactions to reminders of the traumatic event(s).

(C) One (or more) of the following symptoms, representing either persistent avoidance of stimuli associated with the traumatic event(s) or negative alterations in cognitions and mood associated with the traumatic event(s), must be present, beginning after the event(s) or worsening after the event(s):

Persistent Avoidance of Stimuli

    (1) Avoidance of or efforts to avoid activities, places, or physical reminders that arouse recollections of the traumatic event(s).

    (2) Avoidance of or efforts to avoid people, conversations, or interpersonal situations that arouse recollections of the traumatic event(s)..

Negative Alterations in Cognitions

    (3) Substantially increased frequency of negative emotional states (e.g., fear, guilt, sadness, shame, confusion).

    (4) Markedly diminished interest or participation in significant activities, including constriction of play.

    (5) Socially withdrawn behavior.

    (6) Persistent reduction in expression of positive emotions.

(D) Alterations in arousal and reactivity associated with the traumatic event(s), beginning or worsening after the traumatic event(s) occurred, as evidenced by two (or more) of the following:

    (1) Irritable behavior and angry outbursts (with little or no provocation) typically expressed as verbal or physical aggression toward people or objects (including extreme temper tantrums.

    (2) Hypervigilance.

    (3) Exaggerated startle response.

    (4) Problems with concentration.

    (5) Sleep disturbance (e.g., difficulty falling or staying asleep or restless sleep).

(E) The duration of the disturbance is more than a month.

(F) The disturbance causes clinically significant distress or impairment in relationships with parents, siblings, peers, or with school behavior.

(G) The disturbance is not attributable to the physiological effects of a substance (e.g., medication or alcohol) or another medical condition.

Specify if:

With dissociative symptoms: The individual's symptoms meet the criteria for post-traumatic stress disorder, and the individual experiences persistent or recurrent symptoms of either of the following:

    (1) **Depersonalization:** Persistent or recurrent experiences of feeling detached from, and as if one were an outside observer of, one's mental processes or body (e.g., feeling as though one were in a dream; feeling a sense of unreality of self or body or of time moving slowly).

(continues)

(2) Derealization: Persistent or recurrent experiences of unreality of surroundings (e.g., the world around the individual is experienced as unreal, dreamlike, distant, or distorted). **Note:** To use this subtype, the dissociative symptoms must not be attributable to the physiological effects of a substance (e.g., blackouts) or another medical condition (e.g., complex partial seizures).

Specify if:

With delayed expression: If the full diagnostic criteria are not met until at least 6 months after the event (although the onset and expression of some symptoms may be immediate).

Source: Diagnostic and Statistical Manual of Mental Disorders, 5th ed. American Psychiatric Association.

Turner, & Finkelhor, 2010; Copeland et al., 2007). Most do not develop PTSD, except after several traumas or a history of anxiety. Nevertheless, a significant number of children and adolescents who are exposed to trauma develop PTSD, and many others experience some PTSD symptoms as well as other emotional disturbances (Briggs-Gowan et al., 2010; McLaughlin et al., 2010). In a large national sample of over 4,000 adolescents 12 to 17 years of age in the United States, the 6-month prevalence of PTSD was 3.7% for boys and 6.3% for girls. In addition, nearly 75% of youngsters with PTSD displayed a comorbid diagnosis of depression and/or substance abuse (Kilpatrick et al., 2003). Thus, PTSD is a significant problem, especially among children and youths who experience multiple or cumulative forms of trauma such as child maltreatment, exposure to domestic violence, bullying, assaults, and other forms of victimization (Cloitre et al., 2009).

The prevalence of PTSD symptoms is appreciably greater in children who are exposed to life-threatening events or prolonged interpersonal trauma (such as abuse) than children who are exposed to less severe trauma (Furr et al., 2010). For example, nearly 40% of children exposed to the Buffalo Creek Dam collapse in 1972 showed probable PTSD symptoms 2 years after the disaster (Fletcher, 2003). PTSD in children is also strongly correlated with degree of exposure. In children exposed to a schoolyard sniper attack, proximity to the attack was directly related to the risk of developing PTSD symptoms (Pynoos et al., 1987). In effect, traumatic events that have a personal or direct impact on a child are more likely to lead to strong reactions and more persistent symptoms of PTSD (Nader & Fletcher, 2014).

As many as half of victims of maltreatment involving sexual abuse or combined sexual and physical abuse meet criteria for PTSD during childhood or adolescence (Martin et al., 2013; Nooner et al., 2012; Scott, Wolfe, & Wekerle, 2003). The prevalence of PTSD among adults is equally disturbing: About one-third of the childhood victims of sexual abuse, physical abuse, or neglect meet criteria for lifetime PTSD (Koenen &

Widom, 2009; Widom, 1999). Among adults, women are twice as likely to develop PTSD as men, and women's symptoms last up to 4 times longer; but gender differences are less apparent among children and youths (Nader & Fletcher, 2014).

> The child trapped in an abusive environment is faced with formidable tasks of adaptation. She must find a way to preserve a sense of trust in people who are untrustworthy, safety in a situation that is unsafe, control in a situation that is terrifyingly unpredictable, power in a situation of helplessness.
>
> —From Herman (1992)

This statement by prominent clinician and researcher Judith Herman captures the essence of the world of children and youths who have suffered maltreatment or fear. Trauma and maltreatment are more than physical pain and transitory fear; to a child or adolescent, these events often represent threats to their emerging sense of self, their world, and their feelings of safety and well-being. We return to Rosita's case to illustrate this dramatic impact:

ROSITA

Feeling Trapped

At age 6, Rosita was brought to the hospital following two suicidal/self-harm gestures. While camping, she wrapped a rope that hung from a tree around her neck and her foster mother grabbed it and untangled it. She did not appear to be hurt, but she sat and cried for a long time while her foster mother cuddled her.

"Rosita is preoccupied with themes of death and self-harm, in her drawings, stories at school, and even with her classmates," her teacher explained. "She has problems making friends, because she acts silly when she tries to join their games. More than once she's asked other children to touch her vagina, and she has tried to put her finger in one girl's vagina. Needless to say, this

(continues)

has alarmed other parents and teachers. But she's such a needy child—she'll go from a temper tantrum to becoming clingy in a matter of seconds."

Rosita's life became more settled, and by age 9 her school performance had improved noticeably. However, at age 15, her psychological condition rapidly grew worse. She made suicide attempts and began cutting her arm with glass and other sharp objects. When I saw her after her release from the hospital, she was very distraught, and felt unloved and abandoned. Her feelings of depression and anxiety were evident: "I'll jump or get really scared, for no reason. I just want to go somewhere and hide, and get away from people," she explained. "I can't trust anybody except for my friend Mary—but even she thinks I'm weird when I get like this. It's like I'm trapped or caught, and can't get away." My interview went on to reveal Rosita's sleeping problems and her constant crying and sadness.

Rosita had never forgotten the abuse she experienced as a child, and sometimes had intrusive reminders of what happened. "I feel tied in a knot, and I feel like I'm going crazy or something. That's when I might start cutting on my arm or something, just to feel like I'm not dreaming, that I'm real." Sometimes she even blamed herself for losing her family years ago, explaining that "no matter how bad it was I wish no one had ever found out, because it wasn't worth all the pain I'm going through." (Based on authors' case material.)

Rosita lacks a sense of self-esteem and a sense of the future. She is very vulnerable to recurring victimization because she lacks self-awareness and has limited self-protection skills. She feels a terrible loss and ambivalence over her family, sometimes blaming herself for the abuse or wishing it had never been discovered. Although she is a verbal and insightful young woman, she often is overcome with worries, anxiety, fear, and emotional distress related to her current circumstances.

What happens to the development of children who suffered trauma or maltreatment during their important formative years? Normal development follows a predictable, organized course (see Chapter 1), beginning with the child's mastery of physiological regulation (eating, sleeping) and continuing throughout the development of higher skills, such as problem solving and peer relationships. However, under abnormal and highly stressful circumstances, such as abuse and neglect, predictability and organization are disrupted and thrown off course, which often results in developmental impairments and limited adaptation.

Children with histories of trauma or maltreatment not only must face acute and unpredictable parental outbursts or betrayal, but also must adapt to environmental circumstances that pose developmental challenges. These influences include the more dramatic events, such as marital violence and separation of family members, as well as the mundane but important everyday activities that may be disturbing or upsetting, such as unfriendly interactions, few learning opportunities, and a chaotic lifestyle. Children who are sexually abused undergo pronounced interruptions in their developing view of themselves and the world that result in significant emotional and behavioral changes, indicative of their attempts to cope with such events. Because the source of stress and fear is centralized in their family, children who are maltreated are challenged regularly to find ways to adapt that pose the least risk and offer maximum protection and opportunity for growth (Collishaw et al., 2007).

The course of PTSD may begin during childhood with abuse-specific fears, such as fear of being alone and fear of men, as well as idiosyncratic fears related to specific events of abuse, such as fear of sleeping (van der Kolk, 2007). PTSD-related symptoms also are more likely to occur if the abuse was chronic and the perpetrator relied on a method of coercion or trickery to force compliance (Williams, 2003). But child trauma, like other forms of adversity during childhood, does not affect each child in a predictable or consistent fashion. On the contrary, the impact of trauma depends not only on the severity and chronicity of the specific events, but also on how the events interact with the child's individual and family characteristics. Without proper support and assistance, young children who initially may have achieved normal developmental milestones can show a dramatic downturn in their developmental progress as a result of chronic or acute trauma or similar types of stress (Crooks & Wolfe, 2007). Consequently, their core developmental processes are impaired, which results in emotional and behavioral problems ranging from speech and language delays to criminal behavior.

Associated Problems and Adult Outcomes

Longitudinal findings suggest that PTSD can become a chronic psychiatric disorder for some children and youths, persisting for decades and in some cases for a lifetime (Nader & Fletcher, 2014). Children and youths with chronic PTSD may display a developmental course marked by remissions and relapses. In a less common delayed variant, children exposed to a traumatic event may not exhibit symptoms until months or years later, when a situation similar to the original trauma triggers the onset of PTSD (Andrews et al., 2007). For example, attempts to develop sexual intimacy during adulthood may trigger PTSD in a survivor of childhood sexual abuse.

The developmental disruptions and impairments that accompany many forms of trauma and stress set in motion a series of events that increase the likelihood of adaptational failure. As stated earlier, not all children who face these developmental challenges will have psychopathology—let alone the same form of psychopathology—but they are at a much greater risk for significant emotional and adjustment problems.

There are often patterns linking the nature of child or adolescent trauma and subsequent adult expressions of either PTSD or its many associated features relating to fear, emotion regulation, avoidance, and physiological arousal. For example, adolescents and adults with histories of physical abuse and exposure to violence between parents are at increased risk of developing interpersonal problems marked by their own acts of aggression and violence or of violent victimization by others (Berlin, Appleyard, & Dodge, 2011; El-Sheikh & Erath, 2011). This relationship between being abused as a child and becoming abusive toward others as an adult is known as the **cycle-of-violence hypothesis**. Although victims of violence have a greater chance of becoming perpetrators of violence, this relationship is not inevitable and it can be attenuated through early intervention (Berlin et al., 2011).

Persons with histories of sexual abuse, on the other hand, are more likely than nonvictims to develop chronic impairments in self-esteem, to have physical health problems, and to lack emotional and behavioral self-regulation (Hillberg, Hamilton-Giachritsis, & Dixon, 2011; Irish, Kobayashi, & Delahanty, 2010). As adulthood approaches, developmental impairments that stem from child sexual abuse can lead to more pervasive and chronic psychiatric disorders and health problems, including anxiety and panic disorders, depression, eating disorders, sexual problems, and personality disturbances (Chapman et al., 2007; Maniglio, 2009; Paras et al., 2009). As we see below, some of the more significant impairments from which many sexual abuse victims suffer stem from PTSD and associated chronic regulatory problems with mood and affect (Campbell et al., 2008).

Traumatized children frequently exhibit symptoms of disorders other than PTSD, and children with other disorders may have PTSD as a comorbid diagnosis (Famularo et al., 1996). For example, PTSD that occurs in children traumatized by fires, hurricanes, or chronic maltreatment may worsen or lead to disruptive behavior disorders (Amaya-Jackson & March, 1995). In the following sections, we examine four prominent outcomes associated with trauma and PTSD—mood and affect disturbances, emotional and behavioral problems, sexual adjustment, and unhealthy relationships. We discuss these outcomes based on the extant literature on child maltreatment, as they are more generally representative of child victims of trauma and stress.

Mood and Affect Disturbances

Some say that traumatic events, such as maltreatment, affect children to their very soul, since they disrupt and impair so many significant childhood memories and experiences. Perhaps this is why symptoms of depression, emotional distress, and suicidal ideation are common among children with histories of physical, emotional, and sexual abuse and why they often lead to PTSD (Crooks & Wolfe, 2007). As noted, the causes of these longer-term symptoms and problems sometimes can be avoided if children are provided with support by nonoffending family members and are given opportunities to develop healthy coping strategies and social supports. If symptoms of depression and mood disturbance go unrecognized, however, they are likely to increase during late adolescence and adulthood and can lead to suicide attempts and self-mutilating behavior, especially among those who have been sexually or physically abused since childhood (Fitzgerald et al., 2008; Mironova et al., 2011).

Similarly, teens with histories of maltreatment have a much greater risk of substance abuse that, in turn, increases the risk of other adjustment problems (Clark et al., 2010; Jones et al., 2013). Perhaps as a result of their chronic emotional pain, some teens and adults attempt to cope with unpleasant memories and current stressors by abusing alcohol and drugs in a futile effort to reduce or avoid their distress. Substance abuse may also temporarily bolster self-esteem and reduce feelings of isolation. Childhood sexual abuse also can lead to eating disorders, such as anorexia nervosa and bulimia nervosa (Murray, Macdonald, & Fox, 2008).

Many women, as well as men, with histories of childhood sexual abuse face lifelong struggles in establishing close and trusting relationships.

Walled Away

"What I would end up doing was separating from the physical feeling and couldn't comprehend the physical pain and emotional sensation. The only word I can use now—I didn't have the word when I was five—the word I use now is rape, and the only way I could deal with that was I would separate into the wallpaper and the wallpaper was all different ballerinas and different poses and what I could see from them was that they didn't move. They were always smiling or they always had this look on their face and they couldn't be touched. They just stood still. So I would become this ballerina and I couldn't be touched and whatever he did to me I couldn't feel it because I was in the wall."

"The body mends soon enough. The broken spirit, however, takes the longest to heal," by an adult survivor of sexual abuse. Transcribed from *The Nature of Things with David Suzuki*, executive producer, Michael Adler, for the Canadian Broadcasting Corporation, originally aired on October 6, 1994.

PTSD affects a significant number of men and women who have been subjected to severe physical or sexual abuse during childhood, but its expression may vary. Like Rosita, some adults may be haunted by intrusive thoughts or feelings of being trapped or, like Celia, they may dissociate or become emotionally numb, as they did originally to escape from the pain and fear.

In reaction to emotional and physical pain from abusive experiences, children or adults voluntarily or involuntarily may induce an altered state of consciousness known as **dissociation**, which can be adaptive when neither resistance nor escape are possible (Valentino et al., 2008). The process allows the victim to feel detached from the body or self, as if what is happening is not happening to him or her. Almost all people dissociate in minor ways, such as daydreaming, but abuse victims may rely on this form of psychological escape to the extent that profound disruptions to self and memory can occur (Macfie, Cicchetti, & Toth, 2001). Over time, this fragmentation of experience and affect can progress into borderline disorder, dissociative identity disorder, or chronic pain (Briere, Hodges, & Godbout, 2010; Raphael & Widom, 2011; Widom, Czaja, & Paris, 2009).

Emotional and Behavioral Problems

Girls and boys tend to differ in the ways they process and express their turmoil and symptoms of PTSD. Girls tend to show more internalizing signs of distress, such as shame and self-blame; boys, on the other hand, tend to show heightened levels of physical and verbal aggression (Wekerle et al., 2008).

It comes as no surprise that the relationships children have with their peers and teachers typically mirror the models of relationships they know best. Instead of a healthy sense of autonomy and self-respect, models of relationships among children who experience violence or maltreatment have elements of victim and victimizer—those who rule and those who submit—and during interactions with peers, such children may alternate between being the aggressor and being the victim (Dodge, Pettit, & Bates, 1994a). Their strategies for adaptation, such as hypervigilance and fear, evolve to become highly responsive to threatening or dangerous situations. These strategies conflict, however, with the new challenges of school and peer groups. As a result, some children with histories of maltreatment may be more distracted by aggressive stimuli, and they may misread the intentions of their peers and teachers as being more hostile than they actually are (Dodge et al., 1994a).

The development of empathy and social sensitivity for others during the preschool years are prerequisites for the development of positive, reciprocal peer relationships. Physically abused and neglected children, however, show less skill at recognizing or responding to distress in others, since they have no experience with this (Smetana et al., 1999). Observational studies of the behavior of maltreated children and their nonmaltreated peers reveal that physically abused children engage in more stealing behavior, and neglected children engage in more cheating behavior and less rule-compatible behavior (Cicchetti & Valentino, 2006; Koenig, Cicchetti, & Rogosch, 2004).

Children with histories of physical abuse or neglect stand out as having the most severe and wide-ranging problems in school and interpersonal adjustment. Their performance on standardized tests of reading, language, and math is worse than that of other children (Mills et al., 2011). Teachers who are unaware of their backgrounds describe them as lacking maturity and academic readiness—pointing out their problems with completing schoolwork, lack of initiative, over-reliance on teachers for help, and behavior that is both aggressive toward and withdrawn from their peers (Egeland et al., 2002). This pattern of poor adjustment often persists, contributing to higher rates of physical and mental health problems in later adolescence and adulthood (Clark, Thatcher, & Martin, 2010; Trickett, Negriff et al., 2011).

Longitudinal studies of girls who were sexually abused in childhood or early adolescence reveal deleterious effects across a host of biopsychosocial domains (the impact on men has received less attention, but similar patterns have been reported; Wolfe, Francis, &

Straatman, 2006). The most illustrative of these studies followed a sample of sexually abused girls for 23 years, documenting problems and concerns at home and school and with peers. The pattern and extent of harm to these girls was substantial: compared to a comparison group of girls who were not abused, those with histories of sexual abuse had significant neurodevelopmental differences in their responses to stress; earlier onsets of puberty; greater cognitive deficits; more mental health problems (especially depression and PTSD); higher rates of obesity; and more major illnesses and health-care utilization. They also had higher rates of dropping out of high school, self-mutilation, physical and sexual revictimization, teen motherhood, drug and alcohol abuse, and domestic violence in adulthood (Trickett, Noll et al., 2011).

Sexual Adjustment

Sexual abuse, in particular, can also lead to **traumatic sexualization**, in which a child's sexual knowledge and behavior are shaped in developmentally inappropriate ways. About 35% of preschoolers who have been sexually abused show age-inappropriate sexual behaviors, such as French-kissing, open masturbation, and genital exposure (Friedrich & Trane, 2002).

For some children, the offenders' means of enticement—gifts, privileges, affection, and special attention—teaches them that their own sexual behavior is a means to an end. Thus, the abused child may attempt to sexualize interpersonal relationships by indiscriminately hugging and kissing strange adults and children (i.e., signs of disinhibited social engagement disorder, discussed above), acts that are relatively uncommon among children who were not sexually abused (Cosentino et al., 1995). For others, however, sexual behavior is associated with strong emotions, such as fear, disgust, shame, and confusion. These feelings may translate into distorted views about the body and sexuality, in some cases leading to weight problems, eating disorders, poor physical health care, and physically self-destructive behaviors (Trickett, Noll et al., 2011).

Although sexualized behaviors are more common among younger abused children, they sometimes re-emerge during adolescence or young adulthood in the guise of promiscuity, prostitution, sexual aggression, and victimization of others (Tricket, Noll et al., 2011; Wilson & Widom, 2011). In fact, a history of any type of maltreatment among males is a significant risk factor for inappropriate sexual behaviors, alienation, and social incompetence during adolescence (Salter et al., 2003; Tewksbury, 2007). Women with childhood histories of sexual abuse, in particular, are more likely to report difficulties during adulthood related to sexual adjustment; these difficulties range from low sexual arousal to intrusive flashbacks, disturbing sensations, and feelings of guilt, anxiety, and low self-esteem concerning their sexuality (Merrill et al., 2003).

Because their normal development of self-awareness and self-protection was severely compromised, adult survivors of child sexual abuse may become less capable of identifying risky situations or persons or knowing how to respond to unwanted sexual or physical attention. Consequently, both men and women who were sexually abused as children are more likely to fall victim to further trauma and violence, such as rape or domestic violence, during adulthood (McIntyre & Spatz Widom, 2011; Widom, Czaja, & Dutton, 2008; Wolfe et al., 2006).

Unhealthy Relationships

Does violence beget violence, as predicted by the cycle-of-violence hypothesis discussed above? Although many persons convicted of heinous crimes and violence against others report histories of child abuse and neglect, most children who experience abuse or other traumas do not go on to commit crimes. How do we reconcile this obvious, but complicated, connection between victim and victimizer roles?

Consider the developmental importance of adolescence. This developmental stage may represent a critical transition between being a victim of child maltreatment and the future likelihood of becoming abusive or being abused as an adult (Scott et al., 2003). Social dating, a favorite—and significant—adolescent pastime, can be a testing ground wherein one's knowledge and expectations about relationships are played out. Youths who have learned to adapt to violence and intimidation as a way of life, and who lack suitable alternative role models or experiences, are more likely to enter the social dating arena with inappropriate expectations about relationships.

Indeed, youths (girls as well as boys) who grew up in violent homes report more violence—especially verbal abuse and threats—toward their dating partners and toward themselves (Wolfe et al., 2004). Dating violence that occurs during adolescence, when combined with a history of violence in their own family, is a strong pre-relationship predictor of intimate violence during early adulthood and marriage (White & Widom, 2003). Thus, adolescence may be the middle stage, or initiation period, in the formation of a violent dynamic in intimate partnerships.

As we said, most children with histories of maltreatment or trauma do not become violent offenders or child abusers as young adults. Nonetheless, there is a significant connection between these events and subsequent arrests as a juvenile or an adult, even among girls, or engaging in sexual and physical violence as a young adult, especially for males (Campbell et al., 2008; Lansford et al., 2007). A history of maltreatment is associated with an earlier mean age at first offense and a higher frequency of offenses, as well as a higher proportion of chronic offenses (Widom, 1989). Also, for about one in five mothers, a history of child physical abuse (but not neglect) was associated with physical abuse of their offspring (Berlin et al., 2011).

Growing up with power-based, authoritarian methods—even if they do not result in physical injuries or identified maltreatment—can be toxic to relationships and social patterns. Many investigators believe that the prolonged and significant harm created by acts of child maltreatment by caregivers stems from the emotional and psychological damages implicit in such acts. In other words, child maltreatment involves more than physical harm to a child. Such acts by caregivers undermine the child's basic sense of trust and safety, leading to lifelong struggles in their interpersonal relationships and sense of well-being (Wekerle & Wolfe, 2014; Wolfe & McIsaac, 2011). Even the amount of routine violence—frequently being hit with objects or physically punished—that one experiences as a child is significantly associated with violent delinquent behavior later in life (Straus, 2001). A study that links childhood violence and adult criminal behavior is described in A Closer Look 12.2.

A CLOSER **LOOK** 12.2

What Are the Long-Term Criminal Consequences of Child Maltreatment?

This important question has plagued the general public and the field of child maltreatment, from therapists and educators to policy makers and criminal justice officials. Cathy Widom (1996) addressed this question by examining the criminal records of over 900 individuals subjected as children to physical or sexual abuse or neglect prior to age 12, along with a matched cohort of children who were not maltreated. Both groups were followed into adolescence and early adulthood to determine whether they engaged in criminal or delinquent behavior as adolescents or adults.

The results are telling: Of the people who experienced any type of child maltreatment (physical abuse, sexual abuse, or neglect), 27% were arrested as juveniles, as compared with 17% of their nonabused counterparts. The same pattern continued into adulthood: 42% of the abused/neglected group, as compared with 33% of the controls, had arrest records as adults. Consistent with the cycle-of-violence hypothesis, those with histories of physical abuse (21%), neglect (20%), or both (16%) were particularly likely to be arrested for committing a violent crime (Maxfield & Widom, 1996).

One disturbing result is that women with histories of physical abuse and neglect were significantly more likely than women who were not maltreated to be arrested for a violent act (7% vs. 4%), whereas this relationship was barely significant for men (26% vs. 22%). Notably, persons with histories of sexual abuse were no different from the other maltreated children in their rates of criminal offenses.

But what about sex crimes? Are persons who were sexually abused during childhood more likely to commit sexual offenses, as suggested by the backgrounds of the known sexual offenders? If all types of abuse and neglect are combined, the odds of being arrested for a sex crime were 2 times greater for victims of maltreatment than for nonvictims. However, if maltreatment backgrounds were broken down by type, only those with physical abuse and neglect backgrounds had increased arrests for sex crimes; those with sexual abuse backgrounds did not (this finding remained when only male subjects were compared). Children who were sexually abused were about as likely as the controls to be arrested later for any sex crime, and less likely than victims of physical abuse and neglect (see the accompanying figure).

Thus, although any type of maltreatment puts victims at higher risk for criminal behavior, persons who were sexually abused in childhood are less likely than victims of physical abuse or neglect to commit a sex crime, and no more likely than demographically similar individuals.

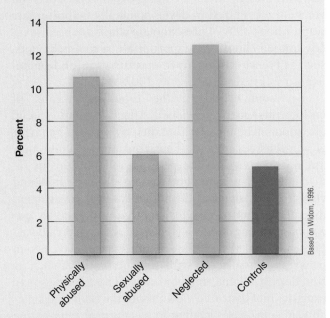

Sex crimes and maltreatment backgrounds

Causes

By definition, PTSD originates from severe trauma and/or threat that overwhelms a person's emotional, social, and biological capabilities. In this section, we examine the ways in which trauma affects critical homeostatic functions that, in turn, cause PTSD. Full- or partial-symptom PTSD can strike at any time throughout the life span. Its course depends on the age of the child or adolescent when trauma event(s) occurred and the nature of those events.

Because traumatic experience is filtered cognitively and emotionally before it can be appraised as an extreme threat, how trauma is experienced depends on a number of factors, including the child's developmental level and pre-disaster characteristics, such as level of anxiety and stress; cognitive appraisal of the threat and coping style; and characteristics of the disaster or traumatic experience, among other factors (Furr et al., 2010; Weems et al., 2007). In one study of children 6 years of age or younger who had PTSD, it was found that symptoms continued for 2 years after the event even with treatment (Scheeringa et al., 2005). This finding raises the troubling possibility that very young children who are vulnerable to developing PTSD after experiencing trauma may have an increased vulnerability to a more chronic course of the disorder, perhaps related to the impact of trauma on the developing brain (Bremner, 2007; Lyons-Ruth et al., 2014). Despite these differences related to age and timing, exposure to horrific or frightening events is traumatic to nearly all children.

Understanding the major factors that influence the development of PTSD requires consideration of the basic psychological and developmental processes that are impaired or delayed because of trauma, stress, or maltreatment. We examine the primary factors that contribute to adjustment after trauma, beginning with early attachment and affect regulation—the building blocks of the development of important self-regulatory and interpersonal competencies that can be compromised by trauma, stress, maltreatment, or related events. Whereas the diagnosis of PTSD may apply to only a minority of maltreated or traumatized children, PTSD *symptoms* in childhood, rather than a PTSD *diagnosis,* may serve to interfere with important psychological and neurobiological mechanisms. Over time, these symptoms may develop into delays and impairments that increase the likelihood of PTSD, as discussed below. Again, we reference the adjustment of maltreated children to illustrate these processes.

A common postulate of psychological causes of PTSD centers on the child's efforts to integrate a traumatic event into his or her existing cognitive view of the world, especially in cases in which the trauma stems from someone who cares for them and is in a position of trust. In simple learning terms, a traumatic experience can result in an individual's long-term response that continues well beyond the original stressor (Baum, O'Keefe, & Davidson, 1990). The process of conditioning—that is, the manner by which traumatic episodes become associated with particular eliciting stimuli such as odors, locations, or situations—can lead to overreactions that interfere with normal daily activities. In addition to the original event(s), major and minor stressful life events often occur as a result of the original traumatic event. For example, disclosure of sexual abuse gives rise to both immediate events (e.g., change in living arrangements, arrest of the perpetrator) and long-term events (e.g., loss of contact with the perpetrator) that can also reduce an individual's coping resources. These additional stressors can create a chronic, stress-filled lifestyle that disguises the original source of trauma or maltreatment.

Poor Emotion Regulation

Trauma, stress, and maltreatment can disrupt the important process of parent–child attachment and can interfere with children's ability to seek comfort and to regulate their own physiological and emotional processes. Parent–child attachment and the home climate play a critical role in emotion regulation, another early developmental milestone. As noted in Chapter 2, **emotion regulation** refers to the ability to modulate or control the intensity and expression of feelings and impulses, especially intense ones, in an adaptive manner (Kim & Cicchetti, 2010). For example, without consistent stimulation, comfort, and routine to aid in the formation of a secure attachment, maltreated infants and toddlers have considerable difficulty establishing a reciprocal, consistent pattern of interaction with their caregivers. Instead, they show a pattern described as *insecure–disorganized attachment,* characterized by a mixture of approach and avoidance, helplessness, apprehension, and a general disorientation (Cyr et al., 2010). The lack of a secure, consistent basis for relationships places maltreated children at greater risk of falling behind in their cognitive and social development and can result in problems regulating their emotions and behavior with others. Emotions serve as important internal monitoring and guidance systems; they are designed to appraise events as beneficial or dangerous and to provide motivation for action. Poor emotion regulation, in contrast, is at the heart of PTSD.

Because emotions provide important signals about our internal and external worlds, children must learn to interpret and respond to them appropriately. Most children learn this naturally through the emotional expressions and explanations given by their caregivers. Maltreated children, on the other hand, live in a world of emotional turmoil and extremes, making it difficult for them to understand, label, and regulate their internal states (Shipman et al., 2007). Expressions of affect, such as crying or signals of distress, may trigger disapproval, avoidance, or abuse, so maltreated youngsters tend to inhibit their emotional expression and regulation and remain more fearful and on alert. Similarly, they show increased attention to anger- and threat-related signals such as facial expressions, and less attention to other emotional expressions (Masten et al., 2008; Shackman, Shackman, & Pollak, 2007). When a new situation that involves a stranger or peer triggers emotional reactions, these children do not have the benefit of a caring smile or words from a familiar adult to assure them that things are okay (El-Sheikh & Erath, 2011).

Difficulties modulating emotions can be expressed as depressive reactions as well as intense angry outbursts. Accordingly, as maltreated children grow older and face new situations involving peers and other adults, poor emotional regulation becomes more and more problematic, resulting in unusual and self-harmful behaviors, such as Rosita's attempts to cut herself (Mironova et al., 2011). Over time, this inability to regulate emotions is associated with PTSD as well as other internalizing disorders, such as depression and fearfulness, and externalizing disorders, such as hostility, aggression, and various forms of acting out (Brensilver et al., 2011; Teisl & Cicchetti, 2008).

Emerging View of Self and Others

As normal development progresses, regulation of affect and behavior becomes less dependent on the caregiver and more and more autonomous (parents often use the vernacular expression, "terrible twos"). Toddlers' developing self-regulation is now applied to new situations, which further strengthens their emerging view of themselves and others. Importantly, children form complex mental representations of people, relationships, and the world during this developmental period. Their emerging view of themselves and their surroundings is fostered by healthy parental guidance and control that invoke concern for the welfare of others. To the degree that these opportunities are available to children with PTSD or with histories of maltreatment, emotional and behavioral problems are more likely to appear as a result of their maladaptive view of themselves and others.

Representational models of oneself and others are significant because they contain experience, knowledge, and expectations that carry forward to new situations (Cicchetti & Lynch, 1995). For example, consider how a child's internalized belief that "My mother is usually there for me when I need her" or that "I am loved and worthy of love" shapes his basic beliefs about himself and others, and how these ideas reflect a sense of well-being and connection. Maltreated children, in contrast, often lack these core positive beliefs about themselves and their world. Instead, they may develop negative representational models of themselves and others based on a sense of inner "badness," self-blame, shame, or rage, all of which further impair their ability to regulate their affective responses (Simon, Feiring, & McElroy, 2010; Valentino et al., 2008).

Feelings of powerlessness and betrayal often are described by children and adults who have been victims of maltreatment—feelings that become salient components of their self-identity (van der Kolk, 2007; Wolfe et al., 2003). In a situation of powerlessness, the child's will, desire, and sense of self-efficacy are thwarted and rebuked; these circumstances are often linked to fears, worries, and depression. In the words of one survivor, "It's as if the world was evil, it's coming to get you, and you could do almost nothing to defend from it" (Lisak, 1994, p. 533). Betrayal involves the degree to which the child feels the perpetrator gained his confidence through manipulation and coercion, as well as the position of trust or authority held by the perpetrator. As a consequence, the child's emotional needs may be compromised by intense and contradictory feelings of the need for closeness and the fear of it.

One's sense of personal power or self-efficacy can be undermined by significant trauma, stress, or maltreatment, as such events may devalue the child as a person. Feelings of betrayal can also challenge an individual's sense of self, because the person the individual depended on violated that trust and confidence. Such feelings may not be identified until years later, once the individual reaches an age at which he or she can recognize this betrayal dynamic as the source of feelings of self-blame, guilt, and powerlessness (Freyd, DePrince, & Gleaves, 2007; Williams, 2003). Thus, they are a significant aspect of the criteria for a diagnosis of PTSD.

Emotional reactions elicited by harsh punishment or sexual exploitation require the child to search for an answer to a fundamental question concerning responsibility and blame: "Why did this happen to me?" The previous quotes about self-esteem illustrate how some sexually abused children feel responsible for failing to recognize the abuse, for participating in the abuse, for causing their families' reactions to disclosure, for failing to avoid or control the abuse, and for failing to protect themselves. Rather than acknowledge or believe that one's own parents or a trusted adult could be the person at fault, some maltreated children may ascribe nonmalevolent intentions to the offender that can then be used to explain and justify to others their family problems and disruption. Shifting the blame to themselves or to situational factors that are less important than one's own parents provides a more acceptable explanation (McGee, Wolfe, & Olson, 2001). One male survivor describes this attribution of blame: "I had to make sense out of what was going on. And the sense I made out of this was that I'm not really a good person. There's something different about me and something wrong" (Lisak, 1994, p. 541).

Neurobiological Changes

Stressful childhood life experiences can influence brain development and lead to both anatomical and functional brain changes that underlie symptoms of PTSD. Neuroscientists have connected the behavioral signs of poor emotion regulation among children with PTSD to alterations in the developing brain, resulting in abnormalities in their ability to manage stress (Danese et al., 2011). For example, the concept of "limbic irritability" has been coined to account for symptoms of internalizing psychopathology after maltreatment because of its impact on the limbic system. Symptoms of limbic irritability include somatic, sensory, and behavioral phenomena believed to be due to increased excitatory neurotransmission after maltreatment in early childhood (Dackis et al., 2012).

The brain undergoes its most rapid growth and organization early in development, especially from birth to 2 years of age. The changes that occur during this sensitive period of rapid growth may become permanent and thus influence further development. In the case of PTSD, this means that exposure to trauma or maltreatment early in life could influence further development even when that adversity is no longer present, leading to enduring effects. For example, long-term alterations in the hypothalamic–pituitary–adrenal (HPA) axis and norepinephrine systems are found among maltreated children and adults with a history of childhood abuse, which have a pronounced effect on their responsiveness to stress (McCrory, De Brito, & Viding, 2010). The brain areas implicated in the stress response that can lead to long-term mental health problems include the hippocampus (learning and memory), the prefrontal cortex (planning and decision-making), and the amygdala (emotion regulation) (Cicchetti et al., 2010; Nunes et al., 2010; Roth & Sweatt, 2011).

In effect, acute and chronic forms of stress associated with maltreatment may cause changes in brain development and structure from an early age (Danese et al., 2011). The neuroendocrine system is designed to handle sudden stressful events by releasing cortisol to produce a fight-or-flight response (see Chapter 2). Elevated levels of stress hormones can act on structures in the brain such as the hippocampus and the amygdala to disrupt learning and memory and can lead to adverse brain development through accelerated neuronal loss, myelination delays, inhibition of neurogenesis, and decreased brain growth factors (McCrory et al., 2010). However, after prolonged and unpredictable stressful episodes associated with most forms of chronic childhood trauma and maltreatment, cortisol levels become depleted and the feedback systems that control hormone levels in the brain may not function correctly. Stress floods the brain with cortisol; the brain, in turn, resets the threshold at which cortisol is produced so that ultimately it circulates at a dramatically low level. As a result, the neuroendocrine system becomes highly sensitive to stress (Davies et al., 2009; Nunes et al., 2010).

Late childhood and adolescence are considered to be critical periods for the brain's prefrontal cortical development. These regions are responsible for the maturation of executive functioning, including attention and cognitive flexibility, and are among the last areas of the brain to develop (Anderson et al., 2001). Therefore, because executive skills develop later in life, difficulties in executive functioning would not become apparent until children are older. The neurobiological changes that occur in response to untoward early-life stress may partially account for PTSD and related disorders that emerge throughout the lives of children and youths exposed to maltreatment or trauma.

Section Summary

Trauma and Stressor-Related Disorders

- Children with reactive attachment disorder show little effort to seek comfort from a caregiver or adult,
- Children with disinhibited social engagement disorder show a pattern of overly familiar and culturally inappropriate behavior with relative strangers,
- Children with either disorder of social neglect show developmental delays that may persist for several years.
- Youngsters with post-traumatic stress disorder (PTSD) display persistent frightening thoughts after experiencing overwhelming traumatic events such as threatened death or injury, natural disasters, or maltreatment.
- Children with PTSD reexperience the traumatic event, avoid associated stimuli, and display symptoms of extreme arousal.
- Stress and trauma can result in significant PTSD-related symptoms at any time from childhood to adulthood, including mood disturbances, emotional and behavioral problems, difficulties in sexual adjustment, and unhealthy relationships.
- Causes of PTSD in children focus on psychological factors (such as emotion regulation and their view of self and others), as well as neurobiological factors that affect various brain areas and reactivity to stress.

TREATMENT AND PREVENTION

Violence against children is never justifiable. Nor is it inevitable. If its underlying causes are identified and addressed, violence against children is entirely preventable.

—Kofi Annan

Adults play a critical role in assisting children's recovery from traumatic events.

Children who are maltreated or who experience violence at home, children who witness serious harm to others, or those who face other severe forms of stress and trauma will need some degree of help to restore their trust of others and feelings of safety and to cope with their fear and anxiety. Fortunately, there are well-supported intervention methods available to restore their healthy development (e.g., after being abused or neglected) and reduce immediate- and long-term problems that may arise from early stress or trauma (Thompson, 2014).

By providing proper knowledge and support, families and communities often play the most critical role in assisting children and youths who directly or indirectly experience traumatic or stressful events. Children may be protected, in part, from the effects of trauma or severe stress by a positive, supportive relationship with at least one important and consistent person in their lives who provides support and protection, such as other family members or peers (Haskett et al., 2006; Skopp et al., 2007). Paradoxically, this person could be a maltreating parent, a notion that at first may be hard to comprehend. Many maltreated children do not think of their parents as abusive; rather, they adapt to their own experiences as best as possible. Loyalty to one's parents is a powerful emotional tie—so from the child's point of view, a parent who at times yells, hits, and castigates, may at other times be a source of connection, knowledge, or love (Wekerle & Wolfe, 2003). In addition to the importance of supportive relationships, personality characteristics such as positive self-esteem and sense of self also are related to fewer negative outcomes among maltreated children (Afifi & MacMillan, 2011).

Exposure-Based Therapy

We begin our discussion of intervention by considering single-episode events, such as school shootings or other loss of life. Such events are a reality for some and a concern for everyone, so most school boards and communities have developed well-structured plans to be put into action in the event of tragedy or loss. Notably, a school's response can be instrumental in the immediate aftermath of traumatic events involving children or youths. Children can be affected by dire news or by witnessing tragic events, so schools play a crucial role in maintaining a reasonable routine, allowing for appropriate expression of grief or loss, identifying students who might be at risk, and helping students who need it to access available resources for assistance (Steele & Malchiodi, 2012).

Effective intervention and prevention for children who have been exposed to trauma or maltreatment generally takes the form of structured therapy involving the child directly and/or programs for parents to assist them in supporting the child or changing their child-rearing methods (as in the case of maltreatment). Efforts to help children cope with their feelings and reactions after a disaster focus on helping the child acknowledge the experience and their reactions, and addressing pre- and post-disaster factors that are known to affect the child's adjustment, such as their developmental level, anxiety, coping style, and available social support (Gerson & Rappaport, 2013). Cognitive–behavioral treatment involving imagined or real-life exposure to feared stimuli, discussed below, has been shown to be effective treatment in helping children with PTSD and related symptoms after trauma or loss (AACAP, 2010; Silverman, Ortiz, et al., 2008).

Following acute stress or trauma, such as motor vehicle accidents, shootings, bombings, and hurricanes, the use of an early exposure intervention has reduced acute stress symptoms. Many of these interventions are brief, ranging from 1 to 10 sessions, and are often delivered in groups to reach as many children as possible. Psychological First Aid (PFA), for example, is based on the theory that children need information and support to reintegrate back into their school routine. PFA strives to provide safety and practical assistance, stability, and connection with needed supports for everyone affected by the event(s). This form of brief therapy is intended for secondary victims—children who have learned of harm to others such as classmates or community members—and to address the post-disaster reactions among victims, such as feeling displaced or at a loss (Forbes et al., 2011).

In-depth psychological interventions are available for children who are severely affected by a traumatic event. The child or youth typically begins by describing a particular traumatic incident (such as a classmate's suicide) and their feelings, thoughts, or attitudes

AP Images/Mike Gullett, File

about it. With the aid of the therapist, the child examines the incident, including aspects such as the time and duration, awareness of and connectedness to each incident, and a verbal report of the incident. In Grief and Trauma Intervention for Children (GTI), sessions address topics that are common to children who are experiencing grief and trauma, such as dreams (nightmares), questioning, anger, and guilt. The techniques are based on cognitive–behavioral therapy (CBT) and narrative therapy and include narrative exposure to the trauma through drawing, discussing, and writing. A child is encouraged to develop an in-depth, coherent narrative of what happened while expressing their thoughts and feelings, developing positive coping strategies, and making meaning of losses (Salloum & Overstreet, 2012). Through such graded exposure to memories and feelings stemming from the event, the child becomes more able to talk about the traumatic incident with a sense of emotional control without the intrusion of negative emotions and other reactions elicited by the incident. However, researchers are finding that children or adults who show signs of dissociation at the time at which treatment starts do not respond as well to such early intervention, most likely because of their degree of shock and disconnection (Price et al., 2014).

Trauma-focused cognitive–behavioral therapy (TF-CBT) is the most widely studied and supported form of exposure therapy for childhood trauma or stress. TF-CBT is a components-based psychosocial treatment model that incorporates elements of cognitive-behavioral, attachment, humanistic, empowerment, and family therapy models. This method has helped children and adults cope with the emotions and intrusive thoughts related to sexual abuse, domestic violence, traumatic loss, acts of violence and terrorism, and many other traumatic or stressful events (Barrera et al., 2013; Gerson & Rappaport, 2013).

TF-CBT involves a combination of exposure therapy and skill building to allow the individual to practice more effective ways of coping with intrusive memories and emotions (Cohen et al., 2010). Exposure strategies essentially involve having children or youths talk about the traumatic event and their feelings about it at a speed that is not too distressing for them. Children or youths are encouraged to create a coherent "narrative," or story of what happened, at their own pace, which enables them to master painful feelings about the event and to resolve the impact the event has on their life. During this process they are able to correct any untrue or distorted ideas about what happened, such as feeling they are to blame or could have done something to prevent it. Throughout each session, they are taught stress management and relaxation skills to help them cope with unpleasant feelings or intrusive memories about the trauma (see A Closer Look 12.3).

Some children have reactions to trauma that consist of more complex patterns extending beyond typical PTSD-related symptoms. **Complex trauma** often manifests as problems with attachment to others, emotion regulation, dissociation, behavior problems, and distorted self-concept. For example, we saw how children who have been sexually abused report engaging in health-compromising behaviors such as substance abuse, unsafe sex, and conduct problems (Fergusson et al., 2013; Homma et al., 2012). To meet these needs, TF-CBT has additional time allotted to teaching coping skills that incorporate safety and appropriate gradual exposure. Such modifications also allow for an adequate treatment-closure phase that includes traumatic grief components and ensures ongoing safety and trust (Cohen et al., 2012).

Special Needs of Maltreated Children

It should come as no surprise that child maltreatment exacts an enormous toll on society, in terms of both human suffering and economic loss. The total lifetime economic costs of medical, legal, educational, and child welfare services related to maltreatment are estimated to be a staggering $124 billion a year in the United States (Fang et al., 2012). Accordingly, there is a sense of urgency in addressing this issue at all levels of prevention and intervention (Wekerle, 2011a).

Consider these obstacles to intervention and prevention services for maltreating families: (1) Those most in need are least likely to seek help on their own; (2) these children are brought to the attention of professionals as a result of someone else's concern, usually after they have violated expected norms or laws; and (3) parents do not want to admit to problems because they fear losing their children or being charged with a crime (fears that are, of course, realistic).

Many children and adults who seek treatment related to child abuse and neglect are under some form of legal constraint. Similar to other psychological interventions, child-abuse treatments are based on the principle of beneficial assistance—but who wants assistance for something they will not admit is a problem? Therefore, treatments for child abuse and neglect have languished because of this basic dilemma: Access to treatment and prevention depends on admitting to or recognizing one's own culpability (Azar & Wolfe, 2006).

Despite these obstacles, through treatment, children and youths who have grown up with violence can make major shifts in how they relate to others, especially if treatment is begun early. Seeing their strengths and abilities, rather than their deficits, is a plausible approach to preventing physical abuse, neglect, and related social problems. Fifteen years after receiving pre- and postnatal home-visitation services to establish resource linkages and learn about their child's developmental needs, first-time parents—who were initially at risk of maltreating their child based on either low socioeconomic status, young age (under 19 years), or unmarried status—gained controls on important dimensions such as better family planning with regard to the number and spacing of children, less need for welfare, less child maltreatment, and fewer arrests of their children during adolescence (Eckenrode et al., 2010; Kitzman et al., 2010; Olds et al., 1997). As a result of intensive research, home-visitation programs to prevent child abuse and neglect have become widespread in many parts of North America (MacMillan et al., 2009).

Clearly, efforts to enhance positive experiences at an early stage in the development of the parent–child relationship hold considerable promise for prevention of child maltreatment and the reduction of its consequences. As shown in ● Figure 12.4, child-abuse

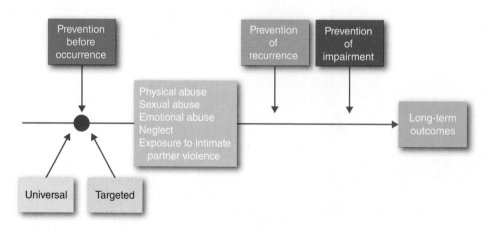

● **FIGURE 12.4** | A continuum depicting opportunities for preventing child abuse or its long-term outcomes.

Based on MacMillan et al., 2009

interventions include efforts to prevent such acts altogether (i.e., universal and targeted prevention), as well as efforts to prevent recurrence or significant impairments.

Similarly, programs that instruct children and their parents on how to avoid and report sexual abuse will improve children's responses to victimization, especially programs that encourage children to participate actively in prevention activities (Finkelhor, 2009). Formal treatment efforts also increase the chances of overcoming the harmful effects of abuse and neglect. We discuss treatments for physical abuse and neglect in the same section because of their close connection to child-rearing disturbances. Treatment of child sexual abuse is presented separately because of its unique nature and course.

Physical Abuse and Neglect

The results of any traumatic experience, such as abuse, can only be resolved by experiencing, articulating, and judging every facet of the original experience within a process of careful therapeutic disclosure.

—Alice Miller

Treatment of child abuse and neglect can be delivered in many ways: to individual parents, to children, to parents and children together, or to the entire family. Although most interventions emphasize desired changes in parental behavior, such changes can have a pronounced effect on their children's development as well.

Interventions for physical abuse usually involve ways to change how parents teach, discipline, and attend to their children, most often by training parents in basic child-rearing skills, accompanied by cognitive–behavioral methods that target specific anger patterns or distorted beliefs. Treatment for child neglect also focuses on parenting skills and expectations, coupled with teaching parents how to improve their skills in organizing important family needs—such as home safety, finances, and medical needs, among others—as well as drug and alcohol counseling (Azar & Wolfe, 2006). Similarly, children who have witnessed violence in the home benefit from interventions that address their needs in the context of their family circumstances. For example, their nonoffending mothers may attend treatment with them, so that mothers learn ways to deal with problematic child behavior while also providing appropriate maternal support (Graham-Bermann et al., 2007; Jaffe et al., 2011).

Because maltreating parents place too much emphasis on control and discipline, or ways to avoid contact and responsibilities, they seldom know how to enjoy their child's company. Therefore, treatment often begins with efforts designed to increase positive parent–child interactions and pleasant experiences. Parents are shown—through modeling, role playing, and feedback—how to engage with their children in daily activities that serve to strengthen the child's areas of deficiency and to promote adaptive functioning (Wolfe, 1991). Activities are selected to maximize the child's attention and provide ample opportunity for pleasant interchanges. Milton's treatment plan illustrates this important initial step:

MILTON'S TREATMENT

Session 1

It didn't take long to see what Brenda faced at home. Partway through our first session, Milton (age 4) wanted his mother's attention and became quite angry when she was asked to leave the room for a few minutes. During this outburst, he pushed an easy chair over and tried to hit Brenda with a rolled-up poster. She happily left for the observation room, leaving him and me together for the first time. I found a game and some puppets that he liked, and began the process of establishing a relationship. As soon as Milton started to lose interest, I switched to a new activity. I modeled for Brenda some ways simply to observe Milton's behavior and express my interest:

"Milton likes to explore everything! Look! I have a talking doll! Can you make him say something? Excellent—he spoke to you!" (Milton starts to go for the toy chest). "Look, Milton! I have a puppet. Would you like to hold him? Good, you're coming back to play with me. After we play with the puppet, mommy will come in and play too! When we're all done, we'll go get a drink. Can you stack these blocks? Oops, you knocked them down; that looked like fun. Let's try again; only this time, you put one on here for me." I closely guided Milton to new activities to reduce his distractibility, all the time talking aloud so that his mother could hear in the adjoining room where she was observing the interaction. (Based on authors' case material.)

Once parents learn a more flexible, adaptive teaching style that suits their child's development, efforts are begun to strengthen the child's compliance and self-control. Parents observe while the therapist models positive ways to encourage the child's attention and appropriate behavior, followed by practice and feedback. Therapists model for the parent how to express positive affect—with smiles, hugs, physical affection, and praise—and how to show dismay or concern when necessary with appropriate facial expression, firmer voice tone, and similar cues that express disapproval.

Parent training seldom goes smoothly, especially with families who have multiple problems. What do you do when a child just "acts himself" and doesn't follow your directions, while his parent watches? These situations often are valuable for helping a parent apply the new skills under naturalistic, this-is-what-it's-really-like conditions. Serendipitously, the value of modeling how to handle such a challenge was discovered a few sessions later:

MILTON'S TREATMENT

Session 4

Milton was tired of following my directions. Unaware that his mother was watching, he seized the opportunity to have some fun. He picked up toys and tossed them, and turned the light switch off and on. I thought I could simply get Milton to settle down by taking him down from his chair (which he was using to reach the light switch) and bringing him back to the couch. I was wrong. He started throwing a tantrum and screaming violently. With no other choice (child psychologists know when they're licked), I decided to talk above the noise so that his mother could hear how I was feeling and what I thought I might do: "I'm not sure just what to do yet. Milton seems to be uninterested in listening at the moment. Rather than getting angry, I think I'll wait a minute or two and try again. I've seen my 3-year-old do this, and I know you can't always expect kids to listen."

Brenda, familiar with this behavior at home, thought the situation was priceless—"Now you know what I have to deal with!" In lighthearted defense, I explained how there may not be an easy solution for these situations, which is why it is so important to maintain your composure and not expect or demand cooperation from Milton immediately. Tongue-in-cheek, I reminded her of Murphy's law of child behavior—"Anything that can go wrong, will"—and its corollary, "Just because it worked last time doesn't mean it will work every time!" (Based on authors' case material.)

From this and similar misadventures, we discovered how familiar problems that emerge during treatment delivery will add authenticity for parents (and conveniently happen whether or not we plan them!). These situations, as well as less stressful ones, also are used to teach parents how to manage themselves calmly, yet firmly. Therapists model how parents can express frustration and annoyance without becoming abusive and harsh, and parents then are encouraged to discuss and rehearse how they can handle the situation.

Gradually, they learn to replace physical punishment or apathy with more positive approaches. This process takes time, and parental frustration and impatience are to be anticipated. Cognitive–behavioral methods have been successful at teaching coping and problem-solving skills to abusive and neglectful parents as well as to parents at risk for maltreating their children (Mikton & Butchart, 2009; Thomas & Zimmer-Gembeck, 2011).

In addition to learning new ways to stimulate child development and structure child activities, neglectful parents often require very basic education and assistance in managing everyday demands, such as financial planning and home cleanliness (Allin, Wathen, & MacMillan, 2005). Programs like Project SafeCare provide multicomponent interventions, such as marital counseling, financial planning, and lessons on cleanliness and similar concerns, that address the various needs of neglectful and multiproblem families (Gershater-Molko, Lutzker, & Wesch, 2003). Treatment services for abused or neglected children are less common than parent-oriented interventions, largely because parental behavior is often the primary concern. We have seen, however, that maltreated children often lag in important developmental competencies, which is a strong rationale for focusing additional attention on these areas.

The wave of the future in preventing child abuse and neglect is likely to involve public health approaches that offer comprehensive assistance to parents and families based on their level of need and proper timing of assistance. For example, the well-supported Triple P program offers five tiers of assistance to best meet the needs of all parents in a community, from brief sessions to intense training and one-on-one assistance (Prinz et al., 2009). Similarly, information and guidance for parents of younger children can be readily provided by pediatric primary care providers as part of regular health visits (Dubowitz, Feigelman, Lane, & Kim, 2009).

Sexual Abuse

What allowed this to happen was that so many people were silent about it.

—Adult sexually abused as a child

Sexually abused children have experienced a world of secrecy, silence, and isolation. After they break that silence by disclosing the abuse, or the abuse is discovered by accident, the path toward healing can be difficult. They must access not only unpleasant memories, but also buried feelings of guilt, confusion, fear, and low self-worth. Sexual abuse, like many other problems of childhood, occurs in the context of other individual, family, and community problems that affect its impact and treatment. Elements of family functioning, especially maternal support and help-seeking in response to the crisis, are known to affect children's levels of distress and aid in their recovery, so treatment often must address these situational issues as well.

Treatment programs for children who have been sexually abused usually provide several crucial elements to restore the child's sense of trust, safety, and guiltlessness (Cohen, Mannarino, & Murray, 2011; Johnson, 2008). One major element of treatment involves education and support to help these children understand why this happened to them and how they can learn to feel safe once again. Information and education about the nature of sexual abuse helps clarify false beliefs that might lead to self-blame, and children's feelings of stigma and isolation often are addressed through reassurance or group therapy that involves other child victims. Animated films and videos offer ways for child victims to acknowledge and validate their feelings and to help them talk about their feelings, allowing these children to move toward the future with a sense of hope and empowerment. Children also are taught ways to prevent sexual abuse and restore their sense of personal power and safety. Through the use of animated films and behavioral rehearsal, children learn how to distinguish appropriate from inappropriate touches.

Cognitive–behavioral methods are particularly valuable in achieving these goals (Cohen et al., 2010, 2012). Preferably, education and support are provided not only to the child victim, but to (nonoffending) parents as well. The secretive betrayal that underlies the nature of sexual abuse causes some parents to feel ambivalent about whether to believe their child or how they feel about the alleged perpetrator, whom they may have trusted. Parents may need advice on ways to understand and manage their child's behavior, which because of the abuse may involve regressive or sexual behaviors. Parents often experience their own fears and worries as a result of the disclosure, and discussion with other parents and therapists can provide valuable support.

In conjunction with education and support, sexually abused children must express their feelings about the abuse and its aftermath—anger, ambivalence, fear—within a safe and supportive context. Younger children, for example, often cannot report their psychological reactions to the trauma unless they are asked specifically about the aspects of the trauma (Wolfe, Sas, & Wekerle, 1994). Sexual abuse elicits attempts by children to cope with powerful and confusing feelings, and it is understandable that some will use every method possible to avoid these feelings.

However, attempts to escape or avoid internal states of fear and anxiety, paradoxically, can make them worse.

For these reasons, TF-CBT has been adapted for child sexual abuse victims and others with complex trauma symptoms. The child is asked to recall gradually her memories of events, often to the point of feeling distressed, to allow the powerful emotions to be extinguished with repeated exposure. In addition, she learns to cope with negative thoughts and feelings about the abuse by using positive statements and imagery. Overall, gradual exposure, modeling, education, coping, and prevention-skills training have shown positive effects in the treatment of PTSD and other common outcomes of sexual abuse (Harvey & Taylor, 2010; Trask, Walsh, & DiLillo, 2011).

There is strong agreement that successful interventions for sexually abused children should result in several important outcomes (Berliner & Elliott, 2002). Treatment services should help children understand that what happened to them was abuse, that it was wrong, and that it may have caused them some temporary problems. Emotional and behavioral problems that may have arisen from the abuse should subside, and children should have the personal resources to handle future problems. Importantly, they should have supportive relationships in place, especially with parents and other caregivers who have received adequate knowledge and assistance to understand the possible impact the abuse may have on their children's behavior and adjustment. Finally, successful treatment results in children's regaining their normal rate of development.

A generation ago, psychology textbooks rarely discussed child sexual abuse. We had little knowledge of the devastating developmental, mental health, and societal consequences of abuse and neglect, and very few treatments were available. Since that time, considerable progress has been made in understanding and helping children who have been abused and neglected and their families. Most importantly, broader efforts at prevention and family support may help reduce or eliminate the likelihood of such unnecessary and harmful mistreatment of children and youths.

Section Summary

Treatment and Prevention

- Several factors appear to be important in children's course of recovery from PTSD, including the nature of the traumatic event, preexisting child characteristics, and family/social support.

(continues)

Section Summary (continued)

- Trauma-focused cognitive–behavioral therapy involves a combination of exposure therapy and skill building to allow the individual to practice more effective ways of coping with intrusive memories and emotions.
- Prevention of maltreatment holds considerable promise, especially if attempts are begun early in the formation of the parent–child relationship.
- Treatment of physical abuse involves training parents in more positive child-rearing skills, accompanied by cognitive–behavioral methods to target specific anger patterns or distorted beliefs.
- Treatment for child neglect focuses on parenting skills and expectations, coupled with training in social competence and household management.
- Interventions for children who have been sexually abused emphasize the children's needs for safety, understanding, and expression of emotional consequences.
- Cognitive–behavioral methods have shown value in working with sexually abused children, especially when accompanied by education and support for nonoffending, supportive caregivers.

Study Resources

SECTION SUMMARIES

KEY TERMS

13

Health-Related and Substance-Use Disorders

It is health that is real wealth and not pieces of gold and silver.

—Mahatma Gandhi

JEREMIAH

Breath Is Life

Jeremiah Jager, age 4, loves blue. He drinks blue soda pop, picks the blue marshmallows out of his Magic Stars cereal, and grabs the blue crayon. But when he got croupy and turned his favorite color this past winter—lips, cheeks, nose—his mother panicked. It was Jeremiah's eighth visit to the ER. And the scariest. "When he turned blue, I said 'I want some answers,'" says Cathy, who figured that—like relatives on both sides of his family—Jeremiah was developing asthma. She called the 800 number for Lung Line at the National Jewish Medical and Research Center in Denver. "This is going to cost twice as much as our car," says Cathy. "But why give birth to them if you're not going to do all you can for them?" Within a week, the Jagers left Alliance, Nebraska, for the long drive to Denver. They had to find out what was wrong with their child.

From "An Epidemic of Sneezing and Wheezing," by C. G. Dowling and A. Hollister, Life Magazine, May 1997, p. 79.

Jeremiah was thoroughly tested for allergies. The test results were all negative.

Similarly, Freddie's sleep problems are intermingled with worries brought on by his father's comments about him failing to get enough sleep. What role, if any, do psychological factors play in Jeremiah's and Freddie's development and adaptation to their health-related problems?

FREDDIE

Too Worried to Sleep

Freddie, age 12, had considerable difficulty falling asleep. Each night it would take him an hour or two to fall asleep, which made it very difficult for him to get up for school at 6:00 A.M. the next morning. His typical nighttime routine was to watch television downstairs until 9:00 p.m. and then get ready for bed. Once in bed, he read for a while before turning out the lights. He explains: "I start to get sleepy when I'm reading, but as soon as I turn off the lights I'm wide awake. I can't stop from thinking about things, especially stuff that bothers me at school, like homework and making friends. My dad told me I would get sick because I don't sleep enough, and now I'm afraid I'll catch 'mono' like a friend of mine has at school. No matter what I do, I can't seem to just fall asleep like I used to."

Adapted from Bootzin & Chambers, 1990.

WHAT DO JEREMIAH AND Freddie have in common? To varying degrees, these children must face situations that affect their health and well-being; as a result, they and their family members are continually distressed and worried. Jeremiah's parents want answers for his breathing problems, which seem to occur without warning. Because doctors are unable to explain his episodes, Jeremiah's parents secretly wonder whether his breathing problems may be due to psychological causes.

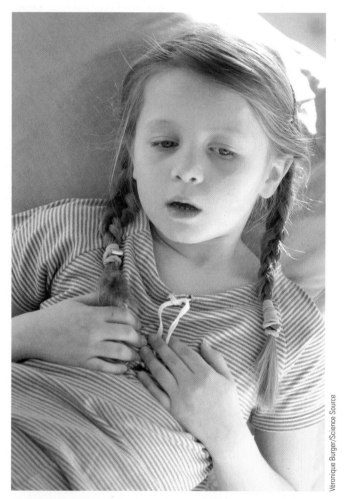

Children's health problems can affect their psychological adjustment.

Children, parents, and other family members are all deeply affected by children's health-related problems, which is why they have considerable psychological importance. The problems discussed in this chapter are not typically viewed as mental health disorders, rather they are viewed as health-related problems and medical stressors. Some stressors are mild, such as Freddie's problems falling asleep and sleeping through the night, but problems such as Jeremiah's asthma can be life-threatening and highly disruptive, and they may involve complicated and intrusive medical interventions.

Pediatric health-related disorders are a distinct area of specialization, but cover a wide range of concerns, from relatively minor, such as enuresis (bed-wetting) and encopresis (soiling), to chronic illnesses such as cancer and diabetes (Jackson, Alberts, & Roberts, 2010; Prinstein & Roberts, 2006). Health-related disorders are different from other mental disorders largely because children's adjustment problems are more directly connected to the impact of the physical illness. Moreover, the field of pediatric psychology stresses the interaction between physical and mental health because the various disorders and developmental problems all share medical, psychological, and psychosocial components (Peterson, Reach, & Grube, 2003). The involvement of psychologists and other mental health professionals in children's health-related problems has led to many highly successful ways to assist children and family members in coping with and adapting to their circumstances.

HISTORY

Psychological approaches to aiding children with health-related problems have gained considerable momentum over the past two decades, but a long history preceded these developments. Ever since Greek philosophers first suggested that pain and disease were caused by an imbalance in the body's basic elements of fire, air, water, and earth, various cultures have been both fascinated and perplexed by the interrelationship between the mind and the body. During the medieval period, these early philosophies were overshadowed by the belief that mental and physical illnesses were caused by demonic possession and required a quick and gruesome dispatch of the afflicted person.

Most new theories and research related to emotional and physical well-being remained dormant until the late 19th century. Charcot and Freud introduced their theories on the nature of hysteria and conversion disorders. However, debates about the importance of the mind–body connection dichotomy caused a clash between psychodynamic theory and modern medicine in the early 20th century (Siegel, Smith, & Wood, 1991).

Partially as a result of these controversies, an early distinction emerged between disorders caused by physical factors and those caused by emotional or psychological factors (Peterson et al., 2003). Physical disorders caused or affected by psychological and social factors were referred to as *psychosomatic*. Later, the term *psychosomatic* was replaced by the term *psychophysiological*, meaning that psychological factors affected somatic (physical) function. These terms are no longer used, however, because they wrongly implied that a person's physical symptoms were caused solely by mental problems.

Until 50 years ago, attention was rightfully placed on the acute, infectious diseases—such as smallpox, tuberculosis, diphtheria, and typhus—that claimed the lives of one in four children before their ninth birthday (Pollock, 1987). This statistic—simple, unemotional, impartial—belies the emotional toll this high infant and child mortality rate must have had on our ancestors. In fact, some historians argue that prior to the mid-19th century, children's highly unpredictable life spans contributed to a diminished emotional investment in children among parents and society (Garrison & McQuiston, 1989). In Western society today, it is difficult to conceive of these circumstances, even though high child mortality rates still exist in other countries around the world.

Sleep–wake disorders, elimination disorders, chronic illness, and substance-use disorders—all health-related problems addressed in this chapter—are good examples of how poorly understood physical symptoms can be misattributed to psychological causes. Moreover, diverse childhood experiences underscore how reliance on fashionable cures and untested folk wisdom, rather than on scientific findings, can be viewed by subsequent generations as unwise and sometimes harmful.

Consider children's sleep and elimination disorders. For centuries, these relatively common afflictions were unfairly attributed to children's inherent stubbornness and laziness. Societal attitudes toward addressing bedwetting ranged from severe to lenient. By the turn of the 20th century, according to professional and public opinion, enuresis, like childhood masturbation, was a potential sign of emotional and behavioral disturbance. Early psychodynamic theory was gaining in popularity and proposed that toileting difficulties reflected unconscious conflicts that, if unresolved, could turn into troublesome personality styles. The sources of the underlying conflict were numerous: lack of parental love, the guilt value of feces, separation anxiety, pregnancy wishes, response to family problems, and traumatic separation from mother between the oral and anal stages of psychosexual development (Fielding & Doleys, 1988).

By the 1920s, the *Infant Care Bulletin,* the official publication of the U.S. Children's Bureau, reflected the harsh stance of society toward children's developmental problems. It advised parents to force their children to have bowel movements on a strict, regular schedule and to complete toilet training by 8 months of age at the latest! If the baby did not go along with this plan, elimination was induced by inserting a stick of soap into the rectum (Achenbach, 1982).

Fortunately, by the 1940s this advice mellowed toward more natural, developmentally sensitive approaches that allowed children's maturity to dictate when parents could shift from diapers to toileting, which occurred between 12 and 30 months of age. Toilet-training issues once again emerged during the rebellious 1960s, when renowned pediatrician Benjamin Spock was blamed for many social problems in North America because his advice on toileting and early childhood discipline from the 1940s was considered too lenient. Spock (1945) made it clear, though, that "the child supplies the power but the parents have to do the steering."

The Society of Pediatric Psychology was organized in 1968 to connect psychology and pediatrics, and it established the *Journal of Pediatric Psychology* in 1976. These two landmark events broadened the research and theory on physical outcomes of child health disorders to encompass the psychosocial effects of illness and the interplay between the two (Roberts & Steele, 2009).

How children adapt to the many situational, developmental, and chronic stressors affecting their health and well-being is a primary interest of pediatric health psychology. We begin by discussing sleep–wake disorders, pausing to consider how important sleep is to our psychological and physical development and its regulation from birth onward. Then we discuss elimination disorders and chronic illness in children and adolescents, areas in which monumental gains have been made in recent years in helping children overcome or adapt to these challenges. Finally, we describe substance-use disorders and related health-compromising behaviors that emerge in adolescence. How health-related problems interact with children's and adolescents' psychological well-being, and how they and their families adapt in response, are central themes throughout this chapter.

Section Summary

History

- For centuries, poorly understood physical symptoms have been misattributed to psychological causes.
- Today, pediatric health psychologists study how children's health-related problems interact with their psychological well-being and how they and their families adapt in response.

SLEEP–WAKE DISORDERS

People who say they sleep like a baby usually don't have one.

—Leo J. Burke

We all have problems sleeping at one time or another. Usually, the problems are not serious and do not interfere with the next day's activities, but sometimes sleep problems can seriously affect our physical and psychological health and well-being. As any parent, sibling, or roommate can attest, these problems can have a major impact on them as well. In fact, problems such as resistance at bedtime, difficulty settling at bedtime, night waking, difficulty waking up, and fatigue are among the most common concerns expressed by parents of young children (Meltzer & Mindell, 2007).

Arguably, sleep is the *primary* activity of the brain during the early years of development. Consider this: By 2 years of age the average child has spent almost 10,000 hours (nearly 14 months) asleep, and approximately 7,500 hours (about 10 months) in waking activities (Anders, Goodlin-Jones, & Sadeh, 2000). During those 2 years, the brain has reached 90% of its adult size and the child has attained remarkable complexity in cognitive skills, language, concept of self, socioemotional development, and physical skills (Dahl, 2007; Dahl & El-Sheikh, 2007). And most of these maturational advances occurred while the child was asleep.

By age 5 or so, a more even balance gradually emerges between sleep and wakefulness. Still, by the time they begin school, children have spent more time asleep than in social interactions, exploration of the environment, eating, or any other single waking activity. Why has evolution favored sleep over these important activities? Wouldn't it be to our advantage to have more waking time to learn language, acquire knowledge, and develop similar adaptive skills? Apparently, sleep serves a fundamental role in brain development and regulation (Dahl, 2007). This role explains why sleep disturbances can affect overall physical and mental health and well-being and why sleep disorders are important to abnormal child psychology.

Perhaps you have noticed how sleep problems co-occur with many different disorders, including attention-deficit/hyperactivity disorder (ADHD), depression, anxiety, conduct problems, and developmental disorders (Chorney et al., 2008; Kelly & El-Sheikh, 2013). This connection raises an important consideration: Do sleep problems cause other disorders, or do they result from them? The answer to this question requires an understanding of how sleep problems interact with a person's psychological well-being. Since sleep problems commonly arise from particular stressors— an upcoming exam or a relationship problem—we tend to think that sleep difficulties are secondary symptoms of a more primary problem. However, the relationship between sleep problems and psychological adjustment is bidirectional.

Sleep problems may cause emotional and behavioral problems among children and adolescents, and they may be caused by a psychological disorder. An underlying factor common to both sleep problems and other disorders may cause sleep issues in some cases. Problems in the brain's arousal and regulatory systems can cause increased anxiety and can affect sleep (see Chapter 11). Stress-related events, especially those that affect the child's safety—such as war, disaster, and family conflict—both increase arousal and interfere with normal sleep patterns (El-Sheikh, Bub, et al., 2013; Kelly & El-Sheikh, 2013). Simply stated, sleep–wake disorders can cause other psychological problems or they can result from other disorders or conditions. Sleep–wake disorders have considerable importance to abnormal child psychology because they mimic or worsen many of the symptoms of major disorders.

The Regulatory Functions of Sleep

We tend to think that sleep is a time when not much is happening—the "lights are on but nobody's home." This lack of activity and nearly complete loss of awareness during sleep suggests that sleep regulation has little to do with psychological processes such as attention, arousal, emotions, and behavior. So why does the brain—particularly, the developing brain—require long periods of relative inactivity?

Sleep, arousal, affect, and attention are all closely intertwined in a dynamic regulatory system (Dahl, 1996). This at odds with the popular image of sleep as simply rest. When the central nervous system (CNS) must increase arousal in response to possible danger,

Children's sleep patterns help regulate their mood and behavior.

the system must recover soon thereafter and restore the balance between sleep and arousal. It is fascinating how the system changes with development: During infancy, the balance is skewed in favor of more sleep, because safety and other needs are provided for by the child's caregivers. As children mature, they start looking after their own needs, becoming more alert and attentive to danger. Gradually, the cycle between sleep and arousal becomes skewed more in favor of arousal, which by then is adaptive and necessary, and the dynamic patterns of sleep help restore the balance.

Most college students suffer sleep loss or disruption as a result of all-night study sessions or late-night partying. So you are probably familiar with sleep's important role in regulating states of emotional arousal and restoration. The giddiness, silliness, and impulsive behaviors children and adults show if sleep-deprived signify impairment in the prefrontal cortex functions. The prefrontal cortex is an important *executive control* center in the brain—it is in charge of processing emotional signals and making critical decisions for response—so impairment results in signs of decreased concentration and diminished ability to inhibit, or control, basic drives, impulses, and emotions (Talbot et al., 2010).

The prefrontal cortex is uniquely situated in the brain where it can integrate thoughts (higher cortical functions) with emotions (basic CNS functions). If a person is sleep-deprived or otherwise impaired, the first functions affected are the more complex, demanding tasks that require integrating cognitive, emotional, and social input rapidly and accurately (Dahl, 1996). Ask any parent or teacher and they can tell you: Children with disrupted or inadequate sleep show less executive control the next day; they are more cranky, impulsive, distractible, and emotionally labile (meaning they switch abruptly from, say, laughing to crying). These symptoms are easily confused with those of ADHD, although sleep-related problems usually self-correct within a day or two (Cortese et al., 2013).

The physiology of sleep also has a fascinating connection to developmental problems that occur during childhood, and it further underscores the crucial role of sleep in restoring balance (Gregory et al., 2008). Specific stages of sleep are believed to produce an active *uncoupling*, or disconnection, of neurobehavioral systems (Dahl, 1996). In effect, separate aspects of the CNS take a break from their constant duty. Think about how your nervous system must use electrical signals to continuously maintain an active, close connection while you are awake. These signals require that our neurobehavioral systems maintain precise timing and frequency. (See our discussion of communication and learning disorders in Chapter 7.)

© Zits Partnership. Reprinted with special permission of King Features Syndicate

Sleep researcher R. E. Dahl describes the uncoupling process by comparing sleep's role to that of tuning instruments in a large orchestra: Tuning cannot be accomplished while the instrument is continuously playing, or "coupling," with the other instruments in the orchestra. Likewise, retuning or recalibration of the components of the CNS may require temporary uncoupling, or disconnection from other systems. Further, the uncoupling may be particularly critical for children. As children mature, regions of the brain rapidly differentiate and establish specific functions and patterns of interconnection within the CNS (Dahl, 1996, 2007), which requires considerable recalibration or retuning. In Dahl's music analogy, a new instrument must be retuned more often than one that has been broken in.

Maturational Changes

Our sleep patterns and needs change dramatically during the first few years of life, then gradually settle into a stable pattern as we reach adulthood. Newborns sleep about 16 to 17 hours each day, and 1-year-olds sleep about 13 hours a day, including daytime naps that range from 1 to over 2 hours (Acebo et al., 2005; Anders & Eiben, 1997). These maturational changes partially explain why the sleep problems of infants and children are different from those of older children, adolescents, and adults. Infants and toddlers have more night-waking problems, preschoolers have more falling-asleep problems, and younger school-age children have more going-to-bed problems. In contrast, sleep problems among adolescents and adults typically involve difficulty going to or staying asleep (insomnia) or not having enough time to sleep (Roberts, Roberts, & Xing, 2011).

Paradoxically, adolescents have an increased physiological need for sleep, but many get significantly less sleep than they did during early childhood. This results in many teens being chronically sleep-deprived, with daytime symptoms of fatigue, irritability, emotional lability, difficulty concentrating, and falling asleep in class (Roberts et al., 2011). The bottom line? Let sleeping teens lie—they need to catch up on their sleep!

Features of Sleep–Wake Disorders

Primary sleep–wake disorders are likely a result of abnormalities in the body's ability to regulate sleep–wake mechanisms and the timing of sleep, as opposed to sleep problems related to a medical disorder, a mental disorder, or the use of medications. There are 10 sleep–wake disorders in the *Diagnostic and Statistical of Mental Disorders*, 5th ed. (DSM-5), reflecting the increasing research and clinical overlap between sleep problems and mental health disorders (Reynolds & O'Hara, 2013). Only the major sleep–wake disorders most relevant to children and youths are discussed herein; for simplicity, these are divided into two categories: dyssomnias and parasomnias (Voderholzer & Guilleminault, 2012). **Dyssomnias** are disorders of initiating or maintaining sleep, characterized by difficulty getting enough sleep, not sleeping when you want to, not feeling refreshed after sleeping, and so forth. **Parasomnias**, in contrast, are sleep disorders in which behavioral or physiological events intrude on ongoing sleep. Whereas dyssomnias involve disruptions in the sleep process, parasomnias involve physiological or cognitive arousal at inappropriate times during the sleep–wake cycle, which can result in sleepwalking or in nightmares that jolt someone from sleep. Persons suffering from parasomnia sleep disorders often report unusual behaviors while asleep, rather than sleepiness or insomnia.

Dyssomnias

Dyssomnias, many of which are common during certain stages of development, are disturbances in the amount, timing, or quality of sleep. Freddie, for example, suffered from a common form of childhood insomnia in which he had difficulty getting to sleep. Fortunately, many sleep problems resolve themselves as the child matures, especially if parents are given basic information and guidance, such as to refrain from yelling at the child to go to sleep and instead to adhere to a bedtime routine (U.S. Department of Health and Human Services, 2011).

Table 13.1 provides a descriptive overview of childhood dyssomnias. For the most part, dyssomnias are common childhood afflictions, with the exception of narcolepsy, which is uncommon but may be underdiagnosed in children (Nevsimalova, 2009). Breathing-related sleep disorders can affect children of various ages as a result of allergies, asthma, or swollen tonsils and adenoids. Although relatively common, dyssomnias can sometimes have a significant impact on

TABLE 13.1 | Dyssomnias

Sleep Disorder	Description	Prevalence and Age	Treatment
Insomnia Disorder	Difficulty initiating or maintaining sleep, or sleep that is not restorative; in infants, repetitive night waking and inability to fall asleep	25% to 50% of 1-to 3-year-olds	Behavioral treatment, family guidance
Hypersomnolence Disorder	Excessive sleepiness that is displayed as either prolonged sleep episodes or daytime sleep episodes	Common among young children	Behavioral treatment, family guidance
Narcolepsy	Irresistible attacks of refreshing sleep occurring daily, accompanied by brief episodes of loss of muscle tone (cataplexy)	<1% of children and adolescents	Structure, support, psychostimulants, antidepressants
Breathing-Related Sleep Disorder	Sleep disruption leading to excessive sleepiness or insomnia that is caused by sleep-related breathing difficulties	1% to 2% of children; preschool, elementary ages	Removal of tonsils and adenoids
Circadian Rhythm Sleep Disorder	Persistent or recurrent sleep disruption leading to excessive sleepiness or insomnia due to a mismatch between the sleep–wake schedule required by a person's environment and his or her internal sleep cycle (circadian rhythm); late sleep onset (after midnight), difficulty awakening in morning, sleeping in on weekends, resistance to change	Unknown; possibly 7% of adolescents	Behavioral treatment, chronotherapy

Source: Based on authors' case material.

children's behavior and emotional state, much like they impact adult behavior (Reid, Huntley, & Lewin, 2009).

Parasomnias

Parasomnias are somewhat common afflictions during early to mid-childhood and, we might add, are a bit easier to understand because of their more familiar terms and our own experiences. They include **nightmares** (repeated awakenings, with frightening dreams that you usually remember), **sleep terrors** (abrupt awakening, accompanied by autonomic arousal but no recall), and **sleepwalking** (getting out of bed and walking around, but with no recall the next day). Nightmares occur during rapid-eye-movement (REM) (dream) sleep, usually during the second half of the sleep period, whereas sleep terrors and sleep walking occur during non-REM (NREM) sleep (for this reason, DSM-5 combines sleep terrors and sleepwalking into one category: NREM sleep arousal disorders). Sleep terrors and sleepwalking occur during deep sleep in the first third of the sleep cycle, when the person is so soundly asleep that he or she is difficult to arouse and has no recall of the episode the next morning (Reid et al., 2009). Although girls and boys report similar rates of nightmares in childhood, by adolescence, girls report more nightmares

than boys, a pattern that continues into adulthood (Schredl & Reinhard, 2011). Fortunately, as with the dyssomnias, children typically grow out of parasomnias or recover from sleep disruption or sleep loss and do not develop a chronic condition that interferes with daily activities. Characteristics of parasomnia sleep disorders are shown in Table 13.2.

DSM-5 criteria for sleep disorders typically are not met in full by younger children because of the transitory nature of their sleep problems (Goodlin-Jones et al., 2009). Refer to Tables 13.1 and 13.2, in lieu of the specific criteria for children, to aid in understanding the major features and differences of the various sleep disorders. Also, note two considerations concerning diagnostic criteria: In addition to the symptoms pertaining to each sleep disorder, as listed in Tables 13.1 and 13.2, DSM-5 diagnostic criteria for all sleep-related disorders emphasize: (1) the presence of clinically significant distress or impairment in social, occupational, or other important areas of functioning; and (2) the requirement that the sleep disturbance cannot be better accounted for by another mental disorder, the direct physiological effects of a substance, or a general medical condition (other than a breathing-related disorder) (APA, 2013). These considerations apply to all the disorders discussed in this chapter.

TABLE 13.2 | Parasomnias

Sleep Disorder	Description	Prevalence and Age	Treatment
Nightmare Disorder	Repeated awakenings with detailed recall of extended and extremely frightening dreams, usually involving threats to survival, security, or self-esteem; generally occurs during the second half of the sleep period	Common between ages 3 and 8	Provide comfort, reduce stress
NREM Sleep Arousal Disorders			
Sleep Terrors	Recurrent episodes of abrupt awakening from sleep, usually occurring during the first third of the major sleep episode and beginning with a panicky scream; accompanied by autonomic discharge, racing heart, sweating, vocalized distress, glassy-eyed staring; difficult to arouse, inconsolable, disoriented; no memory of episodes in morning	3% of children; ages 18 months to 6 years	Reduce stress and fatigue; add late afternoon nap
Sleepwalking	Repeated episodes of arising from bed during sleep and walking about, usually during the first third of the major sleep episode; poorly coordinated, difficult to arouse, disoriented; no memory of episode in morning	15% of children have one attack; 1% to 6% have one to four attacks per week; age 4 to 12 years, rare in adolescence	Take safety precautions, reduce stress and fatigue, add late afternoon nap

Source: Based on authors' case material.

Treatment

Sleeping difficulties in infants and toddlers often subside on their own, but any parent who has been awakened night after night by a screaming child can attest that "waiting for them to grow out of it" seems like forever. If going to sleep or staying asleep becomes difficult, the goal of behavioral interventions is to teach parents to attend to the child's need for comfort and reassurance, but to gradually withdraw more quickly from the child's room after saying goodnight. (This is an example of *extinction*, since parental attention is being removed.)

Parents also can be taught to establish good sleep hygiene appropriate to their child's developmental stage and the family's cultural values. Once established, positive reinforcement methods, such as praise or star charts, can be used to reward the child for efforts to follow the bedtime routine. Sleep hygiene may involve identifying suspected causes of disrupted sleep and involving other family members in maintaining a chosen routine. For example, individualized bedtime rituals, such as reading, singing, or playing a quiet game, establish a positive transition to bedtime, and regular bedtimes and waking times establish a consistent routine (Reid et al., 2009).

Treatment of circadian rhythm sleep disorders requires a highly motivated adolescent and a supportive family, because there are no shortcuts or medications that can easily restore a disrupted sleep–wake cycle. The goal of behavioral intervention is twofold: to eliminate the sleep deprivation and to restore a more normal sleep–wake routine. The adolescent is asked to keep a sleep–wake and daily activity log, with regular bedtimes and rise times. If begun early in the disorder, such supportive behavioral methods are often effective (Hasler et al., 2012). In addition to behavioral methods, melatonin (a natural hormone) supplements have shown to be effective with children and adolescents in advancing the sleep–wake rhythm and restoring the sleep cycle (van Geijlswijk, Korzilius, & Smits, 2010).

In contrast to treatment for some dyssomnias, prolonged treatment of child and adolescent parasomnias is usually not necessary, particularly if the episodes of sleep intrusion occur infrequently (Moturi & Avis, 2010; Sullivan, 2012). Treatment of nightmares consists of providing comfort at the time of occurrence and attempting to reduce daytime stressors. If nightmares or sleep terrors are intense and persistent, daytime stresses at school, family conflicts, or emotional disturbance may be implicated (El-Sheikh, Kelly, & Rauer, 2013; Keller et al., 2014). If sleepwalking is suspected, parents usually are asked to record episodes at home on video.

If sleepwalking is confirmed, parents must take precautions to reduce the chance of injury to a child who may fall or bump into objects. Because of the possibility of fire or other emergencies, children should never be locked in their rooms. Excessive fatigue or unusual stresses during the daytime often precipitate sleepwalking. Therefore, brief afternoon naps can be beneficial.

Section Summary

Sleep–Wake Disorders

- Sleep disorders are important to abnormal child psychology because they mimic or worsen many symptoms of the major disorders.

- Sleep disorders can cause psychological problems, result from other disorders, or be a symptom of trauma or stress in the child's life.

- Dyssomnias are disorders of initiating or maintaining sleep, and include hypersomnia, narcolepsy, breathing-related sleep disorders, and circadian rhythm disorder.

- Parasomnias are sleep disorders in which behavioral or physiological events intrude on ongoing sleep, arousing the sleeper. They include nightmares, sleep terrors, and sleepwalking.

- Although most dyssomnias and parasomnias of childhood are common and often disappear with maturity, they still may have a negative impact on the child's daily activity and adjustment. Effective psychological treatments for most childhood sleep disorders involve the establishment and regulation of bedtime routines.

ELIMINATION DISORDERS

"Step 1: Before you begin, remove all stubbornness from the child." These instructions were provided by a popular toilet training manual years ago, apparently without a hint of irony. For generations, parents have half-jokingly referred to the bathroom, and toilet training in particular, as the "combat zone," where parental right meets child's might. Teaching toddlers how to use the toilet is one of the more significant challenges of parenting, but it is unlikely that it deserved the disproportionate amount of attention it received in the early abnormal child psychology literature.

Thanks to a better understanding of the biological and psychological underpinnings of elimination disorders, attention has been directed away from the child's personality or emotional trauma. However, for a significant minority of children, the problems associated with toileting continue well past the age when most children have achieved freedom and independence. Elimination problems can turn into distressing and chronic difficulties, and can affect participation in educational and social activities, camps, sleepovers, and so forth. In extreme cases, toileting accidents can precipitate physical child abuse (Herrenkohl, Herrenkohl, & Egolf, 1983).

Two elimination problems that occur during childhood and adolescence are **enuresis**, the involuntary discharge of urine during the day or night, and **encopresis**, the passage of feces in inappropriate places, such as in clothing or on the floor. Child psychologists have studied and treated these elimination problems among children because they can have strong implications on the development of self-competence and self-esteem. Even though most children eventually outgrow problems of enuresis or encopresis by age 10 or so, they may have suffered years of embarrassment and peer rejection that remain troublesome. Fortunately, in most instances the problems can be alleviated through education and retraining efforts involving both parents and children. These disorders are one of the few areas of abnormal child psychology in which early referral and treatment can virtually eliminate long-term consequences.

Enuresis

As many as 7 million children in the United States and Canada go through the same routine each night: turn off the lights, go to sleep, wet the bed. Most of the time the child cannot control the discharge, but on occasion it may be intentional. Although the problem is relatively common, it is stressful for parents and children.

Concerns about correcting children's bed-wetting have perplexed professionals and parents for generations. Here is how Thomas Phaer, "the father of English pediatrics," explained the early cure to physicians under the heading "Of Pyssying in the Bedde" in his *Boke of Children* (1544):

> Many times for debility of vertus retentive of the reines or blader, as wel olde men as children are often-times annoyed, whan their urine issueth out either in theyre slepe or waking against theyr wylles, having no power to reteine it whan it cometh, therfore yf they will be holpen, fyrst they must avoid al fat meates, til ye vertue be restored againe, and to use this pouder in their meates and drynkes. (Cited in Glicklich, 1951, p. 862)

The "pouder" was derived from the trachea of a cock or the "stones of a hedge-hogge." This remedy seems tame in view of more "enlightened" mechanical and surgical approaches to enuresis that emerged by the 18th century—yokes made of iron (mercifully covered with velvet) that prevented urination and steel spikes placed on the child's back to prevent lying on the back, because that position was believed to stimulate bladder function during sleep. If you did not want your child to be outfitted for one of these devices, other forms of treatment were available. Medicinals such as strychnine, belladonna, sacral plasters, and chloral hydrate were used presumably to stimulate the bladder (regardless of poisonous side effects), or the orifice of the urethra was cauterized (partially closed) with silver nitrate to make it more tender and responsive to the passage of urine (Glicklich, 1951). Throughout history, the treatment of childhood bed-wetting reflects society's generally poor understanding of and sensitivity to children's needs and problems at the time.

Most children have bed-wetting accidents until age 5 or so, therefore DSM-5 has narrowed the criteria to reflect the developmental nature of this disorder (see Table 13.3). The criteria stipulate that the problem must be frequent (at least twice a week for 3 consecutive months) or accompanied by significant distress or impairment in social, academic, or other important areas of functioning. A chronological age of 5 years, or the equivalent developmental level, was arbitrarily chosen as a developmental benchmark for the point at which most children achieve urinary continence. Finally, the voiding of urine into bed or clothes must not be due exclusively to a general medical condition or the result of a diuretic, which is a drug that reduces water retention.

DSM-5 distinguishes between three subtypes of enuresis (APA, 2013). *Nocturnal only* is the most common subtype, in which wetting occurs only during sleep at night, typically during the first third of the night. Nocturnal enuresis is significantly more common among boys than girls (Su et al., 2011). Sometimes the child is dreaming of urinating, which indicates that the voiding took place during REM sleep. *Diurnal only* is defined as the passage of urine during waking hours, most often during the early afternoon on school days (APA, 2013). Diurnal enuresis is more common in females than males and is uncommon after age 9. Because of these features, suspected causes of diurnal enuresis often indicate a child's reluctance to use the toilet because of social anxiety or a preoccupation with a school event. Finally, *nocturnal* and *diurnal* can exist in combination.

Prevalence and Course

Because it is common for young children to wet the bed occasionally, it is not seen as a clinical problem unless it occurs more than once a month (Brown et al., 2008). Using one or more episodes a month as a cutoff, the incidence of nocturnal enuresis varies from about 4% to 13% for children 10 years of age or younger (Su et al., 2011). The prevalence of enuresis declines rapidly as children mature: By age 10, only 3% of males and 2% of females are affected, and this evens out to 1% of males and less than 1% of females by late adolescence (Mellon & Houts, 2006). Diurnal enuresis is much less common; it is estimated to affect 3% of 6-year-olds (Peterson et al., 2003). However, prevalence of both forms of enuresis is higher among those who are less educated, members of lower socioeconomic groups, and institutionalized children, perhaps due to less structure in their daily routines and added environmental stressors (APA, 2000).

Approximately 85% of children with enuresis have *primary enuresis,* because they have never attained at least 6 months of continuous nighttime control. By definition, primary enuresis starts at age 5. In contrast, *secondary enuresis* is less common and refers to children who have previously established urinary continence but then relapse, usually between the ages of 5 and 8 years (APA, 2013). Children with secondary enuresis often take a longer time establishing initial nighttime continence or have a higher number of stressful life events (Mellon & Houts, 2006). Most children do eventually stop wetting the bed, but for those who do not attain this on their own, treatment is particularly beneficial in preventing a lengthy and disruptive problem.

You can imagine how younger children are treated when peers discover that they have wet themselves in class or while sleeping over a friend's house. Teasing, name calling, and social stigmatization are common peer reactions to this unfortunate problem. Although

TABLE 13.3 | Diagnostic Criteria for Enuresis

DSM-5

(A) Repeated voiding of urine into bed or clothes, whether involuntary or intentional

(B) The behavior is clinically significant as manifested by either a frequency of at least twice a week for at least 3 consecutive months or the presence of clinically significant distress or impairment in social, academic (occupational), or other important areas of functioning.

(C) Chronological age is at least 5 years (or equivalent developmental level)

(D) The behavior is not attributable to the physiological effects of a substance (e.g., a diuretic, an antipsychotic medication) or another medical condition (e.g., diabetes, spina bifida, a seizure disorder)

Specify if:

Nocturnal only: Passage of urine only during nighttime sleep

Diurnal only: Passage of urine during waking hours

Nocturnal and diurnal: A combination of the two subtypes above

Source: *Diagnostic and Statistical Manual of Mental Disorders,* 5th ed. American Psychiatric Association.

enuresis is a physical condition, it is often accompanied by some degree of psychological distress (Joinson et al., 2007; Van Hoecke et al., 2006). The impact of this distress often depends on three features related to the nature of the enuresis: (1) limitations imposed on social activities, such as sleeping away from home; (2) effects on self-esteem, including the degree of social ostracism imposed by peers; and (3) parental reactions, such as anger, punishment, and rejection (Christophersen & VanScoyoc, 2013; Houts, 2010). Parents are often poorly informed about the nature of enuresis and may respond by punishing or humiliating the child who suffers from it. Fortunately, these consequences are not inevitable or long-lasting. Many children with enuresis are able to establish their self-esteem and peer relationships despite their occasional embarrassment or anxiety. For others, treatment for bed-wetting usually has a positive impact on their self-concept and peer relations (Brown, Pope, & Brown, 2011).

Waking up to a wet bed is upsetting, and it can affect a young child's self-confidence if poorly managed.

sodapix/Getty images

Causes and Treatment

For most children with enuresis, one specific etiology cannot be identified (Fritz, Rockney, & the Work Group on Quality Issues, 2004). Children with nocturnal enuresis need to urinate at night, but they do not wake up when they need to urinate. By age 5 or so, most children have made the transition from urinating around the clock, as they did in infancy, to urinating only during waking hours.

Children who continue to need to urinate at night may have a deficiency during sleep of an important hormone known as *antidiuretic hormone (ADH)*. ADH helps concentrate urine during sleep hours, meaning that the urine contains less water and has therefore decreased volume. For normal children, this decreased volume usually means that their bladders do not overfill while they are asleep, unless they drank excessive fluids before bed. Children with enuresis, however, do not show the usual increase in ADH during sleep (Norgaard, Pederson, & Djurhuus, 1985). They continue to produce more urine during the hours of sleep than their bladders can hold, and if they fail to wake up, bedwetting results.

The reason children with enuresis fail to wake up when they need to urinate can also be explained by developmental and biological factors. Older children and adolescents are able to sense a full bladder at night, which activates a nerve impulse from the bladder to the brain. This signal may initiate dreams about water or going to the toilet, which usually wakes them up. This signaling mechanism matures during early childhood, so infants understandably have very little ability to detect the need to urinate. Some children with primary enuresis, however, lack normal development of this signal processing in the brain (Ornitz et al., 1999).

Primary enuresis, the most common type, is decidedly not due to stress or child obstinacy. On the contrary, this trait appears to be inherited. If both parents were enuretic, 77% of their children are too; if only one parent was enuretic, then 44% of their offspring are also. If neither parent had this problem, only about 15% of their children develop enuresis. Concordance rates of enuresis for monozygotic (68%) and dizygotic (36%) twins also verify this connection (Bakwin, 1973; Sethi, Bhargava, & Phil, 2005).

Treatments for children with nocturnal enuresis have perhaps the most comprehensive track record of evaluation for any psychological intervention for childhood problems (Mellon & Houts, 2006). Dozens of promising behavioral methods have been investigated by hundreds of studies over several decades; they are joined by many other studies of pharmacological agents. Fortunately, these efforts have led to some strong conclusions as to what works best. (This example provides a good lesson in how long it often takes to verify successful treatment methods for psychological disorders.)

The standard behavioral intervention, based on classical conditioning principles, is using an alarm that sounds at the first detection of urine. Bed-wetting alarms have been around since Mowrer and Mowrer (1938) first invented the "bell and pad" (a battery-operated device that produced a loud sound as soon as a drop of urine closed the electrical circuit), and they are among the safest and most effective treatments. Modern alarms have a simple moisture sensor that snaps into a child's pajamas, with a small speaker attached to the shoulder to awaken the child. A single drop of urine completes the electronic circuit, setting off a piercing alarm that causes the child to tense and reflexively stop urinating. The one drawback to this method is the alarm's unpopularity with other household members. For the alarm to be effective, an adult must wake the child up, which usually is not easy; walk him to the bathroom; get him to finish urinating in the toilet; and then reset the alarm. If this ritual is carefully followed, the alarm will begin to wake the child directly within 4 to 6 weeks, and by 12 weeks he will likely master nighttime bladder control and no longer need the alarm. The modern urine alarm, when used in conjunction with other behavioral activities (e.g., monitoring and intermittent reinforcement), has been recommended by the American Academy of Child and Adolescent Psychiatry as a minimal standard in the treatment of enuresis (i.e., should apply in at least 95% of enuresis cases) (Fritz et al., 2004).

Another behavioral method, based on operant conditioning principles, involves variations of *dry-bed training*. Children, like adults, wake up more easily when the day holds promise and excitement. Reward systems, such as star charts or other tokens, capitalize on this anticipation. Dry-bed training was originally developed as a brief but intensive intervention in response to parents' frustration over the more intrusive and drawn-out urine alarm. During a single office visit, parents are instructed in bladder retention control training by having their child drink more and more fluids during the day, and then delay urination for longer periods (in an effort to strengthen bladder control); hourly wakings for trips to the toilet; a cleanup routine for accidents (overcorrection, or having the child clean more than just the sheets); and positive reinforcement for dry nights. This routine is practiced nightly for 1 or 2 weeks.

Dry-bed training methods combined with an alarm (referred to today as *full-spectrum home training*) are still commonly used, resulting in a success rate of about three in four children and a relapse rate of 10% after 1 year (Brown et al., 2011; Friman, 2008). In less severe or prolonged cases of primary enuresis, a simple incentive such as earning stars or similar tokens for dry nights is often enough to make children responsive to nighttime bladder fullness. Other children, however, may require the alarm treatment to get the message firmly implanted, coupled with close professional monitoring to help parents adhere to the training methods.

In the mid-1980s, desmopressin, a synthetic ADH administered by nasal spray before bedtime, became available as a treatment for enuresis. About 70% of children using desmopressin can avoid bed-wetting within a few days, and another 10% or so show significant improvement in the number of dry nights (Brown et al., 2011). Although desmopressin works very well while

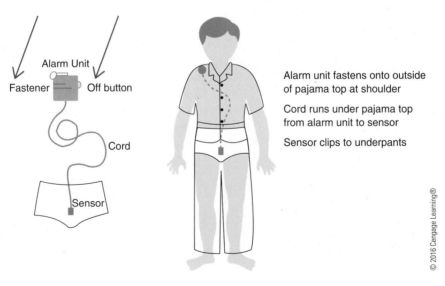

● **FIGURE 13.1** | The urine alarm: Moisture closes a circuit in a battery-powered alarm unit that wakens the child and stops the flow of urine.

children are taking the medicine, the difficulty comes in keeping them dry when they stop taking it: the relapse rate can be as high as 80% (Fritz et al., 2004). Unlike alarm systems, which have most children cured of bed-wetting within 12 weeks, treatment with medication often requires some additional behavioral treatment before children are able to stop taking the medicine.

Psychological treatments for enuresis, especially the urine alarm, have been more effective overall than pharmacological treatments (Campbell, Cox, & Borowitz, 2009; Houts, 2010). In particular, treatment using the urine alarm was found to be superior to any other type of intervention. At the end of treatment, which generally lasts 12 weeks, children who used a urine alarm were equally as likely to have ceased bed-wetting as those who took desmopressin; however, at their 3-month follow-up visit, children using a urine alarm are almost twice as likely to have ceased bed-wetting as children who received other treatments, including desmopressin. On average, almost half of all children who used alarms remain dry at follow-up, compared with about one-third treated with other behavior therapies and one-quarter treated with tricyclic medications (an antidepressant that sometimes prevents bed-wetting) (Mellon & Houts, 2006). Enuresis is one of the few disorders for which treatments using psychological interventions are clearly superior to those using drugs; therefore, psychological interventions should be used instead of waiting for the child to grow out of the problem because of the distress it causes the child and family.

Encopresis

Encopresis refers to the passage of feces in inappropriate places, such as in clothing or on the floor. Like enuresis, this act is usually involuntary, but may occasionally be done intentionally. The diagnostic criteria stipulate that this event must occur at least once per month for at least 3 months, and that the child must be 4 years old or older (if the child is developmentally delayed, a mental age of at least 4 years is used). Fecal incontinence must not be due to an organic or general medical condition (see Table 13.4).

Two subtypes of encopresis are described in DSM-5: with or without constipation and overflow incontinence. Essentially, encopresis results from constipation that produces fecal impaction. Liquid stool above the impaction gradually develops sufficient pressure to leak around the impaction, thereby producing overflow incontinence in most cases (Christophersen & VanScoyoc, 2013).

Prevalence and Course

An estimated 1% of 5-year-old children have encopresis (APA, 2013). Similar to enuresis, encopresis is

TABLE 13.4 | Diagnostic Criteria for Encopresis

(A) Repeated passage of feces in inappropriate places (e.g., in clothing, on floor), whether involuntary or intentional.

(B) At least one such event occurs each month for at least 3 months.

(C) Chronological age is at least 4 years (or equivalent developmental level).

(D) The behavior is not attributable to the physiological effects of a substance (e.g., laxatives) or another medical condition, except through a mechanism involving constipation

Specify if:

With constipation and overflow incontinence: There is evidence of constipation on physical examination or by history.

Without constipation and overflow incontinence: There is no evidence of constipation or physical examination or by history.

Source: *Diagnostic and Statistical Manual of Mental Disorders*, 5th ed. American Psychiatric Association.

more common in boys than in girls, decreases rapidly with age, and involves primary and secondary types. Children with primary encopresis have reached age 4 without establishing fecal continence, whereas children with secondary encopresis had established a period of continence before the current episode of encopresis began.

As many as one in five children with encopresis show significant psychological problems, but these problems more likely result from, rather than initially cause, the encopresis (Mikkelsen, 2010; Peterson et al., 2003). Understandably, they may feel ashamed and try to avoid situations, such as camp or school, that might lead to embarrassment. As with enuresis, the degree of children's impairment and associated psychological distress is partially a function of social ostracism by peers, as well as anger, punishment, and rejection on the part of caregivers.

Causes and Treatment

Overly aggressive or early toilet training, family disturbance and stress, and child psychopathology have all been thought, at one time or another, to cause encopresis (Burket et al., 2006; Peterson et al., 2003). However, like enuresis, encopresis is a physical disorder that can lead to psychological factors, but it seldom results from these factors alone. The sooner it is diagnosed and treated, the less likely it is that the child will suffer any lasting emotional scars or disruptions in social relationships. Exceptions, of course, are children with oppositional defiant and conduct disorders (discussed in Chapter 9), in which encopresis and enuresis may occur as secondary symptoms of broader behavior patterns.

Understanding the etiology of encopresis leads to a discussion of toilet training, during which children first learn to control bowel movements. Children must learn how to recognize signals from the muscles and nerves that tell them when it is time for a bowel movement. Sometimes they try to avoid or suppress these signals, especially if something more enjoyable is going on. Some children attempt to suppress passing feces to avoid having an accident; this allows feces to build up in the colon over time, causing *megacolon*. If uncleared, the feces that stay in the bowel become large, hard, and dry, which causes later bowel movements to be painful. Over time, the stretched muscles and nerves give fewer and fewer signals to the child about the need to have a bowel movement. This decrease in signals results in stool accidents, and the colon and rectum often do not empty as they should.

About half of all children who develop this pattern of avoidance also have abnormal *defecation dynamics*; that is, they contract rather than relax the external sphincter when they attempt to defecate (Campbell et al., 2009). Combined with avoidance tactics, an increased risk of chronic constipation and encopresis develops. In case you're wondering how such dynamics develop, consider how some children (and adults) avoid using a bathroom if they are in a strange place or if they have been told that public toilets should be avoided because they are germ-infested. Anxiety about defecating in a particular place, or stressful and harsh toileting experiences, can cause chronic constipation. Without reversing this pattern of retention, the child becomes less able to perform the many skills required for successful toileting, including recognizing body cues, undressing, going into the bathroom, sitting on the toilet chair, and relaxing the appropriate muscles (Peterson et al., 2003).

Optimal treatment of encopresis involves both medical and behavioral interventions to help the child learn to empty the colon to allow it to return to normal size and function (Christophersen & VanScoyoc, 2013). To get the process moving, fiber, enemas, laxatives, or lubricants may be given to disimpact the fecal mass (Kuhl et al., 2010). Then, to establish a better routine and healthy pattern of elimination, behavioral methods are used in combination with laxatives or similar agents. Laxatives alone do not address the underlying behavioral mechanisms. Children who have large and impacted stools will find defecation frightening and painful, which further encourages them to ignore early rectal distention cues (the urge to defecate) and avoid going to the toilet.

Behavioral methods involve teaching a toilet-training procedure that encourages detection of and response to rectal distention cues, parental efforts to praise the child's clean pants and toilet use, and regularly scheduled toilet times after meals. During these times, children practice tensing and relaxing their external anal sphincter for several minutes; the practice time often is followed by fun time of reading or playing games to desensitize children to sitting on the toilet. Then they are taught to strain and attempt to have a bowel movement. With a combination of laxatives and behavioral treatment, most children improve significantly within the first 2 weeks of treatment, and over 75% maintain these improvements (Campbell et al., 2009; Houts, 2010). Internet-based behavioral treatments for encopresis have also shown success and have the advantage of wider access for families (Ritterband et al., 2013).

Section Summary

Elimination Disorders

- Enuresis is the involuntary discharge of urine during the day or night.
- Encopresis is the passage of feces in inappropriate places, such as in clothing or on the floor.
- Primary enuresis has a strong genetic component, whereas encopresis results from children's efforts to avoid defecation, resulting in chronic constipation.
- Combined pharmacological and psychological treatments of elimination problems are often very successful.

CHRONIC ILLNESS

Who has not feared that the very worst could somehow single out a family member? Who does not worry as a toddler wanders toward the curb, as a preschooler climbs a playground ladder, or as a teenager suddenly begins having severe headaches and dizziness? Chronic illnesses and medical conditions affect over 12 million children and adolescents in North America, so it is likely that we frequently will hear about these sad events. Here is one mother's reflection:

> When does the pain go away? I don't think ever. It is a lifetime mourning for what could have been. It has nothing to do with lack of acceptance or understanding and everything to do with things we hold close in our hearts; the celebrations never realized. Sharing in the joy of watching others trying out for sports, having a first date, graduate, get accepted at university, or watch a beloved daughter walk down the aisle to be married, will never be experienced. Different experiences are ours. Instead of reflecting on what

could have been, look for what's right with your child, not what's wrong. Be proud of all accomplishments. Different joys are ours. Celebrate each achievement, each milestone. They are great motivators for yourself, your child, and others. (Reprinted with permission from Greey, 1995.)

A **chronic illness** is one that persists longer than 3 months in a given year or that requires a period of continuous hospitalization of more than 1 month. Chronic medical conditions—the wide range of complications relating to physical growth, function, and development, such as a visual or hearing impairment—are part of this picture as well. About 10% to 20% of youths under the age of 18 years will experience one or more chronic health conditions, with approximately 5% of these children suffering from a disease so severe that it regularly interferes with their daily activities, such as forming friendships, attending school, and simply pursuing a normal quality of life (Brown, Daly, & Rickel, 2007).

Children and adolescents whose health and functional ability are compromised by a chronic medical condition face numerous challenges to their development and adjustment. Each day, children with insulin-dependent diabetes must monitor their blood-glucose level and diet and inject insulin. Children with asthma cautiously navigate new situations, on the alert for an attack that can literally leave them breathless, and children with cancer must cope with the stares or comments from peers who have little understanding or compassion for why another child looks different or seems frail. Like other developmental disorders, these conditions impact not only the child but also peers and family members. This impact, in turn, affects the child's ability to adapt to the condition (Havermans et al., 2011; Sharpe & Rossiter, 2002).

The DSM-5 addresses the mental health issues pertaining to health-related disorders in children and adults indiscriminately. However, there has been considerable effort to redirect the focus of health-related symptoms and disorders away from the absence of a medical cause and more toward the presence of distressing physical symptoms. **Somatic symptom and related disorders** (previously called "somatoform disorders") are a group of related problems involving distressing somatic symptoms, such as pain and dizziness, that interfere with daily activities. These somatic or health concerns are accompanied by excessive thoughts, feelings, and behaviors, such as anxiety or worry about the seriousness of the symptoms (APA, 2013).

For somatic symptom and related disorders, the emphasis is on the way a child or youth presents with and interprets their symptoms, rather than on the symptoms per se. For example, younger children may frequently complain of aches and pain, which is common; however, worrying day and night that something is not right about one's health might be indicative of a somatic symptom disorder if this pattern continues for more than 6 months. These symptoms are not intentionally produced or feigned, and they are real enough to cause the child significant distress or impairment. Because the etiology of these symptoms is unknown, there is no longer a presumption that they are caused by psychological factors. Rather, the DSM-5 has revised their take on somatic symptom and related disorders by recognizing the potential influence of genetic and biological vulnerability (such as increased sensitivity to pain), early traumatic experiences (such as those discussed in Chapter 12), and cultural norms that may stigmatize psychological suffering as compared with physical suffering (APA, 2013).

Somatic symptom disorders have been studied largely in adults, especially because they imply a chronic, established pattern that is often not detected until young adulthood (Abramowitz & Braddock, 2011). Thus, their diagnostic applicability in reference to children and adolescents is questionable and seldom used (Eminson, 2007; Schulte & Petermann, 2011). Nonetheless, we raise this topic primarily because the multiple somatic symptoms in children, especially recurrent abdominal pain, may be developmental precursors to adult somatic symptom disorders (Essau, 2007).

Somatic symptom and related disorders include a new category known as **psychological factors affecting other medical conditions.** This category may be relevant to children and youths with existing medical symptoms or conditions because psychological factors, such as distress or poor coping, may influence their physical condition or its treatment. For example, a child with diabetes who is depressed and refuses to monitor and regulate her glucose level can affect her

Chronic illness and medical conditions affect over 12 million children and adolescents in North America.

health condition significantly. However, this diagnostic category does not apply to most children with chronic health conditions because it is the medical condition and its limitations that affect their psychological adjustment, not the other way around. In other words, psychological symptoms may develop in response to the stress of having or being diagnosed with a general medical condition. Rather than depression affecting the course of diabetes, as in the previous example, it is more likely that diabetes causes adjustment difficulties, which sometimes (but by no means always) include clinical disorders, such as depression. Thus, some children and adolescents with chronic illness accompanied by significant adjustment or behavioral problems may receive a diagnosis of *adjustment disorder*, which better accounts for the nature of the stressor (APA, 2013).

Progress in the development of effective medical treatments and cures for children with chronic illness has been spectacular over the past three decades, greatly prolonging the lives of many who previously would have died during infancy or childhood. Remarkably, the survival rate for certain types of cancer, such as acute lymphoblastic leukemia, has increased from about one in five children in the 1950s to four in five children today (Brown et al., 2007). At the same time, however, these advances and improved survival rates have led to greater child and adult morbidity. **Morbidity** refers to the various forms of physical and functional consequences and limitations that result from an illness. Increased morbidity implies that more children and adolescents are adapting to the challenges of a chronic illness. For these children, illness has become a chronic life situation and stressor, and it can have repercussions well into adulthood.

As children's survival has improved and life-threatening illnesses are better controlled, attention has moved away from the acute, infectious diseases to a broader emphasis on promoting children's health and development and assisting in the care of children with chronic illness or handicapping conditions (Canter & Roberts, 2012). Pediatric health psychologists are particularly active in helping children with chronic health disorders to successfully adapt and to attain an optimal quality of life.

To increase our awareness of the ways children with chronic disease learn to cope and adapt to physical and social challenges, we take a look at how children normally think of and express health concerns. This helps distinguish between adaptive and maladaptive coping reactions among children with chronic illness.

Normal Variations in Children's Health

We now recognize that children can communicate about their pain and discomfort about as well as adults

do, but this was not always true. It was once thought that infants did not experience pain at all and that children were far less sensitive to pain than adults. Because children seemed less able to communicate about their pain, it was wrongly concluded that they had higher pain thresholds than adults. However, children do have a good concept of what pain is and how to express that they are feeling it (McAlpine & McGrath, 1999). Their concepts of pain and its causes, their descriptions of pain, and their specific pain experiences seem remarkably well formed by an early age, both for boys and girls. Consider this comment:

> It [stomachache] was like bees in your stomach—stinging your stomach, yellow jackets going ping, pong, bop inside—like something just chopped down your stomach. [6-year-old boy].

> It [earache] felt like something is inside your ear like a sticker from a rose bush poking deep inside your ear, like way harder than just pricking. [9-year-old boy] (Ross & Ross, 1984, p. 184)

It is unlikely that children simply pick up pain descriptions from their parents or others. Consider the childlike imagery used by a 7-year-old boy in describing a headache:

> Like there's this big monster in there, see, and he's growing like crazy and there's no room and he's pulling the two sides of my head apart he's getting so big. (Ross & Ross, 1984, p. 189).

Now picture this common scene: Since age 6, Jackie has informed her parents from time to time that she was "too sick" to go to school. She then would carefully provide them with a list of her symptoms: "My tummy hurts; I feel hot, my throat hurts; I can't feel my toes." Careful questioning would usually result in a further list of symptoms—in fact, most were suggested by one of her parents: "Does your leg hurt too?" [yes]; "How does your head feel?" [achy]; "What does your skin feel like?" [stingy]. The astute reader might note that these symptoms emerged at about the time Jackie was entering the first grade. Would you consider this situation to be typical of how children learn about physical symptoms and their connection to life's responsibilities?

Are somatic symptoms in children (such as those expressed by Jackie) normal and commonplace? To no one's surprise, about a third of typical school-aged children report using pain for secondary gains, such as increased parental and peer attention, and avoidance of school and athletic activities. Undeniably, one of the most common ways children express their fears, dislikes, and avoidance is to complain of aches and pains, often of uncertain or dubious origin.

Girls and boys show interesting differences in this respect. When they are asked, girls report more symptoms of pain and anxiety than boys do (Kröner-Herwig et al., 2011). Under stressful circumstances, girls are more likely to cry, cling, and seek emotional support, and boys are more likely to be uncooperative, avoidant, and stoic. Similarly, excessive somatic symptoms are associated with emotional disorders in girls and disruptive behavior disorders in boys (Egger et al., 1999; Jellesma et al., 2011; Rose & Rudolph, 2006). Does this imply that girls are somehow more sensitive to pain or less able to manage their fear and anxiety than boys? Yes and no. These gender differences stem from socialization expectations as well as biological differences. We are all familiar with the ways boys are encouraged to adopt stoic attitudes about pain, whereas girls are reinforced for passive, affective expression. Both boys and girls react to distress, but they express it according to how they have been taught and what they wish to receive. Therefore, these complaints are within the normal developmental range and do not merit a psychiatric label.

Some children may be more likely than others to experience recurrent pain and physical symptoms because of their family influences. For example, children with functional abdominal pain and similar forms of recurrent unexplained pain are more likely to identify someone in their family who often expresses pain than are children whose pain is due to known organic causes (Marshall et al., 2007). In addition, children of mothers with a somatic disorder are 4 times more likely to express physical symptoms when emotionally upset (Craig, Cox, & Klein, 2002; Guite et al., 2007). These unexplained, recurrent pain symptoms among children, therefore, seem to originate primarily from family *pain models* (Peterson et al., 2003). Children also learn healthy adaptational patterns at home and elsewhere. Children with well-developed social and academic competence, for instance, are less likely to respond to negative life events, such as divorce or hospitalizations, with amplified stress and pain reactions (Walker et al., 2007).

Let's turn our attention now to children who have chronic health problems or conditions. Each chronic illness has unique challenges. Children with diabetes face daily medical routines, but they have a relatively predictable prognosis; children with cancer experience unpleasant side effects of treatment and must also cope with the uncertain prognosis of their illness.

The one important thing that all chronic illnesses and medical conditions have in common is that they constitute a major stressor that challenges and absorbs both the child's and the family's available coping resources. Viewing chronic illness in this way—as a form of major stress requiring adaptation—has allowed researchers to identify factors that promote successful adaptation to chronic illness. This view also has advanced new ways to assist children in coping with these challenges, as we will see.

It is estimated that in North America, 10% to 20% of the child population suffers from some form of chronic health-related disorder or condition (including obesity, diabetes, asthma, and others), and the rate has been rising dramatically in recent years (Brown et al., 2007; Van Cleave, Gortmaker, & Perrin, 2010). Of these children, about two-thirds have mild conditions; the remainder have conditions that result in moderate to severe activity restrictions and bothersome treatment regimens (Peterson et al., 2003). Asthma is the most common chronic illness in childhood, followed by neurological and developmental disabilities and behavioral disorders. Fortunately, severe forms of chronic illnesses—those that pose major physical and intellectual limitations that interfere with children's daily lives—are relatively rare, but their combined rates are sizable.

Table 13.5 shows the incidence rates (i.e., number of new cases occurring in a specified population during a year) of selected chronic childhood diseases and medical conditions. Survival rates for many of these illnesses have greatly improved in recent years (Jemal et al., 2009); therefore, these rates reflect a large proportion of children who have survived these childhood illnesses until 20 years of age or older. The impact of living with HIV and AIDS, currently the sixth leading cause of death among 15- to 24-year-olds in the United States, likely will be a major health issue in the years to come (Garvie et al., 2009; Howland et al., 2007).

TABLE 13.5 | Incidence Rates of Selected Chronic Illnesses in U.S. Children and Adolescents, Ages 0 to 19

Illness	Incidence (per population annually)
Asthma	19.6% of child population[a]
Cancers and tumors	16/100,000 children diagnosed each year[b]
Diabetes mellitus	24/100,000 children diagnosed each year[c]
Sickle-cell anemia	1/500 African American newborns[d]

[a]Prevalence of the total child/youth population (Akinbami, Moorman, & Liu, 2011).
[b]Bloom, Cohen, and Freeman (2011).
[c]Centers for Disease Control and Prevention (CDC) (2011a).
[d]Amendah et al. (2010).

Most chronic childhood illnesses do not discriminate in terms of social class and ethnicity—they can affect children from all walks of life. However, there are certain exceptions to how illnesses affect children, such as the specific conditions genetically determined by racial or ethnic descent. For example, cystic fibrosis affects primarily whites, and sickle-cell disease affects primarily persons of African descent (Thompson & Gustafson, 1996). African American children are about 3 times more likely to be hospitalized for asthma than are their white peers; this difference may be due to the conditions associated with low income and disadvantage (Brown et al., 2007).

Also, a troubling connection exists between socioeconomic status (SES), ethnicity, and survival rates among children and adults with cancer in particular (Wich et al., 2011). Despite attempts to achieve more equitable health care delivery, residents of poorer communities still may receive inferior quality of care, even in universal health care systems like those in Canada (Booth, et al., 2010), Korea (Son et al., 2011), and the United Kingdom (Stringhini et al., 2010). In addition, the poor may have other ailments that make cancer survival more difficult, or parents may be less inclined to seek medical attention if they have other major life stressors or if they are not aware of critical symptoms. In general, children in poor families are 5 times as likely to be in fair or poor health as children in families that are not poor (Bloom et al., 2011). People with adequate means generally have more options and control over their lives, which translates into greater opportunities for proper medical care for their children. Later in this chapter, we consider some ways to empower families and achieve a greater balance in their roles and available resources.

We now take a closer look at two specific illnesses—diabetes mellitus and childhood cancer—that are representative of the course and patterns of adaptation faced by children with chronic illness.

Diabetes Mellitus

AMANDA

Daily Struggle with Diabetes

Amanda, age 14, was diagnosed with insulin-dependent diabetes mellitus about a year ago. Like most teenagers, she leads an active life, and eating the proper foods is difficult enough without the added burden of daily glucose monitoring and insulin injections. She shared with us some of the ways this disease has affected her life, and how she copes with its demands and limitations:

Becoming diabetic has completely changed my life. My best friend is the insulin I take and the machine. I use the machine to test my blood sugar four times a day by poking my finger and putting blood on a test strip.

From the reading I am able to adjust my insulin and what I must eat. I am forced to eat a healthy balanced meal regularly about six times every day. I try not to have a negative attitude because I now realize just how lucky I am. I do not know what I would do if I did not have my machine or all of the sugar-free foods that are now available. Not only did diabetes change my physical life, but it altered my mental life as well. It helped me look at my life and realize what was important to me. My close friend, Germaine, helped me get through the first year at school, when some of the other kids wondered why I had to use needles and couldn't eat the same things they do. My parents have been great, and even my younger brother lays off me when he knows I'm having a particularly bad day. In a way, I'm more aware of how important health is to us than most kids at school, and I don't take things for granted the way I used to. (Based on authors' case material.)

Amanda suffers from **insulin-dependent diabetes mellitus,** a lifelong metabolic disorder in which the body is unable to metabolize carbohydrates because the pancreas releases inadequate amounts of insulin. This lack of insulin has a domino effect on the body's ability to regulate appetite, metabolize carbohydrates into necessary energy, and maintain a balance of blood chemistry. The lack of insulin prohibits glucose from entering the cells, which forces glucose to accumulate in the bloodstream and cause *hyperglycemia*. Glucose also tells the regulatory cells of the hypothalamus when a person is hungry or full, so without this information, the person tends to eat constantly but does not gain weight (Thompson & Gustafson, 1996). A treatment regimen consisting of insulin injections, diet, and exercise is necessary to approximate a normal metabolic state. Although current treatment regimens have greatly improved the health status of people with diabetes, the condition is still associated with significant morbidity and mortality.

Diabetes affects boys and girls equally, and its incidence is increasing: a child born in North America in 2000 stands a one in three chance of being diagnosed with diabetes in his or her lifetime (Canadian Diabetes Association, 2014). Initial symptoms often include fatigue, thirst, hunger, frequent urination, and weight loss despite excessive eating. It is a progressive disease; the more chronic complications that occur during young adulthood or beyond, including circulatory problems, can lead to blindness, kidney failure, and accelerated cardiovascular disease (Siegel, 2008). Individuals with

Adolescents with chronic illness, such as diabetes, must adhere carefully to a daily treatment regimen.

diabetes have an increased risk of illness and death, including a risk of cardiovascular disease double that for the population without diabetes (Franco et al., 2007). Given the seriousness of the illness and the long-standing, intrusive treatment requirements, it is understandable that children with diabetes and their families have an increased risk for conflict and adjustment problems (Ellis et al., 2007).

Children with diabetes face daily treatment tasks to maintain their metabolic control, such as blood-glucose monitoring, dietary restraints, insulin injections, and learning how to balance energy demands and insulin needs (Peterson et al., 2003). **Metabolic control** is the degree to which the patient's glucose levels are maintained within the normal range. Children and adolescents must carefully monitor their insulin levels—too little insulin can result in a diabetic coma, too much insulin can result in an insulin reaction called *hypoglycemia*. Hypoglycemic episodes are extremely unpleasant and can include irritability, headaches, and shakiness. Adding to the complexity is the fact that illness and

stress can upset the relationship between glucose and required insulin levels (Schwartz et al., 2011).

Children and teens must carefully follow the instructions given to them by their physicians; that is, they must practice careful *regimen adherence*. Good regimen adherence and metabolic control are linked to the individuals' correct knowledge about their disease and its treatment, their belief that adherence is important, and adequate problem-solving skills (Drotar, 2013; Rasmussen et al., 2011). As we saw with Amanda, adolescence is a particularly difficult period because of the impact that the illness can have on self-esteem and social and educational experiences—adolescence is difficult enough without the added burden of these daily treatment tasks. Therefore, psychologists have become active in developing ways to promote regimen adherence and metabolic control by helping family members adapt to the demands of the condition (Schwartz et al., 2011). Behavioral strategies have been quite successful in this regard, especially with methods that reinforce symptom reduction or medication use and self-control methods that teach patients to regulate dosage and monitor their symptoms, blood glucose, and medications (Drotar, 2006; Elkin & Stoppelbein, 2008; Jaser & White, 2011).

Childhood Cancer

CHEN

A Determined Boy Fighting Leukemia

Chen, age 9, explains his feelings about childhood leukemia and its impact on his family and peer relations:

I've had cancer now for 3 years. They're still trying to fight it with the right medicine but nothing has worked yet. My friends come visit me—they're pretty OK with everything. But sometimes if you try and tell other kids about it they don't understand because they don't have it. To them we're normal. They don't have any kind of problems that hold them back from doing things. They don't have to worry about being in the hospital, checkups and things, to see how you're doing. You can tell your friends why you have to stop and rest awhile, but they don't really understand—they don't really want to—they want to keep on going. I've got lots of family who care about me and I worry for them. I guess I'm used to all the doctors and medicines I take. Not that I like them but I know it's the only thing that might help. But I liked having the ability to do anything with my friends (or even my parents). I want to be able to get up and go. I'd tell someone else going through this to stay strong and keep the faith. And speak up when you need something!

(continues)

(continued)

Chen's mother explains the ordeal he and his family have undergone since his diagnosis:

Chen received a bone marrow transplant from his brother over a year ago and, thankfully, his leukemia went into remission. But when we went back 1 year later for a checkup, we were told Chen had suffered a relapse—the cancer had overtaken the bone marrow, and his prognosis is poor. Now our family focuses on enjoying our time together and doing things with Chen. We are fortunate—my employer has gone out of his way to help me stay at home with Chen. Their support over the past year has been incredible. In fact, our whole community has shown tremendous support to our family. But his turn for the worse has made it difficult for us to do the things we have done over the past few months. We are angry, hopeful, depressed, joyous, saddened all the time. It is the worst roller coaster that we have ever ridden. Yet, Chen's medical condition has made us more determined to do more than we had ever hoped for, and the kindness shown toward our family has been overwhelming. (Based on authors' case material.)

It is difficult for most of us to imagine what Chen and his family have experienced. Their words acknowledge the importance of their strength and determination and their human kindness when faced with a serious childhood illness, which in this case was terminal. Cancer can strike children very suddenly, more so than with adults, and children are often at a more advanced stage of cancer when they are first diagnosed (Brown et al., 2007). White children suffer the highest rates of cancer as compared to other ethnic groups, but reasons for this disparity are not known. Incidence rates for Hispanic and Asian/Pacific

One out of every 330 children in North America will get cancer before age 20. Despite remarkable research progress, cancer still kills more children than any other disease (National Childhood Cancer Foundation, 2014).

Islander children fall between those for African Americans and whites, while rates for American Indians are much lower than for any other group (Bloom et al., 2011).

The most common form of childhood cancer is acute lymphoblastic leukemia (ALL), which accounts for close to half of all forms of childhood cancer (U.S. Cancer Statistics Working Group, 2013). ALL is actually a group of heterogeneous diseases in which there is a malignancy of the bone marrow, which produces blood cells. In ALL, the bone marrow produces malignant cells called "lymphoblasts" that progressively replace normal bone marrow with fewer red blood cells and more white blood cells, causing anemia, infection, and easy bruising or excessive bleeding (Friedman, Latham, & Dahlquist, 1998). Childhood cancer used to be fatal, but advances in medical treatment have resulted in dramatic improvements in survival rates. Still, long-term complications such as recurrent malignancy, growth retardation, neuropsychological deficits, cataracts, and infertility pose a risk to survival and quality of life.

Like those with diabetes, children with cancer undergo complicated medical treatment regimens, especially during the first 2 to 3 years after diagnosis. In addition, they face school absences, significant treatment side effects, and an uncertain prognosis. Chemotherapy and radiation therapy can cause hair loss and weight changes, as well as nausea, vomiting, increased fatigue, endocrine and growth retardation, and a depressed immune system (Friedman et al., 1998). Children with cancer also must cope with painful medical procedures, such as venipuncture, bone marrow aspiration, and lumbar puncture. Treatment requires children to be away from friends and some family members, which hinders their psychosocial development. Therefore, the psychosocial aspects of pediatric cancer have focused on managing the distress related to the multiple diagnostic and treatment procedures these children face.

Although approximately 80% of pediatric cancer patients survive, about half of the survivors will have a serious physical or mental illness as adults (Krull et al., 2010; Kwak et al., 2013; Zebrack et al., 2002). The most common illnesses include infertility, chronic anxiety, and recurrent cancers (Cantrell, 2011; Stuber et al., 2011). Many patients require long-term care into adulthood because they never learned the life-skills necessary for self-care.

Development and Course

Children with chronic illnesses are more likely than their healthy peers to suffer emotional and behavioral adjustment problems stemming from the burden of their disease and its treatment, especially children with chronic illness accompanied by disability (Hysing et al., 2009). Understandably, children whose normal functional abilities are limited face the greatest challenges in everyday activities; these challenges, in turn, increase behavioral, social, and school-adjustment difficulties. These problems are most often expressed as internalizing symptoms, such as anxiety, depression, or post-traumatic stress disorder, or a combination of both internalizing and externalizing problems (Pao & Bosk, 2011; Pinquart & Shen, 2011; Wechsler & Sánchez-Iglesias, 2013).

To keep these symptoms in perspective, one must recognize that the adjustment of children with chronic illness typically is better than that of children referred to mental health clinics for non-health-related problems (Wechsler & Sánchez-Iglesias, 2013). For the most part, children with chronic illness are exhibiting stress-related symptoms; the incidence of DSM-5-type disorders among these children is actually low. For example, a meta-analysis of 340 studies revealed that symptoms of depression among children with various chronic health conditions are only slightly higher than those of their healthy peers, an encouraging indication of successful adaptation among the vast majority of these children (Pinquart & Shen, 2011). Moreover, children with diabetes and children with cancer on average report symptoms of anxiety, depression, and low self-esteem within the normal range for their age and gender (Brown et al., 2007; Wechsler & Sánchez-Iglesias, 2013).

Although populations of chronically ill children are at risk for initial adjustment difficulties, it is difficult to say what causes particular symptoms or why some children adapt more successfully than others. When one considers how these children must cope with un-predictable events and challenges almost every day, it is understandable that they would have increased stress-related symptoms. It is especially encouraging to know that most can adapt successfully to the course and consequences of their illness. Symptoms of anxiety, depression, and anger can be thought of as normal responses to stressful experiences associated with the long-term illness and treatment regimens, rather than as psychiatric disorders (Wechsler & Sánchez-Iglesias, 2013). This is similar to the adjustment problems faced by children with intellectual disabilities and children who have been abused or neglected. Most children with chronic illness show considerable resilience in the face of stressful experiences associated with their condition, and we should exercise caution in applying psychiatric labels or descriptors that fail to capture the context and nature of their circumstances.

Effect on Family Members

The field of pediatric health psychology has clearly adopted a focus on the important role of family functioning in the adjustment of children with chronic illness.

The child's circumstances may result in family cohesion and support, as we saw in Amanda's and Chen's families, or it may result in family disruption and crisis. As parents try to understand and cope with the news of their child's diagnosis, they must at the same time start to accept that their child might always be different from other children. How they react and accept these realities determines, to a large extent, how their child and other siblings will react and adapt. Parents who fail to resolve this crisis are more likely to have problems with attachment and child-rearing, which further complicates the stressful nature of the child's illness (Mullins et al., 2007).

Learning that a child has a life-threatening disease causes trauma and stress to all family members and, in fact, qualifies as a traumatic event that can precipitate post-traumatic stress disorder (PTSD) (Kwak et al., 2013). A mother of an infant born with a chronic disability describes her initial reaction:

> I felt like I was bouncing around on a raft in the middle of a terrible storm. I didn't know where I was, where I was going, or what wave was going to break over my head next. Most of the time, I just hung on. Hanging on, I discovered, is the key to survival. (Medvescek, 1997, p. 67)

Many parents of children with chronic illness report that their fears resurface and memories return whenever their child has only a common illness, like a cold or flu (Pai et al., 2007). About 10% of mothers and fathers suffer symptoms of PTSD, a rate that is comparable to that for other types of traumatic stress exposure (Barakat, Hocking, & Kazak, 2013). Fortunately, the children themselves do not typically suffer PTSD-related symptoms upon learning of their disorder, probably because they are very young at the time of diagnosis. However, children's memories of stressful procedures play a role in their experience of distress, and some survivors of childhood cancer recall disturbing memories of the medical procedures many years later (Stuber & Shemesh, 2006).

Families affect the behavior of children with chronic health problems, as they do the behavior of the healthy children. No one type of chronic illness poses a significantly greater risk of adjustment than another. Thus, factors associated with children's situations—such as family stress and resources—may be more critical to their adaptation than the challenges posed by the illness alone (Peterson & Drotar, 2006). The degree to which parents can assist their older children in developing more autonomy and control over their treatment regimens in a nonconflictual manner predicts the likelihood that the teen will adhere to the treatment regimen. The normal conflict observed in parent–teenager relationships is heightened in families in which the teen is trying to incorporate a treatment regimen into a changing lifestyle. For example, drinking alcohol is a significant risk for teens with diabetes; therefore, conversations and parental expectations regarding experimentation with substance use often are heightened because alcohol use is more deleterious (Jaser & White, 2011).

The amount of concordance between parent and teen perceptions of who is making decisions about treatment is not what predicts adherence to treatments—it is the degree of conflict in the parent–teen relationship (Drotar, 2013). Thus, parents who can help their teen in a nonconfrontational manner to maintain adherence (regardless of whether they agree with their child about who is in fact making treatment decisions) will increase their teen's health and adaptation. In general, the following stress factors that parents face are quite similar across all types of pediatric chronic illness: financial and physical burdens, changes in parenting roles, sibling resentment, child adjustment problems, social isolation, frequent hospitalizations, and grief (Alriksson-Schmidt, Wallander, & Biasini, 2007). It comes as no surprise, therefore, that couples with chronically ill children report more marital conflict, poor communication, role incongruity, and a lack of intimacy and positive affect (Rodrigues & Patterson, 2007).

The point is worth repeating: Despite these psychological and tangible repercussions, many children with chronic illness adapt favorably to these challenges, as do their families (Long & Marsland, 2011). Perceived social support and parental adaptation are key components aiding the child's adaptation, since primary caregivers play an important role in their children's stress and coping abilities. Specifically, mothers who perceive lower levels of illness-related stress, use more adaptive and active ways to cope with stress and problems, and perceive their families as more supportive than conflictual are more likely to show normal adjustment levels themselves (Thompson & Gustafson, 1996). Regardless of the circumstances, we often see this connection: When maternal abilities remain intact, child and family functioning is less impaired. This illustrates the reciprocal relationship between children's adjustment and parental stress and distress—healthy parental adjustment is related to healthy child adjustment, and vice versa. (Most research has considered only the role of mothers on child adjustment, but the specific influence of fathers on children's coping and adaptation to chronic illness is being recognized [Ware & Raval, 2007].) Thus, parental adjustment is one of the important correlates of children's adjustment to chronic illness.

Siblings of children with a chronic illness also experience heightened social and mental health problems.

They tend to have more internalizing symptoms, such as depression and anxiety, lower cognitive scores, and fewer peer activities (Bellin & Kovacs, 2006). These outcomes are worse for chronic illnesses that require daily treatment regimens, which suggests that the increased caregiving demands faced by parents and the subsequent decreased amounts of parental attention for siblings contribute to their maladjustment. Despite these problems, many children with a chronic illness benefit from sibling relationships, and vice versa, because of the positive bond that is often formed between them (Havermans et al., 2011; Long & Marsland, 2011).

Social Adjustment and School Performance

Children's adjustment to chronic illness is reflected not only in terms of psychological distress, but also through developmental accomplishments in social adjustment, peer relationships, and school performance. Because chronic illness results in lifestyle interruptions that interfere with opportunities for social interaction, children with more severe, disruptive illnesses tend to suffer in social adjustment (La Greca, Bearman, & Moore, 2002). This maladjustment often is expressed by children displaying more submissive behavior with their peers and engaging in fewer social activities overall (Meijer et al., 2002).

Consider the peer relationships of children with cancer. Chen explained how the other children did not understand why he could not join in or behave the same as they did—to them he looked normal, so he must be okay. Negative or ill-informed reactions from peers and others are, unfortunately, a fact of life for some children with chronic illness. In a longitudinal study of children with cancer, adolescents were perceived by their teachers as less sociable, less prone toward leadership, and more socially isolated and withdrawn than their peers (Noll et al., 1991). Similar problems in social adjustment are evident among children with illnesses that affect primarily the CNS—cerebral palsy, spina bifida, and brain tumors—because of the impact of these disorders on cognitive abilities such as social judgment (Hysing et al., 2009).

School adjustment and performance is another domain in which children and adolescents with chronic illness are at increased risk for adjustment difficulties. Risk may stem from two sources: primary effects of the illness or its treatment, and secondary consequences of the illness, such as fatigue, absenteeism, or psychological stress (Witt, Riley, & Coiro, 2003). Primary effects of the illness on school performance are especially evident among children with brain-related illnesses. They must undergo aggressive treatment regimens that put a heavy toll on the CNS, especially for younger children (Brown et al., 2007). The most common neurocognitive effects appear in nonverbal abilities and attention or concentration functions (Mulhern et al., 2004; Reeves et al., 2006). Short-term memory, speed of processing, visuomotor coordination, and sequencing ability also frequently are affected (Reeves et al., 2006). Thus, about half of the children with brain-related illnesses are placed in special education settings or do not attend school. In contrast, children with physical, non-brain-related illnesses tend to have normal educational placements; however, they continue to have problems with reading, which may be one indirect effect of chronic illness and school absence (Witt et al., 2003).

How Children Adapt: A Biopsychosocial Model

We have described the adjustment difficulties of children with chronic illness in general terms, but we know that each child's illness and family situation is different. Some children, like Amanda and Chen, have supportive families with adequate resources, but others may not. Countless events can influence children's adaptation to chronic illness; no single factor explains why some children adjust more readily than others.

How do we make sense of the numerous factors influencing children's adjustment? When a single-factor theory is not a sufficient explanation, researchers often develop multifactorial theories that link the most important variables in conceptual and meaningful ways. The *transactional stress and coping model* explains how children's adaptation to chronic illness is influenced not only by the nature of the illness itself, but also by personal and family resources (Gustafson et al., 2006; Thompson et al., 1994). This model helps make sense of the complicated processes that shape children's outcomes.

The transactional stress and coping model emphasizes the stressful nature of chronic illness, which compels the child and family members to adapt. How they accomplish the adaptation is a key factor in children's outcomes.

Illness parameters encompass the type of illness and the severity of the illness, including visible disfigurement and functional impairment. Demographic parameters include the gender, age, and SES of the child, which also can affect the impact of the illness. The model then proposes that important child and family processes mediate the illness–outcome relationship, beyond the illness and demographic factors. Important psychological mediators involve parental adjustment, child adjustment, and their interrelationship, as described next.

Family support plays a crucial role in helping children cope with chronic illness.

Illness Parameters

One would expect that children's psychosocial adjustment varies as a function of their medical condition. Some illnesses have an uncertain course and others have dire effects on everyday activities, adding stress along the way. Different chronic illnesses have many features in common, though, so it often makes sense to study children's adjustment in relation to illness-related dimensions, or parameters, rather than their adjustment to specific illnesses. The common dimensions that vary among different illnesses include things such as the extent to which the illness:

- Is visible to others, or involves physical deformity.
- Is severe and life-threatening.
- Has a worsening or fatal prognosis versus a stable or improving prognosis.
- Requires intrusive or painful procedures.
- Affects the child's functional status, such as physical or cognitive impairments that affect performance of everyday tasks. (Thompson & Gustafson, 1996)

Children with chronic illness face different challenges along each of these dimensions, so naturally their adjustment may be affected accordingly. Across all medical conditions, the illness parameters that play the most significant role in children's adjustment are *severity, prognosis*, and *functional status* (Lavigne & Faier-Routman, 1993). Functional status seems to be especially important in terms of cognitive impairments, such as conditions that involve the brain and CNS.

Personal Characteristics

Chronic medical conditions require both children and family members to accept and cope with considerable stress and uncertainty. Which child characteristics and resources might favor successful adaptation? A child's sex is one consideration: Boys with chronic illness show more adjustment problems overall than girls. However, this sex difference depends on the dimension of adjustment and who is reporting the information. Boys are described by parents and teachers as having more behavior problems than girls; however, girls are more likely than boys to self-report anxiety, depression, and negative perceptions of physical appearance (Miller & La Greca, 2005).

Although children's overall adjustment seldom differs as a function of current age or age at the onset of the illness, economic and health disparities that exist among ethnic minority children and their families play a contributing role. These disparities not only affect the course and treatment of chronic illnesses, but also have a pronounced effect on quality of life and risk of disease and disability. Being poor is a risk factor for many stressful life events, but being poor and having a health problem greatly increases distress and adjustment problems (Greenberg, Raymond, & Leeder, 2011). Similarly, treatment studies on chronic illness in children and adolescents have not addressed important cultural issues that affect treatment outcome, especially compliance with the treatment regimen (Clay, Mordhorst, & Lend, 2002; Elkin & Stoppelbein, 2008).

Not surprisingly, children with greater intellectual ability and acquired strengths in their self-concept and coping skills also show more positive psychological adjustment, regardless of their medical condition. Specifically, children's accurate appraisal of perceived stress—how they interpret and react to daily events and hassles associated with illness management—leads to a better sense of well-being and fewer symptoms of distress and maladjustment (Pai et al., 2006). Chen states this well:

> I now realize that life is full of a series of tests. You never know what is around the corner, but you have to take it as it comes. A positive attitude, and remembering that I have friends and family for support, helps me get through some of the rough days.

Family Adaptation and Functioning

If chronic illness is considered a stressor affecting all family members to some extent, then child adjustment depends in part on the degree of stress and symptoms experienced by other family members, especially the primary caregiver. Undeniably, the family environment assumes greater importance in the lives of children with a chronic illness, in part because a closer parent–child interaction often is necessary to manage the disease.

The transactional model considers parental adaptation to be a key mediator of the relationship between child illness and adjustment for both child and parent. How does a parent "adapt" in a way that favors healthy outcomes? According to the model, parental adaptation is a function of three major processes: (1) how they manage daily stress and view their self-efficacy, as seen with Chen's mother; (2) whether they use active, solution-focused coping; and (3) family functioning and perceived support. Successful parental adaptation, in turn, leads to better parental adjustment and healthier family communication and conflict-resolution skills (Wysocki et al., 2008). Ultimately, of course, parents' positive adjustment greatly increases the likelihood of more positive child outcomes. Parents' perceptions of illness are one aspect of parental adaptation that plays a key role in promoting their child's health. Perceptions of child vulnerability are related to increased social anxiety in their children and more school absences (Long & Marsland, 2011).

Family functioning often is defined in terms of the availability of two types of primary family resources: *utilitarian* and *psychological*. Utilitarian family resources relate to the practical demands of caring for a child with a disability, such as financial resources and parental education, which influence their ability to understand the illness and seek beneficial assistance for their child. Psychological resources are less tangible but often are considered far more important—how family members support one another, relate to each other and to persons outside the family, and resolve conflicts. Together these two types of family resources account for considerable variance in the behavioral and social adjustment of chronically ill children (Robinson et al., 2007).

Intervention

The psychological impact of chronic illness occurs through the disruption of normal processes of child development and family functioning. Fortunately, this impact can be lessened and adaptation can be strengthened by the use of psychosocial interventions that reduce stress, enhance social problem-solving skills, and promote effective child-rearing methods. These various methods often entail stress-management and skill-building components to assist children and family members in their continuous process of adaptation.

The basic goal of intervention is to enhance the quality of life for the children and their families. Ways to achieve this goal have taken a dramatic shift over the past four decades, given the strong interest of pediatric and health psychologists. Prior to the mid-1970s, intervention efforts primarily were based on a child-centered, medically based model. The health professional was the expert, the child was the patient, and parents were passive observers. Today, parents are expected to participate in the decision-making process and their child's educational planning, which has led to family-centered interventions. In effect, families are now recognized as important resources, and they are seen as part of the solution; they are kept in the forefront of children's intervention needs, not in the background.

Empowering Families

This underlying philosophy of family empowerment reduces stress and dependency and enables families to obtain the necessary information to make informed decisions and take competent actions. Chen's family members, for example, took an active role in enhancing his quality of life and were not frightened away or uninformed about his needs and their opportunities. His mother explains:

> Physiotherapy has helped Chen be less dependent on mom and dad. The goal is for him to think ahead and be prepared to do things on his own. An example is at bedtime getting his clothes out and onto the bed for the following morning. Then in the morning he can get himself dressed and transferred into his chair by himself.

Support groups and educational programs of various types offer considerable benefits to children and other family members. Helping families connect with one another and share their common experiences and concerns generates both personal power and important resources for change (Barakat et al., 2013; Drotar, 2006). Participation is the active agent in empowerment, and a cooperative health professional–family model encourages individuals to support one another while providing a venue for modeling positive attitudes and values. Similarly, educational programs that provide information and skills training to family members often are beneficial. The most beneficial programs promote knowledge and self-management of the illness, reintegration of children into the school setting, and support and coordination of care among parents of children with chronic illness (Canter & Roberts, 2012; Drotar & Bonner, 2009). Gaining more knowledge about their child's disease promotes greater parental understanding of the child and the overall effect of the disease on the family.

In short, treatment-related activities for children with chronic illness often are based on the needs of the entire family. However, these efforts must fit the degree to which parents want to be—and realistically can be—involved in their child's overall care. Intervention methods that favor these adaptive processes adhere to medical regimens and psychologically based approaches to help children cope with the pain that is associated with invasive medical procedures and illness, as described in the next section.

Helping Children Cope

Throughout our discussion of children with chronic illness, we have seen how they must cope with numerous stressful circumstances, ranging from painful medical procedures to peer rejection and functional limitations. For this reason, considerable effort has been placed on ways to enhance their successful coping through support groups (see A Closer Look 13.1) and recreational activities (see A Closer Look 13.2). Much of this work focuses on coping with painful medical procedures, yet these methods also apply to other settings and circumstances, including at school or during home routines. Parental involvement and adaptation are, once again, key components in children's coping; to effectively assist their children, parents must maximize their sense of control over the outcome and progress of their children's health (Robinson et al., 2007).

Enhancing adaptation and quality of life of children with chronic illness similarly requires that children comply as much as possible with medical regimens, both inside and outside the doctor's office. Since children often do not comply with even simpler tasks—like following directions, eating what they should, or getting ready for school—how can we expect them to comply with the unpleasant demands of medical procedures? The significance of these procedures has caused the emphasis in pediatric health psychology to shift to helping children and their parents cope with necessary protocols, rather than developing ways to make them comply.

Evidence suggests that most children and adults do best if a stressful medical procedure is explained first and they are given an opportunity to see what is going to happen. Accordingly, interventions for reducing stress and managing pain during pediatric procedures have applied behavioral and cognitive approaches that emphasize *coping and stress management* (Hermann, 2011). Children who actively seek information about impending painful events show improved adjustment and less distress (Williams, Blount, & Walker, 2011).

"insatiable voracity, morbid or canine appetite, with or without vomiting" (Parry-Jones & Parry-Jones, 1994, p. 288). Interestingly, almost all of these historical cases described males, perhaps because overeating was socially accepted as a sign of wealth or success. Ideal body sizes change with the times and with cultural preferences. Rubenesque figures were considered highly attractive and desirable until the late 19th century, when body image preferences were usurped by major cultural changes. During the Victorian period, refusing food was in keeping with prevailing social pressures. A hearty appetite was considered a wanton expression of sexuality and lack of self-restraint; women were expected to be passively uninterested in both sex and food. Thus, it became morally, spiritually, and socially desirable for women to refuse food, in response to shifting cultural norms for women's appearance and behavior (Brumberg, 1988).

According to physicians around the turn of the 20th century, anorexia nervosa was a symptom of inappropriate romantic choices, blocked educational or social opportunities, and conflicts with parents. Slimness symbolized asexuality and gentility, which implied a respectable amount of social distance from the working classes (Attie & Brooks-Gunn, 1995). Since the 1930s, attitudes and beliefs about women's ideal body size and appearance have been shaped by advertisers, film stars, clothing designers, and similar forces, resulting in a prevailing cultural preference for slimness.

The meaning of food and eating for gender identity, the role of family and social class in determining body image and food choices, and the use of weight regulation as a substitute for self-regulation and control in adolescence remain salient causes of eating disorders to this day. Within the past quarter century, additional aspects of eating disorders, such as the chronic refusal of food, emphasis on overactivity, and bulimic symptoms of bingeing and purging, have gained recognition as significant and potentially dangerous complications (von Ranson & Wallace, 2014).

Anorexia Nervosa

SOOKI

Obsessed with Food and Weight

Sooki is a 19-year old Asian-American college student who is 5 feet 4 inches tall and weighs 90.3 pounds. Friends have not noticed that Sooki has lost so much weight over the past year (25 pounds!) because she wears baggy clothes. About a year ago, Sooki became extremely afraid of becoming fat. She was convinced that weight gain would be the worst thing possible and that her college life would be ruined if she gained weight. Sooki began skipping meals and, when she did eat once or twice a day, consumed only a "salad" of small items. Her salad consists of four lettuce leaves, part of a carrot, an apple slice, and no dressing. Sooki is preoccupied with food and calories. Every bite of food she eats is carefully considered, and she carries charts that list calories per serving of many different foods. She drinks only water and diet soda.

Sooki is obsessed with how much she weighs and how she looks. She owns two scales: one is near her bed and one is in her bathroom. She weighs herself 10 or more times a day. Sooki has told others her butt is too big and her stomach is "poochy." Sooki is markedly underweight but frequently checks her body in the mirror to make sure she is not becoming fat. Her self-esteem depends heavily on her body weight. When Sooki weighs more than 90 pounds she feels bad about herself; when she weighs less than 90 pounds she is perkier. Sooki views weight loss as an impressive achievement in self-discipline. Family members have noticed her weight change and have told Sooki she is underweight. Sooki has not had her menstrual period for 6 months. Still, Sooki does not see her eating and low weight as a problem. She hopes to lose more weight by eliminating "fattening" foods from her diet such as apple slices and diet soda. Sooki has kept to herself recently and leaves her room only to attend class.

From Kearney/Trull. Cengage Advantage Books: Abnormal Psychology and Life, 1E

Sooki is suffering from **anorexia nervosa**, an eating disorder characterized by:

▶ the refusal to maintain a minimally normal body weight.

▶ an intense fear of gaining weight.

▶ a significant disturbance in the individual's perception and experiences of his or her own size.

As Sooki's story shows, anorexia is a severe eating disorder with serious physical and mental health consequences if left untreated. One of the most notable features of the psychopathology of the disease is that persons who have it deny that they are too thin or that they have a weight problem. As a result, friends or family members often must insist on taking them to see a physician. Diagnostic criteria for anorexia are shown in Table 14.1.

Although the word *anorexia* literally means "loss of appetite," that definition is misleading because the

19 year-old Sooki worries about being fat and weighs herself 10 or more times a day.

TABLE 14.1 | **Diagnostic Criteria for Anorexia Nervosa**

(A) Restriction of energy intake relative to requirements, leading to a significantly low body weight in the context of age, sex, developmental trajectory, and physical health. *Significantly low weight* is defined as a weight that is less than minimally normal or, for children and adolescents, less than that minimally expected. **DSM-5**

(B) Intense fear of gaining weight or of becoming fat, or persistent behavior that interferes with weight gain, even though at a significantly low weight.

(C) Disturbance in the way in which one's body weight or shape is experienced, undue influence of body weight or shape on self-evaluation, or persistent lack of recognition of the seriousness of the current low body weight.

Specify if:

Restricting type: During the past 3 months, the individual has not engaged in recurrent episodes of binge eating or purging behavior (i.e., self-induced vomiting or the misuse of laxatives, diuretics, or enemas). This subtype describes presentations in which weight loss is accomplished primarily through dieting, fasting, and/or excessive exercise.

Binge eating/purging type: During the past 3 months, the individual has engaged in recurrent episodes of binge eating or purging behavior (i.e., self-induced vomiting or the misuse of laxatives, diuretics, or enemas).

Specify if:

In partial remission: After full criteria for anorexia nervosa were previously met, Criteria A (low body weight) has not been met for a sustained period, but either Criterion B (intense fear of gaining weight or becoming fat or behavior that interferes with weight gain) or Criterion C (disturbances in self-perception of weight and shape) is still met.

Specify current severity:

For children and adolescents the minimum level of severity is based on current body mass index (BMI; the weight in kilograms divided by the square of the height in meters) percentile. The level of severity may be increased to reflect clinical symptoms, the degree of functional disability, and the need for supervision.

Mild: BMI ≥17
Moderate: BMI 16 to 16.99
Severe: BMI 15 to 15.99
Extreme: BMI <15

Source: Diagnostic and Statistical Manual of Mental Disorders, 5th ed. American Psychiatric Association.

person with this disorder rarely suffers appetite loss. Weight loss is accomplished deliberately through a very restricted diet, purging, and/or exercise. Although many persons occasionally use these methods to lose weight, the individual with anorexia intensely fears obesity and pursues thinness relentlessly.

Young persons who suffer from anorexia show a major distortion in how they experience their weight and shape. They may become obsessed with measuring themselves to see whether the "fat" has been eliminated. Thus, how they see themselves and how they relate to others is often a function of their perceived shape and weight. To such an individual, weight loss is a triumph of self-discipline. But with anorexia there is never enough weight loss: The person always wants to lose more weight to be on the safe side, and if not enough weight is lost one day, the person may panic and work extra hard to lose weight the next day.

The DSM-5 specifies two subtypes of anorexia based on the methods used to limit caloric intake. In the **restricting type,** individuals seek to lose weight primarily through diet, fasting, or excessive exercise;

in the **binge eating/purging type**, the individual regularly engages in episodes of binge eating or purging, or both. Compared with persons with bulimia, those with the binge eating/purging type of anorexia eat relatively small amounts of food and commonly purge more consistently and thoroughly. Because studies have failed to find significant evidence of the differences between the binge–purge and restricting subtypes of anorexia, subtypes are used mostly to describe current symptoms rather than a distinctive pattern or course (Eddy et al., 2009; Forbush et al., 2010).

Bulimia Nervosa

PHILLIPA

A Well-Kept Secret

Phillipa developed bulimia nervosa at 18. Her strange eating behavior began when she started to diet. Phillipa began gaining weight because she was eating a lot at night. With the extra weight came self-loathing. "I felt like my body was in the way of me being successful at school, and getting dates. I looked in the mirror several times a day, thinking 'I don't even want to be in this body.' There wasn't a minute in my life that I didn't think about some aspect of how I looked."

Although Phillipa dieted and exercised to lose weight, she regularly ate huge amounts of food and maintained her normal weight by forcing herself to vomit. Phillipa often felt like an emotional powder keg—angry, frightened, and depressed. Unable to understand her own behavior, Phillipa thought no one else would either. She felt isolated and lonely. Typically, when things were not going well, she would be overcome with an uncontrollable desire for sweets. She would eat pounds of candy and cake at a time and often not stop until she was exhausted or in severe pain. Then, overwhelmed with guilt and disgust, she would make herself vomit.

Her eating habits so embarrassed her that she kept them secret until, depressed by her mounting problems, she attempted suicide. Fortunately, she didn't succeed. While recuperating in the hospital, Phillipa was referred to an eating disorders clinic where she became involved in group therapy. There she received medications to treat the illness and the understanding and help she so desperately needed from others who had the same problem. With a smile, Phillipa explains: "It taught me that my self-worth is not absolutely correlated with my appearance or what others may think of me."

National Institute of Mental Health [NIMH], 1994b.

Of the two major forms of eating disorders afflicting adolescents and young adults, **bulimia nervosa** is far more common than anorexia. The DSM-5 diagnostic criteria listed in Table 14.2 note that the primary hallmark of bulimia is binge eating. Because most of us overeat certain foods at certain times, you may ask "What exactly is a binge?" As noted in the criteria, a **binge** is an episode of overeating that must involve: (1) an objectively large amount of food (more than most people would eat under the circumstances), and (2) lack of control over what or how much food is eaten.

No specific quantity of food constitutes a binge—the context of the behavior that must also be considered.

TABLE 14.2 | **Diagnostic Criteria for Bulimia Nervosa**

DSM-5

(A) Recurrent episodes of binge eating. An episode of binge eating is characterized by both of the following:

(1) Eating, in a discrete period of time (e.g., within any 2-hour period), an amount of food that is definitely larger than most people would eat during a similar period of time and under similar circumstances

(2) A sense of lack of control over eating during the episode (e.g., a feeling that one cannot stop eating or control what or how much one is eating)

(B) Recurrent inappropriate compensatory behavior in order to prevent weight gain, such as self-induced vomiting; the misuse of laxatives, diuretics or enemas, or other medications; fasting; or excessive exercise.

(C) The binge eating and inappropriate compensatory behaviors both occur, on average, at least once a week for 3 months.

(D) Self-evaluation is unduly influenced by body shape and weight.

(E) The disturbance does not occur exclusively during episodes of anorexia nervosa.

Specify if:

In partial remission: After full criteria for bulimia nervosa were previously met, some, but not all, of the criteria have been met for a sustained period of time.

In full remission: After full criteria for bulimia nervosa were previously met, none of the criteria have been met for a sustained period of time.

Specify current severity:

The minimum level of severity is based on the frequency of inappropriate compensatory behaviors (see below). The level of severity may be increased to reflect other symptoms and the degree of functional disability.

Mild: an average of 1 to 3 episodes of inappropriate compensatory behaviors per week.

(continues)

TABLE 14.2 | **Diagnostic Criteria for**
Bulimia Nervosa (continued)

Moderate: an average of 4 to 7 episodes of inappropriate compensatory behaviors per week.

Severe: an average of 8 to 13 episodes of inappropriate compensatory behaviors per week.

Extreme: an average of 14 or more episodes of inappropriate compensatory behaviors per week.

Source: Diagnostic and Statistical Manual of Mental Disorders, Fifth Edition. American Psychiatric Association.

Overeating at celebrations or holiday feasts, for example, is not considered bingeing. Although most binge eaters report overeating junk food rather than fresh fruits and vegetables, the amounts of food they consider a binge vary widely. On average, binge episodes range from 1000 to 4,500 calories, (Wolfe et al., 2009).

Persons with bulimia attempt to conceal binge eating out of shame. Although binges are not planned, a ritual may form wherein the person, sensing no one around, makes a split-second decision (on the way

Like African American women, Latinas were thought to possess a kind of cultural immunity to eating disorders, but current trends disprove that.

David J. Green - lifestyle themes/Alamy

home from a late-night party, for example) to stop, purchase, and consume massive quantities of food. Typically, binge eating follows changes in mood or interpersonal stress, but it also may be related to intense hunger from dieting or to feelings about personal appearance or body shape. Although these feelings may dissipate for awhile, the depressed mood and self-criticism usually return (Smyth et al., 2007).

The second important part of the diagnostic criteria involves the individual's attempts to compensate somehow for a binge. **Compensatory behaviors** are intended to prevent weight gain following a binge episode, and include self-induced vomiting, fasting, exercising, and the misuse of diuretics, laxatives, enemas, or diet pills. By far the most common compensatory technique after an episode of binge eating is induced vomiting—stimulating the gag reflex with the fingers or another instrument. Vomiting produces immediate relief from physical discomfort and reduces fear of gaining weight.

Research with community (nonclinical) samples has not identified any significant differences between persons with bulimia who purge and those who do not (Tanofsky-Kraff et al., 2004). Dietary symptoms (e.g., restraint, purging) are central features of bulimia, but a subset of people with bulimia exhibit both dietary restraint and depressive affect. Young women who have the dietary–depressive pattern exhibit more eating pathology, social impairment, psychiatric comorbidity, and persistence of bulimic symptoms over 5 years than women with only the dietary subtype (Stice & Fairburn, 2003).

Like those with anorexia, adolescents and adults with bulimia often are described as rigid and absolutistic (displaying an all-or-nothing attitude) in their thinking (Joiner, Katz, & Heatherton, 2000; Thompson-Brenner et al., 2008). They see themselves as either completely in control or completely out of control and view everyday events in extremes of either black or white. Phillipa expressed absolutistic thinking, attributing her woes to one thing and one thing only: "I felt like my body was in the way of me being successful at school, and getting dates." These beliefs relate to the DSM-5 criteria, which stress the importance of body shape and weight to self-evaluation. Young women with bulimia, as well as those with anorexia, have greater dissatisfaction with their body proportions and distort their true body size, behaviors that are more strongly connected to cognitive factors, such as biases in attention and memory, and selective interpretation or judgment, than with any actual problem with perceptual ability (Striegel-Moore & Bulik, 2007).

The medical consequences of chronic bulimia can be significant, although they are not as severe as the consequences that can result from anorexia. Common physical symptoms include fatigue, headaches, and puffy cheeks (due to enlarged salivary glands). The permanent or significant loss of dental enamel, especially from the inside surface of the front teeth, is due to the contact of the acidic stomach contents with the teeth. Among females, menstrual irregularity or amenorrhea may occur, although it is not clear whether these disturbances are related to weight fluctuations, other nutritional deficiencies, or stress. Electrolyte imbalances due to purging behavior are sometimes severe enough to cause significant medical problems.

Binge Eating Disorder

Binge eating disorder (BED) has become increasingly widespread during this age of abundant fast food and obesity. Although similar to the binge eating found in bulimia, BED does not include the compensatory behaviors (see Table 14.3). It involves periods of eating more than other people would, accompanied by a feeling of a loss of control (APA, 2013). Researchers differ about whether binge episodes are objective overeating (e.g., over 1,000 calories) or an individual, subjective feeling of losing control (e.g., eating two cookies on a strict diet). Youths define overeating in a variety of ways, including the amount and types of food eaten, emotional consequences after the binge (e.g., feeling guilty), and the individual's reasons for overeating (Neumark-Sztainer et al., 2006). In contrast to individuals with bulimia nervosa, who tend

(C) Marked distress regarding binge eating is present.

(D) The binge eating occurs, on average, at least once a week for 3 months.

(E) The binge eating is not associated with the recurrent use of inappropriate compensatory behavior as in bulimia nervosa and does not occur exclusively during the course of bulimia nervosa or anorexia nervosa.

Specify if:

In partial remission: After full criteria for binge eating disorder were previously met, binge eating occurs at an average frequency of less than one episode per week for a sustained period of time.

In full remission: After full criteria for binge eating disorder were previously met, none of the criteria have been met for a sustained period of time.

Specify current severity:

The minimum level of severity is based on the frequency of episodes of binge eating (see below). The level of severity may be increased to reflect other symptoms and the degree of functional disability.

Mild: 1 to 3 binge eating episodes per week.

Moderate: 4 to 7 binge eating episodes per week.

Severe: 8 to 13 binge eating episodes per week.

Extreme: 14 or more binge eating episodes per week.

Source: Diagnostic and Statistical Manual of Mental Disorders, Fifth Edition. American Psychiatric Association.

to be normal weight to overweight, individuals with BED are often overweight or obese (von Ranson & Wallace, 2014).

The mounting concern over BED is justified not only by the higher rates of obesity and weight loss attempts, but also by the negative mental health correlates. Youths with BED score lower on body satisfaction and self-esteem, score higher on depressive mood, and are more likely to report that weight and shape are very important to their overall feelings about themselves (Stice et al., 2009; Stice et al., 2013).

Diagnosing eating disorders is especially difficult among youths, who are still maturing physically, cognitively, and emotionally. As a result, criteria for eating disorders may not be fully met (Eddy et al., 2009; Eddy, Doyle et al., 2008). To accommodate this disparity, DSM-5 includes the categories Other Specified Feeding or Eating Disorder and Other Unspecified Feeding or Eating Disorder. These categories of eating disorders are used for individuals who are deemed to have a clinically significant eating disorder but who do not meet the full criteria for anorexia, bulimia, or BED (sometimes termed *subthreshold*). These "other"

TABLE 14.3 | **Diagnostic Criteria for Binge Eating Disorder**

(A) Recurrent episodes of binge eating. An episode of binge eating is characterized by both of the following: `DSM-5`

   (1) Eating, in a discrete period of time (e.g., within any 2-hour period), an amount of food that is definitely larger than what most people would eat in a similar period of time under similar circumstances.

   (2) A sense of lack of control over eating during the episode (e.g., a feeling that one cannot stop eating or control what or how much one is eating).

(B) The binge eating episodes are associated with three (or more) of the following:

   (1) Eating much more rapidly than normal

   (2) Eating until feeling uncomfortably full

   (3) Eating large amounts of food when not feeling physically hungry

   (4) Eating alone because of feeling embarrassed by how much one is eating

   (5) Feeling disgusted with oneself, depressed, or very guilty afterward.

categories are less stringent, and therefore are sometimes more appropriate for adolescents (Keel et al., 2010). Because the majority of adolescents with eating problems do not meet the diagnostic criteria for bulimia, anorexia, or BED, professional organizations such as the Society for Adolescent Medicine have advised clinicians to set lower thresholds for diagnosing adolescents with eating disorders (i.e., not requiring that they meet all the DSM-5 criteria).

An overview of key features of anorexia, bulimia, and binge eating disorder is shown in Table 14.4 for ease of comparison.

Prevalence and Development

A large nationwide U.S. sample showed that the lifetime prevalence of anorexia and bulimia among adolescents is 0.3% and 0.9%, respectively (Swanson et al., 2011). Although BED is more prevalent in young adulthood, it affects about 1.5% to 3% of adolescents (Stice, Marti, & Rohde, 2013; Swanson et al., 2011). Distinguishing between the major eating disorders of adolescence and young adulthood can be difficult because anorexia, bulimia, and BED share many features. Adolescents with anorexia or bulimia

TABLE 14.4 | Overview of Anorexia, Bulimia, and Binge Eating Disorders

	Anorexia	Bulimia	Binge Eating Disorder
Key Diagnostic Criteria	• Food restriction leading to significantly low body weight • Fear of or interference with weight gain • Disturbance in self-perceived weight or shape (distorted body perception)	• Recurrent binge eating • Recurrent compensatory behaviors to prevent weight gain • View of self unduly influenced by body shape and weight	• Recurrent episodes of binge eating (similar to bulimia but differs in terms of eating more rapidly, eating alone, eating large amounts when not hungry, and feeling disgusted or guilty afterward) • Marked distress regarding binge eating • Binge eating not associated with compensatory behaviors, as in bulimia
Prevalence in Adolescents and Young Adults	~0.3%	~1%	~1.5–3%
Sex Ratio	Girls affected significantly more than boys (~90%)	Girls affected significantly more than boys (~90%)	Girls more than boys (to a lesser degree than anorexia and bulimia)
Mortality	~5% per decade	~2% per decade	Unknown (overlaps with complications of obesity)
Weight	Markedly reduced	Usually normal	Can be normal, overweight, or obese
Onset	Early to mid-adolescence	Mid- to late adolescence	Late adolescence
Menstrual Irregularity or Amenorrhea	Common	Common	Not present
Comorbidity	Common: bipolar; depression; anxiety; suicide risk Less common: obsessive–compulsive disorder, substance-use disorder	Common: mood disturbance and depression; anxiety Less common: substance-use disorder; suicide risk	Comparable to anorexia and bulimia
Remission	Majority in remission after 5 years	Can be chronic or intermittent, with periods of remission	Similar to bulimia in severity and duration

these areas hopefully will contribute to understanding and managing eating disorders, which now are increasingly recognized in individuals from all cultural and ethnic backgrounds (Pike, Dunne, & Addai, 2013).

Developmental Course

Anorexia usually appears during adolescence, between the ages of 14 and 18, although it occasionally does affect older women, men, and prepubertal children. It often begins insidiously, with dieting that gradually leads to life-threatening starvation (Lock & Le Grange, 2006). Sometimes the onset of this dieting and starvation pattern is linked to stressful events, such as being teased about weight, onset of menses, school transitions, and so forth.

Although the symptoms of anorexia are quite specific and well defined, its developmental course and outcome are highly variable. Findings averaged across 119 studies of persons with anorexia show that the rate of mortality is significant (5%); of the survivors, fewer than one-half show full recovery, one-third show fair improvement, and one-fifth continue on a chronic course (Franko et al., 2013; Steinhausen, 2009).

Most common is a fluctuating pattern that involves a restoration of normal weight followed by relapse (Fichter, Quadflieg, & Hedlund, 2006). Although the majority of young persons with anorexia go into remission in 5 years (APA, 2013), those with worse outcomes show more bingeing and purging, and comorbid affective or anxiety disorders (Steinhausen, 2009). Once an individual loses weight and becomes dangerously malnourished, she is hospitalized and begins to show signs of improvement. Nonetheless, a significant number of patients—between 6% and 10%—die from medical complications or suicide (Arcelus et al., 2011; Bulik et al., 2008). Although anorexia is rare, it has the highest mortality rate of any psychiatric disorder and is a leading cause of death for females 15 to 24 years old in the general population (Preti et al., 2011; Striegel-Moore & Bulik, 2007).

Full-blown symptoms of bulimia usually emerge in late adolescence and young adulthood, although episodes of bingeing and purging and a preoccupation with weight begin much earlier (Lock & Le Grange, 2006). A noteworthy aspect of bulimia is that binge eating often develops during or after a period of restrictive dieting (Treasure, Claudino, & Zucker, 2010). Because of the guilt and discomfort caused by binge eating, purging follows as compensation. Bulimia either can follow a chronic course or occur intermittently, with periods of remission alternating with binge eating and purging (Fairburn et al., 2000). However, it is not easy to reverse the developmental course. Because the habits and cultural influences that led to the disorder are so powerful, a chronic pattern of disturbed eating may be established, such as secretive bingeing at social gatherings, which in turn leads to further problems.

Follow-up studies of patients with bulimia indicate that they have a greater chance of recovery than patients with anorexia—between 50% and 75% show full recovery or significant improvement over several years (Chavez & Insel, 2007; Steinhausen & Weber, 2009). The best predictors of a more favorable outcome were younger age at onset and higher social class. Importantly, bulimia responds favorably to treatment that disrupts its cyclical course (Keel et al., 2010).

Similar to the study of long-term outcomes of persons with bulimia, studies of eating behaviors and attitudes among populations of college students suggest that maturing into adulthood and getting away from powerful social pressures that emphasize thinness help many women escape from chronic dieting and abnormal eating. A 20-year follow-up study of body weight, dieting, and symptoms of eating disorders among male and female college students found both encouraging and discouraging results (Keel et al., 2007). On a positive note, women reduced their eating disorder behaviors and increased their body satisfaction ratings. However, body dissatisfaction and desires to lose weight still remained relatively high. Men, on the other hand, were prone to weight gain after college, and many reported increased dieting or disordered eating in the 20 years following college. Although disordered eating tends to decline during the transition to early adulthood, body dissatisfaction remains an issue for many young adults (Keel et al., 2007).

Causes

Why would people starve themselves to near emaciation or eat to the point of illness? The dramatic effects on physical and psychological well-being that can result from eating disorders have inspired many theories. No single factor has been isolated as the major cause of any type of eating disorder, and searching for causes is complicated by the "chicken and egg" problem of causation: Do neurobiological processes disrupt eating patterns, or do eating problems lead to changes in neurobiology?

The single best predictor of risk for developing an eating disorder is being female, and adolescence marks the period of the greatest risk for onset (Striegel-Moore & Bulik, 2007). But not all women or all adolescents develop eating disorders. Thus, explaining the gradual degenerative process of developing an eating disorder requires acknowledging the contribution of all three major etiological domains—biological, sociocultural (including family and peers), and psychological—which can operate singly or in combination to disturb self-regulation in any given individual. Too often, discussions of the etiology of eating disorders become polarized into "cultural" versus "biological" explanations that often ignore the fact that biological and environmental variables are inextricably linked (Striegel-Moore & Bulik, 2007). While the field has made great leaps in understanding the risk factors for the "prototypical" eating disorder case, which is often a young, white, middle- or upper-class North American woman, our knowledge about risk factors unique to diverse cultural populations remains incomplete.

The Biological Dimension

There is reasonable agreement that neurobiological factors play only a minor role in precipitating anorexia and bulimia. However, these factors may contribute to the maintenance of the disorder because of their effects on appetite, mood, perception, and energy regulation (Lock & Le Grange, 2006).

It makes sense to suspect that biological mechanisms (a gene? a neurochemical process?) acting together or alone are responsible for corrupting normal regulatory functions. A slight twist of this scenario places the problem on the individual who disrupts his or her normal regulatory processes in an ill-conceived attempt to achieve weight or diet goals. This disruption may cause biological changes throughout the central nervous and neuroendocrine systems that, in turn, create more disruption. Thus, it also makes sense that success at controlling important bodily functions such as hunger or appetite may lead to unnatural eating habits, resulting in an abusive eating pattern.

Genetic and Constitutional Factors

Eating disorders tend to run in families. Research has found that relatives of patients with anorexia or bulimia, especially female relatives, are 4 to 5 times more likely than persons in the general population to develop an eating disorder (Strober et al., 2000). A large-scale study of 31,406 Swedish twins born between 1935 and 1956 indicates that anorexia and bulimia moderately overlap in genetic and environmental contributors, with heritability playing the larger role in both disorders (Bulik et al., 2010). In this study, the contribution of the shared environment was found to be negligible, and the remaining variance was primarily attributable to unique environmental factors.

If eating disorders are connected to genetic factors, what exactly is inherited? Some people may have a biological vulnerability that interacts with social and psychological factors to increase their chances of developing an eating disorder (Trace et al., 2013). For example, inherited personality traits, such as emotional instability and poor self-control, would predispose an individual to be emotionally reactive to stress, which, in turn, could lead to impulsive eating in an attempt to relieve the feelings associated with stress (Thompson-Brenner et al., 2008). Genomewide association studies currently under way will likely identify genes and pathways involved in eating disorders in the near future (Scherag, Hebebrand, & Hinney, 2010).

Neurobiological Factors

Because serotonin regulates hunger and appetite, studies have focused on this neurotransmitter as a possible cause of anorexia, bulimia, and BED (Calati et al., 2011). Essentially, the presence of serotonin leads to a feeling of fullness and a desire to decrease food intake, so a decrease in serotonin leads to continuous hunger and greater consumption of food at one time—the perfect condition for bingeing. This explanation stems from a gene–environment interaction: children with a genetic risk factor in a serotonin transporter gene are more susceptible to high parental control, which in turns interferes with the child's ability to regulate stress; by adolescence, life events could more easily trigger the onset of anorexia (Karwautz et al., 2011).

One of the strongest findings in support of the serotonin explanation for bulimia comes from studies investigating the relationship of diet to the availability in the brain of the serotonin precursor *tryptophan*. Meals that are rich in protein or low in carbohydrates decrease tryptophan; carbohydrate-rich meals increase it. Put another way, bingeing on sweet and starchy foods creates conditions in the brain that produce more serotonin, which, eventually, leads to a sense of fullness. Binge eating (which usually involves high-carbohydrate food), especially for women, may increase the availability of tryptophan, thereby temporarily increasing brain serotonin (Scherag et al., 2010). It is still not known, however, whether problems related to the availability of serotonin in the brain are due to dieting or are a premorbid characteristic (Trace et al., 2013).

In addition to connections between depression and eating disorders, scientists have found biochemical similarities between people with eating disorders and people with obsessive–compulsive disorder (OCD). Just as serotonin levels are known to be abnormal in people with depression and people with eating disorders, they also are abnormal in patients with OCD (Lock, et al, 2011). Moreover, many persons with bulimia show obsessive–compulsive behavior as severe as that shown among patients diagnosed with OCD, and patients with OCD often have abnormal eating behaviors (Sallet et al., 2010).

fou
at p
are
star
hov
turl
logi

Soc
The
con
free
abil
sior
loss
Gu
nes
the
anc
nat
of a
trol
& 1

cha
exa
"fi
eati
wit
este
beg
(wh
abc
of
styl
sive
tha
bee
wh
pro

So
Ad
ov
Wl
lik
rhy
rou

in
nes
cal
an

double depression An instance in which a major depressive episode is superimposed on the individual's previous persistent depressive disorder, causing the individual to present with both disorders.

Down syndrome A chromosomal abnormality in which there are three copies chromosome 21 rather than the normal two. Children with Down syndrome typically function at the moderate level of intellectual disability, have an increased likelihood of medical problems, and have unusual physical features. This syndrome is also called trisomy 21.

drive for thinness A motivational variable underlying dieting and body image, among young females in particular, whereby the individual believes that losing more weight is the answer to overcoming her troubles and achieving success.

dyslexia Disorder of reading not due to low intelligence.

dysphoria A negative mood state characterized by prolonged bouts of sadness.

dyssomnias A category of sleep disorders involving difficulties initiating or maintaining sleep. Such disorders are often characterized by problems with getting enough sleep, not sleeping when one wants to, and not feeling refreshed after sleeping.

dysthymic disorder (DD) or dysthymia (See *persistent depressive disorder [P-DD]*).

echolalia A child's immediate or delayed parrot-like repetition of words or word combinations.

educational neglect Failure to provide for a child's basic educational needs, including allowing chronic truancy, failing to enroll a child of mandatory school age in school, and failing to attend to a special educational need.

electroencephalogram (EEG) An electrophysiological measure of brain functioning whereby electrodes are taped to the surface of the subject's scalp to record the electrical activity of the brain. EEG recordings are sensitive to changes in state and emotionality, thereby making them particularly useful for studying social and emotional processes.

emotion reactivity A dimension of emotional processes associated with individual differences in the threshold and intensity of emotional experience.

emotion regulation The processes by which emotional arousal is redirected, controlled, or modified to facilitate adaptive functioning.

emotional neglect Failure to provide for a child's basic emotional needs, including

marked inattention to the child's needs for affection, refusal of or failure to provide needed psychological care, spousal abuse in the child's presence, and permission for drug or alcohol use by the child.

encopresis The passage of feces in inappropriate places, such as in clothing, whether involuntary or intentional.

enuresis Involuntary discharge of urine occurring in persons over 5 years of age or the developmental equivalent.

epidemiological research The study of the incidence, prevalence, and co-occurrence of childhood disorders and competencies in clinic-referred and community samples.

epigenetic The underlying biological changes to genetic structure resulting from environmental factors, such as toxins, diet, stress, and many others.

epinephrine A hormone produced by the adrenal glands that is released into the bloodstream in response to stress in order to energize and prepare the body for a possible threat. This hormone is also known as adrenaline.

equifinality The concept that similar outcomes may stem from different early experiences.

etiology The study of the causes of disorders. With respect to childhood disorders, etiology considers how biological, psychological, and environmental processes interact.

eugenics First defined by Sir Francis Galton in 1883 as "the science which deals with all influences that improve the inborn qualities of a race." In the early 1900s, public and professional emphasis shifted away from the needs of persons with intellectual disability toward a consideration of the needs of society; society was to be protected from the presumable harm done by the presence of these persons in the community. This misdirected view provided justification for restricting the rights of individuals with intellectual disability and their opportunities for advancement.

euphoria An exaggerated sense of well-being.

evidence-based treatments (EBTs) Clearly specified treatments shown to be effective in controlled research studies with specific populations.

excoriation disorder (skin-picking disorder) Disorder characterized by recurrent skin picking resulting in skin lesions, repeated attempts to stop skin picking, and significant distress or impairment in important areas of life functioning.

executive functions Higher-order mental processes that enable a child to maintain a problem-solving orientation in order to

attain a future goal. Examples of executive functions include working memory, mental computation, flexibility of thinking, internalization of speech, response inhibition, motor coordination, self-regulation of arousal level, and mature moral reasoning, among others.

expectable environment External conditions or surroundings that are considered to be fundamental and necessary for healthy development. The expectable environment for infants includes protective and nurturing adults and opportunities for socialization; for older children it includes a supportive family, contact with peers, and ample opportunities to explore and master the environment.

exposure A behavioral therapy technique for treating anxiety disorders that exposes the subject to the source of his or her fear while providing appropriate and effective ways of coping with the fear (other than through escape and avoidance).

expressive language disorder A form of communication disorder characterized by deficits in expression despite normal comprehension of speech.

external validity The degree to which findings can be generalized, or extended to people, settings, times, measures, and characteristics other than the ones in the original study.

externalizing behavior A continuous dimension of behavior that includes a mixture of impulsive, overactive, aggressive, and delinquent acts.

externalizing problems Problem behaviors that begin during childhood and encompass acting-out behaviors such as aggression and delinquent behavior.

failure to thrive (FTT) Disorder characterized by weight below the fifth percentile for age, and/or deceleration in the rate of weight gain from birth to the present of at least 2 standard deviations, using standard growth charts for comparison.

family history Using a background questionnaire or interview, information is obtained from the parents regarding potentially significant developmental milestones and historical events that might have a bearing on the child's current difficulties.

family systems Theory that the behavior of an individual can be most accurately understood in the context of the dynamics of his or her family.

fear An alarm reaction to current danger or life-threatening emergencies; marked by strong escape-oriented tendencies and a surge in the sympathetic nervous system.

fetal alcohol syndrome A disorder stemming from extensive prenatal exposure to alcohol. Children with this disorder typically suffer from problems in intellectual functioning, central nervous system dysfunction, cranial feature defects, behavior problems, growth retardation, and physical abnormalities of the face.

fight/flight response The immediate reaction to perceived danger or threat whereby efforts are directed toward protecting against potential harm, either by confronting the source of danger (fight), or by escaping from the situation (flight).

flooding A procedure for treating anxiety that involves prolonged and repeated exposure to the anxiety-provoking situation until the subject's level of anxiety has diminished.

fragile-X syndrome A chromosomal abnormality in which one area on the X chromosome is pinched. Children with fragile-X syndrome typically suffer from moderate intellectual disability.

frontal lobe Area of the brain located at the front of each cerebral hemisphere; responsible for the functions underlying much of our thinking and reasoning abilities, including memory.

frontostriatal circuitry of the brain A structure of the brain consisting of the prefrontal cortex and the basal ganglia; associated with attention, executive functions, delayed response, and response organization. Abnormalities within this structure have been linked to ADHD.

functional analysis of behavior (See *behavior analysis*.)

gene–environment interaction (G×E) Complex interplay of nature and nurture to account for genetic and environmental influences and their timing.

general intellectual functioning One's general level of intellectual ability, defined by an intelligence quotient (IQ or equivalent) derived from an assessment with one or more of the standardized, individually administered intelligence tests.

generalized anxiety disorder (GAD) A form of anxiety disorder in which the subject experiences chronic or exaggerated worry and tension, almost always anticipating disaster, even in the absence of an obvious reason to do so. The worrying is often accompanied by physical symptoms such as trembling, muscle tension, headache, and nausea.

genotype An individual's specific genetic makeup.

goodness of fit The extent to which two things are suited. For instance, with respect to child psychopathology, one might use the term to refer to the extent to which the child's early temperament and the parent's style of interaction are suited to each other.

graded exposure Gradual exposure of a subject to a feared situation.

hallucinations Disturbances in perception in which things are seen, heard, or otherwise sensed even though they are not real or present.

health promotion An approach to the prevention of disease that involves education, public policy, and similar actions to promote health.

heritability The proportion of the variance of a trait that is attributable to genetic influences.

hoarding disorder Disorder characterized by persistent difficulty discarding or parting with possessions, regardless of their actual value.

hopelessness theory The view that depression-prone individuals make internal, stable, and global attributions to explain the causes of negative events and external, unstable, and specific attributions about positive events. This attributional style results in the individual taking personal blame for negative events in his or her life and leads to helplessness, avoidance, and hopelessness about the future, which promotes further depression.

hostile attributional bias The tendency of aggressive children to attribute negative intent to others, especially when the intentions of another child are unclear (e.g., when a child accidentally bumps into them, they are likely to think the other child did it on purpose).

hyperactive Displaying an unusually high level of energy and an inability to remain still or quiet.

hyperactivity–impulsivity A core feature of ADHD that involves the undercontrol of motor behavior, poor sustained inhibition of behavior, the inability to delay a response or defer gratification, or an inability to inhibit dominant responses in relation to ongoing situational demands.

hypothalamic–pituitary–adrenal (HPA) axis A regulatory system of the brain made up of the hypothalamus control center and the pituitary and adrenal glands; it influences a person's response to stress and his or her ability to regulate emotions.

idiographic case formulation An approach to case formulation or assessment that emphasizes the detailed representation of the individual child or family as a unique entity. This approach is in contrast to the nomothetic approach, which instead emphasizes the general laws that apply to all individuals.

impulsive Prone to acting with little or no consideration of possible consequences. This term is frequently used to describe children who suffer from attention-deficit/hyperactivity disorder.

inattentive Lacking the ability to focus or sustain one's attention. Children who are inattentive find it difficult to sustain mental effort during work or play and behave carelessly, as if they are not listening.

incidence rate The rate at which new cases of a disorder appear over a specified period of time.

incidental training A method of teaching readiness skills or other desired behaviors that works to strengthen the behavior by capitalizing on naturally occurring opportunities.

inclusion Education strategies based on the premise that the abilities of children with special needs will improve from associating with normally developing peers and being spared the effects of labeling and special placements.

inclusion movement The integration of individuals with disabilities into regular classroom settings, regardless of the severity of the disability. The school curriculum must be adaptable to meet the individual needs and abilities of these children.

information-processing disturbances Cognitive misperceptions and distortions in the way events are perceived and interpreted.

informed consent An individual's expressed willingness to participate in a research study, based on his or her understanding of the nature of the research, the potential risks and benefits involved, the expected outcomes, and possible alternatives.

insulin-dependent diabetes mellitus A lifelong metabolic disorder in which the body is unable to metabolize carbohydrates because the pancreas releases inadequate amounts of insulin.

interdependent Applies to the assumption that abnormal child behavior is determined by both the child and his or her environment, and that these two factors are interconnected. (Also see *transaction*.)

internal validity The extent to which an intended manipulation of a variable, rather than extraneous influences, accounts for observed results, changes, or group differences.

internalizing problems Problem behaviors that begin during childhood and include anxiety, depression, somatic symptoms, and withdrawn behavior.

intervention A broad concept that encompasses many different theories and methods with a range of problem-solving strategies directed at helping the child and family adapt more effectively to their current and future circumstances.

irritability A common symptom of major depressive disorder and disruptive mood dysregulation disorder characterized by easy annoyance and touchiness, an angry mood, and temper outbursts.

joint attention   The ability to coordinate one's focus of attention on another person and an object of mutual interest.

juvenile delinquency   A broad term used to describe children who have broken a law, anything from sneaking into a movie without a ticket to homicide.

language disorder   A communication disorder characterized by difficulties in the comprehension or production of spoken or written language.

learning disabilities   A general term that refers to significant problems in mastering one or more of the following skills: listening, speaking, reading, writing, reasoning, and mathematics.

learning disorders   A diagnostic term that refers to specific problems in reading (disorder of reading), math (disorder of mathematics), or writing ability (disorder of written expression) as determined by achievement test results that are substantially below what would be expected for the child's age, schooling, and intellectual ability.

life-course–persistent (LCP) path   A developmental pathway to antisocial behavior in which the child engages in antisocial behavior at an early age and continues to do so into adulthood.

longitudinal research   A method of research whereby the same individuals are studied at different ages/stages of development.

maintenance   Efforts to increase adherence to treatment over time in order to prevent a relapse or recurrence of a problem.

major depressive disorder (MDD)   A form of depressive disorder characterized by five or more mood, cognitive (e.g., indecisiveness, inability to think or concentrate), psychomotor (e.g., agitation or retardation), or somatic (e.g., weight loss, sleep disturbances) symptoms that have been present during the same 2-week period; at least one of the symptoms is either depressed mood most of the day, nearly every day, or markedly diminished interest or pleasure in all, or almost all, activities most of the day, nearly every day.

mania   An abnormally elevated or expansive mood.

mediator variables   The process, mechanism, or means through which a variable produces a specific outcome.

mentalization   Awareness of other people's and one's own mental states. Also referred to as *theory of mind*.

metabolic control   The degree to which an individual's glucose level is maintained within the normal range (in reference to diabetes mellitus).

metabolic rate   The body's balance of energy expenditure. Metabolic rate is determined by genetic and physiological makeup, along with eating and exercise habits.

methylphenidate   The stimulant medication most commonly used in treating children with attention-deficit/hyperactivity disorder. It is sold under the name Ritalin.

mild intellectual disability   Children with mild intellectual disability often show small delays in development during the preschool years, but typically are not identified until academic or behavior problems emerge during the early elementary years.

moderate intellectual disability   Children and adolescents at this level of impairment are more intellectually and adaptively impaired than someone with mild intellectual disability, and usually they are identified during the preschool years, when they show delays in reaching early developmental milestones.

moderator variables   A factor that influences the direction or strength of a relationship between variables.

molecular genetics   The methods of genetics that directly assess the association between variations in DNA sequences and variations in particular traits. More than an association, variations in genetic sequences are thought to cause the variations in the trait(s). These methods offer more direct support for genetic influences on child psychopathology.

mood disorder   A disorder in which the subject suffers from extreme, persistent, or poorly regulated emotional states. DSM-5 mood disorders include disruptive mood dysregulation disorder, major depressive disorder, persistent depressive disorder, and bipolar disorder.

morbidity   The various forms of physical and functional consequences and limitations that result from an illness.

multifinality   The concept that various outcomes may stem from similar beginnings.

multimethod assessment approach   A clinical assessment that emphasizes the importance of obtaining information from different informants, in a variety of settings, using a variety of procedures that include interviews, observations, questionnaires, and tests.

multiple-baseline design   A single-case experimental design in which the effect of a treatment is shown by demonstrating that behaviors in more than one baseline change as a result of the institution of a treatment.

multisystemic treatment (MST)   An approach to treatment that attempts to address the multiple determinants of problematic behavior by involving family members, school personnel, peers, juvenile justice staff, and others in the child's life, and by drawing on multiple techniques such as parent management training, cognitive problem-solving skills training, and marital therapy, as well as specialized interventions such as special education placements, referral to substance abuse treatment programs, or referral to legal services.

natural experiments   Experiments in which comparisons are made between preexisting conditions or treatments (i.e., random assignment is not used).

naturalistic observation   The unstructured observation of a child in his or her natural environment.

negative affectivity   A persistent negative mood evidenced by nervousness, sadness, anger, and guilt.

negative cognitive schemata   Stable structures in memory, including self-critical beliefs and attitudes, that guide information processing in a way that is consistent with the negative self-image of the subject. These cognitive schemata are rigid and resistant to change even in the face of contradictory evidence.

negative cognitive triad   Negative views about oneself, the world, and the future that are characteristic of youngsters with depression. These views maintain feelings of helplessness, undermine the child's mood and energy level, and are related to the severity of depression.

neural plasticity   The malleable nature of the brain, evidenced throughout the course of development (use-dependent). Although infants are born with basic brain processes, experience leads to anatomical differentiation. That is, certain synapses of the brain are strengthened and stabilized, while others regress and disappear.

neurodevelopmental model of schizophrenia   A model in which a genetic vulnerability and early neurodevelopmental insults result in impaired connections between many brain regions, including the cerebral cortex, white matter, hippocampus, cerebellum, and parts of the limbic system. This defective neural circuitry creates a vulnerability to dysfunction that is revealed by developmental processes and events during puberty (e.g., synaptic and hormonal changes) and by exposure to stress. The neurodevelopmental model is consistent with findings that infants and children who later develop schizophrenia often display developmental impairments in motor, language, cognitive, and social functioning well before the onset of their psychotic symptoms.

neuroimaging   A method of examining the structure and/or function of the brain.

Neuroimaging procedures include magnetic resonance imaging (MRI), computed tomographic (CT) scan, positron-emission tomography (PET), functional magnetic resonance imaging (fMRI), and diffusion MRI (dMRI).

neuropsychological assessment   A form of assessment that attempts to link brain functioning with objective measures of behavior known to depend on an intact central nervous system.

neurotic paradox   The pattern of self-perpetuating behavior in which children who are overly anxious in various situations, even while being aware that the anxiety may be unnecessary or excessive, find themselves unable to abandon their self-defeating behaviors.

nightmares   A form of parasomnia that occurs during rapid-eye-movement (REM) sleep and is characterized by repeated awakenings with detailed recall of extended and extremely frightening dreams, usually involving threats to survival, security, or self-esteem.

nomothetic formulation   An approach to case formulation or assessment that emphasizes general principles that apply to all people. This approach contrasts with the idiographic approach, which instead emphasizes a detailed representation of the individual or family as a unique entity.

nondisjunction   The failure of the 21st pair of the mother's chromosomes to separate during meiosis. In most cases of Down syndrome, the extra chromosome results from this failure of the chromosomes to separate.

nonshared environment   A subtype of environmental influences that refers to the environmental factors that produce behavioral differences among siblings living in the same household. Nonshared environmental influence can be estimated and is calculated by subtracting the MZ twin correlation from 1.0.

nonverbal learning disabilities (NLD) Learning disabilities characterized by deficits related to right-hemisphere brain functioning, such as problems in social skills, spatial orientation, and problem solving.

nosologies   Efforts to classify psychiatric disorders into descriptive categories.

obsessions   Persistent, intrusive, and irrational thoughts, ideas, impulses, or images that focus on improbable or unrealistic events or on real-life events that are greatly exaggerated.

obsessive–compulsive disorder (OCD)   A disorder in which the individual experiences recurrent and persistent thoughts, urges, or images that are experienced as intrusive and unwanted and that in most individuals cause marked anxiety or distress; the individual attempts to ignore or suppress such thoughts, urges, or images or to neutralize them with some other thought or action (i.e., by performing a compulsion).

operant speech training   A strategy used to help children use language more appropriately. It involves a step-by-step approach that successively increases the child's vocalizations; teaches the child to imitate sounds and words; teaches the meanings of words; and teaches the child to use language expressively to label objects, make verbal requests, and express desires. This training is often employed for children with autism.

oppositional defiant disorder (ODD)   A pattern of angry/irritable mood, argumentative/defiant behavior, or vindictiveness lasting at least 6 months and exhibited during interaction with a least one individual who is not a sibling.

organic group   Intellectual disability stemming from clear organic (physical) causes such as brain damage or improper central nervous system development.

organization of development   The assumption that early patterns of adaptation evolve over time and transform into higher-order functions in a structured manner. For instance, infant eye contact and speech sounds evolve and transform into speech and language.

overt–covert dimension   An independent dimension consisting of a continuum of antisocial behavior ranging from overt forms such as physical aggression at one end, to covert forms (i.e., hidden or sneaky acts) at the other. The overt forms of antisocial behavior correspond roughly to those on the aggressive subdimension of the externalizing dimension, whereas the covert behaviors correspond roughly to those on the delinquent subdimension of the externalizing dimension.

panic   A group of unexpected physical symptoms of the fight/flight response that occur in the absence of any obvious threat or danger.

panic attack   An abrupt surge of intense fear or intense discomfort that reaches a peak within minutes and during which time is accompanied by four (or more) physical and cognitive symptoms (e.g., palpitations, sweating, trembling, shortness of breath, chest pain, dizziness, chills, numbness, fear of losing control, fear of dying).

panic disorder (PD)   A form of anxiety disorder characterized by panic attacks and sudden feelings of terror that strike repeatedly and without warning. Physical symptoms include chest pain, heart palpitations, shortness of breath, dizziness, and abdominal stress. There is also persistent concern about having additional attacks and the possible implications and consequences they would bring and a significant maladaptive change in behavior related to these attacks (e.g., avoidance of unfamiliar situations, avoidance of exercise).

parasomnias   A category of sleep disorders in which behavioral or physiological events intrude on ongoing sleep. Persons suffering from parasomnias often report unusual behaviors during sleep, such as sleepwalking and nightmares.

parent management training (PMT)   A program aimed at teaching parents to cope effectively with their child's difficult behavior and their own reactions to it.

persistent depressive disorder (P-DD), or dysthymia/dysthymic disorder   A depressive disorder associated with depressed or irritable mood; generally fewer, less severe, but longer-lasting symptoms (a year or more in children) than seen in major depressive disorder (MDD); and significant impairment in functioning.

personality disorder   An enduring pattern of inner experience and behavior that deviates noticeably from the expectations of the individual's culture, resulting in clinically significant distress or impairment in functioning.

phenotype   An individual's observable characteristics or behavior (the expression of one's genotype in the environment).

phonemes   The basic sounds that make up language.

phonological awareness   A broad construct that includes recognition of the relationship that exists between sounds and letters, detection of rhyme and alliteration, and awareness that sounds can be manipulated within syllables in words.

phonological disorder   A form of communication disorder characterized by difficulties in articulation or sound production, but not necessarily in word expression.

phonology   The ability to learn and store phonemes as well as the rules for combining the sounds into meaningful units or words. Deficits in phonology are a chief reason that most children and adults with communication and learning disorders have problems in language-based activities such as learning to read and spell.

physical abuse   The infliction or risk of physical injury as a result of punching, beating, kicking, biting, burning, shaking, or otherwise intentionally harming a child.

physical neglect   Failure to provide for a child's basic physical needs, including refusal of or delay in seeking health care, inadequate provision of food, abandonment, expulsion from the home or refusal to allow a runaway to return home, inadequate supervision, and inadequate provision of clean clothes.

pica A form of eating disorder in which the infant or toddler persists in eating inedible, nonnutritive substances. This disorder is one of the more common and usually less serious eating disorders found among very young children.

positive affectivity A persistent positive mood as reflected in states such as joy, enthusiasm, and energy.

positive bias A person's report of higher self-esteem than is warranted by his or her behavior. This exaggeration of one's competence may, for example, cause a child with ADHD to perceive their relationships with their parents no differently than do control children, even though their parents see things in a more negative light.

post-traumatic stress disorder (PTSD) A form of trauma- and stressor-related disorder wherein the child displays persistent anxiety following exposure to or witnessing of an overwhelming traumatic or stressful event that is outside the range of usual human experience.

Prader–Willi syndrome A complex genetic disorder associated with an abnormality of chromosome 15. Children with Prader–Willi syndrome typically suffer from short stature, intellectual disability or learning disabilities, incomplete sexual development, certain behavior problems, low muscle tone, and an involuntary urge to eat constantly.

pragmatics The aspect of language that focuses on its appropriate use in social and communicative contexts.

predominantly hyperactive–impulsive presentation (ADHD-HI) (See under *ADHD*.)

predominantly inattentive presentation (ADHD-PI) (See under *ADHD*.)

presentation type A term used to describe a group of individuals with something in common—symptoms, etiology, problem severity, or likely outcome—that makes them distinct from other groups.

preservation of sameness A characteristic of children with autism spectrum disorder who show an anxious and obsessive insistence on the maintenance of sameness that no one but the child may disrupt. Changes in daily routine, arrangement of objects, or the wording of requests, or the sight of anything broken or incomplete will produce tantrums or despair.

prevalence rates The number of cases of a disorder, whether new or previously existing, that are observed during a specified period of time.

prevention Activities directed at decreasing the chances that undesired future outcomes will occur.

problem-solving skills training (PSST) Instruction aimed at targeting the cognitive deficiencies and distortions displayed by children and adolescents who experience conduct problems in interpersonal situations, particularly those children who are aggressive.

profound intellectual disability Individuals with this disability are typically identified in infancy because of marked delays in development and biological anomalies such as asymmetrical facial features.

prognosis The prediction of the course or outcome of a disorder.

projective test A form of assessment that presents the child with ambiguous stimuli, such as inkblots or pictures of people. The hypothesis is that the child will "project" his or her own personality onto the ambiguous stimuli of other people and things. Without being aware, the child discloses his or her unconscious thoughts and feelings to the clinician.

pronoun reversal The repetition of personal pronouns exactly as heard, without changing them according to the person being referred to. For example, if asked "Are you hungry?" one might reply, "You are hungry," rather than, "I am hungry."

protective factor A variable that precedes a negative outcome of interest and decreases the chances that the outcome will occur.

protodeclarative gestures Gestures or vocalizations that direct the visual attention of other people to objects of shared interest, such as pointing to a dog; done with the prime purpose of engaging another person in interaction.

protoimperative gestures Gestures or vocalizations used to express needs, such as pointing to an object that one desires but cannot reach.

psychological abuse Abusive behavior that involves acts or omissions by parents or caregivers that cause, or could cause, serious behavioral, cognitive, emotional, or mental disorders. (Also known as *emotional abuse*.)

psychological disorder A pattern of behavioral, cognitive, or physical symptoms that includes one or more of the following prominent features: (a) some degree of distress in the subject; (b) behavior indicating some degree of disability; and (c) an increased risk of suffering, death, pain, disability, or an important loss of freedom.

psychological factors affecting other medical conditions Psychological disorders or conditions that are presumed to cause or exacerbate a physical condition.

psychopathic features A pattern of deceitful, callous, manipulative, and remorseless behavior.

purging Behavior aimed at ridding the body of consumed food, including self-induced vomiting and the misuse of laxatives, diuretics, or enemas. (Also see *compensatory behavior*.)

qualitative research Research for which the purpose is to describe, interpret, and understand the phenomenon of interest in the context in which it is experienced.

quality of life A person's subjective perception of their position in life as evidenced by their physical, psychological, and social functioning.

random assignment The assignment of research participants to treatment conditions whereby each participant has an equal chance of being assigned to either condition. Random assignment increases the likelihood that characteristics other than the independent variable will be equally distributed across treatment groups.

randomized controlled trials (RCT) A design used to evaluate treatment outcomes in which children with a particular problem are randomly assigned to various treatment and control conditions.

reactive attachment disorder (RAD) Disorder characterized by a pattern of disturbed and developmentally inappropriate attachment behaviors, likely due to social neglect in early childhood.

real-time prospective designs Research designs in which the research sample is identified and then followed longitudinally over time, with data collected at specified time intervals.

reciprocal influence The theory that the child's behavior is both influenced by and itself influences the behavior of other family members.

relational aggression A form of indirect aggression in which harm is caused through damage to one's relationships or social status rather than direct physical harm. It may involve the use of verbal insults, gossip, tattling, ostracism, threatening to withdraw one's friendship, getting even, or third-party retaliation.

relational disorders Disorders that occur in the context of relationships, such as child abuse and neglect. Relational disorders signify the connection between children's behavior patterns and the availability of a suitable child-rearing environment.

reliability The extent to which the result of an experiment is consistent or repeatable.

research Generally viewed as a systematic way of finding answers to questions—a method of inquiry that follows certain rules.

research designs These are the strategies used to examine questions of interest. They detail the ways in which a researcher arranges conditions to draw valid inferences about the variables of interest.

residential care A living arrangement in which a child whose family or school cannot adequately provide for him or her is cared for in a specialized out-of-home setting.

resilience The ability to avoid negative outcomes despite being at risk for psychopathology.

response prevention A procedure used in the treatment of anxiety that prevents the child from engaging in escape or avoidance behaviors. This procedure is usually used in conjunction with flooding.

response-cost procedure A technique for managing a subject's behavior that involves the loss of reinforcers such as privileges, activities, points, or tokens in response to inappropriate behavior.

restricted and repetitive behaviors Behaviors that are characterized by their high frequency, repetition in a fixed manner, and desire for sameness in the environment.

restricting type A type of anorexia in which the individual uses dieting, fasting, or excessive exercise to lose or avoid gaining weight. During the current episode of anorexia, the person has not engaged in binge-eating or purging behavior.

retrospective design A research design in which people in the research sample are asked to provide information relating to an earlier time.

risk factor A variable that precedes a negative outcome of interest and increases the chances that the outcome will occur.

schizophrenia A form of schizophrenia spectrum disorder that involves characteristic disturbances in thinking (delusions), perception (hallucinations), speech, emotions, and behavior.

school refusal behavior A form of anxious behavior in which the child refuses to attend classes or has difficulty remaining in school for an entire day.

screening Identification of subjects at risk for a specific negative outcome.

selective attention The ability to concentrate exclusively on relevant stimuli and ignore task-irrelevant stimuli in the environment.

selective mutism An anxiety disorder involving a consistent failure to speak in specific social situations in which there is an expectation for speaking (e.g., at school) despite speaking in other situations.

self-injurious behavior (SIB) Severe and sometimes life-threatening acts that cause damage to the subject's own body, such as head banging, eye gouging, severe scratching, rumination, some types of pica, and inserting objects under the skin.

self-instructional training Teaching children to use verbal cues to process information, which are initially taught by the therapist or teacher, to keep themselves on task.

self-stimulatory behaviors Repetitive body movements or movements of objects, such as hand flapping or spinning a pencil.

semistructured interviews Interviews that include specific questions designed to elicit information in a relatively consistent manner regardless of who is conducting the interview. The interview format usually ensures that the most important aspects of a particular disorder are covered.

sensitive periods Windows of time during which environmental influences on development (both good and bad) are heightened, thus providing enhanced opportunities to learn.

separation anxiety disorder (SAD) A form of anxiety disorder in which the individual displays age-inappropriate, excessive, and disabling anxiety about being apart from his or her parents or away from home.

set point A comfortable range of body weight that the body tries to "defend" and maintain.

severe intellectual disability Most of these individuals suffer one or more organic causes of impairment, such as genetic defects, and are identified at a very young age because they have substantial delays in development and visible physical features or anomalies.

sexual abuse Abusive acts that are sexual in nature, including fondling a child's genitals, intercourse, incest, rape, sodomy, exhibitionism, and commercial exploitation through prostitution or the production of pornographic materials.

shared environment A subtype of environmental influences that refers to the environmental factors that produce similarities in developmental outcomes among siblings living in the same household. If siblings are more similar than expected from only their shared genetics, this implies an effect of the environment both siblings share, such as being exposed to marital conflict or poverty, or being parented in a similar manner.

single-case experimental design A type of research design most frequently used to evaluate the impact of a clinical treatment on a subject's problem. Single-case experimental design involves repeated assessment of behavior over time, the replication of treatment effects on the same subject over time, and the subject serving as his or her own control by experiencing all treatment conditions.

sleep terrors A form of parasomnia that occurs during deep sleep and is characterized by abrupt awakening, accompanied by autonomic arousal but no recall.

sleepwalking A form of parasomnia that occurs during deep sleep, in which the individual gets out of bed and walks around but has no recall of such activity upon awakening.

social anxiety (See *social anxiety disorder*.)

social anxiety disorder (SOC) or social phobia A marked and persistent fear of social or performance requirements that expose the individual to scrutiny and possible embarrassment. These individuals go to great lengths to avoid these situations, or they may face the challenge with great effort, wearing a mask of fearlessness.

social cognition A construct to describe how people think about themselves in relation to others, and how they interpret ambiguous events and solve problems.

social–cognitive abilities The skills involved in attending to, interpreting, and responding to social cues.

social learning A theoretical approach to the study of behavior that is interested in both overt behaviors and the role of possible cognitive mediators that may influence such behaviors directly or indirectly.

social phobia (See *social anxiety disorder*.)

social selection hypothesis The premise that people tend to select environments in which there are other people similar to themselves.

somatic symptoms and related disorders Disorders involve distressing somatic symptoms and concerns, such as pain and dizziness, that interfere with daily activities and are accompanied by anxiety or worry about the seriousness of the symptoms.

specific learning disorder A diagnostic term that refers to specific problems in learning and using academic skills

specific phobia An extreme and disabling fear about objects or situations that in reality pose little or no danger or threat; those with a specific phobia go to great lengths to avoid these objects or situations. They experience extreme fear or dread, physiological arousal to the feared stimulus, and fearful anticipation and avoidance when confronted with the object of their fear.

specifier A term used in DSM-5 to describe more homogeneous subgroups of individuals with the disorder who share particular features (e.g., age at onset, severity) and to communicate information that is relevant to treatment of the disorder (e.g., a co-occurring condition).

spectrum disorder   A disorder whose symptoms, abilities, and characteristics are expressed in many different combinations and in any degree of severity.

speech sound disorder   A disorder in which children have trouble controlling their rate of speech or lag behind playmates in learning to articulate certain sounds.

standardization   The process by which a set of standards or norms is specified for a measurement procedure so that it can be used consistently across different assessments.

stigma   A cluster of negative attitudes and beliefs that motivates fear, rejection, avoidance, and discrimination against people with mental illnesses.

stimulant medications   Drugs that alter the activity in the frontostriatal region of the brain by impacting three or more neurotransmitters important to the functioning of this region—dopamine, norepinephrine, and epinephrine, and possibly serotonin. Stimulant medications are commonly used for the management of symptoms of ADHD and its associated impairments.

stressful events   Events that are less extreme than traumatic events and stem from single events or multiple or ongoing stressful situations or events.

structured observation   Observation of a subject, usually occurring in a clinic or laboratory, in which the subject is given specific tasks or instructions to carry out, and researchers look for specific information.

subclinical levels of symptoms   Troubling symptoms too few in number to qualify for a categorical diagnosis.

substance abuse   A problematic pattern of substance use over the past 12 months leading to significant impairment or distress.

substance dependence   *Psychological dependence* refers to the subjective feeling of needing the substance to adequately function. *Physical dependence* occurs when the body adapts to the substance's constant presence, and *tolerance* refers to requiring more of the substance to experience an effect once obtained at a lower dose. Physical dependence can lead to symptoms of withdrawal, an adverse physiological symptom that occurs when

consumption of an abused substance is ended abruptly and is thus removed from the body.

substance-related and addictive disorders   These disorders encompasses 10 separate classes of drugs, including alcohol, caffeine, cannabis, hallucinogens, inhalants, opioids, sedatives, stimulants, tobacco, and other (or unknown) substances.

substance-use disorders (SUDs)   Disorders that occur during adolescence and include substance dependence and substance abuse that result from the self-administration of any substance that alters mood, perception, or brain functioning.

sustained attention or vigilance   The ability to maintain a persistent focus of attention over time on unchallenging, uninteresting tasks or activities or when fatigued.

systematic desensitization   A three-step behavior therapy technique for treating anxiety whereby: (1) the child is taught to relax, (2) an anxiety hierarchy is constructed, and (3) the anxiety-provoking stimuli are presented sequentially while the child remains relaxed.

target behaviors   Behaviors that are the primary problems of concern.

temperament   The child's innate reactivity and self-regulation with respect to the domains of emotions, activity level, and attention; the child's organized style of behavior that appears early in development, such as fussiness or fearfulness, that shapes the child's approach to his or her environment, and vice versa.

test   A task or set of tasks given under standard conditions with the purpose of assessing some aspect of the subject's knowledge, skill, personality, or condition.

theory of mind (ToM)   The cognition and understanding of mental states that cannot be observed directly, such as beliefs and desires, both in one's self and in others. Also referred to as *mentalization*.

tic disorders   Disorders characterized by sudden, repetitive, nonrhythmic motor movements or sounds, such as eye blinking, facial grimacing, throat clearing, and grunting or other sounds.

transaction   The process by which the subject and environment interact in a dynamic fashion to contribute to the expression of a disorder. (Also see *interdependent*.)

traumatic event   Exposure to actual or threatened harm or fear of death or injury and are considered uncommon or extreme stressors.

trauma-focused cognitive–behavioral therapy (TF-CBT)   A form of exposure therapy that incorporates elements of cognitive–behavioral, attachment, humanistic, empowerment, and family therapy models.

traumatic sexualization   One possible outcome of child sexual abuse, wherein the child's sexual knowledge and behavior are shaped in developmentally inappropriate ways.

treatment   Corrective actions that will permit successful adaptation by eliminating or reducing the impact of an undesired outcome that has already occurred.

treatment effectiveness   The degree to which a treatment can be shown to work in actual clinical practice, as opposed to under controlled laboratory conditions.

treatment efficacy   The degree to which a treatment can produce changes under well-controlled conditions that depart from those typically used in clinical practice.

treatment planning and evaluation   The process of using assessment information to generate a treatment plan and evaluate its effectiveness.

trichotillomania (hair-pulling disorder)   Hair loss from compulsive pulling out or twisting of one's own hair.

true experiment   An experiment in which the researcher has maximum control over the independent variable or conditions of interest and in which the researcher can use random assignment of subjects to groups, can include needed control conditions, and can control possible sources of bias.

two-factor theory   Theory used to explain the learning and maintenance of fears through a combination of classical and operant conditioning.

unexpected discrepancy   A basic premise of definitions of learning disorders that denotes a disparity or discrepancy between an individual's measured ability and actual performance.

validity   The extent to which a measure actually assesses the dimension or construct that the researcher sets out to measure.

"with limited prosocial emotions" specifier   A term used in DSM-5 to describe youths with conduct disorder (CD) who display a persistent and typical pattern of interpersonal and emotional functioning involving at least two of the following three characteristics: lack of remorse or guilt; callous–lack of empathy; and unconcerned about performance.

References

AAIDD Ad Hoc Committee on Terminology and Classification. (2010). *Intellectual disability: Definition, classification, and systems of supports* (11th ed.). Washington, DC: American Association on Intellectual and Developmental Disabilities.

Aase, H., & Sagvolden, T. (2006). Infrequent, but not frequent, reinforcers produce more variable responding and deficient sustained attention in young children with attention-deficit/hyperactivity disorder. *Journal of Child Psychology and Psychiatry, 47,* 457–471.

Abbass, A. A., Rabung, S., Leichsenring, F., Refseth, J. S., & Midgley, N. (2013). Psychodynamic psychotherapy for children and adolescents: A meta-analysis of short-term psychodynamic models. *Journal of the Academy of Child & Adolescent Psychiatry, 52,* 863–875.

Abebe, D. S., Lien, L., & von Soest, T. (2012). The development of bulimic symptoms from adolescence to young adulthood in females and males: A population-based longitudinal cohort study. *International Journal of Eating Disorders, 45,* 737–745.

Abel, C. G., Osborn, C. A., & Twigg, D. A. (1993). Sexual assault through the life span: Adult offenders with juvenile histories. In H. E. Barbaree, W. L. Marshall, & S. M. Husdon (Eds.), *The juvenile sex offender* (pp. 104–117). New York: Guilford Press.

Abel, K. M., Drake, R., & Goldstein, J. M. (2010). Sex differences in schizophrenia. *International Review of Psychiatry, 22,* 417–428.

Abela, J. R. Z., & Hankin, B. J. (2008a). Cognitive vulnerability in children and adolescents. In J. R. Z. Abela & B. L. Hankin (Eds.), *Handbook of depression in children and adolescents* (pp. 35–78). New York: Guilford Press.

Abela, J. R. Z., & Hankin, B. L. (Eds.). (2008b). *Handbook of depression in children and adolescents.* New York: Guilford Press.

Abela, J. R. Z., & Hankin, B. L. (2011). Rumination as a vulnerability factor to depression during the transition from early to middle adolescence: A multiwave longitudinal study. *Journal of Abnormal Psychology, 120,* 259–271.

Aber, J. L., Jones, S. M., & Raver, C. C. (2007). Poverty and child development: New perspectives on a defining issue. In J. L. Aber, S. J. Bishop-Josef, S. M. Jones, K. T. McLearn, & D. A. Phillips (Eds.), *Child development and social policy: Knowledge for action* (pp. 149–166). Washington, DC: American Psychological Association.

Abikoff, H. (2009). ADHD psychosocial treatments: Generalization reconsidered. *Journal of Attention Disorders, 13,* 207–210.

Abikoff, H., Courtney, M., Pelham, W., & Koplewicz, H. (1993). Teachers' ratings of disruptive behaviors: The influence of halo effects. *Journal of Abnormal Child Psychology, 21,* 519–533.

Abikoff, H., Gallagher, R., Wells, K. C., Murray, D. W., Huang, L., Lu, F., & Petkova, E. (2013). Remediating organizational functioning in children with ADHD: Immediate and long-term effects from a randomized controlled trial. *Journal of Consulting and Clinical Psychology, 81,* 113-128.

Abramowitz, J. S., & Braddock, A. E. (2011). *Hypochondriasis and health anxiety.* Cambridge, MA: Hogrefe & Huber.

Abramson, L. Y., Metalsky, G. I., & Alloy, L. B. (1989). Hopelessness depression: A theory-based subtype of depression. *Psychological Review, 96,* 358–372.

Abramson, L. Y., Seligman, M. E., & Teasdale, J. D. (1978). Learned helplessness in humans: Critique and reformulation. *Journal of Abnormal Psychology, 37,* 49–74.

Acebo, C., Sadeh, A., Seifer, R., Tzischinsky, O., Hafer, A., & Carskadon, M. A. (2005). Sleep/wake patterns derived from activity monitoring and maternal report for healthy 1- to 5-year-old children. *Sleep, 28,* 1568–1577.

Achenbach, T. M. (1982). *Developmental psychopathology* (2nd ed.). New York: Wiley.

Achenbach, T. M. (1991a). *Manual for the Child Behavior Checklist/4-18 and 1991 Profile.* Burlington: University of Vermont, Department of Psychiatry.

Achenbach, T. M. (1991b). *Manual for the Youth Self-Report and 1991 Profile.* Burlington: University of Vermont, Department of Psychiatry.

Achenbach, T. M. (2009). *The Achenbach System of Empirically Based Assessment (ASEBA): Development, findings, theory, and applications.* Burlington: University of Vermont, Research Center for Children, Youth, & Families.

Achenbach, T. M. (2010). Multicultural evidence-based assessment of child and adolescent psychopathology. *Transcultural Psychiatry, 47,* 707–726.

Achenbach, T. M., Becker, A., Dopfner, M., Heiervang, E., Roessner, V., Steinhausen, H., … Rothenberger, A. (2008). Multicultural assessment of child and adolescent psychopathology with ASEBA and instruments: Research findings, applications, and future directions. *Journal of Child Psychology and Psychiatry, 49,* 251–275.

Achenbach, T. M., McConaughy, S., Ivanova, M. Y., & Rescorla, L. A. (2011). *Brief Problem Monitor: For normed multiinformant assessment of children's functioning & responses to interventions (RTIs).* Burlington: University of Vermont, Research Center for Children, Youth, & Families.

Achenbach, T. M., & Rescorla, L. A. (2001). *Manual for the ASEBA school-age forms & profiles.* Burlington: University of Vermont, Research Center for Children, Youth, & Families.

Achenbach, T. M., & Rescorla, L. A. (2006). *Developmental issues in assessment, taxonomy, and diagnosis of psychopathology: Life span and multicultural perspectives.* Hoboken, NJ: Wiley.

Achenbach, T. M., & Rescorla, L. A. (2007). *Multicultural understanding of child and adolescent psychopathology: Implications for mental health assessment.* New York: Guilford Press.

Adams, D., & Oliver, C. (2011). The expression and assessment of emotions and internal states in individuals with severe or profound intellectual disabilities. *Clinical Psychology Review, 31,* 293–306.

Addington, J., & Heinssen, R. (2012). Prediction and prevention of psychosis in youth at clinical high risk. *Annual Review of Psychology, 8,* 269-289.

Addington, J., Piskulic, D., & Marshall, C. (2010). Psychosocial treatments for schizophrenia. *Current Directions in Psychological Science, 19,* 260–263.

Afifi, T. O., & MacMillan, H. L. (2011). Resilience following child maltreatment: A review of protective factors. *Canadian Journal of Psychiatry, 56,* 266–272.

Agency for Healthcare Research and Quality. (2011). *Minority health: Recent findings.* AHRQ Publication No. 00-PO41. Rockville, MD: Author. Retrieved from http://www.ahrq.gov/research/minorfind3.htm#health

Agoston, A. M., & Rudolph, K. D. (2013). Pathways from depressive symptoms to low social status. *Journal of Abnormal Child Psychology, 41,* 295–308.

Agras, W. S. (2010). *The Oxford handbook of eating disorders.* New York: Oxford University Press.

Ainsworth, M. D. S., Blehar, M. C., Waters, E., & Wall, S. (1978). *Patterns of attachment: A psychological study of the Strange Situation.* Hillsdale, NJ: Erlbaum.

Ajdacic-Gross, V., Vetter, S., Müller, M., Kawohl, W., Frey, F., Lupi, G., … Rössler, W. (2010). Risk factors for stuttering: A secondary analysis of a large data base. *European Archives of Psychiatry and Clinical Neuroscience, 260,* 279–286.

Akinbami, L. J., Liu, X., Pastor, P. N., & Reuben, C. A. (2011). Attention deficit hyperactivity disorder among children aged 5–17 years in the United States, 1998–2009. *NCHS Data Brief, 70,* 1–8.

Akinbami, L. J., Moorman, J. E., & Liu, X. (2011, January 12). Asthma prevalence, health care use, and mortality: United States,

2005–2009. *National Health Statistics Reports, 32,* 1–15.

Alarcón, R. D. (2009). Culture, cultural factors and psychiatric diagnosis: Review and projections. *World Psychiatry, 8,* 131–139.

Albano, A. M. (1995). Treatment of social anxiety in adolescents. *Cognitive and Behavioral Practice, 2,* 271–298.

Albano, A. M. (2003). Treatment of social anxiety disorder. In M. A. Reinecke & F. M. Dattilio (Eds.), *Cognitive therapy with children and adolescents: A casebook for clinical practice* (2nd ed., pp. 128–161). New York: Guilford Press.

Albano, A. M., Chorpita, B. F., & Barlow, D. H. (2003). Childhood anxiety disorders. In E. J. Mash & R. A. Barkley (Eds.), *Child psychopathology* (2nd ed., pp. 279–329). New York: Guilford Press.

Albano, A. M., Detweiler, M. F., & Logsdon-Conradsen, S. (1999). Cognitive-behavioral interventions with socially phobic children. In S. W. Russ & T. H. Ollendick (Eds.), *Handbook of psychotherapies with children and families* (pp. 255–280). New York: Plenum Press.

Albano, A. M., & DiBartolo, P. M. (2007). *Cognitive-behavioral therapy for social phobia in adolescents: Stand up, speak out* [Therapist guide]. New York: Oxford University Press.

Albano, A. M., Knox, L. S., & Barlow, D. H. (1995). Obsessive-compulsive disorder. In A. R. Eisen, C. A. Kearney, & C. A. Schaefer (Eds.), *Clinical handbook of anxiety disorders in children and adolescents* (pp. 282–316). Northvale, NJ: Aronson.

Albano, A. M., Miller, P. P., Zarate, R., Côté, G., & Barlow, D. H. (1997). Behavioral assessment and treatment of PTSD in pre-pubertal children: Attention to developmental factors and innovative strategies in the case study of a family. *Cognitive and Behavioral Practice, 4,* 245–262.

Albaugh, M. D., Harder, V. S., Althoff, R. R., Rettew, D. C., Ehli, E. A., Lengyel-Nelson, T., … Hudziak, J. J. (2010). COMT Val158Met genotype as a risk factor for problem behaviors in youth. *Journal of the American Academy of Child & Adolescent Psychiatry, 49,* 841–849.

Alegria, M., Vallas, M., & Pumariega, A. J. (2010). Racial and ethnic disparities in pediatric mental health. *Child and Adolescent Psychiatric Clinics of North America, 19,* 759–774.

Alfano, C. A., Beidel, D. C., & Turner, S. M. (2002). Cognition in childhood anxiety: Conceptual, methodological, and developmental issues. *Clinical Psychology Review, 22,* 1209–1238.

Alfano, C. A., Ginsburg, G. S., & Kingery, J. N. (2007). Sleep-related problems among children and adolescents with anxiety disorders. *Journal of the American Academy of Child & Adolescent Psychiatry, 46,* 224–232.

Ali, Z. (2001). Pica in people with intellectual disability: A literature review of aetiology, epidemiology and complications. *Journal of Intellectual & Developmental Disability, 26,* 205–215.

Allen, J. L., Lavallee, K. L., Herren, C., Ruhe, K., & Schneider, S. (2010). DSM-IV criteria for childhood separation anxiety disorder: Informant, age, and sex differences. *Journal of Anxiety Disorders, 24,* 946-952.

Allin, H., Wathen, C. N., & MacMillan, H. (2005). Treatment of child neglect: A systematic review. *Canadian Journal of Psychiatry, 50,* 497–504.

Alriksson-Schmidt, A. I., Wallander, J., & Biasini, F. (2007). Quality of life and resilience in adolescents with a mobility disability. *Journal of Pediatric Psychology, 32,* 370–379.

Alsabban, S., Rivers, M., & McGuffin, P. (2011). Genome-wide searches for bipolar disorder genes. *Current Psychiatry Reports, 13,* 522–527.

Alwell, M., & Cobb, B. (2009). Social and communicative interventions and transition outcomes for youth with disabilities: A systematic review. *Career Development for Exceptional Individuals, 32,* 94–107.

Amaya-Jackson, L., & March, J. S. (1995). Posttraumatic stress disorder. In J. S. March (Ed.), *Anxiety disorders in children and adolescents* (pp. 276–300). New York: Guilford Press.

Amendah, D. D., Grosse, S. D., & Bertrand, J. (2011). Medical expenditures of children in the United States with fetal alcohol syndrome. *Neurotoxicology and Teratology, 33,* 322–324.

Amendah, D. D., Mvundura, M., Kavanagh, P. L., Sprinz, P. G., & Grosse, S. D. (2010). Sickle cell disease–related pediatric medical expenditures in the U.S. *American Journal of Preventive Medicine, 38,* S550–S556.

American Academy of Child and Adolescent Psychiatry (AACAP). (2001). Practice parameter for the assessment and treatment of children and adolescents with suicidal behavior. *Journal of the American Academy of Child & Adolescent Psychiatry, 40*(Suppl.), 24S–51S. Retrieved from http://www.aacap.org/

American Academy of Child and Adolescent Psychiatry. (AACAP). (2004/2012). *Psychiatric medication for children and adolescents Part II: Types of medications.* (Facts for Families, #29, updated May 2012). Retrieved from http://www.aacap.org

American Academy of Child and Adolescent Psychiatry (AACAP). (2007a). AACAP official action: Practice parameter on child and adolescent mental health care in community systems of care. *Journal of the American Academy of Child & Adolescent Psychiatry, 46,* 284–299.

American Academy of Child and Adolescent Psychiatry (AACAP). (2007b). Practice parameter for the assessment and treatment of children and adolescents with anxiety disorders. *Journal of the American Academy of Child & Adolescent Psychiatry, 46,* 267–283.

American Academy of Child and Adolescent Psychiatry (AACAP). (2007c). Practice parameter for the assessment and treatment of children and adolescents with attention-deficit/hyperactivity disorder. *Journal of the American Academy of*

Child & Adolescent Psychiatry, 46, 894–921.

American Academy of Child and Adolescent Psychiatry (AACAP). (2007d). Practice parameter for the assessment and treatment of children and adolescents with bipolar disorder. *Journal of the American Academy of Child & Adolescent Psychiatry, 46,* 107–125.

American Academy of Child and Adolescent Psychiatry (AACAP). (2007e). Practice parameter for the assessment and treatment of children and adolescents with depressive disorders. *Journal of the American Academy of Child & Adolescent Psychiatry, 46,* 1503–1526.

American Academy of Child and Adolescent Psychiatry (2009a). *Code of ethics.* Retrieved from http://www.aacap.org/App_Themes/AACAP/docs/about_us/transparency_portal/aacap_code_of_ethics_2012.pdf

American Academy of Child and Adolescent Psychiatry (AACAP). (2009b). Practice parameter on the use of psychotropic medication in children and adolescents. *Journal of the American Academy of Child & Adolescent Psychiatry, 48,* 961–973.

American Academy of Child and Adolescent Psychiatry (AACAP). (2010). Practice parameter for the assessment and treatment of children and adolescents with posttraumatic stress disorder. *Journal of the American Academy of Child & Adolescent Psychiatry, 49,* 414–430.

American Academy of Child and Adolescent Psychiatry (AACAP). (2012). Practice parameter for psychodynamic psychotherapy with children. *Journal of the American Academy of Child & Adolescent Psychiatry, 51,* 541-557.

American Academy of Child and Adolescent Psychiatry (AACAP). (2013). Parent's Medication Guide (Revised July 2013). Retrieved from http://www.aacap.org

American Psychiatric Association. (1952). *Diagnostic and statistical manual of mental disorders.* Washington, DC: Author.

American Psychiatric Association. (1968). *Diagnostic and statistical manual of mental disorders* (2nd ed.). Washington, DC: Author.

American Psychiatric Association. (1980). *Diagnostic and statistical manual of mental disorders DSM-III* (3rd ed.). Washington, DC: Author.

American Psychiatric Association. (1987). *Diagnostic and statistical manual of mental disorders DSM-III-R* (3rd ed., rev.). Washington, DC: Author.

American Psychiatric Association. (1994). *Diagnostic and statistical manual of mental disorders DSM-IV* (4th ed.). Washington, DC: Author.

American Psychiatric Association. (2000). *Diagnostic and statistical manual of mental disorders DSM-IV-TR* (text revision). Washington, DC: Author.

American Psychiatric Association. (2013). *Diagnostic and statistical manual of mental disorders DSM-5* (5th ed.). Washington, DC: Author.

American Psychological Association. (1996/2007). Violence and the family. *Report of the American Psychological Association Presidential Task Force on Violence and the Family*. Washington, DC: Author. Retrieved from http://www.apa.org/pi/viol&fam.html

American Psychological Association (2002). Ethical principles of psychologists and code of conduct. *American Psychologist, 57*, 1060–1073.

American Psychological Association. (2010). *Ethical principles of psychologists and code of conduct: 2010 Amendments*. Retrieved from http://www.apa.org/ethics/code/principles.pdf

American Speech–Language–Hearing Association (ASHA). (2008). Incidence and prevalence of communication disorders and hearing loss in children—2008 edition. Retrieved from http://www.asha.org/members/research/reports/children.htm

Anders, T., Goodlin-Jones, B., & Sadeh, A. (2000). Sleep disorders. In C. H. Zeanah Jr. (Ed.), *Handbook of infant mental health* (2nd ed., pp. 326–338). New York: Guilford Press.

Anders, T. F., & Eiben, L. A. (1997). Pediatric sleep disorders: A review of the past 10 years. *Journal of the American Academy of Child & Adolescent Psychiatry, 36*, 9–20.

Anderson, C. A., & Bushman, B. J. (2002). The effects of media violence on society. *Science, 295*, 2377–2379.

Anderson, E. (1994, May). The code of the streets. *Atlantic Monthly, 273*, 81–94.

Anderson, E. R., & Hope, D. A. (2008). A review of the tripartite model for understanding the link between anxiety and depression in youth. *Clinical Psychology Review, 28*, 275–287.

Anderson, E. R., & Mayes, L. C. (2009). Race/ethnicity and internalizing disorders in youth: A review. *Clinical Psychology Review, 30*, 338–348.

Anderson, E. R., & Mayes, L. C. (2010). Race/ethnicity and internalizing disorders in youth: A review. *Clinical Psychology Review, 30*, 338–348.

Anderson, J. S., Druzgal, T. J., Froehlich, A., BuBray, M. B., Lange, N., Alexander., A. L., … Lainhart, J. E. (2011). Decreased interhemispheric functional connectivity in autism. *Cerebral Cortex, 21*, 1134–1146.

Anderson, K. E., Lytton, H., & Romney, D. M. (1986). Mothers' interactions with normal and conduct-disordered boys: Who affects whom? *Developmental Psychology, 22*, 604–609.

Anderson, K. G., Ramo, D. E., Schulte, M. T., Cummins, K., & Brown, S. A. (2007). Substance use treatment outcomes for youth: Integrating personal and environmental predictors. *Drug and Alcohol Dependence, 88*, 42–48.

Anderson, V.A., Anderson, P., Northam, E., Jacobs, R., & Catroppa, C. (2001). Development of executive functions through late childhood and adolescence in an Australian sample. *Developmental Neuropsychology, 20*, 385–406.

Anderson-Fye, E. (2009). Cross-cultural issues in body image among children and adolescents. In L. Smolak, & J. K. Thompson (Eds.), *Body image, eating disorders, and obesity in youth: Assessment, prevention, and treatment.* (2nd ed., pp. 113–133). Washington, DC: American Psychological Association.

Andersson, U. (2010). Skill development in different components of arithmetic and basic cognitive functions: Findings from a 3-year longitudinal study of children with different types of learning difficulties. *Journal of Educational Psychology, 102*, 115–134.

Andrade, A. R., Lambert, E. W., & Bickman, L. (2000). Dose effect in child psychotherapy: Outcomes associated with negligible treatment. *Journal of the American Academy of Child & Adolescent Psychiatry, 39*, 161–168.

Andrews, B., Brewin, C. R., Philpott, R., & Stewart, L. (2007). Delayed-onset posttraumatic stress disorder: A systematic review of the evidence. *American Journal of Psychiatry, 164*, 1319–1326.

Andrews, G., Hobbs, M. J., Borkovec, T. D., Beesdo, K., Craske, M. G., Heimberg, R. G., … & Stanley, M. A. (2010). Generalized worry disorder: A review of DSM-IV generalized anxiety disorder and options for DSM-V. *Depression and Anxiety, 27*, 134–147.

Andrews, G., Pine, D. S., Hobbs, M. J., Anderson, T. M. & Sunderland, M. (2009). Neurodevelopmental disorders: Cluster 2 of the proposed meta-structure for DSM-V and ICD-11. *Psychological Medicine, 39*, 2013–2023.

Andreyeva, T., Puhl, R. M., & Brownell, K. D. (2008). Changes in perceived weight discrimination among Americans, 1995–1996 through 2004–2006. *Obesity, 6*, 1129–1134.

Angold, A., Costello, E. J., Burns, B. J., Erkanli, A., & Farmer, E. M. Z. (2000). Effectiveness of nonresidential specialty mental health services for children and adolescents in the "real world." *Journal of the American Academy of Child & Adolescent Psychiatry, 39*, 154–160.

Angold, A., Costello, E. J., & Erkanli, A. (1999). Comorbidity. *Journal of Child Psychology and Psychiatry, 40*, 57–88.

Angold, A., Worthman, C., & Costello, E. J. (2003). Puberty and depression. In C. Hayward (Ed.), *Gender differences at puberty* (pp. 137–164). New York: Cambridge University Press.

Anney, R., Klei, L., Pinto, D., Almeida, J., Bacchelli, E., Baird, G., … Wijsman, E. M. (2012). Individual common variants exert weak effects on the risk for autism spectrum disorders. *Human Molecular Genetics, 21*, 4781–4792.

Anthony, J. L., Lonigan, C. J., & Hecht, S. A. (1999). Dimensionality of posttraumatic stress disorder symptoms in children exposed to disaster: Results from confirmatory factor analyses. *Journal of Abnormal Psychology, 108*, 326–336.

Antrop, I., Roeyers, H., Van Oost, P., & Buysse, A. (2000). Stimulation seeking and hyperactivity in children with ADHD. *Journal of Child Psychology and Psychiatry, 41*, 225–231.

Antshel, K. M., & Arnold, G. (2007). Inborn errors of metabolism. In M. M. Mazzocco & J. L. Ross (Eds.), *Neurogenetic developmental disorders: Variation of manifestation in childhood* (pp. 297–334). Cambridge, MA: MIT Press.

Antshel, K. M., & Barkley, R. (2008). Psychosocial interventions in attention deficit hyperactivity disorder. *Child and Adolescent Psychiatric Clinics of North America, 17*, 421–437.

Antshel, K. M., Faraone, S. V., Maglione, K., Doyle, A., Fried, R., Seidman, L., & Biederman, J. (2008). Temporal stability of ADHD in the high-IQ population: Results from the MGH longitudinal family studies of ADHD. *Journal of the American Academy of Child & Adolescent Psychiatry, 47*, 817–825.

Apter-Levy, Y., Feldman, M., Vakart, A., Ebstein, R. P., & Feldman, R. (2013). Impact of maternal depression across the first 6 years of life on the child's mental health, social engagement, and empathy: The moderating role of oxytocin. *American Journal of Psychiatry, 170*, 1161–1168.

Arcelus, J., Haslam, M., Farrow, C., & Meyer, C. (2013). The role of interpersonal functioning in the maintenance of eating psychopathology: A systematic review and testable model. *Clinical Psychology Review, 33*, 156–167.

Arcelus, J., Mitchell, A. J., Wales, J., & Nielsen, S. (2011). Mortality rates in patients with anorexia nervosa and other eating disorders: A meta-analysis of 36 studies. *Archives of General Psychiatry, 68*, 724–731.

Aries, P. (1962). *Centuries of childhood.* New York: Vintage.

Arnett, A. B., MacDonald, B., & Pennington, B. F. (2013). Cognitive and behavioral indications of ADHD symptoms prior to school age. *Journal of Child Psychology and Psychiatry, 54*, 1284–1294.

Arnold, L. E., Aman, M. G., Li, X., Butter, E., Humphries, K., Scahill, L., … Stigler, K. A. (2012). Research units of pediatric psychopharmacology (RUPP) autism network randomized clinical trial of parent training and medication: One-year follow-up. *Journal of the American Academy of Child & Adolescent Psychiatry, 51*, 1173–1184.

Arnold, L. E., & DiSilvestro, R. A. (2005). Zinc in attention-deficit/hyperactivity disorder. *Journal of Child and Adolescent Psychopharmacology, 15*, 619–627.

Arseneault, L., Cannon, M., Fisher, H. L., Polanczyk, G., & Moffitt, T. E. (2011). Childhood trauma and children's emerging psychotic symptoms: A genetically sensitive longitudinal cohort study. *American Journal of Psychiatry, 168*, 65–72.

Arsenio, W. F., & Lemerise, E. A. (Eds.). (2010). *Emotions, aggression, and morality in children: Bridging development and psychopathology.* Washington, DC: American Psychological Association.

Asarnow, J. R., & Asarnow, R. F. (2003). Childhood-onset schizophrenia. In E. J. Mash & R. A. Barkley (Eds.), *Child psychopathology* (2nd ed., pp. 455–485). New York: Guilford Press.

Asarnow, J. R., Goldstein, M. J., & Ben-Meir, S. (1988). Parental communication deviance in childhood-onset schizophrenia spectrum and depressive disorders.

Journal of Child Psychology and Psychiatry, 29, 825–838.

Asarnow, J. R., Tompson, M. C., & McGrath, E. P. (2004). Childhood-onset schizophrenia: Clinical and treatment issues. *Journal of Child Psychology and Psychiatry, 45,* 180–194.

Asarnow, R. F., & Asarnow, J. R. (1994). Childhood-onset schizophrenia. *Schizophrenia Bulletin, 20,* 591–598.

Asarnow, R. F., Nuechterlein, K. H., Fogelson, D., Subotnik, K. L., Payne, D. A., Russell, A. T., ... Kendler, K. S. (2001). Schizophrenia and schizophrenia-spectrum personality disorders in the first-degree relatives of children with schizophrenia: The UCLA family study. *Archives of General Psychiatry, 58,* 581–588.

Ashkenazi, S., Mark-Zigdon, N., & Henik, A. (2013). Do subitizing deficits in developmental dyscalculia involve pattern recognition weakness? *Developmental Science, 16,* 35–46.

Asperger, H. (1944). Die autistischen Psychopathen im Kindesalter [The autistic psychopathy of childhood]. *Archiv für Psychiatrie und Nervenkrankheiten, 117,* 76–136.

Atalay, A., & McCord, M. (2011). Characteristics of failure to thrive in a referral population: Implications for treatment. *Clinical Pediatrics, 51,* 219–225.

Atkinson, A. P. (2009). Impaired recognition of emotions from body movements is associated with elevated motion coherence thresholds in autism spectrum disorders. *Neuropsychologia, 47,* 3023–3029.

Attie, I., & Brooks-Gunn, J. (1995). The development of eating regulation across the life span. In D. Cicchetti & D. J. Cohen (Eds.), *Developmental psychopathology: Vol. 2. Risk, disorder, and adaptation* (pp. 332–368). New York: Wiley.

Austin, S. B., Ziyadeh, N., Kahn, J. A., Camargo, C. A., Jr., Colditz, G. A., & Field, A. E. (2004). Sexual orientation, weight concerns, and eating-disordered behaviors in adolescent girls and boys. *Journal of the American Academy of Child & Adolescent Psychiatry, 43,* 1115–1123.

Autism Speaks (2013). *How common is autism?* Retrieved from http://www.autismspeaks.org/what-autism

Avenevoli, S., Knight, E., Kessler, R. C., & Merikangas, K. R. (2008). Epidemiology of depression in children and adolescents. In J. R. Z. Abela & B. L. Hankin (Eds.), *Handbook of depression in children and adolescents* (pp. 6–32). New York: Guilford Press.

Averill, J. R. (2001). Studies on anger and aggression: Implications for theories of emotion. In W. Parrott (Ed.), *Emotions in social psychology: Essential readings* (pp. 337–352). Philadelphia: Psychology Press.

Axelson, D. A., Birmaher, B., Findling, R. L., Fristad, M. A., Kowatch, R. A., Youngstrom, E. A., ... Diler, R. S. (2011). Concerns regarding the inclusion of temper dysregulation disorder with dysphoria in the Diagnostic and Statistical Manual of Mental Disorders, Fifth Edition. *Journal of Clinical Psychiatry, 72,* 1257–1262.

Axelson, D., Birmaher, B., Strober, M., Gill, M. K., Valeria, S., Chiappetta, L., ... Keller, M. (2006). Phenomenology of children and adolescents with bipolar spectrum disorders. *Archives of General Psychiatry, 63,* 1139–1148.

Axline, V. M. (1947). *Play therapy: The inner dynamics of childhood.* Boston: Houghton Mifflin.

Azar, S., & Wolfe, D. (2006). Child physical abuse and neglect. In E. J. Mash & R. A. Barkley (Eds.), *Treatment of childhood disorders* (3rd ed., pp. 595–646). New York: Guilford.

Babinski, D. E., Pelham, W. E., Molina, B. S. G., Gnagy, E. M., Waschbusch, D. A., Yu, J., ... Karch, K. M. (2010). Late adolescent and young adult outcomes of girls diagnosed with ADHD in childhood: An exploratory investigation. *Journal of Attention Disorders, 15,* 204–214.

Bagner, D. M., & Eyberg, S. M. (2007). Parent-child interaction therapy for disruptive behavior in children with mental retardation: A randomized controlled trial. *Journal of Clinical Child & Adolescent Psychology, 36,* 418–429.

Bagner, D. M., Pettit, J. W., Lewinsohn, P. M., & Seeley, J. R. (2011). Effect of maternal depression on child behavior: A sensitive period? *Journal of the American Academy of Child and Adolescent Psychiatry, 49,* 699–707.

Bailey, A. J. (2012). Editorial: Autism in adults. *Autism Research, 5,* 1–2.

Bailey, A., Phillips, W., & Rutter, M. (1996). Autism: Towards an integration of clinical, genetic, neuropsychological, and neurobiological perspectives. *Journal of Child Psychology and Psychiatry, 37,* 89–126.

Bakermans-Kranenburg, M. J., & Van Ijzendoorn, M. H. (2011). Differential susceptibility to rearing environment depending on dopamine-related genes: New evidence and a meta-analysis. *Development and Psychopathology, 23,* 39–52.

Bakwin, H. (1973). The genetics of enuresis. In I. Kolvin, R. C. MacKeith, & R. Meadow (Eds.), *Bladder control and enuresis* (pp. 73–77). Philadelphia: Lippincott.

Baldwin, W. K. (1958). The social position of mentally handicapped children in the regular class in the public schools. *Exceptional Children, 25,* 106–108.

Ball, L. K., Ball, R., & Pratt, D. (2001). An assessment of thimerosal use in childhood vaccines. *Pediatrics, 107,* 1147–1154.

Banaschewski, T., Becker, K., Scherag, S., Franke, B., & Coghill, D. (2010). Molecular genetics of attention-deficit/hyperactivity disorder: An overview. *European Child & Adolescent Psychiatry, 19,* 237–257.

Banaschewski, T., Hollis, C., Oosterlaan, J., Roeyers, H., Rubia, K., Willcutt, E., & Taylor, E. (2005). Towards an understanding of unique and shared pathways in the psychopathophysiology of ADHD. *Developmental Science, 8,* 132–140.

Bandura, A. (1977). *Social learning theory.* Englewood Cliffs, NJ: Prentice Hall.

Bandura, A. (1986). *Social foundations of thought and action: A social cognitive theory.* Englewood Cliffs, NJ: Prentice Hall.

Bandura, A., & Walters, R. H. (1963). *Social learning and personality development.* New York: Holt, Rinehart, & Winston.

Banerjee, T. D., Middleton, F., & Faraone, S. V. (2007). Environmental risk factors for attention-deficit hyperactivity disorder. *Acta Paediatrica, 96,* 1269–1274.

Barakat, L. P., Hocking, M., & Kazak, A. E. (2013). *Child health psychology.* In A. M. Nezu, C. Maguth, P. A. Geller, & I. B. Weiner (Eds.), *Handbook of psychology, Vol. 9: Health psychology* (2nd ed., pp. 413–436). Hoboken, NJ: Wiley.

Barenbaum, J., Ruchkin, V., & Schwab-Stone, M. (2004). The psychosocial aspects of children exposed to war: Practice and policy initiatives. *Journal of Child Psychology and Psychiatry, 45,* 41–62.

Bar-Haim, Y., Lamy, D., Pergamin, L., Bakersman-Kranenburg, M. J., & van IJzendoorn, M. H. (2007). Threat-related attentional bias in anxious and nonanxious individuals: A meta-analytic study. *Psychological Bulletin, 133,* 1–24.

Barker, E. D., Tremblay, R. E., van Lier, P. A. C., Vitaro, F., Nagin, D. S., Assaad, J. M., & Seguin, J. R. (2011). The neurocognition of conduct disorder behaviors: Specificity to physical aggression and theft after controlling for ADHD symptoms. *Aggressive Behavior, 37,* 63–72.

Barkley, R. A. (1988). The effects of methylphenidate on the interactions of preschool ADHD children with their mothers. *Journal of the American Academy of Child & Adolescent Psychiatry, 26,* 336–341.

Barkley, R. A. (1995). *Taking charge of ADHD: The complete, authoritative guide for parents.* New York: Guilford Press.

Barkley, R. A. (2003). Attention-deficit/hyperactivity disorder. In E. J. Mash & R. A. Barkley (Eds.), *Child psychopathology* (pp. 75–143). New York: Guilford Press.

Barkley, R. A. (2006a). *Attention-deficit hyperactivity disorder: A handbook for diagnosis and treatment* (3rd ed.). New York: Guilford Press.

Barkley, R. A. (2006b). Attention-deficit/hyperactivity disorder in adolescents. In D. A. Wolfe & E. J. Mash (Eds.), *Behavioral and emotional disorders in adolescents* (pp. 91–152). New York: Guilford Press.

Barkley, R. A. (2012). *Executive functions: What they are, how they work, and why they evolved.* New York: Guilford Press.

Barkley, R. A. (2013a). *Defiant children: A clinician's manual for assessment and parent training* (3rd ed.). New York: Guilford Press.

Barkley, R. A. (2013b). Distinguishing sluggish cognitive tempo from ADHD in children and adolescents: Executive functioning, impairment, and comorbidity. *Journal of Clinical Child & Adolescent Psychology, 42,* 161–173.

Barkley, R. A. (2013c). *Taking charge of ADHD: The complete, authoritative guide for parents* (3rd ed.). New York: Guilford Press.

Barkley, R. A. (2014a). Comorbid psychiatric disorders and psychological maladjustment in adults. In R. A. Barkley (Ed.),

Attention-deficit hyperactivity disorder: A handbook for diagnosis and treatment (4th ed.). New York: Guilford Press.

Barkley, R. A. (2014b). Educational, occupational, social, and financial impairments in adults. In R. A. Barkley (Ed.), *Attention-deficit hyperactivity disorder: A handbook for diagnosis and treatment* (4th ed.). New York: Guilford Press.

Barkley, R. A. (2014c). Emotional dysregulation is a core component of ADHD. In R. A. Barkley (Ed.), *Attention-deficit hyperactivity disorder: A handbook for diagnosis and treatment* (4th ed.). New York: Guilford Press.

Barkley, R. A. (2014d). Health and related impairments in children and adults. In R. A. Barkley (Ed.), *Attention-deficit hyperactivity disorder: A handbook for diagnosis and treatment* (4th ed.). New York: Guilford Press.

Barkley, R. A. (Ed.). (2014e). History. In R. A. Barkley (Ed.), *Attention-deficit hyperactivity disorder: A handbook for diagnosis and treatment* (4th ed.). New York: Guilford Press.

Barkley, R. A. (2014f). Sluggish cognitive tempo (concentration deficit disorder?): Current status, future directions, and a plea to change the name. *Journal of Abnormal Child Psychology, 42,* 117–125.

Barkley, R. A., & Peters, H. (2012). The earliest reference to ADHD in the medical literature? Melchior Adam Weikard's description in 1775 of "attention deficit" (Mangel der Aufmerksamkeit, attentio volubilis). *Journal of Attention Disorders, 16,* 623–630.

Barkley, R. A., & Pfiffner, L. J. (1995). Off to school on the right foot: Managing your child's education. In R. A. Barkley, *Taking charge of ADHD: The complete, authoritative guide for parents* (pp. 206–221). New York: Guilford Press.

Barkley, R. A., Fischer, M., Smallish, L., & Fletcher, K. (2002). The persistence of attention-deficit/hyperactivity disorder into young adulthood as a function of reporting source and definition of disorder. *Journal of Abnormal Psychology, 111,* 279–289.

Barkley, R. A., Shelton, T. L., Crosswait, C., Moorehouse, M., Fletcher, K., Barrett, S., ... Metevia, L. (2002). Preschool children with high levels of disruptive behavior: Three-year outcomes as a function of adaptive disability. *Development and Psychopathology, 14,* 45–68.

Barlow, D. H. (2002). *Anxiety and its disorders: The nature and treatment of anxiety and panic* (2nd ed.). New York: Guilford Press.

Barlow, D. H., Nock, M. K., & Hersen, M. (2009). *Single case experimental designs: Strategies for studying behavior change.* Boston: Allyn & Bacon.

Barnea-Goraly, N., Lotspeich, L. J., & Reiss A. L. (2010). Similar white matter aberrations in children with autism and their unaffected siblings: A diffusion tensor imaging study using tract-based spatial statistics. *Archives of General Psychiatry, 67,* 1052–1060.

Baron-Cohen, S. (1995). *Mindblindness: An essay on autism and theory of mind.* Cambridge, MA: MIT Press.

Baron-Cohen, S. (2002). The extreme male brain theory of autism. *Trends in Cognitive Sciences, 6,* 248–254.

Baron-Cohen, S. (2009). Autism: The empathizing-systemizing (E-S) theory. *Annals of New York Academy of Science, 1156,* 68–80.

Baron-Cohen, S., & Bolton, P. (1993). *Autism: The facts.* Oxford, England: Oxford University Press.

Baron-Cohen, S., Richler, J., Bisarya, D., Gurunathan, N., & Wheelright, S. (2003). The systemizing quotient: An investigation of adults with Asperger syndrome or high-functioning autism, and normal sex differences. *Philosophical Transactions of the Royal Society: Biological Sciences, 358,* 361–374.

Baron-Cohen, S., Tager-Flusberg, H., & Cohen, D. (2000). *Understanding other minds: Perspectives from developmental cognitive neuroscience.* Oxford, England: Oxford University Press.

Barrera, A. Z., Torres, L. D., & Munoz, R. F. (2007). Prevention of depression: The state of the science at the beginning of the 21st century. *International Review of Psychiatry, 19,* 655–670.

Barrera, T. L., Mott, J. M., Hofstein, R. F., & Teng, E. J. (2013). A meta-analytic review of exposure in group cognitive behavioral therapy for posttraumatic stress disorder. *Clinical Psychology Review, 33,* 24–32.

Barrett, J., & Fleming, A. S. (2011). All mothers are not created equal: Neural and psychobiological perspectives on mothering and the importance of individual differences. *Journal of Child Psychology and Psychiatry, 52,* 368–397.

Barrett, P. M., Dadds, M. R., & Rapee, R. M. (1996). Family treatment of childhood anxiety: A controlled trial. *Journal of Consulting and Clinical Psychology, 64,* 333–342.

Barrett, P. M., Farrell, L. J., Ollendick, T. H., & Dadds, M. (2006). Long-term outcomes of an Australian universal prevention trial of anxiety and depression symptoms in children and youth: An evaluation of the Friends program. *Journal of Clinical Child & Adolescent Psychology, 35,* 403–411.

Barrett, P. M., Farrell, L., Pina, A. A., Peris, T. A., & Piacentini, J. (2008). Evidence-based psychosocial treatments for child and adolescent obsessive-compulsive disorder. *Journal of Clinical Child & Adolescent Psychology, 37,* 131–155.

Barrett, P. M., Rapee, R. M., Dadds, M. M., & Ryan, S. M. (1996). Family enhancement of cognitive style in anxious and aggressive children. *Journal of Abnormal Child Psychology, 24,* 187–203.

Barrios, B. A., & Hartmann, D. P. (1997). Fears and anxieties. In E. J. Mash & L. G. Terdal (Eds.), *Assessment of childhood disorders* (3rd ed., pp. 230–327). New York: Guilford Press.

Barry, M. M. (2009). Addressing the determinants of positive mental health: Concepts, evidence and practice. *International Journal of Mental Health Promotion, 11,* 4–17.

Bartels, M., Beijsterveldt, C. V., Derks, E. M., Stroet, T. M., Polderman, T. J., Hudziak, J. J., & Boomsma, D. I. (2007). Young

Netherlands Twin Register (Y-NTR): A longitudinal multiple informant study of problem behavior. *Twin Research and Human Genetics, 10,* 3–11.

Barter, C., & Renold, E. (2000). "I wanna tell you a story": Exploring the application of vignettes in qualitative research with children and young people. *International Journal of Social Research Methodology: Theory & Practice, 3,* 307–323.

Barth, C., Fein, D., & Waterhouse, L. (1995). Delayed match-to-sample performance in autistic children. *Developmental Neuropsychology, 11,* 53–69.

Barton, M., & Volkmar, F. (1998). How commonly are known medical conditions associated with autism? *Journal of Autism and Developmental Disorders, 28,* 273–278.

Bate, K. S., Malouff, J. M., Thorsteinsson, E. T., & Bhullar, N. (2011). The efficacy of habit reversal therapy for tics, habit disorders, and stuttering: A meta-analytic review. *Clinical Psychology Review, 31,* 865–871.

Batten, L. A., Hernandez, M., Pilowsky, D. J., Stewart, J. W., Blier, P., Flament, M. F., ... Weissman, M. M. (2012). Children of treatment-seeking depressed mothers: A comparison with the sequenced treatment alternatives to relieve depression (STAR*D). *Journal of the American Academy of Child & Adolescent Psychiatry, 51,* 1185–1196.

Bauer, K. W., Laska, M. N., Fulkerson, J. A., & Neumark-Sztainer, D. (2011). Longitudinal and secular trends in parental encouragement for healthy eating, physical activity, and dieting throughout the adolescent years. *Journal of Adolescent Health, 49,* 306–311.

Baughman, F. (2006). *The ADHD fraud: How psychiatry makes "patients" out of normal children.* Oxford, England: Trafford.

Baum, A., O'Keefe, M.K., & Davidson, L.M. (1990). Acute stressors and chronic response: The case of traumatic stress. *Journal of Applied Social Psychology, 20(20),* 1643–1654.

Bauman, M. L., & Kemper, T. L. (2005). Structural brain anatomy in autism: What is the evidence? In M. L. Bauman & T. L. Kemper (Eds.), *The neurobiology of autism* (2nd ed., pp. 121–135). Baltimore: Johns Hopkins University Press.

Baumeister, R. F., Bushman, B. J., & Campbell, W. K. (2000). Self-esteem, narcissism, and aggression: Does violence result from low self-esteem or from threatened egotism? *Current Directions in Psychological Science, 9,* 26–29.

Beardslee, W. R., Brent, D. A., Weersing, R., Clarke, G. N., Porta, G., Hollon, S. D., ... Garber, J. (2013). Prevention of depression in at-risk adolescents: Longer-term effects. *JAMA Psychiatry, 70,* 1161–1170.

Beardslee, W. R., Chien, P. L., & Bell, C. C. (2011). Prevention of mental disorders, substance abuse, and problem behaviors: A developmental perspective. *Psychiatric Services, 62,* 247–254.

Bearman, S. K., & Weisz, J. R. (2009). Primary and secondary control enhancement training (PASCET): Applying the deployment-focused model of treatment development and testing. In C. A. Essau (Ed.), *Treatments for adolescent depression: Theory and practice* (pp. 97–121). New York: Oxford University Press.

Bearman, S. K., Ugueto, A., Alleyne, A., & Weisz, J. R. (2010). Adapting cognitive-behavioral therapy for depression to fit diverse youths and contexts: Applying the deployment-focused model of treatment and testing. In J. R. Weisz & A. E. Kazdin (Eds.), *Evidence-based psychotherapies for children and adolescents* (2nd ed., pp. 466–481). New York: Guilford Press.

Beauchaine, T. P. (2003). Taxometrics and developmental psychopathology. *Development and Psychopathology, 15*, 501–527.

Beauchaine, T. P., Hinshaw, S. P., & Pang, K. L. (2010). Comorbidity of attention-deficit/hyperactivity disorder and early-onset conduct disorder: Biological, environmental, and developmental mechanisms. *Clinical Psychology: Science and Practice, 17*, 327–336.

Beauchaine, T. P., Katkin, E. S., Strassberg, Z., & Snarr, J. (2001). Disinhibitory psychopathology in male adolescents: Discriminating conduct disorder from attention-deficit/hyperactivity disorder through concurrent assessment of multiple autonomic states. *Journal of Abnormal Psychology, 110*, 610–624.

Beck, A. T. (1967). *Depression: Clinical, experimental, and theoretical aspects.* Philadelphia: University of Pennsylvania Press.

Beck, H. P., Levinson, S., & Irons, G. (2009). Finding Little Albert: A journey to John B. Watson's infant laboratory. *American Psychologist, 64*, 605–614.

Beck, S. J., Hanson, C. A., Puffenberger, S. S., Benninger, K. L., & Benninger, W. B. (2010). A controlled trial of working memory training for children and adolescents with ADHD. *Journal of Clinical Child & Adolescent Psychology, 39*, 825–836.

Becker, K. D., Chorpita, B. F., & Daleiden, E. L. (2011). Improvement in symptoms versus functioning: How do our best treatments measure up? *Administration and Policy in Mental Health and Mental Health Services Research, 38*, 440–458.

Becker, S. P., McBurnett, K., Hinshaw, S. P., & Pfiffner, L. J. (2013). Negative social preference in relation to internalizing symptoms among children with ADHD predominantly inattentive type: Girls fare worse than boys. *Journal of Clinical Child & Adolescent Psychology, 42*, 784–795.

Becker-Blease, K. A., Turner, H. A., & Finkelhor, D. (2010). Disasters, victimization, and children's mental health. *Child Development, 81*, 1040–1052.

Becker-Weidman, E. G., Jacobs, R. H., Reinecke, M. A., Silva, S. G., March, J. S. (2010). Social problem-solving among adolescents treated for depression. *Behaviour Research and Therapy, 48*, 11–18.

Bédard, A. C., Schulz, K. P., Cook, Jr., E. H., Fan, J., Clerkin, S. M., Ivanov, I., … Newcorn, J. H. (2010). Dopamine transporter gene variation modulates activation of striatum in youth with ADHD. *Neuroimage, 53*, 935–942.

Beesdo, K., Knappe, S., & Pine, D. S. (2009). Anxiety and anxiety disorders in children and adolescents: Developmental issues and implications for DSM-V. *Psychiatric Clinics of North America, 32*, 483–524.

Beesdo, K., Pine, D. S., Lieb, R., & Wittchen, H.U. (2010). Incidence and risk patterns of anxiety and depressive disorders and categorization of generalized anxiety disorder. *Archives of General Psychiatry, 67*, 47–57.

Beesdo-Baum, K., Knappe, S., Fehm, L., Hofler, M., Lieb, R., Hofmann, S. G., Wittchen, H.-U. (2012). The natural course of social anxiety disorder among adolescents and young adults. *Acta Psychiatrica Scandinavica, 126*, 411–425.

Beidel, D. C., & Turner, S. M. (1997). At risk for anxiety: I. Psychopathology in the offspring of anxious parents. *Journal of the American Academy of Child & Adolescent Psychiatry, 36*, 918–924.

Beidel, D. C., & Turner, S. M. (1998). *Shy children, phobic adults: Nature and treatment of social phobia.* Washington, DC: American Psychological Association.

Beidel, D. C., & Turner, S. M. (2007). *Clinical presentation of social anxiety disorder in children and adolescents.* Washington, DC: American Psychological Association.

Beidel, D. C., Turner, S. M., & Morris, T. L. (1999). Psychopathology of childhood social phobia. *Journal of the American Academy of Child & Adolescent Psychiatry, 38*, 643–650.

Beidel, D. C., Turner, S. M., Young, B. J., Ammerman, R. T., Sallee, F. R., & Crosby, L. (2007). Psychopathology of adolescent social phobia. *Journal of Psychopathology and Behavioral Assessment, 29*, 46–53.

Beintner, I., Jacobi, C., & Schmidt, U. H. (2014). Participation and outcome in manualized self-help for bulimia nervosa and binge eating disorder—A systematic review and metaregression analysis. *Clinical Psychology Review, 34*, 158–176.

Beitchman, J., & Brownlie, E. B. (2014). *Language disorders in children and adolescents.* Cambridge, MA: Hogrefe & Huber.

Belfer, M. L. (2008). Child and adolescent mental disorders: The magnitude of the problem across the globe. *Journal of Child Psychology and Psychiatry, 49*, 226–236.

Belitz, J., & Bailey, R. A. (2009). Clinical ethics for the treatment of children and adolescents: A guide for general psychiatrists. *Psychiatric Clinics of North America, 32*, 243–257.

Bell, A. (1996, March). Dying to win: The shocking stories of eating disorders and female athletes. *Teen*, 34–41.

Bell, B. T., & Dittmar, H. (2011). Does media type matter? The role of identification in adolescent girls' media consumption and the impact of different thin-ideal media on body image. *Sex Roles, 65*, 478–490.

Bell, D. J., Foster, S. L., & Mash, E. J. (Eds.). (2005). *Handbook of behavioral and emotional problems in girls.* New York: Kluwer.

Bellamy, C. (2002). *The state of the world's children 2002: Leadership.* New York: United Nations Children's Fund.

Bellani, M., Moretti, A., Perlini, C., & Brambilla, F. (2011). Language disturbances in ADHD. *Epidemiology and Psychiatric Sciences, 20*, 311–315.

Bellin, M. H., & Kovacs, P. J. (2006). Fostering resilience in siblings of youths with a chronic health condition: A review of the literature. *Health & Social Work, 31*, 209–216.

Belmonte, M. K., Gomot, M., & Baron-Cohen, S. (2010). Visual attention in autism families: 'unaffected' sibs share atypical frontal activation. *Journal of Child Psychology and Psychiatry, 51*, 259–276.

Belsky, J., & de Haan, M. (2011). Parenting and children's brain development: The end of the beginning. *Journal of Child Psychology and Psychiatry, 52*, 409–428.

Bemporad, J. R. (1979). Adult recollections of a formerly autistic child. *Journal of Autism and Developmental Disorders, 9*, 179–197.

Bemporad, J. R. (1994). Dynamic and interpersonal theories of depression. In W. M. Reynolds & H. F. Johnston (Eds.), *Handbook of depression in children and adolescents* (pp. 81–95). New York: Plenum Press.

Benasich, A. A., Curtiss, S., & Tallal, P. (1993). Language, learning, and behavioral disturbances in childhood: A longitudinal perspective. *Journal of the American Academy of Child & Adolescent Psychiatry, 32*, 585–594.

Benassi, M., Simonelli, L., Giovagnoli, S., & Bolzani, R. (2010). Coherence motion perception in developmental dyslexia: A meta-analysis of behavioral studies. *Dyslexia: An International Journal of Research and Practice, 16*, 341–357.

Benes, F. M. (2006). The development of the prefrontal cortex: The maturation of neurotransmitter systems and their interactions. In D. Cicchetti & D. J. Cohen (Eds.), *Developmental psychopathology: Vol. 2. Developmental neuroscience* (2nd ed., pp. 216–258). Hoboken, NJ: Wiley.

Benjamin, C. L., Harrison, J. P., Settipani, C. A., Brodman, D. M., & Kendall, P. C. (2013). Anxiety and related outcomes in young adults 7 to 19 years after receiving treatment for child anxiety. *Journal of Consulting and Clinical Psychology, 81*, 865–876.

Benjamin, L. T., Jr., & Shields, S. A. (1990). Leta Stetter Hollingworth (1886–1939). In A. N. O' Connell & N. F. Russo (Eds.), *Women in psychology: A bio-biographic sourcebook* (pp. 173–183). Westport, CT: Greenwood.

Benjamin, L. T., Jr., Whitaker, J. L., Ramsey, R. M., & Zeve, D. R. (2007). John B. Watson's alleged sex research: An appraisal of the evidence. *American Psychologist, 62*, 131–139.

Bennett, T., Szatmari, P., Bryson, S., Volden, J., Zwaigenbaum, L., Vaccarella, L., … Boyle, M. (2008). Differentiating autism and Asperger syndrome on the basis of language delay or impairment. *Journal of Autism and Developmental Disorders, 38*, 616–625.

Bennett-Gates, D., & Zigler, E. (1998). Resolving the developmental-difference debate: An evaluation of the triarchic and systems theory models. In J. A. Burack, R. M. Hodapp, & E. Zigler (Eds.),

Handbook of mental retardation and development (pp. 115–131). New York: Cambridge University Press.

Benoit, D. (2009). Feeding disorders, failure to thrive, and obesity. In C. H. Zeanah (Ed.), *Handbook of infant mental health* (3rd ed., pp. 377–391). New York: Guilford Press.

Benoit, D., Zeanah, C. H., & Barton, L. M. (1989). Maternal attachment disturbances in failure to thrive. *Infant Mental Health Journal, 10,* 185–202.

Benson, N., Hulac, D. M., & Bernstein, J. D. (2013). An independent confirmatory factor analysis of the Wechsler Intelligence Scale for Children—Fourth Edition (WISC–IV) Integrated: What do the process approach subtests measure? *Psychological Assessment, 25,* 692–705.

Ben-Zeev, D., Young, M. A., Corrigan, P. W. (2010). DSM-V and the stigma of mental illness. *Journal of Mental Health, 19,* 318–327.

Berger, A., & Berger, A. (2011). Individual differences in self-regulation. In A. Berger (Ed.), *Self-regulation: Brain, cognition, and development.* (pp. 61–90). Washington, DC: American Psychological Association.

Bergman, R. L., Piacentini, J., & McKracken, J. T. (2002). Prevalence and description of selective mutism in a school-based sample. *Journal of the American Academy of Child & Adolescent Psychiatry, 41,* 938–946.

Berlin, L. J., Appleyard, K., & Dodge, K. A. (2011). Intergenerational continuity in child maltreatment: Mediating mechanisms and implications for prevention. *Child Development, 82,* 162–176.

Berliner, L., & Elliot, D. (2002). Sexual abuse of children. In J. E. B. Myers, L. Berliner, J. Briere, C. T. Hendrix, C. Jenny, & T. A. Reid (Eds.), *The APSAC handbook on child maltreatment* (2nd ed., pp. 55–78). Thousand Oaks, CA: Sage.

Berman, A. L., & Jobes, D. A. (1991). *Adolescent suicide: Assessment and intervention.* Washington, DC: American Psychological Association.

Bernstein, G. A., & Victor, A. M. (2010). Separation anxiety disorder and school refusal. In M. K. Dulcan (Ed.), *Dulcan's textbook of child and adolescent psychiatry* (pp. 325–338). Arlington, VA: American Psychiatric Publishing.

Bernstein, G. A., Bernat, D. H., Davis, A. A., & Layne, A. E. (2008). Symptom presentation and classroom functioning in a nonclinical sample of children with social phobia. *Depression and Anxiety, 25,* 752–760.

Bernstein, G. A., Borchardt, C. M., & Perwien, A. R. (1996). Anxiety disorders in children and adolescents: A review of the past 10 years. *Journal of the American Academy of Child & Adolescent Psychiatry, 35,* 1110–1119.

Best, J. R., & Miller, P. H. (2010). A developmental perspective on executive function. *Child Development, 81,* 1641–1660.

Bethune, S. (2014). Teen stress rivals that of adults. *Monitor on Psychology, 45*(4), 20–22.

Bettelheim, B. (1967). *The empty fortress: Infantile autism and the birth of the self.* New York: Free Press.

Bexkens, A., Ruzzano, L., Collot D'Escury-Koenigs, A. M., Van der Molen, M.W., & Huizenga, H. M. (2014). Inhibition deficits in individuals with intellectual disability: A meta-regression analysis. *Journal of Intellectual Disability Research, 58,* 3–16.

Biederman, J., Faraone, S. V., Mick, E., Spencer, T., Wilens, T., Kiely, K., … Warburton, R. (1995). High risk for attention deficit hyperactivity disorder among children of parents with childhood onset of the disorder: A pilot study. *American Journal of Psychiatry, 152,* 431–435.

Biederman, J., Mick, E., & Faraone, S. V. (1998). Depression in attention deficit hyperactivity disorder (ADHD) children: "True" depression or demoralization? *Journal of Affective Disorders, 47,* 113–122.

Biederman, J., Monuteaux, M. C., Mick, E., Spencer, T., Wilens, T. E., Klein, K. L., … Faraone, S. V. (2006). Psychopathology in females with attention-deficit/hyperactivity disorder: A controlled five-year prospective study. *Biological Psychiatry, 60,* 1098–1105.

Biederman, J., Petty, C. R., Monuteaux, M. C., Fried, R., Byrne, D., Mirto, T., … Faraone, S. V. (2010). Adult psychiatric outcomes of girls with attention deficit hyperactivity disorder: 11-year follow-up in a longitudinal case-control study. *American Journal of Psychiatry, 167,* 409–417.

Bienvenu, O. J., Samuels, J. F., Wuyek, L. A., Liang, K. Y., Wang, Y., Grados, M. A., … Nestadt, G. (2012). Is obsessive-compulsive disorder an anxiety disorder, and what, if any, are spectrum conditions? A family study perspective. *Psychological Medicine, 42,* 1–13.

Bierman, K. L., Coie, J. D., Dodge, K. A., Greenberg, M. T., Lochman, J. E., McMahon, R. J., … Conduct Problems Prevention Research Group. (2010). The effects of a multiyear universal social–emotional learning program: The role of student and school characteristics. *Journal of Consulting and Clinical Psychology, 78,* 156–168.

Biklen, D. (1990). Communication unbound: Autism and praxis. *Harvard Educational Review, 60,* 291–314.

Biklen, D., & Cardinal, D. N. (Eds.). (1997). *Contested words, contested science: Unraveling the facilitated communication controversy.* New York: Teachers College Press.

Bird, H. R., Canino, G. J., Davies, M., Zhang, H., Ramirez, R., & Lahey, B. B. (2001). Prevalence and correlates of antisocial behaviors among three ethnic groups. *Journal of Abnormal Child Psychology, 29,* 465–478.

Birmaher, B., Arbelaez, C., & Brent, D. A. (2002). Course and outcome of child and adolescent major depressive disorder. *Child and Adolescent Psychiatric Clinics of North America, 11,* 619–637.

Birmaher, B., Axelson, D., Strober, M., Gill, M. K., Valeri, S., Chiappetta, L., … Keller, M. (2006). Clinical course of children and adolescents with bipolar spectrum disorders. *Archives of General Psychiatry, 63,* 175–183.

Birmaher, B., Ryan, N. D., Williamson, D. E., Brent, D. A., Kaufman, J., Dahl, R. E., … Nelson, B. (1996). Childhood and adolescent depression: A review of the past 10 years: Part I. *Journal of the American Academy of Child & Adolescent Psychiatry, 35,* 1427–1439.

Birmaher, B., Williamson, D. E., Dahl, R. E., Axelson, D. A., Kaufman, J., Dorn, L. D., & Ryan, N. D. (2004). Clinical presentation and course of depression in youth: Does onset in childhood differ from onset in adolescence? *Journal of the American Academy of Child & Adolescent Psychiatry, 43,* 63–70.

Bishop, D. V. M., Bishop, S. J., Bright, P., James, C., Delaney, T., & Tallal, P. (1999). Different origin of auditory and phonological processing problems in children with language impairment: Evidence from a twin study. *Journal of Speech, Language, & Hearing Research, 42,* 155–168.

Bishop, V. M. (2006). Developmental cognitive genetics: How psychology can inform genetics and vice versa. *Quarterly Journal of Experimental Psychology, 59,* 1153–1168.

Bittner, A., Egger, H. L., Erkanli, A., Costello, J., Foley, D. L., & Angold, A. (2007). What do childhood anxiety disorders predict? *Journal of Child Psychology and Psychiatry, 48,* 1174–1183.

Black, M. M., Dubowitz, H., Krishnakumar, A., & Starr, R. H., Jr. (2007). Early intervention and recovery among children with failure to thrive: Follow-up at age 8. *Pediatrics, 120,* 59–69.

Blair, R. J. R. (2010). Empathy, moral development, and aggression: A cognitive neuroscience perspective. In W. F. Arsenio & E. A. Lemerise (Eds.), *Emotions aggression, and morality in children: Bridging development and psychopathology* (pp. 97–114). Washington, DC: American Psychological Association.

Blair, R. J. R. (2011). Commentary: Are callous unemotional traits all in the eyes? Examining eye contact in youth with conduct problems and callous-unemotional traits-reflections on Dadds et al. (2011). *Journal of Child Psychology and Psychiatry, 52,* 246–247.

Blair, R. J. R., Peschardt, K. S., Budhani, S., Mitchell, D. G. V., & Pine, D. S. (2006). The development of psychopathy. *Journal of Child Psychology and Psychiatry, 47,* 262–275.

Blazei, R. W., Iacono, W. G., & Krueger, R. F. (2006). Intergenerational transmission of antisocial behavior: How do kids become antisocial adults? *Applied and Preventive Psychology, 11,* 230–253.

Blissett, J., Meyer, C., & Haycraft, E. (2007). Maternal mental health and child feeding problems in a non-clinical group. *Eating Behaviors, 8,* 311–318.

Block, J., Block, J. H., & Gjerde, P. F. (1986). The personality of children prior to divorce: A prospective study. *Child Development, 57,* 827–840.

Bloom, B., Cohen, R. C., & Freeman, G. (2011). Summary Health Statistics for U.S. Children: National Health Interview Survey, 2010. *Vital and Health Statistics Series 10* (250). DHHS publication no.

(PHS)-2012-1578. Hyattsville, MD: Department of Health and Human Services, Centers for Disease Control and Prevention, National Center for Health Statistics.

Blumberg, H. P., Kaufman, J., Martin, A., Whiteman, R., Zhang, J. H., Gore, J. C., ... Peterson, B. S. (2003). Amygdala and hippocampal volumes in adolescents and adults with bipolar disorder. *Archives of General Psychiatry, 60,* 1201–1208.

Boada, R., & Pennington, B. F. (2006). Deficient implicit phonological representations in children with dyslexia. *Journal of Experimental Child Psychology, 95,* 153–193.

Bodden, D. H. M., Dirksen, C. D., & Bögels, S. M. (2008). Societal burden of clinically anxious youth referred for treatment: A cost-of-illness study. *Journal of Abnormal Child Psychology, 36,* 487–497.

Boden, J. M., Fergusson, D. M., & Horwood, L. J. (2011). Age of menarche and psychosocial outcomes in a New Zealand birth cohort. *Journal of the American Academy of Child & Adolescent Psychiatry, 50,* 132–140.

Boetsch, E. A., Green, P. A., & Pennington, B. F. (1996). Psychosocial correlates of dyslexia across the life span. *Development and Psychopathology, 8,* 539–562.

Bogdan, R., & Taylor, S. J. (1982). *Inside out: The social meaning of mental retardation.* Toronto, ON: University of Toronto Press.

Bögels, S. M., & Brechman-Toussaint, M. L. (2006). Family issues in child anxiety: Attachment, family functioning, parental rearing and beliefs. *Clinical Psychology Review, 26,* 834–856.

Bögels, S. M., & Phares, V. (2008). Fathers' role in the etiology, prevention and treatment of child anxiety: A review and new model. *Clinical Psychology Review, 28,* 539–558.

Bögels, S. M., Alden, L., Beidel, D. C., Clark, L. A., Pine, D. S., Stein, M. B., & Voncken, M. (2010). Social anxiety disorder: Questions and answers for the DSM-V. *Depression and Anxiety, 27,* 168–189.

Bolton, D., Eley, T. C., O'Connor, T. G., Perrin, S., Rabe-Hesketh, S., Rijsdijk, F., & Smith, P. (2006). Prevalence and genetic and environmental influences on anxiety disorders in 6-year-old twins. *Psychological Medicine, 36,* 335–344.

Bolton, P., Carcani-Rathwell, I., Hutton, J., Goode, S., Howlin, P., & Rutter, M. (2011). Epilepsy in autism: Features and correlates. *British Journal of Psychiatry, 198,* 289–294.

Bongers, I. L., Koot, H. M., van der Ende, J., & Verhulst, F. C. (2003). The normative development of child and adolescent problem behavior. *Journal of Abnormal Psychology, 112,* 179–192.

Booth, C. M., Li, G., Jina Zhang-Salomons, J., & Mackillop, W. J. (2010). The impact of socioeconomic status on stage of cancer at diagnosis and survival: A population-based study in Ontario, Canada. *Cancer, 116,* 4160–4167.

Bootzin, R. R., & Chambers, M. J. (1990). Childhood sleep disorders. In A. M. Gross & R. S. Drabman (Eds.), *Handbook of clinical behavioral pediatrics* (pp. 205–227). New York: Plenum Press.

Boraston, Z. L., Corden, B., Miles, L. K., Skuse, D. H., & Blakemore, S. J. (2008). Brief report: Perception of genuine and posed smiles by individuals with autism. *Journal of Autism and Developmental Disorders, 38,* 574–580.

Borawski, E. A., Ievers-Landis, C. E., Lovegreen, L. D., & Trapl, E. S. (2003). Parental monitoring, negotiated unsupervised time, and parental trust: The role of perceived parenting practices in adolescent health risk behaviors. *Journal of Adolescent Health, 33,* 60–70.

Bornovalova, M. A., Hicks, B. M., Iacono, W. G., & McGue, M. (2010). Familial transmission and heritability of childhood disruptive disorders. *American Journal of Psychiatry, 167,* 1066–1074.

Borowsky, I. W., Ireland, M., & Resnick, M. D. (2001). Adolescent suicide attempts: Risks and protectors. *Pediatrics, 107,* 485–493.

Borstelmann, L. J. (1983). Children before psychology: Ideas about children from antiquity to the late 1800s. In W. Kessen (Vol. Ed.), *Handbook of child psychology: Vol. 1. History, theory, and methods* (4th ed., pp. 1–40). New York: Wiley.

Bothe, A. K., Davidow, J. H., Bramlett, R. E., & Ingham, R. J. (2006). Stuttering treatment research 1970–2005: I. Systematic review incorporating trial quality assessment of behavioral, cognitive, and related approaches. *American Journal of Speech-Language Pathology, 15,* 321–341.

Boutelle, K., Neumark-Sztainer, D., Story, M., & Resnick, M. (2002). Weight control behaviors among obese, overweight, and nonoverweight adolescents. *Journal of Pediatric Psychology, 27,* 531–540.

Bowlby, J. (1950, March 11). Research into the origins of delinquent behavior. *British Medical Journal, 1*(4653), 570–573.

Bowlby, J. (1961). The Adolf Meyer lecture: Childhood mourning and its implications for psychiatry. *American Journal of Psychiatry, 118,* 481–498.

Bowlby, J. (1973). *Attachment and loss: Vol. 2. Separation: Anxiety and anger.* New York: Basic Books.

Bowlby, J. A. (1988). *A secure base: Parent–child attachment and healthy human development.* New York: Basic Books.

Bowler, P. J. (1989). Holding your head up high: Degeneration and orthogenesis in theories of human evolution. In J. R. Moore (Ed.), *History, humanity, and evolution: Essays for John C. Greene* (pp. 329–353). Cambridge, England: Cambridge University Press.

Bowman, S. A., Gortmaker, S. L., Ebbeling, C. B., Pereira, M. A., & Ludwig, D. S. (2004). Effects of fast-food consumption on energy intake and diet quality among children in a national household survey. *Pediatrics, 113,* 112–118.

Boyle, C. A., Boulet, S., Schieve, L. A., Cohen, R. A., Blumberg, S. J., Yeargin-Allsopp, M., ... Kogan, M. D. (2011). Trends in the prevalence of developmental disabilities in US children, 1997–2008. *Pediatrics, 127,* 1034–1042.

Bradley, R. G., Binder, E. B., Epstein, M. P., Tang, Y., Nair, H. P., Liu, W., ... Ressler, K. J. (2008). Influence of child abuse on adult depression: Moderation by the corticotropin-releasing hormone receptor gene. *Archives of General Psychiatry, 65,* 190–200.

Brame, B., Nagin, D. S., & Tremblay, R. E. (2001). Developmental trajectories of physical aggression from school entry to late adolescence. *Journal of Child Psychology and Psychiatry, 42,* 503–512.

Branstetter, S. A., Low, S., & Furman, W. (2011). The influence of parents and friends on adolescent substance use: A multidimensional approach. *Journal of Substance Use, 16,* 150–160.

Braun, J. M., Kahn, R. S., Froehlich, T., Auinger, P., & Lamphear, P. (2006). Exposures to environmental toxicants and attention deficit hyperactivity disorder in U.S. children. *Environmental Health Perspectives, 114,* 1904–1909.

Brazoria County Sheriff's Department, Narcotic Division. Retrieved from http://www.brazoria-county.com/sheriff/narc/quiz.htm

Brecht, B. (1980). *The life of Galileo/Bertholt Brecht* (1980 translation by H. Brenton). London: Eyre Methuen.

Breggin, P. (2001). *Talking back to Ritalin: What doctors aren't telling you about stimulants for children* (Rev. ed.). Cambridge, MA: Perseus Books.

Brehaut, J. C., Miller, A., Raina, P., & McGrail, K. M. (2003). Childhood behavior disorders and injuries among children and youth. *Pediatrics, 111,* 262–269.

Bremner, J. D. (2007). Does stress damage the brain? In L. J. Kirmayer, R. Lemelson, & M. Barad (Eds.), *Understanding trauma: Integrating biological, clinical, and cultural perspectives* (pp. 118–141). New York: Cambridge University Press.

Brennan, P. A., Grekin, E. R., & Mednick, S. (2003). Prenatal and perinatal influences on conduct disorder and serious delinquency. In B. B. Lahey, T. E. Moffitt, & A. Caspi (Eds.), *Causes of conduct disorder and serious delinquency* (pp. 319–344). New York: Guilford Press.

Brennan, P. A., Hall, J., Bor, W., Najman, J. M., & Williams, G. (2003). Integrating biological and social processes in relation to early-onset persistent aggression in boys and girls. *Developmental Psychology, 39,* 309–323.

Brensilver, M., Negriff, S., Mennen, F. E., & Trickett, P. K. (2011). Longitudinal relations between depressive symptoms and externalizing behavior in adolescence: Moderating effects of maltreatment experience and gender. *Journal of Clinical Child & Adolescent Psychology, 40,* 607–617.

Brent, D. A., & Maalouf, F. T. (2009). Pediatric depression: Is there evidence to improve evidence-based treatments? *Journal of Child Psychology and Psychiatry, 50,* 143–152.

Brent, D. A., McMakin, D. L., Kennard, B. D., Goldstein, T. R., Mayes, T. L., & Douaihy, A. B. (2013). Protecting adolescents from self-harm: A critical review of intervention studies. *Journal of the American Academy of Child & Adolescent Psychiatry, 52,* 1260–1271.

Brent, D. A., Perper, J. A., Goldstein, C. E., Kolko, D. J., Allan, M. J., Allman, C. J., & Zelenak, J. P. (1988). Risk factors for adolescent suicide: A comparison of adolescent suicide victims with suicidal inpatients. *Archives of General Psychiatry, 45,* 581–588.

Brent, D. A., Perper, J. A., Moritz, G., Allman, C., Friend, A., Roth, C., ... Baugher, M. (1993). Psychiatric risk factors for adolescent suicide: A case control study. *Journal of the American Academy of Child & Adolescent Psychiatry, 32,* 521–529.

Brent, D. A., Perper, J. A., Moritz, G., Allman, C., Friend, A., Schweers, J., ... Harrington, K. (1992). Psychiatric effects of exposure to suicide among the friends and acquaintances of adolescent suicide victims. *Journal of the American Academy of Child & Adolescent Psychiatry, 31,* 629–640.

Brent, D. A., Poling, K. D., Goldstein, T. R. (2011). *Treating depressed and suicidal adolescents: A clinician's guide.* New York: Guilford Press.

Breslau, J., Saito, N., Tancredi, D. J., Nock, M., & Gilman, S. E. (2012). Classes of conduct disorder symptoms and their life course correlates in a US national sample. *Psychological Medicine, 42,* 1081–1089.

Bretherton, I., & Munholland, K. A. (2008). Internal working models in attachment relationships: Elaborating a central construct in attachment theory. In J. Cassidy & P. R. Shaver (Eds.), *Handbook of attachment: Theory, research, and clinical applications* (2nd ed., pp. 102–127). New York: Guilford Press.

Bridge, J. A., Iyengar, S., Salary, C. B., Barbe, R. P., Birmaher, B., Pincus, H. A., ... Brent, D. A. (2007). Clinical response and risk for reported suicidal ideation and suicide attempts in pediatric antidepressant medication: A meta-analysis of randomized controlled trials. *JAMA: Journal of the American Medical Association, 297,* 1683–1696.

Briere, J., Hodges, M., & Godbout, N. (2010). Traumatic stress, affect dysregulation, and dysfunctional avoidance: A structural equation model. *Journal of Traumatic Stress, 23,* 767–774.

Briggs-Gowan, M. J., Carter, A. S., Clark, R., Augustyn, M., McCarthy, K. J., & Ford, J. D. (2010). Exposure to potentially traumatic events in early childhood: Differential links to emergent psychopathology. *Journal of Child Psychology and Psychiatry, 51,* 1132–1140.

Briggs-Gowan, M. J., Nichols, S. R., Voss, J., Zobel, E., Carter, A. S., McCarthy, K. J., ... Wakschlag, L. S. (2014). Punishment insensitivity and impaired reinforcement learning in preschoolers. *Journal of Child Psychology and Psychiatry, 55,* 154–161.

Brinkmeyer, M. Y., & Eyberg, S. M. (2003). Parent-child interaction therapy for oppositional children. In A. E. Kazdin & J. R. Weisz (Eds.), *Evidence-based psychotherapies for children and adolescents* (pp. 204–223). New York: Guilford Press.

Britton, J. C., Lissek, S., Grillon, C., Norcross, M. A., & Pine, D. S. (2011). Development of anxiety: The role of threat appraisal and fear learning. *Depression and Anxiety, 28,* 5–17.

Broidy, L. M., Nagin, D. S., Tremblay, R. E., Bates, J. E., Brame, B., Dodge, K. A., ... Vitaro, F. (2003). Developmental trajectories of childhood disruptive behaviors and adolescent delinquency: A six-site, cross-national study. *Developmental Psychology, 39,* 222–245.

Bromberg, M. H., Gil, K. M., & Schanberg, L. E. (2011). Daily sleep quality and mood as predictors of pain in children with juvenile polyarticular arthritis. *Health Psychology, 31,* 202–209.

Bromet, E. J., & Fennig, S. (1999). Epidemiology and natural history of schizophrenia. *Biological Psychiatry, 46,* 871–881.

Bronfenbrenner, U. (1977). Toward an experimental ecology of human development. *American Psychologist, 52,* 513–531.

Brooke, L., & Mussap, A. J. (2013). Brief report: Maltreatment in childhood and body concerns in adulthood. *Journal of Health Psychology, 18,* 620–626.

Brooker, R. J., Buss, K. A., Lemery-Chalfant, K., Aksan, N., Davidson, R. J., & Goldsmith, H. H. (2013). The development of stranger fear in infancy and toddlerhood: Normative development, individual differences, antecedents, and outcomes. *Developmental Science, 16,* 864–878.

Brooks-Gunn, J., Klebanov, P. K., Smith, J., Duncan, G. J., & Lee, K. (2003). The Black-White test score gap in young children: Contributions of test and family characteristics. *Applied Developmental Science, 7,* 239–252.

Brooks-Gunn, J., Schneider, W., & Waldfogel, J. (2013) The Great Recession and the risk for child maltreatment. *Child Abuse & Neglect, 37,* 721–729.

Brooks-Russell, A., Simons-Morton, B., Haynie, D., Farhat, T., & Wang, J. (2013). Longitudinal relationship between drinking with peers, descriptive norms, and adolescent alcohol use. *Prevention Science.* Advance online publication. doi:10.1007/s11121-013-0391-9.

Brosnan, M. J., Gwilliam, L. R., & Walker, I. (2012). Brief report: The relationship between visual acuity, The Embedded Figures Test, and systemizing in autism spectrum disorders. *Journal of Autism and Developmental Disorders, 42,* 2491–2497.

Brossard-Racine, M., Shevell, M., Snider, L., Bélanger, S. A., & Majnemer, A. (2012). Motor skills of children newly diagnosed with attention deficit hyperactivity disorder prior to and following treatment with stimulant medication. *Research in Developmental Disabilities, 33,* 2080–2087.

Brotman, M. A., Rich, B. A., Guyer, A. E., Lunsford, J. R., Horsey, S. E., Reising, M. M., ... Leibenluft, E. (2010). Amygdala activation during emotion processing of neutral faces in children with severe mood dysregulation versus ADHD or bipolar disorder. *American Journal of Psychiatry, 167,* 61–69.

Brown, E. (2011, March 10). *Obama at White House Bullying conference: I wasn't immune.* Retrieved from http://articles.latimes.com/2011/mar/10/news/la-heb-obama-bullying-conference-20110310

Brown, E. C., Hawkins, J. D., Rhew, I. C., Shapiro, V. B., Abbott, R. D., Oesterle, S., ... Catalano, R. F. (2013, July 5). Prevention system mediation of *Communities That Care effects on youth outcomes. Prevention Science.* Advance online publication. doi:10.1007/s11121-013-0413-7.

Brown, J. S., Meadows, S. O., & Elder, G. H., Jr. (2007). Race-ethnic inequality and psychological distress: Depressive symptoms from adolescence to young adulthood. *Developmental Psychology, 43,* 1295–1311.

Brown, M. L., Pope, A. W., & Brown, E. J. (2011). Treatment of primary nocturnal enuresis in children: A review. *Child: Care, Health and Development, 37,* 153–160.

Brown, R. T., Antonuccio, D. O., DuPaul, G. J., Fristad, M. A., King, C. A., Leslie, L. K., ... Vitiello, B. (2008). Elimination disorders. In R. T. Brown, D. O. Antonuccio, G. J. DuPaul, M. A. Fristad, C. A. King, L. K. Leslie... B. Vitiello. (Eds.), *Childhood mental health disorders: Evidence base and contextual factors for psychosocial, psychopharmacological, and combined interventions* (pp. 121–127). Washington, DC: American Psychological Association.

Brown, R. T., Daly, B. P., & Rickel, A. U. (2007). *Chronic illness in children and adolescents. Advances in psychotherapy: Evidence-based practice.* Ashland, OH: Hogrefe & Huber.

Brown, R. T., Ellis, D., Naar-King, S. (2014). Health-related and somatic symptoms disorders. In E. J. Mash & R. A. Barkley (Eds.), *Child psychopathology* (3rd ed., pp. 897–948). New York: Guilford Press.

Brown, S. A., Tomlinson, K., & Winward, J. (2013). Substance use disorders in adolescence. In T. P. Beauchaine & S. P. Hinshaw (Eds.), *Child and adolescent psychopathology* (2nd ed., pp. 489–510). Hoboken, NJ: Wiley.

Brown, T. A., & Keel, P. K. (2013). The impact of relationships, friendships, and work on the association between sexual orientation and disordered eating in men. *Eating Disorders: The Journal of Treatment & Prevention, 21,* 342–359.

Brown, T. E. (2000). Emerging understandings of attention-deficit disorders and comorbidities. In T. E. Brown (Ed.), *Attention-deficit disorders and comorbidities in children, adolescents, and adults* (pp. 3–55). Washington, DC: American Psychiatric Press.

Brownell, K. D., & Rodin, J. (1994). The dieting maelstrom: Is it possible and advisable to lose weight? *American Psychologist, 49,* 781–791.

Brownlie, E. B., Jabbar, A., Beitchman, J., Vida, R., & Atkinson, L. (2007). Language impairment and sexual assault of girls and women: Findings from a community sample. *Journal of Abnormal Child Psychology, 35,* 618–626.

Bruch, H. (1962). Perceptual and conceptual disturbances in anorexia nervosa. *Psychosomatic Medicine, 24,* 187–194.

Bruch, H. (1973). *Eating disorders: Obesity, anorexia nervosa and the person within.* New York: Basic Books.

Brumariu, L. E., & Kerns, K. A. (2010). Parent-child attachment and internalizing symptoms in childhood and adolescence: A review of empirical findings and future directions. *Developmental Psychopathology, 22,* 177–203.

Brumberg, J. J. (1988). *Fasting girls: The emergence of anorexia nervosa as a modern disease.* Cambridge, MA: Harvard University Press.

Bryant-Waugh, R., Markham, L., Kreipe, R. E., & Walsh, B. T. (2010). Feeding and eating disorders in childhood. *International Journal of Eating Disorders, 43,* 98–111.

Bryson, S. E., Rogers, S. J., & Fombonne, E. (2003). Autism spectrum disorders: Early detection, intervention, education, and psychopharmacological management. *Canadian Journal of Psychiatry, 48,* 506–515.

Bryson, S. E., Zwaigenbaum, L., McDermott, C., Rombough, V., & Brian, J. (2008). The Autism Observation Scale for Infants: Scale development and reliability data. *Journal of Autism and Developmental Disorders, 38,* 731–738.

Brytek-Matera, A. (2012). Orthorexia nervosa—An eating disorder, obsessive-compulsive disorder or disturbed eating habit? *Archives of Psychiatry and Psychotherapy, 14,* 55–60.

Bucchianeri, M. M., Eisenberg, M. E., Wall, M. M., Piran, N., & Neumark-Sztainer, D. (2013, December 24). Multiple types of harassment: Associations with emotional well-being and unhealthy behaviors in adolescents. *Journal of Adolescent Health.* Advance online publication. doi:10.1016/jadohealth.2013.10.205.

Buckholtz, J. W., & Meyer-Lindenberg, A. (2008). MAOA and the neurogenetic architecture of human aggression. *Trends in Neurosciences, 31,* 120–129.

Buckles, J., Luckasson, R., & Keefe, E. (2013). A systematic review of the prevalence of psychiatric disorders in adults with intellectual disability, 2003–2010. *Journal of Mental Health Research in Intellectual Disabilities, 6,* 181–207.

Buckner, J. D., Schmidt, N. B., Lang, A. R., Small, J. W., Schlauch, R. C., & Lewinsohn, P. M. (2008). Specificity of social anxiety disorder as a risk factor for alcohol and cannabis dependence. *Journal of Psychiatric Research, 42,* 230–239.

Bufferd, S. J., Dougherty, L. R., Carlson, G. A., Rose, S,, & Klein, D. N. (2012). Psychiatric disorders in preschoolers: Continuity from ages 3 to 6. *American Journal of Psychiatry, 169,* 1157–1164.

Buitelaar, J. K., Barton, J., Danckaerts, M., Friedrichs, E. Gillberg, C., & Hazell, P. L., Hellmans, H., … Zuddas, A. (2006). A comparison of North American and non-North American ADHD study populations. *European Child & Adolescent Psychiatry, 15,* 177–181.

Bulik, C. M., Thornton, L., Pinheiro, A. P., Plotnicov, K., Klump, K. L., Brandt, H., … Kaye, W. H. (2008). Suicide attempts in anorexia nervosa. *Psychosomatic Medicine, 70,* 378–383.

Bulik, C. M., Thornton, L. M., Root, T. L., Pisetsky, E. M., Lichtenstein, P., & Pedersen, N. L. (2010). Understanding the relation between anorexia nervosa and bulimia nervosa in a Swedish national twin sample. *Biological Psychiatry, 67,* 71–77.

Burke, J. D. (2012). An affective dimension within oppositional defiant disorder symptoms among boys: Personality and psychopathology outcomes into early adulthood. *Journal of Child Psychology and Psychiatry, 53,* 1176–1183.

Burke, J. D., Hipwell, A. E., & Loeber, R. (2010). Dimensions of oppositional defiant disorder as predictors of depression and conduct disorder in preadolescent girls. *Journal of the American Academy of Child & Adolescent Psychiatry, 49,* 484–492.

Burke, J. D., & Loeber, R. (2010). Oppositional defiant disorder and the explanation of the comorbidity between behavioral disorders and depression. *Clinical Psychology: Science and Practice, 17,* 319–326.

Burke, J. D., Rowe, R., & Boylan, K. (2014). Functional outcomes of child and adolescent oppositional defiant disorder symptoms in young adult men. *Journal of Child Psychology and Psychiatry, 55,* 264–272.

Burke, J. D., Waldman, I., & Lahey, B. B. (2010). Predictive validity of childhood oppositional defiant disorder and conduct disorder: Implications for the *DSM–V. Journal of Abnormal Psychology, 119,* 739–751.

Burket, R. C., Cox, D. J., Tam, A. P., Ritterband, L., Borowitz, S., Sutphen, J., … Kovatchev, B. (2006). Does "stubbornness" have a role in pediatric constipation? *Journal of Developmental & Behavioral Pediatrics, 27,* 106–111.

Burns, G. L., de Moura, M. A., Beauchaine, T. P., & McBurnett, K. (2014). Bifactor latent structure of ADHD/ODD symptoms: Predictions of dual pathway/trait impulsivity etiological models of ADHD. *Journal of Child Psychology and Psychiatry, 55,* 393–401.

Burns, G. L., Walsh, J. A., Patterson, D. R., Holte, C. S., Somers-Flanagan, R., & Parker, C. M. (1997). Internal validity of the disruptive behavior disorder symptoms: Implications from parent ratings for a dimensional approach to symptom validity. *Journal of Abnormal Child Psychology, 25,* 307–319.

Burt, S. A., Krueger, R. F., McGue, M., & Iacono, W. G. (2001). Sources of covariation among attention-deficit hyperactivity disorder, oppositional defiant disorder, and conduct disorder: The importance of shared environment. *Journal of Abnormal Psychology, 110,* 516–525.

Burt, S. A., McGue, M., DeMarte, J. A., Krueger, R. F., & Iacono, W. G. (2006). Timing of menarche and the origins of conduct disorder. *Archives of General Psychiatry, 63,* 890–896.

Burt, S. A., & Neiderhiser, J. M. (2009). Aggressive versus nonaggressive antisocial behavior: Distinctive etiological moderation by age. *Developmental Psychology, 45,* 1164–1176.

Bush, G. (2008). Neuroimaging of attention deficit hyperactivity disorder: Can new imaging findings be integrated into clinic practice? *Child and Adolescent Psychiatric Clinics of North America, 17,* 385–404.

Bussing, R., Zima, B. T., Gary, F. A., Mason, D. M., Leon, C. E., Sinha, K., & Garvan, C. W. (2003). Social networks, caregiver strain, and utilization of mental health services among elementary school students at high risk for ADHD. *Journal of the American Academy of Child & Adolescent Psychiatry, 42,* 842–850.

Butcher, J. N., Williams, C. L., Graham, J. R., Archer, J. P., Tellegen, A., Ben-Porath, Y. S., & Kaemmer, B. (1992/2006). *Minnesota Multiphasic Personality Inventory-Adolescent (MMPI-A).* Minneapolis: University of Minnesota Press. (Manual, 1992; Manual Supplement, 2006).

Button, T. M. M., Corley, R. P., Rhee, S. H., Hewitt, J. K., Young, S. E., & Stallings, M. C. (2007). Delinquent peer affiliation and conduct problems: A twin study. *Journal of Abnormal Psychology, 116,* 554–564.

Byrd, A. L., Loeber, R., & Pardini, D. A. (2012). Understanding desisting and persisting forms of delinquency: The unique contributions of disruptive behavior disorders and interpersonal callousness. *Journal of Child Psychology and Psychiatry, 53,* 371–380.

Calati, R., De Ronch, D., Bellini, M., & Serretti, A. (2011). The 5-HTTLPR polymorphism and eating disorders: A meta-analysis. *International Journal of Eating Disorders, 44,* 191–199.

Calder, J. (1980). *RLS: A life study.* London: Hamish Hamilton.

Calhoun, C. D., Franklin, J. C., Adelman, C. B., Guerry, J. D., Hastings, P. D., Nock, K., Prinstein, M. J. (2012). Biological and cognitive responses to an in vivo interpersonal stressor: Longitudinal associations with adolescent depression. *International Journal of Cognitive Therapy, 5,* 283–299.

Camp OOCHIGEAS (2006). A camp for children with cancer. Retrieved from http://www.ooch.org/page.aspx?pid=221

Campbell, F. A., Pungello, E. P., Burchinal, M., Kainz, K., Pan, Y., Wasik, B. H., … Ramey, C. T. (2012). Adult outcomes as a function of an early childhood educational program: An Abecedarian Project follow-up. *Developmental Psychology, 48,* 1033–1043.

Campbell, F. A., & Ramey, C. T. (2010). Carolina Abecedarian Project. In A. J. Reynolds, A. J. Rolnick, M. M. Englund, & J. A. Temple (Eds.), *Childhood programs and practices in the first decade of life: A human capital integration* (pp. 76–98). New York: Cambridge University Press.

Campbell, F. A., Ramey, C. T., Pungello, E., Sparling, J., & Miller-Johnson, S. (2002). Early childhood education: Young adult outcomes from the Abecedarian Project. *Applied Developmental Science, 6,* 42–57.

Campbell, L. K., Cox, D. J., & Borowitz, S. M. (2009). Elimination disorders: Enuresis and encopresis. In M. C. Roberts & R. G. Steele (Eds.), *Handbook of pediatric psychology* (4th ed., pp. 481–490). New York: Guilford Press.

Campbell, R., Greeson, M. R., Bybee, D., & Raja, S. (2008). The co-occurrence of childhood sexual abuse, adult sexual assault, intimate partner violence, and sexual harassment: A mediational model of posttraumatic stress disorder and physical health outcomes. *Journal of Consulting and Clinical Psychology, 76,* 194–207.

Campbell, S. B. (2006). *Behavior problems in preschool children: Clinical and developmental issues.* New York: Guilford Press.

Campbell, S. B., Shaw, D. S., & Gilliom, M. (2000). Early externalizing behavior problems: Toddlers and preschoolers at risk for later maladjustment. *Development and Psychopathology, 12,* 467–488.

Campbell, S. B., Spieker, S., Vandergrift, N., Belsky, J., Burchinal, M., & The NICHD Early Child Care Research Network (2010). Predictors and sequelae of trajectories of physical aggression in school-age boys and girls. *Development and Psychopathology, 22,* 133–150.

Campbell, S. B., & von Stauffenberg, C. (2009). Delay and inhibition as early predictors of ADHD in third grade. *Journal of Abnormal Child Psychology, 37,* 1–15.

Canadian Diabetes Association. (2014). *The prevalence and costs of diabetes.* Retrieved from http://www.diabetes.ca/documents/aboutdiabetes/PrevalanceandCost_09.pdf

Canino, G., & Alegria, M. (2008). Psychiatric diagnosis—Is it universal or relative to culture? *Journal of Child Psychology and Psychiatry, 49,* 237–250.

Canino, G., Polanczck, G., Bauermeister, J. J., Rohde, L. A., & Frick, P. J. (2010). Does the prevalence of CD and ODD vary across cultures? *Social Psychiatry and Psychiatric Epidemiology, 45,* 695–704.

Cannon, T. D., Cadenhead, K., Cornblatt, B., Woods, S. W., Addington, J., Walker, E., … Heinssen, R. (2008). Prediction of psychosis in youth at high clinical risk. *Archives of General Psychiatry, 65,* 28–37.

Canter, K. S., & Roberts, M. C. (2012). A systematic and quantitative review of interventions to facilitate school reentry for children with chronic health conditions. *Journal of Pediatric Psychology, 37,* 1065–1075.

Cantor, J. M., & Blanchard, R. (2012). White matter volumes in pedophiles, hebephiles, and teleiophiles. *Archives of Sexual Behavior, 41,* 749–752.

Cantrell, M. A. (2011). A narrative review summarizing the state of the evidence on the health-related quality of life among childhood cancer survivors. *Journal of Pediatric Oncology Nursing, 28,* 75–82.

Capaldi, D. M., & Patterson, G. R. (1994). Interrelated influences of contextual factors on antisocial behavior in childhood and adolescence. In D. Fowles, P. Sutker, & S. Goodman (Eds.), *Psychopathy and antisocial personality: A developmental perspective* (pp. 165–198). New York: Springer.

Caplan, R. (1994). Communication deficits in childhood schizophrenia spectrum disorders. *Schizophrenia Bulletin, 20,* 671–684.

Caplan, R., Guthrie, D., Tang, B., Komo, S., & Asarnow, R. F. (2000). Thought disorder in childhood schizophrenia: Replication and update of concept. *Journal of the American Academy of Child & Adolescent Psychiatry, 39,* 771–778.

Capps, L., Sigman, M., Sena, R., & Henker, B. (1996). Fear, anxiety and perceived control in children of agoraphobic parents. *Journal of Child Psychology and Psychiatry, 37,* 445–452.

Carballo, J. J., Baca-Garcia, E., Blanco, C., Perez-Rodriguez, M. M., Arriero, M. A. J., Group for the Study of Evolution of Diagnosis (SED), & Oquendo, M. A. (2010). Stability of childhood anxiety disorder diagnoses: A follow-up naturalistic study in psychiatric care. *European Child & Adolescent Psychiatry, 19,* 395–403.

Cardoos, S. L., Loya, F., & Hinshaw, S. P. (2013). Adolescent girls' ADHD symptoms and young adult driving: The role of perceived deviant peer affiliation. *Journal of Clinical Child & Adolescent Psychology, 42,* 232–242.

Carlson, E. A., Jacobvitz, D., & Sroufe, L. A. (1995). A developmental investigation of inattentiveness and hyperactivity. *Child Development, 66,* 37–54.

Carlson, E. A., & Sroufe, L. A. (1995). Contribution of attachment theory to developmental psychopathology. In D. Cicchetti & D. J. Cohen (Eds.), *Developmental psychopathology: Vol. 1. Theory and methods* (pp. 581–617). New York: Wiley.

Carlson, G. A. (1994). Adolescent bipolar disorder: Phenomenology and treatment implications. In W. M. Reynolds & H. F. Johnston (Eds.), *Handbook of depression in children and adolescents* (pp. 41–60). New York: Plenum Press.

Carlson, G. A. (2002). Bipolar disorder in children and adolescents: A critical review. In D. Shaffer & B. Waslick (Eds.), *The many faces of depression in children and adolescents* (pp. 105–128). Washington, DC: American Psychiatric Press.

Carlson, G. A. (2011). Will the child with mania please stand up? *British Journal of Psychiatry, 198,* 171–172.

Carlson, G. A., & Klein, D. N. (2014). How to understand divergent views on bipolar disorder in youth. *Annual Review of Clinical Psychology, 10,* 529–551.

Carlson, G. A., Pine, D. S., Nottelmann, E., & Leibenluft, E. (2004). Defining subtypes of childhood bipolar illness: Response and commentary. *Journal of the American Academy of Child & Adolescent Psychiatry, 43,* 3–4.

Carpenter, D. O., & Nevin, R. (2010). Environmental causes of violence. *Physiology & Behavior, 99,* 260–268.

Carper, T. L. M., Negy, C., & Tantleff-Dunn, S. (2010). Relations among media influence, body image, eating concerns, and sexual orientation in men: A preliminary investigation. *Body Image, 7,* 301–309.

Carr, J. (2005). Stability and change in cognitive ability over the life span: A comparison of populations with and without Down's syndrome. *Journal of Intellectual Disability Research, 49,* 915–928.

Carretti, B., Borella, E., Cornoldi, C., & De Beni, R. (2009). Role of working memory in explaining the performance of individuals with specific reading comprehension difficulties: A meta-analysis. *Learning and Individual Differences, 19,* 245–251.

Carter, A. S., Black, D. O., Tewani, S., Connoly, C. E., Kadlec, M. B., & Tager-Flusberg, H. (2007). Sex differences in toddlers with autism spectrum disorders. *Journal of Autism and Developmental Disorders, 37,* 86–97.

Cartwright-Hatton, S., McNally, D., Field, A. P., Rust, S., Laskey, B., Dison, C., & Woodham, A. (2011). A new parenting-based group intervention for young anxious children: Results of a randomized controlled trial. *Journal of the American Academy of Child & Adolescent Psychiatry, 50,* 242–251.

Cartwright-Hatton, S., McNicol, K., & Doubleday, E. (2006). Anxiety in a neglected population: Prevalence of anxiety disorders in pre-adolescent children. *Clinical Psychology Review, 26,* 817–833.

Casey, B. J., Nigg, J. T., & Durston, S. (2007). New potential leads in the biology and treatment of attention deficit-hyperactivity disorder. *Current Opinion in Neurology, 20,* 119–124.

Cash, T. F., & Smolak, L. (2011). Understanding body images: Historical and contemporary perspectives. In T. F. Cash & L. Smolak (Eds.), *Body image: A handbook of science, practice, and prevention* (2nd ed., pp. 3–11). New York: Guilford Press.

Cashel, M. L. (2002). Child and adolescent psychological assessment: Current clinical practices and the impact of managed care. *Professional Psychology: Research and Practice, 33,* 446–453.

Caspi, A., Harrington, H., Milne, B., Amell, J. W., Theodore, R. F., & Moffitt, T E. (2003). Children's behavioral styles at age 3 are linked to their adult personality traits at age 26. *Journal of Personality, 71,* 495–513.

Caspi, A., Langley, K., Milne, B., Moffitt, T. E., O'Donovan, M., Owen, M. J., … Thapar, A. (2008). A replicated molecular genetic basis for subtyping antisocial behavior in children with attention-deficit/hyperactivity disorder. *Archives of General Psychiatry, 65,* 203–210.

Caspi, A., & Moffitt, T. E. (1995). The continuity of maladaptive behavior: From description to understanding in the study of antisocial behavior. In D. Cicchetti & D. J. Cohen (Eds.), *Developmental psychopathology: Vol. 2. Risk, disorder, and adaptation* (pp. 472–511). New York: Wiley.

Castellanos, F. X., Sharp, W. S., Gottesman, R. F., Greenstein, D. K., Giedd, J. N., & Rapoport, J. L. (2003). Anatomic brain abnormalities in monozygotic twins discordant for attention deficit hyperactivity disorder. *American Journal of Psychiatry, 160,* 1693–1696.

Caylak, E. (2011). The auditory temporal processing deficit theory in children with developmental dyslexia. *Journal of Pediatric Neurology, 9,* 151–168.

Center on the Developing Child at Harvard University (2011). *Building the brain's "Air Traffic Control" system: How early experiences shape the development of executive function: Working Paper No. 11.* Retrieved from http://www.developinchild.harvard.edu

Centers for Disease Control and Prevention. (2010). *"Healthy Youth!" Health Topics.*

Retrieved from www.cdc.gov/Healthy Youth/healthtopics/index.htm

Centers for Disease Control and Prevention (CDC). (2011a) *Children and diabetes.* Retrieved from http://www.cdc.gov/diabetes/projects/diab_children.htm#1

Centers for Disease Control and Prevention (CDC). (2011b). *Childhood overweight and obesity.* Retrieved from http://www.cdc.gov/obesity/childhood/index.html

Centers for Disease Control and Prevention (CDC). (2011c). *Tracking fetal alcohol syndrome (FAS).* Retrieved from http://www.cdc.gov/ncbddd/fasd/research-tracking.html

Centers for Disease Control and Prevention. (CDC). (2011d). *Understanding child maltreatment factsheet 2010.* Retrieved from http://www.cdc.gov/violenceprevention/pdf/CM-factsheet-a.pdf

Centers for Disease Control and Prevention (2011e, June 8). Youth risk behavior surveillance—United States 2011. *MMWR: Morbidity and Mortality Weekly Report,* 61(4), 1-45.

Centers for Disease Control and Prevention [CDC]. (2012a). *Prevalence of autism spectrum disorders—Autism and Developmental Disabilities Monitoring Network, 14 sites, United States, 2008. MMWR: Morbidity and Mortality Weekly Report,* 61(3), 1–20. Retrieved from http://www.cdc.gov/mmwr/pdf/ss/ss6103.pdf

Centers for Disease Control and Prevention [CDC]. (2012b). Youth risk behavior surveillance—United States, 2011. *MMWR: Morbidity and Mortality Weekly Report,* 61(4), 1–162. Retrieved from http://www.cdc.gov/HealthyYouth/yrbs/index.htm

Centers for Disease Control and Prevention [CDC]. (2013). *WISQARS fatal injuries: Mortality reports.* Retrieved from http://webappa.cdc.gov/sasweb/ncipc/mortrate10_us.html.

Centers for Disease Control and Prevention (CDC) (2014a). Childhood overweight and obesity. Retrieved from http://www.cdc.gov/obesity/childhood/index.html

Centers for Disease Control and Prevention (CDC). (2014b, March 28). Prevalence of autism spectrum disorder among children aged 8 years—Autism and Developmental Disability Monitoring Network, 11 Sites, United States, 2010, *MMWR: Morbidity and Mortality Weekly Report,* 63(2), 1–21.

Cerel, J., Fristad, M. A., Verducci, J., Weller, R. A., & Weller, E. B. (2006). Childhood bereavement: Psychopathology in the 2 years postparental death. *Journal of the American Academy of Child & Adolescent Psychiatry,* 45, 681–690.

Cha, C. B., & Nock, M. K. (2014). Suicidal and non suicidal self-injurious thoughts and behaviors. In E. J. Mash & R. A. Barkley (Eds.), *Child psychopathology* (3rd ed., pp. 317–342). New York: Guilford Press.

Chacko, A., Allan, C., Uderman, J., Cornwell, M., Anderson, L., & Chimiklis, A. (2014). Training parents of youth with ADHD. In R. A. Barkley (Ed.), *Attention-deficit hyperactivity disorder: A handbook for diagnosis and treatment* (4th ed.). New York: Guilford Press.

Chaidez, V., Hansen, R. L., & Hertz-Picciotto, I. (2014). Gastrointestinal problems in children with autism, developmental delays or atypical development. *Journal of Autism and Developmental Disorders,* 44, 1117–1127.

Challman, T. D., Barbaresi, W. J., Katusic, S. K., & Weaver, A. (2003). The yield of the medical evaluation of children with pervasive developmental disorders. *Journal of Autism and Developmental Disorders,* 33, 187–192.

Chan, E., Zhan, C., & Homer, C. J. (2002). Health care use and costs for children with attention-deficit/hyperactivity disorder: National estimates from the medical expenditure panel study. *Archives of Pediatrics and Adolescent Medicine,* 156, 504–512.

Chan, J., Merriman, B., Parmenter, T., & Stancliffe, R. (2012). Rethinking respite policy for people with intellectual and developmental disabilities. *Journal of Policy and Practice in Intellectual Disabilities,* 9, 120–126.

Chang, Z., Lichtenstein, P., Halldner, L., D'Onofrio, B., Serlachius, E., Fazel, S., … Larsson, H. (2013). Stimulant ADHD medication and risk for substance abuse. *Journal of Child Psychology and Psychiatry.* Advance online publication. doi:10.1111/jcpp.12164.

Chansky, T. E., & Kendall, P. C. (1997). Social expectancies and self-perceptions in anxiety-disordered children. *Journal of Anxiety Disorders,* 11, 347–363.

Chaplin, T. M., & Aldao, A. (2013). Gender differences in emotion expression in children: A meta-analytic review. *Psychological Bulletin,* 213, 735–765.

Chapman, D. A., Scott, K. G., & Stanton-Chapman, T. L. (2008). Public health approach to the study of mental retardation. *American Journal on Mental Retardation,* 113, 102–116.

Chapman, D. P., Dube, S. R., & Anda, R. F. (2007). Adverse childhood events as risk factors for negative mental health outcomes. *Psychiatric Annals,* 37, 359–364.

Charach, A., Yeung, E., Climans, T., & Lillie, E. (2011). Childhood attention deficit/hyperactivity disorder and future substance use disorders: Comparative meta-analyses. *Journal of the American Academy of Child & Adolescent Psychiatry,* 50, 9–21.

Charman, T. (2003). Why is joint attention a pivotal skill in autism? *Philosophical Transactions of the Royal Society: Biological Sciences,* 358, 315–324.

Charman, T. (2011). Commentary: Glass half full or half empty? Testing social communication interventions for young children with autism—reflections on Landa, Holman, O'Neill, and Stuart (2011). *Journal of Child Psychology and Psychiatry,* 52, 22–23.

Charman, T., Pickles, A., Simonoff, E., Chandler, S., Loucas, T., & Baird, G. (2011). IQ in children with autism spectrum disorders: Data from the Special Needs and Autism Project (SNAP). *Psychological Medicine,* 41, 619—627.

Chassin, L., Bountress, K., Haller, M. & Wang, F. (2014). Adolescent substance use disorders. In E. J. Mash & R. A. Barkley (Eds.), *Child psychopathology* (3rd ed., pp. 180–222). New York: Guilford Press.

Chassin, L., Presson, C., Il-Cho, Y., Lee, M., & Macy, J. (2013). *Developmental factors in addiction: Methodological considerations.* In J. MacKillop & H. de Wit (Eds.), *The Wiley-Blackwell handbook of addiction psychopharmacology* (pp. 7–26). Hoboken, NJ: Wiley-Blackwell.

Chavez, M., & Insel, T. R. (2007). Eating disorders: National Institute of Mental Health's perspective. *American Psychologist [Special issue: Eating disorders],* 62, 159–166.

Chavira, D. A., Shipon-Blum, E., Hitchcock, C., Cohan, S., & Stein, M. B. (2007). Selective mutism and social anxiety disorder: All in the family? *Journal of the American Academy of Child & Adolescent Psychiatry,* 46, 1464–1472.

Chen, J., Li, X., & McGue, M. (2013). The interacting effect of the BDNF Val66Met polymorphism and stressful life events on adolescent depression is not an artifact of gene–environment correlation: Evidence from a longitudinal twin study. *Journal of Child Psychology and Psychiatry,* 54, 1066–1073.

Chen, M. H., Su, T. P., Chen, Y. S., Hsu, J. W., Huang, K. L., Chang, W. H., … Bai, Y. M. (2013). Asthma and attention-deficit/hyperactivity disorder: A nationwide population-based prospective cohort study. *Journal of Child Psychology and Psychiatry,* 54, 1208–1214.

Chen, X., Rubin, K. H., Li, B., & Li, D. (1999). Adolescent outcomes of social functioning in Chinese children. *International Journal of Behavioral Development,* 23, 199–223.

Chen, X., Rubin, K. H., & Li, Z. Y. (1995). Social functioning and adjustment in Chinese children: A longitudinal study. *Developmental Psychology,* 31, 531–539.

Chesley, E. B., Alberts, J .D., Klein, J. D., & Kreipe, R. E. (2003). Pro or con? Anorexia nervosa and the Internet. *Journal of Adolescent Health,* 32, 123–124.

Chess, S. (1960). Diagnosis and treatment of the hyperactive child. *New York State Journal of Medicine,* 60, 2379–2385.

Chess, S., & Thomas, A. (1984). *Origins and evolution of behavior disorders.* New York: Brunner/Mazel.

Chethik, M. (2000). *Techniques of child therapy: Psychodynamic strategies* (2nd ed.). New York: Guilford Press.

Cheung, A. H., Kozloff, N., & Sacks, D. (2013). Pediatric depression: An evidence-based update on treatment interventions. *Current Psychiatry Reports,* 15, 381.

Cheung, A. H., Zuckerbrot, R. A., Jensen, P. S., Ghalib, K., Laraque, D., Stein, R. E. K., & GLAD-PC Steering Group. (2007). Guidelines for adolescent depression in primary care (GLAD-PC): II. Treatment and ongoing management. *Pediatrics,* 120, e1313–e1326.

Chiang, H.-M., & Carter, M. (2008). Spontaneity of communication in individuals with autism. *Journal of Autism and Developmental Disorders,* 38, 693–705.

Child Medication Safety Act. (2007). *Child medication safety act of 2007.* 110th U.S. Congress, 1st Session, S 891 IS 1170 (Report No. 108–121, Union Calendar No. 62). Introduced March 15, 2007.

Child Welfare Information Gateway. (2011). *Definitions of child abuse and neglect in federal law.* Retrieved from http://www.childwelfare.gov/can/defining/federal.cfm

Children's Defense Fund (2007). *America's cradle to prison pipeline: A report of the Children's Defense Fund.* Washington, DC: Author. Retrieved from www.childrensdefense.org/child-research-data-publications/data/cradle-prison-pipeline-report-2007-full-highres.html

Children's Defense Fund (2012). *The State of America's Children Handbook.* Washington, DC: Author. Retrieved from www.childrensdefense.org/child-research-data-publications/data/soac-2012-handbook.html

Chirdkiatgumchai, V., Xiao, H., Fredstrom, B. K., Adams, R. E., Epstein, J. N., Shas, S. S., … Froelich, T. (2013). National trends in psychotropic use in young children. 1994-2009. *Pediatrics, 132,* 615–623.

Chorney, D. B., Detweiler, M. F., Morris, T. L., & Kuhn, B. R. (2008). The interplay of sleep disturbance, anxiety, and depression in children. *Journal of Pediatric Psychology, 33,* 339–348.

Chorpita, B. F. (2002). The tripartite model and dimensions of anxiety and depression: An examination of structure in a large school sample. *Journal of Abnormal Child Psychology, 30,* 177–190.

Chorpita, B. F. (2007). *Modular cognitive-behavioral therapy for childhood anxiety disorders.* New York: Guilford Press.

Chorpita, B. F., Albano, A. M., & Barlow, D. H. (1996). Cognitive processing in children: Relation to anxiety and family in influences. *Journal of Clinical Child Psychology, 25,* 170–176.

Chorpita, B. F., & Daleiden, E. L. (2014). Structuring the collaboration of science and service in pursuit of a shared vision. *Journal of Clinical Child & Adolescent Psychology, 43,* 323–338.

Chorpita, B. F., Daleiden, E. L., Ebesutani, C., Young, J., Becker, K. D., Nakamura, B. J., & Storace, N. (2011). Evidence-based treatments for children and adolescents: An updated review of indicators of efficacy and effectiveness. *Clinical Psychology: Science and Practice, 18,* 154–172.

Chorpita, B. F., Reise S., Weisz, J. R., Grubbs, K., Becker, K. D., Krull, J. L., & The Research Network on Youth Mental Health. (2010). Evaluation of the Brief Problem Checklist and caregiver interviews to measure clinical progress. *Journal of Consulting and Clinical Psychology, 78,* 4, 526–536.

Chorpita, B. F., & Southam-Gerow, M. A. (2006). Fears and anxieties. In E. J. Mash & R. A. Barkley (Eds.), *Treatment of childhood disorders* (3rd ed., pp. 271–335). New York: Guilford Press.

Chorpita, B. F., Tracey, S. A., Brown, T. A., Collica, T. J., & Barlow, D. A. (1997). Assessment of worry in children and adolescents: An adaptation of the Penn State Worry Questionnaire. *Behaviour Research and Therapy, 35,* 569–581.

Christian, L. M., Glaser, R., Porte, K., & Iams, J. D. (2013). Stress-induced inflammatory responses in women: Effects of race and pregnancy. *Psychosomatic Medicine, 75,* 658–669.

Christophersen, E. R., & VanScoyoc, S. M. (2013). Diagnosis and management of encopresis. In E. R. Christophersen & S. M. VanScoyoc *(Eds.), Treatments that work with children: Empirically supported strategies for managing childhood problems* (2nd ed., pp. 109–128). Washington, DC: American Psychological Association.

Chronis, A. M., Chacko, A., Fabiano, G. A., Wymbs, B. T., & Pelham, W. E., Jr. (2004a). Enhancements to the behavioral parent training paradigm for families of children with ADHD: Review and future directions. *Clinical Child and Family Psychology Review, 7,* 1–27.

Chronis, A. M., Fabiano, G. A., Gnagy, E. M., Onyango, A. N., Pelham, W. E., Lopez-Williams, A., … Seymour, K. E. (2004b). An evaluation of the summer treatment program for children with ADHD using a treatment withdrawal design. *Behavior Therapy, 35,* 561–585.

Chronis-Tuscano, A., Chacko, A., & Barkley, R. A. (2013). Letter to the editor: Key issues relevant to the efficacy of behavioral treatment for ADHD. *American Journal of Psychiatry, 170,* 799.

Chronis-Tuscano, A., Degnan, K. A., Pine, D. S., Pérez-Edgar, K., Henderson, H. A., Diaz, Y., & Fox, N. A. (2009). Stable early maternal report of behavioral inhibition predicts lifetime social anxiety disorder in adolescence. *Journal of the American Academy of Child & Adolescent Psychiatry, 48,* 928–935.

Chronis-Tuscano, A., Molina, B. S. G., Pelham, W. E., Applegate, B., Dahlke, A., Overmyer, M., & Lahey, B. B. (2010). Very early predictors of adolescent depression and suicide attempts in children with attention-deficit/hyperactivity disorder. *Archives of General Psychiatry, 67,* 1044–1051.

Chronis-Tuscano, A., Raggi, V. L., Clarke, T. L., Rooney, M. E., Diaz, Y., & Pian, J. (2008). Associations between maternal attention-deficit/hyperactivity disorder symptoms and parenting. *Journal of Abnormal Child Psychology, 36,* 1237–1250.

Churches, O., Baron-Cohen, S., & Ring, H. (2012). The psychophysiology of narrower face processing in autism spectrum conditions. *NeuroReport, 23,* 395–399.

Cicchetti, D. (2006). Development and psychopathology. In D. Cicchetti & D. J. Cohen (Eds.), *Developmental psychopathology: Vol. 1. Theory and method* (2nd ed., pp. 1–23). Hoboken, NJ: Wiley.

Cicchetti, D., & Cannon, T. D. (1999). Neurodevelopmental processes in the ontogenesis and epigenesis of psychopathology. *Development and Psychopathology, 11,* 375–393.

Cicchetti, D., & Curtis, W. J. (2006). The developing brain and neural plasticity: Implications for normality, psychopathology, and resilience. In D. Cicchetti & D. J. Cohen (Eds.), *Developmental psychopathology: Vol. 2. Developmental neuroscience* (pp. 1–64). Hoboken, NJ: Wiley.

Cicchetti, D., & Hinshaw, S. P. (2003). Conceptual, methodological, and statistical issues in developmental psychopathology: A special issue in honor of Paul E. Meehl. *Development and Psychopathology, 15,* 497–499.

Cicchetti, D., & Lynch, M. (1995). Failures in the expectable environment and their impact on individual development: The case of child maltreatment. In D. Cicchetti & D. J. Cohen (Eds.), *Developmental psychopathology: Vol. 2. Risk, disorder, and adaptation* (pp. 32–71). New York: Wiley.

Cicchetti, D., & Rogosch, R. A. (2002). A developmental psychopathology perspective on adolescence. *Journal of Consulting and Clinical Psychology, 70,* 6–20.

Cicchetti, D., Rogosch, F. A., Gunnar, M. R., & Toth, S. L. (2010). The differential impacts of early physical and sexual abuse and internalizing problems on daytime cortisol rhythm in school-aged children. *Child Development, 81,* 252–269.

Cicchetti, D., Rogosch, F. A., Howe, M. L., & Toth, S. L. (2010). The effects of maltreatment and neuroendocrine regulation on memory performance. *Child Development, 81,* 1504–1519.

Cicchetti, D., & Valentino, K. (2006). An ecological-transactional perspective on child maltreatment: Failure of the average expectable environment and its influence on child development. In D. Cicchetti & D. J. Cohen (Eds.), *Developmental psychopathology, Vol. 3: Risk, disorder, and adaptation* (2nd ed., pp. 129–201). Hoboken, NJ: Wiley.

Clark, D. B., Thatcher, D. L., & Martin, C. S. (2010). Child abuse and other traumatic experiences, alcohol use disorders, and health problems in adolescence and young adulthood. *Journal of Pediatric Psychology, 35,* 499–510.

Clark, D. B., Thatcher, D. L., & Tapert, S. F. (2008). Alcohol, psychological dysregulation, and adolescent brain development. *Alcohol, Clinical and Experimental Research, 32,* 375–385.

Clark, L. S., & Tiggemann, M. (2006). Appearance culture in 9- to 12-year-old girls: Media and peer influences on body dissatisfaction. *Social Development, 15,* 628–643.

Clark, L. S., & Tiggemann, M. (2007). Sociocultural influences and body image in 9- to 12-year-old girls: The role of appearance schemas. *Journal of Clinical Child & Adolescent Psychology, 36,* 76–86.

Clark, R. W. (1971). *Einstein: The life and times.* New York: World.

Clarke, G. N., & DeBar, L. L. (2010). Group cognitive-behavioral treatment for adolescent depression. In J. R. Weisz & A. E. Kazdin (Eds.), *Evidence-based psychotherapies for children and adolescents* (2nd ed., pp. 110–125). New York: Guilford Press.

Clarke, G. N., Lewinsohn, P. M., & Hops, H. (2001). *Instructor's manual for adolescent coping with depression course.* Retrieved from http://www.kpchr.org/public/acwd/acwd.html

Clauss, J. A., & Blackford, J. U. (2012). Behavioral inhibition and risk for developing social anxiety disorder: A meta-analytic study. *Journal of the American*

Academy of Child & Adolescent Psychiatry, 51, 1066–1075.

Clay, D., Vignoles, V. L., & Dittmar, H. (2005). Body image and self-esteem among adolescent girls: Testing the influence of sociocultural factors. Journal of Research on Adolescence, 15, 451–477.

Clay, D. L., Mordhorst, M. J., & Lend, L. (2002). Empirically supported treatments in pediatric psychology: Where is the diversity? Journal of Pediatric Psychology, 27, 325–337.

Clifford, S. M., & Dissanayake, C. (2008). The early development of joint attention in infants with autistic disorder using home video observations and parental interview. Journal of Autism and Developmental Disorders, 38, 791–805.

Cloitre, M., Stolbach, B. C., Herman, J. L., van, d. K., Pynoos, R., Wang, J., & Petkova, E. (2009). A developmental approach to complex PTSD: Childhood and adult cumulative trauma as predictors of symptom complexity. Journal of Traumatic Stress, 22, 399–408.

Cobb, B., Sample, P. L., Alwell, M., & Johns, N. R. (2006). Cognitive-behavioral interventions, dropout, and youth with disabilities: A systematic review. Remedial and Special Education, 27, 259–275.

Coccaro, E. F., Sripada, C. S., Yanowitch, R. N., & Phan, K. L. (2011). Corticolimbic function in impulsive aggressive behavior. Biological Psychiatry, 69, 1153–1159.

Cogan, J. C., Bhalla, S. K., Sefa-Dedeh, A., & Rothblum, E. D. (1996). A comparison study of United States and African students on perceptions of obesity and thinness. Journal of Cross Cultural Psychology, 27, 98–113.

Coghill, D., Nigg, J., Rothenberger, A., Sonuga-Barke, E., & Tannock, R. (2005). Whither causal models in the neuroscience of ADHD? Developmental Science, 8, 105–114.

Cohan, S. L., & Chavira, D. A. (2008). Refining the classification of children with selective mutism: A latent profile analysis. Journal of Clinical Child & Adolescent Psychology, 37, 770–784.

Cohan, S. L., Chavira, D. A., Shipon-Blum, E., Hitchcock, C., Roesch, S. C., & Stein, M. B. (2008). Refining the classification of children with selective mutism: A latent profile analysis. Journal of Clinical Child & Adolescent Psychology, 37, 770–784.

Cohen, J., Mannarino, A., & Murray, L. (2011). Trauma-focused CBT for youth who experience ongoing traumas. Child Abuse and Neglect, 35, 637–646.

Cohen, J. A., Bukstein, O., Walter, H., Benson, R. S., Chrisman, A., Farchione, T. R., … Stock, S. (2010). Practice parameter for the assessment and treatment of children and adolescent with posttraumatic stress disorder. Journal of the American Academy of Child & Adolescent Psychiatry, 49, 414–430.

Cohen, J. A., Mannarino, A. P., Kliethermes, M., & Murray, L. A. (2012). Trauma-focused CBT for youth with complex trauma. Child Abuse & Neglect, 36, 528–541.

Cohen, M. A., & Piquero, A. R. (2009). New evidence on the monetary value of saving a high risk youth. Journal of Quantitative Criminology, 25, 25–49.

Cohen, P., Cohen, J., & Brook, J. S. (1993). An epidemiological study of disorders in late childhood and adolescence: II. Persistence of disorders. Journal of Child Psychology and Psychiatry, 34, 869–877.

Coker, T. R., Austin, S. B., & Schuster, M. A. (2010). The health and health care of lesbian, gay, and bisexual adolescents. Annual Review of Public Health, 31, 457–477.

Colapinto, J. (1993, November). The trouble with Nick. Redbook, 121–123, 145, 151–153.

Colder, C. R., Lochman, J. E., & Wells, K. C. (1997). The moderating effects of children's fear and activity level on relations between parenting practices and childhood symptomatology. Journal of Abnormal Child Psychology, 25, 251–263.

Colder, C. R., Scalco, M., Trucco, E. M., Read, J. P., Lengua, L. J., Wieczorek, W. F., & Hawk, L. W., Jr. (2013). Prospective associations of internalizing and externalizing problems and their co-occurrence with early adolescent substance use. Journal of Abnormal Child Psychology, 41, 667–677.

Cole, D. A. (1990). The relation of social and academic competence to depressive symptoms in childhood. Journal of Abnormal Psychology, 99, 422–429.

Cole, D. A., Ciesla, J. A., Dallaire, H., Jacquez, F. M., Pineda, A. Q., Lagrange, B., … Felton, J. W. (2008). Emergence of attributional style and its relation to depressive symptoms. Journal of Abnormal Psychology, 117, 16–31.

Cole, D. A., Martin, J. M., Peeke, L., Henderson, A., & Harwell, J. (1998). Validation of depression and anxiety measures in White and Black youths: Multitrait-multimethod analyses. Psychological Assessment, 10, 261–276.

Cole, P. M., & Hall, S. E. (2008). Emotion dysregulation as a risk factor for psychopathology. In T. P. Beauchaine & S. P. Hinshaw (Eds.), Child and adolescent psychopathology (pp. 265–298). Hoboken, NJ: Wiley.

Cole, T. J. (2007). Early causes of child obesity and implications for prevention. Acta Paediatrica, 96(Suppl. 454), 2–4.

Coll, C. G., Akerman, A., & Cicchetti, D. (2000). Cultural influences on developmental processes and outcomes: Implications for the study of development and psychopathology. Development and Psychopathology [Special issue: Reflecting on the past and planning for the future of developmental psychopathology], 12, 333–356.

Collishaw, S., Maughan, B., Goodman, R., & Pickles, A. (2004). Time trends in adolescent mental health. Journal of Child Psychology and Psychiatry, 45, 1350–1362.

Collishaw, S., Pickles, A., Messer, J., Rutter, M., Shearer, C., & Maughan, B. (2007). Resilience to adult psychopathology following childhood maltreatment: Evidence from a community sample. Child Abuse & Neglect, 31, 211–229.

Comer, J. S., Furr, J. M., Cooper-Vince, C. E., Kerns, C. E., Chan, P. T., Edson, A. L., … Freeman, J. B. (2014). Internet-delivered, family-based treatment for early-onset OCD: A preliminary case series. Journal of Clinical Child & Adolescent Psychology, 43, 74–87.

Comer, J. S., & Kendall, P. C. (2007). Terrorism: The psychological impact on youth. Clinical Psychology: Science and Practice, 14, 179–212.

Comer, J. S., Olfson, M., & Mojtabai, R. (2010). National trends in child and adolescent psychotropic polypharmacy in office-based practice, 1996–2007. Journal of the American Academy of Child & Adolescent Psychiatry, 49, 1001–1010.

Comer, J. S., Pincus, D. B., & Hofmann, S. G. (2012). Generalized anxiety disorder and the proposed associated symptoms criterion change for DSM-5 in a treatment-seeking sample of anxious youth. Depression and Anxiety, 29, 994–1003.

Compas, B. E., & Andreotti, C. (2013). Risk and resilience in child and adolescent psychopathology. In T. P. Beauchaine & S. P. Hinshaw (Eds.), Child and adolescent psychopathology (2nd ed., pp. 143–169). Hoboken, NJ: Wiley.

Compas, B. E., Connor-Smith, J. K., Saltzman, H., Thomsen, A. H., & Wadsworth, M. E. (2001). Coping with stress during childhood and adolescence: Problems, progress, and potential in theory and research. Psychological Bulletin, 127, 87–127.

Compas, B. E., Forehand, R., Thigpen, J. C., Keller, G., Hardcastle, E. J., Cole, D. A., … Roberts, L. (2011). Family group cognitive–behavioral preventive intervention for families of depressed parents: 18- and 24-month outcomes. Journal of Consulting and Clinical Psychology, 79, 488–499.

Compas, B. E., & Hammen, C. L. (1994). Child and adolescent depression: Covariation and comorbidity in development. In R. J. Haggerty, L. R. Sherrod, N. Garmezy, & M. Rutter (Eds.), Stress, risk, and resilience in children and adolescents: Processes, mechanisms, and interventions (pp. 225–267). New York: Cambridge University Press.

Compton, S. N., Nelson, A. H., & March, J. S. (2000). Social phobia and separation anxiety symptoms in community and clinical samples of children and adolescents. Journal of the American Academy of Child & Adolescent Psychiatry, 39, 1040–1046.

Compton, S. N., Peris, T. S., Almirall, D., Birmaher, B., Sherill, J., Kendall, P. C., … Albano, A. M. (2014). Predictors and moderators of treatment response in childhood anxiety disorders: Results from the CAMS trial. Journal of Consulting and Clinical Psychology, 82, 212–224.

Conduct Problems Prevention Research Group. (2007). Fast track randomized controlled trial to prevent externalizing psychiatric disorders: Findings from grades 3 to 9. Journal of the American Academy of Child & Adolescent Psychiatry, 46, 1250–1262.

Conduct Problems Prevention Research Group. (2010). The Fast Track Project:

The prevention of severe conduct problems in school-age youth. In R. C. Murrihy, A. D. Kidman, & T. H. Ollendick (Eds.), *Clinical handbook of assessing and treating conduct problems in youth* (pp. 407–433). New York: Springer.

Conduct Problems Prevention Research Group. (2011). The effects of the Fast Track preventive intervention on the development of conduct disorder across childhood. *Child Development, 82,* 331–345.

Conger, R. D., Ge, X., Elder, G. H., Lorenz, F. O., & Simons, R. L. (1994). Economic stress, coercive family process, and developmental problems of adolescents. *Child Development, 65,* 541–561.

Connell, A. M., & Goodman, S. H. (2002). The association between psychopathology in fathers versus mothers and children's internalizing and externalizing behavior problems: A meta-analysis. *Psychological Bulletin, 128,* 746–773.

Connell, A. M., Hughes-Scalise, A., Klostermann, S., & Azem, T. (2011). Maternal depression and the heart of parenting: Respiratory sinus arrhythmia and affective dynamics during parent-adolescent interactions. *Journal of Family Psychology, 25,* 653–662.

Conner, B. T., & Lochman, J. E. (2010). Comorbid conduct disorder and substance use disorders. *Clinical Psychology: Science and Practice, 17,* 337–349.

Conners, K., Epstein, J., March, J., Angold, A., Wells, K. C., Klaric, J., ... Wigal, T. (2001). Multimodal treatment of ADHD in the MTA: An alternative outcome analysis. *Journal of the American Academy of Child & Adolescent Psychiatry, 40,* 168–179.

Connolly, J., Furman, W., & Konarski, R. (2000). The role of peers in the emergence of heterosexual romantic relationships in adolescence. *Child Development, 71,* 1395–1408.

Connor, D. F. (2014). Stimulant and nonstimulant medications for childhood ADHD. In R. A. Barkley (Ed.), *Attention-deficit hyperactivity disorder: A handbook for diagnosis and treatment* (4th ed.) New York: Guilford Press.

Conrod, P. J., Castellanos-Ryan, N., & Mackie, C. (2011). Long-term effects of a personality-targeted intervention to reduce alcohol use in adolescents. *Journal of Consulting and Clinical Psychology, 79,* 296–306.

Constantino, J. N., & Charman, T. (2012). Editorial: Gender bias, female resilience, and the sex ratio in autism. *Journal of the American Academy of Child & Adolescent Psychiatry, 51,* 756-758.

Conway, K. P., Vullo, G. C., Nichter, B., Wang, J., Compton, W. M., Iannotti, R. J., & Simons-Morton, B. (2013). Prevalence and patterns of polysubstance use in a nationally representative sample of 10th graders in the United States. *Journal of Adolescent Health, 52,* 716–723.

Cook, F., & Oliver, C. (2011). A review of defining and measuring sociability in children with intellectual disabilities. *Research in Developmental Disabilities, 32,* 11–24.

Cooley-Strickland, M., Quille, T. J., Griffin, R. S., Stuart, E. A., Bradshaw, C. P., & Furr-Holden, D. (2009). Community violence and youth: Affect, behavior, substance use, and academics. *Clinical Child and Family Psychology Review, 12,* 127–156.

Coolidge, F. L., Thede, L. L., & Young, S. E. (2000). Heritability and the comorbidity of attention deficit hyperactivity disorder with behavioral disorders and executive function deficits: A preliminary investigation. *Developmental Neuropsychology, 17,* 273–287.

Cooper, P. J., Fearn, V., Willets, L., Seabrook, H., & Parkinson, M. (2006). Affective disorders in the parents of a clinical sample of children with anxiety disorders. *Journal of Affective Disorders, 93,* 205–212.

Cooper, S. W., Estes, R. J., Giardino, A. P., Kellogg, N. D., & Vieth, V. I. (2005). Medical, legal, & social science aspects of child sexual exploitation: A comprehensive review of pornography, prostitution, and internet crimes, Vol. 1. St. Louis: GW Medical.

Cooper-Vince, C. E., Emmert-Aronsom, B. O., Pincus, D. B., & Comer, J. S. (2014). The diagnostic utility of separation anxiety disorder symptoms: An item response theory analysis. *Journal of Abnormal Child Psychology, 42,* 417–428.

Copeland, W., Shanahan, L., Costello, E. J., & Angold, A. (2011). Cumulative prevalence of psychiatric disorders by young adulthood: A prospective cohort analysis from the great smoky mountains study. *Journal of the American Academy of Child & Adolescent Psychiatry, 50,* 252–261.

Copeland, W. E., Keeler, G., Angold, A., & Costello, E. J. (2007). Traumatic events and posttraumatic stress in childhood. *Archives of General Psychiatry, 64,* 577–584.

Copeland, W. E., Keeler, G., Angold, A., & Costello, E. J. (2010). Posttraumatic stress without trauma in children. *American Journal of Psychiatry, 167,* 1059–1065.

Copeland, W. E., Wolke, D., Angold, A., & Costello, E. J. (2013). Adult psychiatric outcomes of bullying and being bullied by peers in childhood and adolescence. *JAMA Psychiatry, 70,* 419–426.

Corbett, B. A., Constantine, L. J., Hendren, R., Rocke, D., & Ozonoff, S. (2009). Examining executive functioning in children with autism spectrum disorder, attention deficit hyperactivity disorder and typical development. *Psychiatry Research, 166,* 210–222.

Cornelius, J. R., Maisto, S. A., Pollock, N. K., Martin, C. S., Salloum, I. M., Lynch, K. G., & Clark, D. B. (2003). Rapid relapse generally follows treatment for substance use disorders among adolescents. *Addictive Behaviors, 28,* 381–386.

Cornier, M. (2011). Is your brain to blame for weight regain? *Physiology & Behavior, 104,* 608–612.

Corning, A. F., Gondoli, D. M., Bucchianeri, M. M., & Salafia, E. H. B. (2010). Preventing the development of body issues in adolescent girls through intervention with their mothers. *Body Image, 7,* 289–295.

Cornish, K., Cole, V., Longhi, E., Karmiloff-Smith, A., & Scerif, G. (2013). Mapping developmental trajectories of attention and working memory in fragile X syndrome: Developmental freeze or developmental change? *Development and Psychopathology, 25,* 365–376.

Corrales, M., & Herbert, M. (2011). Autism and environmental genomics: Synergistic systems approaches to autism complexity. In D. Amaral, G. Dawson, & D. Geschwind (Eds.), *Autism spectrum disorders* (pp. 875–892). New York: Oxford University Press.

Corrigan, P. W. (2000). Mental health stigma as social attribution: Implications for research methods and attitude change. *Clinical Psychology: Science and Practice, 7,* 48–67.

Cortese, S., Brown, T. E., Corkum, P., Gruber, R., O'Brien, L. M., Stein, M., & Owens, J. (2013). Assessment and management of sleep problems in youths with attention-deficit/hyperactivity disorder. *Journal of the American Academy of Child & Adolescent Psychiatry, 52,* 784–796.

Cortese, S., Faraone, S. V., Konofal, E., & Lecendreux, M. (2009). Sleep in children with attention-deficit/hyperactivity disorder: Meta-analysis of subjective and objective studies. *Journal of the American Academy of Child & Adolescent Psychiatry, 48,* 894–908.

Cortese, S., Kelly, C., Chabernaud, C., Proal, E., Di Martino, A., Milham, M. P., & Castellanos, F. X. (2012). Toward systems neuroscience of ADHD: A meta-analysis of 55 fMRI studies. *American Journal of Psychiatry, 169,* 1038–1055.

Cosentino, C. E., Meyer-Bahlburg, H. F., Alpert, J., Weinberg, S. L., & Gaines, R. (1995). Sexual behavior problems and psychopathology symptoms in sexually abused girls. *Journal of the American Academy of Child and Adolescent Psychiatry, 34,* 1033–1042.

Cosmopolitan. (2001, August). "Why models got so skinny." Retrieved from http://www.highbeam.com/doc/1G1-76667021.html

Costello, E. J., & Angold, A. (2006). Developmental epidemiology. In D. Cicchetti & D. J. Cohen (Eds.), *Developmental psychopathology: Vol. 1. Theory and method* (2nd ed., pp. 41–75). Hoboken, NJ: Wiley.

Costello, E. J., Egger, H., & Angold, A. (2005a). 10-year research update review: The epidemiology of child and adolescent psychiatric disorders: I. Methods and public health burden. *Journal of the American Academy of Child & Adolescent Psychiatry, 44,* 972–986.

Costello, E. J., Egger, H., & Angold, A. (2005b). The developmental epidemiology of anxiety disorders: Phenomenology, prevalence, and comorbidity. *Child and Adolescent Psychiatric Clinics of North America, 14,* 631–648.

Costello, E. J., Erkanli, A., & Angold, A. (2006). Is there an epidemic of child or adolescent depression? *Journal of Child Psychology and Psychiatry, 47,* 1263–1271.

Costello, E. J., Erkanli, A., Fairbank, J. A., & Angold, A. (2002). The prevalence of potentially traumatic events in childhood and adolescence. *Journal of Traumatic Stress, 15,* 99–112.

Costello, E. J., Farmer, E. M. Z., Angold, A., Burns, B. J., & Erkanli, A. (1997). Psychiatric disorders among American Indian and white youth in Appalachia: The Great Smoky Mountains Study. *American Journal of Public Health, 87,* 827–832.

Costello, E. J., Worthman, C., Erkanli, A., & Angold, A. (2007). Prediction from low birth weight to female adolescent depression. *Archives of General Psychiatry, 64,* 338–344.

Côté, S. M., Vaillancourt, T., Barker, E. D., Nagin, D., & Tremblay, R. E. (2007). The joint development of physical and indirect aggression: Predictors of continuity and change during childhood. *Development and Psychopathology, 19,* 37–55.

Courchesne, E., Carper, R., & Akshoomoff, N. (2003). Evidence of brain overgrowth in the first year of life in autism. *JAMA: Journal of the American Medical Association, 290,* 337–344.

Courchesne, E., Pierce, K., Schumann, C. M., Redcay, E., Buckwalter, J. A., Kennedy, D. P., … Morgan, J. (2007). Mapping early brain development in autism. *Neuron, 56,* 399–413.

Cowan, P. A., & Cowan, C. P. (2006). Developmental psychopathology from family systems and family risk factors perspectives: Implications for family research, practice, and policy. In D. Cicchetti & D. Cohen (Eds.), *Developmental psychopathology: Vol. 1. Theory and method* (2nd ed., pp. 530–587). Hoboken, NJ: Wiley.

Cox, D. J., Madaan, V., & Cox, B. S. (2011, July). Adult attention-deficit/hyperactivity disorder and driving: Why and how to manage it. *Current Psychiatry Reports, 13,* 345–350.

Cox, M. J., Mills-Koonce, R., Propper, C., & Gariépy, J. (2010). Systems theory and cascades in developmental psychopathology. *Development and Psychopathology. Special Issue: Developmental Cascades: Part 1, 22,* 497–506.

Craig, T. K., Cox, A. D., & Klein, K. (2002). Intergenerational transmission of somatization behaviour: A study of chronic somatizers and their children. *Psychological Medicine, 32,* 805–816.

Crapanzano, A.M., Frick, P.J., & Terranova, A.M. (2010). Patterns of physical and relational aggression in a school-based sample of boys and girls. *Journal of Abnormal Child Psychology, 38,* 433–445.

Craske, M. G., & Rowe, M. K. (1997). Nocturnal panic. *Clinical Psychology: Science and Practice, 4,* 153–174.

Craske, M. G., Kircanski, K., Epstein, A., Wittchen, H-U., Pine, D. S., Lewis-Fernández, R., … Posttraumatic and Dissociative Disorder Work Group. (2010). Panic disorder: A review of DSM-IV panic disorder and proposals for DSM-V. *Depression and Anxiety, 27,* 93–112.

Crawford, A. M., Pentz, M. A., Chou, C., Li, C., & Dwyer, J. H. (2003). Parallel developmental trajectories of sensation seeking and regular substance use in adolescents. *Psychology of Addictive Behaviors, 17,* 179–192.

Creswell, C., & Cartwright-Hatton, S. (2007). Family treatment of child anxiety: Outcomes, limitations and future directions. *Clinical Child and Family Psychology Review, 10,* 232–252.

Creswell, C., Murray, L., Stacey, J., & Cooper, P. (2011). Parenting and child anxiety. In W. K. Silverman & A. Field (Eds.), *Anxiety disorders in children and adolescents: Research, assessment, and intervention* (2nd ed., pp. 299–322). Cambridge, England: Cambridge University Press.

Crick, N. R. (1995). Relational aggression: The role of intent attributions, feelings of distress, and provocation type. *Development and Psychopathology, 7,* 313–322.

Crick, N. R. (1997). Engagement in gender normative versus nonnormative forms of aggression: Links to social-psychological adjustment. *Developmental Psychology, 33,* 610–617.

Crick, N. R., & Dodge, K. A. (1994). A review and reformulation of social-information-processing mechanisms in children's social adjustment. *Psychological Bulletin, 115,* 74–101.

Crick, N. R., & Dodge, K. A. (1996). Social information-processing mechanisms on reactive and proactive aggression. *Child Development, 67,* 993–1002.

Crick, N. R., Bigbee, M. A., & Howes, C. (1996). Gender differences in children's normative beliefs about aggression: How do I hurt thee? Let me count the ways. *Child Development, 67,* 1003–1014.

Crick, N. R., Nelson, D. A., Morales, J. R., Cullerton-Sen, C., Casas, J. F., & Hickman, S. E. (2001). Relational victimization in childhood and adolescence: I hurt you through the grapevine. In J. Juvonen & S. Graham (Eds.), *Peer harassment in school: The plight of the vulnerable and victimized* (pp. 196–214). New York: Guilford Press.

Crick, N. R., Ostrov, J. M., & Werner, N. E. (2006). A longitudinal study of relational aggression, physical aggression, and children's social-psychological adjustment. *Journal of Abnormal Child Psychology, 34,* 131–142.

Crick, N. R., & Rose, A. J. (2000). Toward a gender-balanced approach to the study of social-emotional development: A look at relational aggression. In P. H. Miller & E. K. Scholnick (Eds.), *Toward a feminist developmental psychology* (pp. 153–168). Florence, KY: Taylor & Francis/Routledge.

Crijnen, A. A. M., Achenbach, T. M., & Verhulst, F. C. (1997). Comparisons of problems reported by parents of children in 12 cultures: Total problems, externalizing, and internalizing. *Journal of the American Academy of Child & Adolescent Psychiatry, 36,* 1269–1277.

Crisp, A. H. (1997). Anorexia nervosa as flight from growth: Assessment and treatment based on the model. In D. M. Garner & P. E. Garfinkel (Eds.), *Handbook of treatment for eating disorders* (2nd ed., pp. 248–277). New York: Guilford Press.

Crisp, R. J., & Turner, R. N. (2011). Cognitive adaptation to the experience of social and cultural diversity. *Psychological Bulletin, 137,* 242–266.

Croen, L. A., Grether, J. K. Yoshida, C. K., Odouli, R., & Hendrick, V. (2011). Antidepressant use during pregnancy and childhood spectrum disorders. *Archives of General Psychiatry, 68,* 1104–1112.

Crooks, C. V., & Wolfe, D. A. (2007). Child abuse and neglect. In E. J. Mash & R. A. Barkley (Eds.), *Assessment of childhood disorders* (4th ed., pp. 639–684). New York: Guilford Press.

Cross-Disorder Group of the Psychiatric Genomics Consortium (2013). Genetic relationship between five psychiatric disorders estimated from genome-wide SNPs. *Nature Genetics, 45,* 984–994.

Cuccaro, M. L., Brinkley, J., Abramson, R. K., Hall, A., Wright, H. H., Hussman, J. P., … Pericak-Vance, M. A. (2007). Autism in African American families: Clinical-phenotypic findings. *American Journal of Medical Genetics Part B: Neuropsychiatric Genetics, 144,* 1022–1026.

Cuéllar, I. (2000). Acculturation as a moderator of personality and psychological assessment. In R. H. Dana (Ed.), *Handbook of cross-cultural and multicultural personality assessment* (pp. 113–129). Mahwah, NJ: Erlbaum.

Cuffe, S. P., Moore, C. G., & McKeown, R. E. (2005). Prevalence and correlates of ADHD symptoms in the National Health Interview Survey. *Journal of Attention Disorders, 9,* 392–401.

Cuijpers, P., Muñoz, R. F., Clarke, G. N., & Lewinsohn, P. M. (2010). Psychoeducational treatment and prevention of depression: The "coping with depression" course thirty years later. *Clinical Psychology Review, 29,* 449–458.

Culbertson, F. M. (1997). Depression and gender: An international review. *American Psychologist, 52,* 25–31.

Culverhouse, R. C., Bowes, L., Breslau, N., Numberger, J. I., Jr., Burmeister, M., Fergusson, D. M., … The 5-HTTLPR, Stress and Depression Consortium. (2013), *BMC Psychiatry, 13:304,* 1–12. Retrieved from www.biomedcentral.com/1471-244X/13/304

Cummings, C. M., Caporino, N. E., & Kendall, P. C. (2014). Comorbidity of anxiety and depression in children and adolescents: 20 years after. *Psychological Bulletin, 140,* 816–845.

Cummings, E. M., & Davies, P. T. (2002). Effects of marital conflict on children: Recent advances and emerging themes in process-oriented research. *Journal of Child Psychology, 43,* 31–63.

Cummings, J. R., & Druss, B. G. (2011). Racial/ethnic differences in mental health service use among adolescents with major depression. *Journal of the American Academy of Child & Adolescent Psychiatry, 50,* 160–170.

Cunningham, C. E., McHolm, A. E., & Boyle, M. H. (2006). Social phobia, anxiety, oppositional behavior, social skills, and self-concept in children with specific selective mutism, generalized selective mutism, and community controls. *European Child & Adolescent Psychiatry, 15,* 245–255.

Cunningham, P. B., Henggeler, S. W., Brondino, M., & Pickrel, S. G. (1999).

Testing underlying assumptions of the family empowerment perspective. *Journal of Child and Family Studies, 8,* 437–449.

Curry, J., Silva, S., Rohde, P., Ginsburg, G., Kratochvil, C., Simons, A., ... March, J. (2011). Recovery and recurrence following treatment for adolescent major depression. *Archives of General Psychiatry, 68,* 263–270.

Cuthbert, B. (2010). Editorial: Early prevention in childhood anxiety disorders. *American Journal of Psychiatry, 167,* 1428–1430.

Cuthbert, B. N., & Kozak, M. J. (2013). Commentary: Constructing constructs for psychopathology: The NIMH Research Domain Criteria. *Journal of Abnormal Psychology, 122,* 928-937.

Cyr, C., Euser, E. M., Bakermans-Kranenburg, M., & Van Ijzendoorn, M. H. (2010). Attachment security and disorganization in maltreating and high-risk families: A series of meta-analyses. *Development and Psychopathology, 22,* 87–108.

Cytryn, L., & McKnew, D. H. (1974). Factors influencing the changing clinical expression of the depressive process in children. *American Journal of Psychiatry, 131,* 879–881.

Cytryn, L., & McKnew, D. H. (1996). *Growing up sad: Childhood depression and its treatment.* New York: Norton.

D'Augelli, A. R. (2006). Developmental and contextual factors and mental health among lesbian, gay, and bisexual youths. In A. M. Omoto & H. S. Kurtzman (Eds.), *Sexual orientation and mental health: Examining identity and development in lesbian, gay, and bisexual people. Contemporary perspectives on lesbian, gay, and bisexual psychology* (pp. 37–53). Washington, DC: American Psychological Association.

Dackis, M. N., Rogosch, F. A., Oshri, A., & Cicchetti, D. (2012). The role of limbic system irritability in linking history of childhood maltreatment and psychiatric outcomes in low-income, high-risk women: Moderation by FK506 binding protein 5 haplotype. *Development and Psychopathology, 24,* 1237–1252.

Dadds, M. R., Jambrak, J., Pasalich, D., Hawes, D. H., & Brennan, J. (2011). Impaired attention to the eyes of attachment figures and the developmental origins of psychopathy. *Journal of Child Psychology and Psychiatry, 52,* 238–245.

Dagne, G. A., & Snyder, J. (2011). Relationship of maternal negative moods to child emotion regulation during family interaction. *Development and Psychopathology, 23,* 211–223.

Dahl, R. E. (1996). The regulation of sleep and arousal: Development and psychopathology. *Development and Psychopathology, 8,* 3–27.

Dahl, R. E. (2006). Sleeplessness and aggression in youth. *Journal of Adolescent Health, 38,* 641–642.

Dahl, R. E. (2007). Sleep and the developing brain. *Sleep, 30,* 1079–1080.

Dahl, R. E., & El-Sheikh, M. (2007). Considering sleep in a family context: Introduction to the special issue. *Journal of Family Psychology [Special issue: Carpe noctem: Sleep and family processes], 21,* 1–3.

Dahlquist, L. M. (1999). *Pediatric pain management.* New York: Plenum Press.

Daley, S. E., Hammen, C., Burge, D., Davila, J., Paley, B., Lindberg, N., & Herzberg, D. S. (1999). Depression and Axis II symptomatology in an adolescent community sample: Concurrent and longitudinal associations. *Journal of Personality Disorders, 13,* 47–59.

Daly, K. J. (2007). *Qualitative methods for family studies & human development.* Thousand Oaks, CA: Sage.

Damasio, H., Tranel, D., Grabowskia, T., Adolphs, R., & Damasio, A. (2004). Neural systems behind word and concept retrieval. *Cognition [Special issue: Towards a new functions anatomy of language], 92,* 179–229.

Danckaerts, M., Sonuga-Barke, E. J. S., Banaschewski, T., Buitelaar, J., Dopfner, M., Hollis, C., ... Coghill, D. (2010). The quality of life of children with attention deficit/hyperactivity disorder: A systematic review. *European Child & Adolescent Psychiatry, 19,* 83–105.

Dandreaux, D. M., & Frick, P. J. (2009). Developmental pathways to conduct problems: A further test of the childhood and adolescent-onset distinction. *Journal of Abnormal Child Psychology, 37,* 375–385.

Danese, A., Caspi, A., Williams, B., Ambler, A., Sugden, K., Mika, J., ... Arseneault, L. (2011). Biological embedding of stress through inflammation processes in childhood. *Molecular Psychiatry, 16,* 244–246.

Daniels, A. M., Halladay, A. K., Shih, A., Elder, L. M., & Dawson, G. (2014). Approaches to enhancing the early detection of autism spectrum disorders: A systematic review of the literature. *Journal of the American Academy of Child & Adolescent Psychiatry, 53,* 141–152.

Dardennes, R. M., Al Anbar, N. N., Prado-Netto, A., Kaye, K., Contejean, Y., & Al Anbar, N. N. (2011). Treating the cause of the illness rather than the symptoms: Parental causal beliefs and treatment choices in autism spectrum disorder. *Research in Developmental Disabilities, 32,* 1137–1146.

Daughton, J. M., & Kratochvil, C. J. (2009). Review of ADHD pharmacotherapies: Advantages, disadvantages, and clinical pearls. *Journal of the American Academy of Child & Adolescent Psychiatry, 48,* 240–248.

David, C. F., & Kistner, J. A. (2000). Do positive self-perceptions have a "dark side"? Examination of the link between perceptual bias and aggression. *Journal of Abnormal Child Psychology, 28,* 327–337.

David, C. N., Greenstein, D., Clasen, L., Gochman, P., Miller, R., Tossell, J. W., ... Rapoport, J. L. (2011). Childhood onset schizophrenia: High rate of visual hallucinations. *Journal of the American Academy of Child and Adolescent Psychiatry, 50,* 681–686.

David-Ferdon, C., & Kaslow, N. J. (2008). Evidence-based psychosocial treatments for child and adolescent depression. *Journal of Clinical Child & Adolescent Psychology, 37,* 62–104.

Davidson, R. J., Pizzagalli, D., & Nitschke, J. (2002). The representation and regulation of emotion in depression: Perspectives from affective neuroscience. In I. H. Gotlib & C. L. Hammen (Eds.), *Handbook of depression* (pp. 219–244). New York: Guilford Press.

Davies, P. T., Sturge-Apple, M., Cicchetti, D., Manning, L. G., & Zale, E. (2009). Children's patterns of emotional reactivity to conflict as explanatory mechanisms in links between interpartner aggression and child physiological functioning. *Journal of Child Psychology and Psychiatry, 50,* 1384–1391.

Davis, A. M., Bennett, K. J., Befort, C., & Nollen, N. (2011). Obesity and related health behaviors among urban and rural children in the United States: Data from the national health and nutrition examination survey 2003–2004 and 2005–2006. *Journal of Pediatric Psychology, 36,* 669–676.

Davis, E. P., Glynn, L. M., Waffarn, F., & Sandman, C. A. (2011). Prenatal maternal stress programs infant stress regulation. *Journal of Child Psychology and Psychiatry, 52,* 119–129.

Davis, N., Barquero, L., Compton, D. L., Fuchs, L. S., Fuchs, D., Gore, J. C., & Anderson, A. W. (2011). Functional correlates of children's responsiveness to intervention. *Developmental Neuropsychology, 36,* 288–301.

Davis, O. S. P., Arden, R., & Plomin, R. (2008). *g* in middle childhood: Moderate genetic and shared environmental influence using diverse measures of general cognitive ability at 7, 9, and 10 years in a large population sample of twins. *Intelligence, 36,* 68–80.

Daviss, W. B. (2008). A review of co-morbid depression in pediatric ADHD: Etiologies, phenomenology, and treatment. *Journal of Child and Adolescent Psychopharmacology, 18,* 565–571.

Dawson, G. (1996). Neuropsychology of autism: A report on the state of the science. *Journal of Autism and Developmental Disorders, 2,* 179–181.

Dawson, G. (2008). Early behavioral intervention, brain plasticity, and the prevention of autism spectrum disorder. *Development and Psychopathology, 20,* 775–803.

Dawson, G. (2010). *Autism Treatment Network: Improving the quality of medical care for children with ASD.* Presentation to the IACC on the Autism Treatment Network (ATN), April 30, 2010, Washington, DC. Retrieved from http://iacc.hhs.gov/events/2010/full-committee-mtg-minutes-april30.shtml#geraldine-dawson

Dawson, G., & Toth, K. (2006). Autism spectrum disorders. In D. Cicchetti & D. J. Cohen (Eds.), *Developmental psychopathology: Vol. 3. Risk, disorder, and adaptation* (2nd ed., pp. 317–357). Hoboken, NJ: Wiley.

Dawson, G., Frey, K., Panagiotides, H., Osterling, J., & Hessl, D. (1997). Infants of depressed mothers exhibit atypical frontal brain activity: A replication and extension of previous findings. *Journal of Child Psychology and Psychiatry, 38,* 179–186.

Dawson, G., Jones, E. J. H., Merkle, K., Venema, K., Lowy, R., Faja, S., … Webb, S. J. (2012). Early behavioral intervention is associated with normalized brain activity in young children with autism. *Journal of the American Academy of Child & Adolescent Psychiatry, 51,* 1150–1159.

Dawson, G., Munson, J., Webb, S. J., Nalty, T., Abbott, R., & Toth, K. (2007). Rate of head growth decelerates and symptoms worsen in the second year of life in autism. *Biological Psychiatry, 15,* 458–464.

Dawson, G., Rogers, S., Munson, J., Smith, M., Winter, J., Greenson J., … Varley, J. (2010). Randomized, controlled trial of an intervention for toddlers with autism: The Early Start Denver Model. *Pediatrics, 125,* e17–e23.

Dawson, G., Webb, S. J., & McPartland, J. (2005). Understanding the nature of face processing impairment in autism: Insights from behavioral and electrophysiological studies. *Developmental Neuropsychology, 27,* 403–424.

Dawson, G., Webb, S., Schellenberg, G. D., Dager, S., Friedman, S., Aylward, E., & Richards, T. (2002). Defining the broader phenotype of autism: Genetic, brain, and behavioral perspectives. *Development and Psychopathology, 14,* 581–611.

Dawson, M., Soulieres, I., Gernsbacher, M. A., & Mottron, L. (2007). The level and nature of autistic intelligence. *Psychological Science, 18,* 657–662.

Day, N. L., Leech, S. L., Richardson, G. A., Cornelius, M. D., Robles, N., & Larkby, C. (2002). Prenatal alcohol exposure predicts continued deficits in offspring size at 14 years of age. *Alcoholism: Clinical and Experimental Research, 26,* 1584–1591.

De Bellis, M. D., Keshavan, M. S., Frustaci, K., Shifflett, H., Iyengar, S., Beers, S. R., & Hall, J. (2002). Superior temporal gyrus volumes in maltreated children and adolescents with PTSD. *Biological Psychiatry, 51,* 544–552.

De Bellis, M. D., Keshavan, M. S., Shifflett, H., Iyengar, S., Dahl, R. E., Axelson, D. A., & Ryan, N. D. (2002). Superior temporal gyrus volumes in pediatric generalized anxiety disorder. *Biological Psychiatry, 51,* 553–562.

De Bolle, M., & De Fruyt, F. (2010). The tripartite model in childhood and adolescence: Future directions for developmental research. *Child Development Perspectives, 4,* 174–180.

de Koning, N. D., Moreland, F., Valenti, R. J., & Dosen, A. (2007). Feeding and eating disorders. In R. Fletcher, E. Loschen, C. Stavrakaki, & M. First (Eds.), *Diagnostic manual—intellectual disability: A textbook of diagnosis of mental disorders in persons with intellectual disability* (pp. 145–155). Kingston, NY: National Association for the Dually Diagnosed.

de Lacy, N., & King, B. H. (2013). Revisiting the relationship between autism and schizophrenia: Toward an integrated neurobiology. *Annual Review of Clinical Psychology, 9,* 555–587.

De Los Reyes, A., & Kazdin, A. E. (2005). Informant discrepancies in the assessment of childhood psychopathology: A critical review, theoretical framework,

and recommendations for further study. *Psychological Bulletin, 131,* 483–509.

De Los Reyes, A., Thomas, S. A., Goodman, K. L., & Kundey, S. M. A. (2013). Principles underlying the use of multiple informants' reports. *Annual Review of Clinical Psychology, 9,* 123–149.

de Onis, M., Blössner, M., & Borghi, E. (2010). Global prevalence and trends of overweight and obesity among preschool children. *American Journal of Clinical Nutrition, 92,* 1257–1264.

de Ruiter, K. P., Dekker, M. C., Douma, J. C. H., Verhulst, F. C., & Koot, H. M. (2008). Development of parent- and teacher-reported emotional and behavioural problems in young people with intellectual disabilities: Does level of intellectual disability matter? *Journal of Applied Research in Intellectual Disabilities, 21,* 70–80.

Dean, K. L., Langley, A. K., Kataoka, S. H., Jaycox, L. H., Wong, M., & Stein, B. D. (2008). School-based disaster mental health services: Clinical, policy, and community challenges. *Professional Psychology: Research and Practice, 39,* 52–57.

Dean, R. R., Kelsey, J. E., Heller, M. R., & Ciaranello, R. D. (1993). Structural foundations of illness and treatment: Receptors. In D. L. Dunner (Ed.), *Current psychiatric therapy.* Philadelphia: Saunders.

Deater-Deckard, K., & Dodge, K. A. (1997). Externalizing behavior problems and discipline revisited: Nonlinear effects and variation by culture, context, and gender. *Psychological Inquiry, 8,* 161–175.

Deater-Deckard, K., Mullineaux, P. Y., Beekman, C., Petrill, S. A., Schatschneider, C., & Thompson, L. A. (2009). Conduct problems, IQ, and household chaos: A longitudinal multi-informant study. *Journal of Child Psychology and Psychiatry, 50,* 1301–1308.

Defoe, I. N., Keijsers, L., Hawk, S. T., Branje, S., Semon Dubas, J., Buist, K., Frijns, T. et al. (2013). Siblings versus parents and friends: Longitudinal linkages to adolescent externalizing problems. *Journal of Child Psychology and Psychiatry, 54,* 881–889.

Degnan, K. A., Almas, A. N., & Fox, N. A. (2010). Temperament and the environment in the etiology of childhood anxiety. *Journal of Child Psychology and Psychiatry, 51,* 497–517.

DeGrandpre, R. J. (2000). A science of meaning: Can behaviorism bring meaning to psychological science? *American Psychologist, 55,* 721–739.

Del'Homme, M., Kim, T. S., Loo, S. K., Yang, M. H., & Smalley, S. L. (2007). Familial association and frequency of learning disabilities in ADHD sibling pair families. *Journal of Abnormal Child Psychology, 35,* 55–62.

DelBello, M. P., Carlson, G. A., Tohen, M., Bromet, E. J., Schwiers, M., & Strakowski, S. M. (2003). Rates and predictors of developing a manic or hypomanic episode 1 to 2 years following a first hospitalization for major depression with psychotic features. *Journal of Child and Adolescent Psychopharmacology, 13,* 173–185.

DelBello, M. P., Hanseman, D., Adler, C. M., Fleck, D. E., & Strakowski, S. M. (2007). Twelve-month outcome of adolescents with bipolar disorder following first hospitalization for a manic or mixed episode. *American Journal of Psychiatry, 164,* 582–590.

Denzin, N. K., & Lincoln, Y. S. (Eds.). (2011). *The Sage handbook of qualitative research* (4th ed.). Thousand Oaks, CA: Sage.

Depla, M., ten Have, M. L., van Balkom, A. J. L. M., de Graaf, R. (2008). Specific fears and phobias in the general population: Results from the Netherlands Mental Health Survey and Incidence Study (NEMESIS). *Social Psychiatry and Psychiatric Epidemiology, 43,* 200–208.

Deren, D. M. (1996). *A childhood without laughter.* Retrieved from http://members.aol.com/depress/children/htm#Introduction

Derosier, M. E., Swick, D. C., Davis, N. O., McMillen, J. S., & Matthews, R. (2010). The efficacy of a social skills group intervention for improving social behaviors in children with high functioning autism spectrum disorders. *Journal of Autism and Developmental Disorders, 41,* 1033–1043.

Dervic, K., Brent, D. A., & Oquendo, M. A. (2008) Completed suicide in childhood. *Psychiatric Clinics of North America, 31,* 271–291.

Desmond, A. J., & Moore, J. (1991). *Darwin.* New York: Warner Books.

Despert, J. L. (1955). Differential diagnosis between obsessive-compulsive neurosis and schizophrenia in children. In P. Hoch & J. Zubins (Eds.), *Psychopathology of childhood* (pp. 241–253). New York: Grune & Stratton.

Devers, P. L., Cronister, A., Ormond, K. E., Facio, F., Brasington, C. K., & Flodman, P. (2013). Noninvasive prenatal testing/noninvasive prenatal diagnosis: The position of the national society of genetic counselors. *Journal of Genetic Counseling, 22,* 291–295.

Devlin, B., Daniels, M., & Roeder, K. (1997). The heritability of IQ. *Nature, 388,* 468–471.

Diamond, A. (2005). Attention-deficit disorder (attention-deficit/hyperactivity disorder without hyperactivity): A neurobiologically and behaviorally distinct disorder from attention-deficit/hyperactivity disorder (with hyperactivity). *Development and Psychopathology, 17,* 808–825.

Diamond, A. (2012). Activities and programs that improve children's executive functions. *Current Directions in Psychological Science, 21,* 335–341.

Dick, D. (2007). Identification of genes influencing a spectrum of externalizing psychopathology. *Current Directions in Psychological Science, 16,* 331–335.

Dick, D. M., Aliev, F., Latendresse, S. J., Hickman, M., Heron, J., Macleod, J., … Kendler, K. S. (2013). Adolescent alcohol use is predicted by childhood temperament factors before age 5, with mediation through personality and peers. *Alcoholism: Clinical and Experimental Research, 37,* 2108–2117.

Dickens, W. T., & Flynn, J. R. (2006). Black Americans reduce the racial IQ gap: Evidence from standardization samples. *Psychological Science, 17,* 913–920.

Dickson, H., Laurens, K. R., Cullen A. E., & Hodgins, S. (2012). Meta-analyses of cognitive and motor function in youth aged 16 years and younger who subsequently develop schizophrenia. *Psychological Medicine, 42,* 743–755.

DiClemente, C. C., Marinilli, A. S., Singh, M., & Bellino, L. E. (2001). The role of feedback in the process of health behavior change. *American Journal of Health Behavior, 25,* 217–227.

Didden, R., Sigafoos, J., Korzilius, H., Baas, A., Lancioni, G. E., O'Reilly, M. F., & Curfs, L. M. G. (2009). Form and function of communicative behaviours in individuals with Angelman syndrome. *Journal of Applied Research in Intellectual Disabilities, 22,* 526–537.

Dillon, K. M. (1993). Facilitated communication, autism, and Ouija. *Skeptical Inquirer, 17,* 281–287.

DiPasquale, L. D., & Petrie, T. A. (2013). Prevalence of disordered eating: A comparison of male and female collegiate athletes and nonathletes. *Journal of Clinical Sport Psychology, 7,* 186–197.

Dishion, T. J., & Andrews, D. W. (1995). Preventing escalation in problem behaviors with high-risk young adolescents: Immediate and 1-year outcomes. *Journal of Consulting and Clinical Psychology, 63,* 538–548.

Dishion, T. J., Brennan, L. M., Shaw, D. S., McEachern, A. D., Wilson, M. N., & Jo, B. (2014). Prevention of problem behavior through annual family check-ups in early childhood: Intervention effects from home to early elementary school. *Journal of Abnormal Child Psychology, 42,* 343–354.

Dishion, T. J., Bullock, B. M., & Granic, I. (2002). Pragmatism in modeling peer influence: Dynamics, outcomes and change processes. *Development and Psychopathology, 14,* 969–981.

Dishion, T. J., & Dodge, K. A. (2005). Peer contagion in interventions for children and adolescents: Moving toward an understanding of the ecology and dynamics of change. *Journal of Abnormal Child Psychology, 33,* 395–400.

Dishion, T. J., & Granic, I. (2004). Naturalistic observation of relationship processes. In S. N. Haynes & E. M. Heiby (Eds.), *Comprehensive handbook of psychological assessment: Vol. 3. Behavioral assessment* (pp. 143–161). New York: Wiley.

Dishion, T. J., & Kavanagh, K. (2003). *Intervening in adolescent problem behavior: A family-centered approach.* New York: Guilford Press.

Dishion, T. J., & Patterson, G. R. (1992). Age effects in parent training outcome. *Behavior Therapy, 23,* 719–729.

Dishion, T. J., & Patterson, G. R. (2006). The development and ecology of antisocial behavior in children and adolescents. In D. Cicchetti & D. J. Cohen (Eds.), *Developmental psychopathology: Vol. 3. Risk, disorder, and adaptation* (2nd ed., pp. 503–541). New York: Wiley.

Dishion, T. J., & Stormshak, E. A. (2007a). Ethical and professional standards in child and family interventions. In T. J. Dishion & E. A. Stormshak, *Intervening in children's lives: An ecological, family-centered approach to mental health care* (pp. 241–264). Washington, DC: APA Books.

Dishion, T. J., & Stormshak, E. (2007b). *Intervening in children's lives: An ecological, family-centered approach to mental health care.* Washington, DC: APA Books.

Dissanayake, C., & Sigman, M. (2000). Attachment and emotional responsiveness in children with autism. *International Review of Research in Mental Retardation, 23,* 239–266.

Dodge, K. A. (2009). Mechanisms of gene-environment interaction effects in the development of conduct disorder. *Perspectives on Psychological Science, 4,* 408–414.

Dodge, K. A. (2011). Context matters in child and family policy. *Child Development, 82,* 433–442.

Dodge, K. A., Coie, J. D., & Lynam, D. (2006). Aggression and antisocial behavior in youth. In N. Eisenberg, W. Damon, & R. M. Lerner (Eds.), *Handbook of child psychology: Vol. 3. Social emotional and personality development* (6th ed., pp. 719–788). Hoboken, NJ: Wiley.

Dodge, K. A., Godwin, J., & The Conduct Problems Prevention Research Group (2013). Social-information-processing patterns mediate the impact of preventive intervention on adolescent antisocial behavior. *Psychological Science, 24,* 456–465.

Dodge, K. A., & McCourt, S. N. (2010). Translating models of antisocial behavioral development into efficacious intervention policy to prevent adolescent violence. *Developmental Psychobiology, 52,* 277–285.

Dodge, K. A., & Pettit, G. S. (2003). A biopsychosocial model of the development of chronic conduct problems in adolescence. *Developmental Psychology, 39,* 349–371.

Dodge, K. A., Pettit, G. S., & Bates, J. E. (1994a). Effects of physical maltreatment on the development of peer relations. *Development and Psychopathology, 6,* 43–55.

Dodge, K. A., Pettit, G. S., & Bates, J. E. (1994b). Socialization mediators of the relation between socioeconomic status and child conduct problems. *Child Development, 65,* 649–665.

Doerfler, L. A., Connor, D. F., Volungis, A. M., & Toscano, P. F. (2007). Panic disorder in clinically referred children and adolescents. *Child Psychiatry and Human Development, 38,* 57–71.

Domitrovich, C. E., Bradshaw, C. P., Greenberg, M. T., Embry, D., Poduska, J. M., & Ialongo, N. S. (2010). Integrated models of school-based prevention: Logic and theory. *Psychology in the Schools, 47,* 71–88.

Dong, Q., Yang, B., & Ollendick, T. H. (1994). Fears in Chinese children and adolescents and their relations to anxiety and depression. *Journal of Child Psychology and Psychiatry, 35,* 351–363.

Donnellan, A. M. (1988, February). Our old ways just aren't working. *Dialect* [Newsletter of the Saskatchewan Association for the Mentally Retarded]. Available from Saskatchewan Association for Community Living, 3031 Louise Street, Saskatoon, SK S7J 3L1.

D'Onofrio, B. M., Goodnight, J. A., Van Hulle, C. A., Rodgers, J. L., Rathouz, P. J., Waldman, I. D., & Lahey, B. B. (2009). Maternal age at childbirth and offspring disruptive behaviors: Testing the causal hypothesis. *Journal of Child Psychology and Psychiatry, 50,* 1018–1028.

D'Onofrio, B. M., Singh. A. L., Iliadou, A., Lambe, M., Hultman, C. M., Grann, M., … Lichtenstein, P. (2010a). Familial confounding of the association between maternal smoking during pregnancy and offspring criminality: A population-based study in Sweden. *Archives of General Psychiatry, 67,* 529–538.

D'Onofrio, B. M., Singh, A. L., Iliadou, A., Lambe, M., Hultman, C. M., Neiderhiser, J. M., … Lichtenstein, P. (2010b). A quasi-experimental study of maternal smoking during pregnancy and offspring academic achievement. *Child Development, 81,* 80–100.

D'Onofrio, B. M., Van Hulle, C. A., Waldman, I. D., Rodgers, J. L., Harden, K. P., Rathouz, P. J., & Lahey, B. B. (2008). Smoking during pregnancy and offspring externalizing problems: An exploration of genetic and environmental confounds. *Development and Psychopathology, 20,* 139–164.

D'Onofrio, B. M., Van Hulle, C. A., Waldman, I. D., Rodgers, J. L., Rathouz, P. J., & Lahey, B. B. (2007). Causal inferences regarding prenatal alcohol exposure and childhood externalizing problems. *Archives of General Psychiatry, 64,* 1296–1304.

Donohue, B., Hersen, M., & Ammerman, R. T. (2000). Historical overview. In M. Hersen & R. Ammerman (Eds.), *Abnormal child psychology* (2nd ed., pp. 3–14). Mahwah, NJ: Erlbaum.

Doshi, J. A., Hodgkins, P., Kahle, J., Sikirica, V., Cangelosi, M. J., Setyawan, J., … Neumann, P. J. (2012). Economic impact of childhood and adult attention-deficit/hyperactivity disorder in the United States. *Journal of the American Academy of Child and Adolescent Psychiatry, 51,* 990–1002.

dosReis, S., Barksdale, C. L., Sherman, A., Maloney, K., & Charach, A. (2010). Stigmatizing experiences of parents of children with a new diagnosis of ADHD. *Psychiatric Services, 61,* 811–816.

Dougherty, L. R., Smith, V. C., Bufferd, S. J., Stringaris, A., Leibenluft, E., Carlson, G. A., & Klein, D. N. (2013). Preschool irritability: Longitudinal associations with psychiatric disorders at age 6 and parental psychopathology. *Journal of the American Academy of Child & Adolescent Psychiatry, 52,* 1304–1313.

Douglas, V. I. (1972). Stop, look, and listen: The problem of sustained attention and impulse control in hyperactive and normal children. *Canadian Journal of Behavioural Science, 4,* 259–282.

Douglas, V. I. (1999). Cognitive control processes in attention deficit/hyperactivity disorder. In H. C. Quay & A. E. Hogan (Eds.), *Handbook of disruptive behavior disorders* (pp. 105–138). New York: Kluwer/Plenum Press.

Dowell, K. A., & Ogles, B. M. (2010). The effects of parent participation on child psychotherapy outcome: A meta-analytic review. *Journal of Clinical Child & Adolescent Psychology, 39,* 151–162.

Dowling, C. (1992, January 20). Rescuing your child from depression. *New York Magazine,* 45–51.

Dowling, C. G., & Hollister, A. (1997, May). An epidemic of sneezing and wheezing. *Life Magazine,* 79.

Down, J. L. H. (1866). Observations on an ethnic classification of idiots. *Clinical Lectures and Reports (London Hospital), 3,* 259–262.

Dozois, D. J. A. (1997). *A developmental cognitive model of unipolar major depression.* Unpublished manuscript, Department of Psychology, University of Calgary, Calgary, Alberta T2N 1N4.

Drabick, D. A. G., & Kendall, P. C. (2010). Developmental psychopathology and the diagnosis of mental health problems among youth. *Clinical Psychology: Science and Practice, 17,* 272–280.

Drabick, D. A. G., Ollendick, T. H., & Bubier, J. L. (2010). Co-occurrence of ODD and anxiety: Shared risk processes and evidence for a dual pathway model. *Clinical Psychology: Science and Practice, 17,* 307–318.

Drotar, D. (1999). Child neglect in the family context: Challenges and opportunities for management in pediatric settings. *Children's Health Care, 28,* 109–121.

Drotar, D. (2006). *Psychological interventions in childhood chronic illness.* Washington, DC: American Psychological Association.

Drotar, D. (2013). Strategies of adherence promotion in the management of pediatric chronic conditions. *Journal of Developmental and Behavioral Pediatrics, 34,* 716–729.

Drotar, D., & Bonner, M. S. (2009). Influences on adherence to pediatric asthma treatment: A review of correlates and predictors. *Journal of Developmental and Behavioral Pediatrics, 30,* 574–582.

Drury, S. S., Theall, K. P., Smyke, A. T., Keats, B. J. B. Keats, Egger, H. L., … Zeanah, C. H. (2010). Modification of depression by COMT val158met polymorphism in children exposed to early severe psychosocial deprivation. *Child Abuse & Neglect, 34,* 387–395.

Du Rocher Schudlich, T. D., Youngstrom, E. A., Calabrese, J. R., Findling, R. L. (2008). The role of family functioning in bipolar disorder in families. *Journal of Abnormal Child Psychology, 36,* 849–863.

Duax, J. M., Youngstrom, E. A., Calabrese, E. A., & Findling, R. L. (2007). Sex differences in pediatric bipolar disorder. *Journal of Clinical Psychiatry, 68,* 1565–1573.

Dubowitz, H., & Bennett, S. (2007). Physical abuse and neglect of children. *Lancet, 369*(9576), 1891–1899.

Dubowitz, H., Feigelman, S., Lane, W., & Kim, J. (2009). Pediatric primary care to help prevent child maltreatment: The Safe Environment for Every Kid (SEEK) model. *Pediatrics, 123,* 858–886.

Duerden, E. G., Oatley, H. K., Mak-Fan, K. M., McGrath, P. A. Taylor, M. J., Szatmari, P., & Roberts, S. W. (2012). Risk factors associated with self-injurious behaviors in children and adolescents with autism spectrum disorders. *Journal of Autism and Developmental Disorders, 42,* 2460–2470.

Duff, F. J., & Clarke, P. J. (2011). Practitioner review: Reading disorders: What are the effective interventions and how should they be implemented and evaluated? *Journal of Child Psychology and Psychiatry, 52,* 3–12.

Dummit, E. S., Klein, R. G., Tancer, N. K., Asche, B., Martin, J., & Fairbanks, J. A. (1997). Systematic assessment of 50 children with selective mutism. *Journal of the American Academy of Child & Adolescent Psychiatry, 36,* 653–660.

Duncan, A. B., Velasquez, S. E., & Nelson, E.-L. (2014). Videoconferencing to provide psychological services to rural children and adolescents: A review and case example. *Journal of Clinical Child & Adolescent Psychology, 43,* 115–127.

Dunlap, K. (1932). *Habits: Their making and unmaking.* New York: Liveright.

Dunning, D. L., Holmes, J., & Gathercole, S. E. (2013). Does working memory training lead to generalized improvements in children with low working memory? A randomized controlled trial. *Developmental Science, 16,* 915–925.

DuPaul, G. J., Eckert, T. L., & Vilardo, B. (2012). The effects of school-based interventions for attention-deficit hyperactivity disorder: A meta-analysis 1996-2010. *School Psychology Review, 41,* 387–412.

DuPaul, G. J., Gormley, M. J., & Laracy, S. D. (2013). Comorbidity of LD and ADHD: Implications of DSM-5 for assessment and treatment. *Journal of Learning Disabilities, 46,* 43–51.

DuPaul, G. J., & Langberg, J. M. (2014). Educational impairments in children with ADHD. In R. A. Barkley (Ed.), *Attention-deficit hyperactivity disorder: A handbook for diagnosis and treatment* (4th ed.) New York: Guilford Press.

DuPaul, G. J., & Stoner, G. (2003). *ADHD in the schools* (2nd ed.). New York: Guilford Press.

Durbin, C. E., & Shafir, D. M. (2008). Emotion regulation and risk for depression. In J. R. Z. Abela & B. L. Hankin (Eds.), *Handbook of depression in children and adolescents* (pp. 149–176). New York: Guilford Press.

Durkin, K., & Conti-Ramsden, G. (2010). Young people with specific language impairment: A review of social and emotional functioning in adolescence. *Child Language Teaching and Therapy, 26,* 105–121.

Durlak, J. A., Weissberg, R. P., Dymnicki, A. B., Taylor, R. D., & Schellinger, K. B. (2011). The impact of enhancing students' social and emotional learning: A meta-analysis of school-based universal interventions. *Child Development, 82,* 405–432.

Dworzynski, K., Remington, A., Rijsdijk, F., Howell, P., & Plomin, R. (2007). Genetic etiology in cases of recovered and persistent stuttering in an unselected longitudinal sample of young twins. *American Journal of Speech-Language Pathology, 16,* 169–178.

Dworzynski, K., Ronald, A., Bolton, P., & Happé, F. (2012). How different are girls and boys above and below the diagnostic threshold for autism spectrum disorders? *Journal of the American Academy of Child & Adolescent Psychiatry, 51,* 788–797.

Dykens, E. M. (2013). Aging in rare intellectual disability syndromes. *Developmental Disabilities Research Reviews, 18,* 75–83.

Dykens, E. M., Cassidy, S. B., & DeVries, M. L. (2011). *Prader-Willi syndrome.* New York: Guilford Press.

Dykens, E. M., Hodapp, R. M., & Evans, D. W. (2006). Profiles and development of adaptive behavior in children with Down syndrome. *Down Syndrome: Research & Practice, 9,* 45–50.

Dykens, E. M., & Volkmar, F. (1997). Medical conditions associated with autism. In D. J. Cohen & F. R. Volkmar (Eds.), *Handbook of autism and pervasive developmental disorders* (pp. 388–410). New York: Wiley.

Earleywine, M. (2009). *Substance use problems.* Ashland, OH: Hogrefe & Huber.

Eaves, L. C., & Ho, H. H. (2008). Young adult outcome of autism spectrum disorders. *Journal of Autism and Developmental Disorders, 38,* 739–747.

Eaves, L., Silberg, J., & Erkanli, A. (2003). Resolving multiple epigenetic pathways to adolescent depression. *Journal of Child Psychology and Psychiatry, 44,* 1006–1014.

Ebesutani, C., Bernstein, A., Chorpita, B. F., & Weisz, J. R. (2012). A transportable assessment protocol for prescribing youth psychosocial treatments in real-world settings: Reducing assessment burden via self-report scales. Reducing assessment burden via self-report scales. *Psychological Assessment, 24,* 141–155.

Ebesutani, C., Bernstein, A., Nakamura, B. J., Chorpita, B. F., Higa-McMillan, C. K., … The Research Network on Youth Mental Health (2010). Concurrent validity of the Child Behavior Checklist DSM-oriented scales: Correspondence with DSM diagnoses and comparison to syndrome scales. *Journal of Psychopathology and Behavioral Assessment, 32,* 373–384.

Ebstein, R. P., Novick, O., Umansky, R., Priel, B., Osher, Y., Blaine, D., … Belmaker, R. H. (1996). Dopamine D4 receptor (D4DR) exon III polymorphism associated with the human personality trait of novelty seeking. *Nature Genetics, 12,* 78–80.

Eckenrode, J., Campa, M., Luckey, D., Henderson, C., Cole, R., Kitzman, H., … Olds, D. (2010). Long-term effects of prenatal and infancy nurse home visitation on the life course of youths: 19-year follow-up of a randomized trial. *Archives* of *Pediatrics & Adolescent Medicine, 164*, 9–15.

Eddy, K. T., Crosby, R. D., Keel, P. K., Wonderlich, S. A., le Grange, D., Hill, L., ... Mitchell, J. E. (2009). Empirical identification and validation of eating disorder phenotypes in a multisite clinical sample. *Journal of Nervous and Mental Disease, 197*, 41–49.

Eddy, K. T., Doyle, A. C., Hoste, R. R., Herzog, D. B., & le Grange, D. (2008). Eating disorder not otherwise specified in adolescents. *Journal of the American Academy of Child & Adolescent Psychiatry, 47*, 156–164.

Edelbrock, C., Crnic, K., & Bohnert, A. (1999). Interviewing as communication: An alternative way of administering the Diagnostic Interview Schedule for Children. *Journal of Abnormal Child Psychology, 27*, 447–453.

Eden, G. F., & Moats, L. (2002). The role of neuroscience in the remediation of students with dyslexia. *Nature Neuroscience [Special issue: Beyond the bench: The practical promise of neuroscience], 5*, 1080–1084.

Eden, G. F., VanMeter, J. W., Rumsey, J. M., Maisog, J. M., Woods, R. P., & Zeffiro, T. A. (1996). Abnormal processing of visual motion in dyslexia revealed by functional brain imaging. *Nature, 382*, 66–69.

Edleson, J. L. (1999). The overlap between child maltreatment and woman battering. *Violence Against Women, 5*, 134–154.

Education for All Handicapped Children Act. (1975). *Public law 94–142*. Washington, DC: Government Printing Office.

Edwards, A. C., Dodge, K. A., Latendresse, S. J., Lansford, J. E., Bates, J. E., Pettit, G. S., Dick, D. M. (2010). MAOA-uVNTR and early physical discipline interact to influence delinquent behavior. *Journal of Child Psychology and Psychiatry, 51*, 679–687.

Edwards, S. L., Rapee, R. M., & Kennedy, S. (2010). Prediction of anxiety symptoms in preschool-aged children: Examination of maternal and paternal perspectives. *Journal of Child Psychology and Psychiatry, 51*, 313–321.

Egeland, B., Yates, T., Appleyard, K., & van Dulmen, M. (2002). The long-term consequences of maltreatment in the early years: A developmental pathway model to antisocial behavior. *Children's Services: Social Policy, Research, & Practice, 5*, 249–260.

Egger, H. L., & Angold A. (2006). Common emotional and behavioral disorders in preschool children: Presentation, nosology, and epidemiology. *Journal of Child Psychology and Psychiatry, 47*, 313–337.

Egger, H. L., Costello, E. J., Erkanli, A., & Angold, A. (1999). Somatic complaints and psychopathology in children and adolescents: Stomach aches, musculoskeletal pains, and headaches. *Journal of the American Academy of Child & Adolescent Psychiatry, 38*, 852–860.

Egley, A., Jr., & Howell, J. C. (2013). Highlights of the 2011 National Youth Gang Survey. *OJJDP Fact Sheet* (September). Washington, DC: Department of Justice, Office of Juvenile Justice and Delinquency Prevention. Retrieved from http://www.ojjdp.gov/pubs/242884.pdf

Ehntholt, K. A., & Yule, W. (2006). Practitioner review: Assessment and treatment of refugee children and adolescents who have experienced war-related trauma. *Journal of Child Psychology and Psychiatry, 47*, 1197–1210.

Ehringer, M. A., Rhee, S. H., Young, S., Corley, R., & Hewitt, J. K. (2006). Genetic and environmental contributions to common psychopathologies of childhood and adolescence: A study of twins and their siblings. *Journal of Abnormal Child Psychology, 34*, 1–17.

Ehrmantrout, N., Allen, N. B., Leve, C., Davis, B., & Sheeber, L. (2011). Adolescent recognition of parental affect: Influence of depressive symptoms. *Journal of Abnormal Psychology, 120*, 628–634.

Eikeseth, S., Smith, T., Jahr, E., & Eldevik, S. (2007). Outcome for children with autism who began behavioral treatment between ages 4 and 7: A comparison controlled study. *Behavior Modification, 31*, 264–278.

Einfeld, S. L. (2005). Behaviour problems in children with genetic disorders causing intellectual disability. *Educational Psychology, 25*, 341–346.

Einfeld, S. L., Ellis, L. A., & Emerson, E. (2011). Comorbidity of intellectual disability and mental disorder in children and adolescents: A systematic review. *Journal of Intellectual and Developmental Disability, 36*, 137–143.

Einfeld, S. L., Gray, K. M., Ellis, L. A., Taffe, J., Emerson, E., Tonge, B. J., & Horstead, S. K. (2010). Intellectual disability modifies gender effects on disruptive behaviors. *Journal of Mental Health Research in Intellectual Disabilities, 3*, 177–189.

Eisenberg, L. (2007). Commentary with a historical perspective by a child psychiatrist: When "ADHD" was the "brain-damaged child." *Journal of Child and Adolescent Psychopharmacology, 17*, 279–283.

Eisenberg, M. E., Berge, J. M., Fulkerson, J. A., & Neumark-Sztainer, D. (2012). Associations between hurtful weight-related comments by family and significant other and the development of disordered eating behaviors in young adults. *Journal of Behavioral Medicine, 35*, 500–508.

Eisenberg, M., Neumark-Sztainer, D., & Story, M. (2003). Associations of weight-based teasing and emotional well-being among adolescents. *Archives of Pediatric and Adolescent Medicine, 157*, 733–738.

Eisenberg, N., Smith, C. L., & Spinrad, T. L. (2011). *Effortful control: Relations with emotion regulation, adjustment, and socialization in childhood*. New York: Guilford Press.

Eley, T. C., & Lau, J. Y. F. (2005). Genetics and the family environment. In J. L. Hudson & R. M. Rapee (Eds.), *Psychopathology and the family* (pp. 3–19). New York: Elsevier.

Eley, T. C., Lichtenstein, P., & Moffitt, T. E. (2003). A longitudinal behavioral genetic analysis of the etiology of aggressive and nonaggressive antisocial behavior. *Development and Psychopathology, 15*, 383–402.

Eley, T. C., Napolitano, M., Lau, J. Y. F., & Gregory, A. M. (2010). Does childhood anxiety evoke maternal control? A genetically informed study. *Journal of Child Psychology and Psychiatry, 51*, 772–779.

Eley, T. C., & Stevenson, J. (2000). Specific life events and chronic experiences differentially associated with depression and anxiety in young twins. *Journal of Abnormal Child Psychology, 28*, 383–394.

El-Fishawy, P., & State, M. W. (2010). The genetics of autism: Key issues, recent findings, and clinical implications. *Psychiatric Clinics of North America, 33*, 83–105.

Elkin, T. D., & Stoppelbein, L. (2008). Evidence-based treatments for children with chronic illnesses. In R. G. Steele, T. D. Elkin, & M. C. Roberts (Eds.), *Handbook of evidence-based therapies for children and adolescents: Bridging science and practice. Issues in clinical child psychology* (pp. 297–309). New York: Springer.

Elliott, D. S., Huizinga, D., & Ageton, S. S. (1985). *Explaining delinquency and drug use*. Beverly Hills, CA: Sage.

Elliott, D. S., Huizinga, D., & Menard, S. (1989). *Multiple problem youth: Delinquency, substance use, and mental health problems*. New York: Springer.

Elliott, M., Browne, K., & Kilcoyne, J. (1995). Child sexual abuse prevention: What offenders tell us. *Child Abuse and Neglect, 19*, 579–594.

Ellis, B. J., & Boyce, W. T. (2011). Special section editorial: Differential susceptibility to the environment: Toward an understanding of sensitivity to developmental experiences and context. *Development and Psychopathology, 23*, 1–5.

Ellis, B. J., Boyce, W. T., Belsky, J., Bakermans-Kranenburg, M. J., & Van Ijzendoorn, M. H. (2011). Differential susceptibility to the environment: An evolutionary–neurodevelopmental theory. *Development and Psychopathology, 23*, 7–28.

Ellis, D. A., Templin, T., Naar-King, S., Frey, M. A., Cunningham, P. B., Podolski, C., & Cakan, N. (2007). Multisystemic therapy for adolescents with poorly controlled type I diabetes: Stability of treatment effects in a randomized controlled trial. *Journal of Consulting and Clinical Psychology, 75*, 168–174.

Ellis, D. M., & Hudson, J. L. (2010). The metacognitive model of generalized anxiety disorder in children and adolescents. *Clinical Child and Family Psychology Review, 13*, 151–163.

Elsabbagh, M., Divan, G., Koh, Y-J., Kim, Y. S., Kauchali, S., Marcin, C., ... Fombonne, E. (2012). Global prevalence of autism and other pervasive developmental disorders. *Autism Research, 5*, 160–179.

El-Sheikh, M., Bub, K. L., Kelly, R. J., & Buckhalt, J. A. (2013). Children's sleep and adjustment: A residualized change analysis. *Developmental Psychology, 49*, 1591–1601.

El-Sheikh, M., & Erath, S. A. (2011). Family conflict, autonomic nervous system functioning, and child adaptation: State of the science and future directions. *Development and Psychopathology, 23,* 703–721.

El-Sheikh M., Keiley, M., Erath, S., & Dyer, J. W. (2013). Marital conflict and growth in children's internalizing symptoms: The role of autonomic nervous system activity. *Developmental Psychology, 49,* 92–108.

El-Sheikh, M., Kelly, R., & Rauer, A. (2013). Quick to berate, slow to sleep: Inter-partner psychological conflict, mental health, and sleep. *Health Psychology, 32,* 1057–1066.

Ember, C. R., & Ember, M. (1994). War, socialization, and interpersonal violence: A cross-cultural study. *Journal of Conflict Resolution, 38,* 620–646.

Eme, R. F. (2007). Sex differences in child-onset, life-course persistent conduct disorder: A review of biological influences. *Clinical Psychology Review, 27,* 607–627.

Emerson, E. (2012). Deprivation, ethnicity, and the prevalence of intellectual and developmental disabilities. *Journal of Epidemiology and Community Health, 66,* 218–224.

Emery, R. E. (1999). Postdivorce family life for children: An overview of research and some implications for policy. In R. A. Thompson & P. R. Amato (Eds.), *The postdivorce family: Children, parenting, and society* (pp. 3–27). Thousand Oaks, CA: Sage.

Eminson, D. M. (2007). Medically unexplained symptoms in children and adolescents. *Clinical Psychology Review, 27,* 855–871.

Ensor, R., Marks, A., Jacobs, L., & Hughes, C. (2010). Trajectories of antisocial behavior towards siblings predict antisocial behavior towards peers. *Journal of Child Psychology and Psychiatry, 51,* 1208–1216.

Erhardt, D., & Hinshaw, S. P. (1994). Initial sociometric impressions of attention-deficit hyperactivity disorder and comparison boys: Predictions from social behaviors and from nonbehavioral variables. *Journal of Consulting and Clinical Psychology, 62,* 833–842.

Erickson, M. R., & Egeland, B. (2002). Child neglect. In John E. B. Myers, L. Berliner, J. Briere, C. T. Hendrix, C. Jenny, & T. A. Reid (Eds.), *The APSAC handbook on child maltreatment* (pp. 3–20). Thousand Oaks, CA: Sage.

Erlich, N., Lipp, O. V., & Slaughter, V. (2013). Of hissing snakes and angry voices: Human infants are differentially responsive to evolutionary fear-relevant sounds. *Developmental Science, 16,* 894–904.

Erskine, H. E., Ferrari, A. J., Nelson, P., Polanczyk, G. V., Flaxman, A. D., Vos, T., … Scott, J. G. (2013). Research review: Epidemiological modelling of attention-deficit/hyperactivity disorder and conduct disorder for the Global Burden of Disease Study 2010. *Journal of Child Psychology and Psychiatry, 54,* 1263–1274.

Esbjørn, B. H., Lønfeldt, N. N., Nielsen, S. K., Reinholdt-Dunne, M. L., Sømhovd, M. J., & Cartwright-Hatton, S. (2014). Meta-worry, worry, and anxiety in children and adolescents: Relationships and interactions. *Journal of Clinical Child & Adolescent Psychology.* Advance online

publication. doi:10.1080/15374416.2013.873980.

Essau, C. A. (2007). Course and outcome of somatoform disorders in non-referred adolescents. *Psychosomatics, 48,* 502–509.

Essau, C. A., Conradt, J., & Petermann, F. (1999). Frequency and comorbidity of social phobia and social fears in adolescents. *Behaviour Research and Therapy, 37,* 831–843.

Essau, C. A., Conradt, J., & Petermann, F. (2000). Frequency, comorbidity, and psychosocial impairment of specific phobia in adolescents. *Journal of Clinical Child Psychology, 29,* 221–231.

Essex, M. J., Klein, M.H., Slattery, M. J., Goldsmith, H. H., & Kalin, N. H. (2010). Early risk factors and developmental pathways to chronic high inhibition and social anxiety disorder in adolescence. *American Journal of Psychiatry, 167,* 40–46.

Estes, A., Vismara, L., Mercado, C., Fitzpatrick, A., Elder, L., Greenson, J., … Rogers, S. (2014). The impact of parent-delivered intervention on parents of very young children with autism. *Journal of Autism and Developmental Disorders, 44,* 353–365.

Evans, D. W., Gray, F. L., & Leckman, J. F. (1999). The rituals, fears and phobias of young children: Insights from development, psychopathology and neurobiology. *Child Psychiatry and Human Development, 29,* 261–276.

Evans, D. W., & Leckman, J. F. (2006). Origins of obsessive-compulsive disorder: Developmental and evolutionary perspectives. In D. Cicchetti & D. J. Cohen (Eds.), *Developmental psychopathology: Vol. 3. Risk, disorder, and adaptation* (2nd ed., pp. 404–435). New York: Wiley.

Evans, D. W., Leckman, J. F., Carter, A., Reznick, J. S., Henshaw, D., King, R. A., & Pauls, D. (1997). Ritual, habit, and perfectionism: The prevalence and development of compulsive-like behavior in normal young children. *Child Development, 68,* 58–68.

Evans, G. W., Li, D., Whipple, S. S. (2013). Cumulative risk and child development. *Psychological Bulletin, 139,* 1342–1396.

Evans, S., Owens, J. S., Bunford, N. (2013). Evidence-based psychosocial treatments for children and adolescents with attention-deficit/hyperactivity disorder. *Journal of Clinical Child & Adolescent Psychology.* Advance online publication. doi:10.1080/15374416.2013.850700.

Eyberg, S. M., Nelson, M. M., & Boggs, S. R. (2008). Evidence-based psychosocial treatments for children and adolescents with disruptive behavior. *Journal of Clinical Child & Adolescent Psychology, 37,* 215–237.

Fabiano, G. A., Pelham, W. E., Coles, E. K., Gnagy, E. M., Chronis-Tuscano, A., & O'Connor, B. B. (2009). A meta-analysis of behavioral treatments for attention deficit/ hyperactivity disorder. *Clinical Psychology Review, 29,* 129–140.

Fabricius, W. V., & Luecken, L. J. (2007). Postdivorce living arrangements, parent conflict, and long-term physical health correlates for children of divorce. *Journal of Family Psychology, 21,* 195–205.

Fagan, P. J., Wise, T. N., Schmidt, C. W., Jr., & Berlin, F. S. (2002). Pedophilia. *JAMA: Journal of the American Medical Association, 288,* 2458–2465.

Fair, D. A., Bathula, D., Nikolas, M. A., & Nigg, J. T. (2012). Distinct neuropsychological subgroups in typically developing youth inform heterogeneity in children with ADHD. *Proceedings of the National Academy of Sciences USA, 109,* 6769–6774.

Fair, D. A., Posner, J., Nagel, B. J., Bathula, D., Costa Dias, T. G., Mills, K. L., … Nigg, J. T. (2010). Atypical default network connectivity in youth with attention-deficit/hyperactivity disorders. *Biological Psychiatry, 68,* 1084–1091.

Fairburn, C. G., Cooper, Z., Doll, H., Norman, P., & O'Connor, M. (2000). The natural course of bulimia nervosa and binge eating disorder in young women. *Archives of General Psychiatry, 57,* 659–665.

Fairchild, G., Passamonti, L., Hurford, G., Hagan, C. C., von dem Hagen, E. A. H., van Goozen, S. H. M., … Calder, A. J. (2011). Brain structural abnormalities in early-onset and adolescent-onset conduct disorder. *American Journal of Psychiatry, 168,* 624–633.

Fairchild, G., Van Goozen, S. H. M., Calder, A. J., Stollery, S. K., & Goodyer, I. M. (2009). Deficits in facial expression recognition in male adolescents with early-onset or adolescence-onset conduct disorder. *Journal of Child Psychology and Psychiatry, 50,* 627–636.

Fairchild, S. R. (2002). Women with disabilities: The long road to equality. *Journal of Human Behavior in the Social Environment, 6,* 13–28.

Faja, S., & Dawson, G. (2013). Autism spectrum disorders. In T. P. Beauchaine & S. P. Hinshaw (Eds.), *Child and adolescent psychopathology* (2nd ed., pp. 649–684). Hoboken, NJ: Wiley.

Falicov, C. J. (2003). Culture, society and gender in depression. *Journal of Family Therapy, 25,* 371–387.

Fallucca, E., MacMaster, F. P., Haddad, J., Easter, P., Dick, R., May, G., … Rosenberg, D. R. (2011). Distinguishing between major depressive disorder and obsessive-compulsive disorder in children by measuring regional cortical thickness. *Archives of General Psychiatry, 68,* 527–533.

Famularo, R., Fenton, T., Kinscherff, R., & Augustyn, M. (1996). Psychiatric comorbidity in childhood posttraumatic stress disorder. *Child Abuse and Neglect, 20,* 953–961.

Fang, X., Brown, D. S., Florence, C. S., & Mercy, J. A. (2012). The economic burden of child maltreatment in the united states and implications for prevention. *Child Abuse & Neglect, 36,* 156–165.

Farah, M. J., Shera, D. M., Savage, J. H., Betancourt, L., Giannetta, J. M., Brodsky, N. L., … Hurt, H. (2006). Childhood poverty: Specific associations with neurocognitive development. *Brain Research, 1110,* 166–174.

Faraone, S. V. (2014). Etiologies. In R. A. Barkley (Ed.), *Attention-deficit hyperactivity disorder: A handbook for diagnosis and treatment* (4th ed.). New York: Guilford Press.

Faraone, S. V., & Buitelaar, J. (2010). Comparing the efficacy of stimulants for ADHD in children and adolescents using meta-analysis. *European Child & Adolescent Psychiatry, 19,* 353–364.

Faraone, S. V., & Mick, E. (2010). Molecular gene tics of attention deficit hyperactivity disorder. *Psychiatric Clinics of North America, 33,* 159–180.

Faraone, S. V., Biederman, J., & Mick, E. (2006). The age-dependent decline of attention deficit hyperactivity disorder: A meta-analysis of follow-up studies. *Psychological Medicine, 36,* 159–165.

Farrell, L. J., & Barrett, P. M. (2007). Prevention of childhood emotional disorders: Reducing the burden of suffering associated with anxiety and depression. *Child and Adolescent Mental Health, 12,* 58–65.

Farrington, D. P., & Ttofi, M. M. (2009). *School-based programs to reduce bullying and victimization.* Systematic review for the Campbell Collaboration Crime and Justice Group. Retrieved from www.ncjrs.gov/pdffiles1/nij/grants/229377.pdf

Fasmer, O. B., Riise, T., Eagan, T. M., Lund, A., Dilsaver, S. C. Hundal, Ø., & Oedegaard, K. J. (2011). Comorbidity of asthma with ADHD. *Journal of Attention Disorders, 15,* 564–571.

Fatemi, S. H., & Folsom, T. D. (2011). The role of fragile X mental retardation protein in major mental disorders. *Neuropharmacology, 60,* 1221–1226.

Fein, D., Barton, M., Eigsti, I-M., Kelley, E., Naigles, L., Schultz, R. T., ... Tyson, K. (2013). Optimal outcome in individuals with a history of autism. *Journal of Child Psychology and Psychiatry, 54,* 195–205.

Feinberg, M. E., Button, T. M. M., Neiderhiser, J. M., Reiss, D., & Hetherington, E. M. (2007). Parenting and adolescent antisocial behavior and depression. *Archives of General Psychiatry, 64,* 457–465.

Feldman, H. S., Jones, K. L., Lindsay, S., Slymen, D., Klonoff-Cohen, H., Kao, K., ... Chambers, C. (2012). Prenatal alcohol exposure patterns and alcohol-related birth defects and growth deficiencies: A prospective study. *Alcoholism: Clinical and Experimental Research, 36,* 670–676.

Feldman, L., Harvey, B., Holowaty, P., & Shortt, L. (1999). Alcohol use beliefs and behaviors among high school students. *Journal of Adolescent Health, 24,* 48–58.

Feldman, M. B., & Meyer, I. H. (2007). Childhood abuse and eating disorders in gay and bisexual men. *International Journal of Eating Disorders, 40,* 418–423.

Felton, R. H. (1993). Effects of instruction on the decoding skills of children with phonological-processing problems. *Journal of Learning Disabilities, 26,* 583–589.

Fergusson, D. M., Boden, J. M., & Horwood, J. (2007). Recurrence of major depression in adolescence and early adulthood, and later mental health, educational, and economic outcomes. *British Journal of Psychiatry, 191,* 335–342.

Fergusson, D. M., Boden, J. M., & Horwood, L. J. (2010). Classification of behavior disorders in adolescence: Scaling methods, predictive validity, and gender differences. *Journal of Abnormal Psychology, 119,* 699–712.

Fergusson, D. M., Boden, J. M., & Horwood, L. J. (2013). Child self-control and adult outcomes: Results from a 30-year longitudinal study. *American Journal of Child & Adolescent Psychiatry, 53,* 709–717.

Fergusson, D. M., & Horwood, L. J. (2002). Male and female offending trajectories. *Development and Psychopathology, 14,* 159–177.

Fergusson, D. M., Horwood, L. J., & Lynskey, M. T. (1993). Early dentine lead levels and subsequent cognitive and behavioural development. *Journal of Child Psychology and Psychiatry, 34,* 215–227.

Fergusson, D. M., Horwood, L. J., Miller, A. L., & Kennedy, M. A. (2011). Life stress, 5-HTTLPR and mental disorder: Findings from a 30-year longitudinal study. *British Journal of Psychiatry, 198,* 129–135.

Fergusson, D. M., Horwood, L. J., & Ridder, E. M. (2005). Show me the child at seven: The consequences of conduct problems in childhood for psychosocial functioning in adulthood. *Journal of Child Psychology and Psychiatry, 46,* 837–849.

Fergusson, D. M., Horwood, L. J., & Ridder, E. M. (2007). Conduct and attentional problems in childhood and adolescence and later substance use, abuse, and dependence: Results of a 25-year longitudinal study. *Drug and Alcohol Dependence, 88,* S14–S26.

Fergusson, D. M., McLeod, G. F. H., & Horwood, L. J. (2013). Childhood sexual abuse and adult developmental outcomes: Findings from a 30-year longitudinal study in New Zealand. *Child Abuse & Neglect, 37,* 664–674.

Fernandez-Ballesteros, R. (2004). Self-report questionnaires. In S. N. Haynes & E. M. Heiby (Eds.), *Comprehensive handbook of psychological assessment: Vol. 3. Behavioral assessment* (pp. 194–221). New York: Wiley.

Ferrer, E., Shaywitz, B. A., Holahan, J. M., Marchione, K., & Shaywitz, S. E. (2010). Uncoupling of reading and IQ over time: Empirical evidence for a definition of dyslexia. *Psychological Science, 21,* 93–101.

Ferris, T. (1998, July 20). Not rocket science. *The New Yorker, 74*(20), 4–5.

Fialko, L., Bolton, D., & Perrin, S. (2012). Applicability of a cognitive model of worry to children and adolescents. *Behaviour Research and Therapy, 50,* 341–349.

Fichman, L., Koestner, R., & Zuroff, D. C. (1996). Dependency, self-criticism, and perceptions of inferiority at summer camp: I'm even worse than you think. *Journal of Youth and Adolescence, 25,* 113–126.

Fichter, M. M., Quadflieg, N., & Hedlund, S. (2006). Twelve year course and outcome predictors of anorexia nervosa. *International Journal of Eating Disorders, 39,* 87–100.

Fidalgo, T. M., da Silveira, E. D., & da Silveira, D. X. (2008). Psychiatric comorbidity related to alcohol use among adolescents. *American Journal of Drug and Alcohol Abuse, 34,* 83–89.

Field, A. P. (2006). The behavioral inhibition system and the verbal information pathway to children's fears. *Journal of Abnormal Psychology, 115,* 742–752.

Field, A. P., Hadwin, J. A., & Lester, K. J. (2011). Information processing biases in child and adolescent anxiety: A developmental perspective. In W. K. Silverman & A. Field (Eds.), *Anxiety disorders in children and adolescents: Research, assessment, and intervention* (2nd ed., pp. 103–128). Cambridge, England: Cambridge University Press.

Fielding, D. M., & Doleys, D. M. (1988). Elimination problems: Enuresis and encopresis. In E. J. Mash & L. G. Terdal (Eds.), *Behavioral assessment of childhood disorders* (2nd ed., pp. 586–623). New York: Guilford Press.

Filipek, P. A., Semrud-Clikeman, M., Steingard, R. J., Renshaw, P. F., Kennedy, D. N., & Beiderman, J. (1997). Volumetric MRI analysis comparing subjects having attention-deficit hyperactivity disorder with controls. *Neurology, 48,* 589–601.

Filippi, R., & Karmiloff-Smith, A. (2013). What can neurodevelopmental disorders teach us about typical development? In C. R. Marshall (Ed.), *Current issues in developmental disorders* (pp. 193–209). New York: Psychology Press.

Findling, R. L., Connor, D. F., Wigal, T., Eagan, C., & Onofrey, M. N. (2009). A linguistic analysis of in-office dialogue among psychiatrists, parents, and child and adolescent patients with ADHD. *Journal of Attention Disorders, 13,* 78–86.

Findling, R. L., Drury, S. S., Jensen, P. S., Rapoport, J. L., American Academy of Child and Adolescent Psychiatry (AACAP) Committee on Quality Issues (CQI), ... Stock, S. (2014). Practice parameter for the use of atypical antipsychotic medications in children and adolescents. *Journal of the American Academy of Child & Adolescent Psychiatry.* Retrieved from www.aacap.org

Fine, J. G., Semrud-Clikeman, M., Bledsoe, J. C., & Musielak, K. A. (2013). A critical review of the literature on NLD as a developmental disorder. *Child Neuropsychology, 19,* 190–223.

Finger, E. C., Marsh, A. A., Blair, K. S., Reid, M. E., Sims, C., Ng, P., ... Blair, R. J. R. (2011). Disrupted reinforcement signaling in the orbitofrontal cortex and caudate in youths with conduct disorder or oppositional defiant disorder and a high level of psychopathic traits. *American Journal of Psychiatry, 168,* 152–162.

Finkelhor, D. (2008). *Child victimization: Violence, crime, and abuse in the lives of young people.* New York: Oxford University Press.

Finkelhor, D. (2009). The prevention of childhood sexual abuse. *The Future of Children, 19,* 169–194.

Finkelhor, D. (2011). Prevalence of child victimization, abuse, crime, and violence exposure. In J. W. White, M. P. Koss, & A. E. Kazdin (Eds.), *Violence against women and children, Vol. 1: Mapping the terrain.* (pp. 9–29). Washington, DC: American Psychological Association.

Finkelhor, D., Turner, H., Ormrod, R., & Hamby, S. L. (2009). Violence, abuse, and crime exposure in a national sample of children and youth. *Pediatrics, 124,* 1411–1423.

Finn, P., Bothe, A. K., & Bramlett, R. E. (2005). Science and pseudoscience in communication disorders: Criteria and applications. *American Journal of Speech-Language Pathology, 14,* 172–186.

Fischer, M., Barkley, R. A., Smallish, L., & Fletcher, K. (2002). Young adult follow-up of hyperactive children: Self-reported psychiatric disorders, comorbidity, and the role of childhood conduct problems and teen CD. *Journal of Abnormal Child Psychology, 30,* 463–476.

Fisher, C. B., Brunnquell, D. J., Hughes, D. L., Liben, L. S., Maholmes, V., Plattner, S., … Susman, E. J. (2013). Responsible conduct of research involving children and youth: A response to proposed changes in federal regulations. *Social Policy Report, 27*(1), 1–22.

Fisher, M. H., Moskowitz, A. L., & Hodapp, R. M. (2013). Differences in social vulnerability among individuals with autism spectrum disorder, Williams syndrome, and Down syndrome. *Research in Autism Spectrum Disorders, 7,* 931–937.

Fitzgerald, D. A., Angstadt, M., Jelsone, L. M., Nathan, P. J., & Phan, K. L. (2006). Beyond threat. *NeuroImage, 30,* 1441–1448.

Fitzgerald, K. D., Liu, Y., Stern, E. R., Welsh, R. C., Hanna, G. L., Monk, C. S., … Taylor, S. F. (2013). Reduced error-related activation of dorsolateral prefrontal cortex across pediatric anxiety disorders. *Journal of the American Academy of Child & Adolescent Psychiatry, 52,* 1183–1191.

Fitzgerald, M. (2014). Overlap between autism and schizophrenia: History and current status. *Advances in Mental Health and Intellectual Disabilities, 8,* 15–23.

Fitzgerald, M. M., Schneider, R. A., Salstrom, S., Zinzow, H. M., Jackson, J., & Fossel, R. V. (2008). Child sexual abuse, early family risk, and childhood parentification: Pathways to current psychosocial adjustment. *Journal of Family Psychology, 22,* 320–324.

Flax, J. F., Realpe-Bonilla, T., Hirsch, L. S., Brzustowicz, L. M., Bartlett, C. W., & Tallal, P. (2003). Specific language impairment in families: Evidence for co-occurrence with reading impairments. *Journal of Speech, Language, & Hearing Research, 46,* 530–543.

Fletcher, J. M., Shaywitz, S. E., & Shaywitz, B. A. (1999). Comorbidity of learning and attention disorders: Separate but equal. *Pediatric Clinics of North America, 46,* 885–897.

Fletcher, K. E. (2003). Childhood posttraumatic stress disorder. In E. J. Mash & R. A. Barkley (Eds.), *Child psychopathology* (2nd ed., pp. 330–371). New York: Guilford Press.

Fliers, E. A., Franke, B., Lambregts-Rommelse, N. N. J., Altink, M. E., Buschgens, C. J. M., Nijhuis-van der Sanden, M W. G., … Buitelaar, J. K. (2010). *Child and Adolescent Mental Health, 15,* 85–90.

Fliers, E. A., Vasquez, A. A., Poelmans, G., Rommelse, N., Altink, M., Buschgens, C., … Franke, B. (2012). Genome-wide association study of motor coordination problems in ADHD identifies genes for brain and muscle function. *The World Journal of Biological Psychiatry, 13,* 211–222.

Flynn, J. R. (2007). *What is intelligence? Beyond the Flynn effect.* Cambridge, England: Cambridge University Press.

Flynn, J. R. (2012). *Are we getting smarter? Rising IQ in the twenty-first century.* New York: Cambridge University Press.

Fombonne, E. (2003). Epidemiological surveys of autism and other pervasive developmental disorders: An update. *Journal of Autism and Developmental Disorders, 33,* 365–382.

Fombonne, E. (2005). The changing epidemiology of autism. *Journal of Applied Research in Intellectual Disabilities, 18,* 281–294.

Fombonne, E. (2008). Thimerosal disappears but autism remains. *Archives of General Psychiatry, 65,* 15–16.

Fombonne, E., Wostear, G., Cooper, V., Harrington, R., & Rutter, M. (2001a). The Maudsley long-term follow-up of child and adolescent depression: 1. Psychiatric outcomes in adulthood. *British Journal of Psychiatry, 179,* 210–217.

Fombonne, E., Wostear, G., Cooper, V., Harrington, R., & Rutter, M. (2001b). The Maudsley long-term follow-up of child and adolescent depression: 2. Suicidality, criminality and social dysfunction in adulthood. *British Journal of Psychiatry, 179,* 218–223.

Fombonne, E., & Zinck, S. (2008). Psychopharmacological treatment of depression in children and adolescents. In J. R. Z. Abela & B. L. Hankin (Eds.), *Handbook of depression in children and adolescents* (pp. 207–223). New York: Guilford Press.

Fonagy, P., Target, M., & Gergely, G. (2006). Psychoanalytic perspectives on developmental psychopathology. In D. Cicchetti & D. J. Cohen (Eds.), *Developmental psychopathology: Vol. 1. Theory and method* (2nd ed., pp. 701–749). Hoboken, NJ: Wiley.

Fontaine, N. M. G., McCrory, E. J. P., Boivin, M., Moffitt, T. E., & Viding, E. (2011, February 21). Predictors and outcomes of joint trajectories of callous-unemotional traits and conduct problems in childhood. *Journal of Abnormal Psychology, 120,* 730–742.

Fontaine, R. G., Tanha, M., Yang, C., Dodge, K. A., Bates, J. E., & Pettit, G. S. (2010). Does response evaluation and decision (RED) mediate the relation between hostile attributional style and antisocial behavior in adolescence. *Journal of Abnormal Child Psychology, 38,* 615–626.

Forbes, D., Lewis, V., Varker, T., Phelps, A., O'Donnell, M., Wade, D. J., … Creamer, M. (2011). Psychological first aid following trauma: Implementation and evaluation framework for high-risk organizations. *Psychiatry: Interpersonal and Biological Processes, 74,* 224–239.

Forbes, E. E., May, C., Siegle, G. J., Ladouceur, C. D., Ryan, N. D., Carter, C. S., … Dahl, R. E. (2006). Reward-related decision-making in pediatric major depressive disorder: An fMRI study. *Journal of Child Psychology and Psychiatry, 47,* 1031–1040.

Forbes, E. E., Shaw, D. S., Silk, J. S., Feng, X., Cohn, J., Fox, N. A., & Kovacs, M. (2008). Children's affect expression and frontal EEG asymmetry: Transactional associations with mothers' depressive symptoms. *Journal of Abnormal Child Psychology, 36,* 207–221.

Forbush, K. T., South, S. C., Krueger, R. F., Iacono, W. G., Clark, L. A., Keel, P. K., … Watson, D. (2010). Locating eating pathology within an empirical diagnostic taxonomy: Evidence from a community-based sample. *Journal of Abnormal Psychology, 119,* 282–292.

Forehand, R. L., & Kotchik, B. A. (1996). Cultural diversity: A wake-up call for parent training. *Behavior Therapy, 27,* 187–206.

Foreyt, J. P., & Cousins, J. H. (1987). Obesity. In M. Hersen & V. B. Van Hasselt (Eds.), *Behavior therapy with children and adolescents: A clinical approach* (pp. 485–511). New York: Wiley.

Forgatch, M. S., & Patterson, G. R. (2010). Parent management training—Oregon model: An intervention for antisocial behavior in children and adolescents. In J. R. Weisz & A. E. Kazdin (Eds.), *Evidence-based psychotherapies for children and adolescents* (pp. 159–178). New York: Guilford Press.

Foster, E. M., Jones, D. E., and The Conduct Problems Prevention Research Group. (2005). The high costs of aggression: Public expenditures resulting from conduct disorder. *American Journal of Public Health, 95,* 1767–1772.

Foster, S. L. (2005). Aggression and antisocial behavior in girls. In D. J. Bell, S. L. Foster, & E. J. Mash (Eds.), *Handbook of behavioral and emotional problems in girls* (pp. 149–180). New York: Kluwer/Plenum Press.

Fowles, D. C. (2001). Biological variables in psychopathology: A psychobiological perspective. In P. Sutker & H. E. Adams (Eds.), *Comprehensive handbook of psychopathology* (3rd ed., pp. 85–104). New York: Kluwer/Plenum Press.

Fox, S. E., Levitt, P., & Nelson, C. A. (2010). How the timing and quality of early experiences influence the development of brain architecture. *Child Development, 81,* 28–40.

Fox, T. L., Barrett, P. M., & Shortt, A. L. (2002). Sibling relationships of anxious children: A preliminary investigation. *Journal of Clinical Child & Adolescent Psychology, 31,* 375–383.

Francis, K. J., & Wolfe, D. A. (2008). Cognitive and emotional differences between abusive and non-abusive fathers. *Child Abuse & Neglect, 32,* 1127–1137.

Francis, S. E., & Chorpita, B. F. (2004). Behavioral assessment of children in outpatient settings. In S. N. Haynes &

E. M. Heiby (Eds.), *Comprehensive handbook of psychological assessment: Vol. 3. Behavioral assessment* (pp. 291–319). New York: Wiley.

Franco, O. H., Steyerberg, E. W., Hu, F. B., Mackenbach, J., & Nusselder, W. (2007). Associations of diabetes mellitus with total life expectancy and life expectancy with and without cardiovascular disease. *Archives of Internal Medicine, 167,* 1145–1151.

Frangou, S. (2013). Neurocognition in early-onset schizophrenia. *Child and Adolescent Psychiatric Clinics of North America, 22,* 715–726.

Franic, S., Middeldorp, C. M., Dolan, C. V., Ligthart, L., & Boomsma, D. I. (2010). Childhood and adolescent anxiety and depression: Beyond heritability. *American Journal of Child & Adolescent Psychiatry, 49,* 820–829.

Franko, D. L., Keshaviah, A., Eddy, K. T., Krishna, M., Davis, M. C., Keel, P. K., & Herzog, D. B. (2013). A longitudinal investigation of mortality in anorexia nervosa and bulimia nervosa. *American Journal of Psychiatry, 170,* 917–925.

Frazier, J. A., McClellan, J., Findling, R. L., Vitiello, B., Anderson, R., Zablotsky, B., … Sikich, L. (2007). Treatment of early-onset schizophrenia spectrum disorders (TEOSS): Demographic and clinical characteristics. *Journal of the American Academy of Child and Adolescent Psychiatry, 46,* 979–988.

Frazier, T. W., Demaree, H. A., & Youngstrom, E. (2004). Meta-analysis of intellectual and neuropsychological test performance in attention-deficit/hyperactivity disorder. *Neuropsychology, 18,* 543–555.

Frazier, T. W., & Hardan, A. Y. (2009). A meta-analysis of the corpus callosum in autism. *Biological Psychiatry, 66,* 935–941.

Frazier, T. W., Youngstrom, E. A., Haycook, T., Sinoff, A., Dimitriou, F., Knapp, J., & Sinclair, L. (2010). Effectiveness of medication combined with intensive behavioral intervention for reducing aggression in youth with autism spectrum disorder. *Journal of Child and Adolescent Psychopharmacology, 20,* 167–177.

Frazier, T. W., Youngstrom, E. A., Speer, L., Embacher, R., Law, P., Constantino, J., … Eng, C. (2012). Validation of proposed DSM-5 criteria for Autism Spectrum Disorder. *Journal of the American Academy of Child & Adolescent Psychiatry, 51,* 28–40.

Freeman, J. B., Garcia, A. M., Coyne, L., Ale, C., Przeworski, A., Himle, M., … Leonard, H. L. (2008). Early childhood OCD: Preliminary findings from a family-based cognitive-behavioral approach. *Journal of the American Academy of Child & Adolescent Psychiatry, 47,* 593–602.

Freeman, J., Garcia, A., Frank, H., Benito, K., Conelea, C., Walther, M., & Edmunds, J. (2014). Evidence base update for psychosocial treatments for pediatric obsessive-compulsive disorder. *Journal of Clinical Child & Adolescent Psychology, 43,* 7–26.

Freitag, C. M., Staal, W., Klauck, S. M., Duketis, E., & Waltes, R. (2010). Genetics of autistic disorders: Review and clinical implications. *European Child & Adolescent Psychiatry, 19,* 169–178.

French, D. C., & Dishion, T. (2003). Predictors of early initiation of sexual intercourse among high-risk adolescents. *Journal of Early Adolescence, 23,* 295–315.

French, S. A., Story, M., Downes, B., Resnick, M. D., & Blum, R. W. (1995). Frequent dieting among adolescents: Psychosocial and health behavior correlates. *American Journal of Public Health, 85,* 695–710.

French, V. (1977). History of the child's influence: Ancient Mediterranean civilizations. In R. Q. Bell & L. V. Harper (Eds.), *Child effects on adults* (pp. 3–29). Hillsdale, NJ: Erlbaum.

Freud, S. (1909/1953). Analysis of a phobia in a five-year-old boy. In J. Strachey (Ed.), *The standard edition of the complete psychological works of Sigmund Freud* (Vol. 10, pp. 3–149). London: Hogarth Press.

Freyd, J. J., DePrince, A. P., & Gleaves, D. H. (2007). The state of betrayal trauma theory: Reply to McNally—conceptual issues and future directions. *Memory, 15,* 295–311.

Frick, P. J. (2000). A comprehensive and individualized treatment approach for children and adolescents with conduct disorders. *Cognitive and Behavioral Practice, 7,* 30–37.

Frick, P. J., Cornell, A. H., Bodin, S. D., Dane, H. E., Barry, C. T., & Loney, B. R. (2003). Callous–unemotional traits and developmental pathways to severe conduct problems. *Developmental Psychology, 39,* 246–260.

Frick, P. J., Lahey, B. B., Loeber, R., Tannenbaum, L., Van Horn, Y., Christ, M. A. G., … Hanson, K. (1993). Oppositional defiant disorder and conduct disorder: A meta-analytic review of factor analyses and cross-validation in a clinic sample. *Clinical Psychology Review, 13,* 319–340.

Frick, P. J., Lilienfeld, S. O., Ellis, M., Loney, B., & Silverthorn, P. (1999). The association between anxiety and psychopathy dimensions in children. *Journal of Abnormal Child Psychology, 27,* 383–392.

Frick, P. J. & Nigg, J. T. (2012). Current issues in the diagnosis of attention-deficit hyperactivity disorder, oppositional defiant disorder, and conduct disorder. *Annual Review of Clinical Psychology, 8,* 77–107.

Frick, P. J., Ray, J. V., Thornton, L. C., & Kahn, R. E. (2014). Can callous-unemotional traits enhance the understanding, diagnosis, and treatment of serious conduct problems in children and adolescents? A comprehensive review. *Psychological Bulletin, 140,* 1–57.

Frick, P. J., Van Horn, Y., Lahey, B. B., Christ, M. A. G., Loeber, R., Hart, E. A., Tannenbaum, L., Hanson, K. (1993). Oppositional defiant disorder and conduct disorder: a meta-analytic review of factor analyses and cross-validation in a clinic sample. *Clinical Psychology Review, 13,* 319–340.

Frick, P. J., & Viding, E. (2009). Antisocial behavior from a developmental psychopathology perspective. *Development and Psychopathology, 21,* 111–1131.

Frick, P. J., & White, S. F. (2008). Research review: The importance of callous-unemotional traits for developmental models of aggressive and antisocial behavior. *Journal of Child Psychology and Psychiatry, 49,* 359–375.

Fried, E. J., & Nestle, M. (2002). The growing political movement against soft drinks in schools. *JAMA: Journal of the American Medical Association, 288,* 2181.

Friedlander, L., & Desrocher, M. (2006). Neuroimaging studies of obsessive-compulsive disorder in adults and children. *Clinical Psychology Review, 26,* 32–49.

Friedman, A. G., Latham, S. A., & Dahlquist, L. M. (1998). Childhood cancer. In T. H. Ollendick & M. Hersen (Eds.), *Handbook of child psychopathology* (3rd ed., pp. 435–461). New York: Plenum Press.

Friedman, H. S., Tucker, J. S., Schwartz, J. E., Tomlinson-Keasey, C., Martin, L. R., Wingard, D. L., & Criqui, M. H. (1995). Psychosocial and behavioral predictors of longevity: The aging and death of the "termites." *American Psychologist, 50,* 69–78.

Friedrich, W. N., & Trane, S. T. (2002). Sexual behavior in children across multiple settings. *Child Abuse & Neglect, 26,* 243–245.

Friman, P. C. (2008). Evidence-based therapies for enuresis and encopresis. In R. G. Steele, T. D. Elkin, & M. C. Roberts (Eds.), *Handbook of evidence-based therapies for children and adolescents: Bridging science and practice. Issues in clinical child psychology* (pp. 311–333). New York: Springer.

Fristad, M. A., & Algorta, G. P. (2013). Future directions for research on youth with bipolar spectrum disorders. *Journal of Clinical Child & Adolescent Psychology, 42,* 734–747.

Fristad, M. A., Goldberg Arnold, J. S., & Leffler, J. M. (2011). *Psychotherapy for children with bipolar and depressive disorders.* New York: Guilford Press.

Fristad, M. A., & MacPherson, H. A. (2014). Evidence-based psychosocial treatments for child and adolescent bipolar spectrum disorders. *Journal of Clinical Child & Adolescent Psychology, 43,* 339–355.

Fristad, M. A., Verducci, J. S., Walters, K., & Young, M. E. (2009). Impact of multi-family psychoeducational psychotherapy in treating children aged 8 to 12 years with mood disorders. *Archives of General Psychiatry, 66,* 1013–1021.

Frith, U. (1993, June). Autism. *Scientific American,* 108–114.

Frith, U. (1997). Autism [Special issue]. *Scientific American,* 92–98. Retrieved from http://www.scientificamerican.com

Frith, U. (2003). *Autism: Explaining the enigma* (2nd ed.). Oxford, England: Blackwell.

Frith, U., & Happé, F. (1994). Autism: Beyond "theory of mind." *Cognition, 50,* 115–132.

Fritz, G., Rockney, R., and the Work Group on Quality Issues. (2004). Summary of the practice parameter for the assessment and treatment of children and adolescents with enuresis. *Journal of the American Academy of Child & Adolescent Psychiatry, 43,* 123–125.

Froehlich, T. E., Anixt, J. S., Loe, I. M., Chirdkiatgumchai, V., Kuan, L., & Gilman, R. C. (2011). Update on environmental risk factors for attention-deficit/hyperactivity disorder. *Current Psychiatry Reports, 13,* 333–344.

Froehlich, T. E., Lanphear, B. P., Auinger, P., Hornung, R., Epstein, J. N., Braun, J., & Kahn, R. (2009). Association of tobacco and lead exposures with attention-deficit/hyperactivity disorder. *Pediatrics, 124,* 1054–1063.

Furniss, F., & Biswas, A. B. (2012). Recent research on aetiology, development and phenomenology of self-injurious behaviour in people with intellectual disabilities: A systematic review and implications for treatment. *Journal of Intellectual Disability Research, 56,* 453–475.

Furr, J. M., Comer, J. S., Edmunds, J. M., & Kendall, P. C. (2010). Disasters and youth: A meta-analytic examination of posttraumatic stress. *Journal of Consulting and Clinical Psychology, 78,* 765–780.

Gaab, N., Gabrieli, J. D. E., Deutsch, G. K., Tallal, P., & Temple, E. (2007). Neural correlates of rapid auditory processing are disrupted in children with developmental dyslexia and ameliorated with training: An fMRI study. *Restorative Neurology and Neuroscience, 25,* 295–310.

Gabbay, V., Ely, B. A., Li, Q., Bangaru, S. D., Panzer, A. M., Alonso, C. M., ... Milham, M. P. (2013). Striatum-based circuitry of adolescent depression and anhedonia. *Journal of the American Academy of Child & Adolescent Psychiatry, 52,* 628–641.

Gadow, K. D., & Nolan, E. E. (2002). Differences between preschool children with ODD, ADHD and ODD+ADHD symptoms. *Journal of Child Psychology and Psychiatry, 43,* 191–201.

Gadow, K. D., & Sprafkin, J. (1993). Television "violence" and children with emotional and behavioral disorders. *Journal of Emotional and Behavioral Disorders, 1,* 54–63.

Gaffrey, M. S., Barch, D. M., Singer, J., Shenoy, R., & Luby, J. L. (2013). Disrupted amygdala reactivity in depressed 4- to 6-year-old children. *Journal of the American Academy of Child & Adolescent Psychiatry, 52,* 737–746.

Gaffrey, M. S., Luby, J. L., Beldon, A. C., Hirshberg, J. S., Volsche, J., & Barch, D. M. (2011). Association between depression severity and amygdala reactivity during sad face viewing in depressed preschoolers: An fMRI study. *Journal of Affective Disorders, 129,* 364–370.

Galaburda, A. M., Sherman, G. F., Rosen, G. D., & Geschwind, A. F. (1985). Developmental dyslexia: Four consecutive patients with cortical anomalies. *Annals of Neurology, 18,* 222–223.

Galatzer-Levy, R. M., Bachrach, H., Skolnikoff, A., & Waldron, S. (2000). *Does psychoanalysis work?* New Haven, CT: Yale University Press.

Galsworthy-Francis, L., & Allan, S. (2014). Cognitive behavioural therapy for anorexia nervosa: A systematic review. *Clinical Psychology Review, 34,* 54–72.

Ganz, M. L. (2007). The lifetime distribution of the incremental societal costs of autism. *Archives of Pediatric Adolescent Medicine, 161,* 343–349.

Gao, T., Raine, A., Venables, P. H., Dawson, M. E., & Mednick, S. A. (2010). Association of poor childhood fear conditioning and crime. *American Journal of Psychiatry, 167,* 56–60.

Garber, J., & Cole, D. A. (2010). Intergenerational transmission of depression: A launch and grow model of change across adolescence. *Development and Psychopathology, 22,* 819–830.

Garber, J., & Flynn, C. (2001). Vulnerability to depression in childhood and adolescence. In R. E. Ingram & J. M. Price (Eds.), *Vulnerability to psychopathology: Risk across the lifespan* (pp. 175–225). New York: Guilford Press.

Garber, J., & Horowitz, J. L. (2002). Depression in children. In I. H. Gotlib & C. Hammen (Eds.), *Handbook of depression* (pp. 510–540). New York: Guilford Press.

Garber, J., & Kaminsky, K. M. (2000). Laboratory and performance-based measures of depression in children and adolescents. *Journal of Clinical Child Psychology, 29,* 509–525.

Garber, J., & Weersing, V. R. (2010). Comorbidity of anxiety and depression in youth: Implications for treatment and prevention. *Clinical Psychology: Science and Practice, 17,* 293–306.

Garcia, A. M., Sapyta, J. J., Moore, Reinblatt P. S., Freeman, J. B., Franklin, M. E., March, J. S., & Foa, E. B. (2010). Outcome in the pediatric obsessive compulsive treatment study (POTS I). *Journal of the American Academy of Child & Adolescent Psychiatry, 49,* 1024–1033.

Garcia-Perez, R. M., Hobson, R. P., & Lee, A. (2008). Narrative role taking in autism. *Journal of Autism and Developmental Disorders, 38,* 156–168.

Gardener, H., Spiegelman, D., & Buka, S. L. (2009). Prenatal risk factors for autism: Comprehensive meta-analysis. *British Journal of Psychiatry, 195,* 7–14.

Gardener, H., Spiegelman, D., & Buka, S. L. (2011). Perinatal and neonatal risk factors for autism: A comprehensive meta-analysis. *Pediatrics, 128,* 344–355.

Gardner, D. M., & Gerdes, A. C. (2013). A review of peer relationships and friendships in youth with ADHD. *Journal of Attention Disorders.* Advance online publication. doi:10.1177/1087054713501552.

Garfinkel, P. E., Lin, E., Goergin, P., Spegg, C., Goldbloom, D. S., Kennedy, S., ... Woodside, D. B. (1995). Bulimia nervosa in a Canadian community sample: Prevalence and comparison of subgroups. *American Journal of Psychiatry, 152,* 1052–1058

Garn, S. M., Clark, D. C., Lowe, C. U., Forbes, G., Garn, S., Owen, G. M., ...

Rowe, N. (1976). Trends in fatness and the origins of obesity: Ad hoc committee to review the ten-state nutrition survey. *Pediatrics, 57,* 443–456.

Garner, D. M. (1993). Pathogenesis of anorexia nervosa. *Lancet, 341,* 1631–1635.

Garrett, A., & Chang, K. (2008). The role of the amygdala in bipolar disorder development. *Development and Psychopathology, 20,* 1285–1296.

Garrett, A. S., Reiss, A. L., Howe, M. E., Kelley, R. G., Singh, M. K., Adleman, N. E., ... Chang, K. D. (2012). Abnormal amygdala and prefrontal cortex activation to facial expressions in pediatric bipolar disorder. *Journal of the American Academy of Child & Adolescent Psychiatry, 51,* 821–831.

Garrison, W. T., & McQuiston, S. (1989). *Chronic illness during childhood and adolescence: Psychological aspects.* Newbury Park, CA: Sage.

Garvie, P. A., Lawford, J., Banet, M. S., & West, R. L. (2009). Quality of life measurement in paediatric and adolescent populations with HIV: A review of the literature. *Child Care, Health and Development, 35,* 440.

Gathje, R. A., Lewandowski, L. J., & Gordon, M. (2008). The role of impairment in the diagnosis of ADHD. *Journal of Attention Disorders, 11,* 529–537.

Gatt, J. M., Nemeroff, C. B., Schofield, P. R., Paul, R. H., Clark, C. R., Gordon, E., & Williams, L. M. (2010). Early life stress combined with serotonin 3A receptor and brain-derived neurotrophic factor valine 66 to methionine genotypes impacts emotional brain and arousal correlates of risk for depression. *Biological Psychiatry, 68,* 818–824.

Gaudin, J. M., Polansky, N.A., Kilpatrick, A.C., & Shilton, P. (1996). Family functioning in neglectful families. *Child Abuse & Neglect, 20,* 363–377.

Gaysina, D., Fergusson, D. M., Leve, L. D., Horwood, J., Reiss, D., Shaw, D. S., ... Harold, G. T. (2013). Maternal smoking during pregnancy and offspring of conduct problems: Evidence from 3 independent genetically sensitive research designs. *JAMA Psychiatry, 70,* 956–963.

Geary. D. C. (2013). Learning disabilities in mathematics: Recent advances. In H. L. Swanson, K. R. Harris, & S. Graham (Eds.), *Handbook of learning disabilities* (2nd ed., pp. 239–255). New York: Guilford Press.

Gejman, P. V., Sanders, A. R., & Duan, J. (2010). The role of genetics in the etiology of schizophrenia. *Psychiatric Clinics of North America, 33,* 35–66.

Gelb, S. A. (1995). The beast in man: Degenerationism and mental retardation, 1900–1920. *Intellectual and Developmental Disabilities, 33,* 1–9.

Geller, B., & DelBello, M. P. (Eds.). (2003). *Bipolar disorder in childhood and early adolescence.* New York: Guilford Press.

Geller, B., & DelBello, M. P. (2008). *Treatment of bipolar disorder in children and adolescents.* New York: Guilford Press.

Geller, B., & Luby, J. (1997). Child and adolescent bipolar disorder: A review of the past 10 years. *Journal of the American Academy of Child & Adolescent Psychiatry, 36*, 1168–1176.

Geller, B., Sun, K., Zimerman, B., Luby, J., Frazier, J., & Williams, M. (1995). Complex and rapid cycling in bipolar children and adolescents. *Journal of Affective Disorders, 34*, 259–268.

Geller, D. A., Biederman, J., Jones, J., Park, K., Schwartz, S., Shapiro, S., & Coffey, B. (1998). Is juvenile obsessive–compulsive disorder a developmental subtype of the disorder? A review of the pediatric literature. *Journal of the American Academy of Child & Adolescent Psychiatry, 37*, 420–427.

Geller, D. A., March, J. M., & the AACAP Committee on Quality Issues. (2012). Practice parameter for the assessment and treatment of children and adolescents with obsessive-compulsive disorder. *Journal of the American Academy of Child & Adolescent Psychiatry, 51*, 98–113.

George, M. S., Ketter, T. A., Parekh, P. I., Herscovitch, P., & Post, R. M. (1996). Gender differences in regional cerebral blood flow during transient self-induced sadness or happiness. *Biological Psychiatry, 40*, 859–871.

Gerdes, A. C., Hoza, B., & Pelham, W. E. (2003). Attention-deficit/hyperactivity disordered boy's relationships with their mothers and fathers: Child, mother, and father perceptions. *Development and Psychopathology, 15*, 363–382.

Gerdts, J. A., Bernier, R., Dawson, G., & Estes, A. (2013). The broader autism phenotype in simplex and multiplex families. *Journal of Autism and Developmental Disorders, 43*, 1597–1605.

Gerenser, J., & Forman, B. (2007). *Speech and language deficits in children with developmental disabilities.* In J. W. Jacobson, J. A. Mulick, & J. Rojahn (Eds.), *Handbook of intellectual and developmental disabilities* (pp. 563–579). New York: Springer.

Gershater-Molko, R. M., Lutzker, J. R., & Wesch, D. (2003). Project SafeCare: Improving health, safety, and parenting skills in families reported for, and at-risk for child maltreatment. *Journal of Family Violence, 18*, 377–386.

Gershoff, E. T. (2013). Spanking and child development: We know enough now to stop hitting our children. *Child Development Perspectives, 7*, 133–137.

Gerson, R., & Rappaport, N. (2013). Traumatic stress and posttraumatic stress disorder in youth: Recent research findings on clinical impact, assessment, and treatment. *Journal of Adolescent Health, 52*, 137–143.

Gerstein, E. D., Crnic, K. A., Blacher, J., & Baker, B. L. (2009). Resilience and the course of daily parenting stress in families of young children with intellectual disabilities. *Journal of Intellectual Disability Research, 53*, 981–997.

Gevensleben, H., Kleemeyer, M., Rothenberger, L. G., Studer, P., Flaig-Rohr, A., Moll, G. H., … Heinrich, H. (2014). Neurofeedback in ADHD: Further pieces of the puzzle. *Brain Topography, 27*, 20–32.

Gewirtz, A. H., & Edleson, J. L. (2007). Young children's exposure to intimate partner violence: Towards a developmental risk and resilience framework for research and intervention. *Journal of Family Violence, 22*, 151–163.

Ghaemi, S. N., & Martin, A. (2007). Defining the boundaries of childhood bipolar disorder. *American Journal of Psychiatry, 164*, 185–188.

Ghezzi, P. M. (2007). Discrete trials teaching. *Psychology in the Schools, 44*, 667–679.

Ghuman, J. K., Aman, M. G., Lecavalier, L., Riddle, M. A., Gelenberg, A., Wright, R., … Fort, C. (2009). Randomized, placebo-controlled, crossover study of methylphenidate for attention-deficit/hyperactivity disorder symptoms in preschoolers with developmental disorders. *Journal of Child and Adolescent Psychopharmacology, 19*, 329–339.

Giarelli, E., Wiggins, L. D., Rice, C. E., Levy, S. E., Kirby, R. S., Pinto-Martin, J., & Mandell, D. (2010). Sex differences in the evaluation and diagnosis of autism spectrum disorders among children. *Disability and Health Journal, 3*, 107–116.

Gibbons, R. D., Brown, C. H., Hur, K., Davis, J. M., & Mann, J. J. (2012). Suicidal thoughts and behavior with antidepressant treatment: Reanalysis of the randomized placebo-controlled studies of fluoxetine and venlafaxine. *JAMA Psychiatry, 69*, 580–587.

Gibbons, R. D., Brown, C. H., Hur, K., Marcus, S. M., Bhaumik, D. K., Erkens, J. A., … Mann, J. J. (2007). Early evidence on the effects of regulators' suicidality warnings on SSRI prescriptions and suicide in children and adolescents. *American Journal of Psychiatry, 164*, 1356–1363.

Gibbons, R. D., Hur, K., Bhaumik, D. L., & Mann, J. J. (2006). The relationship between antidepressant prescription rates and rate of early adolescent suicide. *American Journal of Psychiatry, 163*, 1898–1904.

Gibson, J., Adams, C., Lockton, E., & Green, J. (2013). Social communication disorder outside autism? A diagnostic classification approach to delineating pragmatic language impairment, high functioning autism and specific language impairment. *Journal of Child Psychology and Psychiatry, 54*, 1186–1197.

Gilbert, A. R., Akkal, D., Almeida, J. R.C., Mataix-Cols, D., Kalas, C., Devlin, B., … Phillips, M. L. (2009). Neural correlates of symptom dimension in pediatric obsessive-compulsive disorder: A functional magnetic resonance imaging study. *Journal of the American Academy of Child & Adolescent Psychiatry, 48*, 936–944.

Gilbert, S. C., Crump, S., Madhere, S., & Schutz, W. (2009). Internalization of the thin ideal as a predictor of body dissatisfaction and disordered eating in African, African-American, and Afro-Caribbean female college students. *Journal of College Student Psychotherapy, 23*, 196–211.

Gillberg, C., & de Souza, L. (2002). Head circumference in autism, Asperger syndrome, and ADHD: A comparative study. *Developmental Medicine & Child Neurology, 44*, 296–300.

Gillham, J. E., & Reivich, K. J. (1999). Prevention of depressive symptoms in school children: A research update. *Psychological Science, 10*, 461–462.

Gilman, S. E., Kawachi, I., Fitzmaurice, G. M., & Buka, S. (2003). Family disruption in childhood and risk of adult depression. *American Journal of Psychiatry, 160*, 939–946.

Gilvarry, E. (2000). Substance abuse in young people. *Journal of Child Psychology and Psychiatry, 41*, 55–80.

Ginsburg, G. S., & Silverman, W. (1996). Phobic and anxiety disorders in Hispanic and Caucasian youth. *Journal of Anxiety Disorders, 10*, 517–528.

Ginsburg, G. S., & Silverman, W. K. (2000). Gender role orientation and fearfulness in children with anxiety disorders. *Journal of Anxiety Disorders, 14*, 57–67.

Gladstone, T., Marko-Holguin, M., Henry, J., Fogel, J., Diehl, A., & Van Voorhees, B. W. (2014). Understanding adolescent response to a technology-based depression prevention program. *Journal of Clinical & Adolescent Psychology, 43*, 102–114.

Glascoe, F. P., & Leew, S. (2010). Parenting behaviors, perceptions, and psychosocial risk: Impacts on young children's development. *Pediatrics, 125*, 213–319.

Glaser, D. (2011). How to deal with emotional abuse and neglect—further development of a conceptual framework (FRAMEA). *Child Abuse & Neglect, 35*, 866.

Glass, K., Flory, K., & Hankin, B. L. (2012). Symptoms of ADHD and close friendships in adolescence. *Journal of Attention Disorders, 16*, 406–417.

Gleason, M. M., Egger, H. L., Emslie, G. J., Greenhill, L. L., Kowatch, R. A., Lieberman, A. F., … Zeanah, C. H. (2007). Psychopharmacological treatment for very young children: Contexts and guidelines. *Journal of the American Academy of Child & Adolescent Psychiatry, 46*, 1532–1572.

Gleason, M. M., Fox, N. A., Drury, S., Smyke, A., Egger, H. L., Nelson, C. A., … Zeanah, C. H. (2011). Validity of evidence-derived criteria for reactive attachment disorder: Indiscriminately social/disinhibited and emotionally withdrawn/inhibited types. *Journal of the American Academy of Child & Adolescent Psychiatry, 50*, 216–231.

Glicklich, L. B. (1951). An historical account of enuresis. *Pediatrics, 8*, 859–876.

Glover, S. H., & Pumariega, A. J. (1998). The importance of children's mental health epidemiological research with culturally diverse populations. In M. Hernandez & M. R. Isaacs (Eds.), *Promoting cultural competence in children's mental health services* (pp. 271–303). Baltimore: Brookes.

Glover, V. (2011). Prenatal stress and the origins of psychopathology: An evolutionary perspective. *Journal of Child Psychology and Psychiatry, 52*, 356–367.

Goddard, H. H. (1912). *The Kallikak family: A study in the heredity of feeble-mindedness.* New York: MacMillan.

Godley, M. D., Godley, S. H., Dennis, M. L., Funk, R. R., Passetti, L. L., & Petry, N. M. (2014). A randomized trial of assertive continuing care and contingency management for adolescents with substance use disorders. *Journal of Consulting and Clinical Psychology, 82,* 40–51.

Gogtay, N., Ordonez, A., Herman, D. H., Hayashi, K. M., Greenstein, D., Vaituzis, C., … Rapoport, J. L. (2007). Dynamic mapping of cortical development before and after the onset of pediatric bipolar illness. *Journal of Child Psychology and Psychiatry, 48,* 852–862.

Goin-Kochel, R. P., Myers, B. J., & Mackintosh, V. H. (2007). Parental reports on the use of treatments and therapies for children with autism spectrum disorders. *Research in Autism Spectrum Disorders, 1,* 195–209.

Goldentyer, T. (1994). *Gangs.* Austin, TX: Steck-Vaughn.

Goldstein, B. I., Liu, S.-M., Schaffer, A., Sala, R., & Blanco, C. (2013). Obesity and the three-year longitudinal course of bipolar disorder. *Bipolar Disorders, 15,* 284–293.

Goldstein, B. I., Sassi, R., & Diler, R. S. (2012). Pharmacologic treatment of bipolar disorder in children and adolescents. *Child and Adolescent Psychiatric Clinics of North America, 21,* 911–939.

Goldstein, T. R., Axelson, D. A., Birmaher, B., & Brent, D. A. (2007). Dialectical behavior therapy for adolescents with bipolar disorder: A 1-year open trial. *Journal of the American Academy of Child & Adolescent Psychiatry, 46,* 820–830.

Goldstein, T. R., Ha, W., Axelson, D. A., Goldstein, B. I., Liao, F., Gill, M. K., … Birmaher, B. (2012). Predictors of prospectively examined suicide attempts among youth with bipolar disorder. *Archives of General Psychiatry, 69,* 1113–1122.

Goldston, D. B., Daniel, S. S., & Arnold, E. M. (2006). Suicidal and non-suicidal self-harm behaviors. In D. A. Wolfe & E. J. Mash (Eds.), *Behavioral and emotional disorders in adolescents: Nature, assessment, and treatment* (pp. 343–380). New York: Guilford Press.

Goldston, D. B., Molock, S. D., Whitbeck, L. B., Murakami, J. L., Zayas, L. H., & Hall, G. C. N. (2008). Cultural considerations in adolescent suicide: Prevention and psychosocial treatment. *American Psychologist, 63,* 14–31.

Goldston, D. B., Walsh, A., Arnold, E. M., Reboussin, B., Daniel, S. S., Erkanli, A., … Wood, F. B. (2007). Reading problems, psychiatric disorders, and functional impairment from mid- to late adolescence. *Journal of the American Academy of Child & Adolescent Psychiatry, 46,* 25–32.

Golombek, A. A., & King, B. (2010). Pharmacotherapy. In R. C. Dryden-Edwards & L. Combrinck-Graham (Eds.), *Developmental disabilities from childhood to adulthood: What works for psychiatrists in community and institutional settings* (pp. 271–295). Baltimore: Johns Hopkins University Press.

Gooch, D., Hulme, C., Nash, H. M. and Snowling, M. J. (2013). Comorbidities in preschool children at family risk of dyslexia. *Journal of Child Psychology and Psychiatry, 44,* 237–246.

Gooch, D., Snowling, M., & Hulme, C. (2011). Time perception, phonological skills and executive function in children with dyslexia and/or ADHD symptoms. *Journal of Child Psychology and Psychiatry, 52,* 195–203.

Goodkind, J. R., LaNoue, M. D., & Milford, J. (2010). Adaptation and implementation of cognitive behavioral intervention for trauma in schools with American Indian youth. *Journal of Clinical Child & Adolescent Psychology, 39,* 858–873.

Goodlad, J. K., Marcus, D. K., & Fulton, J. J. (2013). Lead and attention-deficit/hyperactivity disorder (ADHD) symptoms: A meta-analysis. *Clinical Psychology Review, 33,* 417–425.

Goodlin-Jones, B., Schwichtenberg, A. J., Iosif, A., Tang, K., Liu, J., & Anders, T. F. (2009). Six-month persistence of sleep problems in young children with autism, developmental delay, and typical development. *Journal of the American Academy of Child & Adolescent Psychiatry, 48,* 247–254.

Goodman, S. (2014). Commentary: The multifaceted nature of maternal depression as a risk factor for child psychopathology—reflections on Sellers et al. (2014). *Journal of Child Psychology and Psychiatry, 55,* 121–123.

Goodman, S. H. (2007). Depression in mothers. *Annual Review of Clinical Psychology, 3,* 107–135.

Goodman, S. H., & Brand, S. R. (2009). Infants of depressed mothers: Vulnerabilities, risk factors, and protective factors for the later development of psychopathology. In C. H. Zeanah, Jr. (Ed.), *Handbook of infant mental health* (3rd ed., pp. 153–170). New York: Guilford Press.

Goodman, S. H., Rouse, M. H., Connell, A. M., Broth, M. R., Hall, C. M., & Heyward, D. (2011). Maternal depression and child psychopathology: A meta-analytic review. *Clinical Child and Family Psychology Review, 14,* 1–27.

Goodman, S. H., Schwab-Stone, M., Lahey, B., Shaffer, D., & Jensen, P. (2000). Major depression and dysthymia in children and adolescents: Discriminant validity and differential consequences in a community sample. *Journal of the American Academy of Child & Adolescent Psychiatry, 39,* 761–770.

Goodman, S. H., & Tully, E. (2008). Children of depressed mothers: Implications for etiology, treatment, and prevention of depression in children and adolescents. In J. R. Z. Abela & B. L. Hankin (Eds.), *Handbook of depression in children and adolescents* (pp. 415–440). New York: Guilford Press.

Goodyer, I. M. (1999). The influence of recent life events on the onset and outcome of major depression in young people. In C. Essau & F. Petermann (Eds.), *Depressive disorders in children and adolescents: Epidemiology, risk factors, and treatment* (pp. 237–260). Northvale, NJ: Aronson.

Goodyer, I. M. (2008). Emanuel Miller Lecture: Early onset depressions—meanings, mechanisms and processes. *Journal of Child Psychology and Psychiatry, 49,* 1239–1256.

Goodyer, I. M., Dubicka, B., Wilkinson, P., Kelvin, R., Roberts, C., Byford, S., … Harrington, R. (2007). Selective serotonin reuptake inhibitors (SSRIs) and routine specialist care with and without cognitive behaviour therapy in adolescents with major depressive disorder: Randomized controlled trial. *British Medical Journal, 335,* 142–146.

Goodyer, I. M., Herbert, J., Tamplin, A., Secher, S. M., & Pearson, J. (1997). Short-term outcome of major depression: II. Life events, family dysfunction, and friendship difficulties as predictors of persistent disorder. *Journal of the American Academy of Child & Adolescent Psychiatry, 36,* 474–480.

Gortmaker, S. L., & Story, M. (2012). Nutrition policy research that can lead to reduced childhood obesity in the United States *American Journal of Preventive Medicine, 43*(3), S149–S151.

Gotlib, I. H., Lewinsohn, P. M., & Seeley, J. R. (1995). Symptoms versus a diagnosis of depression: Differences in psychosocial functioning. *Journal of Consulting and Clinical Psychology, 63,* 90–100.

Gotlib, I. H., Lewinsohn, P. M., & Seeley, J. R. (1998). Consequences of depression during adolescence: Marital status and marital functioning in early adulthood. *Journal of Abnormal Psychology, 107,* 686–690.

Gottfredson, D. C. (2010). Deviancy training: Understanding how preventive interventions harm: The Academy of Experimental Criminology 2009 Joan McCord Award Lecture. *Journal of Experimental Criminology, 6,* 229–243.

Gottfredson, D. C., Gottfredson, G. D., & Hybel, L. G. (1993). Managing adolescent behavior: A multi-year, multi-school study. *American Educational Research Journal, 30,* 179–215.

Gowers, S., & Bryant-Waugh, R. (2004). Management of child and adolescent eating disorders: The current evidence base and future directions. *Journal of Child Psychology and Psychiatry 45,* 63–83.

Graber, J. A., Brooks-Gunn, J., Paikoff, R. L., & Warren, M. P. (1994). Prediction of eating problems: An 8-year study of adolescent girls. *Developmental Psychology, 30,* 823–834.

Gracious, B. L., Findling, R. L., Seman, C., Youngstrom, E. A., Demeter, C. A., & Calabrese, J. R. (2004). Elevated thyrotropin in bipolar youths prescribed both lithium and divalproex sodium. *Journal of the American Academy of Child & Adolescent Psychiatry, 43,* 215–220.

Grafodatskaya, D., Chung, B., Szatmari, P., & Weksberg, R. (2010). Autism spectrum disorders and epigenetics. *Journal of the American Academy of Child & Adolescent Psychiatry, 49,* 794–809.

Graham, J., Banaschewski, T., Buitelaar, J., Coghill, D., Danckaerts, M., Dittmann, R. W., … Taylor, E. (for the European Guidelines Group). (2011). European guidelines on managing adverse effects of medication for ADHD. *European Child & Adolescent Psychiatry, 20,* 17–37.

Graham, S., MacArthur, C., Schwartz, S., & Voth, T. (1992). Improving LD student's compositions using a strategy involving product and process goal-setting. *Exceptional Children, 58*, 322–334.

Graham-Bermann, S. A., Castor, L. E., Miller, L. E., & Howell, K. H. (2012). The impact of intimate partner violence and additional traumatic events on trauma symptoms and PTSD in preschool-aged children. *Journal of Traumatic Stress, 25*, 393–400.

Graham-Bermann, S. A., Lynch, S., Banyard, V., DeVoe, E. R., & Halabu, H. (2007). Community-based intervention for children exposed to intimate partner violence: An efficacy trial. *Journal of Consulting and Clinical Psychology, 75*, 199–209.

Grandin, T., & Panek, R. (2013). *The autistic brain: Thinking across the spectrum.* Boston: Houghton Mifflin Harcourt.

Granic, I., & Patterson, G. R. (2006). Toward a comprehensive model of antisocial development: A dynamic systems approach. *Psychological Review, 113*, 101–131.

Grant, B. F., Stinson, F. S., & Harford, T. C. (2001). Age of onset of alcohol use and DSM-IV alcohol abuse and dependence: A 12-year follow-up. *Journal of Substance Abuse, 13*, 493–504.

Grant, G., Ramcharan, P., & Flynn, M. (2007). Resilience in families with children and adult members with intellectual disabilities: Tracing elements of a psychosocial model. *Journal of Applied Research in Intellectual Disabilities, 20*, 563–575.

Gray, J. A. (1987). *The psychology of fear and stress* (2nd ed.). New York: Cambridge University Press.

Gray, K. M., Piccinin, A. M., Hofer, S. M., Mackinnon, A., Bontempo, D. E., Einfeld, S. L., … Tonge, B. J. (2011). The longitudinal relationship between behavior and emotional disturbance in young people with intellectual disability and maternal mental health. *Research in Developmental Disabilities, 32*, 1194–1204.

Grayson, A., Emerson, A., Howard-Jones, P., & O'Neil, L. (2012). Hidden communicative competence: Case study evidence using eye-tracking and video analysis. *Autism, 15*, 75–86.

Green, S. A., Rudie, J. D., Colich, N. L., Wood, J. J., Shirinyan, D., Hernandez, L., … Bookheimer S. Y. (2013). Overreactive brain response to sensory stimuli in youth with autism spectrum disorders. *Journal of the American Academy of Child & Adolescent Psychiatry, 52*, 1158–1172.

Greenberg, H., Raymond, S. U., & Leeder, S. R. (2011). The prevention of global chronic disease: Academic public health's new frontier. *American Journal of Public Health, 101*, 1386–1391.

Greene, R. W., & Doyle, A. E. (1999). Toward a transactional conceptualization of oppositional defiant disorder: Implications for assessment and treatment. *Clinical Child and Family Psychology Review, 2*, 129–148.

Greene, R. W., Biederman, J., Faraone, S. V., Ouellette, C. A., Courtney, P., & Griffin, S. M. (1996). Toward a new psychometric definition of social disability in children with attention-deficit hyperactivity disorder. *Journal of the American Academy of Child & Adolescent Psychiatry, 35*, 571–578.

Greenhill, L. L., Posner, K., Vaughan, B. S., & Kratochvil, C. J. (2008). Attention deficit hyperactivity disorder in preschool children. *Child and Adolescent Psychiatric Clinics of North America, 17*, 347–366.

Greenspan, S. I., & Wieder, S. (2006). *Engaging autism: Using the floortime approach to help children relate, communicate, and think.* Cambridge, MA: Da Capo Lifelong Books.

Greey, M. (1995, November). Special families, special needs: The rigours and rewards of raising children with disabilities. *Today's Parent, 97*.

Gregg, N. (2011). Adults with learning disabilities: Barriers and progress. In S. Goldstein, J. A. Naglieri & M. DeVries (Eds.), *Learning and attention disorders in adolescence and adulthood: Assessment and treatment* (2nd ed., pp. 87–111). Hoboken, NJ: Wiley.

Gregory, A. M., Caspi, A., Moffitt, T. E., Koenen, K. Eley, T. C., & Poulton, R. (2007). Juvenile mental health histories of adults with anxiety disorders. *American Journal of Psychiatry, 164*, 301–308.

Gregory, A. M., & Eley, T. C. (2007). Genetic influences on anxiety in children: What we've learned and where we're heading. *Clinical Child and Family Psychology Review, 10*, 199–212.

Gregory, A. M., & Eley, T. C. (2011). The genetic basis of child and adolescent anxiety. In W. K. Silverman & A. Field (Eds.), *Anxiety disorders in children and adolescents: Research, assessment, and intervention* (2nd ed., pp. 161–178). Cambridge, England: Cambridge University Press.

Gregory, A. M., Van der Ende, J., Willis, T. A., & Verhulst, F. C. (2008). Parent-reported sleep problems during development and self-reported anxiety/depression, attention problems, and aggressive behavior later in life. *Archives of Pediatric and Adolescent Medicine, 162*, 330–335.

Gremillion, M. L., & Martel, M. M. (2013). Merely misunderstood? Receptive, expressive, and pragmatic language in young children with disruptive behavior disorders. *Journal of Clinical Child & Adolescent Psychology.* Advance online publication. doi:10.1080/15374416.2013.822306.

Gresham, F. M., & MacMillan, D. L. (1997). Autistic recovery? An analysis and critique of the empirical evidence. *Behavioral Disorders, 22*, 185–201.

Grether, J. K., Anderson, M. C., Croen, L. A., Smith, D., & Windham, G. C. (2009). Risk of autism and increasing maternal and paternal age in a large North American population. *American Journal of Epidemiology, 170*, 1118–1126.

Griffin, K. W., & Botvin, G. J. (2010). Evidence-based interventions for preventing substance use disorders in adolescents. *Child and Adolescent Psychiatric Clinics of North America, 19*, 505–526.

Griffith, E. M., Pennington, B. F., Wehner, E. A., & Rogers, S. J. (1999). Executive functions in young children with autism. *Child Development, 70*, 817–832.

Grigorenko, E. L. (2007). Triangulating developmental dyslexia: Behavior, brain, and genes. In D. Coch, G. Dawson, & K. W. Fischer (Eds.), *Human behavior, learning, and the developing brain: Atypical development* (pp. 117–144). New York: Guilford Press.

Grigorenko, E. L., Geiser, C., Slobodskaya, H. R., & Francis, D. J. (2010). Cross informant symptoms from CBCL, TRF, and YSR: Trait and method variance in a normative sample of Russian youths. *Psychological Assessment, 22*, 893–911.

Grinker, R. R. (2007). *Unstrange minds: Remapping the world of autism.* New York: Basic Books.

Groen, W., Teluij, M., Buitelaar, J., & Tendolkar, I. (2010). Amygdala and hippocampus enlargement during adolescence in autism. *Journal of the American Academy of Child & Adolescent Psychiatry, 49*, 552–560.

Gross, M. D. (1995). Origin of stimulant use for treatment of attention deficit disorder. *American Journal of Psychiatry, 152*, 298–299.

Grossbard, J. R., Atkins, D. C., Geisner, I. M., & Larimer, M. E. (2013). Does depressed mood moderate the influence of drive for thinness and muscularity on eating disorder symptoms among college men? *Psychology of Men & Masculinity, 14*, 281–287.

Guedeney, A. (2007). Withdrawal behavior and depression in infancy. *Infant Mental Health Journal, 28*, 393–408.

Guerra, N. G., Williams, K. R., & Sadek, S. (2011). Understanding bullying and victimization during childhood and adolescence: A mixed methods study. *Child Development, 82*, 295–310.

Guerrero, A. P. S., Hishinuma, E. S., Andrade, N. N., Bell, C. K., Kurahara, D. K., Lee, T. G., … Stokes, A. J. (2003). Demographic and clinical characteristics of adolescents in Hawaii with obsessive-compulsive disorder. *Archives of Pediatric and Adolescent Medicine, 157*, 665–670.

Guimarães, A. P., Schmitz, M., Polanczyk, G. V., Zeni, C., Genro, J. Roman, T., … Hutz, M. H. (2009). Further evidence for the association between attention deficit/hyperactivity disorder and the serotonin receptor 1B gene. *Journal of Neural Transmission, 116*, 1675–1680.

Guite, J. W., Lobato, D. J., Shalon, L., Plante, W., & Kao, B. T. (2007). Pain, disability, and symptoms among siblings of children with functional abdominal pain. *Journal of Developmental & Behavioral Pediatrics, 28*, 2–8.

Gullone, E. (1999). The assessment of normal fear in children and adolescents. *Clinical Child and Family Psychology Review, 2*, 91–106.

Gulsuner, S., Walsh, T., Watts, A. C., Lee, M. K., Thornton, A. M., Casadei, S., … McClellan, J. M. (2013). Spatial and temporal mapping of de novo mutations in schizophrenia to a fetal prefrontal cortical network. *Cell, 154*, 518–529.

Guralnick, M. J., Connor, R. T., & Johnson, L. C. (2011). The peer social networks of young children with down syndrome in classroom programmes. *Journal of Applied Research in Intellectual Disabilities, 24,* 310–321.

Gurley, D., Cohen, P., Pine, D. S., & Brook, J. (1996). Discriminating depression and anxiety in youth: A role for diagnostic criteria. *Journal of Affective Disorders, 39,* 191–200.

Gustafson, K. E., Bonner, M. J., Hardy, K. K., & Thompson, R. J., Jr. (2006). Biopsychosocial and developmental issues in sickle cell disease. In R. T. Brown (Ed.), *Comprehensive handbook of childhood cancer and sickle cell disease: A biopsychosocial approach* (pp. 431–448). New York: Oxford University Press.

Guthrie, W., Swineford, L. B., Wetherby, A. M., & Lord, C. (2013). Comparison of DSM-IV and DSM-5 factor structure models for toddlers with autism spectrum disorder. *Journal of the American Academy of Child & Adolescent Psychiatry, 52,* 797-805.

Guttmann-Steinmetz, S., Gadow, K. D., & DeVincent, C. J. (2009). Oppositional defiant and conduct disorders in boys with autism spectrum disorder with and without attention-deficit hyperactivity disorder versus several comparison samples. *Journal of Autism and Developmental Disorders, 39,* 976–985.

Guyer, A. E., Chaote, V. R., Grimm, K. J., Pine, D. S., & Keenan, K. (2011). Emerging depression is associated with face memory deficits in adolescent girls. *Journal of the American Academy of Child and Adolescent Psychiatry, 50,* 180–190.

Guyer, A. E., McClure-Tone, E., Shiffrin, N. D., Pine, D. S., & Nelson, E. E. (2009). Probing the neural correlates of anticipated peer evaluation in adolescence. *Child Development, 80,* 1000–1015

Gzowski, P. (1993, April). Gzowski's Canada: Extraordinary guests. *Canadian Living,* 91.

Haager, D., Klingner, J., & Vaughn, S. (Eds.). (2007). *Evidence-based reading practices for response to intervention.* New York: Brookes.

Haas, S. M., Irr, M. E., Jennings, N. A., & Wagner, L. M. (2011). Communicating thin: A grounded model of online negative enabling support groups in the pro-anorexia movement. *New Media & Society, 13,* 40–57.

Hadwin, J. A., Garner, M., & Perez-Olivas, G. (2006). The development of information processing biases in childhood anxiety: A review and exploration of its origins in parenting. *Clinical Psychology Review, 26,* 876–894.

Haedt-Matt, A. A., & Keel, P. K. (2011). Revisiting the affect regulation model of binge eating: A meta-analysis of studies using ecological momentary assessment. *Psychological Bulletin, 137,* 660–681.

Hafeman, D., Axelson, D., Demeter, C., Findling, R. L., Fristad, M. A., Kowatch, R. A., ... Birmaher, B. (2013). Phenomenology of bipolar disorder, not otherwise specified in youth: A comparison of clinical characteristics across the spectrum of manic symptoms. *Bipolar Disorders, 15,* 240–252.

Häfner, H., an der Heiden, W., Behrens, S., Gattaz, W. F., Hambrecht, M., Löffler, W., ... Stein, A. (1998). Causes and consequences of the gender difference in age of onset of schizophrenia. *Schizophrenia Bulletin, 24,* 99–113.

Hagerman, R. (2011). Review of neurogenetic syndromes: Behavioral issues and their treatment. *American Journal of Psychiatry, 168,* 216–217.

Hajcak, G., Franklin, M. E., Foa, E. B., & Simons, R. F. (2008). Increased error-related brain activity in pediatric obsessive-compulsive disorder before and after treatment. *American Journal of Psychiatry, 165,* 116–123.

Halbfinger, D. M. (2012, December 15). A gunman, recalled as intelligent and shy, who left few footprints in life. *New York Times,* p. A18.

Hale, W. M., Raaijmakers, Q., Muris, P., van Hoof, A., & Meeus, W. (2008). Developmental trajectories of adolescent anxiety disorder symptoms: A 5-year prospective community study. *Journal of the American Academy of Child & Adolescent Psychiatry, 47,* 556–564.

Hallahan, D. P., Pullen, P. C., & Ward, D. (2013). A brief history of the field of learning disabilities. In H. L. Swanson, K. R. Harris, & S. Graham (Eds.), *Handbook of learning disabilities* (2nd ed., pp. 15–32). New York: Guilford Press.

Haller, M., Handley, E., Chassin, L., & Bountress, K. (2010). Developmental cascades: Linking adolescent substance use, affiliation with substance use promoting peers, and academic achievement to adult substance use disorders. *Development and Psychopathology, 22,* 899–916.

Hallett, V., Ronald, A., Colvert, E., Ames, C., Woodhouse, E., Lietz, S., ... Happé, F. (2013). Exploring anxiety symptoms in a large-scale twin study of children with autism spectrum disorders, their co-twins and controls. *Journal of Child Psychology and Psychiatry, 54,* 1176–1185.

Halliday-Boykins, C. A., Schoenwald, S. K., & Letourneau, E. J. (2005). Caregiver-therapist ethnic similarity predicts youth outcomes from an empirically based treatment. *Journal of Consulting and Clinical Psychology, 73,* 808–818.

Hallmayer. J., Cleveland, S., Torres, A., Phillips, J., Cohen, B., Torigoe, T., ... Risch N. (2011). Genetic heritability and shared environmental factors among twin pairs with autism. *Archives of General Psychiatry, 68,* 1095–1102.

Hallowell, E. M., & Ratey, J. J. (1994). *Answers to distraction.* New York: Pantheon Books.

Halmøy, A., Johansson, S., Winge, I., McKinney, J. A., Knappskog, P. M., & Haavik, J. (2010). Attention-deficit/hyperactivity disorder symptoms in offspring of mothers with impaired serotonin production. *Archives of General Psychiatry, 67,* 1033–1043.

Hamalainen, M., & Pulkkinen, L. (1996). Problem behavior as a precursor of male criminality. *Development and Psychopathology, 8,* 443–455.

Hammad, T. A., Laughren, T., & Racoosin, J. (2006). Suicidality in pediatric patients treated with antidepressant drugs. *Archives of General Psychiatry, 63,* 323–329.

Hammen, C. (1999). The emergence of an interpersonal approach to depression. In T. Joiner & J. Coyne (Eds.), *The interactional nature of depression: Advances in interpersonal approaches* (pp. 22–36). Washington, DC: American Psychological Association.

Hammen, C. (2002). Context of stress in families of children with depressed parents. In S. H. Goodman & I. H. Gotlib (Eds.), *Children of depressed parents: Mechanisms of risk and implications for treatment* (pp. 175–202). Washington, DC: American Psychological Association.

Hammen, C., Brennan, P. A., & Le Brocque, R. (2011). Youth depression and early childrearing: Stress generation and intergenerational transmission of depression. *Journal of Consulting and Clinical Psychology, 79,* 353–363.

Hammen, C., Brennan, P. A., Keenan-Miller, D., & Herr, N. R. (2008). Early onset recurrent subtype of adolescent depression: Clinical and psychosocial correlates. *Journal of Child Psychology and Psychiatry, 49,* 433–440.

Hammen, C., & Rudolph, K. D. (2003). Childhood mood disorders. In E. J. Mash & R. A. Barkley (Eds.), *Child psychopathology* (2nd ed., pp. 233–278). New York: Guilford Press.

Hammen, C., Rudolph, K. D., & Abaied, J. (2014). Child and adolescent depression. In E. J. Mash & R. A. Barkley (Eds.), *Child psychopathology* (3rd ed., pp. 225–263). New York: Guilford Press.

Hammermess, P., Geller, D., Petty, C., Lamb, A., Bristol, E., & Biederman, J. (2010). Does ADHD moderate the manifestation of anxiety disorders in children? *European Child & Adolescent Psychiatry, 19,* 107–112.

Hammill, D. D. (1993). A brief look at the learning disabilities movement in the United States. *Journal of Learning Disabilities, 26,* 295–310.

Hammill, D. D., Mather, N., Allen, E. A., & Roberts, R. (2002). Using semantics, grammar, phonology, and rapid naming tasks to predict word identification. *Journal of Learning Disabilities, 35,* 121–136.

Hampton, T. (2007). Reports help identify and manage autism. *JAMA: Journal of the American Medical Association, 298,* 2610.

Hamshere, M. L., Langley, K., Martin, J., Agha, S. S., Stergiakouli, E., Anney, R. J., ... Thapar, A. (2013). High loading of polygenic risk for ADHD in children with comorbid aggression. *American Journal of Psychiatry, 170,* 909–916.

Handen, B. L. (2007). Intellectual disability (mental retardation). In E. J. Mash & R. A. Barkley (Eds.), *Assessment of childhood disorders* (4th ed., pp. 551–597). New York: Guilford Press.

Handen, B. L., McAuliffe, S., Janosky, J., Feldman, H., & Breaux, A. M. (1998). A playroom observation procedure to assess children with mental retardation and ADHD. *Journal of Abnormal Child Psychology, 26,* 269–277.

Handley, E. D., & Chassin, L. (2013). Alcohol-specific parenting as a mechanism of parental drinking and alcohol use disorder risk on adolescent alcohol use onset. *Journal of Studies on Alcohol and Drugs, 74,* 684–693.

Hankin, B. L., & Abramson, L. Y. (2001). Development of gender differences in depression: An elaborated cognitive vulnerability-transactional stress theory. *Psychological Bulletin, 127,* 773–796.

Hankin, B. L., Gibb, B. E., Abela, J. R. Z., & Flory, K. (2010). Selective attention to affective stimuli and clinical depression among youths: Role of anxiety and specificity of emotion. *Journal of Abnormal Psychology, 119,* 491–501.

Hankin, B. L., Jenness, J., Abela, J. R. Z., & Smolen, A. (2011). Interaction of 5-HTTLPR and idiographic stressors predicts prospective depressive symptoms specifically among youth in a multiwave design. *Journal of Clinical Child & Adolescent Psychology, 40,* 572–585.

Hankin, B. L., Wetter, E., & Cheely, C. (2008). Sex differences in child and adolescent depression. In J. R. Z. Abela & B. L. Hankin (Eds.), *Handbook of depression in children and adolescents* (pp. 377–414). New York: Guilford Press.

Hanley, G. P., Iwata, B. A., & McCord, B. E. (2003). Functional analysis of problem behavior: A review. *Journal of Applied Behavior Analysis, 36,* 147–185.

Hannesdottir, D. K., & Ollendick, T. H. (2007). The role of emotion regulation in the treatment of child anxiety disorders. *Clinical Child and Family Psychology Review, 10,* 275–293.

Hanson, E., Cerban, B. M., Slater, C. M., Caccamo, L. M., Bacic, J., & Chan, E. (2013). Brief report: Prevalence of attention deficit/hyperactivity disorder among individuals with an autism spectrum disorder. *Journal of Autism and Developmental Disorders, 43,* 1459–1464.

Happé, F. G. E. (1995a). The role of age and verbal ability in the theory of mind task performance of subjects with autism. *Child Development, 66,* 843–855.

Happé, F. G. E. (1995b, March). *Wechsler IQ profile and theory of mind in autism.* Paper presented at the biennial meeting of the Society for Research in Child Development, Indianapolis, IN.

Happé, F .G. E., & Frith, U. (1996). The neuropsychology of autism. *Brain, 119,* 1377–1400.

Harada, C. M., Siperstein, G. N., Parker, R. C., & Lenox, D. (2011). Promoting social inclusion for people with intellectual disabilities through sport: Special Olympics international, global sport initiatives and strategies. *Sport in Society, 14,* 1131–1148.

Harden, K. P., D'Onofrio, B. M., Van Hulle, C., Turkheimer, E., Rodgers, J. L., Waldman, I. D., & Lahey, B. B. (2009). Population density and youth antisocial behavior. *Journal of Child Psychology and Psychiatry, 50,* 999–1009.

Harden, K. P., & Mendle, J. (2012). Gene-environment interplay in the association between pubertal timing and delinquency in adolescent girls. *Journal of Abnormal Psychology, 121,* 73–87.

Hare, R. D. (1993). *Without conscience: The disturbing world of the psychopaths among us.* New York: Pocketbooks.

Harkness, K. L., Lumley, M. N., & Truss, A. E. (2008). Stress generation in adolescent depression: The moderating role of child abuse and neglect. *Journal of Abnormal Child Psychology, 36,* 421–432.

Harmon, H., Langley, A., & Ginsburg, G. S. (2006). The role of gender and culture in treating youth with anxiety disorders. *Journal of Cognitive Psychotherapy, 20,* 301–310.

Harrington, J. A., Rosen, L., Garneco, A., & Patrick, P. A. (2006). Parental perceptions and use of complementary and alternative medicine practices for children with autistic spectrum disorders in private practice. *Journal of Developmental and Behavioral Pediatrics, 27*(Suppl.), S156–S161.

Harris, J. C. (2006). *Intellectual disability: Understanding its development, causes, classification, evaluation, and treatment.* Oxford, England: Oxford University Press.

Harris, S. L., Handleman, J. S., & Jennett, H. K. (2005). Models of educational intervention for students with autism: Home, center, and school based programming. In F. R. Volkmar, R. Paul, A. Klin, & D. Cohen (Eds.), *Handbook of autism and pervasive developmental disorders: Vol. 2. Assessment, interventions, and policy* (3rd ed., pp. 1043–1054). Hoboken, NJ: Wiley.

Harrison, P., and Oakland, T. (2003). *Adaptive Behavior Assessment System* (2nd ed.). (ABAS-II). New York: The Psychological Corp.

Hart, H., Radua, J., Nakao, T., Mataix-Cols, D., & Rubia, K. (2013). Imaging studies of inhibition and attention in attention-deficit/hyperactivity disorder: Exploring task-specific, stimulant mediation, and age effects. *JAMA Psychiatry, 70,* 185–198.

Hart, L. M., Granillo, M. T., Jorm, A. F., & Paxton, S. J. (2011). Unmet need for treatment in the eating disorders: A systematic review of eating disorder specific treatment seeking among community cases. *Clinical Psychology Review, 31,* 727–735.

Hart, S., Jones, N. A., & Field, T. (2003). Atypical expressions of jealousy in infants of intrusive- and withdrawn-depressed mothers. *Child Psychiatry and Human Development, 33,* 193–207.

Hartmann, D. P., Pelzel, K. E., & Abbott, C. B. (2011). Design, measurement, and analysis in developmental research. In M. H. Bornstein & M. E. Lamb (Eds.), *Cognitive development: An advanced textbook* (pp. 125–213). New York: Psychology Press.

Hartmann, T. (1993). *Attention deficit disorder: A different perception.* Lancaster, PA: Underwood-Miller.

Hartung, C. M., & Widiger, T. A. (1998). Gender differences in the diagnosis of mental disorders. Conclusions and controversies of DSM-IV. *Psychological Bulletin, 123,* 260–278.

Hartup, W. W. (1996). The company they keep: Friendships and their developmental significance. *Child Development, 67,* 1–13.

Harvey, S. T., & Taylor, J. E. (2010). A meta-analysis of the effects of psychotherapy with sexually abused children and adolescents. *Clinical Psychology Review, 30,* 517–535.

Haskett, M. E., Nears, K., Ward, C. S., & McPherson, A. V. (2006). Diversity in adjustment of maltreated children: Factors associated with resilient functioning. *Clinical Psychology Review, 26,* 796–812.

Haskett, M. E., Scott, S. S., & Ward, C. S. (2004). Subgroups of physically abusive parents based on cluster analysis of parenting behavior and affect. *American Journal of Orthopsychiatry, 74,* 436–447.

Hasler, B. P., & Clark, D. B. (2013). Circadian misalignment, Reward-related brain function, and adolescent alcohol involvement. *Alcoholism: Clinical and Experimental Research, 37,* 558–565.

Hasler, B. P., Dahl, R. E., Holm, S. M., Jakubcak, J. L., Ryan, N. D., Silk, J. S., … Forbes, E. E. (2012). Weekend–weekday advances in sleep timing are associated with altered reward-related brain function in healthy adolescents. *Biological Psychology, 91,* 334–341.

Hastings, P. D., Zahn-Waxler, C., Robinson, J., Usher, B., & Bridges, D. (2000). The development of concern for others in children with behavior problems. *Developmental Psychology, 36,* 531–546.

Hatch, M. L., Friedman, S., & Paradis, C. M. (1996). Behavioral treatment of obsessive-compulsive disorder in African Americans. *Cognitive and Behavioral Practice, 3,* 303–315.

Hatch, S. L., Harvey, S. B., & Maughan, B. (2010). A developmental-contextual approach to understanding mental health and well-being in early adulthood. *Social Science & Medicine, 70,* 261–268.

Hatcher, P. J., Hulme, C., Miles, J. N. V., Carroll, J. M., Hatcher, J., Gibbs, S., … Snowling, M. J. (2006). Efficacy of small group reading intervention for beginning readers with reading-delay: A randomised controlled trial. *Journal of Child Psychology and Psychiatry, 47,* 820–827.

Hauser, M., Galling, B., & Correll, C. U. (2013). Suicidal ideation and suicide attempts in children and adolescents with bipolar disorder: A systematic review of prevalence and incidence rates, correlates, and targeted interventions. *Bipolar Disorders, 15,* 507–523.

Havermans, T., Wuytack, L., Deboel, J., Tijtgat, A., Malfroot, A., De Boeck, C., & Proesmans, M. (2011). Siblings of children with cystic fibrosis: Quality of life and the impact of illness. *Child: Care, Health and Development, 37,* 252–260.

Hay, I., Elias, G., Fielding-Barnsley, R., Homel, R., & Freiberg, K. (2007). Language delays, reading delays, and learning difficulties: Interactive elements requiring multidimensional programming. *Journal of Learning Disabilities, 40,* 400–409.

Hay, P. (2013). A systematic review of evidence for psychological treatments in eating disorders: 2005–2012. *International Journal of Eating Disorders, 46,* 462–469.

Hayden, E. P., & Mash, E. J. (2014). Child psychopathology: A developmental systems approach. In E. J. Mash & R. A. Barkley (Eds.), *Child psychopathology* (3rd ed., pp. 3–72). New York: Guilford Press.

Hayden, E. P., Olino, T. M., Mackrell, S. V. M., Jordan, P. L., Desjardins, J., & Katsiroumbas, P. (2013). Cognitive vulnerability to depression during middle childhood: Stability and association with maternal affective styles and parental depression. *Personality and Individual Differences, 55,* 892–897.

Haynes, S. N., & Heiby, E. M. (Eds.). (2004). *Comprehensive handbook of psychological assessment: Vol. 3. Behavioral assessment.* New York: Wiley.

Haynes, S. N., Mumma, G. H., & Pinson, C. (2009). Idiographic assessment: Conceptual and psychometric foundations of individualized behavioral assessment. *Clinical Psychology Review, 29,* 179–191.

Haynes, S. N., Smith, G. T., & Hunsley, J. (2011). *Scientific foundations of clinical assessment.* New York: Routledge, Taylor, & Francis.

Haynos, A. F., & Fruzzetti, A. E. (2011). Anorexia nervosa as a disorder of emotional dysregulation: Evidence and treatment implications. *Clinical Psychology: Science and Practice, 18,* 183–202.

Hayward, C., Gotlib, I. H., Schraedley, P. K., & Litt, I. F. (1999). Ethnic differences in the association between pubertal status and symptoms of depression in adolescent girls. *Journal of Adolescent Health, 25,* 143–149.

Hayward, C., Killen, J. D., Hammer, L. D., Litt, I. F., Wilson, D. M., Simmonds, B., & Taylor, C. B. (1992). Pubertal stage and panic attack history in sixth- and seventh-grade girls. *American Journal of Psychiatry, 149,* 1239–1243.

Hayward, C., Killen, J. D., Wilson, D. M., & Hammer, L. D. (1997). Psychiatric risk associated with early puberty in adolescent girls. *Journal of the American Academy of Child & Adolescent Psychiatry, 36,* 255–262.

Hazlett, H. C., Hammer, J., Hooper, S. R., & Kamphaus, R. W. (2011). *Down syndrome.* New York: Guilford Press.

Health Resources and Services Administration. (2010). *Health professional shortage areas: Mental health designated populations. Rural Assistance Center.* Retrieved from www.raconline.org/maps/mapfiles/hpsa_mental.png

Healy, S. J., Murray, L. Cooper, P. J., Hughes, C., & Halligan, S. L. (2013). A longitudinal investigation of maternal influences on the development of hostile attributions and aggression. *Journal of Clinical Child & Adolescent Psychology.* Advance online publication. doi:10.1080/15374416.2013.850698.

Hebebrand, J., Schrag, A., Schimmelmann, B. G., & Hinney, A. (2010). Child and adolescent psychiatric genetics. *European Child & Adolescent Psychiatry, 19,* 259–279.

Hechtman, L. (2006). Long-term treatment of children and adolescents with attention-deficit/hyperactivity disorder (ADHD). *Current Psychiatry Reports, 8,* 398–408.

Hedley, A. A., Ogden, C. L., Johnson, C. L., Carroll, M. D., Curtin, L. R., Flegal, K. M. (2004). Prevalence of overweight and obesity among US children, adolescents, and adults, 1999-2002. *JAMA: Journal of the American Medical Association, 291,* 2847–2850.

Hedley, M. (2002). The geometry of gendered conflict in popular film: 1986–2000. *Sex Roles, 47*(5–6), 201–217.

Heflinger, C. A., & Hinshaw, S. P. (2010). Stigma in child and adolescent mental health services research: Understanding professional and institutional stigmatization of youth with mental health problems and their families. *Administration and Policy in Mental Health and Mental Health Services Research, 37*(1–2), 61–70.

Heim, C., & Nemeroff, C. B. (2001). The role of childhood trauma in the neurobiology of mood and anxiety disorders: Preclinical and clinical studies. *Biological Psychiatry, 49,* 1023–1039.

Heim, C., Shugart, M., Craighead, W. E., & Nemeroff, C. B. (2010). Neurobiological and psychiatric consequences of child abuse and neglect. *Developmental Psychobiology, 52,* 671–690.

Heim, S., & Benasich, A. A. (2006). Developmental disorders of language. In D. Cicchetti & D. J. Cohen (Eds.), *Developmental psychopathology, Vol. 3. Risk, disorder, and adaptation* (2nd ed., pp. 268–316). Hoboken, NJ: Wiley.

Helland, W. A., Biringer, E., Helland, T., & Heimann, M. (2012). Exploring language profiles for children with ADHD and children with Asperger syndrome. *Journal of Attention Disorders, 16,* 34–43.

Hendren, R. L., De Backer, I., & Pandina, G. J. (2000). Review of neuroimaging studies of child and adolescent psychiatric disorders from the past 10 years. *Journal of the American Academy of Child & Adolescent Psychiatry, 39,* 815–828.

Henggeler, S. W. (1996). Treatment of violent juvenile offenders—We have the knowledge: Comment on Gorman-Smith et al. (1996). *Journal of Family Psychology, 10,* 137–141.

Henggeler, S. W., Chapman, J. E., Rowland, M. D., Halliday-Boykins, C. A., Randall, J., Shackelford, J., & Schoenwald, S. K. (2008). Statewide adoption and initial implementation of contingency management for substance-abusing adolescents. *Journal of Consulting and Clinical Psychology, 76,* 556–567.

Henggeler, S. W., Cunningham, P. B., Rowland, M. D., & Schoenwald, S. K. (2012). *Contingency management for adolescent substance abuse: A practitioner's guide* New York: Guilford Press.

Henggeler, S. W., Melton, G. B., & Smith, L. A. (1992). Family preservation using multisystemic therapy: An effective alternative to incarcerating serious juvenile offenders. *Journal of Consulting and Clinical Psychology, 60,* 953–961.

Henggeler, S. W., & Santos, A. B. (Eds.). (1997). *Innovative approaches for difficult-to-treat populations.* Washington, DC: American Psychiatric Press.

Henggeler, S. W., & Schaeffer, C. (2010). Treating serious antisocial behavior using multisystemic therapy. In J. R. Weisz & A. E. Kazdin (Eds.), *Evidence-based psychotherapies for children and adolescents* (2nd ed., pp. 259–276). New York: Guilford.

Henggeler, S. W., Schoenwald, S. K., Borduin, C. M., Rowland, M. D., & Cunningham, P. B. (2009). *Multisystemic therapy for antisocial behavior in children and adolescents* (2nd ed.). New York: Guilford Press.

Herba, C. M., Roza, S. J., Govaert, P., van Rossum, J., Hofman, A., Jaddoe, V., … Tiemeier, H. (2010). Infant brain development and vulnerability to later internalizing difficulties: The Generation R Study. *Journal of the American Academy of Child & Adolescent Psychiatry, 49,* 1053–1063.

Herba, C. M., Tremblay, R. E., Boivin, M., Liu, X., Mongeau, C., Séguin, J. R., & Côté, S. M. (2013). Can early child care help children of depressed mothers? *JAMA Psychiatry, 70,* 830–838.

Herman, J. L. (1992). *Trauma and recovery: The aftermath of violence—from domestic abuse to political terror.* New York: Basic Books.

Hermann, C. (2011). Psychological interventions for chronic pediatric pain: State of the art, current developments and open questions. *Pain Management, 1,* 473–483.

Herndon, R. W., & Iacono, W. G. (2005). Psychiatric disorder in the children of antisocial parents. *Psychological Medicine, 35,* 1815–1824.

Herrenkohl, R. C., Herrenkohl, E. C., & Egolf, B. P. (1983). Circumstances surrounding the occurrence of child maltreatment. *Journal of Consulting and Clinical Psychology, 51,* 424–431.

Herrmann, E., Call, J., Hernández-Lloreda, M. V., Hare, B., & Tomasello, M. (2007). Humans have evolved specialized skills of social cognition: The cultural intelligence hypothesis. *Science, 317,* 1360–1366.

Hersh, J., Curry, J. F., & Becker, S. J. (2013). The influence of comorbid depression and conduct disorder on MET/CBT treatment outcome for adolescent substance use disorders. *International Journal of Cognitive Therapy, 6,* 325–341.

Hertz-Picciotto, I. (2011). Environmental risk factors in autism: Results from large-scale epidemiologic studies. In D. G. Amaral, G. Dawson, & D. Geschwind (Eds.), *Autism spectrum disorders* (pp. 827–862). New York: Oxford University Press.

Herzog, D. B., & Eddy, K. T. (2007). Diagnosis, epidemiology, and clinical course of eating disorders. In J. Yager & P. Powers (Eds.), *Clinical manual of eating disorders* (pp. 1–29). Washington, DC: American Psychiatric Press.

Hetherington, E. M., Bridges, M., & Insabella, G. M. (1998). What matters? What does not? Five perspectives on the association between marital transitions and children's adjustment. *American Psychologist, 53,* 167–184.

Hetrick, S. E., McKenzie, J. E., & Merry, S. N. (2010). The use of SSRIs in children and adolescents. *Current Opinion in Psychiatry, 23,* 53–57.

Higa-McMillan, C. K., Francis, S. E., & Chorpita, B. F. (2014). Anxiety disorders. In E. J. Mash & R. A. Barkley (Eds.), *Child psychopathology* (3rd ed., pp. 345–428). New York: Guilford Press.

Hildebrandt, T. B. (2005). A review of eating disorders in athletes: Recommendations for secondary school prevention and intervention programs. *Journal of Applied School Psychology, 21,* 145–167.

Hildyard, K., & Wolfe, D. A. (2002). Child neglect: Developmental issues and outcomes. *Child Abuse & Neglect, 26,* 679–695.

Hildyard, K., & Wolfe, D. A. (2007). Understanding child neglect: Cognitive processes underlying neglectful parenting. *Child Abuse & Neglect, 31,* 895–907.

Hill, E. L. (2004). Executive dysfunction in autism. *Trends in Cognitive Sciences, 8,* 26–32.

Hillberg, T., Hamilton-Giachritsis, C., & Dixon, L. (2011). Review of meta-analyses on the association between child sexual abuse and adult mental health difficulties: A systematic approach. *Trauma, Violence, & Abuse, 12,* 38–49.

Hinshaw, S. P. (1992). Externalizing behavior problems and academic underachievement in childhood and adolescence: Causal relationships and underlying mechanisms. *Psychological Bulletin, 111,* 127–155.

Hinshaw, S. P. (2007a). *The mark of shame: Stigma of mental illness and an agenda for change.* New York: Oxford University Press.

Hinshaw, S. P. (2007b). Moderators and mediators of treatment outcome for youth with ADHD: Understanding for whom and how treatments work. *Ambulatory Pediatrics, 7*(Suppl. 1), 91–100.

Hinshaw, S. P. (2008). Lessons from research on the developmental psychopathology of girls and women. *Journal of the American Academy of Child & Adolescent Psychiatry, 47,* 359–361.

Hinshaw, S. P. (2013). Developmental psychopathology as a scientific discipline: Rationale, principles, and advances. In T. P. Beauchaine & S. P. Hinshaw (Eds.), *Child and adolescent psychopathology* (2nd ed., pp. 3–27). Hoboken, NJ: Wiley.

Hinshaw, S. P., & Blachman, D. R. (2003). Attention-deficit/hyperactivity disorder in girls. In D. Bell, S. L. Foster, & E. J. Mash (Eds.), *Handbook of behavioral and emotional problems in girls* (pp. 117–147). New York: Kluwer.

Hinshaw, S. P., & Lee, S. S. (2003). Conduct and oppositional defiant disorders. In E. J. Mash & R. A. Barkley (Eds.), *Child psychopathology* (2nd. ed., pp. 144–198). New York: Guilford Press.

Hinshaw, S. P., Owens, E. B., Zalecki, C., Huggins, S. P., Montenegro-Nevado, A. J., Schrodek, E., & Swanson, E. N. (2012). Prospective follow-up of girls with attention-deficit/hyperactivity

disorder into early adulthood: Continuing impairment includes elevated risk for suicide attempts and self-injury. *Journal of Consulting and Clinical Psychology, 80,* 1041–1051.

Hinshaw, S. P., & Stier, A. (2008). Stigma as related to mental disorders. *Annual Review of Clinical Psychology, 4,* 367–393.

Hinton, E. C., Isles, A. R., Williams, N. M., & Parkinson, J. A. (2010). Excessive appetitive arousal in Prader-Willi syndrome. *Appetite, 54,* 225–228.

Hirschi, T., & Gottfredson, M. (1983). Age and the explanation of crime. *American Journal of Sociology, 89,* 552–583.

Hirshfeld, D. R., Biederman, J., & Rosenbaum, J. F. (1997). Expressed emotion toward children with behavioral inhibition: Associations with maternal anxiety disorder. *Journal of the American Academy of Child & Adolescent Psychiatry, 36,* 910–919.

Hirshfeld-Becker, D. R., Masek, B., Henin, A., Blakely, L. R., Pollock-Wurman, R. A., McQuade, J., ... Biederman, J. (2010). Cognitive behavior therapy for 4- to 7-year-old children with anxiety disorders: A randomized clinical trial. *Journal of Consulting and Clinical Psychology, 78,* 498–510.

Ho, H. Y., Cheung, M. C., & Chan, A. S. (2003). Music training improves verbal but not visual memory: Cross-sectional and longitudinal explorations in children. *Neuropsychology, 17,* 439–450.

Ho, T. C., Wu, J., Shin, D. D., Liu, T. T., Tapert, S. F., Yang, G., ... Yang, T. T. (2013). Altered cerebral perfusion in executive, affective, and motor networks during adolescent depression. *Journal of the American Academy of Child & Adolescent Psychiatry, 52,* 1076–1091.

Hoagwood, K. E., & Cavaleri, M. A. (2010). Ethical issues in child and adolescent psychosocial treatment research. In J. R. Weisz & A. E. Kazdin (Eds.), *Evidence-based psychotherapy for children and adolescents* (2nd ed., pp. 10–27). New York: Guilford Press.

Hobson, R. P. (2002/2004). *The cradle of thought.* London/New York: Macmillan/ Oxford University Press.

Hodapp, R. M., & Burack, J. A. (2006). Developmental approaches to children with mental retardation: A second generation? In D. Cicchetti & D. J. Cohen (Eds.), *Developmental psychopathology, Vol. 3: Risk, disorder, and adaptation* (2nd ed., pp. 235–267). Hoboken, NJ: Wiley.

Hodapp, R. M., & Dykens, E. M. (2003). Mental retardation (intellectual disabilities). In E. J. Mash & R. A. Barkley (Eds.), *Child psychopathology* (2nd ed., pp. 486–519). New York: Guilford Press.

Hodapp, R. M., & Dykens, E. M. (2009). Intellectual disabilities and child psychiatry: Looking to the future. *Journal of Child Psychology and Psychiatry, 50,* 99–107.

Hodapp, R. M. & Dykens, E. M. (2012). Genetic disorders of intellectual disability: Expanding our concepts of phenotypes and of family outcomes. *Journal of Genetic Counseling, 21,* 761–769.

Hodapp, R. M., Griffin, M. M., Burke, M. M., & Fisher, M. H. (2011). Intellectual

disabilities. In R. M. Hodapp, M. M. Griffin, M. M. Burke, & M. H. Fisher (Eds.), *The Cambridge handbook of intelligence* (pp. 193–209). New York: Cambridge University Press.

Hodapp, R. M., Kazemi, E., Rosner, B. A., & Dykens, E. M. (2006). Mental retardation. In D. A. Wolfe & E. J. Mash (Eds.), *Behavioral and emotional disorders in adolescents: Nature, assessment, and treatment* (pp. 383–409). New York: Guilford Press.

Hodge, S. M., Makris, N., Kennedy, D. N., Caviness, V. S., Jr., Howard, J., McGrath, L., ... Harris, G. J. (2010). Cerebellum, language and cognition in autism and specific language impairment. *Journal of Autism and Developmental Disorders, 40,* 300–316.

Hodgins, S., Faucher, B., Zarac, A., & Ellenbogen, M. (2002). Children of parents with bipolar disorder: A population at high risk for major affective disorders. *Child and Adolescent Psychiatric Clinics of North America, 11,* 533–553.

Hodgins, S., Kratzer, L., & McNeil, T. F. (2001). Obstetrical complications, parenting, and risk of criminal behavior. *Archives of General Psychiatry, 58,* 746–752.

Hoeve, M., Blokland, A., Dubas, J. S., Loeber, R., Gerris, J. R. M., & van der Laan, P. H. (2008). Trajectories of delinquency and parenting styles. *Journal of Abnormal Child Psychology, 36,* 223–235.

Hoffer, R. H. (1997, June 30). Lovestruck. *Sports Illustrated.* pp. 22–35.

Hoffman, E. C., & Mattis, S. G. (2000). A developmental adaptation of panic control treatment for panic disorder in adolescence. *Cognitive and Behavioral Practice, 7,* 253–261.

Hoffmann, H. (1845). *Struwwelpeter.* London: Blackie.

Holland, L. A., Bodell, L. P., & Keel, P. K. (2013). Psychological factors predict eating disorder onset and maintenance at 10-year follow-up. *European Eating Disorders Review, 21,* 405–410.

Hollway, J. A., & Aman, M. G. (2011). Sleep correlates of pervasive developmental disorders: A review of the literature. *Research in Developmental Disabilities, 32,* 1399–1421.

Holmans, P., Weissman, M. M., Zubenko, G. S., Scheftner, W. A., Crowe, R. R., Depaulo, J. R., Jr., ... Levinson, D. F. (2007). Genetics of early-onset major depression (GenRED): Final genome scan report. *American Journal of Psychiatry, 164,* 248–258.

Holmbeck, G. N., Friedman, D., Abad, M., & Jandasek, B. (2006). Development and psychopathology in adolescence. In D. A. Wolfe & E. J. Mash (Eds.), *Behavioral and emotional disorders in adolescents: Nature, assessment, and treatment* (pp. 21–55). New York: Guilford Press.

Holmboe, K., Rijsdijk, F. V., Hallett, V., Happé, F., Plomin, R., & Ronald, A. (2014). Strong genetic influences on the stability of autistic traits in childhood. *Journal of the American Academy of Child & Adolescent Psychiatry, 53,* 221–230.

Holmes, F. B. (1936). An experimental investigation of a method of overcoming children's fears. *Child Development, 7*, 6–30.

Holmes, J., Gathercole, S. E., Place, M., Alloway, T. P., Elliott, J. G., & Hilton, K. A. (2010). The diagnostic utility of executive function assessments in the identification of ADHD in children. *Child and Adolescent Mental Health, 15*, 37–43.

Holtom-Viesel, A., & Allan, S. (2014). A systematic review of the literature on family functioning across all eating disorder diagnoses in comparison to control families. *Clinical Psychology Review, 34*, 29–43.

Holzer, S. R., Uppala, S., Wonderlich, S. A., Crosby, R. D., & Simonich, H. (2008). Mediational significance of PTSD in the relationship of sexual trauma and eating disorders. *Child Abuse & Neglect, 32*, 561–566.

Homma, Y., Wang, N., Saewyc, E., & Kishor, N. (2012). The relationship between sexual abuse and risky sexual behavior among adolescent boys: A meta-analysis. *Journal of Adolescent Health, 51*, 18–24.

Hooper, S. R., Costa, L. C., McBee, M., Anderson, K. L., Yerby, D. C., Childress, A., & Knuth, S. B. (2013). A written language intervention for at-risk second grade students: A randomized controlled trial of the process assessment of the learner lesson plans in a tier 2 response-to-intervention (RtI) model. *Annals of Dyslexia, 63*, 44–64.

Hooper, S. R., Costa, L., McBee, M., Anderson, K. L., Yerby, D. C., Knuth, S. B., & Childress, A. (2011). Concurrent and longitudinal neuropsychological contributors to written language expression in first and second grade students. *Reading and Writing, 24*, 221–252.

Hoover, D. W., & Milich, R. (1994). Effects of sugar ingestion expectancies on mother-child interactions. *Journal of Abnormal Child Psychology, 22*, 501–514.

Hopfer, C., Salomonsen-Sautel, S., Mikulich-Gilbertson, S., Min, S.-J., McQueen, M., Crowley, T., ... Hewitt, J. (2013). Conduct disorder and initiation of substance use: A prospective longitudinal study. *Journal of the American Academy of Child & Adolescent Psychiatry, 52*, 511–518.

Horowitz, J. L., & Garber, J. (2006). The prevention of depressive symptoms in children and adolescents: A meta-analytic review. *Journal of Consulting and Clinical Psychology, 74*, 401–415.

Horst, R. (2009). Diagnostic issues in childhood bipolar disorder. *Psychiatric Clinics of North America, 32*, 71–80.

Houts, A. C. (2010). Behavioral treatment for enuresis. In J. R. Weisz & A. E. Kazdin (Eds.), *Evidence-based psychotherapies for children and adolescents* (2nd ed., pp. 359–374). New York: Guilford Press.

Howard, A. L., Robinson, M., Smith, G. J., Ambrosini, G. L., Piek, J. P., & Oddy, W. H. (2011). ADHD is associated with a "Western" dietary pattern in adolescents. *Journal of Attention Disorders, 15*, 403–411.

Howard, J. S., Sparkman, C. R., Cohen, H. G., Green, G., & Stanislaw, H. (2005). A comparison of intensive behavior analytic and eclectic treatment for young children with autism. *Research in Developmental Disabilities, 26*, 359–383.

Howell, P. (2011). *Recovery from stuttering*. New York: Psychology Press.

Howell, P., & Davis, S. (2011). Predicting persistence of and recovery from stuttering by the teenage years based on information gathered at age 8 years. *Journal of Developmental and Behavioral Pediatrics, 32*, 196–205.

Howes, O. D., & Falkenberg, I. (2011). Early detection and intervention in bipolar affective disorder: Targeting the development of the disorder. *Current Psychiatry Reports, 13*, 493–499.

Howland, L. C., Storm, D. S., Crawford, S. L., Ma, Y., Gortmaker, S. L., & Oleske, J. M. (2007). Negative life events: Risk to health-related quality of life in children and youth with HIV infection. *JANAC: Journal of the Association of Nurses in AIDS Care, 18*, 3–11.

Howlin, P. (2013). Social disadvantage and exclusion: Adults with autism lag far behind in employment prospects. *Journal of the American Academy of Child & Adolescent Psychiatry, 52*, 897–899.

Howlin, P., Goode, S., Hutton, J., & Rutter, M. (2004). Adult outcome for children with autism. *Journal of Child Psychology and Psychiatry, 45*, 212–229.

Howlin, P., Moss, P., Savage, S., & Rutter, M. (2013). Social outcomes in mid- to later adulthood among individuals diagnosed with autism and average nonverbal IQ as children. *Journal of the American Academy of Child and Adolescent Psychiatry, 52*, 572–581.

Hoza, B., Murray-Close, D., Arnold, L. E., Hinshaw, S. P., Hechtman, L., and the MTA Cooperative Group (2010). Time-dependent changes in positively biased self-perceptions of children with attention-deficit/hyperactivity disorder: A developmental psychopathology perspective. *Development and Psychopathology, 22*, 375–390.

Hoza, B., Vaughn, A., Waschbusch, D. A., Murray-Close, D., & McCabe, G. (2012). Can children with ADHD be motivated to reduce bias in self-reports of competence? *Journal of Consulting and Clinical Psychology, 80*, 245–254.

Hoza, B., Waschbusch, D. A., Pelham, W. E., Molina, B. S. G., & Milich, R. (2000). Attention-deficit/hyperactivity disordered and control boys' responses to social success and failure. *Child Development, 71*, 432–446.

Huck, S., Kemp, C., & Carter, M. (2010). Self-concept of children with intellectual disability in mainstream settings. *Journal of Intellectual and Developmental Disability, 35*, 141–154.

Hudson, J. I., Hiripi, E., Pope, H. G., & Kessler, R. C. (2007). The prevalence and correlates of eating disorders in the National Comorbidity Survey Replication. *Biological Psychiatry, 61*, 348–358.

Hudson, J. L., & Dodd, H. F. (2012). Informing early intervention: Preschool predictors of anxiety disorders in middle childhood. *PLoS ONE, 7*(8), e42359.

Hudziak, J. J., & Novins, D. K. (2013). Illuminating the complexities of developmental psychopathology: Special series on longitudinal and birth cohort studies. *Journal of the American Academy of Child & Adolescent Psychiatry, 52*, 6–7.

Huebner, T., Vloet, T. D., Marx, I., Konrad, K., Fink, G. R., Herpertz, S. C., & Herpertz-Dahlmann, B. (2008). Morphometric brain abnormalities in boys with conduct disorder. *Journal of the American Academy of Child & Adolescent Psychiatry, 47*, 540–547.

Huemer, J., Erhart, F., & Steiner, H. (2010). Posttraumatic stress disorder in children and adolescents: A review of psychopharmacological treatment. *Child Psychiatry and Human Development, 41*, 624–640.

Huerta, M., Bishop, S. L., Duncan, A., Hus, V., & Lord, C. (2012). Application of DSM-5 criteria for autism spectrum disorder to three samples of children with DSM-IV diagnoses of pervasive developmental disorders. *American Journal of Psychiatry, 169*, 1056–1064.

Huesmann, L. R., Eron, L. D., Lefkowitz, M. M., & Walder, L. O. (1984). Stability of aggression over time and generations. *Developmental Psychology, 20*, 1120–1134.

Huesmann, L. R., Moise-Titus, J., Podolski, C., & Eron, L. D. (2003). Longitudinal relations between children's exposure to TV violence and their aggressive and violent behavior in young adulthood: 1977–1992. *Developmental Psychology, 39*, 201–221.

Huey, S. J., & Polo, A. J. (2008). Evidence-based treatment for minority youth: A review and meta-analysis. *Journal of Clinical Child & Adolescent Psychology, 37*, 262–301.

Huizink, A. C., Mulder, E. J. H., & Buitelaar, J. K (2004). Prenatal stress and risk for psychopathology: Specific effects or induction of general susceptibility. *Psychological Bulletin, 130*, 115–142.

Hulme, C., & Snowling, M. J. (2009). *Developmental disorders of language learning and cognition*. Malden, MA: Blackwell.

Hummel, A., Shelton, K. H., Heron, J., Moore, L., & van den Bree, M.D.M. (2013). A systematic review of the relationships between family functioning, pubertal timing and adolescent substance use. *Addiction, 108*, 487–496.

Humphreys, K. L., Eng, T., & Lee, S. S. (2013). Stimulant medication and substance use outcomes: A meta-analysis. *JAMA Psychiatry, 70*, 740–749.

Hunsley, J., & Mash, E. J. (Eds.). (2008). *A guide to assessments that work*. New York: Oxford University Press.

Hurlbert, R. T., Happé, F., & Frith, U. (1994). Sampling the form of inner experience in three adults with Asperger syndrome. *Psychological Medicine, 24*, 385–395.

Hurt, E. A., & Arnold, L. E. (2014). Dietary management of ADHD. In R. A. Barkley (Ed.), *Attention-deficit hyperactivity disorder: A handbook for diagnosis and treatment* (4th ed.). New York: Guilford Press.

Huss, M., Verney, J. P., Fosker, T., Mead, N., & Goswami, U. (2011). Music, rhythm, rise time perception and developmental dyslexia: Perception of musical meter predicts reading and phonology. *Cortex: A Journal Devoted to the Study of the Nervous System and Behavior, 47,* 674–689.

Hussong, A., Bauer, D., & Chassin, L. (2008). Telescoped trajectories from alcohol initiation to disorder in children of alcoholic parents. *Journal of Abnormal Psychology, 117,* 63–78.

Hussong, A. M., Flora, D. B., Curran, P. J., Chassin, L. A., & Zucker, R. A. (2008). Defining risk heterogeneity for internalizing symptoms among children of alcoholic parents. *Development and Psychopathology, 20,* 165–193.

Hysing, M., Elgen, I., Gillberg, C., & Lundervold, A. J. (2009). Emotional and behavioural problems in subgroups of children with chronic illness: Results from a large-scale population study. *Child: Care, Health and Development, 35,* 527–533.

Ialongo, N., Edelsohn, G., Werthamer-Larsson, L., Crockett, L., & Kellam, S. (1995). The significance of self-reported anxious symptoms in first grade children: Prediction to anxious symptoms and adaptive functioning in fifth grade. *Journal of Child Psychology and Psychiatry, 36,* 427–437.

Ialongo, N. S., Rogosch, F. A., Cicchetti, D., Toth, S. L., Buckley, L., Petras, H., & Neiderhiser, J. (2006). A developmental psychopathology approach to the prevention of mental health disorders. In D. Cicchetti & D. J. Cohen (Eds.), *Developmental psychopathology: Vol. 1. Theory and method* (2nd ed., pp. 968–1018). New York: Wiley.

Illick, J. E. (1974). Childrearing in seventeenth century England and America. In L. deMause (Ed.), *The history of childhood* (pp. 303–350). New York: Psychohistory Press.

Ilott, N., Saudino, K. J., Wood, A., & Asherson, P. (2010). A genetic study of ADHD and activity level in infancy. *Genes, Brain, and Behavior, 9,* 296–304.

Inderbitzen-Nolan, H. M., & Walters, K. S. (2000). Social anxiety scale for adolescents: Normative data and further evidence of construct validity. *Journal of Clinical Child Psychology, 29,* 360–371.

Individuals with Disabilities Education Improvement Act (IDEA). (2004). *Public Law No. 104–446.* Retrieved from http://idea.ed.gov/explore/view/p/%2Croot%2Cstatute%2CJ

Ingman, K. A., Ollendick, T. H., & Akande, A. (1999). Cross-cultural aspects of fears in African children and adolescents. *Behaviour Research and Therapy, 37,* 337–345.

Innocenti, G. M. (1982). Development of interhemispheric cortical connections. *Neurosciences Research Program Bulletin, 20,* 532–540.

Insel, T. (2010, October 7). *Brain scans: Not quite ready for prime time.* NIMH, Director's Blog. Retrieved from http://www.nimh.nih.gov/about/director/2010/brain-scans-not-quite-ready-for-prime-time.shtml

Insel, T. (2013). *Transforming diagnosis* [Weblog post, April 29, 2013]. Retrieved from http://www.nimh.nih.gov/about/director/index.shtml

Insel, T., Cuthbert, B., Garvey, M., Heinssen, R., Pine, D.S., Quinn, K., ... Wang, P. (2010). Research domain criteria (RDoC): Toward a new classification framework for research on mental disorders. *American Journal of Psychiatry, 167,* 748–751.

Institute of Education Sciences. (2010, August). Early childhood education intervention for children with disabilities: Lovaas Model of Applied Behavior Analysis. *WWC Intervention Report,* pp. 1–10, U.S. Department of Education. Retrieved from http://ies.ed.gov/ncee/wwc/reports/ece_cd/lovaas_model/effectiveness.asp

Institute of Medicine. (2004). *Immunization safety review: Vaccines and autism.* Washington, DC: Author.

Institute of Medicine. (2011). *Clinical practice guidelines we can trust.* Washington, DC: National Academies Press. Retrieved from www.nap.edu/download.php?record_id=13058

Interactive Autism Network. (2011, September). *Interactive Autism Network (IAN): Linking the autism community and researchers.* Retrieved from http://www.ianproject.org

Interagency Autism Coordinating Committee (IACC). (2011, January). *2011 IACC Strategic Plan for Autism Spectrum Disorder Research.* Retrieved from http://iacc.hhs.gov/strategic-plan/2011/index.shtml

International Human Genome Sequencing Consortium. (2004). Finishing the euchromatic sequence of the human genome. *Nature, 431,* 931–945.

International Society for Prevention of Child Abuse and Neglect. (2010). *World Perspectives on Child Abuse* (9th ed.). Aurora, CO: Author.

Irish, L., Kobayashi, I., & Delahanty, D. L. (2010). Long-term physical health consequences of childhood sexual abuse: A meta-analytic review. *Journal of Pediatric Psychology, 35,* 450–461.

Isomaa, R., Isomaa, A. L., Marttunen, M., Kaltiala-Heino, R., & Bjorkqvist, K. (2010). Psychological distress and risk for eating disorders in subgroups of dieters. *European Eating Disorders Review, 18,* 296–303.

Ivarsson, T., Granqvist, P., Gillberg, C., & Broberg, A. G. (2010). Attachment states of mind in adolescent with obsessive compulsive disorder and/or depressive disorders: A controlled study. *European Child & Adolescent Psychiatry, 19,* 845–853.

Ivarsson, T., Rastam, M., Wentz, E., Gillberg, I. C., & Gillberg, C. (2000). Depressive disorders in teenage-onset anorexia nervosa: A controlled longitudinal, partly community-based study. *Comprehensive Psychiatry, 41,* 398–403.

Iwaniec, D., Sheddon, H., & Allen, S. (2003). The outcomes of a longitudinal study of non-organic failure-to-thrive. *Child Abuse Review, 12,* 216–226.

Izard, C. E., Youngstrom, E. A., Fine, S. E., Mostow, A. J., & Trentacosta, C. J. (2006). Emotions and developmental psychopathology. In D. Cicchetti & D. J. Cohen (Eds.), *Developmental psychopathology: Vol. 1. Theory and method* (2nd ed., pp. 244–292). Hoboken, NJ: Wiley.

Jaaniste, T., Hayes, B., & von Baeyer, C. L. (2007). Providing children with information about forthcoming medical procedures: A review and synthesis. *Clinical Psychology: Science and Practice, 14,* 124–143.

Jackson, Y., Alberts, F. L., & Roberts, M. C. (2010). Clinical child psychology: A practice specialty serving children, adolescents, and their families. *Professional Psychology: Research and Practice, 41,* 75–81.

Jacobi, C., Hayward, C., de Zwaan, M., Kraemer, H. C., & Agras, S. (2004). Coming to terms with risk factors for eating disorders: Application of risk terminology and suggestions for a general taxonomy. *Psychological Bulletin, 130,* 19–65.

Jacobson, J. W., Mulick, J. A., & Schwartz, A. A. (1995). A history of facilitated communication: Science, pseudoscience, and antiscience. *American Psychologist, 50,* 750–765.

Jaffe, P., Lemon, N., Sandler, J., & Wolfe, D. (1996). *Working together to end domestic violence.* Tampa, FL: Mancorp.

Jaffe, P., Wolfe, D. A., & Campbell, M. (2011). *Growing up with domestic violence: Assessment, intervention & prevention strategies for children & adolescents.* Cambridge. MA: Hogrefe & Huber.

Jaffee, S. R., Moffitt, T. E., Caspi, A., & Taylor, A. (2003). Life with (or without) father: The benefits of living with two biological parents depend on the father's antisocial behavior. *Child Development, 74,* 109–126.

Jaffee, W. B., & D'Zurilla, T. J. (2003). Adolescent problem solving, parent problem solving, and externalizing behavior in adolescents. *Behavior Therapy, 34,* 295–311.

Jakobson, A., & Kikas, E. (2007). Cognitive functioning in children with and without attention-deficit/hyperactivity disorder with and without comorbid learning disabilities. *Journal of Learning Disabilities, 40,* 194–202.

Jamison, K. R. (1997, January). Manic-depressive illness and creativity. *Scientific American, 7,* 44–49.

Jaser, S. S., & White, L. E. (2011). Coping and resilience in adolescents with type 1 diabetes. *Child: Care, Health and Development, 37,* 335–342.

Jaycox, L. H., Stein, B. D., Paddock, S., Miles, J. N. V., Chandra, A., & Burnam, M. A. (2009). Impact of teen depression on academic, social, and physical functioning. *Pediatrics, 125,* e596–e605.

Jellesma, F. C., Rieffe, C., Terwogt, M. M., & Westenberg, P. M. (2011). Children's sense of coherence and trait emotional intelligence: A longitudinal study exploring the development of somatic complaints. *Psychology & Health, 26,* 307–320.

Jemal, A., Siegel, R., Ward, E., Hao, Y., Xu, J., & Thun, M.J. (2009). Cancer statistics,

2009. *CA: A Cancer Journal for Clinicians, 59,* 225–249.

Jencks, C., & Phillips, M. (1998). *The Black–White test score gap.* Washington, DC: Brookings Institution Press.

Jenkins, M. M., Youngstrom, E. A., Washburn, J. J., & Youngstrom, J. K. (2010). Evidence-based strategies improve assessment of pediatric bipolar disorder by community practitioners. *Professional Psychology: Research and Practice, 42,* 121–129.

Jensen, C. D., Cushing, C. C., Aylward, B. S., Craig, J. T., Sorell, D. M., & Steele, R. G. (2011). Effectiveness of motivational interviewing interventions for adolescent substance use behavior change: A meta-analytic review. *Journal of Consulting and Clinical Psychology, 79,* 433–440.

Jensen, P. S. (2000). Commentary. *Journal of the American Academy of Child & Adolescent Psychiatry, 39,* 984–987.

Jensen, P. S., Arnold, L. E., Swanson, J. M., Vitiello, B., Abikoff, H. B., Greenhill, L. L., ... Hur, K. (2007). 3-year follow-up of the NIMH MTA Study. *Journal of the American Academy of Child & Adolescent Psychiatry, 46,* 989–1002.

Jensen, P. S., Goldman, E., Offord, D., Costello, E. J., Friedman, R., Huff, B., ... Roberts, R. (2011). Overlooked and underserved: "Action signs" for identifying children with unmet mental health needs. *Pediatrics, 128,* 970–979.

Jensen, P. S., Hoagwood, K., & Petti, T. (1996). Outcomes of mental health care for children and adolescents: II. Literature review and application of a comprehensive model. *Journal of the American Academy of Child & Adolescent Psychiatry, 35,* 1064–1077.

Jensen, P. S., Kettle, L., Roper, R. S., Sloan, M. T., Dulcan, M. K., Hoven, C., ... Payne, J. D. (1999). Are stimulants overprescribed? Treatment of ADHD in four U.S. communities. *Journal of the American Academy of Child & Adolescent Psychiatry, 38,* 797–804.

Jepsen, J. R. M., Fagerlund, B., & Mortensen, E. L. (2009). Do attention deficits influence IQ assessment in children and adolescents with ADHD? *Journal of Attention Disorders, 12,* 551–562.

Jespersen, A. F., Lalumière, M. L., & Seto, M. C. (2009). Sexual abuse history among adult sex offenders and non-sex offenders: A meta-analysis. *Child Abuse & Neglect, 33,* 179–192.

Johansson, B. B. (2006). Cultural and linguistic influence on brain organization for language and possible consequences for dyslexia: A review. *Annals of Dyslexia, 56,* 13–50.

Johnson, C. J., Beitchman, J. H., & Brownlie, E. B. (2010). Twenty-year follow-up of children with and without speech-language impairments: Family, educational, occupational, and quality of life outcomes. *American Journal of Speech-Language Pathology, 19,* 51–65.

Johnson, J. G., Cohen, P., Smailes, E. M., Kasen, S., & Brook, J. S. (2002). Television viewing and aggressive behavior during adolescence and adulthood. *Science, 295,* 2468–2471.

Johnson, K. C., Brennan, P. A., Stowe, Z. N., Leibenluft, E., & Newport, D. J. (2014). Physiological regulation in infants of women with a mood disorder: Examining associations with maternal symptoms and stress. *Journal of Child Psychology and Psychiatry, 55,* 191–198.

Johnson, M. H., & de Haan, M. (2006). Typical and atypical human functional brain development. In D. Cicchetti & D. J. Cohen (Eds.), *Developmental psychopathology: Vol. 2. Developmental neuroscience* (2nd ed., pp. 197–215). Hoboken, NJ: Wiley.

Johnson, R. J. (2008). Advances in understanding and treating childhood sexual abuse: Implications for research and policy. *Family & Community Health. Special Issue: Advancing Adolescent Health, 31*(Suppl. 1), S24–S34.

Johnson, S., Hollis, C., Kochhar, P., Hennessey, E., Wolke, D., & Marlow, N. (2010). Autism spectrum disorders in extremely preterm children. *Journal of Pediatrics, 156,* 525–531.

Johnson, S. L. M., Wang, L., Alpert, K. I., Greenstein, D., Clasen, L., Lalonde, F., ... Gogtay, N. (2013). Hippocampal shape abnormalities of patients with childhood-onset schizophrenia and their unaffected siblings. *Journal of the American Academy of Child & Adolescent Psychiatry, 52,* 527–536.

Johnston, C., & Chronis-Tuscano, A. (2014). Families and ADHD. In R. A. Barkley (Ed.), *Attention-deficit hyperactivity disorder: A handbook for diagnosis and treatment* (4th ed.). New York: Guilford Press.

Johnston, C., & Freeman, W. (1998). Parent training interventions for sibling conflict. In J. Briesmeister & C. E. Schaefer (Eds.), *Handbook of parent training: Parents as co-therapists for children's behavior problems* (2nd ed., pp. 153–176). New York: Wiley.

Johnston, C., Hommersen, P., & Seipp, C. M. (2009). Maternal attributions and child oppositional behavior: A longitudinal study of boys with and without attention-deficit/hyperactivity disorder. *Journal of Consulting and Clinical Psychology, 77,* 189–195.

Johnston, C., & Leung, D. W. (2001). Effects of medication, behavioral, and combined treatments on parents' and children's attributions for the behavior of children with attention-deficit hyperactivity disorder. *Journal of Consulting and Clinical Psychology, 69,* 67–76.

Johnston, C., & Mah, J. W. T. (2008). Child attention-deficit/hyperactivity disorder. In J. Hunsley & E. J. Mash (Eds.), *A guide to assessments that work* (pp. 17–40). New York: Oxford University Press.

Johnston, C., & Mash, E. J. (2001). Families of children with attention-deficit hyperactivity disorder: A review and recommendations for future research. *Clinical Child and Family Psychology Review, 4,* 183–207.

Johnston, C., Mash, E. J., Miller, N., & Ninowski, J. E. (2012). Parenting in adults with attention-deficit/hyperactivity disorder (ADHD). *Clinical Psychology Review, 32,* 215–228.

Johnston, L. D., O'Malley, P. M., Bachman, J. G., & Schulenberg, J. E. (2013a). *Monitoring the future national results on drug use: 2012 overview, key findings on adolescent drug use.* Ann Arbor: Institute for Social Research, University of Michigan.

Johnston, L. D., O'Malley, P. M., Bachman, J. G., & Schulenberg, J. E. (2013b). Demographic subgroup trends among adolescents for forty-six classes of licit and illicit drugs, 1975–2012 (Monitoring the Future Occasional Paper No. 79). Ann Arbor: Institute for Social Research. Retrieved from http://www.monitoringthefuture.org

Joiner, T. E., Jr. (1999). A test of interpersonal theory of depression in youth psychiatric inpatients. *Journal of Abnormal Child Psychology, 27,* 77–85.

Joiner, T. E., Katz, J., & Heatherton, T. (2000). Personality features differentiate late adolescent females and males with chronic bulimic symptoms. *International Journal of Eating Disorders, 27,* 191–197.

Joinson, C., Heron, J., Emond, A., & Butler, R. (2007). Psychological problems in children with bedwetting and combined (day and night) wetting: A UK population-based study. *Journal of Pediatric Psychology, 32,* 605–616.

Joint Committee on Testing Practices. (2004). *Code of fair testing practices in education.* Washington, DC: Author. Retrieved from http://www.apa.org/science/programs/testing/fair-testing.pdf

Jolliffe, T., & Baron-Cohen, S. (1997). Are people with autism and Asperger syndrome faster than normal on the embedded figures test? *Journal of Child Psychology and Psychiatry, 38,* 527–534.

Jones, D. J. (2014). Future directions in the design, development, and investigation of technology as a service delivery model. *Journal of Clinical Child & Adolescent Psychology, 43,* 128–142.

Jones, D. J., Forehand, R., Cueller, J., Parent, J., Honeycutt, A., Khavjou, O., ... Newey, G. A. (2014). Technology-enhanced program for child disruptive behavior disorders: Development and pilot randomized control trial. *Journal of Clinical Child & Adolescent Psychology, 43,* 88–101.

Jones, D. J., Lewis, T., Litrownik, A., Thompson, R., Proctor, L. J., Isbell, P., ... Runyan, D. (2013). Linking childhood sexual abuse and early adolescent risk behavior: The intervening role of internalizing and externalizing problems. *Journal of Abnormal Child Psychology, 41,* 139–150.

Jones, H. A., Epstein, J. N., Hinshaw, S. P., Owens, E. B., Chi, T. C., Arnold, L. E., ... Wells, K. C. (2010). Ethnicity as a moderator of treatment effects on parent-child interaction for children with ADHD. *Journal of Attention Disorders, 13,* 592–600.

Jones, L. M., Finkelhor, D., & Halter, S. (2006). Child maltreatment trends in the 1990's: Why does neglect differ from sexual and physical abuse? *Child Maltreatment, 11,* 107–120.

Jones, M. C. (1924). The elimination of children's fears. *Journal of Experimental Psychology, 1,* 383–390.

Jones, W., & Klin, A. (2009). Heterogeneity and homogeneity across the autism spectrum: The role of development. *Journal of the American Academy of Child and Adolescent Psychiatry, 48,* 471–473.

Jones, W., & Klin, A. (2013, November 7). Letter: Attention to eyes is present but in decline in 2-6-month-old infants later diagnosed with autism. *Nature, 504,* 427–431.

Jones, W. R., & Morgan, J. F. (2010). Eating disorders in men: A review of the literature. *Journal of Public Mental Health, 9,* 23–31.

Joosten, A. V., Bundy, A. C., & Einfeld, S. L. (2009). Intrinsic and extrinsic motivation for stereotypic and repetitive behavior. *Journal of Autism and Developmental Disorders, 39,* 521–531.

Jordan, A. E., & Cole, D. A. (1996). Relation of depressive symptoms to the structure of self-knowledge in childhood. *Journal of Abnormal Psychology, 105,* 530–540.

Joseph, R. M., & Tanaka, J. (2003). Holistic and part-based face recognition in children with autism. *Journal of Child Psychology and Psychiatry, 44,* 529–542.

Juarascio, A. S., Forman, E. M., Timko, C. A., Herbert, J. D., Butryn, M., & Lowe, M. (2011). Implicit internalization of the thin ideal as a predictor of increases in weight, body dissatisfaction, and disordered eating. *Eating Behaviors, 12,* 207–213.

Juffer, F., & van IJzendoorn, M. H. (2007). Adoptees do not lack self-esteem: A meta-analysis of studies on self-esteem of transracial, international, and domestic adoptees. *Psychological Bulletin, 133,* 1067–1083.

Kagan, J. (2013). Behavioral inhibition as a temperamental vulnerability to psychopathology. In T. P. Beauchaine & S. P. Hinshaw (Eds.), *Child and adolescent psychopathology* (2nd ed., pp. 227–250). Hoboken, NJ: Wiley.

Kagan, J., & Snidman, N. (1999). Early child predictors of adult anxiety disorders. *Biological Psychiatry, 46,* 1536–1541.

Kahn, C. A., Kelly, P. C., & Walker, W. O. (1995). Lead screening in children with attention deficit hyperactivity disorder and developmental delay. *Clinical Pediatrics, 34,* 498–501.

Kahn, R. E., Frick, P. J., Youngstrom, E., Findling, R. L., & Youngstrom, J. K. (2012). The effects of including a callous-unemotional specifier for the diagnosis of conduct disorder. *Journal of Child Psychology and Psychiatry, 53,* 271–282.

Kaiser, N. M., & Pfiffner, L. J. (2011). Evidence-based psychosocial treatments for childhood ADHD. *Psychiatric Annals, 41,* 9–15.

Kaiser, N. M., McBurnett, K., & Pfiffner, L. J. (2011). Child ADHD severity and positive and negative parenting as predictors of child social functioning: Evaluation of three theoretical models. *Journal of Attention Disorders, 15,* 193–203.

Kalarchian, M. A., & Marcus, M. D. (2012). Psychiatric comorbidity of childhood obesity. *International Review of Psychiatry, 24,* 241–246.

Kallman, F. J., & Roth, B. (1956). Genetic aspects of preadolescent schizophrenia. *American Journal of Psychiatry, 112,* 599–606.

Kaminski, K. M., & Garber, J. (2002). Depressive spectrum disorders in high-risk adolescents: Episode duration and predictors of time to recovery. *Journal of the American Academy of Child & Adolescent Psychiatry, 41,* 410–418.

Kanaya, T., Scullin, M. H., & Ceci, S. J. (2003). The Flynn effect and U.S. policies: The impact of rising IQ scores on American society via mental retardation diagnoses. *American Psychologist, 58,* 778–790.

Kane, P., & Garber, J. (2004). The relations among depression in fathers, children's psychopathology, and father-child conflict: A meta-analysis. *Clinical Psychology Review, 24,* 339–360.

Kanner, L. (1943). Autistic disturbances of affective contact. *Nervous Child, 2,* 217–250.

Kanner, L. (1944). Early infantile autism. *Journal of Pediatrics, 25,* 211–217.

Kanner, L. (1962). Emotionally disturbed children: A historical review. *Child Development, 33,* 97–102.

Kanner, L. (1964). *A history of the care and study of the mentally retarded.* Springfield, IL: Thomas.

Kanoski, S. E., Hayes, M. R., Greenwald, H. S., Fortin, S. M., Gianessi, C. A., Gilbert, J. R., & Grill, H. J. (2011). Hippocampal leptin signaling reduces food intake and modulates food-related memory processing. *Neuropsychopharmacology, 36,* 1859–1870.

Kaplan, R. M. (2000). Two pathways to prevention. *American Psychologist, 55,* 382–396.

Kapp, S. K. (2011). Navajo and autism: The beauty of harmony. *Disability & Society, 26,* 583–595.

Karg, K., Burmeister, M., Shedden, K., & Sen, S. (2011). The serotonin transporter promoter variant (5-HTTLPR), stress, and depression meta-analysis revisited: evidence of genetic moderation. *Archives of General Psychiatry, 68,* 444–454.

Karier, C. J. (1986). *Scientists of the mind: Intellectual founders of modern psychology.* Urbana: University of Illinois Press.

Karki, S., Pietilä, A., Länsimies-Antikainen, H., Varjoranta, P., Pirskanen, M., & Laukkanen, E. (2012). The effects of interventions to prevent substance use among adolescents: A systematic review. *Journal of Child & Adolescent Substance Abuse, 21,* 383–413.

Karlsgodt, K. H., Sun, D., Jimenez, A. M., Lutzenhoff, E. S., Willhite, R., van Erp, T. G. M., & Cannon, T. D. (2008). Developmental disruptions in neural connectivity in the pathophysiology of schizophrenia. *Development and Psychopathology, 20,* 1297–1327.

Karna, A., Voeten, M., Little, T. D., Poskiparta, E., Kaljonen, A., & Salmivalli, C. (2011). A large-scale evaluation of the KiVa Antibullying Program: Grades 4–6. *Child Development, 82,* 311–330.

Karwautz, A. F. K., Wagner, G., Waldherr, K., Nader, I. W., Fernandez-Aranda, F., Estivill, X., … Treasure, J. L. (2011). Gene-environment interaction in anorexia nervosa: Relevance of non-shared environment and the serotonin transporter gene. *Molecular Psychiatry, 16,* 590–592.

Kasari, C., & Smith, T. (2013). Interventions in schools for children with autism spectrum disorder: Methods and recommendations. *Autism, 17,* 254–267.

Kasen, S., Cohen, P., Brook, J. S., & Hartmark, C. (1996). A multiple-risk interaction model: Effects of temperament and divorce on psychiatric disorders in children. *Journal of Abnormal Child Psychology, 24,* 121–150.

Kashani, J. H., Allan, W. D., Dahlmeier, J. M., Rezvani, M., & Reid, J. C. (1995). An examination of family functioning utilizing the circumplex model in psychiatrically hospitalized children with depression. *Journal of Affective Disorders, 35,* 65–73.

Kaslow, N. J., Broth, M. R., Smith, C. O., & Collins, M. H. (2012). Family-based interventions for child and adolescent disorders. *Journal of Marital and Family Therapy, 38,* 82–100.

Kates, W. R. (2007). Editorial: Inroads to mechanisms of disease in child psychiatric disorders. *American Journal of Psychiatry, 164,* 547–551.

Kats-Gold, I., Besser, A., & Priel, B. (2007). The role of simple emotion recognition skills among school aged boys at risk of ADHD. *Journal of Abnormal Child Psychology, 35,* 363–378.

Katzmarzyk, P. T., & Ardern, C. I. (2004). Overweight and obesity mortality trends in Canada, 1985–2000. *Canadian Journal of Public Health, 95,* 16–20.

Kaufman, A. S., & Kaufman, N. L. (2004). *KABC-II: Kaufman assessment battery for children* (2nd ed.). Circle Pines, MN: AGS.

Kaufman, J., Martin, A., King, R. A., & Charney, D. (2001). Are child-, adolescent-, and adult-onset depression one and the same disorder? *Biological Psychiatry, 49,* 980–1001.

Kaufman, J., Yang, B.Z., Douglas-Palumberi, H., Grasso, D., Lipschitz, D., Houshyar, S., … Gelernter, J. (2006). Brain-derived neurotrophic factor-5-HTTLPR gene interactions and environmental modifiers of depression in children. *Biological Psychiatry, 59,* 673–680.

Kavale, K. A., & Forness, S. R. (1996). Social skill deficits and learning disabilities: A meta-analysis. *Journal of Learning Disabilities, 29,* 226–237.

Kazak, A. E., Hoagwood, K., Weisz, J. R., Hood, K., Kratochwill, T. R., Vargas, L. A., & Banez, G. A. (2010). A meta-systems approach to evidence-based practice for children and adolescents. *American Psychologist, 65,* 85–97.

Kazdin, A. E. (1992). Overt and covert antisocial behavior: Child and family characteristics among psychiatric inpatient children. *Journal of Child and Family Studies, 1,* 3–20.

Kazdin, A. E. (1995). *Conduct disorders in childhood and adolescence* (2nd ed.). Thousand Oaks, CA: Sage.

Kazdin, A. E. (1996a). Combined and multimodal treatments in child and adolescent psychotherapy: Issues, challenges, and research directions. *Clinical Psychology: Science and Practice, 3,* 69–100.

Kazdin, A. E. (1996b). Problem solving and parent management training in treating aggressive and antisocial behavior. In E. D. Hibbs & P. S. Jensen (Eds.), *Psychosocial treatments for child and adolescent* disorders: *Empirically based strategies for clinical practice* (pp. 377–408). Washington, DC: American Psychological Association.

Kazdin, A. E. (2000). *Psychotherapy for children and adolescents: Directions for research and practice.* New York: Oxford University Press.

Kazdin, A. E. (2007). Psychosocial treatments for conduct disorder in children and adolescents. In P. E. Nathan & J. M. Gorman (Eds.), *A guide to treatments that work* (3rd ed., pp. 71–104). New York: Oxford University Press.

Kazdin, A. E. (2010). Problem-solving skills training and parent management training for oppositional defiant disorder and conduct disorder. In J. R. Weisz & A. E. Kazdin (Eds.), *Evidence-based psychotherapies for children and adolescents* (2nd ed., pp. 211–226). New York: Guilford.

Kazdin, A. E. (2011). *Single case research designs: Methods for clinical and applied settings* (2nd ed.). New York: Oxford University Press.

Kazdin, A. E., & Blase, S. L. (2011). Rebooting psychotherapy research and practice to reduce the burden of mental illness. *Perspectives on Psychological Science, 6,* 21–37.

Kazdin, A. E., & Wassell, G. (1999). Barriers to treatment participation and therapeutic change among children referred for conduct disorder. *Journal of Clinical Child Psychology, 28,* 160–172.

Kearney, C. A. (1995). School refusal behavior. In A. R. Eisen, C. A. Kearney, & C. A. Schaefer (Eds.), *Clinical handbook of anxiety disorders in children and adolescents* (pp. 19–52). Northvale, NJ: Aronson.

Kearney, C. A. (2007). Forms and functions of school refusal behavior in youth: An empirical analysis of absenteeism severity. *Journal of Child Psychology and Psychiatry, 48,* 53–61.

Kearney, C. A., & Albano, A. M. (2004). The functional profiles of school refusal behavior: Diagnostic aspects. *Behavior Modification, 28,* 147–161.

Kearney, C. A., & Albano, A. M. (2007). *When children refuse school: A cognitive-behavioral therapy approach, therapist guide* (2nd ed.). New York: Oxford University Press.

Kearney, C. A., & Silverman, W. K. (1996). The evolution and reconciliation of taxonomic strategies for school refusal behavior. *Clinical Psychology: Science and Practice, 3,* 339–354.

Keehn, B., Lincoln, A. J., Muller, R.-A., & Townsend, J. (2010). Attentional networks in children and adolescents with autism spectrum disorder. *Journal of Child Psychology and Psychiatry, 51,* 1251–1259.

Keel, P. K., Baxter, M. G., Heatherton, T. F., & Joiner, T. E. (2007). A 20-year longitudinal study of body weight, dieting, and eating disorder symptoms. *Journal of Abnormal Psychology, 116,* 422–432.

Keel, P. K., Gravener, J. A., Joiner, T. E., & Haedt, A. A. (2010). Twenty-year follow-up of bulimia nervosa and related eating

disorders not otherwise specified. *International Journal of Eating Disorders, 43,* 492–497.

Keel, P. K., & Klump, K. L. (2003). Are eating disorders culture-bound syndromes? Implications for conceptualizing their etiology. *Psychological Bulletin, 129,* 747–769.

Keenan, K. (2000). Emotion dysregulation as a risk factor for child psychopathology. *Clinical Psychology: Science and Practice, 7,* 418–434.

Keenan, K. (2011). Mind the gap: Assessing impairment among children affected by proposed revisions to the diagnostic criteria for oppositional defiant disorder. *Journal of Abnormal Psychology, 121,* 352–359.

Keenan, K., Boeldt, D. Chen, D., Coyne, C., Donald, R., Duax, J., … Humphries, M. (2011). Predictive validity of DSM-IV oppositional defiant and conduct disorders in clinically referred preschoolers. *Journal of Child Psychology and Psychiatry, 52,* 47–55.

Keenan, K., Wroblewski, K., Hipwell, A., Loeber, R., & Stouthamer-Loeber, M. (2010). Age of onset, symptom threshold, and expansion of the nosology of conduct disorder in girls. *Journal of Abnormal Psychology, 119,* 689–698.

Keenan-Miller, D., Hammen, C. L., & Brennan, P. A. (2007). Health outcomes related to early adolescent depression. *Journal of Adolescent Health, 41,* 256–262.

Kell, C. A., Neumann, K., von Kriegstein, K., Posenenske, C., von Gudenberg, A. W., Euler, H., & Giraud, A. (2009). How the brain repairs stuttering. *Brain: A Journal of Neurology, 132,* 2747–2760.

Keller, M., Lavori, P., Wunder, J., Beardslee, W., Schwartz, C., & Roth, J. (1992). Chronic course of anxiety disorders in children and adolescents. *Journal of the American Academy of Child & Adolescent Psychiatry, 31,* 595–599.

Keller, P. S., Kouros, C. D., Erath, S. A., Dahl, R. E., & El-Sheikh, M. (2014). Longitudinal relations between maternal depressive symptoms and child sleep problems: The role of parasympathetic nervous system reactivity. *Journal of Child Psychology and Psychiatry, 55,* 172–179.

Kelly, R. J., & El-Sheikh, M. (2011). Marital conflict and children's sleep: Reciprocal relations and socioeconomic effects. *Journal of Family Psychology, 25,* 412–422. Kelly, R. J., & El-Sheikh, M. (2014). Reciprocal relations between children's sleep and their adjustment over time. *Developmental Psychology, 50,* 1137–1147.

Kemp, C., Kishida, Y., Carter, M., & Sweller, N. (2013). The effect of activity type on the engagement and interaction of young children with disabilities in inclusive childcare settings. *Early Childhood Research Quarterly, 28,* 134–143.

Kendall, J. (1999). Sibling accounts of attention deficit hyperactivity disorder (ADHD). *Family Process, 38,* 117–136.

Kendall, P. C. (Ed.). (2011a). *Child and adolescent therapy: Cognitive-behavioral procedures* (4th ed.). New York: Guilford Press.

Kendall, P. C. (2011b). Guiding theory for therapy with children and adolescents. In P. C. Kendall (Ed.), *Child and adolescent therapy: Cognitive behavioral procedures* (4th ed., pp. 3–24). New York: Guilford Press.

Kendall, P. C., & Flannery-Schroeder, E. C. (1998). Methodological issues in treatment research for anxiety disorders in youth. *Journal of Abnormal Child Psychology, 26,* 27–38.

Kendall, P. C., Furr, J. M., & Podell, J. L. (2010). Child focused treatment of anxiety. In J. R. Weisz & A. E. Kazdin (Eds.), *Evidence-based therapies for children and adolescents* (2nd ed., pp. 45–60). New York: Guilford.

Kendall, P. C., Panichelli-Mindel, S. M., Sugarman, A., & Callahan, S. A. (1997). Exposure to child anxiety: Theory, research, and practice. *Clinical Psychology: Science and Practice, 4,* 29–39.

Kendall, P. C., Safford, S., Flannery-Schroeder, E., & Webb, A. (2004). Child anxiety treatment: Outcomes in adolescence and impact on substance use and depression at 7.4-year follow-up. *Journal of Consulting and Clinical Psychology, 72,* 276–287.

Kendall, P. C., & Suveg, C. (2006). Treating anxiety disorders in youth. In P. C. Kendall (Ed.), *Child and adolescent therapy: Cognitive-behavioral procedures* (3rd ed., pp. 243–294). New York: Guilford Press.

Kendall-Tackett, K. A., Williams, L. M., & Finkelhor, D. (2001). Impact of sexual abuse on children: A review and synthesis of recent empirical studies. In R. Bull (Ed.), *Children and the law: The essential readings. Essential readings in developmental psychology* (pp. 31–76). Malden, MA: Blackwell.

Kennedy, E. E. (2008). Media representations of attention deficit disorder: Portrayals of cultural skepticism in popular media. *Journal of Popular Culture, 41,* 91–117.

Kennedy, P., Terdal, L., & Fusetti, L. (1993). *The hyperactive child book.* New York: St. Martin's Press.

Kenneson, A., Funderburk, J. S., & Maisto, S. A. (2013). Substance use disorders increase the odds of subsequent mood disorders. *Drug and Alcohol Dependence, 133,* 338–343.

Kent, R. G., Carrington, S. J., Le Couteur, A., Gould, J., Wing, L., Malijaars, J., … Leekam, S. R. (2013). Diagnosing autism spectrum disorder: Who will get a DSM-5 diagnosis? *Journal of Child Psychology and Psychiatry, 54,* 1242–1250.

Kenworthy, L., Anthony, L. G., Naiman, D. Q., Cannon, L., Wills, M. C., Luong-Tran, C., … Wallace, G. L. (2014). Randomized controlled effectiveness trial of executive function intervention for children on the autism spectrum. *Journal of Child Psychology and Psychiatry, 55,* 374–383.

Kerns, K. A., & Brumariu, L. E. (2014). Is insecure parent-child attachment a risk factor for the development of anxiety in childhood or adolescence? *Child Development Perspectives, 8,* 12–17.

Kertz, S. J., & Woodruff-Borden, J. (2011). The developmental psychopathology of worry. *Clinical Child and Family Psychology Review, 14,* 174–197.

Kessler, R. C., Adler, L. A., Barkley, R., Biederman, J., Conners, K., Faraone, S. V., … Zaslavsky, A. M. (2005). Patterns and predictors of attention-deficit/hyperactivity disorder persistence into adulthood: Results from the National Comorbidity Survey replication. *Biological Psychiatry, 57,* 1442–1451.

Kessler, R. C., Aguilar-Gaxiola, S., Alonso, J., Chatterji, S., Lee, S., Ormel, J., et al. (2009). The global burden of mental disorders: An update from the WHO World Mental Health (WMH) Surveys. *Epidemiologia e Psichiatria Sociale, 18,* 23–33.

Kessler, R. C., Avenevoli, S., Costello, E .J., Georgiades, K., Green, J. G., Gruber, M. J., … Merikangas, K. R. (2012a). Prevalence, persistence, and socio-demographic correlates of DSM-IV disorders in the National Comorbidity Survey-Replication Adolescent Supplement. *Archives of General Psychiatry, 69,* 372–380.

Kessler, R. C., Avenevoli, S., Costello, E. J., Green, J. G., Gruber, M. J., McLaughlin, K. A., …& Merikangas, K. R. (2012b). Severity of 12-month DSM-IV disorders in the National Comorbidity Survey-Replication Adolescent Supplement. *Archives of General Psychiatry, 69,* 381–389.

Kessler, R. C., Avenevoli, S., McLaughlin, K. A., Green, J. G., Lakoma, M. D., Petukhova, M., … Merikangas, K. R. (2012c). Lifetime comorbidity of DSM-IV disorders in the NCS-R Adolescent Supplement (NCS-A). *Psychological Medicine, 42,* 1997–2010.

Kessler, R. C., Merikangas, K. R., & Wang, P. S. (2007). Prevalence, comorbidity, and service utilization for mood disorders in the United States at the beginning of the twenty-first century. *Annual Review of Clinical Psychology, 3,* 137–158.

Khanna, M. S., & Kendall, P. C. (2010). Computer-assisted cognitive behavioral therapy for child anxiety: Results of a randomized clinical trial. *Journal of Consulting and Clinical Psychology, 78,* 737–745.

Kieling, C., Gonclaves, R. R. F., Tannock, R., & Castellanos, F. X. (2008). Neurobiology of attention deficit hyperactivity disorder. *Child and Adolescent Psychiatric Clinics of North America, 17,* 285–307.

Kilgus, M. D., Pumariega, A. J., & Cuffe, S. P. (1995). Influence of race on diagnosis in adolescent psychiatric inpatients. *Journal of the American Academy of Child & Adolescent Psychiatry, 34,* 67–72.

Kilpatrick, D. G., Ruggiero, K. J., Acierno, R., Saunders, B. E., Resnick, H. S., & Best, C. L. (2003). Violence and risk of PTSD, major depression, substance abuse/dependence, and comorbidity: Results from the National Survey of Adolescents. *Journal of Consulting and Clinical Psychology, 71,* 692–700.

Kim, J., & Cicchetti, D. (2010). Longitudinal pathways linking child maltreatment, emotion regulation, peer relations, and psychopathology. *Journal of Child Psychology and Psychiatry, 51,* 706–716.

Kim-Cohen, J., Caspi, A., Taylor, A., Williams, B., Newcombe, R., Craig, I. W., & Moffitt, T. E. (2006). MAOA, maltreatment, and gene-environment interaction predicting children's mental health: New evidence and a meta-analysis. *Molecular Psychiatry, 11,* 903–913.

Kim-Cohen, J., & Gold, A. L. (2009). Measured gene-environment interactions and mechanisms promoting resilient development. *Current Directions in Psychological Science, 18,* 138–142.

Kimonis, E. R., Frick, P. J., & McMahon, R. J. (2014). Conduct and oppositional defiant disorders. In E. J. Mash & R. A. Barkley (Eds.), *Child psychopathology* (3rd ed., pp. 145–179). New York: Guilford Press.

King, B. H., & Lord, C. (2011). Is schizophrenia on the autism spectrum? *Brain Research, 1380,* 34–41.

King, B. H., Toth, K. E., Hodapp, R. M., & Dykens, E. M. (2009). Intellectually disability. In B. J. Sadock, V. A. Sadock, & P. Ruis (Eds.), *Comprehensive textbook of psychiatry* (9th ed., pp. 3444–3474). Philadelphia: Lippincott Williams & Wilkins.

King, M., & Bearman, P. (2009). Diagnostic change and the increased prevalence of autism. *International Journal of Epidemiology, 38,* 1224–1234.

King, N. J., Ollendick, T. H., & Mattis, S. G. (1994). Panic in children and adolescents: Normative and clinical studies. *Australian Psychologist, 29,* 89–93.

King, S., St-Hilaire, A., & Heidkamp, D. (2010). Prenatal factors in schizophrenia. *Current Directions in Psychological Science, 19,* 209–213.

Kirby, M. J. L., & Keon, W. J. (2006). *Out of the shadows at last: Transforming mental health, mental illness and addiction services in Canada.* Ottawa, ON: Standing Senate Committee on Social Affairs, Science and Technology. Retrieved from www.parl.gc.ca/39/1/parlbus/commbus/senate/com-e/soci-e/rep-e/rep02may06-e.htm

Kirmayer, L. J., Dandeneau, S., Marshall, E., Phillips, M. K., & Williamson, K. J. (2011). Rethinking resilience from indigenous perspectives. *Canadian Journal of Psychiatry/La Revue Canadienne De Psychiatrie, 56,* 84–91.

Kirsch, V., Wilhelm, F. H., & Goldbeck, L. (2011). Psychophysiological characteristics of PTSD in children and adolescents: A review of the literature. *Journal of Traumatic Stress, 24,* 146–154.

Kiser, L. J. (2007). Protecting children from the dangers of urban poverty. *Clinical Psychology Review, 27,* 211–225.

Kishiyama, M. M., Boyce, W. T., Jimenez, A. M., Perry, L. M., & Knight, R. T. (2009). Socioeconomic disparities affect prefrontal function in children. *Journal of Cognitive Neuroscience, 21,* 1106–1115.

Kitzman, H., Olds, D., Cole, R., Hanks, C., Anson, E., Arcoleo, K., … Holmberg, J. (2010). Enduring effects of prenatal and infancy home visiting by nurses on children: Follow-up of a randomized trial among children at age 12 years. *Archives of Pediatrics & Adolescent Medicine, 164,* 412–418.

Kitzmann, K. M., & Beech, B. M. (2011). Family-based interventions for pediatric obesity: Methodological and conceptual challenges from family psychology. *Couple and Family Psychology: Research and Practice, 1,* 45–62.

Kitzmann, K. M., Dalton, W. T., Stanley, C. M., Beech, B. M., Reeves, T. P., Buscemi, J., … Midgett, E. L. (2010). Lifestyle interventions for youth who are overweight: A meta-analytic review. *Health Psychology, 29,* 91–101.

Kiuru, N., Leskinen, E., Nurmi, J.-E., & Salmela-Aro, K. (2011). Depressive symptoms during adolescence: Do learning difficulties matter? *International Journal of Behavioral Development, 35,* 298–306.

Klahr, A. M., McGue, M., Iacono, W. G., & Burt, S. A. (2011). The association between parent-child conflict and adolescent conduct problems over time: Results from a longitudinal adoption study. *Journal of Abnormal Psychology, 120,* 46–56.

Klein, D. N., Lewinsohn, P. M., & Seeley, J. R. (1997). Psychosocial characteristics of adolescents with a past history of dysthymic disorder: Comparison with adolescents with past histories of major depressive and non-affective disorders, and never mentally ill controls. *Journal of Affective Disorders, 42,* 127–135.

Klein, D. N., Shankman, S. A., & Rose, S. (2008). Dysthymic disorder and double depression: Baseline predictors of 10-year course and outcome. *Journal of Psychiatric Research, 42,* 408–415.

Kleinman, J. M., Ventola, P. E., Pandey, J., Verbalis, A. D., Barton, M., Hodgson, S., … Fein, D. (2008). Diagnostic stability in very young children with autism spectrum disorders. *Journal of Autism and Developmental Disorders, 38,* 606–615.

Klietz, S. J., Borduin, C. M., & Schaeffer, C. M. (2010). Cost–benefit analysis of multisystemic therapy with serious and violent juvenile offenders. *Journal of Family Psychology, 24,* 657–666.

Klin, A., Lin, D. J., Gorrindo, P., Ramsay, G., & Jones, W. (2009). Two-year olds with autism orient to non-social contingencies rather than biological motion. *Nature, 459,* 257–261.

Klinger, L. G., Dawson, G., Burner, K., & Crisler, M. (2014). Autism spectrum disorder. In E. J. Mash & R. A. Barkley (Eds.), *Child psychopathology* (3rd ed., pp. 531–572). New York: Guilford Press.

Klinger, L. G., O'Kelley, S. E., & Mussey, J. L. (2009). Assessment of intellectual functioning in autism spectrum disorders. In S. Goldstein, J. Naglieri, & S. Ozonoff (Eds.), *Assessment of autism spectrum disorders* (pp. 209–252). New York: Guilford Press.

Klintwall, L., Holm, A., Eriksson, Carlsson, L. ., Olsson, B., Hedvall, A., … Fernell, E. (2011). Sensory abnormalities in autism: A brief report. *Research in Developmental Disabilities, 32,* 795–800.

Knapp, M., Romeo, R., & Beechum, J. (2009). Economic cost of autism in the UK. *Autism, 13,* 317–336.

Knappe, S., Beesdo-Baum, K., Fehm, L., Stein, M. B., Lieb, R., & Wittchen, H.-U.

(2011). Social fear and social phobia types among community youth: Differential clinical features and vulnerability factors. *Journal of Psychiatric Research, 45,* 111–120.

Knappe, S., Beesdo-Baum, K., Wittchen, H.-U. (2010). Familial factors in social anxiety disorder: Calling for a family-oriented approach for targeted prevention and early intervention. *European Child & Adolescent Psychiatry, 19,* 857–871.

Knickmeyer, R. C., Wheelwright, S., & Baron-Cohen, S. B. (2008). Sex-typical play: Masculinization/defeminization in girls with an autism spectrum condition. *Journal of Autism and Developmental Disorders, 38,* 1028–1035.

Kochanska, G., De Vet, K., Goldman, M., Murray, K., & Putnam, S. P. (1994). Maternal reports of conscience development and temperament in young children. *Child Development, 65,* 852–868.

Koenen, K. C., & Widom, C. S. (2009). A prospective study of sex differences in the lifetime risk of posttraumatic stress disorder among abused and neglected children grown up. *Journal of Traumatic Stress, 22,* 566–574.

Koenig, A. L., Cicchetti, D., & Rogosch, F. A. (2004). Moral development: The association between maltreatment and young children's prosocial behaviors and moral transgressions. *Social Development, 13,* 97–106.

Koerting, J., Smith, E., Knowles, M. M., Latter, S., Elsey, H., McCann, D. C., ... Sonuga-Barke, E. J. (2013). Barriers to, and facilitators of, parenting programmes for childhood behavior problems: A qualitative synthesis of studies of parents' and professionals' perceptions. *European Child & Adolescent Psychiatry, 22,* 653–670.

Kofler, M. J., Rapport, M. D., & Alderson, R. M. (2008). Quantifying ADHD classroom inattentiveness, its moderators, and variability: A meta-analytic review. *Journal of Child Psychology and Psychiatry, 49,* 59–69.

Kohler, F. W., Strain, P. S., & Goldstein, H. (2005). Learning experiences... An alternative program for preschoolers and parents: Peer-mediated interventions for young children with autism. In E. D. Hibbs & P. S. Jensen (Eds.), *Psychosocial treatments for child and adolescent disorders: Empirically based strategies for clinical practice* (2nd ed., pp. 659–687). Washington, DC: American Psychological Association.

Kokko, K., & Pulkkinen, L. (2000). Aggression in childhood and long-term unemployment in adulthood: A cycle of maladaptation and some protective factors. *Developmental Psychology, 36,* 463–472.

Kolko, D. J. (1987). Depression. In M. Hersen & V. B. Van Hasselt (Eds.), *Behavior therapy with children and adolescents: A clinical approach* (pp. 159–164). New York: Wiley.

Kortlander, E., Kendall, P. C., & Panichelli-Mindel, S. M. (1997). Maternal expectations and attributions about coping in anxious children. *Journal of Anxiety Disorders, 11,* 297–315.

Kosciw, J. G., Greytak, E. A., & Diaz, E. M. (2009). Who, what, where, when, and why: Demographic and ecological factors contributing to hostile school climate for lesbian, gay, bisexual, and transgender youth. *Journal of Youth and Adolescence, 38,* 976–988.

Kossowsky, J., Pfaltz, M. C., Schneider, S., Taeymans, J., Locher, C., & Gaab, J. (2013). The separation anxiety hypothesis of panic disorder revisited: A meta-analysis. *American Journal of Psychiatry, 170,* 768–781.

Kotsopoulos, S. (1986). Aretaeus the Cappadocian on mental illness. *Comprehensive Psychiatry, 27,* 171–179.

Kotte, A., Joshi, G., Fried, R., Uchida, M., Spencer, A., Woodworth, K. Y., ... Biederman, J. (2013). Autistic traits in children with and without ADHD. *Pediatrics, 132*(3), e612-e622.

Kovacs, M. (1996). Presentation and course of major depressive disorder during childhood and later years of the life span. *Journal of the American Academy of Child & Adolescent Psychiatry, 35,* 705–715.

Kovacs, M. (1997). Depressive disorders in childhood: An impressionistic landscape. *Journal of Child Psychology and Psychiatry, 38,* 287–298.

Kovacs, M., Akiskal, H. S., Gatsonis, C., & Parrone, P. L. (1994). Childhood-onset dysthymic disorder: Clinical features and prospective naturalistic outcome. *Archives of General Psychiatry, 51,* 365–374.

Kovacs, M., & Goldston, D. (1991). Cognitive and social cognitive development of depressed children and adolescents. *Journal of the American Academy of Child & Adolescent Psychiatry, 30,* 388–392.

Kovacs, M., Obrosky, D. S., Gatsonis, C., & Richards, C. (1997). First-episode major depressive and dysthymic disorder in childhood: Clinical and sociodemographic factors in recovery. *Journal of the American Academy of Child & Adolescent Psychiatry, 36,* 777–784.

Kovacs, M., & Yaroslavsky, I. (2014). Practitioner review: Dysphoria and its regulation in child and adolescent depression. *Journal of Child Psychology and Psychiatry.* Advance online publication. doi:10.1111/jcpp.12172

Kovshoff, H., Vrijens, M., Thompson, M., Yardley, L., Hodgkins, P., Sonuga-Barke, E. J. S., & Danckaerts, M. (2013). What influences clinicians' decisions about ADHD medication? Initial data from the Influences on Prescribing for ADHD Questionnaire (IPAQ). *European Child & Adolescent Psychiatry, 22,* 533–542.

Kowalski, R. M., Giumetti, G. W., Schroeder, A. N., & Lattanner, M. R. (2014). Bullying in the digital age: A critical review and meta-analysis of cyberbullying research among youth. *Psychological Bulletin.* Advance online publication. doi:10.1037/a0035618

Kowatch, R. A., Fristad, M., Birmaher, B., Wagner, K. D., Findling, R. L., & Hellander, M. (2005). Treatment guidelines for children and adolescents with bipolar disorder. *Journal of the American Academy of Child & Adolescent Psychiatry, 44,* 213–235.

Krain, A. L., & Castellanos, F. X. (2006). Brain development and ADHD. *Clinical Psychology Review, 26,* 433–444.

Krain, A. L., Hefton, S., Pine, D. S., Ernst, M., Castellanos, F. X., Klein, R. G., & Milham, M. P. (2006). An fMRI examination of developmental differences in the neural correlates of uncertainty and decision making. *Journal of Child Psychology and Psychiatry, 47,* 1023–1030.

Krain, A. L., & Kendall, P. C. (2000). The role of parental emotional distress in parent report of child anxiety. *Journal of Clinical Child Psychology, 29,* 328–335.

Kral, T. V. E., & Faith, M. S. (2009). Influences on child eating and weight development from a behavioral genetics perspective. *Journal of Pediatric Psychology, 34,* 596–605.

Kratzer, L., & Hodgins, S. (1997). Adult outcomes of child conduct problems: A cohort study. *Journal of Abnormal Child Psychology, 25,* 65–81.

Krentz, E. M., & Warschburger, P. (2011). Sports-related correlates of disordered eating in aesthetic sports. *Psychology of Sport and Exercise, 12,* 375–382.

Krijn, M., Emmelkamp, P. M. G., Olafsson, R. P., & Biemond, R. (2004). Virtual reality exposure therapy of anxiety disorders: A review. *Clinical Psychology Review, 24,* 259–281.

Kroneman, L. M., Hipwell, A. E., Loeber, R., Koot, H. M., & Pardini, D. A. (2011). Contextual risk factors as predictors of disruptive behavior disorder trajectories in girls: The moderating effect of callous-unemotional features. *Journal of Child Psychology and Psychiatry, 52,* 167–175.

Kröner-Herwig, B., Gassmann, J., van Gessel, H., & Vath, N. (2011). Multiple pains in children and adolescents: A risk factor analysis in a longitudinal study. *Journal of Pediatric Psychology, 36,* 420–432.

Krug, I., Root, T., Bulik, C., Granero, R., Penelo, E., Jiménez-Murcia, S., & Fernández-Aranda, F. (2011). Redefining phenotypes in eating disorders based on personality: A latent profile analysis. *Psychiatry Research, 188,* 439–445.

Kruger, T. H. C., & Schiffer, B. (2011). Neurocognitive and personality factors in homo- and heterosexual pedophiles and controls. *Journal of Sexual Medicine, 8,* 1650–1659.

Krull, K. R., Huang, S., Gurney, J. G., Klosky, J. L., Leisenring, W., Termuhlen, A., ... Hudson, M. M. (2010). Adolescent behavior and adult health status in childhood cancer survivors. *Journal of Cancer Survivorship, 4,* 210–217.

Kuhl, E. S., Hoodin, F., Rice, J., Felt, B. T., Rausch, J. R., & Patton, S. R. (2010). Increasing daily water intake and fluid adherence in children receiving treatment for retentive encopresis. *Journal of Pediatric Psychology, 35,* 1144–1151.

Kuhl, P. K., Stevens, E., Hayashi, A., Deguchi, T., Kiritani, S., & Iverson, P. (2006). Infants show a facilitation effect for native language phonetic perception between 6 and 12 months. *Developmental Science, 9,* F13–F21.

Kumar, A., Sundaram, S. K., Sivaswamy, L., Behen, M. E., Makki, M. I., Ager J., … Chugani, D. C. (2010). Alterations in frontal lobe tracts and corpus callosum in young children with autism spectrum disorder. *Cerebral Cortex, 20,* 2103–2013.

Kumpfer, K. L., Alvarado, R., Smith, P., & Bellamy, N. (2002). Cultural sensitivity and adaptation in family-based prevention interventions. *Prevention Science, 3,* 241–246.

Kuniyoshi, J., & McClellan, J. M. (2014). Early onset schizophrenia. In E. J. Mash & R. A. Barkley (Eds.). *Child psychopathology* (3rd ed., pp. 573–592). New York: Guilford Press.

Kuntsi, J., Pinto, R., Price, T. S., van der Meere, J. J., Frazier-Wood, A. C., & Asherson, P. (2014). The separation of ADHD inattention and hyperactivity-impulsivity symptoms: Pathways from genetic effects to cognitive impairments and symptoms. *Journal of Abnormal Child Psychology, 42,* 127–136.

Kuny, A. V., Althoff, R. R., Copeland, W., Bartels, M., Van Beijsterveldt, C. E., Baer, J., & Hudziak, J. J. (2013). Separating the domains of oppositional behavior: Comparing latent models of the Conners' Oppositional Subscale. *Journal of the American Academy of Child & Adolescent Psychiatry, 52,* 172–183.

Kwak, M., Zebrack, B. J., Meeske, K. A., Embry, L., Aguilar, C., Block, R., … Cole, S. (2013). Prevalence and predictors of post-traumatic stress symptoms in adolescent and young adult cancer survivors: A 1-year follow-up study. *Psycho–Oncology, 22,* 1798–1806.

Kyriakopoulos, M., & Frangou, S. (2007). Pathophysiology of early onset schizophrenia. *International Review of Psychiatry, 19,* 315–324.

La Greca, A. M., Bearman, K. J., & Moore, H. (2002). Peer relations of youth with pediatric conditions and health risks: Promoting social support and healthy lifestyles. *Journal of Developmental & Behavioral Pediatrics, 23,* 271–280.

La Greca, A. M., & Landoll, R. R. (2011). Peer influences. In W. K. Silverman & A. Field (Eds.), *Anxiety disorders in children and adolescents: Research, assessment, and intervention* (2nd ed., pp. 323–348). Cambridge, England: Cambridge University Press.

La Greca, A. M., & Lopez, N. (1998). Social anxiety among adolescents: Linkages with peer relations and friendships. *Journal of Abnormal Child Psychology, 26,* 83–94.

Lachar, D. (1999). Personality Inventory for Children, Second Edition (PIC-2), Personality Inventory for Youth (PIY), and Student Behavior Survey (SBS). In M. E. Maruish (Ed.), *The use of psychological testing for treatment planning and outcomes assessment* (2nd ed., pp. 399–427). Mahwah, NJ: Erlbaum.

LaFreniere, P. J. (2000). *Emotional development: A biosocial perspective.* Belmont, CA: Wadsworth.

LaGrange, B., Cole, D. A., Dallaire, D. H., Ciesla, J. A., Pineda, A. Q., Truss, A. E., & Follmer, A. (2008). Developmental changes in depressive cognitions: A longitudinal evaluation of the cognitive triad inventory for children. *Psychological Assessment, 20,* 217–226.

Lahey, B. B., Goodman, S. H., Waldman, I. D., Bird, H., Canino, G., Jensen, P., … Applegate, B. (1999). Relation of age of onset to type and severity of child and adolescent conduct problems. *Journal of Abnormal Child Psychology, 27,* 247–260.

Lahey, B. B., Loeber, R., Burke, J. D., & Applegate, B. (2005). Predicting future antisocial personality disorder in males from a clinical assessment in childhood. *Journal of Consulting and Clinical Psychology, 73,* 389–399.

Lahey, B. B., Loeber, R., Burke, J., & Rathouz, P. J. (2002). Adolescent outcomes of childhood conduct disorder among clinic-referred boys: Predictors of improvement. *Journal of Abnormal Child Psychology, 30,* 333–348.

Lahey, B. B., Loeber, R., Hart, E. L., Frick, P. J., Applegate, B., Zhang, Q., … Russo, M. F. (1995). Four-year longitudinal study of conduct disorder in boys: Patterns and predictors of persistence. *Journal of Abnormal Psychology, 104,* 83–93.

Lahey, B. B., Loeber, R., Quay, H. C., Frick, P. J., & Grimm, S. (1992). Oppositional defiant and conduct disorders: Issues to be resolved for DSM-IV. *Journal of the American Academy of Child & Adolescent Psychiatry, 31,* 539–546.

Lahey, B. B., Miller, T. L., Gordon, R. A., & Riley, A. W. (1999). Developmental epidemiology of the disruptive behavior disorders. In H. C. Quay & A. E. Hogan (Eds.), *Handbook of disruptive behavior disorders* (pp. 23–48). New York: Kluwer/Plenum Press.

Lahey, B. B., Rathouz, P. J., Lee, S. S., Chronis-Tuscano, A., Pelham, W. E., Waldman, I. E., & Cook, E. H. (2011). Interactions between early parenting and a polymorphism of the child's dopamine transporter gene in predicting future child conduct disorder symptoms. *Journal of Abnormal Psychology, 120,* 33–45.

Lahey, B. B., Van Hulle, C. A., D'Onofrio, B. M., Rodgers, J. L., & Waldman, I. D. (2008). Is parental knowledge of their adolescent offspring's whereabouts and peer associations spuriously associated with offspring delinquency? *Journal of Abnormal Child Psychology, 36,* 807–823.

Lahey, B. B., Van Hulle, C. A., Keenan, K., Rathouz, P. J., D'Onofrio, B. M., Rodgers, J. L., & Waldman, I. D. (2008). Temperament and parenting during the first year of life predict future child conduct problems. *Journal of Abnormal Child Psychology, 36,* 1139–1158.

Lahey, B. B., Van Hulle, C. A., Singh, A. L., Waldman, I. D., & Rathouz, P. J. (2011). Higher order genetic and environmental structure of prevalent forms of child and adolescent psychopathology. *Archives of General Psychiatry, 68,* 181–189.

Lahey, B. B., Van Hulle, C. A., Waldman, L. C., Rodgers, J. L., D'Onofrio, B. M.,

Pedlow, S., … Keenan, K. (2006). Testing descriptive hypotheses regarding sex differences in the development of conduct problems and delinquency. *Journal of Abnormal Child Psychology, 34,* 737–755.

Lahey, B. B., & Waldman, I. D. (2003). A developmental propensity model of the origins of conduct problems during childhood and adolescence. In B. B. Lahey, T. E. Moffitt, & A. Caspi (Eds.), *Causes of conduct disorder and juvenile delinquency* (pp. 76–117). New York: Guilford Press.

Lahey, B. B., & Willcutt, E. G. (2010). Predictive validity of a continuous alternative to nominal subtypes of attention-deficit/hyperactivity disorder for DSM-V. *Journal of Clinical Child & Adolescent Psychology, 39,* 761–775.

Lahti, J., Raikkonen, K., Sovio, U., Miettunen, J., Hartikainen, A.-L., Pouta, A., … Veijola, J. (2009). Early-life origins of schizotypal traits in adulthood. *British Journal of Psychiatry, 195,* 132–137.

Lai, M.-C., Lombardo, M. V., Chakrabarti, B., & Baron-Cohen, S. (2013a). Subgrouping the autism "spectrum": Reflections on DSM-5. *PLOS Biology, 11*(4, e1001544), 1-7. Retrieved from www.plosbiology.org

Lai, M.-C., Lombardo, M. V., Suckling, J., Ruigrok, A. N. V., Chakrabarti, B., Ecker, C., …& Baron-Cohen, S. (2013b). Biological sex affects the neurobiology of autism. *Brain: A Journal of Neurology, 136,* 2799–2815.

Laird, R. D., Jordan, K., Dodge, K. A., Pettit, G. S., & Bates, J. E. (2001). Peer rejection in childhood, involvement with antisocial peers in early adolescence, and the development of externalizing problems. *Development and Psychopathology, 13,* 337–354.

Laird, R. D., Pettit, G. S., Dodge, K. A., & Bates, J. E. (2005). Peer relationship antecedents of delinquent behavior in late adolescence: Is there evidence of demographic group differences in developmental processes? *Development & Psychopathology, 17,* 127–144.

Lakdawalla, Z., Hankin, B. L., & Mermelstein, R. (2007). Cognitive theories of depression in children and adolescents: A conceptual and quantitative review. *Clinical Child and Family Psychology Review, 10,* 1–24.

Lamb, D. J., Middeldorp, C. M., van Beijsterveldt, C. E., Bartels, M., van der Aa, N., Polderman, T. J., & Boomsma, D. I. (2010). Heritability of anxious-depressive and withdrawn behavior: Age-related changes during adolescence. *Journal of the American Academy of Child & Adolescent Psychiatry, 49,* 248–255.

Lambek, R., Tannock, R., Dalsgaard, S., Trillingsgaard, A., Damm, D., & Thomsen, P. H. (2010). ADHD: How do children with and without an executive function deficit differ? *Journal of Child Psychology and Psychiatry, 51,* 895–904.

Lambek, R., Tannock, R., Dalsgaard, S., Trillingsgaard, A., Damm, D., & Thomsen, P. H. (2011). Executive dysfunction in school-age children with ADHD. *Journal of Attention Disorders, 15,* 646–655.

of ADHD type: An argument for continued study of sluggish cognitive tempo. *Journal of Abnormal Child Psychology, 29,* 207–213.

McBurnett, K., Villodas, M., Burns, G. L., Hinshaw, S., Beaulieu, A., & Pfiffner, L. J. (2014). Structure and validity of sluggish cognitive tempo using an expanded item pool in children with attention-deficit/hyperactivity disorder. *Journal of Abnormal Child Psychology, 42,* 37–48.

McCabe, D. P., & Castel, A. D. (2008). Seeing is believing: The effect of brain images on judgments of scientific reasoning. *Cognition, 107,* 343–352.

McCabe, M. A. (1996). Involving children and adolescents in medical decision making: Developmental and clinical considerations. *Journal of Pediatric Psychology, 21,* 505–516.

McCabe, M. A. (2006). Involving children and adolescents in decisions about medical and mental health treatment. *National Register of Health Service Psychologists: The Register Report, Spring 2006.* Retrieved from www.nationalregister.org/trr_spring06_mccabe.html

McCabe, S. E., & West, B. T. (2013). Medical and nonmedical use of prescriptionstimulants: Results from a national multicohort study. *Journal of the American Academy of Child & Adolescent Psychiatry, 52,* 1272–1280.

McCann, D., Barrett, A., Cooper, A., Crumpler, D., Dalen, L., Grimshaw, K., … Stevenson, J. (2007). Food additives and hyperactive behaviour in 3-year-old and 8/9-year-old children in the community: A randomised, double-blinded, placebo-controlled trial. *Lancet, 370,* 1560–1567.

McCary, L. M., & Roberts, J. E. (2013). Early identification of autism in fragile X syndrome: A review. *Journal of Intellectual Disability Research, 57,* 803–814.

McCauley, E., Schloredt, K., Gudmundsen, G., Martell, C., & Dimidjian, S. (2011). Expanding behavioral activation to depressed adolescents: Lessons learned in treatment development. *Cognitive and Behavioral Practice, 18,* 371–383.

McClellan, J., Breiger, D., McCurry, C., & Hlastala, S. A. (2003). Premorbid functioning in early-onset psychotic disorders. *Journal of the American Academy of Child & Adolescent Psychiatry, 42,* 666–672.

McClellan, J., Stock, S., & American Academy of Child and Adolescent Psychiatry (AACAP) Committee on Quality Issues (CQI). (2013). *Journal of the American Academy of Child & Adolescent Psychiatry, 52,* 976–990.

McClure, E. B., Adler, A., Monk, C. S., Cameron, J., Smith, S., Nelson, E. E., … Pine, D. S. (2007a). fMRI predictors of treatment outcome in pediatric anxiety disorders. *Psychopharmacology, 191,* 97–105.

McClure, E. B., Monk, C. S., Nelson, E. E., Parrish, J. M., Adler, A., Blair, R. J. R., … Pine, D. S. (2007b). Abnormal attention modulation of fear circuit activation in pediatric generalized anxiety disorder. *Archives of General Psychiatry, 64,* 97–106.

McClure, E. B., & Pine, D. S. (2006). Social anxiety and emotional regulation: A model for developmental psychopathology perspectives on anxiety disorders. In D. Cicchetti & D. J. Cohen (Eds.), *Developmental psychopathology: Vol. 3. Risk, disorder, and adaptation* (2nd ed., pp. 470–502). Hoboken, NJ: Wiley.

McCluskey, K. K., & McCluskey, A. (2000). Excerpts from Butterfly Kisses: Amber's journey through hyperactivity. *The Canadian, 6,* 11–15.

McConaughey, S. H., Ivanova, M. Y., Antshel, K., & Eiraldi, R. B. (2009). Standardized observational assessment of attention deficit hyperactivity disorder combined and predominantly inattentive subtypes. I. Test Session Observations. *School Psychology Review, 38,* 45–66.

McConkey, R., Truesdale-Kennedy, M., &Cassidy, A. (2009). Mothers' recollections of early features of autism spectrum disorders. *Child and Adolescent Mental Health, 14,* 31–36.

McCracken, J. (2011). Pharmacotherapy for autism spectrum disorders. In D. G. Amaral, G. Dawson, & D. H. Geschwind (Eds.), *Autism spectrum disorders* (pp. 1309–1322). New York: Oxford University Press.

McCrory, E., De Brito, S. A., & Viding, E. (2010). Research review: The neurobiology and genetics of maltreatment and adversity. *Journal of Child Psychology and Psychiatry, 51,* 1079–1095.

McCullough, J. P., Klein, D. N., Borian, F. E., Howland, R. H., Riso, L. P., Keller, M. B., Banks, P. L. C. (2003). Group comparisons of DSM-IV subtypes of chronic depression: Validity of the distinctions, Part 2. *Journal of Abnormal Psychology, 112,* 614–622.

McDermott, P. A. (1996). A nationwide study of developmental and gender prevalence for psychopathology in childhood and adolescence. *Journal of Abnormal Child Psychology, 24,* 53–66.

McDermott, S., Durkin, M. S., Schupf, N., & Stein, Z. A. (2007). Epidemiology and etiology of mental retardation. In J.W. Jacobson, J.A. Mulick, & J. Rojahn (Eds.), *Handbook of intellectual and developmental disabilities* (pp. 3–40). New York: Springer.

McDermott, S., Zhou, L., & Mann, J. (2008). Injury treatment among children with autism or pervasive developmental disorder. *Journal of Autism and Developmental Disorders, 38,* 626–633.

McDonald, R., Jouriles, E. N., Ramisetty-Mikler, S., Caetano, R., & Green, C. E. (2006). Estimating the number of American children living in partner-violent families. *Journal of Family Psychology, 20,* 137–142.

McDonnell, M. G., & Dyck, D. G. (2004). Multiple family group treatment as an effective intervention for children suffering from psychological disorders. *Clinical Psychology Review, 24,* 685–706.

McEwan, K., Waddell, C., & Barker, J. (2007). Bringing children's mental health "out of the shadows." *Canadian Medical Association Journal, 176,* 471–472.

McGee, R., Stanton, W. R., & Sears, M. R. (1993). Allergic disorders and attention deficit disorder in children. *Journal of Abnormal Child Psychology, 21,* 79–88.

McGee, R., Wolfe, D. A., & Olson, J. (2001). Multiple maltreatment, attribution of blame, and adjustment among adolescents. *Development and Psychopathology, 13,* 827–846.

McGee, R. A., Wolfe, D. A., & Wilson, S. K. (1997). Multiple maltreatment experiences and adolescent behavior problems: Adolescents' perspectives. *Development and Psychopathology, 9,* 131–149.

McGrath, L. M., Hutaff-Lee, C., Scott, A., Boada, R., Shriberg, L. D., & Pennington, B. F. (2008). Children with comorbid speech sound disorder and specific language impairment are at increased risk for attention-deficit/hyperactivity disorder. *Journal of Abnormal Child Psychology, 36,* 151–163.

McGrath, L. M., Pennington, B. F., Shanahan, M. A., Santerre-Lemmon, L. E., Barnard, H. F., Willcutt, E. G., … Olson, R. K. (2011). A multiple deficit model of reading disability and attention-deficit/hyperactivity disorder: Searching for shared cognitive deficits. *Journal of Child Psychology and Psychiatry, 52,* 547–557.

McGrath, L. M., Pennington, B. F., Willcutt, E. G., Boada, R., Shriberg, L. D., & Smith, S. D. (2007). Gene × environment interactions in speech sound disorder predict language and preliteracy outcomes. *Development and Psychopathology [Special issue: Gene–environment interaction], 19,* 1047–1072.

McHugh, R. K., Whitton, S. W., Peckham, A. D., Welge, J. A., & Otto, M. W. (2013). Patient preference for psychological vs pharmacologic treatment of psychiatric disorders: A meta-analytic review. *Journal of Clinical Psychiatry, 74,* 595–602.

McInnes, A., Humphries, T., Hogg-Johnson, S., & Tannock, R. (2003). Listening comprehension and working memory are impaired in attention-deficit hyperactivity disorder irrespective of language impairment. *Journal of Abnormal Child Psychology, 31,* 427–443.

McIntosh, V. V. W., Carter, F. A., Bulik, C. M., Frampton, C. M. A., & Joyce, P. R. (2011). Five-year outcome of cognitive behavioral therapy and exposure with response prevention for bulimia nervosa. *Psychological Medicine: A Journal of Research in Psychiatry and the Allied Sciences, 41,* 1061–1071.

McIntyre, J. K., & Spatz Widom, C. (2011). Childhood victimization and crime victimization. *Journal of Interpersonal Violence, 26,* 640–663.

McKnew, D. H., Jr., Cytryn, L., & Yahraes, H. (1983). *Why isn't Johnny crying? Coping with depression in children.* New York: Norton.

McKowen, J. W., Tompson, M. C., Brown, T. A., & Asarnow, J. R. (2013). Longitudinal associations between depression and problematic substance use in the Youth Partners in Care study. *Journal of Clinical*

Child & Adolescent Psychology, 42, 669–680.

McLaughlin, K. A., Fairbank, J. A., Bruber, M. J., Jones, R. T., Osofsky, J. D., Pfefferbaum, B., ... Kessler, R. C. (2010). Trends in serious emotional disturbance among youths exposed to Hurricane Katrina. *Journal of the American Academy of Child & Adolescent Psychiatry, 49*, 990–1000.

McLaughlin, K. A., Hilt, L. M., & Nolen-Hoeksema, S. (2007). Racial/ethnic differences in internalizing and externalizing symptoms in adolescents. *Journal of Abnormal Child Psychology, 35*, 801–816.

McLean, C. P., & Anderson, E. R. (2009). Brave men and timid women? A review of gender differences in fear and anxiety. *Clinical Psychology Review, 29*, 496–505.

McLearn, K. T., Knitzer, J., & Carter, A. S. (2007). Mental health: A neglected partner in the healthy development of young children. In J. L. Aber, S. J. Bishop Josef, S. M. Jones, K. T. McLearn, & D. A. Phillips (Eds.), *Child development and social policy: Knowledge for action* (pp. 233–248). Washington, DC: American Psychological Association.

McLeod, B. D., Jensen-Doss, A., & Ollendick, T. H. (2013). Overview of behavioral and diagnostic assessment. In B. D. McLeod, A. Jensen-Doss, & T. H. Ollendick (Eds.), *Diagnostic and behavioral assessment in children and adolescents: A clinical guide* (pp. 3–33). New York: Guilford Press.

McLeod, B. D., Wood, J. J., & Weisz, J. R. (2007). Examining the association between parenting and childhood anxiety: A meta-analysis. *Clinical Psychology Review, 27*, 155–172.

McLeod, J. D., Fettes, D. L., Jensen, P. S., Pescosolido, B. A., & Martin, J. K. (2007). Public knowledge, beliefs, and treatment preferences concerning attention-deficit hyperactivity disorder. *Psychiatric Services, 58*, 626–631.

McMahon, R. J., & Forehand, R. L. (2003). *Helping the noncompliant child: Family-based treatment for oppositional behavior* (2nd ed.). New York: Guilford Press.

McMahon, R. J., Wells, K. C., & Kotler, J. S. (2006). Conduct problems. In E. J. Mash & R. A. Barkley (Eds.), *Treatment of childhood disorders* (3rd ed., pp. 137–268). New York: Guilford Press.

McMahon, R. J., Witkiewitz, K., Kotler, J. S., & The Conduct Problems Prevention Research Group. (2010). Predictive validity of callous–unemotional traits measured in early adolescence with respect to multiple antisocial outcomes. *Journal of Abnormal Psychology, 119*, 752–763.

McMahon, T. J., & Luthar, S. S. (2007). Defining characteristics and potential consequences of caretaking burden among children living in urban poverty. *American Journal of Orthopsychiatry, 77*, 267–281.

McManis, M. H., Kagan, J., Snidman, N. C., & Woodward, S. A. (2002). EEG asymmetry, power, and temperament in children. *Developmental Psychobiology, 41*, 169–177.

McNamara, N. K., & Findling, R. L. (2008). Guns, adolescents, and mental illness. *American Journal of Psychiatry, 165*, 190–194.

McPheeters, M. L., Warren, Z., Sathe, N., Bruzek, J. L., Krishnaswami, R. N., & Veenstra-Vanderweele, J. and J. (2011). A systematic review of medical treatments for children with autism spectrum disorders. *Pediatrics, 127*, e1312–e1321.

McQuade, J. D., & Hoza, B. (2014). Peer relationships of children with ADHD. In R. A. Barkley (Ed.), *Attention-deficit hyperactivity disorder: A handbook for diagnosis and treatment* (4th ed.). New York: Guilford Press.

McQuade, J. D., Tomb, M., Hoza, B., Waschbusch, D. A., Hurt, E. A., & Vaughn, A. J. (2011). Cognitive deficits and positively biased self-perceptions in children with ADHD. *Journal of Abnormal Child Psychology, 39*, 307–319.

Meaux, J. B., & Bell, P. L. (2001). Balancing recruitment and protection: Children as research subjects. *Issues in Comprehensive Pediatric Nursing, 24*, 241–251.

Medvescek, C. R. (1997, April). Special kids. *Parents*, 67–70.

Meek, S. E., Lemery-Chalfant, K., Jahromi, L. B., & Valiente, C. (2013). A review of gene-environment correlations and their implications for autism: A conceptual model. *Psychological Review, 120*, 497–521.

Meichenbaum, D. (1977). *Cognitive-behavior modification: An integrative approach.* New York: Plenum Press.

Meier, M. H., Slutske, W. S., Heath, A. C., & Martin, N. G. (2011). Sex differences in the genetic and environmental influences on childhood conduct disorder and adult antisocial behavior. *Journal of Abnormal Psychology, 120*, 377–388.

Meijer, S. A., Sinnema, G., Bijstra, J. O., Mellenbergh, G. J., & Wolters, W. H. G. (2002). Coping styles and locus of control as predictors for psychological adjustment of adolescents with a chronic illness. *Social Science & Medicine, 54*, 1453–1461.

Meiser-Stedman, R., Dalgleish, T., Smith, P., Yule, W., & Glucksman, E. (2007). Diagnostic, demographic, memory quality, and cognitive variables associated with acute stress disorder in children and adolescents. *Journal of Abnormal Psychology, 116*, 65–79.

Melby-Lervåg, M., Lyster, S. H., & Hulme, C. (2012). Phonological skills and their role in learning to read: A meta-analytic review. *Psychological Bulletin, 138*, 322–352.

Mellin, E. A. (2010). Children of families affected by a parental mental illness. In M. H. Guindon (Ed.), *Self-esteem across the lifespan: Issues and interventions* (pp. 79–90). New York: Routledge/Taylor & Francis.

Mellon, M. W., & Houts, A. C. (2006). Nocturnal enuresis. In J. E. Fisher & W. T. O'Donohue (Eds.), *Practitioner's guide to evidence-based psychotherapy* (pp. 432–441). New York: Springer.

Melnick, S. M., & Hinshaw, S. P. (1996). What they want and what they get: The social goals of boys with ADHD and comparison boys. *Journal of Abnormal Child Psychology, 24*, 169–185.

Melton, G. B. (2000). Privacy issues in child mental health services. In J. J. Gates & B. S. Arons (Eds.), *Privacy and confidentiality in mental health care* (pp. 47–70). Baltimore: Brookes.

Meltzer, L. J., & Mindell, J. A. (2007). Relationship between child sleep disturbances and maternal sleep, mood, and parenting stress: A pilot study. *Journal of Family Psychology, 21*, 67–73.

Menon, M., Tobin, D. D., Corby, B. C., Menon, M., Hodges, E. V. E., & Perry, D. G. (2007). The developmental costs of high self-esteem for antisocial children. *Child Development, 78*, 1627–1639.

Menting, B., van Lier, P. A. C., & Koot, H. M. (2011). Language skills, peer rejection, and the development of externalizing behavior from kindergarten to fourth grade. *Journal of Child Psychology and Psychiatry, 52*, 72–79.

Menzel, J. E., Schaefer, L. M., Burke, N. L., Mayhew, L. L., Brannick, M. T., & Thompson, J. K. (2010). Appearance-related teasing, body dissatisfaction, and disordered eating: A meta-analysis. *Body Image, 7*, 261–270.

Merikangas, K. R., Akiskal, H. S., Angst, J., Greenberg, P. E., Hirschfeld, R. M. A., Petukhova, M., & Kessler, R. C. (2007). Lifetime and 12-month prevalence of bipolar spectrum disorder in the National Comorbidity Survey Replication. *Archives of General Psychiatry, 64*, 543–552.

Merikangas, K. R., Avenevoli, S., Dierker, L., & Grillon, C. (1999). Vulnerability factors among children at risk for anxiety disorders. *Biological Psychiatry, 46*, 1523–1535.

Merikangas, K. R., Cui, L., Kattan, G., Carlson, G. A., Youngstrom, E. A., & Angst, J. (2012). Mania with and without depression in a community sample of US adolescents. *Archives of General Psychiatry, 69*, 943–951.

Merikangas, K. R., He, J. P., Burstein, M., Swanson, S. A., Avenevoli, S., Cui, L., ... Swendsen, J. (2010). Lifetime prevalence of mental disorders in U.S. adolescents: Results from the National Comorbidity Survey Replication-Adolescent Supplement (NCS-A). *Journal of the American Academy of Child & Adolescent Psychiatry, 49*, 980–989.

Merikangas, K. R., He, J. P., Burstein, M., Swendsen, J., Avenevoli, S., Base, B., ... Olfson, M. (2011). Service utilization for lifetime mental disorders in U.S. adolescents: Results of the National Comorbidity Survey-Adolescent Supplement (NCS-A). *Journal of the American Academy of Child & Adolescent Psychiatry, 50*, 32–45.

Merikangas, K. R., & Pato, M. (2009). Recent Developments in the epidemiology of bipolar disorder in adults and children:

Magnitude, correlates, and future directions. *Clinical Psychology: Science and Practice, 16,* 121–133.

Merrill, L. L., Guimond, J. M., Thomsen, C. J., & Milner, J. S. (2003). Child sexual abuse and number of sexual partners in young women: The role of abuse severity, coping style, and sexual functioning. *Journal of Consulting and Clinical Psychology, 71,* 987–996.

Mervielde, I., & Fruyt, F. D. (2002). Assessing children's traits with the hierarchical personality inventory for children. In B. de Raad (Ed.), *Big five assessment* (pp. 129–142). Ashland, OH: Hogrefe & Huber.

Mesibov, G. B., Shea, V., & Schopler, E. (2005). *The TEACCH approach to autism spectrum disorders.* New York: Kluwer/Plenum Press.

Mesman, E., Nolen, W. A., Reichert, C. G., & Wals, M. (2013). The Dutch bipolar offspring study: 12-year follow-up. *American Journal of Psychiatry, 170,* 542–549.

Messer, J., Goodman, R., Rowe, R., Meltzer, H., & Maughan, B. (2006). Preadolescent conduct problems in girls and boys. *Journal of the American Academy of Child & Adolescent Psychiatry, 45,* 184–191.

Messer, S. C., & Gross, A. M. (1995). Childhood depression and family interaction: A naturalistic observation study. *Journal of Clinical Child Psychology, 24,* 77–88.

Messinger, D., Young, G. S., Ozonoff, S., Dobkins, K., Carter, A., Zwaigenbaum, L., ... Sigman, M. (2013). Beyond autism: A baby siblings research consortium study of high-risk children at three years of age. *Journal of the Academy of Child & Adolescent Psychiatry, 52,* 300–308.

Meyer, K., & Damasio, A. (2009). Convergence and divergence in a neural architecture for recognition and memory. *Trends in Neurosciences, 32,* 376–382.

Micco, J., Henin, A., Mick, E., Kim, S., Hopkins, C., Biederman, J., & Hirshfeld-Becker, D. (2009). Anxiety and depressive disorders in offspring at high risk for anxiety: A meta-analysis. *Journal of Anxiety Disorders, 23,* 1158–1164.

Mick, E., Biederman, J., Faraone, S. V., Sayer, J., & Kleinman, S. (2002). Case-control study of attention-deficit hyperactivity disorder and maternal smoking, alcohol use, and drug use during pregnancy. *Journal of the American Academy of Child & Adolescent Psychiatry, 41,* 378–385.

Mick, E., Biederman, J., Jetton, J., & Faraone, S. V. (2000). Sleep disturbances associated with attention deficit hyperactivity disorder: The impact of psychiatric comorbidity and pharmacotherapy. *Journal of Child and Adolescent Psychopharmacology, 10,* 223–231.

Mick, E., Byrne, D., Fried, R., Monuteaux, M., Faraone, S. V., & Biederman, J. (2011). Predictors of ADHD persistence in girls at 5-year follow-up. *Journal of Attention Disorders, 15,* 183–192.

Mick, E., Santangelo, S. L., Wypij, D., & Biederman, J. (2000). Impact of maternal depression on ratings of comorbid depression in adolescents with attention-deficit/hyperactivity disorder. *Journal of the American Academy of Child & Adolescent Psychiatry, 39,* 314–319.

Mick, E., Todorov, A., Smalley, S., Hu, X., Loo, S., Todd, R. D., ... Faraone, S. V. (2010). Family based genome-wide association scan of attention-deficit/hyperactivity disorder. *Journal of the American Academy of Child & Adolescent Psychiatry, 49,* 898–905.

Midgley, N., & Kennedy, E. (2011). Psychodynamic psychotherapy for children and adolescents: A critical review of the evidence base. *Journal of Child Psychotherapy, 37,* 232–260.

Mihura, J. L., Meyer, G. J., Dumitrascu, N., & Bombel, G. (2013). The validity of individual Rorschach variables: Systematic reviews and meta-analyses of the comprehensive system. *Psychological Bulletin, 139,* 548–605.

Mikami, A. Y. (2014). Social skills training. In R. A. Barkley (Ed.), *Attention-deficit hyperactivity disorder: A handbook for diagnosis and treatment* (4th ed.). New York: Guilford Press.

Mikami, A. Y., Hinshaw, S. P., Patterson, K. A., & Lee, J. C. (2008). Eating pathology among adolescent girls with attention-deficit/hyperactivity disorder. *Journal of Abnormal Psychology, 117,* 225–235.

Mikkelsen, E. J. (2010). Elimination disorders. In M. K. Dulcan (Ed.), *Dulcan's textbook of child and adolescent psychiatry* (pp. 435–447). Arlington, VA: American Psychiatric Publishing.

Miklowitz, D. J., Chang, K. D., Taylor, D. O., George, E. L., Singh, M. K., Schneck, C. D., ... Garber, J. (2011). Early psychosocial intervention for youth at risk for bipolar I or II disorder: A 1-year treatment development trial. *Bipolar Disorders, 13,* 67–75.

Miklowitz, D. J., Schneck, C. D., Singh, M. K., Taylor, D. O., George, E. L., Cosgrove, V. E., ... Chang, K. D. (2013). Early intervention for symptomatic youth at risk for bipolar disorder: A randomized trial of family-focused therapy. *Journal of the American Academy of Child & Adolescent Psychiatry, 52,* 121–131.

Mikton, C., & Butchart, A. (2009). Child maltreatment prevention: A systematic review of reviews. *Bulletin of the World Health Organization, 87,* 353–361.

Milich, R., Balentine, A. C., & Lynam, D. R. (2001). ADHD combined type and ADHD predominantly inattentive type are distinct and unrelated disorders. *Clinical Psychology: Science and Practice, 8,* 463–488.

Milich, R., & Lorch, E. P. (1994). Television viewing methodology to understand cognitive processing of ADHD children. In T. H. Ollendick & R. J. Prinz (Eds.), *Advances in clinical child psychology* (Vol. 16, pp. 177–202). New York: Plenum Press.

Milich, R., Wolraich, M. C., & Lindgren, S. (1986). Sugar and hyperactivity: A critical review of empirical findings. *Clinical Psychology Review, 6,* 493–513.

Miller, A. (2007). Social neuroscience of child and adolescent depression. *Brain and Cognition, 65,* 47–68.

Miller, A. L., & Olson, S. L. (2000). Emotional expressiveness during peer conflicts: A predictor of social maladjustment among high-risk preschoolers. *Journal of Abnormal Child Psychology, 28,* 339–352.

Miller, G. E., Chen, E., & Parker, K. J. (2011). Psychological stress in childhood and susceptibility to the chronic diseases of aging: Moving toward a model of behavioral and biological mechanisms. *Psychological Bulletin, 137,* 959–997.

Miller, K. B., & La Greca, A. M. (2005). Adjustment to chronic illness in girls. In D. J. Bell, S. L. Foster, & E. J. Mash (Eds.), *Handbook of behavioral and emotional problems in girls. Issues in clinical child psychology* (pp. 489–522). New York: Kluwer/Plenum Press.

Miller, M., Sheridan, M., Cardoos, S. L., & Hinshaw, S. P. (2013). Impaired decision-making as a young adult outcome of girls diagnosed with attention-deficit/hyperactivity disorder in childhood. *Journal of the International Neuropsychological Society, 19,* 110–114.

Miller, T. W., Nigg, J. T., & Miller, R. L. (2009). Attention deficit disorder in African American children: What can be concluded from the past 10 years. *Annual Review of Clinical Psychology, 29,* 77–86.

Millichap, J. G., & Lee, M. M. (2012). The diet factor in attention-deficit/hyperactivity disorder. *Pediatrics, 129,* 330–337.

Mills, R., Alati, R., O'Callaghan, M., Najman, J. M., Williams, G. M., Bor, W., & Strathearn, L. (2011). Child abuse and neglect and cognitive function at 14 years of age: Findings from a birth cohort. *Pediatrics, 127,* 4–10.

Milne, A. A. (1926). *Winnie-the-pooh.* London: Methuen.

Milrod, B., Markowitz, J. C., Gerber, A. J., Cyranowski, J., Altemus, M., Shapiro, T., ... Glatt, C. (2014). Childhood separation anxiety and the pathogenesis and treatment of adult anxiety. *American Journal of Psychiatry, 171,* 34–43.

Minshew, N. J., Johnson, C., & Luna, B. (2000). The cognitive and neural basis of autism: A disorder of complex information processing and dysfunction of neocortical systems. *International Review of Research in Mental Retardation, 23,* 112–140.

Minuchin, S., Rosman, B. L., & Baker, L. (1978). *Psychosomatic families: Anorexia nervosa in context.* Cambridge, MA: Harvard University Press.

Mironova, P., Rhodes, A. E., Bethell, J. M., Tonmyr, L., Boyle, M. H., Wekerle, C., ... Leslie, B. (2011). Childhood physical abuse and suicide-related behavior: A systematic review. *Vulnerable Children and Youth Studies, 6,* 1–7.

Mischoulon, D., Eddy, K. T., Keshaviah, A., Dinescu, D., Ross, S. L., Kass, A. E., ... Herzog, D. B. (2011). Depression and eating disorders: Treatment and course. *Journal of Affective Disorders, 130,* 470–477.

Mitchell, K. J., Wolak, J., & Finkelhor, D. (2007). Trends in youth reports of sexual solicitations, harassment and unwanted exposure to pornography on the internet. *Journal of Adolescent Health, 40,* 116–126.

Mitchell, K. S., Mazzeo, S. E., Schlesinger, M. R., Brewerton, T. D., & Smith, B. N. (2012). Comorbidity of partial and subthreshold PTSD among men and women with eating disorders in the National Comorbidity Survey-Replication study. *International Journal of Eating Disorders, 45,* 307–315.

Mitchell, S., Brian, J., Zwaigenbaum, L., Roberts, W., Szatmari, P., Smith, I., & Bryson, S. (2006). Early language and communication development of infants later diagnosed with autism spectrum disorder. *Journal of Developmental and Behavioral Pediatrics, 27*(Suppl.), S69–S78.

MMWR. (2002, May 24). Fetal alcohol syndrome—Alaska, Arizona, Colorado, and New York, 1995–1997. *MMWR: Morbidity and Mortality Weekly Report, 51,* 433–435.

Moffitt, T. E. (1990). Juvenile delinquency and attention deficit disorder in boys' developmental trajectories from age 3 to age 15. *Child Development, 61,* 893–910.

Moffitt, T. E. (1993). Adolescence-limited and life-course-persistent antisocial behavior: A developmental taxonomy. *Psychological Review, 100,* 674–701.

Moffitt, T. E. (2006). Life-course-persistent versus adolescence-limited antisocial behavior. In D. Cicchetti & D. J. Cohen (Eds.), *Developmental psychopathology: Vol. 3. Risk, disorder, and adaptation* (2nd ed., pp. 570–598). New York: Wiley.

Moffitt, T. E., Arseneault, L., Belsky, D., Dickson, N., Hancox, R. J., Harrington, H., … Caspi, A. (2011). A gradient of childhood self-control predicts health, wealth, and public safety. *PNAS Proceedings of the National Academy of Sciences of the United States of America, 108,* 2693–2698.

Moffitt, T. E., Arseneault, L., Jaffee, S. R., Kim-Cohen, L., Koenen, K. C., Odgers, C. L., … Viding, E. (2008). Research review: DSM-V conduct disorder: Research needs for an evidence base. *Journal of Child Psychology and Psychiatry, 49,* 3–33.

Moffitt, T. E., Caspi, A., Belsky, J., & Silva, P. A. (1992). Childhood experience and the onset of menarche: A test of a sociobiological model. *Child Development, 63,* 47–58.

Moffitt, T. E., Caspi, A., Dickson, N., Silva, P., & Stanton, W. (1996). Childhood-onset versus adolescent-onset antisocial conduct problems in males: Natural history from ages 3 to 18 years. *Development and Psychopathology, 8,* 399–424.

Moffitt, T. E., Caspi, A., Harrington, H. L., & Milne, B. J. (2002). Males on the life-course persistent and adolescence-limited antisocial pathways: Follow-up at age 26. *Development and Psychopathology, 14,* 179–207.

Moffitt, T. E., Caspi, A., Rutter, M., & Silva, P. A. (2001). *Sex differences in antisocial behaviour: Conduct disorder, delinquency and violence in the Dunedin Longitudinal Study.* Cambridge, England: Cambridge University Press.

Moffitt, T. E., Caspi, A., Taylor, A., Kokaua, J., Milne, B. J., Polanczyk, G., & Poulton, R. (2010). Evidence that lifetime prevalence rates are doubled by prospective versus retrospective ascertainment. *Psychological Medicine, 40,* 899–909.

Moffitt, T. E., Lynam, D., & Silva, P. A. (1994). Neuropsychological tests predict persistent male delinquency. *Criminology, 32,* 101–124.

Moffitt, T. E., & Melchior, M. (2007). Editorial: Why does the worldwide prevalence of childhood attention deficit disorder matter? *American Journal of Psychiatry, 164,* 856–858.

Moldavsky, M., & Sayal, K. (2013). Knowledge and attitudes about attention-deficit/hyperactivity disorder (ADHD) and its treatment: The views of children, adolescents, parents, teachers and healthcare professionals. *Current Psychiatry Reports, 15,* 377(1–7).

Molina, B. S. G., Flory, K., Hinshaw, S. P., Greiner, A. R., Arnold, L. E., Swanson, J. M., … Wigal, T. (2007). Delinquent behavior and emerging substance abuse in the MTA at 36 months: Prevalence, course, and treatment effects. *Journal of the American Academy of Child & Adolescent Psychiatry, 46,* 1028–1040.

Molina, B. S. G., Hinshaw, S. P., Arnold, L. E., Swanson, J. M., Pelham, W. E., Hechtman, L., Hoza, B., … The MTA Cooperative Group (2013). Adolescent substance use in the Multimodal Treatment Study of Attention-Deficit Hyperactivity Disorder (ADHD) (MTA) as a function of childhood ADHD, random assignment to childhood treatments, and subsequent medication. *Journal of the American Academy of Child & Adolescent Psychiatry, 52,* 250–263.

Molina, B. S. G., Hinshaw, S. P., Swanson, J. M. Arnold, L. E., Vitiello, B., Jensen, P. S., … The MTA Cooperative Group. (2009). The MTA at 8 years: Prospective follow-up of children treated for combined-type ADHD in a multisite study. *Journal of the American Academy of Child & Adolescent Psychiatry, 48,* 484–500.

Mond, J., Van den Berg, P., Boutelle, K., Hannan, P., & Neumark-Sztainer, D. (2011). Obesity, body dissatisfaction, and emotional well-being in early and late adolescence: Findings from the project EAT study. *Journal of Adolescent Health, 48,* 373–378.

Monk, C. S. (2008). The development of emotion-related neural circuitry in health and psychopathology. *Development and Psychopathology, 20,* 1231–1250.

Monk, S., Klein, R. G., Telzer, E. H., Schroth, E. A., Mannuzza, S., Moulton, J. L., … Ernst, M. (2008). Amygdala and nucleus accumbens activation to emotional facial expressions in children and adolescents at risk for major depression. *American Journal of Psychiatry, 165,* 90–98.

Monroe, S. M., Rohde, P., Seeley, J. R., & Lewinsohn, P. M. (1999). Life events and depression in adolescence: Relationship loss as a prospective risk factor for first onset of major depressive disorder. *Journal of Abnormal Psychology, 108,* 606–614.

Montague, C. T., Farooqi, I. S., Whitehead, J. P., Soos, M. A., Rau, H., Wareham, N. J., … O'Rahilly, S. (1997). Congenital leptin deficiency is associated with severe early-onset obesity in humans. *Nature, 387,* 903–907.

Moran, T. H., & Ladenheim, E. E. (2011). Adiposity signaling and meal size control. *Physiology & Behavior, 103,* 21–24.

Moreno, C., Arango, C., Parellada, M., Shaffer, D., & Bird, H. (2007a). Antidepressants in child and adolescent depression: Where are the bugs? *Acta Psychiatrica Scandinavica, 115,* 184–195.

Moreno, C., Laje, G., Blanco, C., Jiang, H., Schmidt, A. B., & Olfson, M. (2007b). National trends in the outpatient diagnosis and treatment of bipolar disorder in youth. *Archives of General Psychiatry, 64,* 1032–1039.

Morgan, P. L., Hillemeier, M. M., Farkas, G., & Maczuga, S. (2014). Racial/ethnic disparities in ADHD diagnosis by kindergarten entry. *Journal of Child Psychology and Psychiatry.* Advance online publication. doi:10.1111/jcpp.12204.

Morgan, R. K. (1999). *Case studies in child and adolescent psychopathology.* Upper Saddle River, NJ: Prentice Hall.

Morgan, W. P. (1896). A case of congenital word-blindness. *British Medical Journal, 2,* 1543–1544.

Morris, A. S., Silk, J. S., Morris, M. D. S., Steinberg, L., Aucoin, K. J., & Keyes, A. W. (2011). The influence of mother–child emotion regulation strategies on children's expression of anger and sadness. *Developmental Psychology, 47,* 213–225.

Morris, R. J., & Kratochwill, T. R. (Eds.). (2007). *The practice of child therapy* (4th ed.). Needham Heights, MA: Allyn & Bacon.

Morrisey-Kane, E., & Prinz, R. J. (1999). Engagement in child and adolescent treatment: The role of parental cognitions and attributions. *Clinical Child and Family Psychology Review, 2,* 183–198.

Mortensen, E. L., Andresen, J., Kruuse, E., Sanders, S. A., & Reinisch, J. M. (2003). IQ stability: The relation between child and young adult intelligence test scores in low-birthweight samples. *Scandinavian Journal of Psychology, 44,* 395–398.

Moss, J., Oliver, C., Arron, K., Burbidge, C., & Berg, K. (2009). The prevalence and phenomenology of repetitive behavior in genetic syndromes. *Journal of Autism and Developmental Disorders, 39,* 572–588.

Mostert, M. P. (2001). Facilitated communication since 1995: A review of published studies. *Journal of Autism and Developmental Disorders, 31,* 287–313.

Mostert, M. P. (2010). Facilitated communication and its legitimacy—twenty-first century developments. *Exceptionality, 18,* 31–41.

Motlagh, M. G., Katsovich, L., Thompson, N., Lin, H., Young-Shin, K., Scahill, L., … Leckman, J. F. (2010). Severe psychosocial stress and heavy cigarette smoking during pregnancy: An examination of the pre- and perinatal risk factors associated with ADHD and Tourette syndrome. *European Child & Adolescent Psychiatry, 19*, 755–764.

Moturi, S., & Avis, K. (2010). Assessment and treatment of common pediatric sleep disorders. *Innovations in Clinical Neuroscience, 7*(6), 24–37.

Mouridsen, S. E., Rich, B., & Isager, T. (2011). A longitudinal study of epilepsy and other central nervous system diseases in individuals with and without a history of infantile autism. *Brain & Development, 33*, 361–366.

Mowrer, O. H. (1947). On the dual nature of learning: A reinterpretation of "conditioning" and "problem solving." *Harvard Educational Review, 17*, 102–148.

Mowrer, O. H. (1950). *Learning theory and the personality dynamics.* New York: Arnold Press.

Mowrer, O. H., & Mowrer, W. M. (1938). Enuresis: A method for its study and treatment. *American Journal of Orthopsychiatry, 8*, 436–459.

MTA Cooperative Group. (1999a). Fourteen-month randomized clinical trial of treatment strategies for attention-deficit hyperactivity disorder. *Archives of General Psychiatry, 56*, 1073–1086.

MTA Cooperative Group. (1999b). Moderators and mediators of treatment response for children with ADHD: The MTA Study. *Archives of General Psychiatry, 56*, 1088–1096.

MTA Cooperative Group. (2004a). National Institute of Mental Health Multimodal Treatment Study of ADHD follow-up: 24-month outcomes of treatment strategies for attention-deficit/hyperactivity disorder. *Pediatrics, 113*, 754–761.

MTA Cooperative Group. (2004b). National Institute of Mental Health Multimodal Treatment Study of ADHD follow-up: Changes in effectiveness and growth after the end of treatment. *Pediatrics, 113*, 762–769.

Muehlenkamp, J. J., Ertelt, T. W., Miller, A. L., & Claes, L. (2011). Borderline personality symptoms differentiate non-suicidal and suicidal self-injury in ethnically diverse outpatients. *Journal of Child Psychology and Psychiatry, 52*, 148–155.

Mufson, L. (2010). Interpersonal psychotherapy for depressed adolescents (IPT-A): Extending the reach from academic to community settings. *Child and Adolescent Mental Health, 15*, 66–72.

Mufson, L., Dorta, K. P., Moreau, D., & Weissman, M. M. (2004). *Interpersonal psychotherapy for depressed adolescents* (2nd ed.). New York: Guilford Press.

Mufson, L. H., Dorta, K. P., Wickramaratne, P., Momura, Y., Olfson, M., & Weissman, M. M. (2004). A randomized effectiveness trial of interpersonal psychotherapy for depressed adolescents. *Archives of General Psychiatry, 61*, 577–584.

Mufson, L. H., Lewis, L. R., Bunlicks-Stoessel, M., & Young, J. F. (2012). Treatment of adolescent depression with interpersonal psychotherapy. In J. C. Markowitz, & M. M. Weissman (Eds.), *Casebook of interpersonal psychotherapy* (pp. 203–222). New York: Oxford University Press.

Mulhern, R. K., Merchant, T. E., Gajjar, A., Reddick, W. E., & Kun, L. E. (2004). Late neurocognitive sequelae in survivors of brain tumours in childhood. *Lancet Oncology, 5*, 399–408.

Mullane, J. C., Corkum, P. V., Klein, R. M., McLaughlin, E. N., & Lawrence, M. A. (2011). Alerting, orienting, and executive attention in children with ADHD. *Journal of Attention Disorders, 15*, 310–320.

Mullins, L. L., Wolfe-Christensen, C., Pai, A. L. H., Carpentier, M. Y., Gillaspy, S., Cheek, J., & Page, M. (2007). The relationship of parental overprotection, perceived child vulnerability, and parenting stress to uncertainty in youth with chronic illness. *Journal of Pediatric Psychology, 32*, 973–982.

Mulqueen, J. M., Bartley, C. A., & Bloch, M. H. (2013). Meta-analysis: Parental interventions for preschool ADHD. *Journal of Attention Disorders.* Advance online publication. doi:10.1177/1087054713504135.

Mundy, P., & Neal, A. R. (2001). Neural plasticity, joint attention, and a transactional social-orienting model of autism. In L. M. Glidden (Ed.), *International review of research in mental retardation: Autism* (Vol. 23, pp. 139--168). San Diego: Academic Press.

Mundy, P., & Newell, L. (2007). Attention, joint attention, and social cognition. *Current Directions in Psychological Science, 16*, 269–274.

Munn, R., Smeltzer, D., Smeltzer, T., & Westin, K. (2010). The most painful gaps: Family perspectives on the treatment of eating disorders. In M. Maine, H. McGilley, & D. Bunnell (Eds.), *Treatment of eating disorders: Bridging the research–practice gap* (pp. 349–364). San Diego: Elsevier Academic Press.

Munsch, S., Roth, B., Michael, T., Meyer, A. H., Biedert, E., Roth, S., ... Margraf, J. (2008). Randomized controlled comparison of two cognitive behavioral therapies for obese children: Mother versus mother-child cognitive behavioral therapy. *Psychotherapy and Psychosomatics, 77*, 235–246.

Muratori, F., Picchi, L., Bruni, G., Patarnello, M., & Romagnoli, G. (2003). A two-year follow-up of psychodynamic psychotherapy for internalizing disorders in children. *Journal of the American Academy of Child & Adolescent Psychiatry, 42*, 331–339.

Muris, P. (2007). *Normal and abnormal fear in children and adolescents.* Burlington, MA: Elsevier.

Muris, P., & Meesters, C. (2002). Attachment, behavioral inhibition, and anxiety disorders symptoms in normal adolescents. *Journal of Psychopathology and Behavioral Assessment, 24*, 97–106.

Muris, P., & Merckelbach, H. (2001). The etiology of childhood specific phobia: A multifactorial model. In M. W. Vasey & M. M. Dadds (Eds.), *The developmental psychopathology of anxiety* (pp. 355–385). New York: Oxford University Press.

Muris, P., Rapee, R., Meesters, C., Schouten, E., & Geers, M. (2003). Threat perception abnormalities in children: The role

of anxiety disorders symptoms, chronic anxiety, and state anxiety. *Journal of Anxiety Disorders, 17*, 271–287.

Murphy, S. M., Faulkner, D. M., & Farley, L. R. (2014). The behaviour of young children with social communication disorders during dyadic interaction with peers. *Journal of Abnormal Child Psychology, 42*, 277–289.

Murphy, T. K., Lewin, A. B., Storch, E. A., Stock S., and the American Academy of Child and Adolescent Psychiatry (AACAP) Committee on Quality Issues (CQI). (2013). Practice parameter for the assessment and treatment of children and adolescents with tic disorders. *Journal of the American Academy of Child & Adolescent Psychiatry, 52*, 1341–1359.

Murphy, W. P., Yaruss, J. S., & Quesal, R. W. (2007). Enhancing treatment for school-age children who stutter: I. Reducing negative reactions through desensitization and cognitive restructuring. *Journal of Fluency Disorders, 32*, 121–138.

Murray, C. D., Macdonald S., & Fox, J. (2008) Body satisfaction, eating disorders and suicide ideation in an Internet sample of self-harmers reporting and not reporting childhood sexual abuse. *Psychology, Health and Medicine, 13*, 29–42.

Murray, J., Irving, B., Farrington, D. P., Colman, I., & Bloxsom, C. A. J. (2010). Very early predictors of conduct problems and crime: Results from a national cohort study. *Journal of Child Psychology and Psychiatry, 51*, 1198–1207.

Murray, L., Creswell, C., & Cooper, P. J. (2009). The development of anxiety disorders in childhood: An integrative review. *Psychological Medicine, 39*, 1413–1423.

Murray-Close, D., Hoza, B., Hinshaw, S. P., Arnold, L. E., Swanson, J., Jenson, P. S., ... Wells, K. (2010). Developmental processes in peer problems of children with attention-deficit/hyperactivity disorder in The Multimodal Treatment Study of Children with ADHD: Developmental cascades and vicious cycles. *Development and Psychopathology, 22*, 785–802.

Myers, N. L. (2011). Update: Schizophrenia across cultures. *Current Psychiatry Reports, 13*, 305–311.

Myers, S. M., Johnson, C. P., and the Council on Children with Disabilities. (2007). Management of children with autism spectrum disorders. *Pediatrics, 120*, 1162–1182.

Naber, F. B. A., Bakersman-Kranenburg, M. J., van IJzendoorn, M. H., Swinkels, S. H. N., Buitelaar, J. K., Dietz, C., ... van Engeland, H. (2008). Play behavior and attachment in toddlers with autism. *Journal of Autism and Developmental Disorders, 38*, 857–866.

Naber, F. B. A., Swinkels, S. H. N., Buitelaar, J. K., Dietz, C., Van Daalen, E., Dietz, C., ... van Engeland, H. (2007). Attachment in toddlers with autism and other developmental disorders. *Journal of Autism and Developmental Disorders, 37*, 1123–1138.

Nadeau, K., Littman, E. B., & Quinn, P. O. (1999). *Understanding girls with AD/HD.* Silver Spring, MD: Advantage Books.

Nader, K., & Fletcher, K. E. (2014). Child-hood posttraumatic stress disorder. In E. J. Mash & R. A. Barkley (Eds.), *Child psychopathology* (3rd ed., pp. 476–528). New York: Guilford Press.

Nagel, B. J., Bathula, D., Herting, M., Schmitt, C., Kroenke, C. D., Fair, D., & Nigg, J. T. (2011). Altered white matter microstructure in children with attention-deficit/hyperactivity disorder. *Journal of the American Academy of Child & Adolescent Psychiatry, 50,* 283–292.

Nagin, D. S., & Tremblay, R. F. (2001). Parental and early childhood predictors of persistent physical aggression in boys from kindergarten to high school. *Archives of General Psychiatry, 58,* 389–394.

Narusyte, J., Neiderhiser, J. M., Andershed, A.-K., D'Onofrio, B. M., Reiss, D., Spotts, E., ... Lichtenstein, P. (2011). Parental criticism and externalizing behavior problems in adolescents: The role of environment and genotype-environment correlation. *Journal of Abnormal Psychology, 120,* 365–376.

Nation, K., Snowling, M. J., & Clarke, P. (2007). Dissecting the relationship between language skills and learning to read: Semantic and phonological contributions to new vocabulary learning in children with poor reading comprehension. *Advances in Speech Language Pathology, 9,* 131–139.

National Center for Educational Statistics (2012). *2012 Revision of NCES Statistical Standards: Final.* Washington, DC: Author. Retrieved from http://nces.ed.gov/statprog/2012

National Center on Addiction and Substance Abuse at Columbia University. (2011). *Adolescent substance use: America's #1 public health problem.* Retrieved from http://www.casacolumbia.org/templates/publications_reports.aspx

National Infant & Toddler Care Initiative. (2010). *Infant/toddler, development, screening and assessment.* Washington, DC: Zero to Three/U.S. Department of Health and Human Services. Retrieved from www.zerotothree.org/public-policy/state-community-policy/nitcci/multidisciplinary-consultant-module-2.pdf

National Institute of Health and Clinical Excellence [NICE]. (2013a). Attention deficit hyperactivity disorder: Diagnosis and management of ADHD in children, adolescents, and adults. *NICE Clinical Guideline 72,* 1-56. Manchester, ENG: Author. Retrieved from http://guidance.nice.org.uk/CG72/NICEGuidance/pdf/English

National Institute of Health and Clinical Excellence [NICE]. (2013b). Psychosis and schizophrenia in children and young people: Recognition and management. *NICE Clinical Guideline 155,* 1-51. Manchester, England: Author. Retrieved from http://publications.nice.org.uk/psychosis-and-schizophrenia-in-children-and-young-people-cg155

National Institutes of Health. (2007). *Fact sheet: Reading difficulty and disability.* Washington, DC: Author.

National Institute of Justice. (1996). *Victim costs and consequences: A new look.* Washington, DC: Author.

National Institute of Mental Health. (1994a). *Attention deficit hyperactivity disorder: Decade of the brain* (NIMH publication no. 94-3572). Washington, DC: Author.

National Institute of Mental Health. (1994b). *Eating disorders* (DHHS publication no. NIMH 94-3477). Washington, DC: Government Printing Office.

National Institute of Mental Health (NIMH). (2003). *Breaking ground, breaking through: The strategic plan for mood disorders research of the National Institute of Mental Health.* Washington, DC: Department of Health and Human Services.

National Society for the Prevention of Cruelty to Children (NSPCC) (2011). *Child abuse and neglect in the UK today.* London, England: Author. Retrieved from http://www.nspcc.org.uk/Inform/research/findings/child_abuse_neglect_research_wda84173.html

NCTSN Core Curriculum on Childhood Trauma Task Force (2012). *The 12 core concepts: Concepts for understanding traumatic stress responses in children and families.* Core Curriculum on Childhood Trauma. Los Angeles, CA, and Durham, NC: UCLA-Duke University National Center for Child Traumatic Stress. Retrieved from http://www.nctsnet.org/sites/default/files/assets/pdfs/tfcbt_general.pdf

Neale, B. M., Medland, S., Ripke, S., Anney, R. J. L., Asherson, P., Buitelaar, J., Franke, B., ...Biederman, J. for the IMAGE II Consortium. (2010). Case-control genome-wide association study of attention-deficit/hyperactivity disorder. *Journal of the American Academy of Child & Adolescent Psychiatry, 49,* 906–920.

Neece, C. L., Baker, B. L., Crnic, K., & Blacher, J. (2013). Examining the validity of ADHD as a diagnosis for adolescents with intellectual disabilities: Clinical presentation. *Journal of Abnormal Child Psychology, 41,* 597–612.

Neece, C. L., Blacher, J., & Baker, B. L. (2010). Impact on siblings of children with intellectual disability: The role of child behavior problems. *American Journal on Intellectual and Developmental Disabilities, 115,* 291–306.

Negriff, S., Ji, J., & Trickett, P. K. (2011). Exposure to peer delinquency as a mediator between self-report pubertal timing and delinquency: A longitudinal study of mediation. *Development and Psychopathology, 23,* 293–304.

Neisser, U., Boodoo, G., Bouchard, T. J., Jr., Boykin, A. W., Brody, N., Ceci, S. J., ... Urbina, S. (1996). Intelligence: Knowns and unknowns. *American Psychologist, 51,* 77–101.

Nelles, W. B., & Barlow, D. H. (1988). Do children panic? *Clinical Psychology Review, 8,* 359–372.

Nelson, C. A. (2011). Neural development and lifelong plasticity. In D. P. Keating (Ed.), *Nature and nurture in early child development.* (pp. 45–69). New York: Cambridge University Press.

Nelson, J. M., & Harwood, H. (2011). Learning disabilities and anxiety: A meta-analysis. *Journal of Learning Disabilities, 44,* 3–17.

Nemeth, M. (1994, April 4). Altered states. *Maclean's,* 48–49.

Neuhaus, E., Beauchaine, T. P., & Bernier, R. (2010). Neurobiological correlates of social functioning in autism. *Clinical Psychology Review, 30,* 733–748.

Neuman, R. J., Lobos, E., Reich, W., Henderson, C. A., Sun, L. W., & Todd, R. D. (2007). Prenatal smoking exposure and dopaminergic genotypes interact to cause a severe ADHD subtype. *Biological Psychiatry, 61,* 1320–1328.

Neumark-Sztainer, D., Eisenberg, M. E., Fulkerson, J. A., Story, M., & Larson, N. I. (2008). Family meals and disordered eating in adolescents: Longitudinal findings from project EAT. *Archives of Pediatric & Adolescent Medicine, 162,* 17–22.

Neumark-Sztainer, D., Story, M., Hannan, P., Beuhring, T., & Resnick, M. (2000). Disordered eating among adolescents: Associations with sexual/physical abuse and other familial/psychosocial factors. *International Journal of Eating Disorders, 28,* 249–258.

Neumark-Sztainer, D., Wall, M., Guo, J., Story, M., Haines, J., & Eisenberg, M. (2006). Obesity, disordered eating, and eating disorders in a longitudinal study of adolescents: How do dieters fare 5 years later? *Journal of the American Dietetic Association, 106,* 559–568.

Neumark-Sztainer, D., Wall, M., Larson, N. I., Eisenberg, M. E., & Loth, K. (2011). Dieting and disordered eating behaviors from adolescence to young adulthood: Findings from a 10-year longitudinal study. *American Dietetic Association Journal of the American Dietetic Association, 111,* 1004.

Nevonen, L., & Norring, C. (2004). Socio-economic variables and eating disorders: A comparison between patients and normal controls. *Eating and Weight Disorders, 9,* 279–284.

Nevsimalova, S. (2009). Narcolepsy in childhood. *Sleep Medicine Reviews, 13,* 169–180.

Newbury, D. F., Paracchini, S., Scerri, T. S., Winchester, L., Addis, L., Richardson, A. J., ... Monaco, A. P. (2011). Investigation of dyslexia and SLI risk variants in reading- and language-impaired subjects. *Behavior Genetics, 41,* 90–104.

Newsom, C., & Hovanitz, C. A. (2006). Autistic spectrum disorders. In E. J. Mash & R. A. Barkley (Eds.), *Treatment of childhood disorders* (3rd ed., pp. 455–511). New York: Guilford Press.

Nguyen, L., Huang, L. N., Arganza, G. F., & Liao, Q. (2007). The influence of race and ethnicity on psychiatric diagnoses and clinical characteristics of children and adolescents in children's services. *Cultural Diversity & Ethnic Minority Psychology, 13,* 18–25.

Niccols, A. (2007). Fetal alcohol syndrome and the developing socio-emotional brain. *Brain and Cognition, 65,* 135–142.

Nichols, M. (1995, January 30). Schizophrenia: Hidden torment. *Maclean's,* 70–74.

Nicolson, R., Lenane, M., Singaracharlu, S., Malaspina, D., Giedd, J. N., Hamburger, S. D., ... Rapoport, J. L. (2000). Premorbid speech and language impairments in

Brown, T. A., 495
Browne, K., 415
Brownell, K. D., 479, 498
Brownlie, E. B., 197, 203, 205, 207, 217, 221
Bruch, H., 500
Bruijnzeel, C., 189
Brumariu, L. E., 390
Brumberg, J. J., 488
Bryant-Waugh, R., 486, 487, 503
Bryson, S. E., 176
Bryson, S. W., 476
Brytek-Matera, A., 498
Bub, K. L., 445
Bubier, J. L., 286
Bucchianeri, M. M., 478
Buckholtz, J. W., 294
Buckles, J., 140
Buckner, J. D., 370
Buckstein, O., 244
Bufferd, S. J., 317
Buitelaar, J., 259
Buitelaar, J. K., 247, 336
Buka, S., 177
Bulik, C. M., 478, 482, 491, 496, 497, 499, 503
Bullock, B. M., 284
Bundy, A. C., 168
Bunford, N., 258
Burack, J. A., 151
Burge, D., 330
Burke, J. D., 271, 272, 275, 278, 286
Burke, Leo J., 444
Burket, R. C., 453
Burns, G. L., 232, 272
Burt, S. A., 53, 244, 256, 289, 293
Burton, E. M., 501
Burwinkle, T. M., 481
Bush, G., 253, 255
Bush, L. D., 94
Bushman, B. J., 285, 302
Bussing, R., 242
Butchart, A., 438
Butcher, J. N., 101
Butler, M. G., 146
Button, T. M. M., 282
Byrd, D. A., 279

Cairney, J., 319
Calati, R., 497
Calhoun, C. D., 326
Calhoun, S. L., 160, 169
Campbell, F. A., 128, 151, 290
Campbell, L. K., 453, 454
Campbell, M., 402, 427
Campbell, R., 430
Campbell, S. B., 248
Campbell, W. K., 285
Canadian Diabetes Association, 458
Canino, G., 87, 287
Cannon, T. D., 36, 190
Canter, K. S., 456, 465, 466b
Cantor, J. M., 415
Cantrell, M. A., 460
Capaldi, D. M., 300
Caplan, R., 189
Caporino, N. E., 317
Capps, L., 387

Carballo, J. J., 356
Cardinal, D. N., 58
Cardoos, S. L., 241, 246
Carlson, C. L., 235
Carlson, E. A., 34, 256
Carlson, G. A., 245, 347, 348, 350, 351, 353
Carpenter, D. O., 295
Carpenter, Karen, 475
Carper, R., 173
Carper, T. L. M., 495
Carr, E. G., 128
Carretti, B., 219
Carroll, Lewis, 108
Carson, A., 471
Carter, A., 2
Carter, A. S., 175
Carter, M., 139, 166
Carter, Shawn Corey (Jay Z), 15, 15b
Cartwright-Hatton, S., 356, 396
Casey, B. J., 265
Cash, T. F., 478
Cashel, M. L., 98, 101
Caspi, A., 48b, 85, 244, 292, 297, 334
Cassidy, A., 175
Cassidy, S. B., 145
Castellanos, F. X., 251, 253
Castellanos-Ryan, N., 473
Cavaleri, M. A., 79
Caylak, E., 203
Ceci, S. J., 128
Cella, M., 193
Centers for Disease Control and Prevention, 22, 148, 169, 174, 175, 268, 270, 328, 401, 480, 481, 483
Cerel, J., 339
Cha, C. B., 313, 328, 329
Chacko, A., 261
Chaidez, V., 173
Challman, T. D., 173
Chan, A. S., 200
Chan, E., 241
Chan, J., 155
Chance, S. A., 171
Chang, K., 352
Chang, M., 218
Chang, S., 377
Chang, Z., 260
Chansky, T. E., 382
Chaplin, T. M., 85
Chapman, D. A., 142
Chapman, D. P., 18, 401, 427
Charach, A., 241
Charman, T., 163, 168, 169, 175, 182, 186
Chassin, L., 469, 470, 471, 472
Chavez, M., 496, 503, 504
Chavira, D. A., 370, 371
Chayaisit, W., 247
Cheely, C., 319
Chen, E., 407
Chen, F., 19
Chen, J., 241, 334
Chen, R., 472
Chen, X., 21, 87
Chen, Y. R., 320
Chess, S., 46, 230, 256

Chetnik, M., 101, 115
Cheung, A. H., 340, 346
Cheung, M. C., 200
Chiang, H. M., 166
Chien, P. L., 22
Children's Defense Fund, 12, 19, 268, 303
Child Welfare Information Gateway, 408
Chirdkiatgumchai, V., 117
Chorney, D. B., 444
Chorpita, B. F., 9, 94, 96, 109, 120, 121, 122, 356, 364, 382, 383, 392, 393, 394
Christian, L. M., 129
Christophersen, E. R., 451, 453, 454
Chronis, A. M., 261, 263
Chronis-Tuscano, A., 241, 242, 245, 256, 261, 386
Churches, O., 163
Churchill, Winston, 197
Cicchetti, D., 18, 21, 22, 31, 33, 34, 35, 36, 59, 139, 330, 404, 407, 410, 412, 428, 431, 432, 433
Cislak, A., 484
Clark, D. B., 427, 428, 471
Clark, L. A., 234
Clark, L. S., 498
Clark, R. W., 200
Clarke, G. N., 343
Clarke, P., 200
Clarke, P. J., 222, 223, 224
Claudino, A. M., 496
Clauss, J. A., 386
Clay, D. L., 464, 498
Clifford, S. M., 163
Cloitre, M., 425
Cobain, Kurt, 467
Cobb, B., 153, 224
Coccaro, E. F., 296
Code, C., 206
Coffino, B., 34
Cogan, J., 499
Coghill, D., 251
Cohan, S. L., 371
Cohen, D., 170
Cohen, J., 376
Cohen, J. A., 435, 435b, 436, 439
Cohen, M. A., 271
Cohen, M. J., 102
Cohen, N. J., 280
Cohen, P., 376
Coie, J. D., 235, 287
Coiro, M. J., 462
Coker, T. R., 22
Colapinto, J., 298
Colder, C. R., 390, 470
Cole, D. A., 324, 326, 331, 338, 384
Cole, P. M., 30, 339
Cole, T. J., 483
Coll, C. G., 21, 30
Collins, L. M., 469
Collishaw, S., 268, 426
Combs, M. P., 112
Comer, J. S., 117, 260, 375, 396, 405
Compas, B. E., 16, 333, 346
Compton, S. N., 384, 396
Conduct Problems Prevention Research Group, The, 235, 271, 306, 308

DSM-5 CLASSIFICATIONS

Neurodevelopmental Disorders

Intellectual Disabilities

Intellectual Disability (Intellectual Developmental Disorder)/Global Developmental Delay/Unspecified Intellectual Disability (Intellectual Developmental Disorder)

Communication Disorders

Language Disorder/Speech Sound Disorder/Childhood-Onset Fluency Disorder (Stuttering)/Social (Pragmatic) Communication Disorder/Unspecified Communication Disorder

Autism Spectrum Disorder

Autism Spectrum Disorder

Attention-Deficit/Hyperactivity Disorder

Attention-Deficit/Hyperactivity Disorder/Other Specified Attention-Deficit/Hyperactivity Disorder/Unspecified Attention-Deficit/Hyperactivity Disorder

Specific Learning Disorder

Motor Disorders

Developmental Coordination Disorder/Stereotypic Movement Disorder

Tic Disorders

Tourette's Disorder/Persistent (Chronic) Motor or Vocal Tic Disorder/Provisional Tic Disorder/Other Specified Tic Disorder/Unspecific Tic Disorder

Other Neurodevelopmental Disorders

Other Specified Neurodevelopmental Disorder/Unspecified Neurodevelopmental Disorder

Schizophrenia Spectrum and other Psychotic Disorders

Schizotypal (Personality) Disorder
Delusional Disorder
Brief Psychotic Disorder
Schizophreniform Disorder
Schizophrenia
Schizoaffective Disorder
Substance/Medication-Induced Psychotic Disorder
Psychotic Disorder Due to Another Medical Condition
Catatonia Associated with Another Mental Disorder
Catatonic Disorder due to Another Medical Condition
Unspecified Catatonia
Other Specified Schizophrenia Spectrum and Other Psychotic Disorder
Unspecified Schizophrenia Spectrum and Other Psychotic Disorder

Bipolar and Related Disorders

Bipolar I Disorder/Bipolar II Disorder/Cyclothymic Disorder/Substance/Medication-Induced Bipolar and Related Disorder/Bipolar and Related Disorder Due to Another Medical Condition/Other Specified Bipolar and Related Disorder/Unspecified Bipolar and Related Disorder

Depressive Disorders

Disruptive Mood Dysregulation Disorder/Major Depressive Disorder/Persistent Depressive Disorder (Dysthymia)/Premenstrual Dysphoric Disorder/Substance/Medication-Induced Depressive Disorder/Depressive Disorder Due to Another Medical Condition/Other Specified Depressive Disorder/Unspecified Depressive Disorder

Anxiety Disorders

Separation Anxiety Disorder/Selective Mutism/Specific Phobia/Social Anxiety Disorder (Social Phobia)/Panic Disorder/Panic Attack Specifier/Agoraphobia/Generalized Anxiety Disorder/Substance/Medication-Induced Anxiety Disorder/Anxiety Disorder Due to Another Medical Condition/Other Specified Anxiety Disorder/Unspecified Anxiety Disorder

Obsessive-Compulsive and Related Disorders

Obsessive-Compulsive Disorder/Body Dysmorphic Disorder/Hoarding Disorder/Trichotillomania (Hair-Pulling Disorder)/Excoriation (Skin-Picking) Disorder/Substance/Medication-Induced Obsessive-Compulsive and Related Disorder/Obsessive-Compulsive and Related Disorder Due to Another Medical Condition/Other Specified Obsessive-Compulsive and Related Disorder/Unspecified Obsessive-Compulsive and Related Disorder

Trauma- and Stressor-Related Disorders

Reactive Attachment Disorder/Disinhibited Social Engagement Disorder/Posttraumatic Stress Disorder (includes Posttraumatic Stress Disorder for Children 6 Years and Younger)/Acute Stress Disorder/Adjustment Disorders/Other Specified Trauma- and Stressor-Related Disorder/Unspecified Trauma- and Stressor-Related Disorder

Dissociative Disorders

Dissociative Identity Disorder/Dissociative Amnesia/Depersonalization/Derealization Disorder/Other Specified Dissociative Disorder/Unspecified Dissociative Disorder

Somatic Symptom and Related Disorders

Somatic Symptom Disorder/Illness Anxiety Disorder/Conversion Disorder (Functional Neurological Symptom Disorder)/Psychological Factors Affecting Other Medical Conditions/Factitious Disorder (includes Factitious Disorder Imposed on Self, Factitious Disorder Imposed on Another)/Other Specified Somatic Symptom and Related Disorder/Unspecified Somatic Symptoms and Related Disorder

Feeding and Eating Disorders

Pica/Rumination Disorder/Avoidant/Restrictive Food Intake Disorder/Anorexia Nervosa (Restricting type, Binge-eating/Purging type)/Bulimia Nervosa/Binge-Eating Disorder/Other Specified Feeding or Eating Disorder/Unspecified Feeding or Eating Disorder

Elimination Disorders

Enuresis/Encopresis/Other Specified Elimination Disorder/Unspecified Elimination Disorder

Sleep-Wake Disorders

Insomnia Disorder/Hypersomnolence Disorder/Narcolepsy

Breathing-Related Sleep Disorders

Obstructive Sleep Apnea Hypopnea/
Central Sleep Apnea/Sleep-Related
Hypoventilation/Circadian Rhythm
Sleep-Wake Disorders

Parasomnias

Non-Rapid Eye Movement Sleep Arousal
Disorders/Nightmare Disorder/
Rapid Eye Movement Sleep Behavior
Disorder/Restless Legs Syndrome/
Substance/Medication-Induced
Sleep Disorder/Other Specified
Insomnia Disorder/Unspecified
Insomnia Disorder/Other Specified
Hypersomnolence Disorder/
Unspecified Hypersomnolence
Disorder/Other Specified Sleep-Wake
Disorder/Unspecified Sleep-Wake
Disorder

Sexual Dysfunctions

Delayed Ejaculation/Erectile Disorder/
Female Orgasmic Disorder/Female
Sexual Interest/Arousal Disorder/
Genito-Pelvic Pain/Penetration
Disorder/Male Hypoactive Sexual
Desire Disorder/Premature (Early)
Ejaculation/Substance/Medication-
Induced Sexual Dysfunction/Other
Specified Sexual Dysfunction/
Unspecified Sexual Dysfunction

Gender Dysphoria

Gender Dysphoria/Other Specified
Gender Dysphoria/Unspecified
Gender Dysphoria

Disruptive, Impulse-Control, and Conduct Disorders

Oppositional Defiant Disorder/
Intermittent Explosive Disorder/
Conduct Disorder/Antisocial
Personality Disorder/Pyromania/
Kleptomania/Other Specified
Disruptive, Impulse-Control, and
Conduct Disorder/Unspecified
Disruptive, Impulse-Control, and
Conduct Disorder

Substance-Related and Addictive Disorders

Substance-Related Disorders

Alcohol-Related Disorders: Alcohol Use
Disorder/Alcohol Intoxication/Alcohol
Withdrawal/Other Alcohol-Induced
Disorders/Unspecified Alcohol-Related
Disorder

Caffeine-Related Disorders: Caffeine
Intoxication/Caffeine Withdrawal/
Other Caffeine-Induced Disorders/
Unspecified Caffeine-Related Disorder

Cannabis-Related Disorders: Cannabis
Use Disorder/Cannabis Intoxication/
Cannabis Withdrawal/Other Cannabis-
Induced Disorders/Unspecified
Cannabis-Related Disorder

Hallucinogen-Related Disorders:
Phencyclidine Use Disorders/
Other Hallucinogen Use Disorder/
Phencyclidine Intoxication/
Other Hallucinogen Intoxication/
Hallucinogen Persisting Perception
Disorder/Other Phencyclidine-Induced
Disorders/Other Hallucinogen-Induced
Disorders/Unspecified Phencyclidine-
Related Disorders/Unspecified
Hallucinogen-Related Disorders

Inhalant-Related Disorders: Inhalant
Use Disorder/Inhalant Intoxication/
Other Inhalant-Induced Disorders/
Unspecified Inhalant-Related Disorders

Opioid-Related Disorders: Opioid Use
Disorder/Opioid Intoxication/Opioid
Withdrawal/Other Opioid-Induced
Disorders/Unspecified Opioid-Related
Disorder

Sedative-, Hypnotic-, or Anxiolytic-
Related Disorders: Sedative, Hypnotic,
or Anxiolytic Use Disorder/Sedative,
Hypnotic, or Anxiolytic Intoxication/
Sedative, Hypnotic, or Anxiolytic
Withdrawal/Other Sedative-, Hypnotic-,
or Anxiolytic-Induced Disorders/
Unspecified Sedative-, Hypnotic-, or
Anxiolytic-Related Disorder

Stimulant-Related Disorders: Stimulant
Use Disorder/Stimulant Intoxication/
Stimulant Withdrawal/Other
Stimulant-Induced Disorders/
Unspecified Stimulant-Related Disorder

Tobacco-Related Disorders: Tobacco
Use Disorder/Tobacco Withdrawal/
Other Tobacco-Induced Disorders/
Unspecified Tobacco-Related Disorder

Other (or Unknown) Substance-Related
Disorders: Other (or Unknown)
Substance Use Disorder/Other (or
Unknown) Substance Intoxication/
Other (or Unknown) Substance
Withdrawal/Other (or Unknown)
Substance-Induced Disorders/
Unspecified Other (or Unknown)
Substance-Related Disorder

Non-Substance-Related Disorders

Gambling Disorder

Neurocognitive Disorders

Delirium

Major and Mild Neurocognitive Disorders

Major or Mild Neurocognitive Disorder
Due to Alzheimer's Disease

Major or Mild Frontotemporal
Neurocognitive Disorder

Major or Mild Neurocognitive Disorder
with Lewy Bodies

Major or Mild Vascular Neurocognitive
Disorder

Major or Mild Neurocognitive Disorder
Due to Traumatic Brain Injury

Substance/Medication-Induced Major or
Mild Neurocognitive Disorder

Major or Mild Neurocognitive Disorder
Due to HIV Infection

Major or Mild Neurocognitive Disorder
Due to Prion Disease

Major or Mild Neurocognitive Disorder
Due to Parkinson's Disease

Major or Mild Neurocognitive Disorder
Due to Huntington's Disease

Major or Mild Neurocognitive Disorder
Due to Another Medical Condition

Major and Mild Neurocognitive
Disorders Due to Multiple Etiologies

Unspecified Neurocognitive Disorder

Personality Disorders

Cluster A Personality Disorders

Paranoid Personality Disorder/Schizoid
Personality Disorder/Schizotypal
Personality Disorder

Cluster B Personality Disorders

Antisocial Personality Disorder/
Borderline Personality Disorder/
Histrionic Personality Disorder/
Narcissistic Personality Disorder

Cluster C Personality Disorders

Avoidant Personality Disorder/
Dependent Personality Disorder/
Obsessive-Compulsive Personality
Disorder

Other Personality Disorders

Personality Change Due to Another
Medical Condition/Other Specified
Personality Disorder/Unspecified
Personality Disorder